WORLD TRADE ORGANIZATION

Dispute Settlement Reports

1998
Volume II

Pages 233-696

CAMBRIDGE
UNIVERSITY PRESS

PUBLISHED BY THE PRESS SYNDICATE OF THE UNIVERSITY OF CAMBRIDGE
The Pitt Building, Trumpington Street, Cambridge, United Kingdom

CAMBRIDGE UNIVERSITY PRESS
The Edinburgh Building, Cambridge CB2 2RU, UK http://www.cup.cam.ac.uk
40 West 20th Street, New York, NY 10011–4211, USA http://www.cup.org
10 Stamford Road, Oakleigh, Melbourne 3166, Australia
Ruiz de Alarcón 13, 28014 Madrid, Spain

Printed in the United Kingdom at the University Press, Cambridge

French edition and Spanish edition paperbacks of this title are both available directly from WTO Publications, World Trade Organization, Centre William Rappard, 154 rue de Lausanne, CH-1211 Geneva 21, Switzerland http://www.wto.org

ISBN 0 521 78327 5 hardback
ISBN 0 521 78894 3 paperback

THE WTO DISPUTE SETTLEMENT REPORTS

The *Dispute Settlement Reports* of the World Trade Organization (the "WTO") include panel and Appellate Body reports, as well as arbitration awards, in disputes concerning the rights and obligations of WTO Members under the provisions of the *Marrakesh Agreement Establishing the World Trade Organization*. The *Dispute Settlement Reports* are available in English, French and Spanish.

This volume may be cited as DSR 1998:II

TABLE OF CONTENTS

Page

EUROPEAN COMMUNITIES - MEASURES CONCERNING MEAT AND MEAT PRODUCTS (HORMONES)

(COMPLAINT BY CANADA)

Report of the Panel
WT/DS48/R/CAN

Adopted by the Dispute Settlement Body on 13 February 1998 as modified by the Appellate Body Report

TABLE OF CONTENTS

Page

Page

Page

I. INTRODUCTION

1.1 On 28 June 1996, Canada requested consultations with the European Communities pursuant to Article 4 of the Understanding on Rules and Procedures Governing the Settlement of Disputes ("DSU"), Article 11 of the Agreement on the Application of Sanitary and Phytosanitary Measures ("SPS Agreement"), Article 14 of the Agreement on Technical Barriers to Trade ("TBT Agreement"), Article 19 of the Agreement on Agriculture, and Article XXII of the General Agreement on Tariffs and Trade 1994 ("GATT"), regarding the Council Directive Prohibiting the Use in Livestock Farming of Certain Substances Having a Hormonal Action and related measures which "... adversely affect the importation of livestock and meat from livestock" (WT/DS48/1).

1.2 Pursuant to Article 4.11 of the DSU, Australia requested to be joined in these consultations on 16 July 1997 (WT/DS48/2), the United States on 17 July (WT/DS48/3) and New Zealand on 18 July (WT/DS48/4). The European Communities denied the request of the United States to join consultations. On 25 July 1996, Canada, Australia, and New Zealand held joint consultations with the European Communities but failed to reach a mutually satisfactory solution.

1.3 On 27 September 1996, pursuant to Article XXIII of the General Agreement on Tariffs and Trade 1994, Article 11 of the Agreement on the Application of Sanitary and Phytosanitary Measures, Article 14 of the Agreement on Technical Barriers to Trade, Article 19 of the Agreement on Agriculture and Articles 4 and 6 of the DSU, Canada requested the Dispute Settlement Body ("DSB") to establish a panel with standard terms of reference (WT/DS48/5). Canada claimed that:

"(a) the EC measures are inconsistent with:

(i) the Agreement on the Application of Sanitary and Phytosanitary Measures, and in particular Articles 2, 3 and 5 thereof;

(ii) the General Agreement on Tariffs and Trade 1994, and in particular Articles III or XI thereof;

(iii) the Agreement on Technical Barriers to Trade, and in particular Articles 2 and 5 thereof;

(iv) the Agreement on Agriculture, and in particular Article 4 thereof; and

"(b) the application of the EC measures otherwise nullifies or impairs the benefits accruing to Canada pursuant to the Agreement Establishing the World Trade Organization."

1.4 On 16 October 1996, the DSB established a panel in accordance with the request made by Canada. The agreed terms of reference of the Panel were (WT/DS48/6):

"To examine, in the light of the relevant provisions of the covered agreements cited by Canada in document WT/DS48/5, the matter referred to the DSB by Canada in that document and to make such findings as will assist the DSB in making the recommendations or in giving the rulings provided for in those agreements".

1.5 Australia, New Zealand, Norway and the United States reserved their right to participate in the Panel proceedings as third parties, and all presented arguments to the Panel.

1.6 The parties to the dispute agreed on 4 November 1996 to the following composition of the Panel:

Chairman: Mr. Thomas Cottier
Members: Mr. Peter Palecka
Mr. Jun Yokota

1.7 The Panel met with the parties on 7 January 1997 and 19 February 1997. It met with third parties on 7 January 1997. The Panel consulted with scientific and technical experts on 17-18 February 1997, jointly with the parties to this dispute and the parties to the dispute US-EC Measures Concerning Meat and Meat Products (Hormones).[1]

1.8 The Panel issued its interim report to the parties on 7 May 1997. Following a request made by the European Communities pursuant to Article 15.2 of the DSU, the Panel held a further meeting with the Parties on 4 June 1997. The Panel issued its final report to the Parties to the dispute on 30 June 1997.

[1] WT/DS26/7.

II. FACTUAL ASPECTS

1. The Measures at Issue

2.1 This dispute concerns EC measures, in particular Council Directive 81/602/EEC ("Directive 81/602/EEC"), Council Directive 88/146/EEC ("Directive 88/146/EEC") and Council Directive 88/299/EEC ("Directive 88/299/EEC").[2]

2.2 Directive 81/602/EEC prohibits the administering to farm animals of substances having a *thyrostatic action* or substances having an *oestrogenic, androgenic or gestagenic* action; the placing on the market or slaughtering of farm animals to which these substances have been administered; the placing on the market of meat from such animals; the processing of meat from such animals and the placing on the market of meat products prepared from or with such meat. The Directive provides two exceptions to the prohibition: one exception is provided for substances with an oestrogenic, androgenic or gestagenic action when they are used for therapeutic purposes and administered by a veterinarian. The other exception was provided for five growth promoting hormones - oestradiol-17β, progesterone, testosterone, trenbolone acetate and zeranol - when they were used for growth promotion purposes and their use was governed according to the individual regulatory schemes maintained by member States. This exception was made pending an examination of the effects of these hormones on the health of consumers and the adoption of an EC rule. Member States are obliged to apply their regulatory schemes to imports from third countries in a manner not more favourable than that applied to intra-EC trade.

2.3 Directive 88/146/EEC extends the prohibition imposed by Directive 81/602/EEC to the administration to farm animals of trenbolone acetate and zeranol for any purpose, and oestradiol-17β, testosterone and progesterone for fattening purposes. However, the Directive maintains the permission to administer these three natural hormones to animals for therapeutic and zootechnical purposes under prescribed conditions; in particular, therapeutic treatment is defined to mean the administering to an individual animal of any of the substances which are authorized to treat a fertility problem diagnosed on examination by a veterinarian. The products which are used for therapeutic treatment may by administered only by a veterinarian, in the form of an injection (to the exclusion of implantation) to farm animals which have been clearly identified. Such treatment must be registered by the veterinarian and these animals may not be slaughtered before expiry of the period fixed. In the case of animals at the end of their reproductive career, the treatments are prohibited from being administered during the fattening period following the end of their breeding life. The importation from third countries of animals and meat from animals to which have been administered substances with thyrostatic, oestrogenic, androgenic or gestagenic action is prohibited.[3] However, under certain conditions, Article 7 of Di-

[2] Other measures relevant to the dispute are contained in Directives 72/462/EEC, 81/851/EEC, 81/852/EEC, 85/358/EEC, referenced in Directive 88/146/EEC; the decisions, control programme and derogations referred to in Article 6(2), Article 6(7) and Article 7, respectively, of Directive 88/146/EEC; and any amendments or modifications, including Directives 96/22/EC and 96/23/EC.

[3] Article 6(7) of Directive 88/146/EEC requires the establishment of a control programme as regards imports from third countries to ensure that imports do not receive more favourable treatment

rective 88/146/EEC allows trade in those animals and meat from those animals treated for therapeutic or zootechnical purposes, including imports from third countries.[4] Article 4 of Directive 88/146/EEC explicitly requires that undertakings in the EC member States producing the prohibited hormones, those companies authorized to market these hormones for whatever purposes and undertakings producing pharmaceutical and veterinary products based on those substances, must keep a detailed register recording (in chronological order) the quantities produced or acquired and those sold or used for the production of pharmaceutical and veterinary products.

2.4 Directive 88/299/EEC lays down the conditions for applying the derogations, provided for in Article 7 of Directive 88/146/EEC, from the prohibition on trade in certain categories of animals and their meat. The first derogation of the Directive requires member States to authorize trade in animals intended for reproduction and reproductive animals at the end of their career (and of meat of such animals) which, during their reproductive career, have undergone one of two categories of treatments. first category is therapeutic treatment with one of the following substances: oestradiol-17β, testosterone and progesterone; and those derivatives which readily yield the parent compound on hydrolysis after absorption at the site of application which appear in a list of approved products. The second category is the administration of substances having an oestrogenic, androgenic or gestagenic action for synchronization of oestrus, termination of unwanted gestation, the improvement of fertility and the preparation of donors and recipients for the implantation of embryos, provided that the products in which they are contained appear on a list of approved products and with the respect of strict conditions of use concerning, in particular, the respect of the withdrawal period, the monitoring of those conditions of use and of the means of identification of the animals. In addition, Articles 3 and 4 of this Directive provide that trade between the member States of the European Communities in animals intended for reproduction and reproductive animals and meat from such animals is allowed only if all the conditions laid down in the Directive are respected, in particular as regards the waiting period and the requirement that animals have not received any of the above treatments with any of the above substances during the fattening period following the end of their breeding life. The EC stamp may be affixed

than EC products. This control programme also provides for rules on the frequency of controls on imports from each third country and on guarantees offered by the inspection regulation of third countries. Such checks on imports are now carried out in accordance with Directives 91/496/EEC and 90/675/EEC.

4 Article 7 of Directive 88/146/EEC allows derogations in respect to trade in animals intended for reproduction and reproductive animals at the end of their career (and in respect of meat from these various animals, taking into account the guarantees given), which in the course of their existence have been treated under the provisions of Article 4 of Directive 81/602/EEC. This article authorizes the administration to farm animals of substances with oestrogenic, androgenic or gestagenic action approved in accordance with the Directives on veterinary medical products (other than substances referred to in Article 3 of Directive 81/602/EEC) for therapeutic use, synchronization of oestrus, termination of unwanted gestation, the improvement of fertility and the preparation of donors and recipients for the implantation of embryos. The administering of these substances shall be effected by a veterinarian, however, member States may allow the synchronization of oestrus and the preparation of donors and recipients for the implantation of embryos to be done not by a veterinarian but under his direct responsibility.

to the meat only if the waiting time ended before the animals are slaughtered. The second derogation in Directive 88/299/EEC allows imports from third countries of treated animals and meat of such animals under guarantees equivalent to those for domestic animals and meat.

2.5 Directive 96/22/EC will replace Directives 81/602/EEC, 88/146/EEC and 88/299/EEC as from 1 July 1997. It will maintain the prohibition on the use of these hormones for growth promotion purposes; extend the prohibition on the use of beta-agonists; restrict the use of the hormones at issue for therapeutic or zootechnical purposes, reinforcing in particular the role of the veterinarian; and reinforce the provisions on control and testing. Penalties and sanctions in case of violations are to be increased where checks detect the presence of prohibited substances or products or residues of substances administered illegally. Such substances or products will be confiscated and any treated animals or meat placed under official supervision until penalties have been applied.

2. *The Substances at Issue (hormones)*

2.6 Hormones (chemicals) produced by the bodies of humans and animals are called endogenous or natural hormones. Compounds chemically synthesized to mimic the effect of natural hormones are called synthetic or xenobiotic hormones (phyto-hormones are produced by some plants.) Natural hormones are secreted into the blood stream by specialized cells and travel throughout the body. Hormones act by binding protein receptors present in hormone-responsive tissues. The receptor undergoes a conformational change, binds to specific DNA sequences and regulates specific genes within a cell. Synthetic hormones may differ from endogenous (natural) hormones in their rate of metabolism and excretion.

2.7 Hormones function in four broad areas: reproduction; growth and development; maintenance of the internal environment; and production, utilization and storage of energy. One hormone can have multiple actions. For example, the male hormone testosterone controls many processes from the development of the fetus to libido in the adult. One function may be controlled by multiple hormones: the menstrual cycle involves oestradiol, progesterone, follicle-stimulating hormone and luteinizing hormone.

2.8 Of the six hormones involved in this dispute, three are naturally occurring hormones produced by humans and animals: oestradiol-17β, progesterone and testosterone (hereafter also referred to as natural hormones). Oestradiol-17β is a sex steroidal hormone with oestrogenic action (i.e., responsible for female characteristics); testosterone is a sex steroidal hormone with androgenic action (i.e., responsible for male characteristics); progesterone is a sex steroidal hormone with gestagenic action (i.e., responsible for maintaining pregnancy). These three hormones are produced throughout the lifetime of each individual and are required for normal physiological functioning and maturation. Hormone levels vary with the tissue, with the species of animal and with the sex and individual. Hormone levels vary most dramatically with puberty, pregnancy and castration.

2.9 The other three hormones involved in this dispute are artificially produced hormones: trenbolone, zeranol and melengestrol acetate (MGA) (hereafter also referred to as synthetic hormones). These hormones mimic the biological activity of the natural hormones. Trenbolone mimics the action of testosterone; zeranol mimics the action of oestradiol-17β; and MGA mimics progesterone.

2.10 In Canada, the three natural hormones may be administered to animals to correct certain endocrine disfunctions (hereafter "therapeutic" purposes); oestradiol-17β and progesterone may be administered for breeding purposes such as synchronizing oestrus and preparing female animals for artificial insemination (hereafter "zootechnical" purposes); all six substances at issue are used to increase the feed efficiency and the rate of animal growth (hereafter "growth promotion" purposes). Five of these hormones (except MGA) are formulated as pellets (with approved and fixed amounts of compound) designed to be implanted in the ear of the animal. The ear is discarded at slaughter. MGA is administered as a feed additive.

3. The Codex Alimentarius Standards

2.11 The SPS Agreement makes reference, in a number of provisions, to "the relevant international standards, guidelines and recommendations". Annex A:3(a) of the SPS Agreement states that the international standards, guidelines and recommendations relevant for food safety are those established by the Codex Alimentarius Commission relating to food additives, veterinary drug and pesticide residues, contaminants, methods of analysis and sampling, and codes and guidelines of hygienic practice.

2.12 The Codex Alimentarius Commission ("Codex Commission") is a joint FAO/WHO advisory body established to implement the Joint FAO/WHO Food Standards Programme. The purpose of this programme is to protect the health of consumers and to ensure fair practices in food trade through the elaboration of food standards. These standards, together with notifications received from governments with respect to their acceptance or otherwise of the standards, constitute the Codex Alimentarius. The Codex Alimentarius ("Codex") is thus a collection of internationally adopted food standards presented in a uniform manner.

2.13 Membership of the Codex Commission is open to all member Nations and Associate members of FAO and/or WHO and is composed of government representatives of these members. Most of its members, including Canada and the EC member States, are WTO Members. The European Community has an observer status in the Codex Commission. The Codex Commission has established a number of subsidiary bodies, including the Codex Committee on Residues of Veterinary Drugs in Food ("CCRVDF").

2.14 The technical and scientific analysis of veterinary drugs, food additives and some other substances in foods and beverages is not undertaken by the Codex Commission itself but independently by the Joint FAO/WHO Expert Committee on Food Additives ("JECFA"). The JECFA is composed of independent scientists who serve in their individual capacities as experts, not as representatives of their governments or organizations. The goal of the JECFA evaluation of veterinary drugs is:

"to establish safe levels of intake by setting Acceptable Daily Intakes (ADI) and to develop maximum residue limits when veterinary drugs are used in accordance with good veterinary practice"[5].

(a) The Elaboration of Codex Standards

2.15 The elaboration of Codex standards involves an 8-step process:

Step 1: The Codex Commission decides to elaborate a standard and identifies which subsidiary body or other body should undertake the work, taking into account the "Criteria for the Establishment of Work Priorities and for the Establishment of Subsidiary Bodies". Decisions to elaborate standards may also be taken by subsidiary bodies of the Codex Commission subject to subsequent approval by the Codex Commission or its Executive Committee.

Step 2: The Codex Commission secretariat arranges for the preparation of a "proposed draft standard". In the case of veterinary drugs, JECFA is in charge of preparing recommendations for maximum residue levels.

Step 3: The secretariat distributes the "proposed draft standard" to the members of the Commission for comments.

Step 4: The comments received are sent by the secretariat to the CCRVDF which considers the comments and, if appropriate, amends the proposed draft standard.

Step 5: The proposed draft standard is submitted through the secretariat to the Codex Commission or to the Executive Committee with a view to its adoption as a "draft standard".

Step 6: The "draft standard" is sent by the secretariat to all members and interested international organizations for comments on all aspects, including possible implications of the "draft standard" for their economic interests.

Step 7: The comments received are sent by the secretariat to the CCVDRF, which has the power to consider such comments and amend the "draft standard".

Step 8: The "draft standard" is submitted through the secretariat to the Commission together with any written proposals received from members and interested international organizations for amendments at Step 8 with a view to its adoption as a "Codex standard". Adoption of standards is normally done on the basis of a consensus decision, however, if requested, a vote may be taken. In this case, a decision by the majority of Codex members is required. An accelerated elaboration procedure may be used when there is an urgent need for a standard.

2.16 The Codex Commission keeps under review and may revise Codex standards, generally following procedures similar to those used for the elaboration of standards. Codex standards are published and sent to governments for acceptance and to international organizations to which competence in the matter has been transferred by their member States. Acceptance of the standards is voluntary and Codex members

[5] Codex Alimentarius, Vol.3, Residues of Veterinary Drugs in Foods, p.vi.

are not required to indicate formal acceptance of Codex standards, guidelines or recommendations. The implementation of Codex standards at the national level is the responsibility of members.

(b) Codex Standards for Five Hormones at Issue

2.17 Codex standards for veterinary drugs are normally stated in terms of an Acceptable Daily Intake ("ADI") and a Maximum Residue Limit ("MRL"). An ADI is "an estimate by JECFA of the amount of a veterinary drug, expressed on a body weight basis, that can be ingested daily over a lifetime without appreciable health risk (standard man = 60 kg)".[6] An ADI is derived from the experimental No Observable Effect Level ("NOEL") in the most appropriate animal species, by applying an appropriate safety factor. To account for sensitivity variabilities between humans and animals, and dietary variabilities among humans, a safety factor is typically applied. When data from long-term animal toxicity studies are available, a safety factor of 100 is generally applied. Larger safety factors, up to 1000, may be used in certain cases.

2.18 A Codex MRL is one of the tools for ensuring that intake does not exceed the ADI and that "Good Practice in the use of Veterinary Drugs" ("GPVD") is observed. It is the maximum concentration of residue resulting from the use of a veterinary drug (expressed in µg/kg or µg/kg on a fresh weight basis) that is recommended by the Codex Commission to be legally permitted or recognized as acceptable in or on a food. Test animals are first treated with the drug in accordance with proposed GPVD and, on the basis of this usage, tentative MRLs are set for various tissues. These MRLs are then compared with the ADI, considering dietary food intake. If the MRL established on the basis of proposed GPVD would cause the ADI to be exceeded, the MRL will be lowered to a level which ensures that the ADI is not exceeded, and the proposed GPVD will also be made stricter. If, on the other hand, the proposed MRL would not cause the ADI to be exceeded (as is most frequently the case), the MRL will be proposed for adoption. Thus, MRLs are frequently set at levels below (even far below) the theoretical safe levels determined from an ADI. An MRL may also be reduced to be consistent with the GPVD as approved by national authorities or increased (to a level still below the safe level) to be detectable using practical methods.

2.19 "Good Practice in the Use of Veterinary Drugs" (GPVD), is defined as:

> "the official recommended or authorized usage including withdrawal periods, approved by national authorities, of veterinary drugs under practical conditions."[7]

According to the Codex Commission secretariat, the terms "good veterinary practice" and "good veterinary and husbandry practice", when used in JECFA reports, are synonyms for GPVD.

2.20 For the hormones at issue, JECFA considered five of the six substances (all except MGA) and made recommendations on four of them (excluding trenbolone) during its 32nd Session in 1987. For trenbolone, further data was sought and a JECFA recommendation made in 1989. The CCRVDF considered the JECFA rec-

---

6 Codex Alimentarius, Vol.3, Residues of Veterinary Drugs in Foods, p. 65.

7 *Ibid.*

ommendations at its meetings in 1987 and recommended draft standards for the three endogenous hormones and zeranol. These draft standards were approved by the Codex Commission at Step 5 in 1989. Standards for these four hormones were considered at Step 8 by the Codex Commission in June 1991, but, following a vote on the matter, were not adopted. A draft standard for trenbolone at Step 5 was adopted on 1991. In June 1995, the Codex Commission adopted standards, at Step 8, for the five hormones, on the basis of a vote. These standards apply exclusively with respect to cattle, and meat and meat products of bovine origin, when these hormones are used for growth promotion purposes.

2.21 With respect to the three natural hormones in dispute, oestradiol-17β, progesterone and testosterone, similar Codex standards apply. For these three hormones it was considered "*unnecessary*" to establish an ADI or MRL.[8] Specifically, the Codex states that:

> "Establishing an ADI and an [MRL] for a hormone that is produced endogenously at variable levels in human beings was considered unnecessary by the Committee. Residues resulting from the use of this substance as a growth promoter in accordance with good animal husbandry practice are unlikely to pose a hazard to human health."[9]

2.22 The 32nd JECFA Report of 1988 ("1988 JECFA Report"), on which the Codex standards are based, concluded that residues arising from the use of testosterone and oestradiol-17β as a growth promoter in accordance with good animal husbandry practice are unlikely to pose a hazard to human health and that the amount of exogenous progesterone ingested in meat from treated animals would not be capable of exerting an hormonal effect, and therefore, any toxic effect, in human beings. Since, according to JECFA, the potential toxic effect of residues of these hormones is directly related to their hormonal effect, the Report concluded that the additional residue levels in treated animals are not capable of exerting any toxic effect. On the basis of this safety assessment and in view of the difficulty of determining the levels of residues attributable to the use of these hormones for growth promoting purposes in cattle (residues of endogenous natural hormones in meat cannot be practically distinguished from those exogenously administered), JECFA concluded that it was "unnecessary" to establish an ADI or MRL for these hormones.

2.23 With respect to two of the synthetic hormones at issue, zeranol and trenbolone, the Codex standards are the following: an ADI of 0-0.5 and 0-0.02 μg/kg body weight, respectively, and for both hormones an MRL of 2 μg/kg in bovine muscle and 10 μg/kg in bovine liver.

2.24 The 1988 JECFA Report, on which the Codex standard for zeranol is based, noted that zeranol was a weak oestrogen which mimicked the action of oestradiol-17β. The report concluded that the toxic (*in casu* tumorigenic) effect of zeranol is associated with its hormonal (i.e. oestrogenic) properties and that an ADI could thus be established on the basis of a no-hormonal-effect level. Adopting what it considered to be a conservative approach by using as a basis studies on ovariectomized

---

8 Codex Alimentarius, Vol.3, Residues of Veterinary Drugs in Foods, Section 1, pp.7, 12 and 14.

9 *Ibid.*, Section 1, footnote, pp.7, 12 and 14.

female cynomolgus monkeys (highly sensitive to oestrogenic substances) and using a safety factor of 100, JECFA set an ADI for human beings of 0-0.5 μg/kg of body weight. For a 70 kg person consuming 500 g of meat daily over an entire lifetime, the maximum permissible or safe level of zeranol residues in meat would then, according to JECFA, be 70 μg/kg of edible tissue. However, the report noted that when zeranol is administered to cattle according to good animal husbandry practice, the maximum mean residue levels did not exceed 0.2 μg/kg in muscle, 10 μg/kg in liver, 2 μg/kg in kindney, and 0.3 μg/kg in fat at any time after implantation. These residue levels obtained on the basis of good animal husbandry practice are thus below the maximum permissible level of 70 μg/kg. However, in order to set a level which is detectable by routine residue analysis methods, the Codex MRL was increased to 2 μg/kg in muscle and set at 10 μg/kg in liver.

2.25 Trenbolone acetate is the chemical form or ester used for the administration of trenbolone. Trenbolone, or trenbolone acetate ("TBA"), an androgen which mimics the action of testosterone, is rapidly hydrolysed after administration to cattle. The major metabolite (i.e. compound into which TBA breaks down by chemical activity after entering the body) is α-trenbolone, occurring *inter alia* in liver, and β-trenbolone present in muscle. With respect to TBA, the 1988 JECFA Report concluded that its potential toxic effects only arise as a consequence of its hormonal activity. The report further concluded that, therefore, an ADI could be established on the basis of a no-hormonal-effect level. Adopting what it considered to be a conservative approach by using as a basis studies on castrated male rhesus macaque monkeys (which are highly sensitive to compounds with antigonadotropic activity) and pigs (which are a sensitive model for assessing hormonal effects of TBA) and using a safety factor of 100, JECFA later set an ADI for human beings of 0-0.02 μg/kg of body weight (34th JECFA Report of 1989). The maximum ADI for a 60 kg person would thus be 1.2 μg of TBA residues. JECFA then set MRL's for β-trenbolone in muscle and α-trenbolone in liver of 2 μg/kg and 10 μg/kg, respectively, based on average residue levels in heifers at 15-30 days after implantation of 300 mg TBA, noting that concentrations would be even lower at proposed GPVD. According to JECFA, the MRL's thus obtained on the basis of conservative estimates should not exceed the Codex ADI or safe level at any time after implantation of the drug, that is, irrespective of the withdrawal period used.

4. *History of Events*

2.26 European consumers' concern over the use of hormones for growth promotion purposes in livestock grew steadily throughout the 1970s as the result of the illegal use of dethylstilboestrol, commonly known as DES (see paragraph 4.183, footnote 130), in veal production in France and incidents, particularly in Italy, where adolescents had been reported to be suffering from hormonal irregularities and veal had come under suspicion as a possible cause. European consumer organizations called for a boycott of veal, and the market for veal was severely affected. On 20 September 1980, the EC Council of (Agriculture) Ministers adopted a declaration in favour of a ban on the use of oestrogen and endorsed the principle of greater harmonisation of legislation on veterinary medicines and of greater control on animal rearing, both at the production and slaughtering stages.

2.27 On 31 October 1980, the EC Commission proposed legislation aimed at banning the use of all hormone products (COM (80) 614), except for therapeutic purposes. This proposal was expanded later by documents COM(80)920 and COM(80)922, presented on 6 January 1981. These allowed for the controlled use for therapeutic and zootechnical purposes of three natural hormone products, and introduced a number of control measures on the production and handling of such products, together with proposals on the testing of animals. On 13 February 1981, the European Parliament adopted the "Nielsen Report" approving the Commission proposals. The EC Economic and Social Committee endorsed the proposals in February 1981. However, three member States (Belgium, Ireland and the United Kingdom) sought to have the three natural hormones remain available both as therapeutic drugs and as growth promotion agents, and Ireland and the United Kingdom also argued for the retention of the synthetic hormones, trenbolone and zeranol. Moreover, third countries, including Argentina, Australia, Canada, New Zealand, South Africa and the United States, also raised questions concerning the impact of any ban on their exports to the European Communities.

2.28 The EC Council of Ministers adopted its first Directive on the issue (81/602/EEC) on 31 July 1981. In that Directive, and in regard to five of the hormones at issue (all but MGA), the Council directed the Commission to provide, not later than 1 July 1984, a report on the experience acquired and scientific developments, accompanied, if necessary, by proposals taking into account these developments. Accordingly, the Commission set up a Scientific Group on Anabolic Agents in Animal Production, chaired by Professor G.E. Lamming (the "Lamming Group"). The question addressed to the Lamming Group was:

> "Does the use for fattening purposes in animals of the following substances: oestradiol-17β, testosterone, progesterone, trenbolone and zeranol present any harmful effect to health."[10]
>
> "The Lamming Group issued an interim report on 22 September 1982 (the "Lamming Report"). The Lamming Report concluded as follows:
>
> "The Scientific Working Group is of the opinion that the use of oestradiol-17β, testosterone and progesterone and those derivatives which readily yield the parent compound on hydrolysis after absorption from the site of application would not present any harmful effects to the health of the consumer when used under the appropriate conditions as growth promoters in farm animals.
>
> "Evaluation of data on "trenbolone" and "zeranol" revealed that some data on the hormonal non-effect-level and the toxicology of these compounds and their metabolites are still missing.
>
> "The Scientific Working Group considers it necessary that additional information be provided before a final conclusion can be given on trenbolone and zeranol.

---

[10] Report of the (EC) Scientific Veterinary Committee, Scientific Committee for Animal Nutrition and the Scientific Committee for Food on the Basis of the Report of the Scientific Group on Anabolic Agents in Animal Production, pp. 1 and 12.

> "Proper programmes to control and monitor the use of anabolic agents are essential.
>
> "It is necessary to continue scientific investigations on the relevance of the present use of the "no-hormone-effect" level related to the harmful effects of anabolic agents."

2.29 The EC Scientific Veterinary Committee gave its reaction to the Lamming Report on 9 November 1982, followed by the EC Scientific Committee for Animal Nutrition on 17 November 1982 and by the EC Scientific Committee for Food on 4 February 1983. These Committees supported the conclusions and recommendations of the Lamming Report, but stressed the need to lay down provisions regarding the establishment of proper programmes to control and monitor the use of anabolic agents with regard, in particular, to instructions for use, surveillance programmes and analysis methods. In January 1984, the Commission asked a group of experts within the EC Scientific Committee on Anabolic Agents to review the information on trenbolone and zeranol. On 12 June 1984, the Commission published a proposal (COM(84)295 final) for a Council Directive amending Directive 81/602/EEC, which envisaged the controlled use of the three natural hormones for growth promotion purposes and proposed re-examining the ban on the two synthetic hormones after their scientific evaluation had been completed. However, the European Parliament, the EC Economic and Social Committee and the EC Council of Ministers rejected the Commission's proposal.

2.30 The EC Commission amended its proposal accordingly and on 31 December 1985 the EC Council adopted Directive 85/649/EEC. This Directive confirmed the ban on the use of all the substances concerned for growth promotion purposes and established more detailed provisions concerning authorized therapeutic uses. The Directive was challenged in the European Court of Justice, which annulled it on procedural grounds. The proposals were re-introduced by the EC Commission and re-adopted by the EC Council as Council Directive 88/146/EEC on 16 March 1988.

2.31 Following reports of significant use of illegal growth-promoting hormonal substances in a number of EC member States, on 26 September 1988 the European Parliament established a "Committee of Enquiry into the Problem of Quality in the Meat Sector". The Report of this Committee (the "Pimenta Report") endorsed the ban on the use of hormones and was adopted by the European Parliament on 29 March 1989 (see paragraph 4.19). The essential findings of the Pimenta Report were that the prohibition of hormonal substances for non-therapeutic (i.e. growth-promoting) purposes must be maintained and expanded because:

(i) this was the only way to restore consumer confidence in the meat sector;

(ii) 10 out of 12 national veterinary experts indicated that a total ban would facilitate implementation and control;

(iii) the scientific conclusions regarding the use of natural hormones rested upon strict conditions of use which it believed could not in reality be attained. The Committee was of the opinion that use of the natural/nature-identical hormones carried the risk of inexperienced application, incorrect dosage and unsupervised injection which could pose a risk to the animal and the consumer, and also noted doubts with regard to long-term cumulative and interactive potential carcinogenicity.

In addition, the Committee believed that proven necessity and socio-economic desirability should be criteria of acceptability for the use of (bio)chemical growth promoters in animal-rearing;

(iv) The Committee did not accept the argument that prohibiting the use for growth promotion of some natural or nature-identical hormones would result in an increase in the use of other, more dangerous growth-promoting substances to the detriment of the consumer;

(v) the Committee believed that the Commission should promote the concept of *animal welfare* in agricultural production.

2.32 The European Parliament adopted another report on the issue of use of hormones for animal growth promotion, the "Collins Report" of 7 February 1989.[11] This report argued that:

> "Current licensing systems for the regulation of veterinary medicines (including at present, growth promoting products) require that a new product satisfy three criteria: safety, quality and efficacy. These criteria may well be satisfactory for therapeutic drugs. They are by no means sufficient for growth promoting products. For the latter it is proposed here that the Community's veterinary medicine licensing system be adapted to include a *"fourth hurdle", entailing an objective socio-economic and environmental impact assessment"*. In the Commission's July 1988 draft proposals for the reform of veterinary medicine licensing in the Community this idea was accepted in principle. The final version of the proposals (December 1988) does not include this concept. It is clear, however, that the social, agricultural and environmental implications of the use of growth and yield promoting pharmaceuticals require a licensing system somewhat different from that which exists for these products when used for therapeutic purposes".

2.33 The EC Commission organized a scientific conference on this subject in Brussels from 29 November to 1 December 1996. With regard to the natural hormones, the 1995 EC Scientific Conference on Growth Promotion in Meat Production (the "1995 EC Scientific Conference") concluded that:

> "At present, there is no evidence for possible health risks to the consumer due to the use of natural sex hormones for growth promotion, since:
>
> Residue levels of these substances measured in meat of treated animals fall within the physiological range observed in meat of comparable untreated animals.
>
> The daily production of sex hormones by humans is much higher than the amounts possibly consumed from meat, even in

[11] European Parliament, Committee on the Environment, Public Health and Consumer Protection, Report on "The USA's Refusal to comply with Community legislation on slaughterhouses and hormones and the consequences of this refusal", EP 128 381/B, 7 February 1989, named after its reporter Mr. Collins, MEP.

> the most sensitive humans (prepubertal children and menopausal women).
>
> Due to an extensive first-pass metabolism, the bioavailability of ingested hormones is low, thus providing a further safety margin."[12]

With regard to the synthetic hormones, zeranol and trenbolone, the 1995 EC Scientific Conference concluded that:

> "At the doses needed for growth promotion, residue levels [of trenbolone and zeranol] are well below the levels regarded as safe (the MRLs). There are, at present, no indications of a possible human health risk from the low levels of covalently-bound residues of trenbolone."[13]

III. CLAIMS OF THE PARTIES

3.1 **Canada** claimed that the EC measures were governed by the SPS Agreement and that the European Communities, by banning the importation of meat and meat products from animals to which any of the six hormones had been administered for purposes of promoting the growth of animals, had acted inconsistently with the SPS Agreement, in particular Articles 2, 3 and 5. The EC measures were not based on an appropriate risk assessment; failed to take into account international standards, guidelines and recommendations in the absence of scientific justification; were used, in part, as a means to control domestic production; and were more restrictive than required to meet their appropriate level of protection. These measures were far more restrictive than measures adopted by the European Communities to control the use of other substances used in animal husbandry that presented a demonstrably greater risk to health than the six hormones at issue. The EC level of protection for growth promoting hormones was significantly higher than the EC level of protection for antimicrobial growth promoters and other veterinary drugs, resulting in a discrimination against Canadian beef imports and a disguised restriction on international trade.

3.2 Canada also claimed that the EC measures were contrary to GATT, in particular Article III or XI. Canada argued that the EC measures were either an import prohibition, in contravention of GATT, or internal measures that discriminated in favour of EC cattle and beef products, and against like Canadian cattle and beef products, also contrary to GATT.

3.3 Canada submitted alternative arguments that the measures at issue also failed to meet obligations under the TBT Agreement, in particular Article 2, in the event it was found to be applicable.

---

12 "Assessment of Health Risk - Working Group II", in *1995 EC Scientific Conference Proceedings*, pp.20-21.

13 *Ibid.*

3.4 Canada claimed that the application of the EC measures otherwise nullified or impaired the benefits accruing to Canada pursuant to the Agreement Establishing the World Trade Organization ("WTO Agreement") respecting market access for beef.[14]

3.5 The **European Communities** considered that the analysis of the SPS and/or TBT Agreements should take place only if alleged violations of GATT Articles were found and therefore, in its defense, the European Communities first invoked GATT. With regard to the alleged violation of Article III:4 of GATT, the European Communities argued that the animals to which the hormones at issue had been administered for growth promotion, and meat from those animals, were not "like" other animals and meat from those animals, respectively. Furthermore, the European Communities argued that even if they were found to be "like", imported products were not given "less favourable treatment" than domestic products. Therefore, the European Communities claimed that its measures did not infringe Article III:4 of GATT. With regard to the alleged violation of Article XI of GATT, the European Communities claimed that the EC measures at issue were internal regulations within the scope of Article III of GATT. Therefore, Article XI of GATT did not apply. The European Communities claimed that in case its measures were found to be contrary to Article III:4, it was justified by Article XX(b), which did not affect the power of a Member to adopt a policy in order to protect human and animal health.

3.6 The European Communities claimed that the measures at issue, in any event, did not violate any provision of the SPS Agreement because they satisfied all the conditions imposed by it. The measures were based on scientific principles as required by Article 2.2 of the SPS Agreement, and a risk assessment had been performed which established the scientific basis for regulatory action. The European Communities observed that the SPS Agreement recognized a Member's right to establish the level of protection which the Member determined to be appropriate within its territory. The European Communities claimed that the SPS Agreement did not require Members to change the level of sanitary protection they were applying before its entry into force. The European Communities also claimed that the measures at issue were based on scientific principles and aimed at achieving a level of protection which was higher than could be achieved if the recommendations of Codex for these hormones were followed, because more recent scientific evidence showed that these hormones were genotoxic and carcinogenic. It also claimed that WTO dispute settlement panels were not competent to judge its *level* of sanitary protection nor the scientific evidence upon which it was based, but only whether its *measures* were in conformity with the provisions of the SPS Agreement. It further claimed that the arguments of Canada in fact attacked the EC chosen level of protection, not its measures, because they suggested that residues of these hormones above

[14] *Uruguay Round Schedule LXXX - European Communities*, Part I Most Favoured-Nation Tariff, Section I -Agricultural Products, Section I A Tariffs and Section I B Tariff Quotas, as subsequently modified. Tariff items covered by the EC beef and veal regime are:

02011050; 02012015; 02012035; 02012055; 02012090; 02013000; 02021000; 02022010; 02022030; 02022050; 02022090; 02023010; 02023050; 02023090; 02061010; 02061091; 02061095; 02061099; 02062100; 02062210; 02062290; 02062910; 02062991; 02062999; 02102010; 02102090; 02109041; 02109049; 16025010; 16025090; 16029061; and 16029069.

naturally present levels did not pose any risk to health. The European Communities claimed that the SPS Agreement laid down the objective of avoiding arbitrary or unjustifiable distinctions in *applying* the chosen *levels* of protection (not between *measures* used nor between *risks* presented by other substances), and only if such distinctions resulted in discrimination or a disguised restriction on trade. The European Communities further claimed that its measures were based on the precautionary principle. It maintained that its measures were no more trade restrictive than required to achieve its appropriate level of sanitary protection and applied in exactly the same way to all animals treated with these hormones and meat from such animals, whatever its origin; there was consequently no discrimination nor disguised restriction on international trade. The European Communities also claimed that Canada failed to discharge its burden of proof because it had failed to show on the basis of current scientific evidence that meat containing residues of these hormones was safe for human consumption and that there existed another measure, reasonably available taking into account technical and economic feasibility, which could achieve the EC appropriate level of sanitary protection and was significantly less restrictive on trade.

3.7 The European Communities claimed that the measures at issue fell outside the scope of application of the TBT Agreement because they were sanitary measures within the meaning of the SPS Agreement. In the alternative, the EC claimed that the measures at issue did not violate Articles 2.1 and 2.2 of the TBT Agreement because their legitimate objective was to protect human and animal health and they were not more trade restrictive than necessary to achieve this objective. Finally, the European Communities claimed that its measures did not nullify or impair the benefits accruing to Canada pursuant to the WTO Agreement, because the benefits claimed by Canada were granted after the adoption of the EC measures, could have been reasonably anticipated by Canada and did not upset the competitive relationship between domestic and imported products.

IV. ARGUMENTS OF THE PARTIES

1. Relationship Between GATT and the SPS Agreement

4.1 **Canada** claimed that the SPS Agreement, GATT and the TBT Agreement were agreements of equal status, contained in Annex 1A of the WTO Agreement (as per Article II of the WTO Agreement). Since the SPS Agreement contained rules that were more detailed and more precise than those of the GATT, it was appropriate to examine first the application of the SPS Agreement to the EC measures, followed by GATT.

4.2 The **European Communities** considered that the SPS Agreement would apply only if a violation of the Articles of GATT were to be established. The European Communities argued that the SPS Agreement codified, as the last recital of its preamble stated, the desire of Members "to elaborate rules for the application of the provisions of GATT which relate to the use of sanitary or phytosanitary measures, in particular the provisions of Article XX(b)". Furthermore, it was well established GATT law and practice that GATT 1947 did not affect the power of its members to set up a regulatory *policy* which they deemed necessary in order to protect human, animal or plant health. But the conformity of the *measures* it applied for that purpose could be reviewed under GATT [15] It was, therefore, admitted that a violation of GATT by a *measure* should be established first, before recourse to possible justifications (e.g. under Article XX(b)) could be considered. In such an event, the Panel could review the *measure* but not the underlying policy objective on which it was alleged to be based. The European Communities noted that there were several new provisions in the SPS Agreement that imposed a series of rights and obligations on Members. However, the SPS Agreement reaffirmed the right of Members to adopt or enforce measures the Member deemed to be necessary to protect human, animal or plant health (recitals 1 and 6 of preamble). It could therefore be argued that most of the obligations created by the SPS Agreement were already applied under GATT 1947 through interpretations of Article XX(b) by panel reports and the CONTRACTING PARTIES.

4.3 The European Communities claimed that Article 2.4 of the SPS Agreement established that SPS measures which conformed to the Agreement were "presumed" to be in accordance with the obligations of the Members "under the provisions of GATT which relate to the use of sanitary or phytosanitary measures, *in particular* the provisions of Article XX(b)" (emphasis added). Despite the fact that the words "in particular" appeared in Article 2.4, it was hard to imagine *other* provisions of GATT "which relate to the use of sanitary or phytosanitary measures". Therefore, if the SPS Agreement were to be defined as a *self-standing* agreement this was not because it interpreted provisions of GATT other that Article XX(b), but only because it laid down additional *procedural* requirements. The substantive role of the SPS Agreement was to interpret Article XX(b) of GATT; recourse to the substantive provisions of the SPS Agreement could be made only under the same conditions under which recourse could be made to Article XX of GATT, that was only *after* a violation of another provision of GATT was first established. As far as the additional, procedural obligations laid down by the SPS Agreement, these could be examined by the Panel directly and independently of any need to establish first a violation of the provisions of GATT.

4.4 **Canada** disagreed that the substantive mission of the SPS Agreement was "to interpret Article XX(b) of GATT", with the addition of a few procedural rules, and that "... recourse to the substantive provisions of the SPS Agreement could be made only under the same conditions under which recourse could be made to Article XX GATT, that is only *after* a violation of another provision of GATT was first established". Canada responded that, the SPS Agreement was a self-standing agreement of equal status to the GATT. Article 1 of the SPS Agreement provided that the Agreement "applies to all sanitary and phytosanitary measures which may, directly or indirectly, affect international trade." There was no requirement that a violation of GATT must be established before the SPS Agreement applied. The EC measures had a profound and direct effect on Canadian beef exports to the European Communities, so there was no question that the EC measures directly affected international trade. The

[15] In support of its argument, the European Communities referred to the panel report on "Thailand - Restrictions on Importation of and Internal Taxes on Cigarettes", adopted 5 October 1990, DS10/R.

European Communities agreed that its measures were subject to the SPS Agreement. Thus, in accordance with the ordinary meaning to be given to the terms set out in Article 1, the only condition for applying the SPS Agreement had been met.

4.5 Canada further argued that the SPS Agreement was clearly more than just an interpretation of Article XX(b). For example, Articles 3 and 4, on "Harmonization" and "Equivalence" respectively, did not correspond to any provision in the GATT, and were more than "... additional *procedural* requirements". The broad scope of the SPS Agreement was reflected in the fourth and sixth preambular paragraphs, which stated the desire of the WTO Members to establish "a multilateral framework of rules and disciplines to guide the development, adoption and enforcement of sanitary and phytosanitary measures in order to minimize their negative effects on trade" and to "further the use of harmonized sanitary and phytosanitary measures between Members, on the basis of international standards ...". Finally, the negotiating history confirmed that the SPS Agreement was more than an interpretation of Article XX(b). In the early stages of the Uruguay Round, it had been drafted as a Decision interpreting the GATT 1947, but later evolved to a self-standing agreement in Annex 1A. If the negotiators had intended that the SPS Agreement would be merely an interpretation of Article XX(b), it would have been incorporated into the GATT as an "Understanding on the Interpretation of Article XX(b)", rather than an independent agreement.

2. *The SPS Agreement*

4.6 **Canada** noted that historically the EC measures had been motivated by four sets of concerns: (i) anxiety regarding the danger to human health occasioned by the illegal use of substances, such as DES (see paragraph 4.183, footnote 130); (ii) the pressure of public opinion which, under prevailing circumstances, did not distinguish between products or the conditions of their use; (iii) the economic consequences of a "sensationalist campaign"[16], which had resulted in the collapse of the veal market and a sharp decline in beef consumption throughout the European Communities; and (iv) the distortions in the conditions of competition among the EC member States owing to dissimilar provisions and regulations governing the manufacture, distribution and use of substances.[17]

4.7 Canada recalled the terms of reference and conclusions of the Lamming Report (see paragraph 38). Although the Lamming Group was suspended by the EC Commission before it had completed its terms of reference, it had subsequently produced a second report in October 1987, stating that the levels of trenbolone and zeranol and their major metabolites found in edible tissue, following accepted husbandry practices, were substantially below the hormonally effective doses in animal test systems and therefore did not present a harmful effect to health.

---

[16] J.B. Nielsen (1981), "Report drawn up on behalf of the Committee on Agriculture on the proposals from the Commission to the European Communities to the Council ...", *European Parliament*, Doc. I-840/80 (the "Nielsen Report").

[17] *Ibid.*, Doc. 1-523/80.

4.8 Canada observed that in its proposal published in June 1984 (COM(84)295 final, see paragraph 39), the EC Commission had set out three conditions for the use of these hormones for growth promoting purposes: they could be administered only by implantation in a part of the animal which would be discarded at slaughter; treated animals had to be identified at the time of implantation; and the implants were to be administered by a veterinarian. Canada argued that the EC Commission's proposal had been rejected by the Economic and Social Committee because of concerns that the EC Commission's proposal would overturn what the Economic and Social Committee had seen to be the two central objectives of both the original Directive and the EC Commission's proposed Directive, which "... make the protection of the consumer's health and economic interests priority objectives".[18]

4.9 Canada claimed that in rejecting the proposal to allow the use of the three natural hormones, the Economic and Social Committee had clearly disregarded the findings of the Scientific Working Group. In support of its position, the Economic and Social Committee had pointed to the fact, that "... on 30 September 1980 the Council undertook unanimously, under the pressure of public opinion, to prohibit the administering of all hormones ... in livestock production".[19] The Economic and Social Committee had also noted that, although consumer groups and workers had long been unequivocally opposed to the use of anabolics, neither farmers' organizations nor meat processors and traders had taken an official stand at the EC level on this issue. Professor Lamming himself, in a presentation in 1986, had been unequivocal in his assessment of the reasons behind the suspension of the Lamming Group and the rejection of the EC Commission proposal based on the Lamming Group's findings with respect to the three natural hormones:

> "The British Minister has claimed, and rightly so, that [EC Agriculture Commissioner] Andriessen freely admits that the scientific background or scientific consideration were not taken into account. In other words it was purely a political decision and if you read the speeches that were made in the European Parliamentary debate they are mainly based on the fact the [sic] we have got such a surplus of beef and it costs a heck of a lot to store it, why should we authorize any techniques which are going to increase that productivity. The majority of European parliamentary members could see this as a prevention of an increased production of European beef and that probably motivated them more than the scientific background."[20]

4.10 Moreover, the resolution of the European Parliament (February 1988), had stated that "... the Community, with its directives banning hormones, has adopted consistent legislation both in terms of the necessary control of agricultural production and from the point of view of protecting the interests of consumers".[21] Canada

---

[18] "Opinion on the proposal for a Council Directive amending Directive 81/602/EEC concerning the prohibition of certain substances having a hormonal action and of any substances having a thyrostatic action" (1985), *EC Official Journal* (85/C 44/11) (C 44), p.14.

[19] *Ibid.*, p.15.

[20] "Anabolic Growth Promotants and the EEC," *supra,* note 63, p.11.

[21] "Resolution on the ban on hormones", 1988 *EC Official Journal* (C 68) 103.

pointed out that the preamble of Directive 88/146/EEC set out the rationales for the prohibition. These were: to harmonize the regulatory schemes of the EC member States; remove competitive distortions and barriers to intra-Community trade; meet consumer anxieties and expectations; and bring about an increase in the consumption of meat products.[22] This was keeping with the opinion of the Social and Economic Committee[23], as well as the Resolution of the Parliament of 11 October 1985.[24]

4.11 Canada submitted that Sir John Maddox, Editor of *Nature* and Chairman of the 1995 EC Scientific Conference, had touched on two points that had been at the centre of the argument regarding the EC hormones legislation. He had noted, first, that the 1995 EC Scientific conference had reconfirmed the scientific argument that these hormones "were not damaging to meat-eating consumers".[25] Second, his article had highlighted the politicized nature of this debate within the European Communities and how that had been reflected in the composition and proceedings of the 1995 EC Scientific Conference itself. Scientists were outnumbered by participants from bodies such as the European Parliament, the Economic and Social Committee and various lobby groups, all of which had been long-time advocates of the EC measures at issue. In a brief paper forwarded to the European Communities following publication of the proceedings, two Canadian scientists, one of whom had participated in the EC Conference, commented not only were scientists outnumbered by non-scientists but, as noted in the "Report and Conclusions" of the Conference proceedings "... the final plenary session of the whole conference, apart from a brief statement of the principal conclusions by the chairman, was largely dedicated to statements by those not invited as scientist-participants".[26] Canada further criticized the exclusion of scientists directly employed by commercial companies with an interest in the sale of growth promoters, despite the fact that these companies "hold much

[22] "Resolution on the ban on hormones", 1988 *EC Official Journal* (C 68) 103. The relevant portions of the preamble state:

> "Whereas the administration to farm animals of certain substances having a hormonal action is at present regulated in different ways in the member States; whereas while their immediate effect on animals from the farmer's view is clear, assessments on their effect on human health vary and this is reflected in the variations governing their use; whereas this divergence distorts the conditions of competition in products that are the subject of common market organizations and is a serious barrier to intra-Community trade;
>
> "Whereas these distortions of competition and barriers to trade must therefore be removed by ensuring that all consumers are able to buy the products in question under largely identical conditions of supply and that these products correspond to their anxieties and expectations in the best possible manner; whereas such a course of action is bound to bring about an increase in consumption of the product in question."

[23] "Opinion on the proposal for a Council Directive amending Directive 81/602/EEC" (1985), *EC Official Journal* (85/C44/11) (C 44), p.14.

[24] "Resolution closing the procedure for Consultation of the European Parliament on the proposal from the Commission of the European Communities to the Council for a Directive amending Directive 81/602/EEC" (1985), *EC Official Journal* (C 288), p.158.

[25] J.Maddox, "Contention over growth promoters" (1995) 378 *Nature* 553.

[26] Steering Committee, "Report and Conclusions," in *1995 EC Scientific Conference Proceedings* (Luxembourg: European Commission, 1996), p.3.

of the proprietary information that is required for review by national regulatory agencies and international bodies such as JECFA"; and argued that since the conference papers represented individual opinions, "[t]he scientific validity of these conference papers does not compare with the expert committee reviews and recommendations of JECFA, or with the regulatory review process in a registering country".[27]

4.12 The **European Communities** responded that the Lamming Group had been dissolved because it was overtaken by events. During the deliberations of the Lamming Group, the EC Council had decided to adopt a level of protection which avoided the presence of any added hormones in meat. This had made the work of that group redundant, which was already late in issuing its report. Professor Lamming's 1987 account of further work undertaken by members of his group on zeranol and trenbolone had, similarly to the conclusions in the 1982 Lamming Report (see paragraph 38), concluded that these substances would probably be safe when used in accordance with "accepted husbandry practice" - a term he had not defined.[28] The European Communities contended, furthermore, that these conclusions were based on the unsupported assumption that the carcinogenicity of the substances was related to their hormonal effects and that residues of trenbolone and zeranol and their metabolites did not show "*significant* genotoxic potential". The European Communities argued that the common theme of this scientific advice, therefore, was that proper systems of control and monitoring would be a *pre-requisite* for the use of hormones for growth promotion. However, none of these scientific reports had explained what constituted "appropriate conditions of use" nor had they defined what was "good animal husbandry practice". Instead, they had drawn the attention of the EC Commission to the need to lay down the essential conditions concerning use, detection and control of these hormones if they were to be allowed for growth promotion.

4.13 The European Communities argued that the reported opinion of Professor Lamming, who was relaying information reported to have been made to him by the United Kingdom Minister of Agriculture, did not conform with the official and publicly available views expressed by Mr. Andriessen. The European Communities noted that Mr. Andriessen had said, for example, that "the EC Commission recognizes that some scientists consider that, subject to certain conditions, the hormones could safely be used for fattening purposes in animals. The Commission is, however, of the opinion that these substances must be properly considered as medical substances which are only used for veterinary medical purposes, and only under strict conditions of supervision and control".

4.14 The European Communities asserted that the historical record clearly demonstrated that the purpose of the EC measures was to protect human and animal health from risks arising from the use of the hormones at issue. The European Communities noted that the European Parliament had banned imports of meat from animals treated with growth promoting hormones primarily because "scientific information about these substances is far from complete and that considerable doubt therefore exists

---

27 J.D. MacNeil & Yong, "Canada's Comments on the EU Scientific Conference, *Report and Conclusions*, 23 July 1996.

28 Published in *The Veterinary Record* (24/10/1987, p.389).

about the desirability of their use and of their effect on human health".[29] Serious health concerns had been clearly stated in different MEP reports, including the "Nielsen Report", the "Pimenta Report" and the "Collins Report", and the European Parliament had remained constantly opposed to the authorization of all these hormones for animal growth promoting purposes for reasons of possible hazards to human and animal health.

4.15 When the EC Commission had first proposed in 1980 to take measures in this area, as well as in 1988, it had found itself facing certain factual, legal and scientific situations. From the factual point of view, consumer concerns over the use of hormones for growth promotion in livestock was very high. Despite the traditionally cautious approach to the regulation of dangerous substances followed by the EC member States, consumer confidence in science and regulators (especially among well-informed consumer organisations and groups) was very low. This factual situation had not changed during the entire period that had preceded the adoption of Directive 96/22/EC; consumer concerns were even higher today.

4.16 The European Communities noted that from the legal point of view, the use of hormones in animal growth promotion had long been prohibited in most EC member States, but some of them allowed the use of some of these substances under certain conditions.[30] With the progressive establishment of the common market, the divergence in the legislation of the EC member States was inhibiting free trade within the European Communities in animals and meat from animals treated with some of these hormones, and distorting the conditions of competition among EC meat producers.

4.17 Furthermore, the European Communities observed that from the scientific point of view, the situation was very unclear in the early 1980s. The relevant international organizations - FAO, WHO, the Office international des épizooties (OIE) and Codex - had started to seriously examine the safety of these hormones in meat production only during the 1980s. The first substantive and comprehensive scientific report had been published by OIE in 1983. JECFA had discussed and issued a substantive and comprehensive scientific report on these hormones only in 1988. There were two other international reports comprising collective scientific work: the 1984 Scientific Report published by the European Commission (based on the Lamming Report) and the Proceedings of the 1995 EC Scientific Conference. The European Communities stressed, however, that these reports did *not* constitute the entire body of scientific knowledge on the issue of safe use of these hormones for growth promotion. There were also important studies made by individual scientists, and other specialized institutions like the International Agency for Research on Cancer ("IARC")

---

29 Point E of Parliament's Resolution, *EC Official Journal*, No. 288, 11 November 1985, p.158.

30 The European Communities indicated that there was a number of member States (probably 4 or 5) which did allow the use of some of these hormones for growth promotion until their prohibition at EC level. The information on percentages of use, if it was available at all, would only be known to the individual member States which approved the use of the particular substances. At least one member State (the United Kingdom) had indicated that "anecdotal evidence suggests that growth promoting hormones may have been used on up to 40% of United Kingdom cattle prior to the ban".

4.18 The European Communities recalled that the EC Commission proposal (COM(84)295 final), which finally had led to the adoption of Directive 88/146/EEC, proposed to allow the use of the three "natural" hormones only under the following conditions in order to safeguard public health:

- only in the form of an implant to be administered in a part of the animal discarded at slaughter (usually the ear);
- to an identified animal only, to allow control of the withdrawal period;
- only by a veterinarian, with all treatments recorded;
- substances allowed to be administered must be on a EC list, clearly setting out conditions of use;
- these substances must be shown to be effective and safe; and
- meat produced from treated animals must be identified as such to the final consumer.

The European Communities indicated that the Economic and Social Committee had based its refusal of the EC Commission proposal COM(84)295 final on the need for *scientific evidence* and "particular reference to *health aspects*".[31] Moreover, the European Parliament had eventually decided to reject the EC Commission proposal, considering that "scientific information about these substances is far from complete and that considerable doubts therefore exist about the desirability of their use and of their effect on human health".[32] The proposal of the Commission had also been rejected by the EC Council of Ministers on the additional grounds that the proposal was not technically or economically feasible (see paragraph 4.131).

4.19 The European Communities indicated that in 1988, following discoveries of significant use of illegal growth-promoting hormonal substances in certain EC member States, the European Parliament had established a "Committee of Enquiry into the Problem of Quality in the Meat Sector".[33] This Inquiry Committee had received submissions from a wide range of scientific experts, organisations and institutions, including meat trade and farmers' organisations, third country producers, the pharmaceutical industry and consumers' organizations. The outcome of the work of the Committee of Enquiry into the Problem of Quality in the Meat Sector, the Pimenta Report, was adopted by the European Parliament on 29 March 1989. The report observed that:

"1. The Inquiry Committee considers that the prohibition of hormonal substances for non-therapeutic (i.e. growth-promoting) purposes, as laid down in Directives 81/602/EEC and 88/146/EEC must be maintained and expanded with the following justifications:

(a) the Inquiry Committee believes that the maintenance and reinforcement of the total ban on the use of hormonal and other

[31] "Opinion on the proposal for a Council Directive amending Directive 81/602/EEC concerning the prohibition of certain substances having a hormonal action and of any substances having a thyrostatic action," *EC Official Journal* (C 44), 15 February 1985, p.14.

[32] See point E. of Parliament's Resolution, *EC Official Journal*, No. 288, 11 November 1985, p.15.

[33] See para. 2.31.

growth-promoters is the only way to restore consumer confidence in the meat sector and to clarify this very complex issue for producers and consumers alike;

(b) the Inquiry Committee is convinced that control measures will have to be comprehensive and accepts the opinion of 10 out of 12 national veterinary experts that a total ban will facilitate implementation and control;

(c) the Inquiry Committee takes note of the scientific evidence that has been placed before it, and points out that the conclusions regarding the use of natural and nature-identical hormones rest upon strict conditions of use which it believes cannot in reality be attained. *The Inquiry Committee is of the opinion that use of the natural/nature-identical hormones carries the risk of inexperienced application, incorrect dosage and unsupervised injection which could pose a risk to the animal and the consumer. The Inquiry Committee also notes that residual doubts with regard to long-term cumulative and interactive potential carcinogenicity remain.* In addition, the Inquiry Committee believes that proven necessity and socio-economic desirability should be criteria of acceptability for the use of (bio)chemical growth promoters in animal-rearing;

(d) the Inquiry Committee does not accept the argument that prohibiting the use for growth-promotion substances to the detriment of the consumer, given that substances are already in circulation which are more effective in promoting weight-gain and that a black market exists even in authorized pharmaceutical substances. *The Inquiry Committee therefore believes that protection of public health is best achieved by a total ban*;

(e) the Inquiry Committee notes that great pressure to use illegal growth-promoting substances exists in the context of contract fattening on integrated farms and in undertakings established by the processing industry and is therefore of the opinion that legislation should be introduced to strengthen the individual status and responsibilities of such undertakings" (pages 5-6) (emphasis added).

4.20 The European Communities added that the European Parliament had adopted another important report on the issue of use of hormones for animal growth promotion, the "Collins Report" of 7 February 1989.[34] This report noted that the licensing systems for the regulation of veterinary medicines required that a new product satisfy three criteria: safety, quality and efficacy. However, these criteria, which might be satisfactory for therapeutic drugs, were not sufficient for growth promotion products.

[34] European Parliament, Committee on the Environment, Public Health and Consumer Protection, Report on "The USA's Refusal to comply with EC Legislation on Slaughterhouses and Hormones and the Consequences of this Refusal", EP 128 381/B, 7 February 1989, named after its reporter Mr. Collins, MEP.

The Collins Report proposed that the EC veterinary medicine licensing system be adapted to include a "fourth hurdle", entailing an objective socioeconomic and environmental impact assessment. It argued that the social, agricultural and environmental implications of the use of growth and yield promoting pharmaceuticals required a licensing system different from that which existed for these products when used for therapeutic purposes. The same report also found, *inter alia*, that: "... Whereas the use of growth promotion hormones raises questions not only of public but also of animal health; ... Whereas the Community has a duty to protect the health and defend the interests of its consumers and the farm animals; ... Whereas the Community is opposed to all downward harmonisation of health and hygiene standards with regard to the production and marketing of foodstuffs in the European Community and also at international level".

4.21 The European Communities rejected Canada's criticism of the 1995 EC Scientific Conference. The comments by Sir John Maddox should be read in the light of his conclusions as Chairman of the Steering Committee which organized the conference and the letter he had sent to EC Commissioner Fischler, in which he stated:

> "I have myself been impressed that no single class of growth promoters is at present sufficiently well understood for people to be confident that they know the mechanism by which effects (and side-effects) are produced. While that state of affairs persists, risk-assessment will inevitably remain hesitant, regulation cautious and public opinion suspicious ..."

4.22 As far as the comments by the Canadian scientists were concerned, the European Communities noted that the 1995 EC Scientific Conference was funded by the EC Commission but organized by an independent steering committee. The EC Commission had not interfered in the design of the programme or nomination of participants. Scientists employed by, or linked to, the pharmaceutical industry had not been excluded and one of them was a workshop chairman. The steering committee had been asked to invite those persons whom they considered would be able to contribute scientific expertise on the subject, regardless of national origin. Furthermore, contrary to what was stated in the Canadian letter, no expertise or information was excluded. The steering committee had made every effort to obtain all relevant information, for example by announcing in international journals the possibilities for non-participating scientists to contribute to the debate. Finally, the European Communities rejected the suggestions that persons other than scientists should not have been invited to participate in the Conference. It was a matter of fact that the use of growth promoting hormones was a matter of concern and controversy and the EC Commission believed that it was right to consult policy makers and consumers as widely as possible on issues such as this.

(a) Article 1.1 of the SPS Agreement

4.23 **Canada** recalled that Article 1 provided, in part: "[t]his Agreement applies to all sanitary and phytosanitary measures which may, directly or indirectly, affect international trade". The EC measures had a profound and direct effect on Canadian beef exports to the European Communities.[35] The issue was whether the EC measures were sanitary measures within the terms of the SPS Agreement. Recalling that Annex A of the SPS Agreement defined a sanitary or phytosanitary measure to mean, in part, any measure applied "... to protect human or animal life or health within the territory of the Member from risks arising from additives, contaminants, toxins or disease-carrying organisms in foods, beverages or feedstuffs", Canada noted that contaminants included veterinary drug residues.

4.24 Canada claimed that during WTO consultations, the European Communities had not clearly indicated whether the measures at issue were sanitary measures within the scope of the SPS Agreement or technical regulations within the scope of the TBT Agreement. However, the European Communities had suggested that the legislator's intent could be found in the preambles to the Directives. The preambles to Directive 81/602/EEC[36] and Directive 88/146/EEC[37] suggested that one purpose of the measures was to address a concern for human health arising from the presence of hormone residues in meat. On this basis, Canada submitted that the EC measures were subject to the disciplines of the SPS Agreement.

4.25 The **European Communities** agreed with Canada that the measures challenged were better defined as measures falling within the scope of the SPS Agreement rather than the TBT Agreement. The European Communities noted that an essential link of the SPS disciplines with the regulatory freedom of the parties was that the measures applied were of concern to the SPS Agreement (and the WTO system) only if they affected international trade.

---

35 See para. 4.28.

36 The preamble to Directive 81/602/EEC states, in part:

"Whereas, due to the residues that they leave in meat, certain substances with a thyrostatic, oestrogenic, androgenic or gestagenic action may be dangerous for consumers; whereas these substances may also affect the quality of meat;

"Whereas, moreover, the harmless or harmful effects of the use of oestradiol-17β, Progesterone, testosterone, trenbolone and zeranol still have to be examined in detail; whereas, pending the adoption of a decision relating to these substances, the current measures governing them should be maintained as a precautionary measure with due regard for the general provisions of the Treaty."

37 The preamble to Directive 88/146/EEC states, in part:

"Whereas the administration to farm animals of certain substances having a hormonal action is at present regulated in different ways in the member States; whereas while their immediate effect on animals from the farmer's point of view is clear, assessments of their effect on human health vary and this is reflected in the regulations governing their use; whereas this divergence distorts the conditions of competition in products that are the subject of common market organizations and is a serious barrier to intra-Community trade.

...

"Whereas these distortions of competition and barriers to trade must therefore be removed by ensuring that all consumers are able to buy the products in question under largely identical conditions of supply and that these products correspond to their anxieties and expectations in the best possible manner; whereas such a course of action is bound to bring about an increase in consumption of the product in question...."

(b) *Article 2.1 of the SPS Agreement*

4.26 **Canada** argued that Article 2.1 set out a limited right to take sanitary or phytosanitary measures:

> "Members have the right to take sanitary and phytosanitary measures necessary for the protection of human, animal or plant life or health, provided that such measures are not inconsistent with the provisions of this Agreement."

Canada claimed that since the EC measures were inconsistent with Articles 2, 3, and 5, the European Communities had clearly exceeded this limited right.

4.27 Canada noted that a resolution of the European Parliament, an opinion of the Economic and Social Committee, and the Directives themselves, ascribed several additional purposes to the EC measures which were not contemplated or sanctioned by the SPS Agreement, such as harmonizing the regulatory schemes of the EC member States and thereby removing competitive distortions and barriers to intra-Community trade, meeting consumer anxieties and expectations, and bringing about an increase in the consumption of meat products (see paragraph 4.6). A consequence of these additional motives was that the EC measures were more trade restrictive than necessary to protect human life and health.

4.28 Canada argued that in particular with respect to the objective of encouraging intra-Community trade, the EC measures had proven successful.[38] The price of this success, however, had been paid by exporters such as Canada, who were effectively eliminated from the EC market as a result of the EC measures with respect to hormones, as shown by the following quantities in metric tons: 1984: 5,664; 1985: 4,853; 1986: 4,696; 1987: 3,836; 1988: 2,339; 1989: 648; 1990: 383; 1991: 162; 1992: 479; 1993: 223; 1994: 537; 1995: 287. As a direct result of the implementation of such measures in January 1989, Canada's exports into the EC market had suffered a 72 per cent decline.[39] This was from a level that had already been severely impaired by the implementation of the Third Country Meat Directive in 1987, as a result of which the European Communities had unilaterally abandoned the hitherto accepted practice of mutual recognition of national standards and had insisted that all EC trading partners comply with EC standards. The EC measures at issue and the Third Country Meat Directive had, moreover, both been applied more stringently and more precipitately to third countries than to EC member States.[40]

---

[38] Canada claimed that the production- and export-related measures taken under the CAP, the Third Country Directive and the EC measures at issue all combined to encourage intra-Community trade and boost extra-EC exports, while effectively blocking market access for exporting countries such as Canada.

[39] Canada noted that, based on a five-year average, the number of treated animals in Canada was approximately 76.8 per cent of those entering the food chain, and the number of untreated animals was 23.2 per cent. However, the percentage of exported meat and meat products that originated from treated animals would have differed from those figures because meat from treated steers and heifers is of higher quality than meat from untreated bulls and dairy cows, and Canada's exports of beef under the Hilton Beef Quota and offal for human consumption would have been constituted, in large part, by meat from treated animals.

[40] Canada explained that the EC Third Country Meat Directive required countries exporting to the European Communities to comply fully with EC standards. In contrast, Canada and many other

4.29 In the case of the EC measures at issue, third countries had to meet the EC measures or cease exports into the European Communities. Internally, however, abuses had continued since the measures had entered into force. Consumer anxieties, far from being addressed by the EC measures, had been exacerbated by persistent reports of illegal use of prohibited substances and the EC measures had failed to increase consumption.

4.30 Canada claimed that a major problem confronting the European Communities had been an imbalance in production versus consumption. According to a special report produced by the EC Court of Auditors:

> "A look at the trend in consumption and production since 1980 reveals that Community production, which, admittedly, is cyclical, has always, even at the lowest point of the cycle, exceeded consumption. This structural imbalance, which has persisted over a decade, is growing worse. The surplus needing to be disposed of every year on the world market has, over the past ten years, represented on average about 6 per cent of Community production, which is tending to grow at slightly less than 0,5 per cent a year."[41]

4.31 In 1992, the European Communities had undertaken to address some of these problems by launching a reform of the CAP. Even so, the Court of Auditors had opined that, in the beef and veal sector, "[i]n the long term, the structural surpluses will continue to be a problem, one which the 1992 CAP reform has failed to remedy in the slightest and whose extent is hardly likely to diminish either, unless corrective measures ... are implemented".[42]

4.32 Canada concluded that in the context of persistent over-production and declining consumption, there had been scant incentive within the European Communities to address the trade concerns of its trading partners. The impairment to Canada's trade must be assessed not only against the actual losses it had suffered as a result of the EC measures, but against its increasing export potential, as evidenced by Canada's total exports since the 1980s.

4.33 The **European Communities** rejected Canada's argument that the EC measures had been adopted in order to protect production from foreign competition. The reference to the divergence in the legislation of the EC member States which distorted the conditions of competition and affected free circulation of products in intra-EC trade (1st and 2nd paragraphs of Directive 88/146/EEC), was made for the sole purpose of justifying the need to take action at the EC level. Because of its internal constitutional structure, the European Communities was obliged to take action in

---

countries required an exporting country to meet equivalent, albeit not necessarily identical, standards. According to Canada, the Directive was applied to third country exporters sooner than to the EC member States. In the case of Canada, the Directive was effective 1986, when a first list of establishments eligible to export under the EC Directive had been drawn up. Even as late as 1991, however, most of the Mediterranean EC member States, as well as France, had not been forced to comply with the standards of the Directive.

41 Court of Auditors, Special Report No 3/94 on the implementation of the intervention measures provided for by the organization of the market in beef and veal, together with the commission's replies, (1994), *EC Official Journal* (C 356) 1, p.11.

42 *Ibid.*, p.18.

order to eliminate distortions in the conditions of competition and to increase free intra-EC trade.[43] The preamble of the Directive thus clearly explained that the underlying objective was to respond in a *harmonized way* to the effect of these hormones on human health. This objective, however, was not in itself independent or more important than the objective of safeguarding against risks to human and animal health resulting from the substances at issue. These first three paragraphs of the preamble of the Directive clearly indicated these objectives:

> "Whereas the administration to farm animals of certain substances having a hormonal action is at present regulated in different ways in the member States; whereas while their immediate effect on animals from the farmer's point of view is clear, *assessments of their effect on human health vary* and this is reflected in the regulations governing their use; whereas this divergence distorts the conditions of competition in products that are the subject of common market organizations and is a serious barrier to intra-Community trade;
>
> "Whereas the use of hormonal substances for fattening purposes should therefore be prohibited; whereas the use of certain substances for therapeutic purposes may be authorized but must be strictly controlled in order to prevent any misuse of them."

4.34 The European Communities further argued that action at the EC level was explicitly permitted by Article XXIV:8(a) of GATT. It submitted that when the European Court of Justice examined the object and purpose of Directive 85/649/EEC (invalidated on procedural grounds and subsequently re-enacted in Directive 88/146/EEC) it had noted that "the aim of the directive, according to the recitals in its preamble, is to *protect human health and consumer interests* with a view to eliminating the distortion of conditions of competition and bringing about an increase in consumption of the product in question" (emphasis added). The essential aim of the Directive, therefore, was found to be the protection of human health and of consumer interests. This protection was pursued with a view to improving the quality of meat through regulating the conditions for the production and marketing of meat. This objective, which was expected to increase consumption of the products, came within the objective of the Common Agricultural Policy. This justified action at EC level.

4.35 Furthermore, the European Communities asserted that the historical record clearly demonstrated that the purpose of the EC measures was to protect human and animal health from risks arising from the use of the hormones at issue for animal growth promotion. The European Communities noted that the European Parliament had proposed a ban on imports of meat from animals treated with growth promoting hormones primarily because "scientific information about these substances is far from complete and that considerable doubt therefore exists about the desirability of their use and of their effect on human health".[44] Serious health concerns had been clearly stated in different MEP reports, including the "Nielsen Report", the "Pimenta Report" and the "Collins Report", and the European Parliament as well as the Eco-

---

[43] The European Communities indicated that this obligation resulted from Articles 100 and 100A, in conjunction in this case with Articles 30 and 36 of EC Treaty.

[44] Point E of Parliament's Resolution. *EC Official Journal*, No.288, 11 November 1985, p.158.

nomic and Social Committee, had remained constantly opposed to the authorization of all these hormones for animal growth promoting purposes for reasons of possible hazards to human and animal health.

4.36 The European Communities rejected Canada's reference to the so-called EC third-country meat Directive which it considered to be irrelevant to this case. If Canada had any problems with the conformity of this Directive with the international obligations of the European Communities, it could of course complain to GATT and the WTO, but it had not done so. The increase in the EC intervention stocks of beef was unrelated to the objective and purpose of the challenged measures, because such high intervention stocks of beef did not exist in the EC member States that introduced the prohibition on the use of these hormones as early as 1961; such high intervention stocks of beef did not exist in 1981 when this prohibition was for the first time imposed at EC level; and such high intervention stocks of beef did not exist in April 1996 when the European Communities adopted Directive 96/22/EC which re-enforced the prohibition on the use of these hormones. The European Communities further submitted that the fact that the Directive offered equal access to the EC market for third-country meat was additional proof that there was no protectionist purpose in the EC measures. Statistics showed that the European Communities had continued to import about the same quantities of meat as before the application of the ban, it was, however, meat from animals to which hormones for growth promotion purposes had not been administered. The fact that the Court of Auditors' report found structural surpluses in the Common Agricultural Policy of the European Communities was nothing new.

4.37 The European Communities argued that the EC legislation in question did not impose a ban on Canadian meat or on meat from any other origin (i.e. it was origin neutral). Canada continued to export fresh meat not destined for human consumption. Canada also exported to the EC hormone-free meat products for human consumption on the basis of a mutually agreed arrangement. Furthermore, as regarded illegal use, the European Communities did not see what relevance this argument had to the case before the Panel. Canada was using the argument, sometimes used in favour of legalising or decriminalising the use of narcotic drugs by humans, to the effect that legalising some drugs discouraged the use of others. Whether or not this was the case was open to debate but it was not relevant to the present dispute. In any case, the European Communities was taking very seriously the situation as regarded potential illegal use of these substances for animal growth promotion. This was evidenced from the stricter provisions on detection, control and illegal use applied in the European Communities. Furthermore, Directive 96/23/EC tightened up controls and increased substantially the sanctions and penalties to be applied to persons found to act contrary to the provisions of EC law.

4.38 The European Communities also noted that there were several countries which did not allow the use of any or most of these hormones for animal growth promotion, but some of them did not impose any restrictions on imports of hormone-treated meat because they hardly imported any meat as their domestic production sufficed to cover demand. Argentina, for instance, did not allow the use of the three natural hormones for growth promotion (because residues of these hormones could not easily be detected), but did not apply a prohibition on imports of animals or meat treated with these three hormones as there were virtually no imports taking place. In contrast, the European Communities had always imported large quantities of meat and had to adopt the measures in question in order to ensure that the objectives of its domestic sanitary policy were not circumvented through imports from third countries.

4.39 The European Communities argued that its measures offered equal opportunities of access to the EC market for all third-country animals and meat from animals to which no hormones had been administered for growth promotion purposes. Of the 31 countries which were authorized to export meat to the European Communities, only six apparently allowed the use of some or all of these hormones for growth promotion purposes. All of these 31 countries (including Canada) had continued to export to the European Communities animals and meat from animals to which no hormones had been administered for growth promotion purposes. Thus, overall the same competitive pressure as before was maintained from third-country imports on domestic meat production. The intention of the EC measures at issue, therefore, was not to shield domestic meat production from foreign competition. The EC legislation did distinguish between countries which permitted the use of hormones for growth promotion and those which did not, but this was a justified distinction in view of the EC chosen level of protection, and the argument that its measures were a disguised restriction on trade, was unsubstantiated.

4.40 According to the European Communities, the Canadian exports of fresh and frozen meat (to the European Communities) for the years 1985 to 1995 were as follows: 1985: 312 tonnes, 1986: 571 tonnes, 1987: 457 tonnes, 1988: 28 tonnes, 1989: 7 tonnes, 1990: 87 tonnes, 1991: 106 tonnes, 1992: 25 tonnes, 1993: 40 tonnes, 1994: 53 tonnes, 1995: 58 tonnes.[45]

(c) Article 2.2 of the SPS Agreement

4.41 **Canada** noted that the SPS Agreement indicated the "Basic Rights" of Members in Articles 2.1 and 2.4, and the "Basic Obligations" in Articles 2.2 and 2.3. Article 2.2 set out three conditions:

> "Members shall ensure that any sanitary or phytosanitary measure is applied only to the extent necessary to protect human, animal or plant life or health, is based on scientific principles and is not maintained without sufficient scientific evidence, except as provided for in paragraph 7 of Article 5."

4.42 Canada maintained the EC measures were applied well beyond the extent deemed necessary *by the European Communities* to protect human life and health from comparable risks posed by antimicrobial growth promoters in feed additives, and the demonstrably greater risks posed by some veterinary drugs used for therapeutic purposes. Consequently, the EC measures were not applied only to the extent necessary to protect human life or health. In addition, the EC measures were maintained without sufficient scientific evidence, since study after study had confirmed that the six hormones in question were safe for use in growth promotion (see para-

[45] The European Communities indicated that these figures were based on Eurostat statistics. The figures provided by Canada included offal.

graph 4.134). Consequently, Canada claimed that the EC measures were contrary to Article 2.2.

4.43 The **European Communities** noted that Article 2.2 required that sanitary or phytosanitary measures must be based on *scientific* principles, as opposed to non-scientific ones, such as superstition. If a measure was aimed at reducing or eliminating a risk to health, then it must actually address that risk in a manner which could be scientifically justified. Canada had not shown that the measures complained against were not based on scientific principles. A logical consequence of the requirement for measures to be based on scientific principles was that they must not be *maintained* without scientific *evidence*. The European Communities claimed that all Members had measures in place before the SPS Agreement was drawn up, and in the absence of this requirement it could have been argued that the requirement for basing measures on scientific principles could not be applied retrospectively.

4.44 The European Communities noted that the SPS Agreement had not defined the term "scientific evidence" since its content was relative in terms of time and was dependent on the principles, methods, experiments and data used. What might be an acceptable scientific method for one scientist might not satisfy another, who might be more interested in certain other scientific principles or aspects totally neglected or partially examined by the first scientist. For that reason the SPS only required "sufficient", not clear or certain, scientific evidence.[46] The term "sufficient" was also nowhere defined in the SPS Agreement. The European Communities argued that it was generally agreed that sufficient could not mean other than the minimal level of scientific evidence required.

4.45 The European Communities noted that the SPS Agreement also required Members, in their risk assessment, to take into account "*available* scientific evidence" and argued that from the "available" scientific evidence, a Member was entitled to rely on that which its own scientists said was appropriate and sufficient and disregard other available evidence. It followed that neither the Panel nor any other Member might judge the adequacy of the scientific evidence upon which a Member based its measure in order to achieve its level of sanitary or phytosanitary protection[47]. For the same reasons, a Codex group of scientific experts could not judge the

---

[46] The European Communities argued that the term "scientific evidence" had a different meaning from the requirement to provide "evidence" in a legal trial.

[47] The European Communities noted that this had been explained in the US Statement of Administrative Action as follows: *"It is clear that the requirement in the SPS Agreement that measures be based on scientific principles and not be maintained "without sufficient scientific evidence" would not* authorize a dispute settlement panel to substitute its scientific judgment for that of the government maintaining the sanitary or phytosanitary measure. For example, by requiring measures to be based on scientific principles (rather than, for instance, requiring measures to be based on the "best" science) and not to be maintained without sufficient scientific evidence (rather than, for instance, requiring an examination of the "weight of evidence"), the SPS Agreement recognizes the fact that scientific certainty is rare and many scientific determinations require judgments between differing scientific views. The SPS Agreement preserves the ability of governments to make such judgments" (at page 90, emphasis in the original).

adequacy of the scientific evidence used by a Member.[48] In other words, if the "weight" of available scientific evidence indicated that a substance was not dangerous to human health, but another part of available scientific evidence indicated that there might be potential hazards to human or animal health, a Member was entitled under the SPS Agreement to take a precautionary approach and base its measure on the latter part of the available scientific evidence. It was sufficient if the government maintaining the measure had *a* scientific basis for it. However, the European Communities stressed that this did not mean that Members were obliged to demonstrate a scientifically confirmed adverse effect from a particular hazard before they might take measures.[49] The SPS Agreement could not have been intended to operate in such a way that Members must wait until people were actually sick or dying before being allowed to take measures.

4.46 The European Communities noted that the closest the SPS Agreement came to defining sufficient "scientific evidence" was in the footnote to Article 3.3, where the concept of a "scientific justification" was defined as follows:

> "For the purposes of paragraph 3 of Article 3, there is a scientific justification if, on the basis of an examination and evaluation of available scientific information in conformity with the relevant provisions of this Agreement, a Member determines that the relevant international standards, guidelines or recommendations are not sufficient to achieve its appropriate level of sanitary or phytosanitary protection."

It followed that scientific justification required an examination and evaluation of available scientific information, based on scientific principles. However, at the end it was still the prerogative of the Member in question to decide whether the international standard, guideline or recommendation was sufficient to achieve its appropriate level of sanitary protection. The level of protection was decided by the Member alone and it was not a judgment that must be based on scientific principles or scientific evidence.

4.47 **Canada** rejected the EC interpretation of Article 2.2, that "... neither the Panel nor any other Member of the SPS Agreement may judge the adequacy of the scientific evidence upon which a Member based its measure in order to achieve its level of sanitary or phytosanitary protection", as it would render the obligation in Article 2.2 a nullity, and violate the principle of effectiveness. "Sufficient scientific evidence" was not an empty requirement. It set a threshold that required more than deficient or scanty evidence. If the level of scientific evidence was insufficient, then a Member was entitled to adopt a provisional measure under Article 5.7. Canada noted that the European Community had stated that its measures were not provisional measures, so Article 5.7 did not provide an exception to the EC's obligation under Article 2.2.

---

[48] In support of its argument, the European Communities cited an article by D.A. Wirth (1994), "The Role of Science in the Uruguay Round and the NAFTA Trade Disciplines," Vol.27 *Cornell International Law Journal*, pp.817-859, pp.856-57.

[49] The European Communities noted that, for example, it had been recently reported that it was only now that scientists had discovered the mechanism by which smoking could cause cancer. But governments all over the world had long ago been taking measures to prevent or reduce smoking.

4.48 Canada agreed with and adopted the argument advanced by Australia that Article 11.2 of the *SPS Agreement* explicitly acknowledged that disputes may involve scientific or technical issues. In Canada's view, panels must be able to seek expert advice on these issues when it may be relevant to examining whether a Member has complied with its legal obligations. Indeed, the European Communities had suggested that such advice should be sought in the related US-EC Panel[50], and the experts chosen to assist in that case would also be providing advice to this Panel.

4.49 Canada submitted that the EC measures were maintained without sufficient scientific evidence, and were, therefore, inconsistent with Article 2.2.

4.50 The **European Communities** argued that in the Panel proceedings a number of scientists had explained their views on the potential dangers to human and animal health from the use of these hormones for growth promotion. However, none of the scientific experts advising the Panel had said that the experts advising the European Communities did not employ scientific principles in their research. Article 2.2 of the SPS Agreement did not require the best science nor the weight of scientific evidence to be taken into account; it only stipulated that there should be "scientific principles" and "sufficient" (not absolute) scientific evidence. For example, Dr. Lucier had agreed with the conclusions of the EC scientists that both the natural and synthetic hormones were carcinogenic at low levels (the natural hormones are carcinogenic even at existing physiological levels). Some of the scientists who attended the meetings of the Panel (and those of JECFA 1988) might not agree with the conclusions of the scientists advising the European Communities, but this was not relevant for the purposes of Articles 5.2, 2.2 and 3.3 of the SPS Agreement. What was important was whether, in the scientific research employed by the EC scientists (or the scientific reports to which they made reference in their reports), the *minimal attributes of scientific inquiry* were respected. The European Communities had not heard the opposite from any of the experts advising the Panel nor from Canada. Therefore, the European Communities was allowed to take into account its scientific views (or the views of the scientists to which it referred) in its assessment of the risks of these hormones for growth promotion.

4.51 The European Communities noted that the scientific principles on which the 1988 JECFA Report was based might also be said to be also part of available scientific evidence. But it was not necessarily the best nor the prevailing one. The European Communities was entitled to follow the other part of scientific evidence which showed that these hormones were dangerous to human and animal health when used for growth promotion.

(d) Article 2.3 of the SPS Agreement

4.52 **Canada** observed that Article 2.3 was based on the requirements of the chapeau of Article XX of GATT, clarifying that the point of comparison for "where identical or similar conditions prevail" included the territory of the Member taking the measure. Article 2.3 read as follows:

---

50 US-EC Measures Concerning Meat and Meat Products (Hormones), WT/DS26/7.

> "Members shall ensure that their sanitary and phytosanitary measures do not arbitrarily or unjustifiably discriminate between Members where identical or similar conditions prevail, including between their own territory and that of other Members. Sanitary and phytosanitary measures shall not be applied in a manner which would constitute a disguised restriction on international trade."

4.53 Canada argued that in *Reformulated Gasoline*,[51] the Appellate Body had reviewed the chapeau to GATT Article XX. Stressing the close relationship between the text of the chapeau and the obligation in Article 2.3, Canada submitted that the Appellate Body's interpretation of the requirement that a measure shall "... not be applied in a manner which would constitute a disguised restriction on international trade ..." was relevant to the present case. The Appellate Body had found:

> "Arbitrary discrimination', "unjustifiable discrimination" and "disguised restriction" on international trade may, accordingly, be read side-by-side; they impart meaning to one another. It is clear to us that "disguised restriction" includes disguised discrimination in international trade. It is equally clear that concealed or unannounced restriction or discrimination in international trade does not exhaust the meaning of "disguised restriction". We consider that "disguised restriction", whatever else it covers, may properly be read as embracing restrictions amounting to arbitrary or unjustifiable discrimination in international trade taken under the guise of a measure formally within the terms of an exception in Article XX. Put in a somewhat different manner, the kinds of considerations pertinent in deciding whether the application of a particular measure amounts to "arbitrary or unjustifiable discrimination", may also be taken into account in determining the presence of a "disguised restriction" on international trade. The fundamental theme is to be found in the purpose and object of avoiding abuse or illegitimate use of the exceptions to substantive rules available in Article XX."[52]

4.54 Canada claimed that applying this to the present case, a protectionist measure in the guise of a sanitary measure formally within the terms of the SPS Agreement was the essence of a disguised restriction on international trade. One indication that a measure had been taken for a purpose other than the purpose stated was that the measure was more restrictive than necessary. In the present case, the EC measures had been shown to be far more restrictive than necessary to achieve the level of protection achieved by comparable controls over the use of antimicrobial growth promoters and other veterinary drugs. This was not surprising because, as Canada had previously indicated, the relevant Directives, Resolution of the European Parliament and opinion of the Economic and Social Committee demonstrated that there were several additional purposes to the EC measures which were not contemplated or sanctioned by the SPS Agreement (see paragraph 4.27).

---

51 WT/DS2/AB/R, adopted 20 May 1996, DSR 1996:I, 3.

52 *Ibid.*, p. 23.

4.55 Canada claimed that in harmonizing their regulations on the most restrictive EC member State regulations, the European Communities had virtually eliminated all imports of beef from countries that permitted the use of growth promoting hormones, such as Canada (see paragraph 4.28). Canada submitted that the EC measures were more restrictive than necessary to meet a legitimate SPS Agreement objective, namely to protect human life or health. The EC measures were applied in a manner that controlled domestic production and effectively limited foreign competition, constituting a disguised restriction on international trade.

4.56 The **European Communities** argued that many different kinds of biological, chemical or physical hazards might occur in foods, and governments had to decide to what degree they aimed to protect their populations from these hazards. These decisions were taken, as were any political decisions, in the light of a number of factors including the potential danger to health and the cost and feasibility of achieving effective protection. For example, in the case of a fatally poisonous substance, or one which caused a very serious or fatal condition such as cancer, governments would generally set a very high level of protection, i.e. they aimed to avoid the presence of such a substance in food altogether. However, in the case of a lesser hazard, such as an organism which caused an uncomfortable, but transient and non life-threatening effect, governments might set a level of protection which aimed to minimize, but not necessarily eliminate, the presence of the organism in food. The European Communities stated that its level of protection in this case was no residue of these hormones in meat. This level resulted from the provisions of the EC Directives which prohibited the administration to farm animals, by any means whatsoever, of "substances having a thyrostatic action or substances having an oestrogenic, androgenic or gestagenic action"; or the slaughter or sale of any animal to which these substances had been administered, or of the meat or meat products from such animals. The aim of these provisions was to protect human and animal health by seeking a level of protection which required the presence of no residues in meat from animals to which these hormones had been administered for growth promotion. The European Communities noted furthermore that its measure applied not only to the six hormones in dispute, but to all hormones, substances and combinations thereof which exerted the above-mentioned action on all farm animals (i.e. not only on beef cattle). In reply to the Canadian argument that the level of protection in the case of these hormones was higher than the level of protection the European Communities applied against antimicrobial feed additives and therefore that the objective of the EC measures was to control domestic production and effectively limit foreign competition, the European Communities indicated that there was nothing in the text of the contested measures, the legislative history or in other document to suggest that the purpose for which the measures had been adopted was to protect EC production of meat from foreign competition (paragraphs 2.1-2.5 and ff.).

4.57 The European Communities argued that the "appropriate level" a Member decided to apply in its territory did not have to be expressed in the same technical fashion, i.e. as an MRL. International practice and the SPS Agreement left this choice to the Member concerned as a matter of policy. Thus, a Member might decide instead of imposing a stricter MRL to prohibit altogether the use of the substance in the first place, if this was the only "reasonably available alternative taking into account technical and economic feasibility that achieves its appropriate level of sanitary or phytosanitary protection and is significantly less restrictive on trade". The European Communities had continued to import about the same quantities of meat as it did before the implementation of the ban, with the difference that this was meat from animals not treated with growth promotion hormones. The EC measure did not, therefore, contravene Article 2.3. The European Communities argued that Canada had failed to discharge its burden of proof in this case. In particular, it had failed to establish that, in the face of the overwhelming scientific evidence that the use of hormones for animal growth promotion was potentially very dangerous to public and animal health, there were other type of *measures* which, whilst significantly less restrictive on trade, were capable of ensuring that the *level* of protection which the European Communities had chosen in this case (no residue of hormones in animals and meat) could be effectively achieved. Conversely, the Europeran Communities had gone through that exercise in 1984 and recently in April 1996 and decided that the prohibition on use of these hormones in animal growth promotion was the *only* measure reasonably available and less restrictive of trade. The European Communities noted that in Canada the administration of the implant at a site other than where recommended was not likely to be sufficient proof of adulteration under the Canadian Food and Drugs Act. The Canadian Drugs Directorate recommended that "the liver and kidney of animals implanted with these drugs in areas other than the ear shall not be permitted for sale as food". But as regarded the carcass of the animal, it recommended only that "all the area of implantation and any adjacent areas showing evidence of inflammation are to be destroyed". So, improper administration did not result in the rejection of the entire carcass from the food chain. It was only when an inspector believed that there had been administered products not licensed for use in Canada that the entire carcass was to be taken out of the food chain. The European Communities argued that not only were there obvious risks to human health arising from this type of policy, but there were practically no controls and checks for residues of these hormones taking into account the entire animal production destined for exportation or for human consumption in Canada. The Food and Drug Regulations of Canada (section B.01.046 and B.01.047) did not specify that food containing hormone residues was to be considered "adulterated", thus such food could be sold. Also section B.01.048 thereof listed only two drugs (chloramphenicol and its salts and derivatives, and a 5-nitrofuran compound) whose administration to animals rendered them and meat thereof unsuitable for sale. These facts alone justified the precautionary approach adopted by the European Communities, it showed the reasonable and proportional nature of its measures in the light of the risks involved, and underlined the failure of Canada to show that there was another type of measure available to the European Communities, equally effective and less restrictive on trade.

(e) *Article 2.4 of the SPS Agreement*

4.58 **Canada** submitted that Article 2.4 confirmed one role of the SPS Agreement as an elaboration of the rules for the application of GATT which related to the use of sanitary or phytosanitary measures, and in particular the provisions of Article XX(b):

> "Sanitary or phytosanitary measures which conform to the relevant provisions of this Agreement shall be presumed to be in accordance with the obligations of the Members under the provisions of GATT

which relate to the use of sanitary or phytosanitary measures, in particular the provisions of Article XX(b)."

4.59 Canada argued that since the EC measures did not conform to the provisions of the SPS Agreement, they could not be presumed to be in accordance with the provisions of GATT which related to the use of sanitary measures, and in particular Article XX(b).

4.60 The **European Communities** argued that under Article 3.2, if a sanitary measure conformed to a relevant international standard, guideline or recommendation, it was deemed to be necessary to protect human, animal or plant life or health, and it was presumed to be consistent with the relevant provisions of the SPS Agreement and GATT. However, the fact that a sanitary or phytosanitary measure differed from a relevant international standard, guideline or recommendation did not, in itself, create any adverse presumption concerning that measure. This was all the more the case when there was no such international standard (such as for MGA). The European Communities further argued that the fact that a measure in conformity with a Codex standard was deemed to be consistent with the SPS Agreement was one of the weaknesses of the SPS Agreement, given that many Codex standards, guidelines and recommendations were out of date, having been adopted decades before the development of sophisticated analytical methods.

(f) Article 3.1 of the SPS Agreement

4.61 **Canada** noted that other provisions of the SPS Agreement elaborated the basic rights and obligations set out in Article 2. Article 3 detailed the rights and obligations of Members with respect to harmonization. Article 3.1 provided that:

> "To harmonize sanitary and phytosanitary measures on as wide a basis as possible, Members shall base their sanitary or phytosanitary measures on international standards, guidelines or recommendations, where they exist, except as otherwise provided for in this Agreement, and in particular in paragraph 3."

4.62 For food safety, the standards, guidelines and recommendations established by the Codex applied.[53] In the present case, Codex had adopted MRLs for trenbolone and zeranol, but had not set MRLs for oestradiol, testosterone and progesterone because the estimated consumption of the natural hormones was well below any numerical value that would ordinarily be assigned to them.

4.63 Article 3.1 compelled the European Communities to *base* its sanitary measures on these international standards, except as otherwise provided for in the SPS Agreement. Canada noted that the definition of "base" (usually followed by "on" or "upon") was to "found or establish".[54] A summary of the MRLs allocated by the EC

[53] SPS Agreement, Annex A, para. 3(a).

[54] R.E. Allen, ed., "The Concise Oxford Dictionary of Current English", 8th ed., *Oxford: Clarendon Press*, pp.89-90.

Committee on Veterinary Medicinal Products[55] acknowledged that the EC measures were based on MRLs of zero for zeranol and trenbolone, and were not *based* on the Codex MRLs. Canada further observed that to comply with Regulation 2377/90/EEC, the European Communities was required to determine whether MRLs were necessary for the three natural hormones. The European Communities had determined that oestradiol-17β did not require an MRL (Regulation 3059/94/EC) but did not appear to have yet determined whether MRLs were necessary for the other two natural hormones.

4.64 Canada claimed that although MRLs were not sanitary measures in and of themselves, full acceptance of the Codex MRLs for residues of veterinary drugs in food dictated that distribution of food conforming with the MRLs "will not be hindered" by legal provisions.[56] Since the EC measures *prohibited* the distribution of beef treated with these products for growth promoting purposes, it was clear that the European Communities had not accepted these MRLs and had not *based* its measures on them.

4.65 The **European Communities** responded that international standards, guidelines or recommendations were based on a certain concept of level of sanitary protection. But a different level might require a different type of measure. This was what was applied by the European Communities in the case of the hormones at issue: the EC level of protection aimed to attain no residues in meat of these hormones, in other words, consumers should not be exposed to any level of added hormones in their food. To achieve this level of protection, the only reasonably available and least restrictive measure was to apply a prohibition on the use of these hormones for growth promotion. In the EC view, Canada had not shown that different measures were reasonably available to the European Communities. All that Canada argued was that the European Communities should have followed the Codex recommendations. However, the Codex recommendations were designed to achieve a level of protection which was lower than that applied in the European Communities.

4.66 Furthermore, the European Communities considered that the MRLs laid down by Codex were not *measures* but levels of protection and there was no obligation in the SPS Agreement to adopt Codex recommended levels of protection. The European Communities added that even the measures applied by Canada in its territory were not capable of respecting the level recommended by Codex because Canada tested

---

[55] R.J. Heitzman, ed., "Agriculture - Veterinary Drug Residues - Residues in food-producing animals and their products: Reference materials and methods" (Luxembourg: Office for Official Publications of the European Communities, 1992), p.4.

[56] Canada noted that the "General Principles of the Codex Alimentarius," Paragraph 6.A.(i), *Codex Alimentarius Commission, Procedural Manual*, 9th ed. (Rome: Secretariat of the Joint FAO/WHO Food Standards Programme, 1995), p.45 stated:

> "(i) *Full Acceptance*
>
> Full acceptance of a Codex maximum limit for residues of pesticides or veterinary drugs in foods means that the country concerned will ensure, within its territorial jurisdiction, that a food, whether home-produced or imported, to which the Codex maximum limit applies, will comply with that limit. It also means that the distribution of a food conforming with the Codex maximum limit will not be hindered by any legal or administrative provisions in the country concerned which relate to matters covered by the Codex maximum limit."

only a very small number of animals each year. For zeranol, for example, in 1996 it was foreseen that samples of only 650 animals would be tested. For trenbolone acetate samples of only 325 animals, for MGA samples of 275 animals, and for the three natural hormones samples of only 40 animals. The European Communities argued that no provision of the SPS Agreement obliged the European Communities to lower its level of sanitary protection; on the contrary, the preamble expressly stated that Members were not required to change their level of protection.

4.67 The European Communities considered that there was clearly scientific justification for its measures. The 1988 JECFA Report, on whose "scientific" advice Codex had based its recommended MRLs, had established an ADI for zeranol of 0 - 0.5 μg/kg body weight, and for trenbolone of 0 - 0.02 μg/kg body weight. The European Communities was therefore justified, in respect of zeranol and trenbolone, in accepting the lower limit, *i.e. an ADI of zero*. Codex had made no recommendation for MGA. For the "natural" hormones, it was known that they had adverse effects, which combined with a lack of knowledge of their action, lack of data on the effect of combinations and the lack of a definition of "good veterinary practice", permitted the European Communities to adopt a different level of protection, i.e. ensure EC consumers that there were no residues left other than the ones naturally produced by the animals themselves. In fact, as the scientific opinion of Dr. Liehr and the other scientists advising the European Communities in this case demonstrated, these natural hormones and their metabolites were most likely carcinogenic. The European Communities believed that, in view of the potential hazards to human health presented by the sources of risk referred to in paragraphs 4.151 to 4.209, these hormones should only be administered for the purposes and under the conditions defined in the EC Directives, which were in accordance with the 1993 "Codex Code of Practice for Control of the Use of Veterinary Drugs" ("Codex Code of Practice"). The European Communities further argued that the distinction between agents which acted as "tumour initiators" and "tumour promoters" was clearly over-simplistic and was no longer applicable to these hormones. This distinction permited some scientists to make another prediction by extrapolating tumour incidence observed in test animals at high exposure levels to potential human exposure to low levels of such hormones. However, as shown by Dr. Liehr, hormonal potency was not linked to its carcinogenic activity. Nevertheless, it was on this disputed extrapolation, based on the No Hormonal Observed Level, that JECFA had based its 1988 report and on which Codex had based its recommendations in July 1995. The European Communities argued that the JECFA report had been written in 1988, that it was based on research and experiments carried out about ten to fifteen years earlier, and that its recommendations were adopted by Codex only in 1995. There was a gap of about 18 to 23 years between the performance of the experiments and the adoption of the Codex recommendations.

4.68 The European Communities rejected Canada's statement that the Codex decision not to recommend ADIs and MRLs for the three natural hormones was because residues of these hormones were below any numerical value that would ordinarily be assigned and argued that JECFA could not propose an ADI because when it considered the matter, in the early and mid 1980s, the technology for measuring increases in levels of the natural hormones was not sufficiently advanced to be appropriate for routine use. The prohibition on the administration of natural hormones to animals for growth promotion was enforced in the European Communities in several ways. EC member States had been requested, in accordance with the conclusions of the Standing Veterinary Committee, to include testing on the natural hormones in their annual plans. Thus, they needed to carry out testing for natural sex hormones, in accordance with Directive 86/469/EEC, on *live* bovine animals at the farm or at the slaughterhouse in order to determine whether the levels of these hormones exceeded certain levels. For instance, for oestradiol or testosterone if levels exceeding the levels mentioned below were found in the blood plasma of at least one bovine animal, the measures and investigations provided for in Article 6, paragraphs 1, 2 and 3 of Directive 85/358/EEC[57] should immediately be undertaken:

- 17β-oestradiol:	male bovine ≤ 18 months	0.04ppb
	female bovine non pregnant ≤ 6 months	0.04ppb
- 17β-testosterone:	male bovine ≤ 6 months	10ppb
	male bovine 6 to 18 months	30ppb
	female bovine non pregnant ≤ 18 months	0.5ppb

4.69 In addition to the testing for oestradiol and testosterone, EC member States should control the use of gestagens in bovine animals for fattening, as there was a possibility of misusing gestagens as growth promoters or for camouflaging the application of oestrogens. More than 69,000 analysis of samples for the detection of natural hormones had been carried out by all EC member States during 1995. Moreover, in cases of suspected use, analysis of hormone levels in herds or groups of fattening animals might be used to confirm suspicion even when natural hormones had been used. This was because when these hormones were used for growth promotion this was done usually by administering female hormones to male animals and vice-versa. If, therefore, all or most of the samples taken from male animals showed high levels of female hormones there was a presumption that these hormones were not endogenous but had been administered. Taken in conjunction with other evidence which had given rise to the suspicion, such analytical results could confirm the administration of the hormones.

4.70 The European Communities further indicated that the prohibition was also enforced in practice by EC member States, who maintained controls on the manufacture and distribution of veterinary drugs and maintained surveillance of agricultural practices (Article 4 of Directive 88/146/EEC and now Article 9 of Directive 96/22/EC). Illicit use was deterred by the severe penalties imposed in cases of proven misuse.

4.71 With regard to MGA, the European Communities noted that it was authorized for growth promotion only in the United States and Canada, but apparently nowhere else. Codex had never scientifically examined this hormone and had never recommended any standard. Still, Canada in essence argued that the European Communities should accept meat treated with MGA and check only for residue limits as they were set by Canada. This argument flew in the face of the SPS Agreement, which explicitly allowed the European Communities to adopt a *level* of protection which it

[57] The European Communities drew the attention in particular to Articles 3, 6, 7 and 13 of Directive 96/23, which will enter into force on 1 July 1997.

deemed appropriate (no residue at all). The European Communities questioned whether Health Canada had conducted any new tests on MGA or had simply relied on American data from 1968.

4.72 As regarded Canada, the European Communities indicated that there were two violations reported in 1995/96. Although for MGA there was a withdrawal period of 48 hours prior to slaughter, it should not be taken for granted that this period would always be respected. There were many reasons which might lead to it being disregarded, including label dosage, absence of control by a veterinarian, the sudden spread of a disease or even fluctuations in market prices were some reasons which might precipitate slaughtering while active substances from implants or feedstuffs were still very high. Therefore, the European Communities might choose to adopt a *measure* which was no more trade restrictive than required to achieve its appropriate level of protection, taking into account technical and economic feasibility, i.e. a prohibition of use of MGA for animal growth promotion.

4.73 **Canada** noted that the European Communities had argued that "[t]he MRLs laid down by Codex are levels of protection and there is no obligation in the SPS to adopt Codex recommended levels of protection". Canada submitted that the EC argument was patently contrary to the obligation set out in Article 3.1: "... Members *shall base* their sanitary and phytosanitary measures *on international standards, guidelines or recommendations* ..." Codex adopted *standards* on oestradiol-17β, testosterone, progesterone, zeranol and trenbolone.[58] Thus, there was a clear obligation under Article 3.1 for the European Communities to base its sanitary measures on these standards.

4.74 Canada explained that an ADI was expressed as a range, signifying that an intake within the range would be acceptable. For zeranol, an intake of 0 μg/kg body weight would be acceptable, as would an intake of 0.5 μg/kg body weight. Codex defined an MRL *based on* the type and amount of residue considered to be without toxicological hazard for human health as expressed by the ADI.[59] As the EC MRLs for zeranol and trenbolone were zero ("no residues"), the European Communities had clearly not based its measures on the Codex standards, pursuant to Article 3.1.

4.75 Canada argued that the EC stated level of protection for the three natural hormones, "... i.e. ensure the EC consumers that there are no residues left over other than the naturally produced ones by the animals themselves", reflected a fundamental misunderstanding. Canada stated that this was not a level of protection, nor an MRL. The purported risk posed by residues of the natural hormones would occur regardless of whether the residues were produced endogenously or administered exogenously. Thus, the EC measures did not achieve a higher level of protection with respect to the natural hormones, as required by Article 3.3.

---

[58] ALINORM 91/31, Appendix IV and ALINORM 93/31, Appendix II, as adopted by the 21st Session of Codex.

[59] Codex Alimentarius, Vol. 3: Residues of Veterinary Drugs in Foods," 2nd. ed. (Rome: FAO, 1996) p.76.

(g) Article 3.3 of the SPS Agreement

4.76 The **European Communities** observed that the maintenance of a higher level of protection than that afforded by a Codex standard was explicitly allowed by Article 3.3 of the SPS Agreement. This Article provided an exception to the obligation to base SPS measures on international standards:

> "Members may introduce or maintain sanitary or phytosanitary measures which result in a higher level of sanitary or phytosanitary protection than would be achieved by measures based on the relevant international standards, guidelines or recommendations, if there is a scientific justification, or as a consequence of the level of sanitary or phytosanitary protection a Member determines to be appropriate in accordance with the relevant provisions of paragraphs 1 through 8 of Article 5. Notwithstanding the above, all measures which result in a level of sanitary or phytosanitary protection different from that which would be achieved by measures based on international standards, guidelines or recommendations shall not be inconsistent with any other provision of this Agreement."

A footnote to this paragraph provided that:

> "For the purposes of paragraph 3 of Article 3, there is a scientific justification if, on the basis of an examination and evaluation of available scientific information in conformity with the relevant provisions of this Agreement, a Member determines that the relevant international standards, guidelines or recommendations are not sufficient to achieve its appropriate level of sanitary or phytosanitary protection."

4.77 **Canada** observed that the first sentence of Article 3.3 could be divided into two parts. The first phrase set out a precondition for the departure from the relevant international standards: the Member's measures must result in a higher level of sanitary or phytosanitary protection than would be achieved by measures based on the international (Codex) standards. Any other departure was not contemplated. The second phrase presented two alternative justifications for such a departure: first, scientific justification; second, as a consequence of the level of sanitary or phytosanitary protection a Member determined to be appropriate in accordance with the relevant provisions of paragraphs 1 through 8 of Article 5. The footnote to Article 3.3 provided that there was scientific justification if "... on the basis of an examination and evaluation of available scientific information in conformity with the relevant provisions of this Agreement, a Member determines that the relevant international standards, guidelines or recommendations are not sufficient to achieve its appropriate level of sanitary or phytosanitary protection". Article 3.3 also required that the measures not be inconsistent with any other provision of the SPS Agreement.

4.78 Canada suggested that the two justifications (*i.e.,* situations) were similar, and complementary, but were intended to deal with two different situations. The first justification was intended to deal with situations where an international standard was outdated and needed to be re-evaluated, and that standard did not provide the level of protection it was thought to have provided. Thus, "... an examination and evaluation of available scientific information in conformity with the relevant provisions of this Agreement ..." (*inter alia*, Articles 5.1 and 5.2) revealed that the international standard was "... not sufficient to achieve [the Member's] appropriate level of sanitary or phytosanitary protection." The second justification contemplated a situation when a Member wished to maintain a higher level of protection than that afforded by the international standard, where the scientific analysis underlying the standard was valid. However, the second justification required that the different level of protection be ".... in accordance with the relevant provisions of paragraphs 1 through 8 of Article 5." This would include the risk assessment requirements set out in Articles 5.1 and 5.2, as well as the consistency disciplines of Article 5.5.

4.79 In Canada's view, the EC measures failed to meet these requirements for derogations from the obligation in Article 3.1 in four ways. First, with respect to the three natural hormones, the EC measures failed to provide a higher level of protection than would be achieved by measures based on the Codex standards. Since the levels of natural hormones in beef derived from untreated livestock varied widely, depending upon the sex, age and fertility cycle of an animal, the levels of these hormones in beef derived from hormone-treated livestock were well within the levels of natural variation. Since the European Communities did not regulate the exposure of consumers to higher levels of these hormones occurring in the meat of untreated animals, the EC measures failed to achieve any purported higher level of protection. Canada claimed that the naturally occurring hormones, whether endogenous or exogenous, were identical in chemical structure. The fact that these substances were administered exogenously had no bearing on whether or not they were carcinogenic. Thus the EC stated level of protection for the three natural hormones, "... i.e. ensure EC consumers that there are no residues left over other than the naturally produced ones by the animals themselves" was not a level of protection, nor even a MRL. The purported risk posed by residues of the natural hormones would occur regardless of whether the residues were produced endogenously, or administered exogenously.

4.80 Canada noted, furthermore, that the European Communities did not regulate the exposure of consumers to far higher levels of natural hormones occurring in a variety of foods. Second, there did not appear to be a scientific justification for a higher level of protection. An examination and evaluation of available scientific information in conformity with the relevant provisions of the SPS Agreement revealed that the six hormones in question did not present any harmful effects to the health of the consumer when used under the appropriate conditions as growth promoters in farm animals. Third, since the level of protection determined to be appropriate by the European Communities was *not* in accordance with the relevant provisions of paragraphs 1 through 8 of Article 5, the EC measures could not be a valid consequence of that level. Fourth, the EC measures were inconsistent with Article 5 of the SPS Agreement. Canada submitted, therefore, that the EC measures were contrary to Article 3.

4.81 The **European Communities** argued that the term "appropriate level of protection" appeared in Article 3. The SPS Agreement gave the right to Members, when introducing or maintaining their *measures*, to choose between measures which resulted in a level which was higher than that which would result by measures based on the international standards (Article 3.3), if there was scientific justification, or a level of protection which the member determined to be appropriate. The European Communities argued that the text of the footnote to Article 3.3 confirmed the power, which the SPS Agreement left to Members, to make risk management decisions that reflected societal value choices distinct from the strict scientific process of risk assessment. As it had been said : "the choice of appropriate level of protection appears to be the unilateral prerogative of each WTO member State ..."[60]

4.82 The European Communities observed that in both of the options provided in Article 3.3, which were available to a Member when taking a sanitary or phytosanitary *measure*, there must have existed "a potential risk for adverse effects". In other words, it was implicit that in order to need a level of protection there must have been some hazard against which a Member needed to protect. However, this only implied the *identification* of a hazard, not an assessment of the probability that it would cause damage. The SPS Agreement left Members free to define *the level of probability* they wanted to assume: this might range from zero to infinite; it also left them free to decide the *type of measure* they might choose to ensure that the level of protection considered by them to be appropriate was achieved. The approach adopted by the SPS Agreement was in conformity with previous GATT law and practice, and was a sensible approach for the purpose of establishing multilateral rules and disciplines to guide the development and progressive harmonisation in order to minimize the negative effects on trade from national sanitary and phytosanitary measures. The approach of the SPS Agreement was also in conformity with democratic regulatory procedures, where frequently a dichotomy was operated in the decision making process between: *risk assessment* and *risk management*. The first established strictly the scientific basis for regulatory action. The second (risk management) was the process by which the competent authority of a Member decided what action to take in the face on the assessment submitted to it by the scientists. Such action was based on factors such as public health and environmental protection, relevant legislation and legal precedent, application of social, economic and political values and consumer concerns. The risk management phase, therefore, in a democratic legislative system, expressly recognized the importance of societal value choices.

4.83 The European Communities claimed that this seemed to be also the view of Canada. In its Statement on Implementation for the Agreement Establishing the World Trade Organization (31 December 1994, Canada Gazette, Part I, page 4888), it was stated:

> "... Although it is not necessary for members to base their chosen levels of protection on risk assessment, they should work to minimize negative trade effects when choosing the level".

The above interpretation of the disciplines the SPS Agreement imposed on Members was apparently supported also by the United States, since when the USTR had presented the results of the Uruguay Round for approval to Congress it had stated :

> "The SPS Agreement thus explicitly affirms the right of each government to choose its levels of protection, *including a "zero risk" level if it so chooses. A government may establish its levels of protection by any means available under its law, including by referendum. In the*

60 D.A. Wirth, "The Role of Science in the Uruguay Round and the NAFTA Trade Disciplines", 27 *Cornell International Law Journal*, 817-859, at 826 (1994). The European Communities noted also that the US had put it as follows in the SAA: "In the end, the choice of the appropriate level of protection is a societal value judgment .... The SPS Agreement imposes no requirement to establish a scientific basis for the chosen level of protection because *the choice is not a scientific judgment*".

> *end, the choice of the appropriate level of protection is a societal value judgement.* The Agreement imposes no requirement to establish a scientific basis for the chosen level of protection because the choice is not a scientific judgement"[61] (emphasis added).

The European Communities wondered if Canada agreed with the above statement from the US Statement of Administrative Action.[62]

4.84 In response to the arguments of Canada that the EC measures did not meet the requirements for derogation from the obligation to base the measures on Codex's recommendations, the European Communities responded that it was not possible to limit exposure of its consumers to residues from the hormones occurring naturally in the meat of untreated animals. The European Communities did not know how one could regulate the levels of residues from naturally occurring hormones other than banning all meat and foods from human consumption, but assumed this was not what Canada was suggesting. This argument of Canada also disregarded the fact that hormones naturally occurring in animals and other foods had formed part of the human diet and had entered the metabolism of the human body throughout the course of human evolution. The naturally occurring hormones could not be compared with exogenously administered carcinogenic substances given to animals for growth promotion. As Dr. Liehr had said in his written opinion submitted to the Panel: "as the amount of hormone or metabolite necessary for tumour induction is not known, the amount of exogenous hormone or metabolite necessary for tumour induction in addition to unknown amounts of endogenous hormone or metabolite have not yet been determined".

4.85 The European Communities further contended that this argument of Canada also amounted to dictating the *type of measures* the European Communities should put in place in order to achieve the level of protection it alone might decide. But the SPS Agreement imposed no requirement to establish a scientific basis for the chosen

---

61 US Statement of Administrative Action, point 3(b).

62 The European Communities argued that the same applied also under the NAFTA agreement, whose Article 712, para. 2 provides:

> "*Right to Establish Level of Protection.* Notwithstanding *any* other provision of this Section, *each* Party may, in protecting human, animal or plant life or health, establish *its* appropriate level of protection in accordance with Article 715".

The European Communities indicated that Article 715 of NAFTA laid down a number of elements each Party should take into account in conducting risk assessment, including, *inter alia*, "relevant scientific evidence" (Art. 715(1)(b)). However, paragraph 3 of Article 715 made it clear that, in establishing its appropriate level of protection, each Party should only aim at minimizing negative trade effects and should avoid arbitrary or unjustifiable discrimination or disguised restriction on trade. The choice of the level and the measure to achieve the protection chosen, therefore, was not based on scientific grounds. For example, the former Canadian Minister for international trade, the honourable R. MacLaren had stated that :

> "The agreements [i.e. the SPS and NAFTA] make clear that governments remain free to pursue legitimate regulatory objectives, such as consumer safety and health protection. Every government may establish the levels of protection that it considers appropriate. In other words, nothing in either the North American Free trade Agreement or the World Trade Organization Agreement constraints a government from determining the degree of tolerance or protection it wishes." (Statement made during as address at Cambridge University,United Kingdom, 17 July 1995).

level of protection because the choice was *not* a scientific judgement. Canada's submission, therefore, in fact attacked not only the *level* of protection chosen by the European Communities, but also its measures, by insisting that residues of hormones above naturally present levels did not pose any risk to health and, therefore, did not warrant the application of any measures to control them other than MRLs recommended by Codex Alimentarius. If the Panel were to accept this line of argument, it would in the future be open to any country to oppose any health measure which was based on the precautionary principle. There were very few examples of health hazards where all scientists agreed on the degree of risk, and countries might be allowed to make judgments as to what degree of risk they were willing to accept. But the SPS Agreement recognized the fact that scientific certainty was rare and many scientific determinations required judgments between differing scientific views. The SPS Agreement preserved the ability of governments to make such judgments.

4.86 The European Communities stated that Canada's argument amounted to offering a solution to safeguard against the potential risk to human health from the use of these hormones for growth promotion which the European Communities had considered carefully but rightly rejected, because it did not meet its appropriate level of protection. The European Communities also noted that the MGA was authorized for growth promotion only in Canada and the United States, but apparently nowhere else. The Codex Commission had never examined scientifically this hormone and had never recommended any standard. In the view of the European Communities, Canada in essence argued that the European Communities should accept meat treated with MGA and check only for residue limits as they were set by Canada. The European Communities submitted that this argument would fly in the face of the SPS agreement, which explicitly allowed the European Communities to adopt a *level* of protection which it deemed appropriate (no residue at all). Therefore, the European Communities could choose to adopt a *measure* which was no more trade restrictive than required to achieve its appropriate level of protection, taking into account technical and economic feasibility, i.e. a prohibition of use of MGA for animal growth promotion.

4.87 The European Communities also observed that the remaining three reasons invoked by Canada in its submission were unsubstantiated, because there was a growing part of "available" scientific evidence which argued that these hormones were dangerous to human and animal health and the European Communities was basing its measures on this part of the available scientific evidence, as the SPS Agreement clearly allowed it to do. In its view, there were usually several ways of dealing with any given hazard, and the SPS Agreement did not require Members to change the *type* of measure they chose. For example, one of the many ways of tackling pathogenic organism in food was irradiation, and some Members allowed it to be used for certain foods. Codex had adopted standards for irradiation of foods but this did not mean that every Member was now obliged to allow irradiation of all foods. Similarly, if a Member had chosen a level of protection against a contaminant on the basis of an MRL, this did not mean that it should set its MRL at the level recommended by Codex. Also if a Member had chosen not to allow *any* residue of a dangerous substance in food, this did not mean that it was obliged to base its protection on the concept of an MRL recommended by Codex, if one existed for that substance. The maintenance of a higher level of protection than that afforded by a Codex standard was explicitly allowed by Article 3.3.

4.88 The European Communities claimed that the two situations referred to in Article 3.3 as "scientific justification" and "consequence of the level of sanitary or phytosanitary protection a Member determines to be appropriate ..." clarified the circumstances under which a Member may derogate from the provisions of Article 3.1. In order to understand properly the two possibilities envisaged, it was crucial to note the distinction between appropriate *level* of sanitary protection, on the one hand, and sanitary or phytosanitary *measures* introduced or maintained to achieve the level of protection, on the other. This distinction was important, because paragraph 6 of the preamble to the SPS Agreement made it plainly clear that harmonization of sanitary *measures* with international standards, guidelines and recommendations did *not* require Members to change the appropriate *level* of protection of human, animal or plant life or health which they had been applying before the entry into force of the SPS Agreement.

4.89 The "scientific justification" was applicable to the first type of measures. This followed clearly from the text of Article 3.3, which had a comma (,) after justification and then started with the word "or". A "scientific justification" existed when the international standard, guideline or recommendation was inadequate, faulty or obsolete from the scientific point of view. The footnote to paragraph 3 clarified this very well. The first situation appeared to concentrate on the scientific dimension of the international standard, guideline or recommendation. A Member might determine that measures based on an international standard could not achieve its level of protection, because such standard was based, for example, on only part of the available scientific evidence, or was based on faulty scientific evidence, or was out of date because it had been overtaken by more recent evidence, or was based on different climatic or environmental conditions than those prevailing in the Member concerned. The scientific justification referred only to measures, not to the level of protection. This was also in conformity with the other provisions of the SPS Agreement, in particular Article 2.2.

4.90 The European Communities further argued that an international standard, guideline or recommendation implied a certain level of sanitary protection. There might be several types of measures which could achieve that level of protection. The objective of the SPS Agreement was to harmonize such possible measures. But the objective of the Agreement was not to harmonize the level of protection a Member considered appropriate in its territory. Therefore, if the level of protection implied by the international standard and the level deemed appropriate by a Member were different, the measures to achieve that Member's level were also bound to be different, especially when its level was higher than that implied by the international standard.

4.91 The second situation clarified that a Member was in any case entitled to introduce or maintain measures which aimed at achieving the level of sanitary protection it deemed appropriate in its territory, and that such measures resulted in a higher level of protection than that which would result by measures based on the relevant international standard. In this case, when determining its appropriate level of protection, the Member had to comply with paragraphs 1 to 8 of Article 5. Paragraphs 1, 2, 3, 6, 7 and 8 dealt with the assessment of the risk and the type of measures a Member may take. Paragraphs 4 and 5 dealt with the issue of determining the level of protection. But paragraphs 4 and 5 did not indicate how the level of sanitary protection in itself was to be determined. The European Communities recalled its argument that the level of protection was not a scientific judgment and a Member was free to apply the level of sanitary protection it deemed appropriate in its territory. Paragraph 4 (which was not mandatory) and paragraph 5 (which was only an objective to be implemented through guidelines yet to be developed) attempted to place only certain constraints on the liberty of Members to implement the level of protection they had determined. In other words, they *should* (not *shall*) take into account the objective of minimizing trade effects and *shall* avoid arbitrary or unjustifiable distinctions in the levels, if such distinctions result in discrimination or disguised restriction on international trade. Therefore, none of the paragraphs of Article 5 dealt with setting the level of protection *per se*.

4.92 The European Communities observed that in 1989 the detailed provisions of the SPS Agreement were not in place and the GATT 1947 case law, in particular the Thai Cigarettes Panel report of 1990, had clearly acknowledged the right of Members to take sanitary or phytosanitary measures provided the provisions of the "chapeau" of Article XX were respected. On 1 January 1995, the WTO Agreement and its annexes had entered into force. Still at that time there were no Codex standards, which were adopted only in July 1995. The EC level of protection for these hormones had been the same both before and after the entry into force of the SPS Agreement. The 6th paragraph of the preamble of the SPS Agreement also provided that in harmonizing their *measures* to international standards *Members were not required to change their appropriate level of protection of human, animal or plant life or health*. Therefore, the SPS Agreement could not force the European Communities to change the *level* of protection it had been applying legally since 1989. If the *measures* of a Member did not follow international standards, there should be no negative inference that they violated the provisions of the SPS Agreement or GATT. The burden of proof was on the complaining party to establish the alleged violations. Since Canada argued that the European Communities had no scientific justification, it needed to prove *on the basis of the scientific evidence of today* how the European Communities could achieve its higher level of protection, if it had based its measures on the standards of Codex. The European Communities concluded that when it decided to maintain its *level* and its *measures* for these hormones, there was *no* international standard to compare them with. In addition, on 1 January 1995, the European Communities clearly had *a* scientific justification for its measures. In 1988, the European Communites had examined the available scientific information and found it deficient and inadequate to guarantee its level of sanitary protection. In addition, at the time of entry into force of the SPS Agreement, the European Communities had decided to maintain its *measures* because it was clear that the evidence on which the 1988 JECFA report was based out of date. At that time, the European Communities had decided that the *draft* JECFA MRLs were not sufficient to achieve its appropriate *level* of sanitary protection.

4.93 The European Communities claimed that the legal question of justification arose only after July 1995, when the Codex Commission adopted the recommended MRLs for the two synthetic hormones and decided not to adopt MRLs for the three natural hormones. The decision of the Codex Commission of July 1995 made no difference from the scientific point of view, because it was based on evaluation of scientific information dating from 1987 or earlier. This scientific information had been reviewed and evaluated several times by the relevant bodies of the European Communities as regarded these hormones for growth promotion; and the European Communities had constantly rejected it on scientific as well as other grounds. Such other factors included conditions of use of these hormones for growth promotion, potential for misuse, effectiveness of detection and control, synergistic effects, long-term exposure, etc. It should also be borne in mind that JECFA and Codex had never evaluated these hormones when used for therapeutic or zootechnical purposes.[63] The European Communities had decided again to maintain its *measures* in force because it had both a scientific justification and because its appropriate *level* of sanitary protection for these hormones was the same before and after that date, i.e. higher than that which could be achieved by *measures* based on Codex standards. The scientific information which had been emerging since the mid 1980's had reinforced the scientific basis upon which the European Communities had already decided to prohibit the use of these hormones for growth promotion. The newly emerging evidence supported clearly the view that these hormones (or at least some of them) were genotoxic and carcinogenic and, therefore, no tolerance levels could be fixed. As Dr. Lucier and the scientists advising the European Communities had said, the JECFA Report of 1988 was clearly out of date at that time. This report was certainly in need of review in July 1995, in April 1996 and even more today.

4.94 The European Communities explained that it had started the process of reviewing the scope of application of Directive 88/146 since 1993, in order to expand its application to new substances (like beta-agonists) and to reinforce its provisions on control, testing and, in particular, to increase the fines and penalties for violators. This reinforcement in the legislation was requested by the European Parliament, in the light of the reports it had prepared on these substances. Whilst this proposal was being discussed, the SPS Agreement had entered into force and, consequently, the European Communities had reviewed its *measures* and had decided to maintain the prohibition on the use of these hormones for growth promotion. While the proposal which had led to the adoption of Directive 96/22 was pending, the European Communities had also organized the 1995 Scientific Conference in December 1995, mindful of its international obligations under the SPS Agreement. This conference was in itself not a risk assessment, in the sense of Articles 5.1 and 5.2, because the concept of risk assessment, as explained, was much wider and encompassed the other elements mentioned therein. This was made clear from the discussion with the scientists. But on the basis of some of its scientific conclusions, together with the other pieces of scientific information which were already available on these hormones, and after consulting with the appropriate legislative bodies, the European Communities had decided to maintain the *prohibition* on the use of these hormones for growth promotion (i.e. it had decided to maintain the *measures*) and also to expand their coverage to other substances and to increase controls and the levels of fines. This

[63] The European Communities argued that it followed that the evaluation the European Communities had made in 1993/94 of oestradiol-17β for therapeutic or zootechnical purposes was totally irrelevant to this dispute, because it was not made for, nor did it affect, the risk assessment the European Communities had made for the five of these hormones when used as growth promoters.

was contained in Directive 96/22 of April 1996, which would enter into force on 1 July 1997.

4.95 In the view of the European Communities, Canada had to show on the basis of today's scientific evidence that the *measures* the European Communities maintained in place after July 1995 violated the provisions of the SPS Agreement. However, instead of using the scientific evidence of *today*, Canada had been using the scientific evidence of JECFA 1988 (and the much earlier evidence of the Lamming Committee reports). This scientific evidence was clearly *out of date*, as all the scientists advising the European Communities (and some of the scientists advising the Panel) had pointed out in their reports. As Dr. Ritter had said in one of his replies, "the *current weight* of scientific evidence *would, however, appear to continue to support* the view ... that at present there is no evidence for possible health risks to the consumer due to the use of the natural sex hormones for growth promotion ... ". But this was the personal view of Dr. Ritter about the current weight of scientific evidence. Since 1989, the scientific and legislative bodies of the European Communities viewed the weight of scientific evidence differently. The SPS Agreement did not require unanimity in deciding what was the relevant scientific evidence before a Member was allowed to take sanitary *measures*; people did not have to start dying before a preventive measure could be taken.

4.96 The European Communities considered therefore that it had done all it could to conform with its international obligations. It had reviewed the *measures* and had decided to maintain them, in accordance with the provisions of the SPS Agreement, because it had a scientific justification. The other grounds for maintaining them included conditions of use of these hormones for growth promotion, potential for misuse, effectiveness of detection and control, synergistic effects, long-term exposure, etc. It had also reviewed, even if it did not have to, its *level* of protection in this case, and had decided to maintain it as it was before the entry into force of the SPS Agreement with regard to the use of these hormones for growth promotion. It could not achieve its level of protection by other measures based on the standards adopted by Codex in July 1995, which would have been significantly less restrictive on trade. The extremely small number of controls performed by Canada and the number of violations still discovered within this extremely low number of controls demonstrated that there was no other measure which could achieve its level of protection and which was technically and economically feasible and, in addition, significantly less restrictive on trade. At least Canada had not been able to demonstrate the existence of such an alternative measure. The European Communities had also shown that any type of labelling in this case did not work.

(h) Article 5 of the SPS Agreement

4.97 **Canada** noted that an understanding of how scientists evaluate risk is essential to an overall understanding of the safety of veterinary drugs used in animal husbandry. Risk analysis had been defined by the Joint FAO/WHO Expert Consultation as meaning "... a process consisting of three components: risk assessment, risk management, and risk communication".[64] At the end of the process, a sanitary measure might be put in place to control an identified health risk(s). The type of measure chosen related to the severity of the risk and the least trade restrictive risk management option(s), as identified during the risk analysis process. In its most recent draft, Codex had defined risk as "... a function of the probability of an adverse health effect and the severity of that effect, consequential to a hazard(s) in food".[65] Codex acknowledged that hazards were present in food as a result of chemical contaminants (*e.g.*, pesticides and veterinary drug residues), microbiological contaminants, or naturally occurring substances (*e.g.*, toxins) found in food. These hazards presented a risk to human health. Risk assessment, which was one component in the risk analysis process, permitted an objective evaluation of these hazards.

4.98 Canada noted that the SPS Agreement required that a chosen sanitary measure be based on an appropriate risk assessment. ***Risk assessment*** was a process that recognized the inherent uncertainties in conducting a scientific evaluation of the effects certain hazards posed to human health. Thus, the risk assessment process was designed to be conservative and required extensive testing and analysis when evaluating potential human health hazards. Risk assessment was a specific component of the risk analysis process which, conducted by scientists, included well defined procedures that had been described by Codex and JECFA. In the most recent report of the Joint FAO/WHO Expert Consultation on the application of risk analysis to food standard issues, the risk assessment process was defined as having four components:

(i) hazard identification

(ii) hazard characterization

(iii) exposure assessment

(iv) risk characterization.[66]

4.99 Canada noted that risk assessment systematically organized scientific and technical information to answer specific questions about health risks and required explicit recognition that there might be some uncertainties, owing either to limits in the data, or to alternative interpretations of the data. Canada submitted the following explanation of the four components of the risk assessment process according to the Codex report.

4.100 ***Hazard Identification*** was the identification of biological, chemical and physical agents capable of causing adverse health effects, and which might be present in a particular food or group of foods.[67] Canada indicated that in dealing with

[64] "Application of Risk Analysis to Food Standards Issues: Report of the Joint FAO/WHO Expert Consultation, Geneva, Switzerland, 13-17 March 1995" (Geneva: WHO, 1995) p.6 [hereinafter: "Application of Risk Analysis to Food Standards Issues: Report of the FAO/WHO Expert Consultation"]. Canada submitted that this was the most recent comprehensive international report on risk analysis, but stressed that Codex definitions for risk analysis continued to evolve. In June 1996, Codex had issued revised definitions for interim use. These definitions were found in: Codex Alimentarius Commission, "Terms and Definitions Used in Risk Analysis," Joint FAO/WHO Food Standards Programme, June 1996, p.2 [hereinafter "Terms and Definitions used in Risk Analysis"].

[65] *Ibid.*, "Terms and Definitions used in Risk Analysis".

[66] "Application of Risk Analysis to Food Standards Issues: Report of the FAO/WHO Expert Consultation", *supra* note 64.

[67] "Terms and Definitions used in Risk Analysis", *supra* note 57.

veterinary drug residues, the goal was to identify potential adverse health effects in humans associated with exposure to a veterinary drug. The qualitative likelihood of such effects occurring in exposed human populations, and the certainty or uncertainty associated with such effects, were evaluated using available data. These data might be derived from a number of sources, such as epidemiological studies or animal toxicological studies.[68] If there was any evidence of a hazard, then the hazard characterization process of the risk assessment was undertaken.

4.101 ***Hazard Characterization*** was the qualitative and/or quantitative evaluation of the nature of the adverse health effects associated with biological, chemical and physical agents which might be present in food. For chemical agents, such as veterinary drugs, a dose-response assessment was performed.[69] Canada added that in all cases, the chemicals being considered for hazard characterization were present at very low levels in foods, that is, parts per million ("ppm") or less. Therefore, to obtain adequate sensitivity in humans, animal toxicological studies were often conducted at very high levels, sometimes exceeding several thousand ppm's.[70] A safe level or Acceptable Daily Intake ("ADI") was derived from the experimental No Observable Effect Level ("NOEL") or the No Observed Adverse Effect Level ("NOAEL") by applying an appropriate safety factor. When data from long-term animal toxicity studies were available, a safety factor of 100 was generally applied. Larger safety factors, up to 1000, might be used in certain cases. This meant that there was no significant risk if the chemical was ingested at or below the ADI and the likelihood of adverse health effects was notionally zero.

4.102 Canada submitted that traditionally, toxicologists have accepted the existence of thresholds for adverse effects with the exception of carcinogenicity. This was because *genotoxic carcinogenic* compounds had the ability to produce mutations in genetic material (DNA) leading to tumour formation. In recent years, however, it had been possible to discriminate between genotoxic carcinogens and non-genotoxic carcinogens. The latter were themselves not capable of producing mutations, although there might be an effect on cells that were already in the process of mutating. Hazard characterization now distinguished between genotoxic and non-genotoxic carcinogens.[71] In principle, non-genotoxic carcinogens might be regulated using ADIs derived from an experimental NOEL or NOAEL, and by applying appropriate safety factors (the "threshold approach").

---

68 "Application of Risk Analysis to Food Standards Issues: Report of the FAO/WHO Expert Consultation", *supra* note 64.

69 Dose response assessment was defined as, "...the determination of the relationship between the magnitude of exposure (dose) to a chemical, physical or biological agent and the severity and/or frequency of associated adverse health effects": "Terms and Definitions used in Risk Analysis", *supra*, note 57.

70 "Application of Risk Analysis to Food Standards Issues: Report of the FAO/WHO Expert Consultation", *supra*, note 64.

71 Canada explained that non-genotoxic carcinogens were referred to as "promoters"; that is, they did not cause cancer, but rather they could act as promoters in cells that had already been damaged. Non-genotoxic carcinogens were not capable of producing mutations. In contrast, genotoxic carcinogens were "initiators", and could cause mutations of DNA resulting in tumours in humans or animals.

4.103 For genotoxic carcinogens, the "NOEL-safety factor" approach was generally not considered a suitable method for setting ADIs. Two approaches were available: (i) to ban the chemical from commercial use, or (ii) to establish a level of risk that was sufficiently small to be deemed negligible or insignificant. For genotoxic carcinogens, in establishing a negligible level of risk, a quantitative risk assessment process was used.[72] This approach had been used to establish a MRL for carbadox, which had a metabolite that was a known genotoxic carcinogen. Carbadox was permitted for use in the European Communities as a feed additive. The first approach, to ban the compound, had been adopted by several countries, including the European Communities, for nitrofurans, which were also known genotoxic carcinogens.

4.104 ***Exposure Assessment*** was the qualitative or quantitative evaluation of the likely intake of biological, chemical or physical agents via food, as well as exposures from other sources if relevant.[73] Canada explained that this was usually done by examining the dietary intake of foods and determining if the theoretical dietary intake was below the recommended ADIs.

4.105 ***Risk Characterization*** was the qualitative and/or quantitative estimation of the probability of occurrence, and severity, of known or potential adverse health effects in a given population based on hazard identification, hazard characterization and exposure assessment.[74]

4.106 Canada indicated that *risk management* had been defined by Codex as "... the process of weighing policy alternatives in the light of the results of risk assessment and, if required, selecting and implementing appropriate control options, including regulatory measures".[75] It was the view of the Joint FAO/WHO Expert Consultation that "... risk assessment of chemical hazards in foods usually results in the selection of risk management options to ensure that foodborne risks to consumers are not appreciable ('notionally zero')".[76] The setting of MRLs was a risk management option that was commonly used in controlling the risks arising from chemical contaminants (*e.g.*, veterinary drugs) in foods. Coupled with monitoring and testing programs, it was an example of a comprehensive sanitary control measure that could be used to manage risk effectively.

4.107 Canada noted that *risk communication* was defined by Codex as, "[t]he interactive exchange of information and opinions concerning risk among risk assessors risk managers, consumers and other interested parties".[77] Canada submitted that risk communication must take place at all stages of the risk analysis process to ensure

72 "Application of Risk Analysis to Food Standards Issues: Report of the FAO/WHO Expert Consultation", *supra*, note 64.

73 "Terms and Definitions used in Risk Analysis," *supra*, note 64.

74 *Ibid.*

75 Codex Alimentarius Commission, "Risk Analysis: Definitions, Procedures and Principles, Joint FAO/WHO Food Standards Programme, Codex Committee on General Principles - Twelfth Session", Paris, France, 25-28 November 1996 p.18 (hereinafter "Risk Analysis: Definitions, Procedures and Principles").

76 "Application of Risk Analysis to Food Standards Issues: Report of the FAO/WHO Expert Consultation", *supra*, note 64.

77 "Risk Analysis: Definitions, Procedures and Principles".

open, balanced and meaningful discourse between science experts, policy makers, farmers, industry, consumers and all other interested parties.

4.108 The **European Communities** argued that the scientific evidence on which hormone growth promoters were approved, most of it gathered by drug companies and still secret, was obtained using primitive techniques which would not be acceptable today. For example, the Codex decision of 1995 on the growth promoting hormones had been taken on the basis of scientific papers dating back to the 1940s and, in one case, to 1939. The European Communities argued that the system described under "Application of Risk Analysis to Food Standards issues" had not been approved by Codex. The whole subject of risk analysis had been under discussion in various bodies of Codex for several years but, precisely because there was no international consensus on the subject, nothing had been agreed. Codex had not even been able to agree definitions of the various terms used, let alone procedures for their application. At the Codex Committee on General Principles (Paris, November 1996) it had been agreed to forward a draft list of definitions to the Codex Alimentarius Commission meeting in 1997 for it to agree to their use on an interim basis, pending further clarification. The European Communities submitted that a measure might be applied to protect against a suspected hazard, not only against "an identified health risk" as claimed by Canada. The type of measure need not relate to the severity of the risk, nor need it be the least trade restrictive option. The criteria for the choice of measures were set out in the SPS Agreement, which did not mention the "severity" of the risk. The same type of measure might be used for risks of different severity: for example vaccination was a measure widely used against risks of very different severity.

4.109 The question of trade-restrictiveness was addressed in Article 5.6, which did not require the "least" trade-restrictive option; it required Members to ensure that their measures were "not more trade-restrictive than required to achieve their appropriate level of sanitary or phytosanitary protection, taking into account technical and economic feasibility". In the case of growth hormones, it might appear to be least trade-restrictive to allow trade in all meat from treated animals as long as no residues were present in it. However, once the technical and economic problems of ensuring the absence of residues (control over supply and use, testing of meat, etc.) were taken into account, this option would in fact be more trade-restrictive than the measures applied by the European Communities.

4.110 Noting that there was a perfectly satisfactory definition of risk assessment already in the SPS Agreement, Annex A(4), which expressed risk as "the potential for adverse effects", the European Communities noted that disease and death were not the only adverse health effects which might result from the presence of a residue in food - there might also be unwanted physiological consequences. For example, the European Court of Justice, having referred explicitly to the constitution of the WHO, which defined health as "a state of complete physical, mental and social well-being that does not consist only in the absence of illness or infirmity", had concluded that a broad interpretation should be given accordingly to the concept of health contained in a provision of EC law.[78]

4.111 The European Communities recalled that there was no internationally agreed objective, scientific process which could deliver a mathematically precise risk assessment. The statement in Canada's submission that "there may be some uncertainties" was an understatement, particularly in the assessment of biological hazards to human health where direct testing on humans was not possible and individuals varied greatly in their responses to substances. Hazard identification consisted of exactly that - *identification* of a hazard. The processes of evaluating the likelihood (exposure assessment) and severity of effects (risk characterization) were later stages in risk assessment. The reason Canada tried to introduce these later steps into the hazard identification was that a Member needed only identify a hazard in order to set a level of protection. The SPS Agreement did not require a further assessment of the hazard in quantitative terms, as Canada pretended, in order for a Member to decide that it did not want any of the hazard present in its food.

4.112 The European Communities further argued that a dose-response assessment could not be made for all chemicals in all circumstances. This was the case, for instance for genotoxic substances. It was not correct to assume that the chemicals under consideration were always present only at "very low levels in foods". In some situations, for example implant sites of hormones, they might be present at quite high levels. Finally, the concept that toxicity testing in animals was a valid test of toxicity in humans was not a "principle": it was an assumption based on extrapolations which in the past had not always been justified (e.g. thalidomide, DES, etc.).

4.113 The European Communities noted that on the question of genotoxic carcinogens Canada submitted quotes from page 17 of the Report of the Joint FAO/WHO Expert Consultation on the Application of Risk Analysis to Food Standards Issues, in support of their statement that a quantitative risk assessment "is used" to establish a "negligible or insignificant" risk. However, page 18 of that Report went on to state that, with respect to this approach: "It is acknowledged by many regulatory agencies that actual or probable human risks are not being predicted.", and ".... the choice of a risk level is ultimately a risk management decision for each country to decide."

4.114 The European Communities added that the setting of MRLs was not a "measure" in itself. An MRL was a level of protection - the monitoring, testing and control programmes to enforce the MRL were the "measures" in the sense of the SPS Agreement. The European Communities added that it was interesting to read that Canada was now in favour of "open, balanced and meaningful discourse between scientific experts, policy makers, farmers, industry, consumers and all other interested parties". This was in sharp contrast to the criticism which it made of the EC 1995 Scientific Conference, where it considered that the participation of "non-scientific representatives of various interest groups" led to a "biased process with questionable conclusions".

---

[78] Case C-84/94, *United Kingdom v. Council, judgment* of 12 November 1996 (1996 ECR I-5800, para. 15).

4.115 The European Communities also argued that the 1988 JECFA Report had found that there was a potential risk to human health, because if there were no such potential risk, the JECFA would not have recommended any ADI and MRL for the two synthetic hormones. For the three natural hormones, JECFA had not recommended an ADI and MRL because of problems in detecting the level of residues in the meat on a routine basis.

4.116 The European Communities noted in this regard that scientists had said that "the ADI-model is not a risk model and does not predict the risk of the occurrence of adverse effects, when ADI-values are exceeded".[79] The same was basically true for the MRL-model "which specifies the quantity of a particular residue in meat that, even in dietary extremes, would not exceed the ADI for the particular substance concerned".[80] The European Communities concluded that the MRL was based on the notion that there was a risk, but if the proposed threshold was observed the *probability* of the adverse effect arising from the use of hormones would not materialize. In this case, the JECFA recommended standards would achieve "a level of protection" against the risk. But the SPS Agreement allowed Members to determine *another* level, i.e. the level *they* deemed appropriate. This level might be higher or lower.

4.117 **Canada** recalled that *level of protection* (or level of risk) described the probability of an adverse health effect arising from a certain source. The *appropriate* level of protection (or acceptable level of risk) was the level deemed appropriate (or acceptable) by a Member. It was clear that the European Communities were not unfamiliar with the notion of expressing a level of protection, and its appropriate level of protection, in these terms (paragraph 4.124). However, the European Communities described its appropriate level of sanitary protection in this case to be "... no residues of these hormones in meat destined for human consumption"[81] and had clarified this statement, claiming that it was equivalent to setting maximum residue limits ("MRLs") of zero for the six hormones at issue. Canada rejected the EC argument that MRLs were levels of protection. MRLs did not describe the level of risk that a Member would accept, but, were sanitary measures used to *achieve* an appropriate level of protection from a particular sanitary risk.

4.118 Canada observed that the European Communities had implicitly admitted the difference between a MRL and an appropriate level of protection: "... a member may decide instead of imposing a stricter MRL to prohibit altogether the use of the substance in the first place, if this is the only 'reasonably available alternative taking into account technical and economic feasibility that achieves its appropriate level of sanitary or phytosanitary protection and is significantly less restrictive on trade'".[82] A prohibition on the use of a substance was a sanitary measure used to achieve an appropriate level of protection. In comparing a "stricter MRL" with another sanitary

[79] H.A. Kuiper, "Risk Assessment Strategies for Xenobiotics", *1995 EC Scientific Conference Proceedings*, p.375.

[80] "Report and Conclusions", *1995 EC Scientific Conference Proceedings*, p.4.

[81] Canada noted that the European Communities had also stated that its level of protection with respect to the three natural hormones was to "... ensure the EC consumers that there are no residues left over other than the naturally produced ones by the animals themselves".

[82] Para. 4.57.

measure, it was clear that the European Communities acknowledged that an MRL was a sanitary measure. Canada submitted that the European Communities had failed to articulate a meaningful appropriate level of protection with respect to the purported risk resulting from the presence of hormone residues, including their metabolites, in the meat from animals treated with the six hormones at issue.

4.119 Canada noted that the EC discussion of appropriate level of protection was inaccurate in several respects. First, as a technical matter, the EC terminology was not accurate. Probability ranged from zero (no occurrences) to one (occurrence). It was often expressed as a fraction or a percentage. It could not, however, be greater than one, let alone infinite. Second, while a Member might define the level of probability it wanted to assume (acceptable level of risk), it was clear that in fashioning a measure to meet that level of protection, it was not sufficient merely to identify a hazard. There must be an assessment of the probability that the hazard would cause adverse health effects. This "risk characterization" was an essential part of risk assessment[83], and was integral to the risk assessment obligation set out in Article 5.1. Without this information, the measure taken to achieve the level of protection might well be more trade restrictive than required.[84] Finally, while it was up to a Member to decide on the type of measure used to ensure that the appropriate level of protection was achieved, Article 5.6 and Article 2.2 put limits on the measure chosen.

4.120 The **European Communities** responded that its level of protection in the case of these hormones when used for growth promotion in other countries was no residues in meat destined for human consumption. Many different kinds of biological, chemical or physical hazards might occur in foods, and governments had to decide to what degree they would attempt to protect their populations from these hazards. These decisions were taken, as were any political decisions, in the light of a number of factors including the potential danger to health and the cost and feasibility of achieving effective protection. There would obviously also be differences between governments in their approach to setting a level of protection, as a function of their economic priorities and cultural habits. For example, a developed country might consider it desirable to set a high level of protection against contamination of foods by waste material from the chemical industry, whereas a developing country might consider it a higher priority to encourage the establishment of a chemical industry rather than, for the present, to worry about chemical residues in food. This was particularly the case for countries where food *supply* was more of a problem than food *quality*. Similarly, cultural habits such as the eating of certain foods in a raw state might cause a government to set a higher level of protection against certain pathogens than would be the case for a government whose population tended to cook the same food thoroughly before eating it. The European Communities concluded that for economic and cultural reasons such as these, the decision on where to set the level of protection was not a purely scientific one, and it was not one which could be subject to international rules, given the great diversity among Members. The European Communities argued that the "appropriate level" a member decided to apply in its territory did not

[83] Canada explained that this was risk characterization, as explained in para. 4.105.

[84] Canada submitted that if there was no probability that a hazard would cause damage, there was no need for a sanitary measure.

have to be expressed in the same technical fashion, i.e. as an MRL. International practice and the SPS Agreement left this choice to the Member concerned as a matter of policy. Thus, a member might decide instead of imposing a stricter MRL to prohibit altogether the use of the substance in the first place, if this was the only "reasonably available alternative taking into account technical and economic feasibility that achieves its appropriate level of sanitary or phytosanitary protection and is significantly less restrictive on trade". The European Communities further argued that its level of protection in the case of these hormones when used for growth promotion in other countries was no residues in meat destined for human consumption; it failed to see what was the difference between a level of protection set at no residues from a level of protection set at zero MRLs for these substances. Moreover, it appeared that Canada had fixed a "zero" tolerance level for MGA in horse meat.

4.121 The European Communities argued that there was apparently a profound difference between Canada and itself on the definition of the concept of risk assessment for the purposes of Article 5 of the SPS Agreement. In the EC view, the concept of risk assessment was composed of two parts: the *scientific assessment of the risk* and the *management of that risk*. In the management of the risk, elements other than strict science enter into consideration such as those in Article 5.2. The term "appropriate level of protection" appeared in Article 3 of the SPS Agreement. The European Communities considered that there must exist "a potential risk for adverse effects", i.e. it was implicit that in order to need a level of protection there must be some hazard against which a Member needs to protect. However, this only implies the *identification* of a hazard, not an assessment of the probability that it would cause damage. The SPS Agreement left Members free to define *the level of probability* they wanted to assume: this might range from zero to infinite; it also left them free to decide the *type of measure* they might choose to ensure that the level of protection they considered to be appropriate was achieved. The approach of the SPS Agreement was also in conformity with democratic regulatory procedures, where frequently a dichotomy was operated in the decision making process between *risk assessment* and *risk management*. The first established strictly the scientific basis for regulatory action. The second (risk management) was the process by which the competent authority of a Member decided what action to take in the face on the assessment submitted to it by the scientists. Such action was based on factors such as public health and environmental protection, relevant legislation and legal precedent, application of social, economic and political values and consumer concerns. In a democratic legislative system, the risk management phase, therefore, expressly recognized the importance of social value choices.

(i) Articles 5.1 and 5.2 of the SPS Agreement

4.122 **Canada** recalled that Article 5:1 read as follows:

> "Members shall ensure that their sanitary or phytosanitary measures are based on an assessment, as appropriate to the circumstances, of the risks to human, animal or plant life or health, taking into account risk assessment techniques developed by the relevant international organizations."

Canada emphasized that the essence of this obligation was that when a Member devised and maintained a sanitary or phytosanitary measure to attain an appropriate level of sanitary or phytosanitary protection, the measure must be based on a risk assessment. In this case, the risk assessment would be an evaluation of the potential for adverse effects on human health arising from the presence of hormone residues in meat. Canada claimed that it had been unable to find any evidence of the European Communities having undertaken an appropriate assessment of the risk to human life or health arising from the presence of residues in beef from the six hormones in question. In the WTO consultations, the European Communities had stated that the work of the Lamming Group constituted a risk assessment for their measures. Referring to the terms of reference and the conclusions of the Lamming Group (paragraph 2.28) Canada recalled that the Group had been suspended before it could render a final report on zeranol and trenbolone (see paragraph 4.7). Thus, the work of the Lamming Group could at best be considered a risk assessment only of the three natural hormones.[85] In the absence of a final report, the European Communities did not appear to have based its prohibition on the use of zeranol or trenbolone on any risk assessment. Even if the Lamming Report constituted a risk assessment for the three natural hormones, its conclusions had been that these hormones would *not* present any harmful effects to the health of the consumer when used under the appropriate conditions as growth promoters in farm animals. Professor Lamming, the Chairman of the Group, had himself asserted that the EC measures could not be *based* on that risk assessment.[86] Moreover, it would appear that the European Communities had never conducted a risk assessment of MGA. Canada noted that during the WTO consultations, the European Communities had also stated that it was reviewing its measures, and that the 1995 EC Scientific Conference constituted the beginning of a long process of re-evaluation. Thus, the EC ban was not based on a risk assessment of these hormones when used for growth promoting purposes, and the requirements of Article 5.1 had not been met.

4.123 The **European Communities** responded that the SPS Agreement required Members to take into account risk assessment techniques developed by relevant international organizations; however, Codex was far from developing any such techniques as it was still trying to agree on definitions. The European Communities recalled that "assessment of the risk" was defined in Annex A to the SPS Agreement as follows: "the evaluation of the potential for adverse effects on human or animal health arising from the presence of additives, contaminants, toxins or disease causing organisms in food, beverages or feedstuffs". The European Communities noted that there were, therefore, three different concepts to distinguish: the "adverse effect", the "risk" and its "assessment". For assessing the risk, Article 5.2 provided that:

> "Members shall take into account available scientific evidence, relevant processes and production methods; relevant inspection, sampling and testing methods; prevalence of specific diseases or pests; exis-

[85] The members of the group subsequently published an assessment of zeranol and trenbolone: see G.E. Lamming *et al.*, "Special Report: Scientific report on anabolic agents in animal production", *Veterinary Record* (24 October 1987) p.389.

[86] G.E. Lamming, "Anabolic Growth Promotants and the EEC" (Address given at the Technical Services Centre, Kingston, ACT, 29 April 1986) [unpublished], p.11.

tence of pest-or disease -free areas; relevant ecological and environmental conditions; and quarantine or other treatment."

4.124 The European Communities argued that the concept of "*risk assessment*", in the SPS Agreement was predominantly a scientific process. Its purpose was to establish *the strictly scientific basis* for the regulatory measure the Member would take. There was apparently a profound difference between Canada and the European Communities on the definition of the concept of risk assessment for the purposes of Article 5. In the view of the European Communities, the concept of risk assessment was composed of two parts: the *scientific assessment of the risk* and the *management of that risk*. In the management of the risk, elements other than strict science entered into consideration, such as those mentioned above in paragraph 2 of Article 5. Moreover, the SPS Agreement did not prescribe a *quantitative* risk assessment. A risk assessment might help in setting a standard designed to limit the probability that a human developed cancer after a lifetime of exposure to a particular chemical substance to no more than one chance in a million (1/1,000,000 chance). By contrast, the choice of the 1/1,000,000 *goal*, as opposed to 1/1,000 or 1/100 or zero chance, was a choice of public policy (not of scientific nature). The phrase "as appropriate to the circumstances" in the EC view must refer to the "circumstances" of the Member carrying out the risk assessment. In the case of the European Communities, assessment of risk was part of the complex EC legislative process, with its comprehensive consultations, checks and balances involving a proposal by the EC Commission, the opinions of the Economic and Social Committee and the European Parliament, and the adoption by the Council of Ministers.

4.125 The European Communities disagreed with Canada's account of the arguments of the parties during the consultations. It stressed that the risk assessment carried out for EC Directives 81/602, 88/146 and 96/22 had been based on following scientific evidence:

(i) the 1982 Report of the Scientific Veterinary Committee, Scientific Committee for Animal Nutrition and the Scientific Committee for Food on the basis of the Report of the Scientific Group on Anabolic Agents in Animal Production (the "Lamming Report");

(ii) the 1983 OIE Scientific Conference Report;

(iii) the 1987 JECFA Report;

(iv) various works of relevant international institutions, such as the International Agency for Research on Cancer (IARC);

(v) scientific works by individual scientists relevant to the issue of use of hormones in general and for animal growth in particular; and

(vi) information on the use of these hormones for growth promotion available from other countries, when relevant.

4.126 For the adoption of Directive 96/22 of 29 April 1996, the 1995 EC Scientific Conference Proceedings had also been taken into account. All these scientific data, reports, papers, conferences and other relevant information constituted a body of scientific evidence which had been carefully considered by the competent EC institutions and by EC member States. Furthermore, for the adoption of Directives 81/602/EEC, 88/146/EEC and 92/22/EC, apart from the above scientific evidence, additional scientific and technical information had been taken into account. This information (see paragraphs 4.14, 4.19 and 4.20) consisted mainly of the internal studies of the EC Commission, the reports of the European Parliament, the reports of the Economic and Social Committee and the deliberations of the Council of Ministers. For their deliberations, the Ministers were assisted by scientific groups and individual scientific experts, including experts from the relevant administrations of the EC member States.

4.127 The competent EC institutions had performed a risk assessment in the sense of Articles 5:1 to 5:6 of the SPS Agreement by taking into account the available scientific evidence of risks to humans and animals; relevant processes and production methods; and relevant inspection, sampling and testing methods. These latter two elements confirmed that risk assessment for the purposes of the SPS Agreement was not a purely scientific matter; the practicalities of actual application must also be taken into account.

4.128 The European Communities observed that *none* of the available scientific reports had concluded in favour of an unqualified use of these hormones for animal growth promotion. Some of these reports had concluded that all of these hormones individually were not likely to pose risks to human or animal health, if used in accordance with good agricultural/animal husbandry/veterinary practice. However, other reports had concluded that all of these hormones were dangerous to human and animal health, in general as well as when used for growth promotion, and that no MRLs could be easily applied because they were carcinogenic.

4.129 The 1982 and 1987 Lamming reports and the 1987 JECFA Report had not examined the potential risks arising from these hormones when used in combination with other hormones, and had not explained what constituted good agricultural/animal husbandry practice. For example, the 1982 Lamming Report drew the attention of the EC Commission to the need to lay down certain essential provisions as regarded the control of use:

"(a) *Instructions for use*

(i) specification of the doses, the type of pharmaceutical preparation, the number and frequency of administrations;

(ii) association of anabolic agents;

(iii) localization of implant and ablation of zone treated;

(iv) withdrawal period before slaughter;

(v) identification of animals treated, with indication of the period of treatment.

"(b) *Surveillance programme and analysis methods*

(i) control of production and trade in anabolic agents;

(ii). veterinary control of authorized uses;

(iii) means and methods of control."

4.130 The EC Commission had examined this possibility in 1984, when it had proposed to allow the use of the three natural hormones for growth promotion purposes, under the following conditions to safeguard public health and consumer interests:

(i) products to be on an EC list, setting out conditions of use;

(ii) products must be shown to be effective and safe;

(iii) administration only by implant in a part of the animal discarded at slaughter;

(iv) identification of treated animals, to allow control of the withdrawal period;

(v) administration only by a veterinarian, with all treatments recorded;

(vi) meat produced from treated animals to be identified as such to the final consumer.

4.131 This proposal had been fully discussed but rejected on the additional grounds that it was not technically or economically feasible. The following objections had been raised:

Cost: It would be so expensive to restrict the supply and administration of hormone growth promoters by veterinarians that the costs would outweigh the benefits.

Control: Due to the scale of livestock production and the fact that implantation of growth promoters must be performed at certain restricted times of the growth period, it would be technically impossible to ensure at all times, at reasonable administrative and economic costs, a proper administration of hormones.

Bureaucracy: The recording of the treatment of individual animals and their checking at slaughter for the presence of implants (to ensure they had been correctly administered) would be a heavy and expensive bureaucratic burden and would further add to the cost of the process.

Inspection: The inevitable failure to find remnants of implants at slaughter in some animals (due to migration from the implant site, or mal-administration) would entail further expensive examination and residue testing, adding further to the cost. Residue testing would of course include the same testing and corresponding costs for third-country meat imported into the European Communities, as the European Communities would not be able, in the absence of internationally agreed rules on controls and testing, the widely diverging practices of Members, and the obvious and powerful economic incentives for meat producers to disregard the rules, to rely always on testing and controls carried out by third countries.

Labelling: The installation and control of a labelling system to ensure integrity of identification from the live animal through slaughter and processing to a meat product would also be extremely expensive and laborious. The cost would have to be borne by the product, which again would render the whole process uneconomic. Furthermore, retail premises, including restaurants, which supplied unwrapped meat directly to the consumer would have to carry a prominent warning that they used meat from animals treated with hormones. This would be a strong disincentive to using such meat and would thus amount to a restriction on trade. In addition, consumers would have no control and would not be able to make reliable authentic choices (e.g. of meat served in restaurants).

For these reasons, it had been concluded that a ban on the use of hormones for growth promotion would be less trade-restrictive than the imposition of the control system which would otherwise be required. The European Communities argued that, therefore, it had based its measures on the risk assessment it had conducted for that purpose.

4.132 **Canada** claimed that by including under the "appropriate circumstances" of Article 5.1 "... the complex EC legislative process, with its comprehensive consultations, checks and balances involving a proposal by the EC Commission, the opinions of the Economic and Social Committee and the European Parliament, and the adoption by the Council of Ministers", the European Communities contradicted its own observation that the purpose of a risk assessment "... is to establish the *strictly* scientific basis for the regulatory measure the Member would take ..." and confused two distinct aspects of risk analysis: risk assessment, and risk management. The "complex EC legislative process" was the risk management phase - the process of weighing policy alternatives in light of the results of risk assessment and, if required, selecting and implementing appropriate control options, including regulatory measures. It was not part of the risk assessment. In Canada's view, the phrase "as appropriate to the circumstances" referred to the state of scientific and technical knowledge in the area of concern.

4.133 Canada claimed that the EC measures were not *based* on an appropriate risk assessment. In this case, the risk assessment would be an evaluation of the potential for adverse effects on human health arising from the presence of hormone residues in meat. The European Communities had identified cancer as the adverse effect from which the EC measures purportedly protected humans. In Canada's view, the European Communities took a very selective approach of the evidence upon which it said it had based its risk assessment in pointing to purported gaps in the conclusions, characterizing the conclusions as more tentative than they truly were, and ignoring the need for a scientific basis for its measures.

4.134 Canada stressed that the 1987 Lamming Report unequivocally stated that: "The levels of trenbolone and zeranol and their major metabolites found in edible tissue, following accepted husbandry practices, are substantially below the hormonally effective doses in animal tests and therefore *do not present a harmful effect to health*"[87] (emphasis added). The Lamming Group had also clearly stated that it had examined all the studies available "including both long term carcinogenicity studies and short term tests", and the information on which it had based its work was amply referenced in the report. Finally, it was generally accepted by the scientific community that the carcinogenicity of these hormonal substances was indeed related to their hormonal effect. Canada stated that *none* of the "sources of evidence" identified by the European Communities had determined that, at the levels used for growth promotion in cattle, the six hormones at issue posed a risk to human health. In particular, none had determined that they would cause cancer in humans consuming meat containing the residues of such hormones.

4.135 Canada argued that there were four pieces of evidence to demonstrate that the European Communities had not *based* their measures on an appropriate risk assessment, as required by Article 5.1. First, the response given by the European Commu-

[87] G.E. Lamming *et al.*, "Special Report: Scientific report on anabolic agents in animal production," (24 October 1987), *Veterinary Record*, p.389.

nities as to why the Lamming Group had been suspended before it could submit its report on the xenobiotics, trenbolone and zeranol, was that:

> "It was decided by the Council, during the deliberations of the second Lamming Committee for the additional data concerning only the two synthetic hormones, to adopt a level of protection which avoids the presence of any residues of added hormones in meat."

This clearly demonstrated that, the European Communities had adopted its measures originally without the benefit of a current scientific opinion and, therefore, there was no pretence that the measures were *based* on a scientific assessment. Indeed, it had been suggested by Professor Lamming that they were based on political considerations.

4.136 Second, in reply to a question on the sources they relied upon for their purported risk assessment, the European Communities had stated:

> "The works of IARC are well known ... The individual scientists are so many to cite all of them. In its submissions, the EC has referred to the 1983 OIE Conference Report, the 1995 EC Conference report, the works by Dr. R. Hertz, S.S. Epstein and J. Liehr ..."

Canada argued that the works of IARC, the 1983 OIE Conference, and the 1995 EC Scientific Conference report did not support the EC position. In addition, the European Communities had refused to clarify their reliance on the works of individual scientists. Dr. Hertz had been only *mentioned* in the EC submissions in the reports of other authors. These were hardly the "works" of Dr. Hertz; they were the works of others.

4.137 Third, Canada noted that the European Communities' terms of reference for an opinion obtained from Dr. Liehr made it clear that there was no reliance on the works of Dr. Liehr at the time the EC measures came into effect - even for the most recent revision (Directive 96/22/EC). The letter to Dr. Liehr, provided by the European Communities, stated in part, as follows:

> "The scientists employed by the EC tell me that you are probably one of the very few leading scientists in this area of expertise world-wide who, having carried themselves research fairly recently, suggest that the natural hormones and in particular their metabolites (i.e. catecholestrogens-metabolites of natural hormone oestradiol-17β) are, contrary to the generally held view, *genotoxic* and hence under certain conditions they may cause (not only promote) the genesis of tumours. *If this is correct, we then understand* that no tolerance levels can be established for potentially genotoxic substances, as it was the case in the past for example with DES.
>
> "*If the above information is correct, this would be very valuable scientific information for the EC and of course the GATT Panel to take into account. In a way, it would justify the EC's cautious approach against the use of these hormones for growth promotion,* as potentially carcinogenic substances irrespective of the dose and the conditions under which they may be administered to animals for growth promotion" (emphasis added).

Canada argued that the European Communities were searching, *ex post facto*, for a scientific justification for its measures. Indeed, in performing its risk assessment of oestradiol-17β to determine whether a MRL would be required under Regulation 2377/90, the European Communities did not subscribe to Dr. Liehr's theory of genotoxicity. Rather, the EC public summary stated, "... it is concluded that the toxic effects including carcinogenicity occur as an extension of the physiological effects of oestradiol".[88] Canada recalled too, that one of the EC experts, Dr. Bridges, had asserted that the 1995 EC Scientific Conference did not look at genotoxicity because it was not of current concern. Canada wondered, how could the issue of genotoxicity figure so largely in the risk assessment of a measure passed in April 1996, when the EC scientists attending the November-December 1995 Conference did not think it was a particularly important issue?

4.138 Canada argued that Dr. Liehr's terms of reference also revealed that the European Communities were not interested in an objective opinion on the carcinogenicity of the hormones at issue. The terms of reference stated:

> "*Provided we understand correctly the conclusions of the scientific research carried out by your and/your co-scientists*, the European Communities would be interested in requesting from you a written scientific opinion dealing with the following questions:
>
> > - Are the three natural hormones (oestradiol-17β, testosterone and progesterone) or their metabolites potentially genotoxic?"

Canada suggested that the European Communities had gone so far as to ask Dr. Liehr to find fault with the JECFA report so as to justify the EC departure from the international standards:

> "If you feel that the following two questions also fall within your field of expertise, I would also appreciate a reply:
>
> > - ... what is wrong from a broad scientific point of view with the 1988 FAO/Codex Alimentarius expert group report? On what precise scientific grounds could you criticize it?"

Canada submitted that the opinions of experts retained by the European Communities lacked objectivity and should be considered accordingly.

4.139 Fourth, Canada argued, were the EC evaluations of oestradiol-17β and progesterone under Regulation 2377/90 (which required review of the three natural hormones permitted for therapeutic use). None of these hormones had been placed in Annex IV (list of substances for which no MRL can be fixed). Oestradiol-17β had been placed in Annex II (list of substances not subject to MRLs). For oestradiol, the EC public summary report stated: "... oestradiol does not induce gene mutations *in vitro*, but conflicting results are found in chromosomal aberration assays. Following long term exposure the incidence of tumours in tissues with high level of hormone receptors is increased (e.g. mammary tumours). It is concluded that the toxic effects

[88] Para. 3 of the public summary, cited by Dr. Arnold, answer to Panel question 5, para. 6.54.

including carcinogenicity occur as an extension of the physiological effects of oestradiol ...".[89]

4.140 In considering inclusion of progesterone in Annex II, the European Communities stated in the public summary report:

> "According to the International Agency for Research on Cancer (IARC), progesterone does not exhibit mutagenic activity in most *in vitro* and *in vivo* tests performed, but is known to increase the tumour incidence in endocrine target tissues (ovaries, uterus, mammae) after continuous (parenteral) doses clearly above the physiological levels. Progesterone is not carcinogenic per se, but acts via an epigenetic mechanism associated with its endocrine activity, i.e. its ability to cause a hyperproliferative effect at cellular levels mediated by steroid-hormone receptor interaction. Hence, tumours will not result from ingestion of progesterone at levels that do not produce any hormonal effects."[90]

Furthermore, the public summary stated that, "[a]s the residue studies showed that the milk, tissue and plasma levels after the recommended treatment with progesterone were at or within physiological limits, the conclusion of JECFA that no ADI or MRLs for progesterone need to be established can also be adopted for the therapeutic and zootechnical use of progesterone".[91]

4.141 Thus, Canada noted, the European Communities itself had made the assessment, under Regulation 2377/90, that the natural hormone oestradiol-17β was safe to use. A similar review of progesterone had reached the same conclusion. The European Communities continued to allow the use of oestradiol-17β and progesterone for therapeutic and zootechnical purposes and, thus, had chosen to continue to expose EC consumers to residues of these substances. Canada argued that it was simply incongruent for the European Communities to maintain that its risk assessments had determined that the widespread use of these substances for zootechnical purposes was safe, whereas their use for growth promotion was not.

4.142 The **European Communities** observed that Canada did not appear to argue that the challenged measures had no scientific basis, but that they were not based on an appropriate risk assessment. Canada apparently believed that the only acceptable evidence of risk assessment in this case, on which the European Communities should have based its measures, were the Lamming Reports of 1982 and 1987 and the 1987 JECFA Report. However, in the European Communities' view, neither the 1982 and 1987 Lamming Reports nor the JECFA Report constituted in themselves "risk assessment" in the sense of Articles 5.1 to 5.6 of SPS Agreement. They only formed part of "available scientific evidence". The other factors mentioned in Article 5.2 and in paragraphs 3 to 6 thereof, were not dealt with by the above scientific reports. The assessment of these factors was not a scientific question in the strict sense, and thus

89 Para. 3 of the public summary, cited by Dr. Arnold, answer to Panel question 5, para. 6.54.
90 *Ibid.*, p.12, para. 9.
91 *Ibid.*, para. 16.

they fell within the responsibility of the appropriate political authorities of each Member.

4.143 The European Communities were surprised by the interpretation made by Canada of the words contained in Article 5.1 "as appropriate to the circumstances". If these words meant "the state of scientific and technical knowledge in the area of concern", the remaining phrase in Article 5:1 "taking into account risk assessment techniques developed by the relevant international organizations" would serve no useful purpose. The phrase "as appropriate to the circumstances" was frequently used in legal texts and usually required, as here, to bring close to the concrete circumstances of application the concept under examination. In this case, the risk assessment should take into account the nature of the substances and the type of risks they posed to human and animal health in the territory of each Member. A substance might not be viewed as posing very serious risks in a country, e.g., salmonella in South Africa, whereas the same substance might be viewed as posing a serious risk to humans in the European Communities (and for that reason the European Communities had taken drastic measures to make sure that it was completely eradicated in its territory). Another example might be that some parts of the population of a Member might be viewed to be exposed to different degrees, either higher or lower to risks from a certain substance and there might still be other parts of the population (e.g. young children) which were more vulnerable to a certain type of risk than others. All these were circumstances which needed to be taken into account by a Member when assessing a risk.

4.144 The European Communities stressed that there did not exist yet risk assessment techniques developed by the relevant international organizations. Codex was still discussing different concepts, but there was no agreement yet on these techniques. A Member was, therefore, free to make an assessment of the risk as it thought correct and as was appropriate to the circumstances prevailing in its territory. Canada's definition of the phrase "as appropriate to the circumstances" would devoid it of any useful meaning. Article 5.2 laid down the elements a Member should take into account in an assessment of the risk: available scientific evidence, relevant processes and production methods, relevant inspection, sampling and testing methods, prevalence of specific diseases, etc. Each of the three words "available scientific evidence" had a distinct meaning: the evidence a Member took into account for its risk assessment had to be scientific, i.e. it must have the minimal attributes of scientific inquiry, and it should be part of the body of scientific knowledge in the area of concern, even if it was not the prevailing view among scientists.

4.145 This concept of "available scientific evidence" was also confirmed by the definition of the term "scientific justification" given in the footnote of Article 3.3, where it was explained that there was "... scientific justification if on the basis of an *examination and evaluation of available scientific information* ... a Member determines ...". For systematic purposes, the concept of scientific evidence in the SPS Agreement could not have different meanings in its various provisions. There was apparently a profound difference between Canada and the European Communities on the definition of the concept of risk assessment for the purposes of Article 5. In the view of the European Communities, the concept of risk assessment was composed of two parts: the *scientific assessment of the risk* and the *management of that risk*. In the management of the risk, elements other than strictly science entered into consideration, such as those mentioned above in Article 5.2. The European Communities argued that in the Panel proceedings a number of experts advising the European Communities had explained their views on the potential dangers to human and animal health from the use of these hormones for growth promotion. However, none of the experts advising the Panel had argued that the experts referred to by the European Communities did not employ scientific principles in their research. Article 2.2 of the SPS Agreement did not require the best science nor the weight of scientific evidence to be taken into account; it only stipulated that there should be "scientific principles" and "sufficient" (not absolute) scientific evidence. For example, Dr. Lucier had agreed with the conclusions of the EC scientists that both the natural and synthetic hormones were carcinogenic at low levels (the natural hormones were carcinogenic even at existing physiological levels). Some of the scientists who attended the meeting of experts (and those of JECFA 1988) might not agree with the conclusions of the scientists advising the European Communities. But this was not relevant for the purposes of Article 5.2, 2.2 and 3.3 of the SPS Agreement. What was important was whether, in the scientific research employed by the EC scientists (or the scientific reports to which they made reference in their reports), the *minimal attributes of scientific inquiry* were respected. The European Communities had not heard the opposite from any of the experts advising the Panel nor from Canada. Therefore, the European Communities was allowed to take into account its scientific views (or the views of the scientists to which they referred in their reports) in its assessment of the risks of these hormones for growth promotion.

4.146 The European Communities argued that the first EC Directive dated from 1981 and the second from 1988. The prohibition on the use of these hormones for growth promotion had entered into force on 1 January 1989. At that time, there were no Codex standards for these hormones. The JECFA reports were based on scientific evidence dating from some years before 1988, whilst new scientific evidence started to emerge around 1985 suggesting that these hormones were dangerous to human and animal health because they were carcinogenic. But as with any new discoveries, it had taken time for these new scientific views to get established in the scientific community. In view of that scientific uncertainty, the European Communities had decided not to follow the weight of scientific evidence underlying the JECFA reports for the five hormones. The doubts of the European Communities on the weight of the scientific evidence were explained in the preparatory work of Directive 88/146 and the discussions in the European Parliament, the Economic and Social Committee and the Council of Ministers. The so-called Collins reports and, in particular, the Pimenta reports, established clearly that the European Parliament had heard a very large number of scientists before issuing its reports. It appeared that in Canada's view, risk assessment could only be performed by a number of scientists formally getting together and issuing a formal report within an institutionalized system, like JECFA. Other scientific views not reflected in that report did not seem to be considered by Canada to form part of the scientific evidence. The European Communities did not accept this concept of risk assessment. The SPS Agreement did not provide rules on how the risk assessment should be done; it only indicated the elements that should be taken into account. Until such techniques were developed, each Member was free to decide for itself the procedures it used for assessing the risks in any case. The European Communities had its own system of risk assessment, where there was constant interaction between the scientific committees and experts advising the Commission, the European Parliament and the Council of Ministers. It might take some time to be completed, but that was its system of risk assessment.

4.147 The European Communities further argued that as two of the experts advising the European Communities, Dr. Liehr and Dr. Adlercreutz, had shown in their reports, most of the scientific evidence on the carcinogenic effects of these hormones was based on new research and toxicological methods which had started to appear after the issuance of the 1988 JECFA report. To consider the 1988 JECFA report as representing the state of the art on the hazards to human and animal health from the use of these hormones for growth promotion would amount to voluntarily ignoring the new scientific progress in the name of regulatory stability. To take the fixed view that only the 1988 JECFA report could contain scientific truths on the hazards posed by these hormones, as argued by Canada, was scientifically absurd. As regarded the criteria for inclusion of substances into Annex II of EC Regulation no. 2377/90, the European Communities underlined that in addition to the scientific assessment of the risk, a substance might be put in Annex II (where no MRLs were established) if the animals in question were not sent for slaughter immediately after therapeutic or zootechnical treatment. Animals treated for therapeutic or zootechnical purposes were not slaughtered for human consumption. After such treatment was performed, it took some time before the veterinarian conducting the treatment discovered whether the treatment was effective or not. If after some time, depending on the animal and the therapeutic or zootechnical treatment performed, the veterinarian discovered that the animal could not be maintained as a breeding animal, the possibility of slaughtering was considered. But this meant that in addition to the strict conditions imposed by EC law for such treatment, there was a lapse of time between such treatment and the possibility of slaughtering. The percentage of animals receiving such therapeutic or zootechnical treatment and which might be slaughtered did not represent more than 1 per cent of total bovine animals used for human consumption in the European Communities. This low percentage, along with the conditions imposed for treatments and the time lapsed before possible slaughter, guaranteed that there would be no residues of oestradiol 17β left in meat used for human consumption. Therefore, the level of protection of the European Communities in this case was not affected at all.

4.148 The European Communities claimed that it was necessary to avoid the apparent confusion between the terms "adverse effect", "risk", "risk assessment", "level of protection achieved by measures based on the relevant international standards", and "appropriate level of protection determined by a Member". Noting that it had explained in detail the "risk" (i.e. the "potential for adverse effects on human and animal health") from the use of hormones (see paras. 4.144 and ff.), the European Communities indicated that the 1988 JECFA report had also found that there was a potential risk to human health: if there were no such potential risk, JECFA would have not recommended ADIs and MRLs for the two synthetic hormones. For the three natural hormones the 1988 JECFA report did not recommend ADIs and MRLs essentially because of problems in detecting the level of residues in the meat on a routine basis. Scientists had said that "the ADI-model is not a risk model and does not predict the risk of the occurrence of adverse effects, when ADI-values are exceeded"[92]. The same was true basically for the MRL-model, "which specifies the quantity of a particular residue in meat that, even in dietary extremes, would not exceed the ADI for the particular substance concerned."[93] So, the MRL was based on the notion that there was a risk, but if the proposed threshold was observed the *probability* of the adverse effect arising from the use of hormones would not materialize. Clearly, in this case what the 1988 JECFA report had done was to recommend standards which would achieve "a level of protection" against the potential risks from the use of hormones. But the SPS Agreement allowed Members to determine *another* level, i.e. the level *they* deem appropriate. This level might be higher or lower.

4.149 **Canada** claimed that the SPS Agreement did not define the term "risk". However, its meaning could be deduced from the definition of "risk assessment". Reduced to its components, risk was the *potential for adverse effects on human or animal health arising from certain sources, namely the presence of additives, contaminants, toxins or disease causing organisms in food, beverages or feedstuffs.* Assessment was the *evaluation* of that potential. Canada submitted that, in this case, the only source of risk would be the presence of hormone residues, including their metabolites, in the meat from animals treated with the six hormones at issue. Contrary to the EC arguments, problems linked to the administration of hormones, the detection and control of hormone residues in meat, and so forth, were not *sources* of risk; *i.e.,* they did not fall within "... the presence of additives, contaminants, toxins or disease causing organisms in food, beverages or feedstuffs".

4.150 The **European Communities** contended that available scientific evidence showed the use of the natural and synthetic hormones subject to this dispute could be dangerous to human and animal health. The potential danger resulted from (i) their nature and mode of action; (ii) the action of their metabolites; (iii) combinations of hormones and multiple exposure; (iv) problems linked to their detection and control; and (v) problems linked to their administration. In submitting its supporting arguments, the European Communities indicated that it focused on the potential risks to human beings, but that this did not imply that there were no risks for animal health.

(i) The Nature and Mode of Action of Hormones

4.151 The **European Communities** claimed that even though the precise mode of action of the hormones at issue had only been partly understood, all scientists agreed that these hormones were dangerous. A characteristic of hormones was their extreme potency. They were produced in minute quantities, often at a site distant from their target site but produced significant effects. Hormones had a wide range of actions which affected almost all systems of the body. The principle sex hormone in men, testosterone, contributed to acne, baldness, prostatic disease, coronary heart disease and peptic ulceration. Oestrogens, and to a lesser extent progesterone, exposed women to premenstrual tension, dysmenorrhoea, some disorders of the reproductive system and an increased tendency to develop gallstones. More importantly, these hormones also played a major role in the development of tumours in sex-hormone

---

92 *1995 EC Scientific Conference Proceedings*, p.375.

93 *Ibid.*, p.4.

dependent tissues (for example prostatic cancer, breast cancer, cancer of the uterus and neoplastic liver disease).

4.152 The European Communities noted that the carcinogenic risks from these hormones were well known. For instance, in the 1983 OIE Scientific Report a scientist had concluded that "although it is unlikely that the small amounts of anabolic steroids which might be ingested in agricultural produce could (cause cancer), this possibility should not be ignored entirely" (page 274). Moreover, the same 1983 OIE Scientific Report stated that:

> "... *It is difficult to be entirely confident* about predicting and assessing the toxic and carcinogenic effects of any physical or chemical agent, but in balancing risks and benefits available evidence *strongly favours the view* that residues of anabolic agents present in agricultural produce *do not present any hazard to the human population provided that administration of these agents is properly controlled and that the research for new agents continues*" (page 284).

The European Communities argued that this part of the OIE 1983 Report had now proven to be the most correct prediction of the mode of action and potential toxic and carcinogenic effects of these hormiones. This was in particular the case for oestradiol-17β and the other two natural hormones, which until recently were among those thought to be the most safe to administer to animals and humans.

4.153 The 1987 IARC Report indicated that, in the case of androgens:

> "The fact that castration palliates prostatic cancers suggests that testosterone may be involved *in the genesis* of these tumours, and a number of epidemiological observations suggest that increased testosterone levels may increase the risk for prostatic cancer" (page 96).
>
> "The *evidence* that anabolic steroids can *cause* both benign and malignant liver tumours *is quite strong*. However, because no analytical epidemiological study has been done, the Working Group felt constrained to classify the evidence for carcinogenicity in humans as no more than "limited" (page 97).

In the case of oestrogens, however:

> "A number of studies, utilizing a variety of designs, have shown *a consistent, strongly positive association between exposure to a number of oestrogenic substances and risk of endometrial cancer*, with evidence of positive dose-response relationships both for strength of medication and duration of use" (page 280).

4.154 The IARC did not differentiate between the effects of the substance at high doses versus low doses, as regards the evidence concerning androgenic anabolic steroids. As regards oestrogens, progestins and combinations thereof (i.e. mainly oestradiol-17β, progesterone and MGA), the 1987 IARC Report explained:

> "Steroid hormones are essential for the growth, differentiation and function of many tissues in both animals and humans. It has been established by animal experimentation that modification of the hormonal environment by surgical removal of endocrine glands, by pregnancy or by exogenous administration of steroids can increase or decrease the spontaneous occurrence *of tumours or the induction of tu-*

mours by applied carcinogenic agents .... The incidence of tumours in humans could be altered by exposure to various exogenous hormones, singly or in combination."

"These statements make explicit the facts that oestrogens and progestins occur naturally, and that the hormonal milieu and dose-effect relationships are generally inextricably involved in the carcinogenic effects of oestrogens and progestins.

"In this section, we describe the human epidemiology, carcinogenicity studies in animals, and other relevant data for oestrogens and progestins alone and in combination. The human epidemiological data reflect the patterns of use of oestrogens and progestins and their combinations in medical practice, i.e., the available information concerns specific products used for particular indications. Although may of the products have the same constituents (or a similar class of constituents), doses vary among products and the compounds and doses have changed over time. *The operating principle is to determine the ability of the chemical to produce cancer or other genetic and related effects without the strictures of mode of human use or the magnitude of the doses. Thus, there is a basic incongruity between the human data and the animal carcinogenicity data. As noted earlier, however, the effects of these chemicals in humans appear, at least in most cases, to be linked to the hormonal milieu*" (page 272, emphasis added).

The 1987 IARC Report concluded by saying:

"There is a basic incongruity between the human data and the animal carcinogenicity data. As noted earlier, however, the effects of these chemicals in humans appear, *at least in most cases*, to be linked to the hormonal milieu" (page 272, emphasis added).

The European Communities submitted that the phrase "at least in most cases" did not mean, of course, "in all cases" and under all conditions. It followed from the above that the findings of the IARC reports aim at establishing the carcinogenic or other effects of these substances irrespective of the modes of human use and the magnitude of the doses.

4.155 The European Communities further noted that the carcinogenic effects of hormones on humans (and animals) had been documented by several reports of the IARC. IARC had classified steroidal oestrogens (including oestradiol) in Group 1, meaning the agent *was* carcinogenic to humans; androgenic (anabolic) steroids (including testosterone) in Group 2.A, agents *probably* carcinogenic to humans and progestins in Group 2.B or agents *possibly* carcinogenic to humans.[94]

4.156 There was a body of scientists which believed that the *natural* hormones acted by binding with high affinity and high specificity to protein receptors which were present in hormone-responsive tissues. As a result of hormone binding to the receptor, the receptor underwent a conformational change, bound to specific DNA

[94] *IARC Monographs* (1987), Supplement 7, pp.31, 96 and 280.

sequences and regulated the expression of specific genes with a cell.[95] As regarded the *synthetic* hormones, there were some scientists who thought that these exerted their biological effects via the hormone-receptor mechanism, but had also pharmacokinetic and pharmacodynamic properties which distinguished them from the natural hormones. For example, most of these synthetic agents had oral activity. Tissue distribution was altered because of differences in their relative binding affinity for serum transport proteins. These synthetic agents might also differ from natural hormones in their rate of metabolism and excretion.[96]

4.157 The European Communities submitted that the state of scientific knowledge in 1983 on the way all hormones exerted their biological action had been summarised as follows:

> "Although many studies have been performed in this field over the last few years, the fundamental mode of action at the molecular level has not as yet been fully elucidated."[97]

4.158 The European Communities asserted that the scientific assumption that, despite their carcinogenic potential, these hormones were not likely to cause problems to human health was based on the assumption that "the carcinogenic effect of these hormones is related to the hormonal activity of these compounds, i.e. an increase in tumour incidence in tissues of animals with high levels of specific hormone receptors, which would not occur at normal physiological levels".[98] But scientists could not define what those "normal physiological levels" were since the concentrations of the natural hormones in the body of the animal varied widely according to the animal species, the sex, age, breed, season, nutritional status and the physiological state of the animal. As a consequence, a decision on the "normal" concentration level of these hormones , i.e. a limit at which it was possible to decide whether or not an animal had been treated with a natural occurring hormone, was almost impossible to make. For these reasons, these hormones were considered by some scientists to be "promoters rather that primary inducers of cancer in hormonally sensitive tissues".[99] According to the European Communities, it was on this assumption that was also based the 1988 JECFA Report, on which Codex had based its recommendations. With regard to oestradiol-17β, the 1988 JECFA Report stated that "The results of studies ... (showed that) ... Oral and parenteral administration of oestradiol-17β can increase the incidence of tumours in experimental animals. These tumours largely

[95] M.A. Miller, J.K. Leighton, "Risk Assessment Strategies for Hormones and Hormone-like Substances", *1995 EC Scientific Conference Proceedings*, p.386.

[96] *Ibid.*, p.389.

[97] *1983 OIE Conference Report*, p.54. The European Communities noted that in the same OIE Report (p. 233), three US scientists had explained that "...the published data on oestrogen concentrations in the tissue of food producing animals is scarce. The noticeable lack of such data presents no more than a dim understanding of oestrogen distribution and metabolism in the tissue of food producing animals, such as the cow and pig".

[98] H.A. Kuiper, "Risk Assessment Strategies for Xenobiotics", *1995 EC Scientific Conference Proceedings*, pp.370-371.

[99] H.A. Miller, J.K. Leighton, "Risk Assessment Strategies for Hormones and Hormone-like Substances", *1995 EC Scientific Conference Proceedings*, p.386, and *1983 OIE Scientific Report*, p.339 *et seq.*

occur in tissues with high levels of specific hormone receptors that are normally responsive to stimulation by the particular hormone concerned. The Committee concluded that the carcinogenic response was related to the hormonal activity of oestradiol-17β at levels considerably higher than those required for a physiological response"[100] (page 18).

4.159 The European Communities contended, however, that more recently a number of scientists had suggested that this hormone could be considered to be not only a promoter but also a primary *inducer* of cancer at least in hormonally sensitive tissues[101], and that the 1988 JECFA Report were out of date.

4.160 The European Communities observed, for example, that Dr. Liehr argued that "oestrogens have been implicated for some time in the induction of human cancers, and there is increasing evidence of a similar role for progesterone and testosterone".[102] In particular, Dr. Liehr had stated:

> 4.161 "In the case of oestradiol, experiments have shown that its hormonal potency is *not* linked to its carcinogenic activity. Investigations of the metabolic pathways of oestradiol have revealed that free radicals are continuously produced, and DNA damage by these free radicals, as well as DNA adduct formation, has been demonstrated in a range of tissues. As damage to DNA and DNA adduct formation are known to be associated with tumour formation, these experiments provide strong evidence that oestradiol is a genotoxic carcinogen. In the case of progesterone and testosterone, it is not clear whether their carcinogenic effects are mediated by their action on specific receptors in target tissues or due to mutagenic DNA damage.
>
> "In the present state of knowledge, it is very difficult and in any case not advisable to determine a safe threshold dose of hormone below which tumour formation will not occur. Hormone-associated tumours in the breast, uterus or prostate may be induced by a combination of exogenous and endogenous hormones and/or their metabolites. As the total amount of hormone or metabolite necessary for tumour induction is not known, the amount of exogenous hormone or metabolite necessary for tumour induction in addition to unknown amounts of endogenous hormone or metabolite has not yet been determined. In the 1988 JECFA report, the authors considered only the hormonal receptor-mediated activities of the natural hormones. In view of the considerable amount of scientific evidence which has accumulated since the release of that Report, particularly in respect of the genotoxicity of oestradiol, the Report can no longer be considered applicable to a risk assessment of the use of hormone growth promoters".[103]

---

[100] The European Communities noted that the same assumptions were made in the *1988 JECFA Report* for progesterone (p.20), testosterone (p.2), trenbolone acetate (p.24), and zeranol (p.27).

[101] *Ibid.* 386, and *1983 OIE Scientific Report*, p.339 et seq.

[102] J. Liehr, "Potential genotoxicity of Hormones", 23 December 1996.

[103] *Ibid.*

4.162 In addition the European Communities argued that Dr. Adlercreutz indicated that:

> "... the 1987 JECFA report must now be regarded as too old. The main problem with this report is that it relates any negative effects of hormonal drugs to their hormonal effects, i.e. if a compound occurs in amounts not giving clear "hormonal" responses it is regarded as safe. The anabolic steroid trenbolone has both anabolic and oestrogenic effects and it is not clear which effects are considered. It is frequently used in combination with oestradiol and also with zeranol, which are estrogenic. Furthermore, testosterone and trenbolone seem also to affect the glucocorticoid receptor and testosterone increases growth hormone and growth factor concentrations and both affect steroid biosynthesis. Many other hormonal effects of the five compounds dealt with are known. When studying hormonal effects only gross effects are considered, but nowadays it is obvious that effects may occur at the cellular level at low concentrations of hormones and without being observable by the relatively coarse methods used in toxicology in vivo studies. Such effects may be observable in human subjects first after many years or even longer time. Another problem is that the JECFA report does not deal with or discusses very little the carcinogenicity of metabolites of hormones, particularly those of oestrogens. At the time when the 1987 JECFA Report was written very little was known about the genotoxic effects particularly of estrogen metabolites. Since the report was written it has also been more and more obvious that hormones have nongenomic effects not related to their hormonal effect via the receptors and that steroid hormone metabolites may be as important or even more important with regard to various effects on biochemical or genotoxic events than the parent compound.
>
> "All these hormones have been shown to cause cancer in various experimental systems if given in high amounts but it is obvious that the effect is not always due to their hormonal activity. For oestrogens and trenbolone it has been shown that also other mechanisms occur and the mechanisms by which the other hormones cause cancer is far from clear.
>
> (...)
>
> "Anabolic steroids in meat has been shown to result in positive doping tests. A compound giving positive doping tests cannot be administered for meat production because these may result in lifetime problems for any sportsman or sportswomen who is caught with a positive doping test without having used any doping agents.
>
> "The 1987 JECFA report is definitely too old and does not take into account recent scientific evidence changing our view on the carcinogenicity of oestrogens and does not take into account non-hormonal

and other negative effects of the administration of steroids to animals intended for human consumption".[104]

4.163 The European Communities also presented the argument of Dr. Cavalieri that:

"... the presently available knowledge about tumour induction in hormone-responsive tissues suggests a specific pathway of oestrogen metabolism, namely 4-hydroxylation followed by oxidation to E-3, 4-Q and reaction DNA. This DNA damage is responsible for generating the critical mutations that can lead to tumour formation, if the appropriate mechanisms of promotion occur. Therefore, oestrogens, in particular oestradiol, have genotoxic effects and no threshold dose can be established. In addition, the effects of the other natural and synthetic hormones used for meat production on the metabolism of oestrogens are not known. Thus, Acceptable Daily Intakes and Maximum Acceptable Levels cannot be established for residues of these hormones in meat for human consumption.

"The 1988 and 1990 FAO/Codex Alimentarius expert group reports recommended ADIs and MRLs for these hormones based on their hormonal effects. Genotoxic effects were unknown at that time and, thus, were not considered. In light of the new knowledge about the genotoxic effects of oestrogens, the entire subject of these residues in meat for human consumption must be reassessed."[105]

4.164 Furthermore, the European Communities argued that Dr. Metzler reported that the available data show that:

"17β-oestradiol, 17β-trenbolone and zeranol can be metabolically activated to products capable of covalent DNA binding. The level of DNA binding is low as compared to typical chemical carcinogens, but may have significant toxicological implications, as discussed below.

"17β-oestradiol and some of their metabolites have the potential to cause aneuploid and are therefore chromosomal mutagens. For 17β-trenbolone, the reports about aneuploidogenic potential are controversial. For zeranol and its metabolites, aneuploidogenic potential has not been studied adequately.

"The metabolism of 17β-trenbolone and zeranol in humans and the genotoxicity of the metabolites have not been fully elucidated.

"The mechanisms of hormonal carcinogenesis are not yet fully understood. The hormonal and genotoxic effects of an agent may well act in concert. Therefore, it is conceivable that an hormonally active compound is retained in target cells by the hormone receptor and stimulated cell division, which in turn makes the cell more vulnerable for the induction of gene mutations and aneuploid. Xenobiotic hormones

---

[104] H. Adlercreutz, "Evaluation of the Thirty-Second Report of the Joint FAO/WHO Expert Committee on Food Additives, and Discussion of Dr. J. Liehr's Report on this Topic", 7 January 1997.

[105] E. Cavalieri, "Genotoxicity and Potential Carcinogenicity of Hormones Administered to Animals for Promotion of Growth in Meat Production", 7 February 1997.

have longer half-life and may accumulate to higher levels after repeated exposure.

"The standard systems used in toxicology for assaying genotoxicity may not be suitable to detect the rather subtle genotoxic effects of carcinogenic hormones. As the hormones under consideration and/or some of their metabolites exhibit both DNA-damaging and aneuploidogenic potential, it is not permissible to establish values for No-Adverse-Effect-Levels and for Acceptable Daily Intake. The conclusions and recommendations of the 1988 and 1990 FAO/Codex Alimentarius Reports are solely based on the hormonal activities of the agents under consideration. As the evidence for genotoxic effects of these agents has increased considerably over the past years, an update is required which takes these recent findings into account."[106]

4.165 The European Communities also referred to the report submitted by Dr. Epstein in which he argued that:

"... there is substantial evidence challenging the validity of classifying carcinogens as epigenetic, for which thresholds or Acceptable Daily Intake (ADI) levels are claimed, or genotoxic. Apart from this, hormonal anabolics are mutagenic in mammalian test systems and are thus genotoxic. There is also substantial scientific evidence challenging the existence of thresholds for any carcinogen. This evidence is even more persuasive for exposures involving infants and young children, in view of their enhanced sensitivity to carcinogens and for exposures involving unpredictable synergistic interactions. There is no scientific basis for claims that ADI levels can be set for natural and synthetic anabolic carcinogens, or for claims that ADI levels can be based on "no-hormonal-effect levels" of synthetic anabolic carcinogens (FAO/WHO, 1990).

"These conclusions on the hormonal effects of anabolics are consistent with, and an amplification of, those detailed in an earlier review of endocrine factors in human carcinogenesis. In almost all cases two postulated mechanisms: "alteration of the susceptibility of tissues to the initiation of cancer" and "promotion of the development of cancer from initiated cells", could not be separated. The carcinogenic effects of DES in relation to breast cancer were considered to be "more in keeping with an effect on initiation rather than on promotion". It may further be noted that no mechanism of action, whether promotion, initiation or other, could be determined for the carcinogenic effects of oestrogens on salivary, ovarian, renal and thyroid cancers, and malignant melonoma in humans. A most recent report has further summarized evidence that parent oestrogens and their catecholamine metabolites induce several types of DNA damage, adduct formation, and gene mutations. Additionally, the author concluded, on the basis of

[106] M. Metzler, "Genotoxic Potential of the Natural Sex Hormones 17β-oestradiol and Testosterone, and of the Synthetic Compounds 17β-trenbolone and Zeranol", 6 February 1997.

experimental evidence, that "hormonal activity of oestrogens was considered to be necessary but not sufficient for tumour induction to occur".

"There is no scientific basis for making distinctions between genotoxic and epigenetic carcinogens on the basis of available bioassay data. Thus, there is no basis for attempts to derive threshold levels for hormonal anabolics, or other carcinogens, from such data. ...

"It should further be emphasized that extrapolation from high dose bioassay data is likely to underestimate, rather than overestimate, the carcinogenic effects of low dose chronic human exposure. A recent publication endorsed this conclusion with particular reference to metabolic considerations. "Limited evidence would indicate that proportionately less active metabolite is formed at high concentrations where Phase 2 enzymes predominate, while at lower concentrations pathways leading to active metabolites are favoured. The overall effect would lead to an underestimate of risk from high dose animal experiments when extrapolating to low level, chronic human exposure."

"Apart from the invalidity of distinctions between genotoxic and epigenetic carcinogens, it is generally accepted that threshold levels cannot be determined for genotoxic carcinogens. While hormonal anabolics are inactive in bacterial gene tests, and hence dismissed as epigenetic, they are nevertheless clastogenic in mammalian evidence of genotoxicity is clearly more relevant to human cancer than are data based on bacterial gene tests.

"There are other cogent reasons for rejecting the threshold hypothesis. These include:

- The enhanced sensitivity of neonatal rodents to the carcinogenic effects of anabolic hormones, supported by substantial evidence on the increased susceptibility of infant rodents and humans to a wide range of carcinogens, including natural anabolics and diethylstilbestrol. (IARC, 1989, NRDC, 1989)
- Synergistic interactions between different anabolics administered in combination. Illustrative, are the synergistic effects of oestrogen and progesterone in the induction of mammary tumours in mice. (IARC, 1987)
- The possibility of additive and/or synergistic interactions between natural and synthetic anabolic carcinogens and endogenous hormones, particularly in infants.
- Synergistic interactions, not as yet investigated, between anabolic carcinogens and carcinogenic and/or xenoestrogenic contaminants in meat products, such as chlorinated hydrocarbon pesticides.
- The absence of routine monitoring and residue analysis for parent anabolics following their legal administration, and of sensitive and practical analytic techniques further preclude attempts to estimate threshold or Acceptable Daily Intake levels

for hormonal anabolics. Still further complicating problems of residue analysis is the impracticality of assaying for biologically active oestrogen metabolites."[107]

4.166 The European Communities also presented the arguments of Dr. Pinter that:

"... there is evidence that endogenous and exogenous hormones represent potential carcinogenic risk to humans. The risk is associated with the level of hormones, the time of exerting the hormonal effect and the general status of the hormone-responsive organs. Exogenously administered hormones have been proved to be carcinogenic to experimental animals and there is also evidence for hormones to be casually associated with human tumours. In contrast to many animal carcinogens, in the case of hormones, one has to bear in mind that we deal with "human" carcinogens. Therefore, any consideration should be dealt with more seriously than with "animal" carcinogens. Although the level of endogenous hormones varies greatly during the life time, there is no evidence that low level of additional hormones do not represent additional risk.

"Oestrogens and/or their metabolites can react with DNA causing DNA damages, can alter proteins including tubulin, resulting in aneuploid. There is also evidence that this effect is different from the hormonal one, therefore relying on no-hormonal effect might be inappropriate. Administration of oestrogens and progestins in humans is proved to be tumorigenic. In case of hormone mixtures and their residues, it is possible that similar risks exists. Although the level of administered or ingested mixtures may be different, the tumorigenic hazard should not be excluded.

"All effort should be made to avoid additional hormonal effect unless it is absolutely necessary (mediation, etc.). The risk associated with consumption of hormone-containing meat products can be regarded as unnecessary risk which can be avoided."[108]

4.167 The latest scientific evidence thus indicated that oestrogens were implicated in the induction of human cancers, and there was increasing evidence of a similar role for progesterone and testosterone.[109] In the case of progesterone and testosterone, it was not clear whether their carcinogenic effects were mediated by their action

[107] S.S. Epstein, "Report to the EC on Cancer Risks from Hormonal Meat Products", 5 February 1997.

[108] A. Pinter, "Some Aspects of Hormonal Carcinogenesis", 5 February 1997.

[109] The European Communities cited the following articles: J. G. Liehr (1990), "Genotoxic effects of oestrogens, Mutation Research," pp.269-276; D. Roy and J. G. Liehr (1992), "Target organ-specific inactivation of drug metabolizing enzymes in kidney of hamsters treated with oestradiol", *Molecular and Cellular Biochemistry 110*, pp.31-39; B. T. Zhu, D. Roy and J. G. Liehr (1993), "The carcinogenic activity of ethinyl oestrogens is determined by both their hormonal characteristics and their conversion to catechol metabolites," *132 Endocrinology*, pp.577-583; M. Y. Wang and J. G. Liehr (1994), "Identification of fatty acid hydroperoxide cofactors in the cytochrome P450-mediated oxidation of oestrogens to quinone metabolites," *269 Journal of Biological Chemistry*, pp.284-291.

on specific receptors in target tissues or due to mutagenic DNA damage.[110] In the case of oestradiol, the latest experiments had shown that its hormonal potency was *not* linked to its carcinogenic activity.[111] Investigations of the metabolic pathways of oestradiol had revealed that free radicals were continuously produced, and DNA damage by these free radicals, as well as DNA adduct formation, had been demonstrated in a range of tissues. As damage to DNA and DNA adduct formation were known to be associated with tumour formation, these experiments provided strong evidence that oestradiol was a genotoxic carcinogen.[112]

4.168 The European Communities submitted that the ADI and MRL recommended by the 1988 JECFA Report were equally out of date, since according to the six scientific opinions presented above such levels were difficult to determine given the present insufficient knowledge. The 1987 IARC Monographs also needed to be updated on the hormonal - dose effect level, as explained by the six experts advising the European Communities with regard to the JECFA Report. The European Communities contended that part of the scientific community; whose numbers were increasing steadily in the light of progress made by science, the better understanding of the mode of action of hormones and the development of better analytical methods, placed more attention on the carcinogenic risks arising from the possible genotoxic action of these hormones, irrespective of the dose in which they were administered to animals for growth promotion. In the absence of clear evidence to the contrary, the European Communities considered that it was entitled to follow a cautious approach and side with this body of scientists. This choice was in compliance with the proper definition of the concepts of "risk" and "risk assessment", contained in Articles 5.1 to 5.6 and in paragraph 4 of Annex A, of the SPS Agreement.

4.169 The European Communities referred the reports of Dr. Pérez-Comas in relation to detection, control and administration of hormones. Dr. Pérez-Comas argued that:

> "anomalous sexual development in Puerto Rico is a major and serious public health problem. (..) We have been detecting an increase of such cases since early in 1969 up to the present. Up to this date over 1,500 patients have been documented.
>
> "From our patients, we have deducted that environmental contaminants are a strong factor in etiology of the condition that affects children of both sexes, different races and nationalities residing in PR, and all ages in the form of Anomalous Sexual Development. (...) We have documented clinical evidence of increased serum total oestrogens in a significant number of patients, with over 60 per cent of the

[110] J. G. Liehr (1995), "Induction of a DNA adduct detectable by 32P-postlabeling in the dorsolateral prostate of NBL/Cr rats treated with oestradiol-17β and testosterone," *16 Carcinogenesis*, pp.951-954.

[111] B. T. Zhu, D. Roy and J. G. Liehr (1993), "The carcinogenic activity of ethinyl oestrogens is determined by both their hormonal characteristics and their conversion to catechol metabolites", *132 Endocrinology*, pp.577-583 (1993).

[112] J. G. Liehr (1994), "Mechanisms of metabolic activation and inactivation of catecholestrogens: a basis of genotoxicity," *6 Polycyclic Aromatic Compounds*, pp.229-239.

females with ovarian cysts, variable levels of FSH, LG & Prolactin, that recede or diminish in a significant number of patients after a meat and poultry depletion diet.

"We have been informed that anomalous sexual development cases are increasing in Chile, Bolivia and Colombia. As to our knowledge no definite cause have been found, but poultry and meat contamination is being considered, for in Latinamerica multiple use of growth promoting hormones have been documented. We consider that in PR the Anomalous Sexual Development in children is complex with different etiological factors such as zeranol, other unknown oestrogenic substances, and pesticides. Serious emphasis must be done on the control of these substances and its avoidance in animal husbandry. (...)"[113]

4.170 With regard to the nature and mode of action of hormones, **Canada** stressed that a complete review of the JECFA and IARC materials cited by the European Communities revealed that the carcinogenic effects of the three natural hormones occur only at doses that caused obvious hormonal effects. JECFA had concluded that, as the amount of these hormones ingested in meat from treated animals would be incapable of exerting a hormonal effect, they would be incapable of exerting a toxic effect in humans (see paragraph 2.22). Similarly, JECFA's recommended MRLs for zeranol and trenbolone were based on their no-hormonal-effect level. Humans consumed a range of carcinogens in their diets as illustrated by the fact that 27 natural pesticides that were carcinogenic in rodents were present at levels above 10 ppm in a wide variety of foods, including anise, apple, basil, brussels sprouts, cabbage, carrot, cauliflower, celery, cherries, clovers, coffee (brewed), comfrey herb tea, dill, eggplant, mustard (brown), nutmeg, orange juice, parsley, parsnip, pear, pepper (black), plum, potato, rosemary, sage, sesame seeds (heated), tarragon and thyme. In addition these 27 natural pesticides were present in a large number of other foods.[114] In Canada's view, the key factor was the dose: at the low levels ingested, these substances did not appear to pose a hazard to human health.

4.171 The **European Communities** did not deny that there was probably still a number of scientists who believed that "the carcinogenic effect of these hormones is related to the hormonal activity of these compounds, i.e. an increase in tumour incidence in tissues of animals with high levels of specific hormone receptors, which would not occur at normal physiological levels". However, this view was not held by another part of the scientific community; a part whose numbers were increasing steadily in the light of progress made by science, the better understanding of the mode of action of hormones and the development of better analytical methods. This

---

[113] A. Pérez-Comas and C.A. Saénz, "Anomalous Sexual Development in Puerto Rico: 28 years of Experience", 28 February 1997.

[114] B. Ames, "Human Cancer: Are Pesticides Responsible?" (1992) 45 *Western Society of Weed Science* 15, p.17. Canada submitted that in addition, the cooking of food was also a major dietary source of substances that were carcinogenic in rodents. "Cooking produces about 2000 mg per person per day of mostly untested burnt material that contains many rodent carcinogens -for example, polycyclic hydrocarbons, heterocyclic amines, furfural, nitrosamines - as well as a plethora of mutagens" *Ibid.*, p.18.

was the scientific opinion of Dr. Liehr and of the other scientists cited therein. In the absence of clear evidence to the contrary, the European Communities considered that it was entitled to follow a cautious approach and side with the body of scientists who placed more attention on the carcinogenic risks arising from the possible genotoxic action of these hormones, irrespective of the dose in which they were administered to animals for growth promotion. This choice was in compliance with the proper definition of the concepts of "risk" and "risk assessment", contained in Articles 5.1 to 5.6 and in Annex A.4 of the SPS Agreement.

(ii) Metabolites

4.172 The **European Communities** argued that other risks arose from the hormones at issue because of their metabolites. When drugs were introduced into the body, their pharmacological and toxic effects were directly correlated to their concentration in tissues and fluids. The concentration of a drug was a function of its resorption, excretion and metabolism. Drugs were metabolized (broken down) and their metabolites might also have pharmacological effects, which might differ from the effect of the parent drug. Metabolites might have different side or toxic effects. Anabolic steroids had a large variety of metabolites, some of which were only recently identified. The pharmacological and toxic behaviour of many of these metabolites were still unknown. In addition, the same parent substances might produce different metabolites in different species, making the extrapolation from studies on laboratory animals to humans unreliable.

4.173 The European Communities asserted that there were scientists who argued that knowledge about the toxicity of the metabolites of these hormones was as yet very limited. Moreover, metabolites of such substances which, even in low concentrations, might have highly toxic effects were generated in the human body.[115] These scientists argued that "the use of hormones in growth promotion of animals should not be allowed, as it cannot be excluded that unchanged agents, their metabolites and, above all, unknown highly effective and toxic metabolites are distributed with the meat which is purchased by consumers".[116] Moreover, in some of the experimental studies on which the 1988 JECFA Report was based, no extensive research and risk assessment of the potential risks arising from the metabolites of the hormones under consideration had been carried out.[117] Noting that despite all the uncertainties, JECFA had decided to establish a temporary ADI for trenbolone acetate while requesting additional information to be submitted to it by 1990, the European Communities argued that in light of the arguments advanced by some scientists, it was questionable whether the decision of the JECFA could be regarded as a reasonable one.

[115] W. Schänzer, "The Illegal use of Anabolic Agents in Sport", *1995 EC Scientific Conference Proceedings*, p.352.

[116] *Ibid.*, p.353.

[117] As an example, the European Communities noted that, as regards trenbolone acetate (TBA), the JECFA had stated that "In the absence of satisfactory toxicological data the Committee was unable to establish a separate no-effect level for the a-TBOH metabolite. It also noted that this metabolite was not produced in significant amount in the rat, which made it inadvisable to extrapolate from data generated from ß-epimer, experiments in that species".

4.174 The European Communities added that, as Dr. Liehr[118] and the other scientists advising the European Communities, as well as other scientists[119] had shown, the metabolic pathways of oestradiol had revealed that free radicals were continuously produced, and DNA damage by these free radicals, as well as DNA adduct formation, had been demonstrated in a range of tissues. These experiments with the metabolites of oestradiol provided strong evidence that oestradiol (and possibly the other natural hormones) was a genotoxic carcinogen. Therefore, the 1988 JECFA Report was out of date also in this respect and needed to be updated in the light of the most recent scientific evidence.

4.175 **Canada** claimed that the EC arguments with respect to metabolites did not identify any risk posed by the six hormones at issue when used for growth promoting purposes in animals. The European Communities focused on the conclusions of one paper presented in the 1995 EC Scientific Conference that examined the illegal use of anabolic steroids in athletes and not the use of the six hormones at issue for growth promotion in cattle. Moreover, with regard to the absence of satisfactory toxicological data on trenbolone metabolites in the JECFA Report, the European Communities failed to note that the additional research on these metabolites had been provided to JECFA before it had made its final recommendation.[120]

(iii) Combinations of Hormones and Multiple Exposure

4.176 Referring to scientists' reports at the 1995 EC Scientific Conference of evidence of the illegal use of growth-promoting substances in many European countries and elsewhere[121], the **European Communities** submitted that the illegal use of mixtures of veterinary drugs and growth promoters might result in unpredictable residue levels in edible foods, which might constitute a risk for the consumer. This might be due to variations in physiological and pathological parameters, altering drug disposition and elimination. Biotransformation patterns of synthetic drugs and hormones might differ markedly depending on the animal species and gender. Interactions might occur between compounds as had been reported for sulphadimidine and oestrogenic and androgenic hormones administered to dwarf goats. This might require longer withdrawal times in order to arrive at safe residue levels. For those reasons, the 1995 EC Scientific Conference had concluded that "the use of combinations (or cocktails) of hormones poses serious risks for the health of consumers because the use of mixtures, which usually contain illegal substances, is made in the form of in-

118 J. G. Liehr, (1990), "Genotoxic effects of oestrogens, 238 Mutation Research" 269-276; J. G. Liehr, (1994), "Mechanisms of Metabolic Activation and Inactivation of Catecholestrogens: A basis of genotoxicity, 6 Polycyclic Aromatic Compounds" pp.229-239.

119 B. T. Zhu et al. (1993), "The carcinogenic activity of ethinyl oestrogens is determined by both their hormonal characteristics and their conversion to catechol metabolites," *132 Endocrinology*, pp.577-583; M. L. Winter et al., "Possible mechanism of induction of benign prostatic hyperplasia by oestradiol and dihydrotestosterone in dogs" (1996), *136 Toxicol. Appl. Pharmacol*, pp.211-219.

120 "Evaluation of certain veterinary drug residues in food: Thirty-fourth Report of the Joint FAO/WHO Expert Committee on Food Additives," *Technical Report* Series 788 (Geneva: WHO, 1989), pp.40-42.

121 Steering Committee, "Report and Conclusions", *1995 EC Scientific Conference Proceedings*, p.9.

jections, rather than implants, and this is an impediment to their detection at slaughter. This potentially allows the sale of meat containing very high concentrations of hormones".[122]

4.177 The JECFA Report had pointed clearly to the need to examine the effects of combination:

> "The Committee noted that several of the hormonally active substances on the agenda were used in combination one with another, and recommended that, where substances having similar physiological activities were combined, evidence that their hormonal effects were additive, rather than synergistic, should be provided. The Committee agreed that data on the residues of each of the substances that are used in combination should be available for evaluation, whether or not their physiological activities were similar" (page 7).

However, despite this warning, the JECFA Report had not examined the additive or synergistic effects of any of these hormones, despite the fact that it was fully aware that combinations of these substances were commercially available. Scientists agreed that the concept of ADI was *not* applicable to assess the risk from exposure to mixtures (or cocktails) of compounds. In the EC view, the potentially disastrous effects of cocktails of hormones was now clearly high on the scientific agenda, as had been recently reported for oestrogenic environmental compounds:

> "The relatively low potencies of each of these compounds have suggested that these chemicals alone are unlikely to produce adverse health effects in humans. However, these compounds occur as mixtures in the environment, and their combined action has not been well studied."[123]

4.178 The report referred to scientific research which established that combinations (cocktails) of two weak environmental oestrogens (a natural environmental hormone) were *1000* times more potent than any compound alone. And the report concluded as follows:

> "The possibility for synergistic action of apparently inactive chemicals functioning as hormones may represent a *previously uncharacterized level of receptor-mediated gene regulation*. The interaction of multiple chemicals with the oestrogen receptor suggests a complex interplay between environmental signals and biological systems"[124] (emphasis added).

The European Communities concluded that there was considerable potential hazard arising from the use of combinations, containing authorized or unauthorized hormones, and the existing international rules did not deal adequately with this potential hazard.

---

[122] Steering Committee, "Report and Conclusions", *1995 EC Scientific Conference Proceedings*, p.9, and H.A. Kuiper, "Risk Assessment Strategies for Xenobiotics", *1995 EC Scientific Conference Proceedings*, p.376.

[123] "Synergistic Activation of Oestrogen Receptor with Combinations of Environmental chemicals," 7 June 1996, *Science*, Vol. 272, pp.1489-1492.

[124] *Ibid.*

4.179 **Canada** argued that the EC discussion of combinations and "cocktails" blured the distinctions between combinations of hormones present in legal, approved veterinary products, and mixtures containing illegal drugs such as those sold on the black market in the European Communities. The formulations in approved hormonal implants combined hormones to balance the hormonal effects, achieve optimal growth promotion, and regulate the release rate of the hormones in the implant. In Canada, a veterinary product was approved after a comprehensive review of the drug *as formulated*. Thus, Canada's review of approved hormonal implants containing a combination of hormones examined the safety of these substances *in combination*. In addition, the hormonal implants approved in Canada did not contain combinations of substances that had the same hormonal effect: trenbolone was not combined with testosterone, zeranol was not combined with oestradiol-17β, and MGA was not combined with progesterone.

4.180 In contrast to the combinations of hormones found in legal, approved veterinary products, "cocktails" were mixtures containing illegal substances and Canada agreed that the use of illegal substances, whether used singly or in "cocktails", was dangerous. These substances were not at issue here, and the European Communities had not presented any evidence to show that preventing the use of these illegal substances would also require the complete prohibition on the use of the six hormones at issue.

4.181 Canada referred to the answers of the scientific experts, who noted that legally marketed combinations of growth promoting hormones have been examined, approved and registered by competent national authorities. Moreover, as Dr. Arnold noted in his written answers to the Panel's questions:

> "... the pharmacodynamic and toxic effects of practically all combinations of oestrogens, progestins and androgens one can think about have been studied in whole animals, organs, tissue and cell cultures, and other *in vitro* systems under a great variety of conditions and these effects are known from literature."[125]

Canada recalled that Dr. Arnold stated that legally permitted combinations were used not only for growth promotion purposes, but also for the purposes permitted by the European Communities, such as the synchronization of oestrus.[126]

4.182 Canada stated that on the issue of synergistic effects, Dr. Arnold noted that there were a variety of synergistic and antagonistic interactions among the hormones, but that at the levels of residues present in treated animals, it was not apparent what kind of hazards could arise from maximal changes of less than 0.1 per cent in internal, human hormone pools due to the consumption of meat from a hormone-treated animal.[127] In addition, Canada informed the Panel that the synergistic effects of *environmental oestrogens* cited by the European Communities as reported by *McLachlan*

[125] Dr. Arnold, answer to Panel question 15, para. 6.159.

[126] *Ibid.*, para. 6.159.

[127] *Ibid.*, para. 6.159.

et al.[128] had *not* been found by *four* other laboratories that tried to replicate the experiments.

4.183 Noting that at least nine combinations of hormones for growth promotion were freely available for sale in Canada, the **European Communities** contended that risks may potentially arise from the multiple exposure of humans to hormones and other chemical substances which were similar to those resulting from the illegal use of combinations (or cocktails) of hormones. All foodstuffs, whether of animal or plant origin, were likely to contain trace amounts of several substances derived from various sources, a fact currently not addressed in any risk assessment strategy for food. Because the ADI and MRL assessed the safety of a *single* compound and not the exposure to *mixtures* of compounds, a sufficient protection of humans was only guaranteed if the MRL was not exceeded. Thus, there was a substance-related risk to consumers if the acute ingestion of a residue amount exceeded the established MRL and possibly the ADI. The Codex itself had noted that "Uncertainty in the safety evaluation process is primarily addressed through the use of safety factors. Their respective values are arbitrary and have no measured biological significance, however, their appropriateness is somewhat borne out by experience".[129] The "safety factor", therefore, might not provide the necessary protection, especially in the case of potentially carcinogenic substances whose mode of action was not clear, as the example of the hormone DES[130] had shown. The "safety factor" was in reality no more than a useful tool and applied to those scientific reports which depended on extrapolations from imperfect data on laboratory animals to set ADIs and MRLs for human beings. Although these concepts had served well in the past and would continue to do so in the future, a Member was entitled to deviate from these concepts as used by Codex in establishing recommendations. Codex had proven to be useful in setting guidelines and recommendations for food additives precisely because it had left its members free to decide whether they would accept its recommendations. The SPS Agreement was cast largely on the same basis, because it allowed its Members to depart from international standards, guidelines or recommendations under the conditions laid down therein (e.g. Article 3:3).

4.184 The European Communities further contended that the question also arose on how to protect consumers from a potential adverse effect resulting from long-term treatment with growth- promoting substances. Such adverse effect was the possibility

---

[128] EC first written submission.

[129] "Risk Assessment Procedures used by the Codex Alimentarius Commission and its Subsidiary Advisory Bodies," (1993), *Codex Alimentarius Commission*, p.11.

[130] The European Communities explained that Diethylstilboestrol (DES) was a synthetic hormone which improved both rate of gain and feed efficiency in poultry, cattle and sheep. DES was perhaps the most widely known of oestrogenic growth promoting agents. It was first used in the US therapeutically in pregnant women in the 1940's to prevent abortion. The US Government approved its use as a feed additive for poultry in 1947, for cattle in 1954 and later for sheep. In 1971, its carcinogenic effects in humans and in laboratory animals was clearly established. Additional studies showed that DES had other effects on daughters and sons of mothers treated with it, the most common being vaginal adenosis and other gross abnormalities of the reproductive tract. At the time (1976) these studies were published, an estimated 25 million cattle and 7 million sheep were being treated with DES. Still, its complete withdrawal from the US market was achieved only in 1978, while in the meantime the US FDA was trying to discover and fix acceptable "no residue" limits.

that the biotransformation of other compounds may be altered, as had been shown in the case of steroids. This might result in altered residue kinetics for those compounds.[131] The European Communities claimed that the idea that there may be a risk associated with the long-term exposure to a mixture of substances, resulting in a possible biotransformation of other compounds, was a precursor to the so-called "precautionary" principle and it was at the heart of the policy followed by the European Communities on such issues[132].

4.185 **Canada** argued that in its discussion of multiple exposure, the European Communities had not identified any risk posed by the six hormones at issue. Moreover, if there were any concern over lifetime exposure to a variety of chemicals, it would apply equally well to other veterinary drugs. Yet in its approval procedures for new veterinary drugs, it would appear that the European Communities did not require the testing of new drugs in combination with all existing drugs to ensure there was no "... risk associated with the long-term exposure to a mixture of substances resulting in a possible biotransformation of other compounds ....". This was not surprising, since the number of combinations and permutations of veterinary drugs would render the task impossible. Yet it was a fact that EC farm animals were exposed to a variety of veterinary products throughout their lives.

(iv) Detection and Control

4.186 The **European Communities** argued that difficulties arose because the identification of animals or meat from animals which had been treated with the three natural hormones was difficult due to the wide variation in natural levels of these hormones arising because of factors such as sex, age, diet, physiological condition, etc. While residue analysis for natural hormones in treated animals could experimentally show differences between them and untreated animals, it was currently not possible through routine tests to identify treated animals on the basis of assays of edible tissue samples, and it was also difficult using blood, urine or faeces. A country allowing imports of animals and meat from animals treated with hormones would have to rely largely on checks and controls on use of hormones carried out by the exporting country if trade was not to be impeded, but the importing country would also have to carry out checks and controls in order to ensure that its consumers ate meat which conformed to the requisite standards. Detection and surveillance of hormones was based on screening methods, principally immunoassays (radio or enzyme immunoassays) because they were rapid, relatively low cost and could be applied simultaneously to a large series of samples.[133] However, the European Communities claimed that all the available methods used for detection and control had their limits and drawbacks. Furthermore, although Codex had established an *ad hoc* working group on the matter, there were still no internationally agreed rules for the methods

---

131 "Assessment of Health Risk", Working Group II, *1995 EC Scientific Conference Proceedings*, p.20.

132 See also the reply of Dr. Lucier to question 15, para. 6.161.

133 M-L Scippo and G Maghuin-Rogister, "Methods of Detection and Surveillance of Natural Sex Steroid Hormones", *1995 EC Scientific Conference Proceedings*, p.541 et seq.

to be used for residue control programmes.[134] The European Communities argued that in light of the potential risks to human and animal health resulting from the uncertainties in residue control programmes and the absence of internationally agreed rules, any Member (including the European Communities) was entitled to adopt a regulatory system to achieve the level of protection for its public that it considered to be appropriate.[135]

4.187 The European Communities added that the Codex Alimentarius Commission did not establish MRLs for the three natural hormones essentially because of the difficulty in detecting and measuring the residues, not because their presence at high concentration levels would not pose risks to human health (as did the residues of the synthetic hormones for which MRLs were established). However, Canada's 1996 Plan for the examination of residues in live animals and fresh meat appeared to include testing even for the natural hormones, although the detection limit was said to be "qualitative".

4.188 The European Communities claimed that the hormones were very powerful and genotoxic substances. Risks to consumers' health could not be excluded if hormonally active growth promoters were abusively administered. It was unlikely that authorization of these substances as growth promoters would end their extreme misuse potential. It was obvious that the authorization of a substance distinctly restricted its controllability; thus, the misuse of authorized substances was hardly controllable. Therefore, in the context of a preventive protection of consumers' health it should be self-evident to take the misuse potential of a substance into consideration. If health risks to consumers could not be excluded when a substance was misused, single substances with an extreme misuse potential could also be banned even if the substances were not hazardous in the case of a legal application.[136]

4.189 The European Communities noted that the report of the Food Inspection Directorate of Canada on meat and egg products (Volume 1, fiscal year 1995/96) provided the following information as regarded violations of the MRLs set by Canada: for *zeranol*: 1 violation out of 275 samples of beef bile and liver tested, for *trenbolone*: 1 violation out of 33 samples of beef liver tested, 3 violations out of 155 veal liver and 3 veal muscle tested; for *MGA*: 2 violations out of 69 samples of mares tested. The European Communities argued that had it chosen to apply the MRLs recommended by Codex, it would have exposed itself to possible violations in its market of products which would be legally marketed and used. For that reason, its level of protection could have not been observed. A level of protection of no residues of these hormones in meat destined for human consumption, coupled with the other strict conditions imposed by EC law, were considered by the competent EC authorities to be the only reasonably available measures to safeguard human and animal

[134] The European Communities stressed that in 1991 the Codex Commission had only established *provisional methods* to serve as a potential source of use. See Joint FAO/WHO Food Standards Programme, Residues of Veterinary Drugs in Food, Vol. 3, 2nd Ed., 1993.

[135] The European Communities noted that, for example, Argentina prohibited the use of the three natural hormones (while allowing the use of the two synthetic ones), citing as an essential motive for the restriction the lack of suitable methods for measuring hormone residue levels in meat. *1983 OIE Scientific Report*, at p.411.

[136] See *1995 EC Scientific Conference Proceedings*, pp.537-539.

health in the European Communities. If violations of this level of protection were discovered from time to time, this could result only from illegal use of prohibited substances (a risk inherent in any legal system) and not from the use of authorized products.

4.190 **Canada** claimed that the EC discussion of detection and control failed to identify any risk posed by the six hormones at issue when used for growth promoting purposes in animals. Detection of the misuse of substances was necessary whether products were allowed or not. Presumably, the European Communities sampled and tested meat produced in the European Communities and imported meat for excessive levels of all permitted drugs. The detection of *illegal* substances (such as beta-agonists) was not impaired by permitting the six hormones at issue for growth promotion.

(v) Administration and Use of Hormones

4.191 The **European Communities** observed that all scientists agreed that if the hormones at issue were allowed to be used for animal growth, they must be administered in accordance with good veterinary practice. This requirement was apparently shared also by Canada, which often stated that "hormones are used and regulated as veterinary drugs in several countries, including Canada, the US, Australia and New Zealand". However, the European Communities argued that if the terms "regulated as veterinary drugs" referred to growth promoters, then it was not being used in a sense which the European Communities would recognize. This was apparent from the conditions under which "RALGRO", an hormone implant containing zeranol, was permitted to be used in Canada. According to the 1995 Compendium of Veterinary Products used in Canada, "RALGRO" implanting might be repeated "as often as good husbandry practice allows through the growing and finishing phases of the animal's life". Indeed, it would appear that none of the hormones at issue had to be administered by a veterinarian when used for growth promotion.

4.192 The European Communities shared the view that these hormones should be used in accordance with good veterinary practice when administered for growth promotion, since when the EC Commission considered the alternative of permitting the use of the three natural hormones only for growth promotion in 1984[137], it thought necessary to specify six conditions of administration in order to safeguard public. One of these conditions was administration only by a veterinarian. The JECFA Report required that use patterns be based on data submitted "on the patterns of use of each veterinary drug, including information about what are recognized as good veterinary or animal husbandry practices under different local conditions" (page 11). The 1995 EC Scientific Conference had also concluded that "compliance with Good Agricultural and Good Veterinary Practice are necessary" (page 5). The European Communities pointed out that, as these hormones were veterinary drugs, they had to be used in accordance with good veterinary practice, as laid down in the legislation of each Member. This was provided for by the Codex Code of Practice, which allowed Members to decide whether veterinary products (like the hormones)

---

[137] COM(84)295.

should be used only in accordance with label instructions approved by the authorities, or at least under prescription and instruction of a qualified veterinarian. Canada had choosen the first approach, failing to perform the required number of controls and testing to ensure their respect. After having examined the second approach, the European Communities had decided that the costs of the various elements of control involved would be very high to effectively ensure its level of protection. For these and other reasons, explained in this report, the European Communities had decided against the use of these hormones in food producing animals for growth promotion. As regarded veterinary medicinal products (i.e. all veterinary therapeutic products), the EC legislation conformed to the requirements of the Codex Code of Practice. In the EC view, zootechnical use must also be performed by a veterinarian or under his direct supervision, because it did not differ from the administration point of view from use of these hormones for therapeutic purposes. Indeed, the zootechnical purposes mentioned in the EC legislation did not differ in essence from therapeutic use; if similar treatments were performed on human beings they would be performed by doctors alone. That was the reason why in the European Communities therapeutic or zootechnical use was permitted only if performed by the veterinarian (or under his direct supervision for some types of zootechnical use), with all treatments recorded and the treated animals identified in order to respect withdrawal periods.

4.193 The European Communities observed that the Codex definitions left the responsibility of defining the actual conditions in practice to national authorities. The effect of this was that good practice, veterinary or agricultural, was compliance with national rules. However, nowhere did Codex suggest that countries should accept each other's standards automatically as being in compliance with good practice. As far as the European Communities was concerned, Good Veterinary Practice in the use of hormones was the set of conditions defined in its legislation. The European Communities did not accept that potentially dangerous veterinary drugs could be given to farmers to use in accordance with "Good Agricultural Practice", as they might use pesticides or fertilisers. Good veterinary practice was the proper conduct of a veterinarian, not a sub-set of farming. The terms of reference of JECFA included the obligation to determine acceptable and safe residues levels for veterinary drugs in food "when the drugs in question are administered to animals in accordance with good veterinary and animal husbandry practice". For the hormone growth promoters, the 1988 JECFA seemed to have had forgotten about the veterinary aspect, even though these were veterinary drugs with powerful physiological and toxicological properties. This contrasted sharply with other JECFA reports on veterinary drugs with comparable toxicological properties which provided in their evaluation that treatment of animals should be made in accordance with good practice in the use of veterinary drugs.[138]

4.194 The European Communities argued that although Codex had recommended an International Code of Practice for Control of the Use of Veterinary Drugs in 1993, it was not clear how far and how strictly this Codex Code of Practice was adhered to by countries. Moreover, despite the obvious need to administer hormones in accor-

[138] The European Communities noted that this had been the case, for instance, of the drugs carbadox and olaquindox (1991 JECFA report, 36th meeting, pages 169 and 202, WHO Series 27 (1991)).

dance with good veterinary practice, the JECFA Report considered that five of these hormones were not likely to pose risks to human health if used "in accordance with good animal husbandry practice", a term which it had not defined. The term "Good Animal Husbandry Practice" was assumed to be analogous to "Good Agricultural Practice", but referred specifically to good practice in the care and rearing of animals. It was also used in relation to, for example, feeding and housing of farm animals.

4.195 In the view of the European Communities, the phrase "good animal husbandry practice" did not make sense regarding potentially carcinogenic substances. The difference between "good agricultural practice" and "good veterinary practice" was significant. Good veterinary practice was the proper conduct of a veterinarian, not a sub-set of farming. "Good Practice in the Use of Veterinary Drugs" was the official recommended or authorized usage including withdrawal periods, approved by national authorities, of veterinary drugs under practical conditions. "Good Agricultural Practice in the Use of Pesticides" included the nationally authorized safe uses of pesticides under actual conditions necessary for effective and reliable pest control. It encompassed a range of levels of pesticide applications up to the highest authorized use, applied in a manner which left a residue which was the smallest amount practicable.

4.196 The European Communities argued that for the hormone growth promoters, JECFA had promptly forgotten about the veterinary aspect, even though these were veterinary drugs with powerful physiological and toxicological properties, referring only to "good animal husbandry practice". However, the Codex Commission had stated with regards to zeranol that:

> "The Committee noted that the Acceptable Residue Level, established by JECFA had been based on the maximum residue levels occurring after use of the substance in accordance with Good Practice in the Use of *Veterinary* Drugs and was well below the level which would be of any toxicological significance".[139]

Equally, other JECFA reports on veterinary drugs provided that treatment of animals should be made in accordance with good practice in the use of *veterinary* drugs. This was the case of drugs like carbadox and olaquindox.[140]

4.197 The European Communities noted that the Codex definition of a "veterinary product" was provided in paragraph 3 of the Recommended International Code of Practice for Control of the Use of Veterinary Drugs, which read as follows:

> "Veterinary products (including premixes for manufacture of medicated feedingstuffs) used in food producing animals should be administered (or incorporated into feed) in compliance with the relevant product information approved by national authorities and/or in accordance with a prescription and/or instruction issued by a qualified veterinarian".

---

[139] Alinorm 89/31A, *Codex Commission*, 18th session of 3-12 July 1989, p.10, para. 78.

[140] "Toxicological evaluation of certain veterinary drug residues in food," *1991 JECFA Report, 36th meeting, WHO Food Additives Series 27*, pp.169 and 202.

It followed that a member of Codex was allowed to require that a veterinary product, used for improving animal production, might be used only on prescription and under the direct supervision of a qualified veterinarian. This was clearly not the situation in Canada, where these products were used by farmers without prescription. The European Communities argued that in Canada, the number of animals tested was very small and yet within this extremely small number of samples violations of tolerance levels had been recorded. The question then could be whether this information should be taken into account when performing a risk assessment. In view of the potential for misuse and the powerful incentives for farmers not to respect the conditions of use prescribed in the labels, it could be more appropriate to prohibit the use of these substances for growth promotion. Use on prescription and under the direct supervision of a qualified veterinarian was one of the conditions under which the EC Commission had considered the option of allowing the use of the three natural hormones for growth promotion in 1984, which had been rejected for the reasons explained above (paragraph 4.18) by the competent EC legislative bodies. The European Communities indicated that high costs probably explained the extremely low percentage of tests and controls performed in Canada, because the economic benefit derived from the use of these hormones for growth promotion would probably not suffice to undertake an appropriate level of control.

4.198 The European Communities argued that there were additional risks to human and animal health arising from the administration and potential misuse of hormones. Scientists had argued that:

> "In the present concept of establishing MRLs based on good veterinary practice, the possibilities to detect a misuse of authorized substances are mainly reduced to a direct proof. (...) The profitable misuse of authorized hormonally active growth promoters does not have to lead to a violation of the MRL, either, if an MRL is established at all. In the case of hormonally active growth promoters, too, a misuse could be hazardous to consumers if instead of the authorized implant cheaper black-market products are administered to the animals via injection at undefined parts of the animals' bodies.
>
> "(...) If hormonally active substances were authorized, this would probably also lead to a dramatic reduction of the possibilities to reveal such a misuse with the help of detected injection sites, because there would no longer be indications to select animals during the post-and ante-mortem examination that are considered to be suspicious of a hormonal treatment. On the contrary, each animal would have to be controlled for injecting sites. Since this is completely unrealistic, a randomised selection of the carcasses remains the only control for injection sites. Consumers could thus be subject to the risk of eating undetected, maybe highly contaminated injection sites.
>
> "(...) In the context of a preventive protection of consumers' health it should be self-evident to take the misuse potential of a substance into consideration, when it is assessed for health risks. If health risks to consumers cannot be excluded when a substance is misused, single substances with an extreme misuse potential could also be banned

even if the substances are not hazardous in the case of a legal application (...)."[141]

4.199 The European Communities indicated that the provisions of EC law concerning inspection and control were essentially contained in Directives 85/358/EEC and 86/469/EEC.[142] According to these Directives, the EC member States must present yearly inspection plans and yearly results of their examinations, providing detailed descriptions of, *inter alia*, random sampling of selected live and slaughtered animals; investigation of live suspect animals and meat with details of the substances searched for, the numbers of samples planned and taken, and the analytical methods used. The EC Commission ensured the conformity of the yearly inspection plans with the Directives. On average, about 200,000 samples of animals were checked every year in the European Communities.

4.200 The European Communities claimed that the situation of residue controls and checks in Canada was not entirely clear. It would appear that National Programme Plans existed for each year, but only a very limited number of samples of animals were checked each year. For example, for zeranol it was foreseen that samples of only 650 animals would be tested in 1996. For trenbolone acetate samples of only 325 animals, for MGA samples of 275 animals, and for the three natural hormones samples of only 40 animals.

4.201 The European Communities argued that to state that hormones "are" implanted in the middle third of the animal's ear was to believe that, under practical farm conditions, such precision was a matter of routine. The European Communities claimed that from an examination of the Canadian directives for implantation of "Compudose" implants containing oestradiol and oxytetracycline, published in the 1995 Compendium of Veterinary Products in Canada, it was illusionary to believe that farmers could respect these procedures on a routine basis when administering these hormones for growth promotion. Another example constituted the dosage and implantation directions for "REVALOR-S", an implant containing both trenbolone acetate and oestradiol hormones, with no withdrawal time required, which misleadingly stated that "all implanted animals are visually inspected upon arrival at the slaughterhouse". Other products containing zeranol, oestradiol and testosterone in isolation or in combinations were "Ralgro Ralabol" and "Synovex-H", for which no withdrawal time was required and which improperly used could result in residues of these hormones much higher than the naturally produced hormones, exceeding tolerance levels. In fact, there was no special identification of implanted animals. All animals, implanted or not, should indeed be "visually inspected" upon arrival at a slaughterhouse, but this was part of the normal ante-mortem health inspection; it had nothing to do with hormone implants, which could not usually be detected by visual inspection. Discarding the ear at slaughter was only useful if the implant was still

---

141 B. Jülicher, "Sampling Strategies", in *1995 EC Scientific Conference Proceedings*, pp.537-539. "Detection and Surveillance", Working-Group III, *idem*, pp.33-34.

142 *EC Official Journal* L 191, 23 July 1985, p.46, and *EC Official Journal* L 275, 26 September 1986, p.36. The European Communities noted that these provisions have now been reviewed, improved and re-enacted in new Directive 96/23/EC, of 29 April 1996, which will enter into force on 1 July 1997.

present in the ear, but as a significant proportion of implants migrated to other parts of the body, it might be irrelevant.

4.202 **Canada** claimed that the EC discussion of administration and use failed to identify any risk posed by the six hormones at issue when used for growth promoting purposes in animals. The EC argument focused on the fact that hormone implants were not administered by veterinarians, in the mistaken assumption that farmers were incapable of administering these implants themselves. Referring to procedures for administering hormone implants, the European Communities belittled farmers, asserting that "... it is illusionary to believe that farmers can respect these procedures on a routine basis when administering these hormones for growth promotion". The European Communities provided no evidence to support this assertion.

4.203 Canadian producers routinely and effectively administered treatments and vaccines for which their animals' health depended upon proper application. The application of growth promoting hormone implants was a routine practice that Canadian producers handled with a high level of competence. Moreover, it would appear that the European Communities also trusted its farmers to handle these kinds of repetitious, technical tasks. For example, in some EC member States, farmers did not need a prescription to obtain vaccines that were administered to food-producing animals by injection.[143] In the United Kingdom, farmers did not need a prescription to obtain some local anaesthetics that are administered by injection.[144] Presumably, these injections were administered by the farmer without the supervision of a veterinarian. Similarly, benzylpenicillin must be infused into the udder of a cow to treat mastitis. Benzylpenicillin was available over-the-counter in at least one EC member State. Again, presumably, these treatments were administered without the supervision of a veterinarian.

4.204 Canada stated it was apparent that the EC purported concerns with the abuse and misuse of growth promoting hormones would apply equally, or with greater force, to a variety of veterinary drugs permitted for use in the European Communities. For example, with regard to MGA, administered as an additive in feedstuffs, the European Communities stated that, "[f]or MGA there is a withdrawal period of 48 hours prior to slaughter ... it should not be taken for granted that the prescribed withdrawal period will always be respected. ... substances which are proven to be carcinogenic, *if* allowed to be used, they should be done so only under the most strict conditions possible." In Canada's view, the irony of the EC statements was that the European Communities allowed its farmers to use carbadox and olaquindox in feed additives, without veterinary supervision, and without monitoring the resulting residues (unless a member State chose to do so). Both substances were genotoxic and required a *28 - day* withdrawal period. As the Working Group on the Assessment of Health Risks in the EC 1995 Scientific Conference concluded:

> "The antimicrobial drugs Carbadox and Olaquindox (called quinoxalines), possess genotoxic and/or carcinogenic properties. Ap-

[143] A.R.M. Kidd (September 1992), "Distribution of Veterinary Medicines within the European Community: Final Report prepared for DG III of the Commission of the European Communities" Table 6, p.48.

[144] *Ibid.*, Table 4, p.43.

preciable amounts of residues are found in treated animals. ADI values cannot yet be established. But their restricted use in pigs only during the first four months coupled with the specified 28-day withdrawal period should lead to negligible residues at the time of slaughter and minimize the risk of exposure for consumers. This implied safety feature requires the application of good agricultural/veterinary practice which, however, cannot completely be guaranteed, for example, when slaughtering piglets, there is a potential contradiction between the allowed dosage of the drugs up to 4 months of age and a required withdrawal period of 28 days."[145]

4.205 The **European Communities** noted that with regard to the administration and use of hormones the whole issue of the competing interests involved had been explained by a world expert on this issue. Dr. Roy Hertz, M.D., Director of the National Cancer Institute's Endocrinology Branch for twenty-eight years and now with the Department of Pharmacology at the George Washington University Medical Center, USA, was cited by Orville Schell, in his book *Modern Meat*:

> "(...) to have rigorously defended in 1978 what he called the oestrogen-cancer hypothesis, namely that both exogenous and endogenous oestrogens and their metabolites play a significant and possibly etiologic [disease causing] role in the pathogenesis of cancer in estrogen-responsible tissues of man and animal." (...) When pressed by a colleague to be more specific about the levels of exogenous estrogen that must exist in meat before a risk of cancer to the consumer becomes really meaningful, Hertz replied simply, "The answer to your question is that we do not know. (...) I know that industry people say that the amount of oestrogens they are adding to an animal's system are far below levels that naturally occur after conception. But my response to them is, "Fine. But why add more?" The natural surges of hormones are already enough of a biological burden on the body. We know that these endogenous hormones already play a vital role in the development of malignancies in the female genital tracts and in the breast. So, just because these chemicals are present in the body doesn't justify burdening it with even more, particularly when the amounts that are effective are in microgram quantities. With regard to birth control pills there are two conditions that make the circumstances very different ... the first is that contraceptives are taken under the supervision of a doctor. The second is that when a consumer decides to take them, she is making a free choice, presumably with full knowledge of the alternatives and the possible adverse effects. But in the case of hormonal food additives, the consumer has no idea that he or she is ingesting them. And I simply don't see any reason why a person should be involuntarily exposed to them. I simply take a purist view about these kinds of food additives ... unless there is a compelling need - in the case of famine, for instance - I don't think the actual, or even potential,

145 *1995 EC Scientific Conference Proceedings*, pp.24 to 25.

> risk can be justified. For drug companies to present these compounds as being without risk ... is completely out of order, since we don't really know what their long-term cancer-causing consequences will be."

4.206 The European Communities asserted that for the substances benzylpenicillin and ivermectin, Article 4(3)(b) of Directive 81/851/EEC, as amended by Directive 90/676/EEC[146], required *a prescription by a veterinarian* for the dispensing to the public of veterinary medicinal products in order to avoid risks to consumers of foodstuffs obtained from treated animals. If in some member States no prescription was effectively required, this was not in conformity with the provisions of this Directive. The EC Commission had requested the information from all EC member States, but not all of them had yet replied. The situation of those which had replied was as follows: in Germany and Denmark neither of these two substances could be obtained without prescription. Canada admitted that prescription was also required in France. In the Netherlands, benzylpenicillin was subject to veterinarian prescription. Ireland had not yet replied, but the Commission disposed of information which showed that only benzylpenicillin was available without prescription and only to farmer organisations carrying out a special programme for the prevention of mastitis in cows. This programme was carried out under veterinary supervision to a limited number of animals. The European Communities argued that Canada had made such a wide reference to so many substances, that it was difficult to follow where its argument was leading the legal discussion. Progressively, Canada had confined the issue of consistency to very few substances and it appeared that there were two of them on which Canada had concentrated its arguments: carbadox and olaquindox, because they were said to pose the same type of risks to human and animal health. The European Communities had explained the conditions under which carbadox and olaquindox were allowed to be used in the European Communities. On the basis of the differences stressed by the European Communities, it could be argued that carbadox and olaquindox were different substances from the hormones at issue. They were administered to one type of animals only (piglets) and they acted only indirectly as growth promoters. The conditions imposed by the EC measures guaranteed, however, that there were no residues of carbadox and olaquindox in meat destined for human consumption. So the level of protection was the same with regard to these two substances and the hormones. The European Communities had shown that it would not be able to guarantee the same level of protection for these hormones, had it decided to follow the Codex MRLs. In the case of carbadox and olaquindox, the EC level of protection was also no risks from residues of these hormones in meat destined for human consumption. But the fact that it had choosen to apply this level of protection by measures different from those that it applied to growth hormones was irrelevant to this Panel. The European Communities choose its measures in the light of the specific circumstances in which each substance was used in order to achieve its appropriate level of protection.

4.207 The JECFA scientific report on carbadox and olaquindox was dated from 1991. It had concluded that although carbadox was a carcinogenic chemical sub-

[146] *EC Official Journal* L 373, 31 December 1990, p.15.

stance, the residues of the metabolites which could be detected in the muscle of pig meat, if the conditions of use were respected, were not carcinogenic. It was on this evaluation that JECFA had authorized the use of carbadox. The EC legislation respected all the conditions of use indicated in the JECFA report. On olaquindox, the conclusions of the JECFA report were not conclusive and further studies had been requested. But the provisional use of olaquindox under good practice in the use of veterinary drugs was allowed. The EC legislation respected the conditions of use for olaquindox. The European Communities had allowed the use of carbadox and olaquindox since 1988. At the Council of Ministers of 26 February 1996, the decision had been taken to review the authorizations of a number of substances among which were carbadox and olaquindox. This had been confirmed in the Council of Ministers meeting of 16 December 1996. This showed that the European Communities was already taking action on these two substances on its own initiative.

(vi) Other Parameters

4.208 The **European Communities** argued that a potential source of risk frequently mentioned by scientists stemmed from uncertainty about the nature and reliability of the methods used to establish the relevant data. The procedure for characterising the risk from the use of hormones had remained largely unchanged for 30-40 years and scientists had argued that the process of the scientific assessment of the risk should draw on the science base to assess the risk, then address uncertainties, rather than fuse these two elements together. However, a much sounder scientific approach was to encourage strongly the investigation of the mechanism of toxicity of each new promoter. Unless more effort were directed to understanding why a particular adverse effect of concern occurred (i.e. assessment of the mechanism of toxicity), risk assessment would always be vulnerable to the criticism that its scientific basis was flawed. Science continued to make rapid advances and no risk assessment could be regarded as the definitive statement for all time. A regular review procedure was needed, the frequency of which should be determined by such factors as the availability of new toxicological data; the level of uncertainty identified in the products' risk assessment; and findings from exposure monitoring investigations. All too often, further investigations of the risk ceased at the point at which a particular promoter was either accepted for use or rejected. Means of progressing the knowledge base, in the areas where substantial uncertainties existed, had to be found.[147]

4.209 The European Communities also argued that scientists raised concerns with regard to the confidentiality of data. It had been suggested that a separate risk assessment must be conducted on each growth promoting substance drawing on all the available data, not simply that provided by a company wishing to market a product. This required improved accessibility to information classified as confidential. For this purpose, it had been suggested that a time-limit should be set on the confidentiality of safety data.[148] The European Communities did not dispute the fact that these

[147] Prof. Jim Bridges and Dr. Olga Bridges, "Hazards of Growth Promoting Agents and Strategies of Risk Assessment", *1995 EC Scientific Conference Proceedings*, pp.258-259.
[148] *Ibid.*, p.262.

were limits to science. However, those limits should be taken into account when assessing risks. Members should be able to learn from mistakes of science in the past and take them into account in setting their sanitary policy objectives; should be able to apply a cautious sanitary policy not dictated by narrow economic reasons; and should not be deprived from exercising their sovereign right to take appropriate SPS measures, simply because Codex had decided (by 33 votes in favour and 29 against, with 7 abstentions, out of a total membership of 152 countries) to recommend ADIs and MRLs for these hormones for growth promotion.

(vii) The Precautionary Principle

4.210 The **European Communities** stressed that the difference in degree of regulation between Canada and the European Communities was due to the greater attachment of the European Communities to the precautionary principle.[149] It reflected the different levels of consumer protection adopted by the European Communities and Canada. Where there existed a doubt over the safety of a product, the European Communities had given the benefit of doubt to the consumer, especially in cases where the potential risks might affect very large parts of the population. Canada had, in the case of growth hormones, given it to the producer.

4.211 This difference in degree of regulation was due to the greater attachment of the European Communities to the so-called precautionary principle.[150] This principle was now inscribed in the EC Treaty itself, of which Article 130R on the protection of the environment provided, *inter alia*:

> "Community policy on the environment shall aim at a high level of protection taking into account the diversity of situations in the various regions of the Community. It shall be based on *the precautionary principle* and on the principles that preventive action should be taken, that environmental damage should as a priority be rectified at source and that the polluter should pay. Environmental protection requirements must be integrated into the definition and implementation of other Community policies ..."[151]

4.212 To refer to it as a precautionary "principle"[152] or "approach" was of little importance in the EC view. Its essential features were well known and widely accepted so as to say that it had reached the status of a generally accepted principle of international law, particularly in the area of prevention of risks to human or animal health or the environment. The hazard (cancer) had been identified in this case; lack of scien-

[149] D. Freestone & E. Hey (1996), "The Precautionary Principle and International Law".

[150] *Ibid.*

[151] The European Communities noted that the precautionary principle had acquired recognition in several international law agreements and conventions. E.g., the United Nations Conference on Environment and Development (UNED): Rio Declaration on Environment and Development, 13 June 1992, UN Doc. A/CON. 151/26, Vol. I (1992). In general, Freestone & Hey, above.

[152] The European Communities referred to a chapter of a recent book by D. Freestone and E. Hey, *The Precautionary Principle and International Law*, 1996, which clearly concluded that the precautionary principle had already reached the status of a general principle of international law (Chapter 3 by J. Cameron and J. Abouchar, *The Status of the Precautionary principle in International Law*.

tific knowledge on the exact mechanisms by which it operated was not a sufficient excuse for failing to take strict measures to prevent it.

4.213 The European Communities observed that there was a wider angle from which these risks might be examined and within a broader regulatory context. The crucial role science played in regulating the use of toxic substances and drugs was beyond doubt; the European Communities used science in their regulatory process and promoted its role internationally. But the use of science had its limitations. Scientific certainty in a regulatory process was difficult to achieve and regulating toxic substances had to be done in this context of uncertainty. In the end, the question was how much of that uncertainty a legal system was prepared to accept. The EC precautionary approach was required to avoid situations as those portrayed by many cases of health hazards which only became apparent long after substances or products had been assumed to be safe, such as Cyclamates, saccharin, phehformin, numerous pesticides (e.g., DDT), asbestos, thalidomide, hormone DES. Two cases of recent interest in the European Communities illustrated the desirability of taking a precautionary approach to consumer protection: E. Coli and BSE.[153]

4.214 **Canada** argued that the precautionary principle had not yet attained the status of a general principle of international law, nor that of a rule of customary international law.[154] When the SPS Agreement was being negotiated, governments were

---

[153] The European Community explained that E. Coli was a bacterium which inhabited the intestines of all animals. In the early days of food bacteriology it had been assumed to be ubiquitous and harmless. In the first FAO monograph on meat hygiene, published in 1957, it was stated that: "There are not convincing reports which directly implicate E. Coli in outbreaks of food poisoning". The second report of the Joint FAO/WHO Expert Committee on Meat Hygiene (1962) had considered that knowledge of the importance of E. Coli in causing food-borne disease was lacking and should be investigated. Even in 1974, Thornton's Textbook of Meat Hygiene stated that animal strains of E.Coli were "unlikely to become established in the human bowel". When the European Communities, in 1964, had adopted its first rules on meat hygiene, it had taken a precautionary approach, requiring hygienic structures, equipment and handling procedures with a view to preventing all bacterial contamination of meat.

With regard to BSE, the European Communities noted that this was a new disease of cattle. It had been first recognised in the United Kingdom only 10 years ago. When it had been found to be a member of the group of transmissible spongiform encephalopathies, it had been widely assumed to be the bovine form of scrapie, a disease of sheep recognised for over 250 years. As there was no evidence of a danger to human health from eating meat from scrapie-affected sheep, it had been assumed in some quarters that there would similarly be no danger to humans from BSE. That assumption had recently been challenged by the appearance of a cluster of cases of a new form of Creutzfeldt-Jakob disease, a human spongiform encephalopathy, which experts considered was likely linked to BSE. In this case, it was fortunate that a precautionary approach was taken at an early stage, despite the generally held view that any risk to humans was uncertain or extremely small. The tissues known to contain the BSE agent, as well as some in which infectivity had not been demonstrated but which could possibly be affected, were removed from the human food chain. At the time, this action was criticised in some quarters as an over-reaction but it now appeared to have been far-sighted.

[154] Canada cited Birnie and Boyle, who in their work entitled "International Law and the Environment" (*Oxford: Clarendon Press, 1992*), p.98, arrived at the following conclusion regarding the "precautionary principle":

aware of the precautionary approach as it was being developed in the field of international environmental law. The inclusion of Article 5.7 in the SPS Agreement, which permitted Members to proceed with the adoption of provisional measures on the basis of available pertinent information, was an expression of the precautionary approach in the SPS Agreement Thus the precautionary approach had been taken into account when the internal balance of rights and obligations within the SPS Agreement had been struck.

4.215 The **European Communities** argued that Article 5.7 was not applicable to this case because the EC measures were not temporary. The European Communities knew about the hazards and had taken measures to prevent it. In fact, there was clear evidence, from IARC, JECFA and others that these hormones were carcinogens. The European Communities were therefore justified in acting.

4.216 **Canada** observed that the European Communities had conceded that their import ban was *not* based Article 5.7. However, the European Communities appeared to suggest that the precautionary concept could somehow override certain provisions in the text of the SPS Agreement and Canada rejected any such suggestion. Any intimation by the European Communities that the precautionary concept would somehow justify the adoption of measures under the SPS Agreement that were not based on scientific evidence ran counter to fundamental canons of treaty interpretation laid down in Articles 31 and 32 of the Vienna Convention on the Law of Treaties and would amount to a revision of the SPS Agreement. Thus, the precautionary approach or principle could not be invoked by the European Communities to override the obligations of the SPS Agreement.

(viii) Animal Health Protection

4.217 The **European Communities** argued that one of the aims of the measures at issue was to protect animals from the use of these hormones for growth promotion. In the preparatory discussions, the European Parliament had considered "the possible adverse effects of these substances on the immunity against various diseases of *animals* and that this in turn may lead to an increased use of antibiotics".[155] Furthermore, the preamble and text of Directive 88/146/EEC clearly established that concerns of potential risks to animal health were also taken into account. The strict conditions imposed by the Directive on the use of these hormones for therapeutic and zootechnical purposes had as one of its objectives the protection of animal health from improper administration. Article 5 provided that EC member States must ensure that "no *animals* are dispatched from their territory to that of another Member State which have had administered to them in any way whatsoever substances with a thy-

> Despite its attractions, the great variety of interpretations given to the precautionary principle, and the novel and far-reaching effects of some applications suggest that it is not yet a principle of international law. Difficult questions concerning the point at which it becomes applicable to any given activity remain unanswered and seriously undermine its normative character and practical utility, although support for it does indicate a policy of greater prudence on the part of those states willing to accept it.

Although this was written in 1992, Canada submittted that this conclusion was still valid.

[155] European Parliament's Resolution, *EC Official Journal*, No. C288/158, 11 November 1985.

rostatic, oestrogenic, androgenic or gestagenic action ...", except for therapeutic or zootechnical purposes. Article 6.1 provided that "member States shall prohibit importation from third countries of *animals* and of meat from animals to which have been administered in any way whatsoever substances with a thyrostatic, oestrogenic, androgenic or gestagenic action", except for therapeutic or zootechnical purposes and under conditions equivalent to those applied in the European Communities. One objective of this prohibition was to protect animal health, since the prohibition on trade in such animals clearly discouraged the administration of these hormones in the first place.

4.218 The European Communities claimed that scientists agreed that doses of these hormones at levels which produced a hormonal activity were carcinogenic to laboratory animals. The 1988 JECFA Report had documented these carcinogenic effects. It had reported that oral and parenteral administration of oestradiol-17β could increase the incidence of tumours in experimental animals. These tumours *largely* occurred in tissues with high levels of specific hormone receptors which were *normally* responsive to stimulation by oestradiol-17β. JECFA had also noted that the incidence of tumours of the mammary gland, ovary, uterus and vagina were higher in animals treated with progesterone alone than in control animals. The incidence of uterine tumours was "surprisingly high" and the incidence of prostatic tumours was higher in rodents treated with high doses of testosterone, than in control animals. JECFA concluded that the carcinogenic responses were related to the hormonal activities of each of these three hormones.

4.219 The European Communities noted that JECFA had also found liver hyperplasia and tumours in mice fed high doses of trenbolone acetate and slight increases in the incidence of islet-cell tumours of the pancreas of rats, which JECFA concluded arose as a consequence of the hormonal activity of the trenbolone metabolites. The JECFA review of zeranol noted oestrogenic but not carcinogenic effects in rats. In mice, however, higher incidence of anterior lobe tumours of the pituitary gland occurred than in mice in the negative control group. JECFA reported that such tumours rarely occurred spontaneously in mice but were known to result from administration of oestrogenic hormones. JECFA again concluded that the tumorigenic effect of zeranol was associated with its oestrogenic properties.

4.220 The various carcinogenic effects mentioned by the 1988 JECFA Report on laboratory animals were explained more fully in the reports of the International Agency for Research on Cancer (IARC). IARC Monograph, Supplement 7, 1987, reported sufficient evidence of carcinogenicity to animals from oestradiol-17β and progesterone. IARC noted that "[a]dministration to mice of oestradiol-17β and its esters increased the incidence of mammary, pituitary, uterine, cervical, vaginal, testicular, lymphoid and bone tumours. In rats, there was an increased incidence of mammary and/or pituitary tumours. In hamsters, a high incidence of malignant kidney tumours occurred in intact and castrated males and in ovariectomized females, but not in intact females. In guinea-pigs, diffuse fibromyomatous uterine and abdominal lesions were observed" (page 284). IARC reported that progesterone "increased the incidence of ovarian, uterine and mammary tumours in mice. Dogs treated with progesterone for four years developed a dose-related incidence of mammary-gland nodules" (page 296). Importantly, IARC indicated that there was evidence that *low* doses of progesterone administered over long periods acted in combination with carcinogenic agents, such as some viruses or chemicals, to enhance tumour developments. Therefore, *long-term administration* of synthetic progestins could produce a comparable hazard by increasing the incidence of tumours due to other agents.[156]

4.221 The IARC had also found that zeralenone, a metabolite of zeranol, in the diet of laboratory animals had carcinogenic effects[157], and had caused other effects, including:

> "... atrophy of the seminal vesicles and testes, squamous metaplasia of the prostate gland, osteopetrosis, myelofibrosis of the bone marrow, cytoplasmic vacuolization of the adrenal glands, hyperkeratosis of the vagina and endometrial hyperplasia ... pseudopregnancy [and] infertility."[158]

In addition, consumption of zeralenone by pregnant animals caused a reduction in fetal weight and an increased prevalence of skeletal problems and incidence of stillbirths.[159] As regards the carcinogenic effects of the hormone MGA, published data documented the induction of a statistically significant incidence of mammary tumours in female mice.[160]

4.222 In conclusion, the European Communities submitted that almost all the arguments that were made above (paragraphs 4.151 to 4.209), especially the possible carcinogenic effects and the risks which might arise from an administration of hormones not in accordance with good veterinary practice, were equally applicable to animals.

4.223 **Canada** argued that it emerged from the definition of sanitary measures in Annex A of the SPS Agreement that a sanitary measure was taken to protect human or animal life or health *within the territory of the Member*. The EC prohibition on the importation of hormone-treated beef did not protect the health or life of cattle *in the territory of the European Community*. Thus, the European Communities' references to animal health issues were irrelevant to this dispute and should be given no consideration. Moreover, Canada's complaint was limited to the nullification and impairment of benefits accruing to Canada pursuant to the WTO Agreements respecting market access for meat, and more specifically for beef. Canada exported livestock to the European Communities for breeding purposes only and, since this type of livestock was not treated with hormones for growth promotion, Canada's exports to the European Communities were not affected by the EC measures at issue.

(j) Article 5.4

4.224 The **European Communities** noted that Article 5.4 stated that, in choosing the appropriate level of protection, Members "should ... take into account the objec-

---

156 *21 IARC Monographs*, p.132.
157 *56 IARC Monographs*, p.431; and *31 IARC Monographs*, p.287.
158 *56 IARC Monographs*, p.417.
159 *56 IARC Monographs*, pp.421-422.
160 J.W. Lauderdale et al. (1977), "Studies of a progesterone (MGA) as related to residues and human consumption," Vol.3, pp.5-33.

tive of minimizing negative trade effects". An early draft of this provision required countries to consider the effect on trade of the level they chose, but in the final version of the text the mandatory language had been rejected. A comparison of Articles 5.2 and 5.3 of the SPS Agreement also made it clear that with respect to *human* health risks, economic factors were irrelevant to risk assessment or the determination of the appropriate measures to be used to protect against such risks.

(k) Article 5.5

4.225 **Canada** recalled that Article 5.5 of the SPS Agreement required that "... each Member shall avoid arbitrary or unjustifiable distinctions in the levels it considers to be appropriate in different situations, if such distinctions result in discrimination or a disguised restriction on international trade". Canada claimed, however, that the EC level of sanitary protection for growth promoting hormones was significantly higher than the EC level for antimicrobial growth promoters and other veterinary drugs, resulting in discrimination and a disguised restriction on international trade.

4.226 Canada noted that a veterinary drug was "[a]ny substance applied or administered to any food-producing animal, such as meat or milk producing animals, poultry, fish or bees, whether used for therapeutic, prophylactic, or diagnostic purposes, or for modification of physiological functions or behaviour".[161] A large number of veterinary drugs were used in farm animals and could be categorized into a number of classes, including antimicrobials (*e.g.*, antibiotics), anthelmintics, pesticides, antiprotozoals (*e.g.*, coccidiostats) and hormones. The fate of these veterinary drugs within the animal body was highly variable. Some compounds were metabolized or eliminated quickly, while others, such as some antibiotics, were much more persistent. Hormones were only one type of veterinary drug used for growth promotion. Antimicrobial feed additives were also commonly used as growth promoters in a number of animal species, including cattle. Growth promoters such as ionophores (*e.g.*, monesin) and non-ionophore antibiotics (*e.g.*, avoparcin, carbadox, olaquindox) were used extensively as feed additives in all EC member States.[162]

4.227 Canada argued that the EC measures must be considered in the context of the European Communities' regulation of veterinary drugs in general. The European Communities regulated veterinary drugs under two schemes: products intended for therapeutic use or for the alteration of physiological function[163] and those added to feed for prophylaxis and growth promotion.[164] Canada noted that there appeared to

---

161 *Codex Alimentarius*,Vol. 3: "Residues of Veterinary Drugs in Foods", 2nd ed. (Rome: FAO, 1996) pp.77.

162 Canada explained that feed additives are incorporated into feedingstuffs for oral animal feeding. Substances used in accordance with the Feed Additives Directives are available, in the European Communities, without a veterinary prescription.

163 Regulated under Directives 81/851/EEC and 81/852/EEC and their amendments ("Veterinary Medicines Directives", including: Directive 81/851/EEC; Directive 81/852/EEC and Directive 93/40/EEC.

164 Regulated under Directive 70/524/EEC and its amendments, "Feed Additives Directives", including Directive 70/524/EEC; Directive 84/587/EEC; Directive 93/113/EC; Directive 93/114/EC and Directive 96/51/EC. Directive 91/248/EC appears to contain the most recent consolidation of the annexes to the Feed Additives Directives.

be notable differences between the two schemes. Veterinary drugs governed by the Veterinary Medicines Directives were subject to authorization procedures and Maximum Residue Limit ("MRL") requirements[165] ("MRLs Regulation") and to the residues monitoring requirements.[166] This implies that there was an accepted level of risk in the use of each of these compounds. In contrast, veterinary drugs governed by the Feed Additives Directives did not appear to be subject to these provisions. MRLs were not established for these other products, despite the fact that they posed some human health risks. The three natural hormones at issue - oestradiol-17β, progesterone and testosterone - could only be used for therapeutic and zootechnical purposes in the European Communities. Their use was governed by the Veterinary Medicines Directives, and they were subject to the authorization procedures and MRL requirements set out in the EC MRLs Regulations, and the monitoring requirements set out in Directives 85/348/EEC and 96/23/EC.

4.228 Canada indicated that the EC Veterinary Medicines Directives laid down rules for marketing authorization and distribution of veterinary medicinal products. An application for authorization required studies of toxicity, pharmacological properties, residues and their effects, and data on the emergence of resistant organisms in the case of products used for the prevention or treatment of infectious disease in animals. The Committee for Veterinary Medicinal Products[167] gave opinions on whether a particular medicinal product complied with the Directive's requirements.

4.229 Canada stated that EC member States were obliged to take regulatory measures to control the distribution of veterinary drugs in accordance with the Veterinary Medicines Directives. Canada noted that, nonetheless, implementation differed among EC member States, with some permitting certain veterinary medicines for use in food animals to be available without prescription, while others made it subject to a prescription.[168] There were also divergent views on when it was necessary for a veterinarian to administer a prescribed drug.[169] Although EC Directives dictated that only a veterinarian can administer the three natural hormones, it appeared that the European Communities did not extend that requirement to cover other drugs, such as general anaesthetics, narcotics or psychotropics.[170] In practice, farmers might be administering prescribed veterinary drugs without the veterinarian even seeing the animals being treated.[171]

4.230 Canada noted that under the EC MRLs Regulations, no new veterinary medicinal product might be authorized for use in EC member States until a Community-

---

[165] Set out in Regulation 2377/90/EEC and its amendments.

[166] Set out in Directives 86/469/EEC and 96/23/EC ("Residues Directives").

[167] Established by Directive 81/851/EEC.

[168] A.R.M. Kidd, Distribution of Veterinary Medicines Within the European Community: *Final Report prepared for DG III of the Commission of the European Communities* (September 1992) p.25 (hereinafter Distribution of Veterinary Medicines Within the European Community: Final Report). See also A.R.M. Kidd, "Distribution of veterinary drugs within the European Union" (1994) 8:2 *Vet. Drug Reg. Newsletter* 35, pp.35-38.

[169] Distribution of Veterinary Medecines Within the European Community: *Final Report*, note 33, Table 6, p.47.

[170] Distribution of Veterinary Medicines in the Single Market.

[171] Canada indicated that this was the case in Germany, for example.

wide MRL had been set, and MRLs for existing products were to be established before the end of 1997. All pharmacologically active substances considered must be entered into one of the annexes to the Regulation[172], which were as follows:

(i) substances for which MRLs have been fixed;

(ii) substances not subject to MRLs;

(iii) substances for which provisional MRLs have been fixed;

(iv) substances for which no MRLs can be fixed.

4.231 Substances were included in Annex II where, "... following an evaluation ... it appears that it is not necessary for the protection of public health to establish a maximum residue limit". For substances contained in Annex III, a provisional MRL had been established for a defined period of time "... provided that there are no grounds for supposing that residues of the substance concerned at the level proposed present a hazard to the health of the consumer". Substances were entered in Annex IV where it appeared that a MRL could not be established because residues of the substance, at whatever limit, in foodstuffs constituted a hazard to the health of the consumer. The administration of these substances were prohibited in the European Communities for use in food-producing species. Of the three natural hormones at issue in this dispute, only one appeared to have been considered under this Regulation, oestradiol-17β, which had been included in Annex II. The European Communities had decided that it need not be subject to a MRL.

4.232 Canada indicated that the European Communities had established *requirements for the examination of animals and fresh meat for the presence of veterinary drug residues*[173] which, with respect to hormones, supplemented requirements[174] setting out rules on the detection and monitoring of substances having a hormonal or thyrostatic action. EC member States were required to test for the presence of veterinary drug residues under a "National Plan". EC Reference Laboratories and National Laboratories provided surveillance testing of meat samples. Where an examination of a sample revealed the presence of residues of prohibited substances or quantities of authorized substances exceeding the levels set by EC law or, in their absence, national levels, competent authorities were required to follow up with an investigation and appropriate measures. Canada added that as of 1 July 1997, Council Directive 96/23/EC, would replace the present legislation, setting out measures to monitor listed substances and groups of residues. This Directive appeared to broaden the scope of the repealed Directives "to cover other substances which are used in stockfarming to promote growth and productivity in livestock or for therapeutic purposes and which may prove dangerous to the consumer on account of their residues".[175]

4.233 Canada recalled that the European Communities regulated feed additives differently than other veterinary drugs. However, antimiciobial feed additives were among those animal husbandry drugs, called growth promoters, used for improving animal production without a primary therapeutic objective. Better weight gain and/or

[172] EC Veterinary Medecine Directorate, "Regulation 2377/90: Consolidated Annexes".

[173] Directive 86/469/EEC.

[174] Directive 85/358/EEC.

[175] Council Directive 96/23/EC, preamble.

feed efficiency were the main goals.[176] Antimicrobial feed additives were antimicrobial compounds which changed the population of microorganisms in the alimentary tract of healthy animals, resulting in improved feed conversion efficiency and hence growth rate.[177] Hormones, in contrast, exerted their effects as chemical messengers which bound to specific receptors.[178]

4.234 There were a number of growth promoting antimicrobial compounds that were administered in the feed at low dose rates. These compounds could be subdivided into categories of ionophore antibiotics (*e.g.*, monesin, lasalocid), non-ionophore antibiotics (*e.g.*, carbadox, avoparcin) and gut active growth promoters (*e.g.*, probiotics, enzymes). The ionophore antibiotics altered digestion, whereas the non-ionophore antibiotics might favourably modify the quantity and quality of nutrients entering the body.[179] Coccidiostats were another group of antimicrobial feed additives used for prophylaxis purposes. Coccidiosis was a highly contagious infection of an animal caused by parasitic microbial organisms (*i.e.*, protozoa) collectively known as coccidia. This disease affected mainly poultry, but also cattle, pigs, sheep and game birds. As many of the antimicrobial feed additives were fed to the animals throughout their lives, it was possible that other veterinary drugs would be administered in combination, or at the same time, as the feed additives were being administered.

4.235 Antimicrobial agents were added to animal feeds for two purposes: (1) growth promotion, or (2) to cure or prevent outbreaks of disease. One EC scientist had indicated that "[i]t has been estimated that approximately one-third of all UK feeding stuffs contain medicinal compounds licensed for inclusion without a veterinary prescription, whilst only 5 per cent of feeds contain medicaments for therapeutic use".[180] The primary uses thus were for prophylaxis purposes, that is, to prevent disease outbreaks, or for growth promoting purposes.[181]

4.236 Canada argued that the distinctions made between the EC regulatory schemes governing veterinary drugs on the one hand, and feed additives on the other, were anomalous.[182] At a joint meeting of EC Commission DGIII and DGVI held under the

---

[176] Van Der Wal, P. & Berende, P.L.M. "Effects of anabolic agents on food producing animals" in, "Anabolics in Animal Production: Public health aspects, analytical methods and regulation", *OIE Symposium* (Paris, 15-17 February 1983), p.72.

[177] Crosby, N.T., "Determination of Veterinary Residues in Food", *Ellis Horwood Series in Food Science and Technology*, pp.33-36, p.34 (hereinafter "Determination of Veterinary Residues in Food").

[178] Brander, G.C. *et al.*, eds., "Veterinary Applied Pharmacology & Therapeutics", 5th ed. (London: Bailliere Tindall, 1991), p.279 (hereinafter Veterinary Applied Pharmacology & Therapeutics).

[179] P. Schmidely & M. Hadjipanayiotou, "Growth Promoters for Fattening Kids," in P. Morand-Fehr, ed., "Goat Nutrition" (Pudoc Wageningen, 1991) p.184.

[180] "Determination of Veterinary Residues in Food", *supra*, note 146.

[181] *Ibid.*

[182] "K.N. Woodward & G. Shearer, (Arlington, VA: AOAC International, 1995) "Antibiotic Use in Animal Production in the European Union - Regulation and Current Methods for Residue Detection" in H. Oka *et al.*, eds., *Chemical Analysis for Antibiotics Used in Agriculture*, note 42, p.55.

auspices of the Scientific Committee on Animal Nutrition (SCAN)[183], one EC scientist had commented that:

> "SCAN ... has seen certain benefits in following the MRL route in assuring consumer safety. Not least among these are the use of the MRL for establishing withdrawal periods for 70/524/EEC candidate compounds and for residues surveillance.
>
> This is important now as the JECFA system makes no distinction between veterinary medicines and medicinal feed additives and it recently assessed two drugs, carbadox and olaquindox, currently regulated in the Community under 70/524/EEC and so not subject to MRLs under 2377/90. In doing so it established an MRL for carbadox and identified further work on olaquindox. (...) In viewing MRLs within the Community, it seems only sensible to view medicines as one distinct group - rather than to see them, as is currently the case, largely as therapeutics and feed additives - and to establish MRLs for all. This would introduce some degree of harmonisation on this front with the JECFA/Codex Alimentarius system.[184]

Thus, Canada wondered whether residues in meat arising from the misuse or abuse of substances found in feed additives would be detected under the current EC regulatory scheme.

4.237 Canada also claimed that the EC regulation of the six hormones at issue was also anomalous. In contrast to the prohibition imposed on the three synthetic hormones, some veterinary drugs such as ivermectin and benzylpenicillin were available over-the-counter without a prescription. Similarly, in comparison with the strict control maintained over the administration of the three natural hormones, many classes of prescription drugs might be administered by the farmer, in some instances without the veterinarian even seeing the animals being treated.

4.238 The **European Communities** responded that Canada did not explain the strict conditions under which the use of the three natural hormones for therapeutic and zootechnical use was allowed in the European Communities. The three hormones might be administered only by a veterinarian, only by injection or vaginal spiral (to the exclusion of implantation) and only to farm animals which had been clearly identified. Such treatments must be registered by the veterinarian and these animals could not be slaughtered for meat production before a waiting period long enough to ensure that no residues were present in their meat. All these conditions ensured that the hormones were not administered improperly and that no residues of hormones, other than those naturally produced by the animals themselves, were present in the meat destined for human consumption. The JECFA itself had recognized the need for a clear distinction to be drawn between the use of hormones for therapeutic or zootechnical reasons and animal growth promotion. when it stated:

---

183 Canada indicated that SCAN was an EC independent advisory body which comments on the safety of feed additives and has seen certain benefits in following the MRL route in assuring consumer safety.

184 "Maximum Residue Limits - The Impact of UK and EC Legislation," pp.169-170.

> "The Committee recognized that certain hormonally active substances employed as growth promoters are used in animals for other purposes as well. The Committee concluded that residues left after the use of a drug for growth promotion should be considered *separately* from residues left after the use of that drug for other purposes, because in the latter case (a) the administration of the drug might be by a different route and (b) a different withdrawal period in conformity with good *veterinary* practice might first have to be established and observed. *The Committee therefore did not consider residues of hormonally active drugs used for purposes other than growth promotion*" (page 16, emphasis added).

4.239 The European Communities indicated that the basic provisions in EC law which regulated, at European Community level, the additives in feedingstuffs was Council Directive 70/524/EEC[185] as subsequently amended. In general three types of additives might be used by EC member States in feedingstuffs: antibiotics, growth promoters, coccidiostats and other medicinal substances. The use of any of the three types of additives required advanced authorization by the EC Commission after consultation with the Standing Committee for Feedingstuffs. There were two types of authorizations:

(i) definitive authorization, in which case the additive was placed in Annex I of the Directive and might be used in all EC member States in accordance with the conditions fixed in the authorization; and

(ii) provisional authorization, in which case the additive was placed in Annex II of the Directive. A provisional authorization was valid for a maximum period of five years.

Among the conditions for granting of authorization, particular the European Communities drew attention to those stipulating that the substance must have a favourable effect on the characteristics of those feedingstuffs or on livestock production; that at the level permitted in feedingstuffs, it did not adversely affect human or animal health or the environment, nor harm the consumer by altering the characteristics of livestock products; its presence in feedingstuffs could be controlled; and that at the level permitted in feedingstuffs, treatment or prevention of animal disease was excluded. For the issuance of an authorization to place an additive in Annex I or II, a monograph must be drawn up, indicating the identification process or the criteria for the identification and characterization of the additive, particularly its composition and degree of purity and its physico-chemical and biological properties, taking account of scientific and technical knowledge. A pharmaceutical company applying for the authorization of a substance to be used as an additive in feedingstuffs must provide the information and studies prescribed in Directive 87/153/EEC.[186]

---

185 *EC Official Journal* L 270, 14 December 1970, p.1.

186 *EC Official Journal* L 64, 7 March 1987, p.19. The European Communities added that Directive 95/63/EC of 25.10.95 (EC Official Journal. L 265, 8 November 1995, p.17) laid down the principles relating to official controls of feedingstuffs, and Directive 95/69/EC, of 22 December 19.95 (EC Official Journal L 332, 30 December 1995, p.15) laid down the conditions for the control of establishments producing certain sensitive additives, such as antibiotics and growth promoters.

4.240 The European Communities stressed that the fact that a substance was placed in Annex I or Annex II did not necessarily mean that it was used automatically in all EC member States. The EC member States were free to decide which of those substances could be used in feedingstuffs in their territory. The principle in EC law for all substances permitted as additives in feedingstuffs was that there should be *no residues* of these substances in meat for human consumption.[187] The principle of no residues was achieved with the imposition, if necessary, of appropriate withdrawal periods, as was the case notably for growth-promoting additives, coccidiostats and other medicinal substances. However, when a particular substance was used also as a veterinary medicinal product (i.e. substances administered to food producing animals for medical treatment), the MRLs established in the latter case were also applicable when the substances were used as additives in feedingstuffs. In the European Communities, Council Regulation (EEC) 2377/90 of 26 June 1990[188], laid down the MRLs for veterinary medicinal products which were used in foodstuffs of animal origin. The absence of MRLs for additives in feedingstuffs was explained by the fact that the substances were used in very small quantities and were nearly not absorbed, leaving practically no residues at all in meat destined for human consumption. However, in order to harmonize entirely the EC legislation, the European Commission would shortly propose an amendment to Directive 70/524/EEC, which introduced MRLs also for additives which would need to be established before granting an authorization.

4.241 The European Communities indicated that *monesin* was permitted to be used as an antibiotic in bovine and as coccidiostat in poultry, in which case a withdrawal period of 3 days was required. As an ionophore, it was assumed to have a certain degree of toxicity (headaches, nausea, nosebleeds, skin rashes). But monesin was not genotoxic nor mutagenic. When used as an additive in feedingstuffs, no MRLs were established. The dosage of Monesin authorized as an additive had been evaluated five times. It was concluded that the fact that it was available as a prepared feedingstuff, the dosage permitted and the withdrawal periods fixed eliminated the risks of residues in meat destined for human consumption. Monesin was allowed to be used in Canada for nutritional purposes and the prevention of coccidiosis. *Benzylpenicillin* was an antibiotic substance used mainly against gram-negative bacteria. It was one of the longest-used antibiotics. Penicillins had a very low toxicity in terms of direct effects. In connection with therapeutic use, hypersensitivity reactions were by far the most commonly encountered side effects. The small amounts of penicillin which might be present in food products of animal origin were not able to sensitise humans. For those reasons, benzylpenicillin had been included in Annex I of Regulation 2377/90 for all food producing species and an MRL of 50 µg/kg had been established. *Ivermectin* was an anthelmintic used against various parasites. Its scientific evaluation had shown that it was neither carcinogenic nor mutagenic. It was included in Annex I of Regulation 2377/90 for all food producing animals. MRLs of 100 µg/kg of bovine liver, 40 µg/kg of bovine fat, 15 µg/kg of ovine liver, 20 µg/kg

[187] The European Communities noted that this principle applied also to imports of meat from third countries.

[188] *EC Official Journal* L 224, 18 August 1990, p.1.

of porcine fat had been established. The European Communities added that for monesin, carbadox and olaquindox, the European Commission would shortly propose MRLs even for feed additives. As feed additives, no veterinary control for their use was required. Monesin was not carcinogenic and avoparcin had been recently withdrawn from use. The European Communities noted that in general, the system of surveillance in force in the European Communities had been maintained under the new Directive 96/23/EC, which would enter into force on 1 July 1997. However, the new Directive clarified and improved the procedures for the detection of residues. It required that controls should be based primarily on targeted and unannounced inspections, with less emphasis on the present system of random sampling.

4.242 The European Communities also argued that the argument on consistency which Canada attempted to draw from the fact that oestradiol-17β appeared, as a substance for which no MRL was necessary was misplaced. As stated explicitly in EC Regulation 3059/94, oestradiol-17β was authorized "for therapeutic and zootechnical uses only". This natural hormone (and the other two natural hormones at issue) had to be examined in the context of Regulation 2377/90 because otherwise it could not be used even for therapeutical or zootechnical purposes. No MRL was fixed by the European Communities because it was very difficult to detect such residue limits on a routine basis and without impeding trade. But its administration exclusively for such purposes and under the conditions prescribed in EC Directive 88/299 ensured that there were no residues left in meat destined for human consumption. The European Communities stressed that treatment of animals for therapeutic or zootechnical reasons was *necessary* in exactly the same way treatment of human beings for therapeutic purposes by doctors was necessary. Although new substances for therapeutic purposes were increasingly used, without therapeutic or zootechnical treatment there would be *no* meat production. After such treatment was performed, the European Communities noted that it took some time before the veterinarian discovered whether the treatment was effective or not. If, depending on the animal and the therapeutic or zootechnical treatment performed the veterinarian determined that the animal could not be maintained as a breeding animal, only then the possibility of slaughter was considered. But this meant that, in addition to the strict conditions imposed by EC law for such treatment, there was a lapse of time between such treatment and the slaughter. The percentage of animals receiving such therapeutic or zootechnical treatment and which might be slaughtered did not represent more than 1 per cent of total bovine animals used for human consumption in the European Communities. Therefore, not only the percentage was extremely low but, in addition, the conditions imposed for such treatments and the time which normally lapsed between such treatments and the possibility of slaughtering, guaranteed that there would be no residues of oestradiol-17β left in meat used for human consumption. Therefore, the level of protection of the European Communities was not affected at all. Canada appeared to confuse, as did Dr. Arnold, therapeutic or zootechnical use with use of these hormones for growth promotion. Therapeutic treatment was performed only when the animal was ill. Zootechnical treatment was normally performed *only once* to an animal. It was not performed every year, as Canada seemed to suggest. Animals treated for both of these purposes could not be slaughtered for human consumption while they were under treatment. Withdrawal periods were also fixed. An animal which at the end of its breeding career was fattened to be slaughtered *could not* be treated for therapeutic or zootechnical purposes. It was obvious, therefore, that under the conditions prescribed in EC law, there could be no residues of such hormones in meat when the animals were slaughtered for human consumption. Equally, animals treated for therapeutic or zootechnical reasons and meat of such animals from third countries were allowed to be imported under guarantees which were equivalent to those applied for domestic animals and meat from such animals. Therefore, the provisions of EC law applied regardless of the country of origin of the animals or meat of such animals. The European Communities added that benzylpenicilin, carazolol, anaesthetics and ivermectin could be used only under veterinary prescription in the following EC member States: Germany, Netherlands, Sweden, Italy, Finland and the United Kingdom. Invermectin could be used in the United Kingdom without veterinary prescription but only as a feedingstuff additive only. The use of avoparcin had been prohibited in all EC member States since the end of January 1997.

4.243 **Canada** noted that there was a degree of risk associated with *all* veterinary drugs used for animal husbandry and hormones were as safe as, or safer than, many other veterinary drugs commonly used for therapeutic or non-therapeutic purposes. Moreover, many of these veterinary drugs were used for animal husbandry in the European Communities, such as anthelmintics, pesticides, and some antibiotics, and were administered by producers without a veterinary prescription.

4.244 As one example, Canada noted that *monesin* was an ionophore[189] that had a dual role both as a coccidiostat in poultry and as a growth promoter in cattle. To ensure minimal residues in meat, a three-day withdrawal period was recommended for poultry. Ionophores such as monesin were capable of disturbing biological membranes and affecting action potentials, which presumably accounted for their high toxicity. Additionally, there were high variations in species toxicity. Workers involved in monesin production or feed compounding had reported adverse reactions, such as, headaches, nausea, nosebleeds and skin rashes.[190] Monesin was administered by producers in the European Communities as a feed additive. The use of monesin was governed by the Feed Additives Directive and it appeared that no MRL or safety limit was established for this compound under the MRLs Regulation.

4.245 With regard to non-ionophore antiobiotics, Canada indicated that *carbadox* was a widely available antimicrobial synthetic compound used as a growth promoter in pigs. It was both mutagenic and carcinogenic in animals. Concern had also been expressed about the safety of any residues to the consumer, but evidence suggested that these residues, when present, were devoid of carcinogenic and mutagenic activ-

[189] Canada explained that an ionophore was "an organic substance which binds a polar compound and acts as an ion transfer agent to facilitate movement of monovalent (*i.e.*, sodium and potassium) and divalent ions (*i.e.*, calcium) through cell membranes. The change in electrical charge in membranes influences transport of nutrients and metabolites across the cell membrane, but the exact mechanism by which ionophores improve growth performance in growing ruminants is not known" (D.H. Beermann, "Existing and Emergerging Strategies for Enhancing Efficiency and Composition of Meat Animal Growth", *1995 EC Scientific Conference Proceedings*, p.45).

[190] J. Weissinger, "Miscellaneous Growth Promotants," in L.M. Crawford & D.A. Franco, eds., "*Animal Drugs and Human Health*" (Lancaster: Technomic Publishing Co., 1994) c. 8, p.117.

ity, and any risk was likely to be to the workers handling the drugs.[191] JECFA had evaluated carbadox in 1990, but because of the genotoxic and carcinogenic nature of carbadox and some of its metabolites, JECFA had not be able to establish an ADI. However, JECFA had been able to complete a qualitative risk assessment and concluded that residues resulting from the use of carbadox in pigs were acceptable, provided that MRLs were not exceeded. JECFA had recommended MRLs of 0.03 mg/kg in liver and 0.005 mg/kg in muscle of pig, based on the levels of, and expressed as, quinoxaline-2-carboxylic acid.[192] The JECFA recommendations for carbadox had been adopted as Codex standards.[193] Canada noted that in a study commissioned by the European Communities, concluded in 1991, it was reported that "carbadox shows mutagenic effects in short time tests and in long term experiments and carcinogenic effects on rat-liver that could not be reproduced in experiments with primates. According to today's standards, a NEL [no effect level] cannot be derived nor can a ADI".[194] Carbadox was administered by producers in the European Communities as a feed additive. The use of carbadox was governed by the Feed Additives Directive. It appeared that no MRL or safety limit had been established for this compound under the MRLs Regulation.

4.246 *Olaquindox* was another antimicrobial feed additive used as a growth promoter in pigs, which had been evaluated by the JECFA in 1994. JECFA had concluded that:

> "... because of the genotoxic potential of the parent compound and the absence of specific toxicity studies on the metabolites, it was still unable to allocate an ADI. However, it noted that the parent drug was absent in muscle at the proposed withdrawal time and that the toxicity of the metabolites could be partially evaluated on the basis of toxicity studies in experimental animals because the metabolites are similar to those in the target species. The Committee extended the temporary acceptance of residues resulting from the use of olaquindox in pigs in accordance with good practice in the use of veterinary drugs."[195]

4.247 The 1991 study commissioned by the European Communities described the public safety aspects of olaquindox as follows:

---

[191] K.N. Woodward & G. Shearer, "Antibiotic Use in Animal Production in the European Union - Regulation and Current Methods for Residue Detection" in H. Oka et al., eds., "*Chemical Analysis for Antibiotics Used in Agriculture*" (Arlington, VA: AOAC International, 1995) c. 3, p.54.

[192] "Evaluation of certain veterinary drug residues in food: Thirty-sixth Report of the Joint FAO/WHO Expert Committee on Food Additives", *Technical Report Series 799* (Geneva: WHO, 1990), pp 45-50 (hereinafter "Thirty-Sixth Report").

[193] "Residues of Veterinary Drugs in Foods", *supra*, note 146.

[194] CEAS Consultants (Wye) Ltd. et al., "The Impact on Animal Husbandry in the European Community of the Use of Growth Promoters: *Final Report*,Vol. 1: Growth Promoters in Animal Feed" (February 1991), p.138 (hereinafter "The Impact on Animal Husbandry in the European Community of the Use of Growth Promoters").

[195] "Evaluation of certain veterinary drug residues in food: Forty-second Report of the Joint FAO/WHO Expert Committee on Food Additives", *Technical Report Series 851* (Geneva: WHO, 1995) p.19.

"For Olaquindox a NEL of 1 mg/kg has been determined. Without withdrawal time the residue concentration are above the ADI value. Data concerning kinetics of excretion and practical experience indicate that a withdrawal time of 4 weeks and its use only up to 4 months of age respectively are sufficient to exclude risks for human health."[196]

The study went on to conclude:

"Considering the residues [of the 11 antimicrobial growth promoters studied], all growth permitters approved seem to show a high level of safety, except carbadox and olaquindox. .... The quinoxalines and olaquindox deserve special attention concerning the safety aspects because they are nearly completely absorbed in the gut and are proven to be mutagenic. Carbadox is also carcinogenic. Therefore, a safety evaluation should be extended to the target animal as well as to human beings."[197]

4.248 Canada observed that olaquindox was administered by EC producers as a feed additive. The use of olaquindox was governed by the Feed Additives Directive, and no MRL or safety limit had been established for this compound under the MRLs Regulation.

4.249 Canada indicated that there was a body of scientific evidence suggesting that *avoparcin* presented serious risks to human health, through the development of antibiotic-resistant bacteria. The use of this type of antibiotic at sub-therapeutic levels for growth promoting purposes, could result in resistant strains of bacteria in animals. These resistant strains had the potential to enter the human food chain, causing food borne illness. Other risks included transferring antibiotic resistance to other human disease-causing organisms, thus rendering the traditional therapy of human diseases ineffective.[198] The European Communities had also examined this issue in detail and

---

[196] The Impact of Animal Husbandry in the European Community of the Use of Growth Promoters", *supra*, note 160.

[197] *Ibid.*, pp.140-141.

[198] J. Davies, "Bacteria on the rampage", *Nature*, Vol. 383 (19 September 1996) p.219):

Avoparcin is chemically related to vancomycin (although its name disguises the fact.). In Denmark in 1993, 22 kg of vancomycin were employed in human therapy, while animal use consumed 19,000 kg of avoparcin - inadvertently breaking European Community rules, which state that no agents used in humans and none that cause cross-resistance can be used in animal feed additives. Not surprisingly, resistance to vancomycin sharing the same biochemical mechanisms as that found in humans isolates is now common in farm animals.

Avoparcin was also used in Germany, where vancomycin-resistant enterococci are now widespread and can be detected on supermarket meat products (W.Witte, Robert Goch Inst.). Use of avoparcin is now prohibited in Germany and Denmark, but a powerful lobby is trying to dissuade the European Community from taking general preventative action.

Other difficulties associated with the increase in antibiotic resistant bacteria is an inability to treat human infectious diseases. As reported by S. Kingman ("Resistance a European Problem, Too," *Science*, Vol. 264 (15 April 1994) pp.363-365, the rising level of antibiotic resistance is a real cause for concern, and reports from around Europe show that severe problems already exist in some countries:

The emergence of vancomycin-resistant Enterococci is worrisome because these bacteria are themselves a significant cause of hospital infections. But even more alarming is the possi-

SCAN had recommended further research into the effects of avoparcin, even though there was evidence of a human health risk.[199] Avoparcin was still permitted for use in the European Communities, with the exception of those countries that had implemented a national ban. The scientific community had raised doubts about the safety of avoparcin, particularly with respect to the detrimental effects that the continued use of this drug could have for human therapy and development of pathogenic microbial-resistant strains that could appear in the food chain. Avoparcin was administered by producers as a feed additive, and could be used without veterinary supervision. It was governed by the Feed Additives Directive and, therefore, it appeared that no MRL or safety limit had been established for this compound under the MRLs Regulation.

4.250 Canada submitted that *benzylpenicillin* was one of the most widely used antibiotics in both animals and humans. It was primarily used to control mastitis in dairy cows and for treating infections of the urinary tract, gastrointestinal system and respiratory tract. Benzylpenicillin was also administered as a feed additive to pigs to control streptococcal meningitis, and was included as an additive in the drinking-water of poultry.[200] This drug had been evaluated by JECFA in 1990. The Committee had concluded that allergic reactions in humans was the determining factor in the safety evaluation of residues of benzylpenicillin:

> "Among the adverse reactions which had been reported in people consuming food containing benzylpenicillin residues, hypersensitivity reactions were the most common. The overall prevalence of allergy to penicillin, taking into account various reports of allergic reactions in different populations and using a variety of test procedures, was estimated to be 3-10 per cent."[201]

4.251 Codex had adopted MRLs for meat and for milk.[202] The European Communities had also set MRLs for milk and meat that were the same as the Codex levels.[203] To ensure that the MRLs were attained, proper dosage of the animal was essential. Exceeding the MRLs could result in severe allergic reaction in 3-10 per cent of the population. Canada noted that although proper dose-level was critical to the safety of meat or milk products, benzylpencillin was sold without prescription and administered directly by farmers in certain EC member States.

---

bility that Enterococci will spread vancomycin resistance to other genera of bacteria. Researchers think this will eventually happen because bacteria are very adept at exchanging their antibiotic resistance genes.

[199] Canada noted that *Agra-Europe* had reported that "...evidence had been presented to SCAN by Denmark and Germany that the use of avoparcin in animal feed could cause a resistance to antibiotics in humans but SCAN found that the two countries' evidence was insufficient proof of a link between the additive and increased antibiotic resistance." ("Opposition to avoparcin in EU growing," (25 October 1996), *Agra Europe*, p. E/4).

[200] *Thirty-Sixth Report, supra*, note 158.

[201] *Ibid.*, pp.37-38.

[202] "Residues of Veterinary Drugs in Foods", *supra*, note 147.

[203] R.J. Heitzman, ed., "Agriculture - Veterinary Drug Residues - Residues in food-producing animals and their products: Reference materials and methods" (Luxembourg: Office for Official Publications of the European Communities, 1992), pp.1-7, p.4.

4.252 Canada indicated that *carazolol*, a non-specific β-adrenoceptor-blocking agent, primarily used in pigs to prevent sudden death due to stress during transportation, had been reviewed by JECFA in 1994 at its forty-third meeting. The drug had also been used in cattle for the same reasons and was usually administered to the animals just prior to being loaded for shipment to a slaughter facility. The JECFA Report noted that:

> "The Committee [JECFA] recognized that humans with chronic bronchitis or asthma are highly sensitive to the effects of carazolol. It also recognized that this subgroup forms a substantial part of the general population and that adequate allowance should be made for variations between individuals."[204]

4.253 The JECFA had established an ADI and MRLs for certain tissues. However, the proposed standards had not yet passed through the eight step Codex process and were, therefore, subject to change, based on comments from countries. Nonetheless, concerning the use of this drug, the JECFA Report provided a cautionary note to regulators by stating:

> "The Committee recommended that registration authorities should pay particular attention to the potential risk of residues of carazolol in tissue at the injection site. Considering the potential risk, the Committee concluded that *the use of carazolol in pigs to reduce stress during transportation to slaughter is inconsistent with the safe use of veterinary drugs in food producing animals*"[205] (emphasis added).

4.254 In June 1995, the European Communities had revised its provisional MRLs and had set final MRLs permitting the use of this drug in pigs.[206] In its answer to a question from Canada, the European Communities had stated that, "Carazolol is used in pigs to prevent 'mors subita' during transport". Canada noted that this practice was precisely what JECFA concluded was inconsistent with the safe use of veterinary drugs in food-producing animals.

4.255 Canada noted that i*vermectin* was an antiparasitic agent. It had been evaluated by JECFA in 1990 and again in 1993. Ivermectin was a mixture of two homologous compounds. While the compound was very effective in dealing with parasites, the mode of action in parasites had remained elusive, and the mechanisms of the toxic action of ivermectin in mammalian species had not been elucidated.[207] The typical signs of acute toxicity of ivermectin had been attributed to its effects on the central nervous system. Codex had adopted the JECFA recommended ADIs and MRLs for cattle, sheep and pigs[208] for ivermectin as Codex standards.[209] Ivermectin was approved for use in the European Communities, and an MRL in the target tissues of

---

204 "Evaluation of Certain Veterinary Drug Residues in Food: *Forty-third report of the Joint FAO/WHO Expert Committee on Food Additives*" (Geneva: WHO) Section 3, "Comments on residues of specific veterinary drugs," 3.1 "β-Adrenoceptor-blocking agent." p.6.

205 *Ibid.*, p.8.

206 Regulation 1442/95/EC.

207 *Thirty-sixth Report, supra*, note 158.

208 *Ibid.*, p.30.

209 "Residues of Veterinary Drugs in Foods", *supra*, note 147.

liver and fat had been set for the bovine and porcine species. It was available for use by producers without a veterinarian prescription in some EC member States.

4.256 Canada submitted that in veterinary medicine, a *pesticide* was a compound which was active against parasites that live on the skin of animals or which spend part of their lives in the animal's body (*e.g.*, warble fly larvae). In their larval stage, these parasitic organisms known as ectoparasites, might migrate through the tissue of the host, or burrow into and live in the superficial skin layers. To counter ectoparasites, therefore, it was important to have a compound that could destroy the parasites at every stage of their life cycle, including the larval stage. A range of application modes for the pesticides were available to treat the animals, such as dips, sprays, dusts, feed additives, or subcutaneous injections. Due to environmental concerns, the *organophosphourous compounds* had replaced most of the organochloride compounds for use as pesticides. Unfortunately, the organophosphourous compounds were more toxic to man than the organochlorides, although they were rapidly metabolized and excreted. Compounds such as diazionon were used in the European Communities.[210]

4.257 Canada indicated that because the use of agricultural production aids, such as veterinary drugs, presented a risk, albeit minuscule, to the consumer, the United States Department of Agriculture (USDA) had developed a method to determine the relative risk of various agricultural production aids such as veterinary drugs, naturally occurring toxins, and pesticides. The USDA's Compound Evaluations System ("CES"), developed in 1983, had guided a number of countries in the development of their residue monitoring programmes. This allowed for testing to be targeted at those compounds that were more likely to present a health risk to the consumer.

4.258 The likelihood of a health hazard of compounds which left residues in food was rated A to D or Z. The highest health hazard compounds were scored A and the lowest received a D. Those compounds for which insufficient information was available to conduct a toxicologic or pharmacologic evaluation, received a rating of Z. Each compound was also assigned a rating to evaluate the probability of exposure to the consumer. The categories ranged from 1, meaning a high probability of exposure, to 4, which was negligible probability of exposure. Category Z designated a substance with insufficient information available to estimate the probability of exposure to humans.[211] The CES could thus be used to rank compounds based on their relative risk. The compounds presenting the highest risk to human health would score A1, and the compounds with the lowest risk to human health would be those compounds with a score of D4. Compounds of unknown hazard or exposure risk would receive a Z rating.

4.259 The natural hormones were not ranked by the CES system as they did not leave detectable residues in food and did not present any risk to human health. Canada presented the CES ranking of various veterinary drugs[212], and claimed that it

[210] Regulation 1442/95/EC establishes a MRL for diazinon.

[211] "Compound Evaluation and Analytical Capability: National Residue Program Plan 1993" (Washington: U.S. Department of Agriculture, Food Safety and Inspection Service), pp.1.3-1.7.

[212] "Compound Evaluation and Residue Information 1994" (Washington: U.S. Department of Agriculture, Food Safety and Inspection Service), pp.2.3-2.5.

illustrated that the natural and synthetic hormones were safer than several veterinary drugs commonly used for animal production in the European Communities.

Trenbolone	C-4
Zeranol	C-2
MGA	B-4
Carbadox	A-3
Olaquindox	(Not permitted for use in Canada)
Avoparcin	(Not permitted for use in Canada)
Monesin	B-3
Carazolol	(Not permitted for use in Canada)
Penicillin	A-2
Ivermectin	B-1

4.260 The **European Communities** noted that the basic provisions in EC law which regulated the additives in feedingstuffs was Council Directive 70/524/EEC[213], as subsequently amended several times. There were in general three types of additives which might be used by the EC member States in feedingstuffs: antibiotics, growth promoters, coccidiostats and other medicinal substances. Before any of the three types of additives might be used, an authorization had to be granted by the Commission after consulting the Standing Committee for Feedingstuffs. There were two types of authorization:

(i) definitive authorization, in which case the additive was placed in Annex I of the directive and might be used in all the EC member States in accordance with the conditions fixed in the authorization; and

(ii) provisional authorization, in which case the additive was placed in Annex II of the Directive. A provisional authorization was valid for a maximum period of five years.

4.261 The main conditions for including a substance in Annex I required that:

(i) the substance must have a favourable effect on the characteristics of those feedingstuffs or on livestock production;

(ii) at the level permitted in feedingstuffs, it did not adversely affect human or animal health or the environment, nor harm the consumer by altering the characteristics of livestock products;

(iii) its presence in feedingstuffs could be controlled;

(iv) at the level permitted in feedingstuffs, treatment or prevention of animal disease was excluded.[214]

4.262 For the issuance of an authorization to place an additive in Annex I or II, a monograph must be drawn up, indicating the identification process or the criteria for

[213] *EC Official Journal* L 270, 14 December 1970, p.1.

[214] The European Communities indicated that this condition did not apply to coccidiostats and other medicinal substances.

the identification and characterization of the additive, particularly its composition and degree of purity and its physico-chemical and biological properties, taking account of scientific and technical knowledge (Article 8:1). The fact that a substance was placed in Annex I or Annex II did not necessarily mean that it was used automatically in all EC member States; EC member States were free to decide which of those substances to use in feedingstuffs in their territory.

4.263 The principle in EC law for all substances permitted as additives in feedingstuffs was that there should be *no residues* of these substances in meat for human consumption.[215] The principle of no residues was achieved with the imposition, if necessary, of appropriate withdrawal periods, as was the case notably for growth-promoting additives, coccidiostats and other medicinal substances. However, when a particular substance was used also as veterinary medicinal product (i.e. substances administered to food producing animals for medical treatment), the MRLs established in the latter case were also applicable when the substances were used also as additives in feedingstuffs. Council Regulation (EEC) 2377/90 of 26 June 1990[216], laid down the MRLs for veterinary medicinal products which were used in foodstuffs of animal origin. The absence of MRLs for additives in feedingstuffs was explained by the fact that the substances were used in such small quantities and were little absorbed so that they left practically no residues in meat destined for human consumption. However, in order to harmonize entirely the legislation within the European Communities, the European Commission would shortly propose an amendment to Directive 70/524/EEC, which would require MRLs also for additives before granting an authorization.

4.264 The European Communities stressed that only *two* growth promoting substances could be used: *carbadox and olaquindox* (Annex I (J) of Directive 70/524/EEC).[217] However, certain EC member States had asked the European Commission to review the authorizations of carbadox and olaquindox, and the Commission had agreed, before the Council of Ministers on 26 February 1996, and on 17 December 1996 to review both of these substances shortly after avoparcin, ronidazole and dimetridazole (possibly in the course of 1997). Carbadox, olaquindox and

---

[215] The European Communities indicated that this principle applied also to imports of meat from third countries.

[216] *EC Official Journal* L 224, 18 August 1990, p.1.

[217] The European Communities indicated that a provisional comparison with the situation in Canada, as regards substances used as additives in feedingstuffs for growth - promotion, would appear to indicate that more additives for growth promotion were used in Canada. Thus, although Canada did not allow the use of olaquindox, it did allow (in addition to the hormones at issue) the use of carbadox, chlorotetracycline hydrochloride, oxytetracycline hydrochloride, 3-nitro-4-hydroxyphenylarsonic acid, arsanilic acid, bambermycins, bacitracin, methylene disalicylate, lincomycin, procaine penicillin, etc. Apart from carbadox, olaquindox (and bacitracin zinc for swine only), the other substances were not allowed to be used as growth-promoting feed additives in the European Communities. It should also be noted that the 1991 JECFA report on carbadox and olaquindox concluded that residues resulting from the use of carbadox in pigs were acceptable provided that the recommended MRLs were not exceeded (as was the case in the European Communities), and residues from the use of olaquindox in food-producing animals under conditions of good practice in the use of veterinary drugs were temporarily acceptable.

avoparcin had already been examined and reviewed recently in the SCAN committee and the authorization for avoparcin had already been withdrawn.

4.265 The European Communities added that *at EC level* there were 10 antibiotics which were allowed to be used as additives in feedingstuffs in the EC member States and which might also function as growth-promoters because they stabilized the flora and reduced the pathogenic micro-organisms in the animals and induced a higher feed efficiency and growth rate. Most, if not all, of these substances were also allowed to be used in Canada for nutritional uses (growth promotion). Canada allowed more substances than the European Communities to be used as antibiotics and as coccidiostats in feedingstuffs (only 21 coccidiostats were permitted in the European Communities).

4.266 The European Communities explained that *monesin* was permitted to be used as an antibiotic in bovines and as coccidiostat in poultry, in which case a withdrawal period of 3 days was required. As an ionophore, it was assumed to have a certain degree of toxicity (headaches, nausea, nosebleeds, skin rashes). But monesin was not genotoxic nor mutagenic. When used as an additive in feedingstuffs, no MRLs were established, as explained above (Directive 70/524). The dosage of monesin authorized as an additive had been evaluated five times. It was concluded that its availability as a prepared feedingstuff, the dosage permitted and the withdrawal periods fixed eliminated the risks of residues in meat destined for human consumption. Monesin was allowed to be used in Canada for nutritional purposes and the prevention of coccidiosis. *Avoparcin* was currently allowed to be used as an antibiotic in feedingstuffs. It was not carcinogenic, but it was thought to pose risks because of the development of antibiotic-resistant bacteria which could possibly transfer to humans. Since it was used as a feedingstuff only, there no MRL was fixed. The Commission was in the process of withdrawing its authorization, in accordance with the opinion of the SCAN. *Benzylpenicillin* was an antibiotic substance used mainly against gram-negative bacteria. It was one of the longest-used antibiotics. Penicillins had a very low toxicity in terms of direct effects. In connection with therapeutic use, hypersensitivity reactions were by far the most commonly encountered side effects. The small amounts of penicillin which may be present in food products of animal origin were not able to sensitize humans. For these reasons, benzylpenicillin was included in Annex I of Regulation 2377/90 for all food producing species. An MRL of 50 µg/kg had been established. Ivermectin was an anthelmintic used against various parasites. Its scientific evaluation had shown that it was neither carcinogenic nor mutagenic. It was included in Annex I of Regulation 2377/90 for all food producing animals. MRLs of 100 µg/kg of bovine liver, 40 µg/kg of bovine fat, 15 µg/kg of ovine liver, 20 µg/kg of porcine fat had been established. Although for monesin, carbadox, olaquindox and avoparcin, there were no MRLs, the European Commission would soon propose MRLs for feed additives. As feed additives, no veterinary control for their use was required.

4.267 With regard to benzylpenicillin and ivermectin, the European Communities argued that *a prescription by a veterinarian* was required in order to avoid risks to consumers of foodstuffs obtained from the treated animals. If in some EC member States no prescription was effectively required, this was not in conformity with the provisions of this Directive. The European Commission had already requested the relevant information from all the EC member States. For the moment not all had replied, but the situation of those which had replied showed that in Germany and Denmark neither of these two substances could be obtained without prescription. A prescription was also required in France. In the Netherlands, benzylpenicillin was subject to veterinarian prescription. The Commission had information which showed that in Ireland only benzylpenicillin was available without prescription, and only to farmers organisations carrying out a special programme for the prevention of mastitis in cows. This programme was carried out under veterinary supervision and applied to a limited number of animals.[218]

4.268 The European Communities explained that the measures which EC member States must put in place to ensure that the MRLs for benzylpenicillin and ivermectin were not exceeded. Council Directive 86/469/EEC harmonised controls on residues in live animals (bovines, pigs, sheep, goats and horses) and fresh meat, both of the European Communities and third countries which exported meat to the European Communities. It supplemented Directive 85/358/EEC which set out the rules on the detection and monitoring of substances having a hormonal or thyrostatic action. The aim was to examine animals, their tissues and biological material and fresh meat for the presence of residues of substances having a pharmacological action or of conversion products and other substances transmitted to meat which were likely to be dangerous to human health. The EC member States were allowed to control for residues of *any* substance which might pose a danger to human or animal health.

4.269 The substances and residues to be checked were defined in Annex I of Directive 86/469/EEC. The substances were divided into different groups or sub-groups according to their chemical or pharmacological action. The minimum sampling levels and frequency were also defined in Annex II of the Directive. The samples had to be taken from live animals at farm level or at the slaughterhouse before slaughtering, and from carcasses at slaughterhouse level. A monitoring plan taking into account the specific situation of each EC member State and setting out the national measures to be taken had to be submitted every year to the European Commission (Articles 3 and 4). The Commission examined the plans presented by the EC member States in order to determine wether they conformed to the provisions laid down in Directive 86/469/EEC. These plans were updated each year in the light of experience. For example, on the basis of positive results recorded during a previous year, search for new substances, improvements gained in laboratory techniques, etc. Official samples were examined in approved laboratories for residues (Article 8). National Reference Laboratories coordinated standards and methods of analysis for each group of residues, as defined in the Annex I of the Directive. Four EC Reference Laboratories were designated to help the Commission and the National Reference Laboratories (NRL) to improve the harmonization of the methods of analysis and the quality of the work of each NRL. In case an official sample revealed the presence of residues of *prohibited* substances, or quantities of *authorized* substances exceeding EC or stricter national MRLs, the competent authorities of the EC member States must undertake investigations at the farm of origin without delay, and launch an inquiry into

[218] This type of clinical trials were provided for in Article 14 of regulation 2377/90 of 26 June 1990 (*EC Official Journal*. L 224, 18 August 1990, p.1), on condition that foodstuffs obtained from livestock participating in such trials not contain residues which posed a hazard to human health.

the origin of the substances concerned, as necessary, at the levels of manufacture, handling, storage, transport, administration, distribution or sale. Positive animals (for prohibited substances) were banned from human and animal consumption and additional monitoring took place on the farms of such animals. In the case of *authorized* substances, meat in which the presence of residues in excess of the MRLs was confirmed was excluded from human consumption. All the necessary administrative and penal sanctions had to be taken by competent authorities to ensure that these requirements were strictly observed.

4.270 As regarded imports from third countries, the admission or retention on the list of third countries which were authorized to export animals or meat of animals for human consumption to the European Communities was subject to the submission by the third country concerned of an annual plan detailing of the guarantees for the checking of residues. The effect of these guarantees must be at least equivalent to that resulting from the guarantees provided for in Directive 86/469/EEC. The third country plans were approved by the European Commission in accordance with the opinion of the Standing Veterinary Committee. The annual plans of 25 third countries had currently been approved, and these countries exported meat which respected the MRL requirements of the European Communities, where they existed. In addition, those countries which allowed the use of hormones for growth promotion for their domestic production had all concluded arrangements with the European Communities to ensure that the meat exported to the European Communities was produced without hormones for growth promotion.

4.271 In general, the system of surveillance now in force has been maintained under the new Directive 96/23/EC, which would enter into force on 1 July 1997. However, the new Directive clarified and improved the procedures for the detection of residues. It required that controls should be based primarily on targeted and unannounced inspections, with less emphasis on the present system of random sampling. Under the new Directive, the monitoring plans had to be extended to poultry meat, fish, milk, and some other products (rabbit and game meat, honey eggs). More flexibility was given to sampling plans, according to the specific problems of each EC member State. The new Directive would improve harmonisation of methods of analysis, for both routine and reference methods. It would extend the competence of the four EC Reference Laboratories to products other than meat, and to other types of residues not yet covered by the current residues Directives. Directive 96/23/EC would establish clearly the responsibilities of each operator and would strengthen the sanctions against the farmers and the operators (veterinarians, pharmacists, slaughterhouses, etc.) in case of detection of residues of prohibited substances or residues of authorized but illegally used substances. Serious financial and administrative sanctions would be imposed in case of fraud, without prejudice to possible penal sanctions taken by the competent authorities of the EC member States. The new Directive would also improve transparency on control results since it required their annual publication and as well as the publication of a European Commission report to the Council and to the European Parliament concerning the situation of residues control in the European Communities.

4.272 **Canada** recalled that paragraph 5 of Annex A defined appropriate level of sanitary and phytosanitary protection as "[t]he level of protection deemed appropriate by the Member establishing a sanitary or phytosanitary measure to protect human, animal or plant life or health within its territory" and observed that Article 5.5 of the SPS Agreement limited this choice of an appropriate level of protection by requiring that arbitrary and unjustifiable distinctions in the level of protection considered appropriate in different situations must not result in discrimination, or a disguised restriction on international trade.[219] The European Communities maintained that it was highly risk averse, and that its prohibition on the use of hormones for growth promotion, including the six hormones at issue, was necessary to achieve its high level of sanitary protection. However, as Canada had just demonstrated, EC measures governing the use of other growth promoters and veterinary drugs revealed that a significantly lower level of protection was considered appropriate for the risks to human health posed by those substances. The six hormones in question were as safe as, or safer than, growth promoters commonly used in the European Communities. Moreover, they were demonstrably safer than veterinary drugs that were commonly used in the European Communities.

4.273 Canada submitted that antimicrobial growth promoters distributed as feed additives posed no less risk to human health than the six hormones at issue. Three antimicrobial growth promoters authorized for use in the European Communities were particularly noteworthy: carbadox was known to be both mutagenic and carcinogenic; olaquindox was mutagenic; and there was scientific evidence indicating that the use of avoparcin as a feed additive presented a serious risk to human health because it might lead to the development of vancomycin-resistant strains of bacteria. Yet the EC measures governing the use of feed additives were substantially less restrictive than the complete ban on the use of the six growth promoting hormones for growth promotion purposes. Growth promoters and coccidiostats regulated under the EC Feed Additives Directives could be administered by producers without the supervision of veterinarians, and were not subject to the authorization procedures and MRL requirements set out in the MRLs Regulation or the residues monitoring requirements established under Residues Directives. Canada argued that given that these substances posed no less a risk than that posed by the six growth promoting hormones, it followed that these less restrictive measures could not possibly attain the same level of protection that purportedly lay behind the prohibition on the use of the six hormones for growth promotion purposes. This would be the case even if these substances were subject to MRL requirements and residue monitoring requirements. It was apparent that the EC level of sanitary protection for growth promoting hormones was significantly higher than the level for antimicrobial growth promoters.

4.274 Furthermore, Canada claimed that many veterinary drugs used for therapeutic purposes and governed by the Veterinary Medicines Directives posed demonstrably greater risks to human health when compared to the six hormones.[220] While veteri-

[219] J.J. Barcelo, "Product Standards to Protect the Local Environment - the GATT and the Uruguay Round Sanitary and Phytosanitary Agreement", (1994) 27 *Cornell International Law Journal*,. Vol. 755, pp.765-66.

[220] Canada noted that, for example, in contrast to veterinary drugs with fixed MRLs under Annex I of Directive 2377/90/EEC, or *provisional* MRLs under Annex III, oestradiol-17β was placed in Annex II as a substance for which no MRL was necessary (Regulation 3059/94/EC). Carazolol, on the other hand, poses a significant risk to humans with chronic bronchitis or asthma and has been assigned a MRL.

nary drugs were subject to the authorization procedures and MRL requirements of the MRLs Regulation and the residues monitoring requirements of Residues Directives, under the laws of EC member States some of these substances, such as benzylpenicillin and ivermectin, might be administered by farmers without prescription or the supervision of a veterinarian. Farmers might even administer prescribed veterinary drugs without the veterinarian even seeing the animals being treated. Canada claimed that these less restrictive measures could not possibly attain the same level of protection that purportedly lay behind the prohibition on the use of the six hormones for growth promotion purposes. It was again apparent that the EC level of sanitary protection for growth promotion hormones was significantly higher than the level for other veterinary drugs commonly used in the European Communities.

4.275 Canada argued that these marked distinctions in levels of protection were arbitrary and unjustifiable, and resulted in discrimination and a disguised restriction on international trade.[221] Canadian beef from cattle treated with the six hormones for

[221] J.J. Barcelo, *supra*, note 179, at pp.765-66 provided a useful example:

> A party must "avoid arbitrary or unjustifiable distinctions in the levels it considers to be appropriate in different situations, if such distinctions result in discrimination or a disguised restriction on international trade." The meaning of this language is not immediately apparent, but on its face it could provide a ground for a more searching scrutiny of a party's S&P provisions than any of the other three requirements thus far discussed. We should note, however, that the "arbitrary distinctions" language is tied to the proviso "if such distinctions result in discrimination or a disguised restriction on international trade." That proviso helps to clarify the kind of case envisioned. A good example is the well known German Beer case in EU law decided by the European Court of Justice in 1987.
>
> In the German Beer case, Germany allowed beer to be sold in Germany and labelled "bier" only if it was made from malted barley, hops, yeast, and water. No additives at all were allowed. Most German beer has been made in this manner since the sixteenth century. Beer in other EU countries, however, is frequently made from rice and other cereals. In the case of these beers, additives are needed for technical reasons to produce the beer. The German rule therefore prevented much of the beer made in other EU countries from being imported and sold in Germany as "bier". Germany tried to justify the rule in part on the ground that Germans consume large quantities of beer and that the additives in general would pose a human health risk. The European Court of Justice rejected this argument, however, for one very striking reason: *for all beverages, other than beer, German law specifically allowed some of the very additives that were banned completely in beer.* Thus, the arbitrariness of these distinctions appeared to convince the European Communities that the German regulation was essentially a form of disguised protectionism designed to protect German beer producers from non-German competitors.
>
> Suppose, for example, that the toxicity of pesticides Y and Z are indistinguishable. Suppose further that the United States adopts a rule calling for zero pesticide Z residue on apples. The U.S. provision might run into trouble if, for example, pesticide Z were traditionally used in Canada, pesticide Y in the United States, and the zero pesticide rule applied only to pesticide Z.
>
> Admittedly, judgments could differ about the application of this "arbitrary distinctions" standard. But in its defense, how else could one deal with a situation such as that presented by the German Beer case, apparently a case of disguised protectionism? There is a risk of an inappropriate panel decision under the standard. Without it, how-

growth promotion purposes posed no greater risk to EC consumers than EC beef treated with anti-microbial growth promoters or other veterinary drugs. The prohibition on imports of beef from cattle treated with the six hormones for growth promotion discriminated against Canadian beef imports, and constituted an unwarranted restriction of this trade in the guise of a sanitary measure. Canada claimed, therefore, that the EC measures were contrary to Article 5.5.

4.276 The **European Communities** responded that there was nothing in the text of the contested measures, the legislative history or in any other document to suggest that the purpose for which the measures were adopted was to protect EC production of meat from foreign competition. It was incorrect to conclude that because the European Communities did not, in this case, follow the voluntary MRLs suggested by Codex on the five hormones and because it applied different levels of protection for totally different substances which posed entirely different types of risks to human and animal health, the European Communities must be considered to have violated its obligations under the SPS Agreement. Canada had failed to establish that, in the face of the overwhelming scientific evidence that the use of hormones for animal growth promotion was potentially very dangerous to public and animal health, there were other type of *measures* which, while significantly less restrictive of trade, were capable of ensuring that the *level* of protection which the European Communities had chosen in this case (no residue of hormones in animals and meat) could be effectively achieved. Conversely, the European Communities had gone through that exercise in 1984 and recently in April 1996 and had decided that the prohibition on use of these hormones in animal growth promotion was the *only* measure reasonably available and less restrictive of trade. The European Communities argued that Canada compared things which were not comparable, because the premises on which they were based were different, and that Canada confused the notions of "*risk*", "appropriate *level* of protection", and "*measures* applied to achieve that level of protection".

4.277 The European Communities insisted that under the SPS Agreement, each Member had the right to set its *level* of sanitary protection where and how it chose. The only (minimal) disciplines imposed by the SPS Agreement in respect of the level of protection were in Articles 5.4 and 5.5, as follows:

(i) Members *should* take into account the objective of minimizing negative trade effects (Article 5.4) (emphasis added).

(ii) With the objective of achieving consistency in the *application* of the concept of appropriate level of protection, Members *shall avoid* arbitrary or unjustified distinctions in the levels they consider to be appropriate in different situations, if such distinctions result in discrimination or a disguised restriction on international trade (Article 5.5) (emphasis added).

4.278 The European Communities argued that because there might often be a range of sanitary or phytosanitary measures available to achieve the same level of protec-

ever, there would be a loophole through which very large amounts of disguised protection could be driven.

tion, the measures employed by various Members might differ even where they were designed to achieve the same level of protection. Differences in the type of measures applied might, however, restrict trade without providing any additional protection to human, animal or plant life or health. The European Communities contended that it was for this purpose that Article 5.5 contained the notion of consistency. Article 5.5 did not require Members to achieve consistency between the level of protection which they choose against *different* hazards to human, animal and plant life and health, but only required consistency in terms of avoiding arbitrary or unjustifiable distinctions in *applying* the chosen level of protection, and then only if such distinctions resulted in discrimination or a disguised restriction on trade. It could not be interpreted as requiring consistency in *setting* or *deciding* the level of protection. This interpretation was consistent with the preamble of the SPS Agreement, which stated that the harmonization of SPS measures did not require Members to change their appropriate level of protection.

4.279 The European Communities noted that the text of Article 5.5 did not go further in defining consistency. Consistency was not harmony with past performance, particularly in the context of the SPS Agreement, where new diseases might be emerging and new technologies emerging to deal with old diseases. The definition of consistency which best fit the intention of the SPS Agreement was "constant adherence to the same principles of thought or action".[222] This constant adherence had to be applied to the same substances, which posed the same type of risk under same conditions of use. The European Communities argued that in the context of the SPS Agreement, the factual and legal situation currently existing in Members regarding regulation of dangerous substances should also be taken into account. Consistency was a dynamic process evolving with technology, new risk assessment and the confines of regulatory policies which required years to review existing authorizations of dangerous substances. To infer lack of consistency on 1 January 1995 from the complex situation that existed before the entry into force of the Agreement was to disregard the letter of Article 5.5, to ignore the practical situation in almost all Members and to threaten the credibility of the SPS Agreement.

4.280 The European Communities argued that it was because of this reality that the negotiators had adopted the reasonable approach of developing guidelines "to further practical implementation of this provision" envisaged in Article 5.5. In the European Communities' view, this in itself was indicative of the absence of a consensus on the implications of the provision at the time the Agreement was negotiated and signed. Therefore, the text of paragraph 5 clarified that the concept of consistency was only an objective to be achieved in the application of the appropriate level of sanitary or phytosanitary protection against risks to human, animal or plant life or health. This could also be seen from the drafting history of this provision. On 13 June 1995, the WTO Secretariat had circulated a note[223] on the drafting history of the provision on consistency. The last paragraph of the note stated that:

> "... the purpose of the provision is to ensure that government decisions as to what levels of risk are acceptable in various situations are not

[222] Oxford English Dictionary.

[223] G/SPS/W/16.

> taken in such a manner as to result in discrimination or disguised restrictions on trade. It has been agreed that the mechanism for ensuring that governments avoid arbitrary or unjustifiable distinctions in the levels of risk they accept is to require governments to be consistent in their risk management decisions."

The same note also clarified that during the negotiations, concern had been expressed that what were considered as acceptable levels of risk with regard to animal or plant health could not necessarily be considered as politically acceptable levels of risk in matters regarding human health, or vice - versa. It was also stated that consistency might be desirable and achievable among decisions regarding animal health, or even between plant and animal health issues, however, an across-the-board consistency between decisions regarding human, animal and plant health risks was not acceptable.

4.281 The European Communities observed that the drafting history demonstrated, therefore, that the negotiators of the SPS Agreement had never had in mind a situation similar to the one presented by Canada, where measures applied equally to imported and domestic products were compared with other measures applied to totally different substances which posed different types of risks. Discussions in the SPS Committee had focused on how to ensure consistency, on comparisons between human health on one side and animal and plant health on the other, and on voluntary risks, but had, so far, yielded no concrete guidelines. The only notion that had a legal meaning was the prohibition of arbitrary and unjustifiable distinctions, if they resulted in discrimination or disguised restriction. It should therefore be noted that absolute consistency was not what was implied in Article 5.5, but rather that it was a step-by-step process, an objective which was to be achieved by respecting the legal obligation set out in Article 5.5 of avoiding arbitrary and unjustifiable distinctions.

4.282 The European Communities noted that Canada compared measures adopted with regard to hormones with measures adopted with regard to other substances, and the risks posed by hormones and these other substances, respectively. The European Communities claimed that Article 5.5 dealt with neither of these two notions - neither with measures, nor with risks. Article 5.5 established an obligation to avoid "arbitrary and unjustifiable distinctions in the levels [of sanitary or phytosanitary protection against risks to human life or health, or to animal and plant life or health] it considers to be appropriate in different situations, if such distinctions result ...". In other words, Article 5.5 imposed an obligation not to arbitrarily distinguish between *levels* of protection. No direct comparison of *measures*, nor of *risks* was envisaged. Furthermore, the provision did not prohibit overtly all types of distinctions in the levels of protection, only those distinctions which were arbitrary and unjustifiable, and which resulted in discrimination or disguised restriction. The second could not be assumed to be a consequence of the first; it was a separate qualification. Canada, therefore, was required to prove that the levels of protection were different, that the distinction was arbitrary and unjustifiable, and that it resulted in discrimination or a disguised restriction on international trade.

4.283 The European Communities further argued that the requirement in Article 5.5 to avoid "arbitrary or unjustifiable distinctions in the levels" considered to be appropriate, using "levels" in the plural, indicated that the SPS Agreement accepted that a Member might have more than one level of protection, applicable to different situations. Article 5.5 did not require Members to apply the same level of protection against possible adverse health effects from all pests, diseases and contaminants, as Canada suggested. This would be absurd because the degree of severity of adverse health effects varied according to the pest or disease and because Members could not be expected to provide the same degree of protection to plants which they applied to humans. Moreover, it would be equally unreasonable to interpret Article 5.5, as Canada did, to require Members to choose the same level of protection against residues of all veterinary drugs. Not all veterinary drugs had the same adverse effects on consumers through residues in food, and Members were at liberty to choose different levels of protection for different residues, as long as the level was consistent in different situations for the same residue. This was the essence of the ruling by the European Court of Justice in the *German Beer case*, cited by Canada (footnote to paragraph 4.275, footnote 221) and it was the case with the EC rules on hormones and other veterinary drugs.

4.284 The European Communities admitted that Canada might be justified to claim that the European Communities' level of protection against a particular adverse health effect, e.g. cancer, should be consistent even where that effect was caused by different substances. The European Communities had chosen its measures in the light of the specific circumstances in which each substance was used in order to achieve its appropriate level of protection. A comparison of the hormones with feed additives acting as growth promoters, such as carbadox and olaquindox, had to take into account the following elements:

(i) carbadox and olaquindox were not hormones, although they both acted as growth promoters;

(ii) the hormones at issue, when administered for growth promotion, speeded up directly the feed-weight conversion rate of the animals, whereas carbadox and olaquindox acted as growth promoters only indirectly by combating the development of bacteria and by aiding the intestinal flora of piglets;

(iii) carbadox and olaquindox were commercially available only as prepared feedstuffs, not as injections or implants nor as combinations;

(iv) they were allowed to be administered only to piglets, to the exclusion of any other animal;

(v) there were no commercially alternative products for carbadox and olaquindox which possessed not only the growth promotion aspect but also the medicinal effects of these two substances;

(vi) there were no incentives nor potential for misuse since these two substances could exert growth promotion only in piglets, not in other animals; and

(vii) all substances were said to be genotoxic and carcinogenic.

4.285 On the basis of these elements, the European Communities argued that carbadox and olaquindox were different substances from the hormones at issue, although they posed the same type of risk to human or animal health. The conditions imposed by the European Communities guaranteed, however, that there were no residues of carbadox and olaquindox in meat destined for human consumption. Therefore, the level of protection, "no residues in human food", was the same with regard to these two substances and the hormones.[224] The European Communities recalled that when EC member States made checks for these substances, they were checking to ensure that there were no residues. There was no tolerance level that was permitted for the residues of these two substances in meat for human consumption. But the fact that it had chosen to apply this level of protection by measures different from those it applied to growth hormones was irrelevant. The European Communities choose its measures in the light of the specific circumstances in which each substance was used.

4.286 In summary, the European Communities noted that the SPS Agreement allowed Members to choose their appropriate level of protection by their chosen political process and only required this choice to be "consistent" in respect of the *same* hazard in different situations. The SPS Agreement did not require Members to use the same measures to control the same hazard in different situations. On the contrary, it required measures to be "tailored", by means of risk assessment, to ensure that they were appropriate to the circumstances. To compare measures taken with regard to hormones with measures taken with regard to *other* substances was not relevant nor significant for the purposes of determining the existence of a breach of Article 5.5. More restrictive measures were not necessarily equivalent to a higher level of protection, and more important still, "less restrictive" measures were not at all indicative of a lower level of protection. Measures were taken to achieve the appropriate level of protection. It was, therefore, useless to compare measures which were applied to different products, different risks and in different circumstances. Moreover, the comparison of "risks" was also not correct. Levels of protection were to be compared, and measures taken to achieve such levels were to be based on risk assessment, as appropriate to the circumstances. The EC level of protection was the same in the examples invoked: no residues of the hormones at issue in meat destined for human consumption. The risk against which its measures aimed to protect the EC consumers was also the same: carcinogenicity. The European Communities used different measures as a result of risk assessments appropriate to the circumstances, which took into account the factors outlined in Article 5.2.

4.287 The European Communities argued that although Canada had claimed that "it is apparent that the EC level of protection for growth-promoting hormones is significantly higher than" for other substances, Canada had not demonstrated, first of all, the existence of different levels of protection and second, that the other two conditions were also met. Finally, the European Communities concluded that Canada had stated that there were about 10,000 to 15,000 authorized veterinary medicinal products in the European Communities. Yet, Canada's claim of lack of consistency in the European Communities was limited to five substances. This showed that there was indeed already a very high degree of consistency in the EC legislation.

4.288 **Canada** did not disagree with the EC statement that "Article 5.5 imposes an obligation not to arbitrarily distinguish between *levels* of protection. No direct comparisons of *measures*, nor of *risks* is provided here." Canada argued, however, that it

[224] The European Communities noted that, as it had indicated, it was going to review these two substances shortly and already in the process of withdrawing the authorization for avoparcin, the other substance mentioned by Canada. This showed that the European Communities had already achieved a very high degree of consistency in their legislation.

was not correct to state that "... It is, therefore, useless to compare measures alone which are applied to different products, different risks and in different circumstances". Canada submitted that the Panel was not prevented from looking at the evidence it had presented to infer that the European Communities applied distinctly different levels of protection, and that in the absence of any precise articulation by the European Communities as to what its level of protection was, despite repeated requests by Canada and other WTO Members in consultations, a complaining party and the Panel were left with no other recourse.

4.289 Canada claimed that, contrary to the EC arguments, Article 5.5 addressed precisely the issue of consistency in the *setting* or *deciding* of the appropriate level of protection. The EC interpretation was not consistent with the text of Article 5.5. Nowhere did Article 5.5 speak of "... avoiding arbitrary or unjustifiable distinctions in *applying* the chosen level of protection ....". Rather, it spoke to "... the objective of achieving consistency in the application of the concept of appropriate level of sanitary or phytosanitary protection ....". Moreover, in Canada's view, the EC interpretation was also inconsistent with the negotiating history of the SPS Agreement. As the note by the Secretariat on consistency in risk management decisions made clear, Article 5.5 was drafted with the intention of ensuring some consistency in the decisions of governments when *setting or deciding appropriate levels of protection*:

> "As the following review of the drafting history of the SPS Agreement makes clear, it was agreed at a very early stage in the negotiations that sanitary and phytosanitary measures should not be applied in an arbitrary or unjustifiably discriminatory manner. It was also agreed that sanitary and phytosanitary measures should primarily be based on risk assessment and analysis, and subsequently that *each government was responsible for the determination of what it considered to be its acceptable level of risk* (appropriate level of sanitary or phytosanitary protection). From this it followed that *to ensure that such governmental decisions did not result in arbitrary or unjustifiable discrimination in the application of sanitary or phytosanitary measures, there must be some consistency in the decisions taken*[225] (emphasis added).
>
> Once the concept of governments deciding what was an acceptable level of risk on the basis of an analysis of the actual risks involved was adopted as a basic element of the emerging SPS Agreement, it was recognized that disciplines were needed to ensure that this right to take a sovereign decision not be used to circumvent the obligations of non-arbitrariness or unjustifiable discrimination in the identification and measurement of risks, it was noted that there was still ample scope for governments to succumb to political pressures to protect certain domestic industries from foreign competition through their *decisions regarding acceptable levels of risk/sanitary and phytosanitary protection*"[226] (emphasis added).

[225] "Consistency in Risk Management Decisions", G/SPS/W/16, p.2, para. 4.

[226] *Ibid.*, p.3, para. 7.

4.290 Canada contended that the scope of the phrase "different situations" should be interpreted in the context of the objective of Article 5.5, set out in the opening clause: "With the objective of achieving consistency in the application of the concept of appropriate level of sanitary or phytosanitary protection against risks to human life or health, or to animal and plant life or health ...". As the note of the Secretariat explained:

> "The next concern was that what were considered as acceptable levels of risk with regard to animal or plant health could not necessarily be considered as (politically) acceptable levels of risk in matters regarding human health, or vice-versa. That is, consistency might be desirable and achievable among decisions regarding animal health, or even between plant and animal health issues, however an across-the-board consistency between decisions regarding human, animal and plant health risks was not acceptable."[227]

4.291 Thus, in the present case, it was clear that the appropriate level of protection underlying the EC measures must be compared for consistency only among decisions regarding the appropriate level of protection for other sanitary measures protecting *human health*. In that regard, Canada noted that *all* the examples it had raised identified the potential for adverse health effects in *humans* arising from veterinary drug residues in meat and other animal products. Moreover, the EC interpretation would limit "different situations" to "the same residue" or, at most, "different substances" causing "a particular adverse health effect". The European Communities offered no support for this narrow interpretation, aside from the Note cited above, which only spoke of limiting consistency in this case to human health.

4.292 Canada submitted that the phrase "different situations" captured all the different sanitary risks posed *to human health* contemplated by the *SPS Agreement*, *i.e.*, those arising from different sources, or causing different adverse health effects. Thus, within the terms of the *SPS Agreement*, and drawing upon the applicable paragraphs in the definition of a sanitary measure set in Annex A, (*i.e.*, paragraphs 1(b) and (c)), "different situations" would capture risks posed to human health "... arising from additives, contaminants, toxins or disease-causing organisms in food, beverages or feedstuffs," as well as risks "... arising from diseases carried by animals, plants or products thereof, or from the entry, establishment or spread of pests".[228] In the present case, "different situations" would capture the risks to human health posed by, *inter alia*, contaminants such as veterinary drugs residues, pesticides and heavy metals, by toxins such as botulinum toxin, fumonesin and aflatoxin-B1, and by disease-causing organisms such as salmonella, E. coli and campylobacter.

4.293 In the alternative, if the Panel did not accept this interpretation, Canada submitted that, at the very least, the scope of "different situations" encompassed similar risks and similar products.[229] In this regard, the examples cited by Canada described a

[227] "Consistency in Risk Management Decisions", G/SPS/W/16, p.4, para. 11.

[228] Definition of SPS measure: *SPS Agreement* Annex A, para. 1.

[229] Canada noted that it was interesting to note that the draft guidelines prepared by the Chairman of the SPS Committee suggested that at a minimum this was the scope of "different situations" contemplated by Article 5.5. Guideline 7 stated:

variety of veterinary drugs which were routinely used by EC farmers in animal production and which left residues in meat and milk. Thus, the products were similar. The adverse health effect that was the determining factor in the safety evaluation of each residue might be different: for example, JECFA had concluded that allergic reactions in humans was the determining factor in the safety evaluation of benzylpenicillin. However, these different adverse effects might be no less severe than cancer: for example, allergic reactions to penicillin had caused anaphylactic deaths.[230] Thus, the risks were similar. It was apparent that whatever the EC level of sanitary protection was for the six hormones at issue, it must be significantly higher than its level for antimicrobial growth promoters, in particular carbadox and olaquindox, and for a number of other veterinary drugs. These distinctions were arbitrary and unjustifiable.

4.294 Canada argued that the phrase "each Member shall avoid *arbitrary or unjustifiable* distinctions in the levels it considers to be appropriate" indicated that only some distinctions were to be avoided, *i.e.*, those that were arbitrary or unjustifiable. It followed that other distinctions were permissible, *i.e.*, those that were justifiable. Canada submitted that distinctions might be justified when the severity of the adverse health effects posed by dissimilar risks were significantly different. Thus, if one risk involved acute, anaphylactic shock that may lead to death as the adverse health effect, and another risk involved a mild, transient stomach upset, a higher level of protection for the former when compared to the latter could be justified. However, such a distinction would be arbitrary and unjustifiable if the risks compared involved adverse health effects of comparable severity.

4.295 Canada further submitted that there was no reason to subject consumers to higher risk from the residues of veterinary drugs used for therapeutic purposes, versus those used for other purposes, such as growth promotion: a distinction in the appropriate levels of protection would not be justified. Canada suggested that the distinction between using veterinary drugs for therapeutic purposes, versus using them for other purposes, such as zootechnical or growth promotion purposes, was in many ways a false dichotomy. Using veterinary drugs for therapeutic purposes not only benefited an animal by improving the animal's welfare, it also benefited the farmer because the animal became more productive. Ultimately, whether a farmer would use a veterinary drug to cure a disease in a food producing animal was still an economic question: if the costs outweighed the benefits, the animal probably would not be treated.

4.296 Canada noted that ingesting sufficient quantities of the residues of veterinary drugs commonly used by farmers in the European Communities could cause severe

"A proposed decision on an appropriate level of protection should be compared with previous decisions taken with regard to human health, animal health, or plant health, at least for similar risks or similar products. Any substantive differences in the proposed/accepted level of protection should be duly justified in accordance with the provisions of the Agreement." Draft - "Draft Guidelines to Further the Practical Implementation of Article 5.5", *Note by the Chairman*, 16 September 1996.

[230] W.G. Huber (1986), "Allergenicity of Antibacterial Drug Residues," in A.G. Rico, ed., *Drug Residues in Animals (Orlando: Academic Press)*, pp.46-49.

adverse health effects, *i.e.,* could result in death. Carbadox was a genotoxic carcinogen in animals, as was one of its metabolites. Allergic reactions to benzylpenicillin residues in hypersensitive members of the population could cause anaphylaxis, leading to death. Persons suffering from pulmonary obstructive diseases, such as chronic asthma, were extremely sensitive to non-selective B-adrenoceptor antagonists, such as carazolol; a sufficient dose of carazolol could cause severe bronchial constriction and asphixiation, again leading to death. Organo-phosphate pesticides were powerful neuro-toxins, and some were also carcinogenic.[231] Thus, Canada argued, the severity of the potential adverse health effects of these substances was comparable to, or greater than, that of the six hormones at issue.

4.297 Canada submitted that the phrase "if such distinctions result in discrimination or a disguised restriction on international trade" went to the heart of the purpose of Article 5(5). As the Secretariat Note on the negotiating history stated:

> ... it was noted that there was still ample scope for governments to succumb to political pressures to protect certain domestic industries from foreign competition through their decisions regarding acceptable levels of risk/sanitary and phytosanitary protection.[232]

Canada argued that a disguised restriction could be found when additional factors not relevant to the protection of health led to the introduction of measures that were more restrictive than necessary to meet legitimate sanitary concerns, albeit presented in the guise of a sanitary measure. To paraphrase the note of the Secretariat, without this discipline, there would be ample scope for governments to succumb to political pressures to protect or achieve certain domestic interests, without regard to their impact on international trade, through their decisions regarding acceptable levels of sanitary protection.[233]

4.298 Canada submitted that, on the evidence and arguments presented in its submissions, the Panel could infer distinct appropriate levels of protection for the six hormones at issue and for other veterinary drugs commonly used by farmers in the European Communities. It was apparent that, whatever the EC level of sanitary protection for the six hormones at issue, it must be higher than its level for antimicrobial growth promoters, in particular carbadox and olaquindox, and for a number of other veterinary drugs cited in Canada's submissions. Canada claimed that these distinctions were arbitrary and unjustifiable. There was no objective principle that could justify them, since the severity of the potential adverse effects of these other substances were comparable, if not greater. These distinctions resulted in discrimination against Canadian beef imports, and constituted an unwarranted restriction in this trade in the guise of a sanitary measure. In this regard, the EC submissions were telling:

> "Of the 31 countries which are authorized to export meat to the EC, only 6 allow for the use of some or all of the hormones at issue here as growth promoters (Argentina, Australia, Canada, New Zealand, South

231 Dr. McLean, answer to Panel question 11, para. 6.131.

232 WTO Secretariat, "Consistency in Risk Management Decisions", G/SPS/W/16, p.3, para. 7.

233 *Ibid.*, p.3, para. 7.

Africa and the USA). *These six countries are the main meat producing and exporting countries*"[234] (emphasis added).

4.299 Canada concluded that the EC measures constituted a disguised restriction because additional factors not relevant to the protection of health led to the introduction of measures that were more restrictive than necessary to meet the legitimate sanitary concerns. The European Communities succumbed to political pressures to protect or achieve certain domestic interests, without regard to their impact on international trade, and the effects on exports of Canadian beef to the European Communities had been devastating.

4.300 The **European Communities** considered that the phrase "different situations" could only apply to same substances (or residues from the same substances), if they lead to different levels of protection. The European Communities indicated that that it participated actively in the SPS Committee work on consistency guidelines. But guidelines had not yet been established, and the European Communities submitted that Canada made arguments and advanced interpretations which had not yet been agreed. The European Communities stressed that the guidelines invoked by Canada were no more than draft guidelines, prepared by the Chairman of the SPS Committee after the entry into force of the SPS Agreement, in his attempt to develop the guidelines mentioned in Article 5.5. The text of Article 5.5 was not intended to mean and could not be applied in the way interpreted by Canada. In the EC view, the interpretation of Article 5:5 advanced by Canada in this case was contrary to the customary principles of treaty interpretation, because it disregarded the text, object and purpose of that provision and did not make sense from the systematic point of view as long as the SPS Committee had not agreed on the guidelines for its practical implementation.

4.301 The European Communities argued that Article 5.5 provided for achieving consistency in the levels of protection in "different situations". The situations referred to were mainly trade and marketing situations. The objective was that a Member should apply the same level of protection against the same health hazard whether the hazard arose from domestic production or from imports and, in the case of imports, the same level of protection should be applied in respect of the same hazard in imports from different countries. The words "different situations" could also cover the different elements mentioned in Article 5.2, i.e. process and production methods, inspection, sampling, testing, diseases, ecological and environmental conditions, etc. This did not mean that the measures adopted to achieve the level of protection would always be the same. For example, the European Communities had adopted a high level of protection against foot-and-mouth disease, having eradicated it from its territory by a slaughter policy. However, it imported susceptible animals and their products from many countries, some of which still had the disease. Therefore, in respect of infected countries it imposed conditions on imports which were designed to keep the disease out of its territory. The European Communities did not impose the same measures on domestic production or on imports from other third countries which did not have the disease. Thus, its level of protection was consistent but its measures were different: they were tailored to the risk involved. The European Communities claimed that it had the same policy with regard to hormones. It did not allow the ad-

234 European Communities' first written submission, para. 91.

ministration of these hormones in meat in its territory and meat imported from a variety of third countries, some of which allowed the use of these hormones for growth promotion, others of which did not. For those which did not, no special conditions were imposed on imports. For those which allowed such use, the European Communities imposed measures on imports which were designed to meet its level of protection.

4.302 "Different situations" could not mean that the same level of protection must be applied to similar health hazards, whatever their nature or severity, coming from similar substances. The hazards associated with different diseases and contaminants were different in their nature and severity, and affected different species. It would clearly be unreasonable if the SPS Agreement were to be interpreted as requiring Members to adopt the same level of protection against, for example, ringworm in cattle and cholera in humans. It was, however, reasonable to have the same level of protection against each of these diseases regardless of its origin, i.e. whether it arose inside the territory of the Member or as a result of importation. The same applied to contaminants. Hormones had their own particular effects; some of these effects might be similar to, or the same as, other drugs such as carbadox, but some were different and were unique to hormones. The EC level of protection was chosen for protection against all the undesirable effects of hormones, not only cancer which was the most important one. In any case, its level of protection against carcinogenic substances, whatever their source, was consistent. Article 5.5 clearly stated that "arbitrary or unjustifiable" distinctions were to be avoided if they resulted in discrimination or a disguised restriction on trade. If they did not result in discrimination or a disguised restriction on trade they were not prohibited by the SPS Agreement. In the present dispute, however, this provision was irrelevant since the European Communities did not make any distinction in its level of protection between different situations. Its level of protection was the same irrespective of the source of hormones. Of course, its measures to enforce this level of protection differed according to the circumstances of the risk, which in turn differed according to whether hormones were allowed to be used freely for growth promotion, or whether they were allowed to be used only under strict veterinary control for therapeutic purposes.

4.303 The European Communities argued that its measures resulted in no discrimination. The EC level of protection was designed to protect against particular hazards, not against classes of potential sources of any hazard, such as all "diseases", or, as in this question, all "veterinary drugs". Not all veterinary drugs had the potential to cause adverse health effects in consumers, just as not all human drugs carried the same risks for consumers. For example, morphine and aspirin were both pain-killers but, because of the different degrees of risk associated with them, the former was only available for administration by doctors while the latter was available over the counter, without prescription. Of course the European Communities did not have a level of protection against those hormones produced naturally in the body, any more than it did against any other natural component of the body. As far as other veterinary drugs were concerned, the European Communities had the same level of protection against other carcinogenic drugs as it did for hormones. Its measures were designed to achieve this although, given the different circumstances under which the different drugs were used, they might be different from the measures used for hormones. Nevertheless, they were designed to give the same level of protection. The

European Communities did not, therefore, make any distinctions, arbitrary, unjustifiable or other, in its level of protection against the same hazard arising from the same substances in different situations.

4.304 The European Communities argued that Canada had not shown that there were arbitrary and unjustifiable distinctions in the *levels* of protection the European Communities was applying for these hormones and the other two substances. The levels for these two different groups of substances were the same, not arbitrary. They were also justified, because there was plenty of scientific evidence which showed that these hormones and their metabolites were carcinogenic even at physiological levels, whereas in the case of carbadox the metabolites which could be found in the muscle were not carcinogenic and in the case of olaquindox the studies of JECFA were still inconclusive. The fact that the European Communities did not agree with the conclusions of the JECFA report on hormones but followed the JECFA report in the case of the other two substances, did not necessarily mean lack of consistency. The different situations in the two case justified the difference in the approach, both on technical and scientific grounds, without however affecting the EC levels of protection.

4.305 Canada had not shown that the distinctions resulted in discrimination or a disguised restriction on international trade. Canada did not even discuss this condition in depth, but had simply made an automatic assumption that it was fulfilled in this case. The EC measure did not discriminate against Canada, because Canada could export hormone-free meat to the European Communities like any other country. The production of meat treated with hormones was not a specific characteristic of Canada's production, nor was the production of hormone-free meat a peculiar characteristic of meat production in the European Communities. Therefore, there was no discrimination in effect. In order to show discrimination and disguised restriction Canada had argued that the Members which were suffering from the EC measure were the six principal producers of meat in the world. This type of argument enlarged the elements of comparison in an unacceptable way. But even this class of countries was not treated differently among themselves, on the one hand, and the other meat producing countries (e.g. Argentina) on the other, because any one of them could export hormone-free meat to the European Communities under exactly the same conditions as those applied to all other third countries as well as within the European Communities. In addition, Canada had not shown what other measure, apart from lifting the prohibition, the European Communities could take in this case which would not be disguised and would achieve its appropriate level of protection. Canada had certainly not demonstrated that it had been the intention of the European Communities when adopting its level of protection was to put in place a disguised restriction on international trade. If Canada was affected, it was because of its decision not to comply with the possibilities offered by the EC measures. For instance, the European Communities would import pig meat from Canada treated with carbadox or olaquindox under the same conditions allowed in the European Communities.

(l) *Article 5.6 of the SPS Agreement*

4.306 **Canada** noted that Article 5.6 prescribed how a Member must ensure that any sanitary measure was applied only to the extent necessary to protect human, animal or plant life or health and stressed that in effect, Article 5.6 set out how a Member was to meet this basic requirement of Article 2.2:

> "Without prejudice to paragraph 2 of Article 3, when establishing or maintaining sanitary or phytosanitary measures to achieve the appropriate level of sanitary or phytosanitary protection, Members shall ensure that such measures are not more trade-restrictive than required to achieve their appropriate level of sanitary or phytosanitary protection, taking into account technical and economic feasibility."

A footnote to the paragraph provided that:

> "For the purposes of paragraph 6 of Article 5, a measure is not more trade-restrictive than required unless there is another measure, reasonably available taking into account technical and economic feasibility, that achieves the appropriate level of sanitary and phytosanitary protection and is significantly less restrictive to trade."

4.307 In Canada's view, it was clear that under the Feed Additives Directives, the European Communities maintained regulatory control over antimicrobial growth promoters that was significantly less restrictive to trade than the complete ban on the use for growth promotion of the six hormones at issue. Moreover, the European Communities itself asserted that its appropriate level of protection was the same for carbadox as it was for these hormones. If this was the case, then it was clear that the prohibition on beef from cattle treated with the six hormones at issue was far more trade-restrictive than required. The risks posed by carbadox were greater than those posed by the six hormones at issue and there was no technical or economic reason why a similar scheme could not reasonably be extended to these six hormones. Canada's position was that the EC measures were more trade restrictive than necessary to achieve the level of sanitary protection achieved by the Feed Additives Directives, and therefore the EC measures were contrary to Article 5.6.

4.308 The **European Communities** noted that Article 5.6 required *measures* to be "not more trade-restrictive than required to achieve the appropriate level of protection" and argued that there was no obligation to change the level of protection. The footnote to Article 5.6 explained that a measure was *not* more trade-restrictive than required unless there was *another* measure which was less trade-restrictive and still met the chosen level of protection, taking into account technical and economic feasibility. In these circumstances, it was up to a complaining Member to demonstrate that there was such another measure.

4.309 Noting that labelling might seem to be a reasonable alternative to the prohibition applied by the European Communities on the use of these hormones for growth promotion, the European Communities argued that the starting point to take into account was that the residues of these hormones posed very serious risks to human and animal health, of which cancer was the most important. It might be that the probability of this risk arising was relatively small, as Dr. Lucier, one of the experts advising the Panel had argued, but the SPS Agreement did not require a quantification of the risk and the level of sanitary protection a Member determined to be appropriate could be zero risk. Either there was a risk or not; if there was one, no matter how small, a Member was allowed not to accept that risk. Some parts of the population could not cope with labelling (could not read, could not understand, etc.), so the competent authorities had to assume their responsibilities to the public. Labelling, therefore, was inherently contradictory with a level of no risk from residues of these hormones.

4.310 The European Communities observed that labelling might function in Members which had a lower level of protection than the European Communities in this case. There might indeed be consumers in Canada who would prefer hormone-free meat. In that situation, it was conceivable to think of labelling meat as "hormone-free" meat. Conversely, labelling could not work where the level of protection was higher. Imports of meat labelled treated with hormones, if allowed, would undermine the level of protection in the European Communities as EC farmers would also like to produce meat with the hormones in order to avoid unfair competition from imported cheap labelled meat. But this might expose the entire population in the European Communities to an involuntary risk, because a person could not verify whether meat served in a restaurant was hormone-free. Unlike other pre-packed and labelled food products, where the original producer was indicated and could be traced back in order to impose sanctions in case of violations, labelling was not easily applicable to meat sold for human consumption.

4.311 The European Communities claimed that involuntary exposure to a risk, no matter how small, could not be labelled. This concept was included in Article 5.5, where reference was made to the "exceptional character of human health risks to which people voluntarily expose themselves". Labelling of a packet of cigarettes was not the same as labelling meat. Smoking and eating were not the same type of activity and the voluntary/involuntary nature of the exposure to the risk was very important. When the European Communities imported meat from countries where the use of growth promoting hormones was authorized, it relied first on the guarantees given by the governmental authorities of that Member that the imported meat was hormone-free meat. In addition, the European Communities carried out a number of systematic and random controls and checks in order to verify whether the assurances given by the state authorities were respected. With labelling, there would be no such state assurances, as labelling would be an initiative of private farmers. The number of controls and checks would therefore have to increase substantially without any certainty that there would be no violations of the level of protection.

4.312 In contrast, the European Communities noted that the labelling of meat as BSE-free in no way affected the level of protection a Member had adopted against BSE. It made no difference whether there were incidences of BSE recorded in the country or not, because in both situations the objective was to eradicate or to avoid the potential source of the risk from BSE infected meat. Labelling in this type of situations, therefore, reinforced the level of protection a Member had already put in place and was not likely to undermine it. Conversely, the situation of labelling meat treated or not treated with hormones was completely different.

3. Agreement on Technical Barriers to Trade

4.313 **Canada** submitted the following submissions alternatively, in case the Panel decided that the matters at issue were not governed by the SPS Agreement. Canada argued that the TBT Agreement did not apply to sanitary measures and recalled that Article 1.5 of the TBT Agreement read as follows:

> "The provisions of this Agreement do not apply to sanitary and phytosanitary measures as defined in Annex A of the Agreement on the Application of Sanitary and Phytosanitary Measures."

If the EC measures were not characterized as "sanitary and phytosanitary measures", then they fell within the disciplines of the TBT Agreement as "technical regulations".[235]

4.314 Canada noted that the TBT Agreement set out two basic obligations with respect to technical regulations, in Articles 2.1 and 2.2. Neither of these obligations had been met by the EC measures at issue. Canada had argued that the EC measures had created obstacles to Canadian trade by stopping the importation by the European Communities of Canadian beef produced with growth promoting hormones. What remained to be determined by the Panel was whether these obstacles were more trade-restrictive than necessary to fulfil a legitimate objective.

4.315 Canada recalled its previous arguments that (paragraph 4.6), the EC measures were motivated by four sets of concerns: first, anxiety regarding the danger to human health; second, the pressure of public opinion; third, the economic consequences of a "sensationalist campaign"; and fourth, the distortions in the conditions of competition among the EC member States owing to dissimilar provisions and regulations governing the manufacture, distribution and use of substances. Canada argued that while protection of human health was among the policy objectives listed in Article 2.2, this in itself did not justify a complete import prohibition. As Canada had demonstrated, the EC import prohibition lacked scientific justification. The European Communities had failed to prove that an import prohibition was necessary to provide protection to the health of its consumers. Furthermore, it had also been demonstrated (see paragraphs 4.42, 4 54, 4.225) that the European Communities maintained regulatory control over antimicrobial growth promoters that was significantly less restrictive to trade than the complete ban on the use for growth promotion of the six growth promoting hormones and the import prohibition of beef produced outside the European Communities with the same hormones. Thus the EC measures were more trade restrictive than necessary, in contravention of Article 2.2 of the TBT Agreement.

4.316 Canada claimed that a panel examining a measure under Article 2.1 must determine if the measure in question was a measure to which the provision applied (*i.e.* whether it was a technical regulation), if the products in question were like products, and if the measure resulted in less favourable treatment for the imported Canadian product than for the like domestic and imported products.

4.317 Canada noted that Article 2.1 of the TBT Agreement incorporated the non-discrimination principles set out in GATT Articles I and III but was broader. There was no language in Article 2.1 that qualified or limited the scope of the non-discrimination obligations in the TBT Agreement. While Article 2.1 was broader than GATT Articles I and III, there was an obvious link between these provisions. Although a panel assessing the consistency of a measure with Article 2.1 might be

235 Annex 1 of the *TBT Agreement* defines a technical regulation as a "Document which lays down product characteristics or their related processes and production methods ... with which compliance is necessary ...".

guided generally by the type of analysis that might be conducted under GATT Articles I and III, it was not required to adhere rigidly to the precise form of such analysis. In Canada's view, beef produced with growth promoting hormones was a "like product" to beef produced in the European Communities from animals to which the same growth promoting hormones had been administered for therapeutic reasons, and "like" beef that contained residues of antimicrobial growth promoters and other veterinary drugs. Canada submitted that by excluding Canadian beef from the EC market, the European Communities had treated Canadian products less favourably than like products of EC origin, in contravention of Article 2.2 of the TBT Agreement.

4.318 The **European Communities** reaffirmed that the main purpose of the measures at issue was to protect human health from the risks arising from the consumption of meat from animals treated with growth promoting hormones. In view of the definition of SPS measures under the SPS Agreement, the European Communities considered it to be beyond doubt that the measures at issue were "sanitary measures" within the meaning of the SPS Agreement. Therefore, the EC arguments on TBT were, like the Canadian arguments, presented in the alternative. If, the Panel decided that the measures at issue were not "sanitary measures" but "technical regulations" subject to the TBT Agreement, the European Communities submitted that, contrary to Canada's claims, they did not infringe either Article 2.1 or Article 2.2 of that Agreement.

4.319 Article 2.1 of the TBT Agreement restated the national treatment obligation contained in Article III:4 of GATT and the most favoured nation obligation contained in Article I:1 of GATT. The European Communities claimed that as far as the national treatment obligation was concerned (the only one whose violation had been invoked by Canada), Article 2.1 of the TBT Agreement and Article III:4 of GATT laid down the same type of obligation: not to afford "less favourable treatment" to imported products than to domestic like products. The only difference between the two provisions was that Article 2.1 of the TBT Agreement applied only in respect of technical regulations, while Article III:4 of GATT applied in respect of "all laws, regulations and requirements ...". It followed that no violation of Article 2.1 could be established unless Article III:4 of GATT was simultaneously infringed. For the same reasons that the measures at issue did not infringe Article III:4 of the GATT (paragraph 4.337 ff.), EC measures were consistent with Article 2.1 of the TBT Agreement.

4.320 The primary purpose of the EC measures was to protect human health. This was one of the "legitimate objective" expressly mentioned in Article 2.2 of the TBT Agreement. As evidenced by the precedent discussion on the application of the SPS Agreement, the EC measures were not more "trade restrictive" than necessary in order to fulfil this objective. Therefore, the European Communities maintained its measures were consistent with Article 2.2 of the TBT Agreement.

4. *GATT*

(a) *Article III*

4.321 **Canada** submitted that the EC measures contravened Article III or XI of GATT. Although it considered that there was a threshold question under the GATT whether this matter was governed by Article III by virtue of the Interpretive Note *Ad* Article III, or by Article XI, Canada was of the view that this matter would be more appropriately addressed under Article III than Article XI.

4.322 Canada recalled that Article III:1 of GATT read as follows:

> "The contracting parties recognize that internal taxes and other internal charges, and *laws, regulations and requirements affecting the internal sale, offering for sale, purchase, transportation, distribution or use of products*, and internal quantitative regulations requiring the mixture, processing or use of products in specified amounts or proportions, should not be applied to imported or domestic products so as to afford protection to domestic production" (emphasis added).

4.323 The Appellate Body, in its decision in "Japanese Liquor Tax"[236] had commented on the relationship between Article III:1 and the other paragraphs of Article III as follows:

> "Article III:1 of the GATT articulates a general principle that internal measures should not be applied so as to afford protection to domestic production. This general principle informs the rest of Article III."[237]

4.324 Canada argued that in the present case the most relevant part of Article III:4 was paragraph 4, which provided:

> "The products of the territory of any contracting party imported into the territory of any other contracting party shall be accorded treatment no less favourable than that accorded to like products of national origin in respect of all laws, regulations and requirements affecting their internal sale, offering for sale, purchase, transportation, distribution or use ..."

4.325 The report of the Appellate Body in "Japanese Liquor Tax" had cited with approval the 1970 Working Party Report on "Border Tax Adjustments" as setting out the "... basic approach for interpreting "like or similar products" generally in the various provisions of the GATT 1947".[238] The Appellate Body had quoted the following passage of the report of the Working Party:

> "(...) the interpretation of the terms should be examined on a case-by-case basis. This would allow a fair assessment in each case of the different elements that constitute a 'similar' product. Some criteria were suggested for determining on a case-by-case basis, whether a product is "similar": the product's end-uses in a given market; consumers' tastes and habits, which change from country to country; the product's properties, nature and quality (...)."[239]

236 "Japan - Taxes on Alcoholic Beverages" (AB-1996-2; WT/DS8/AB/R; WT/DS10/AB/R; WT/DS11/AB/R; 4 October 1996), DSR 1996:I, 97.

237 *Idem.*, p.111.

238 *Idem.*, p.113.

239 Report of the Working Party on "Border Tax Adjustments", L/3464, adopted on 2 December 1970, BISD 18S/97, 102, para. 18.

4.326 The Appellate Body, in the same case, had further commented on the tests to determine what constituted a "like product", in particular in the context of Article III:2:

> "No one approach to exercising judgement will be appropriate for all cases. The criteria in "Border Tax Adjustments" should be examined, but there can be no one precise and absolute definition of what is "like". The concept of "likeness" is a relative one that evokes the image of an accordion. The accordion of "likeness" stretches and squeezes in different places as different provisions of the WTO Agreement are applied. The width of the accordion in any one of those places must be determined by the particular provision in which the term "like" is encountered as well as by the context and circumstances that prevail in any given case to which that provision may apply. We believe that, in the context of Article III:2, first sentence of the GATT 1994, the accordion of "likeness" is meant to be narrowly squeezed."[240]

4.327 Applying the flexible approach of the 1970 Working Party Report on "Border Tax Adjustments", different indications of likeness had been invoked by various GATT 1947 Panels, *e.g.* tariff classification[241], end-uses[242] or physical characteristics of the product.[243] Canada argued that the European Communities did not differentiate in its tariff classification between beef produced with growth promoting hormones, antimicrobial growth promoters or any other veterinary drugs, and beef produced without. Similarly, in the EC meat-grading system no such differentiation was made.[244]

4.328 In "Japanese Liquor Tax", the Appellate Body ruled, agreeing with the Panel, that the term "like products" in the first sentence of Article III:2 should be construed narrowly.[245] The rule of Article III:4 of GATT was less specific than the rules of Article III:2. Therefore, the "likeness" test of Article III:4 of GATT was probably intended to be less stringent than that of Article III:2. Even applying the more stringent test of Article III:2, Canada submitted that its beef was a like product when compared with EC beef.

4.329 Canada emphasized that in the present context "likeness" was not the same as "being identical". The burden was not on Canada to prove that beef produced with growth promoting hormones was the same as other beef. Rather, Canada must prove that beef produced with growth promoting hormones was sufficiently similar to EC beef, i.e. beef containing residues of antimicrobial growth promoters and other vet-

240 Appellate Body, "Japan - Taxes on Alcoholic Beverages" (AB-1996-2), DSR 1996:I, 97 at 114.

241 For example, see the 1978 panel report on "EC - Animal Feed Proteins", BISD 25S/49, 63, paras. 5.47-5.49.

242 For example, see the 1987 panel report on "United States - Taxes on Petroleum and Certain Imported Substances", BISD 34S/136, 154-155, para. 5.1.1.

243 For example, see the 1992 panel report on "US - Measures Affecting Alcoholic and Malt Beverages", which held that low alcohol beer and high alcohol beer were like products, BISD 39S/206, 293-294, para. 5.71-5.74.

244 Regulations 1208/81/EEC, 2930/81/EEC and 1026/91/EEC.

245 WT/DS8/AB/R; WT/DS10/AB/R; WT/DS11/AB/R, DSR 1996:I, 97 at 112 and 113.

erinary drugs, to establish that a national treatment violation has occurred. Canada referred to an EC document entitled "Communication from the Commission to the Council and to the European Parliament on control of residues in meat - Hormones - Beta-Agonists - Other Substances", which stated:

4.330 "The results of the enquiry [on residues in meat, initiated by the Commission, following a request of the European Parliament] showed that:

- anabolic substances (hormones and beta-agonists) were generally available, leading to illegal use;
- *antibiotic and sulphonamide residues were frequently found in meat*, especially in the case of intensive livestock rearing systems (veal calves, young fattening bovines, and fattening pigs);
- *other residues were detected occasionally (heavy metals including cadmium, pesticides, antiparasitic substances) ...*"[246] (emphasis added).

4.331 Canada claimed that the physical characteristics of beef produced from animals treated with growth promoting hormones were indistinguishable for the consumer from beef produced without the use of growth promoting hormones. The use of growth promoting hormones resulted in beef of higher quality because the animals concerned had better carcass composition, with a greater lean-to-fat tissue ratio. This had been confirmed in the above-mentioned Communication from the Commission to the Council.[247] Chemical analysis of the beef might be able to identify beef produced from animals treated with growth promoting hormones in certain instances. However, a document commissioned and published by the Commission admitted that this was virtually impossible with regard to oestradiol-17β, testosterone and progesterone. The report commented in this regard:

> "To our present knowledge up to now *distinctions between untreated animals and those treated with oestradiol-17β, testosterone and progesterone can only be made on a quantitative and not a qualitative basis*. This statement is based on the fact that the three steroids mentioned above (oestradiol-17β, testosterone and progesterone) will enter the same metabolic pathways, regardless of whether they are of endogenous or exogenous origin. Thus treated animals can only be identified if their tissue levels significantly exceed those of untreated animals; if such a situation is detected it further has to be verified that the particular animal showing this levels [sic] was clinically sound and that no reproductive problems, such as cystic ovaries or tumours of sex hormone producing organs had been present at slaughter"[248] (emphasis added).

---

[246] Communication from the Commission to the Council and to the European Parliament on Control of Residues in Meat - Hormones - Beta-Agonists - Other Substances COM(93) 167 final 21 April 1993, para. 5.

[247] *Ibid.*, para. 23.

[248] R.J. Heitzman, ed., "Veterinary Drug Residues: Residues in food producing animals and their products: Reference Materials and Methods", 2nd ed., (*Oxford: Blackwell Scientific Publications, 1994*), p.7/5.

4.332 A 1987 Monograph issued by the JECFA had confirmed the above conclusion in respect of progesterone.[249] The difficulty of distinguishing beef produced with the three natural growth promoting hormones from other beef had also been confirmed in a 1994 article by Dr. Stephen F. Sundlof.[250]

4.333 Canada claimed that this showed that it was very difficult, if not impossible, to distinguish, even through chemical analysis, between beef produced with natural growth promoting hormones and beef produced without; and that these differences in production methods did *not* result in products that were "unlike" beef produced in the European Communities. In any event, the European Communities continued to permit the use of oestradiol-17β, progesterone and testosterone for therapeutic purposes and had not prohibited the sale and consumption of the beef derived from animals treated with these hormones. This reinforced the point that it was difficult, if not impossible, to distinguish in the European Communities between beef from cattle that had been treated with these hormones and those that had not.

4.334 Canada argued that given that beef containing residues of antimicrobial growth promoters and other veterinary drugs was widely available in the EC market, it would not be appropriate, in determining the "likeness" of Canadian and EC beef, to limit the comparison of beef produced with growth promoting hormones to beef from cattle that were raised without the use of antimicrobial growth promoters and other veterinary drugs. Canada had shown (see paragraph 4.259) that the use of antimicrobial growth promoters and other veterinary drugs in the European Communities resulted in the presence of residues in beef sold there. The presence of antibiotic and sulphonamide residues, as well as other residues in meat, had been confirmed in the

---

[249] "Residues of some veterinary drugs in animals and foods", Monographs prepared by the Thirty-Second Meeting of the Joint FAO/WHO Expert Committee on Food Additives, Rome, 15-23 June 1987, FAO Food and Nutrition Paper 41 (Rome: FAO, 1988) p.22:

> "As with other endogenous steroid hormones, residue levels of progesterone in tissues are very low. Progesterone levels were measured in tissues from treated steers using a radio-immunoassay technique sensitive at the low ng/kg level, and were found to be about 0.4 μg/kg in muscle, liver and kidney and 3.5 μg/kg in fat; these levels can be compared with normal levels of approximately 0.2 μg/kg in muscle, liver and kidney and approximately 2.5 μg/kg in fat from untreated animals.
>
> "Progesterone, like oestradiol-17β and testosterone, occurs naturally in mammals, and is normally present in the dairy products and the tissues of untreated animals. In the edible tissues of animals treated with progesterone in combination with oestradiol-17β, residue levels are up to twice as high as in the tissue of untreated animals. However, the levels of progesterone found in the meat from animals treated with implants according to good animal husbandry practice are extremely low when compared to the amounts of endogenous progesterone produced daily in human beings. The daily production rate of progesterone in humans is given in Table VII. (Farber and Arcos, 1983). Even in prepubertal boys, the 300 ng additional progesterone derived from a 500 g portion of meat from treated animals is considerably less than the amount of endogenous progesterone produced daily. In addition, for those animal classes studied, the progesterone residue levels in treated animals fell well within the normal range of levels found in untreated bovine animals of different types and ages."

[250] S.F. Sundlof, "Human Health Risks Associated with Drug Residues in Animal-Derived Foods" (1994) 1:2 *Journal of Agromedicine* 5, pp.12-13.

Communication from the EC Commission to the EC Council. The European Communities themselves, in their grading system of beef, did not distinguish between beef produced with and without growth hormones, or between beef with residues of antimicrobial growth promoters and other veterinary drugs and that without.

4.335 Canada submitted that given the other residues present in beef produced in the European Communities, Canadian beef produced with the six growth promoting hormones at issue was a "like product" within the meaning of Article III:4 of the GATT as compared to beef produced in the European Communities; and that Canadian beef had been accorded treatment that was less favourable than EC beef, in contravention of Article III:4 of the GATT.

4.336 The **European Communities** argued that the measures at issue had their domestic counterpart in the prohibition on the administration of the same types of hormones to animals reared in the European Communities and in the prohibition on the marketing of those animals and of meat from those animals. The measures applied to domestic products had identical scope and were subject to the same exceptions as the measures applied to the imported products. The only difference between the measures applied to domestic products and those applied to imported products was that while the former were applied at the stage of production and sale, the latter were enforced at the point of importation. Furthermore, the measures applied to both domestic and imported products as "products", even if their scope was defined in terms of processes and production methods ("PPMs") rather than in terms of product characteristics. The present case was to be distinguished from the situation considered by the panel report on "US - Restrictions on Imports of Tuna I", in which the panel had reasoned that the Note ad Article III covered only those measures which were "applied to products as such". Yet, according to the panel, the US internal regulations "could not possibly affect tuna "*as a product*".[251] In contrast, in the present case the reason for prohibiting the importation of animals which had been treated with certain hormones, and of meat from those animals (as well as their domestic production and sale) was precisely that this treatment, unlike the PPMs for fishing tuna prescribed by the US regulations, modified the physical characteristics and biological composition of the products.

4.337 The European Communities disagreed with the Canadian interpretation of "like products". In the EC view, a determination of "likeness" must be exclusively based on objective criteria related to the characteristics of the products. The purpose of a regulatory distinction between "like products" might only become relevant in deciding whether a measure which was inconsistent with Article III:4 could be justified under any of the general exceptions provided for under Article XX of the GATT. The European Communities contended that the purpose of the measures at issue was not to afford protection to domestic production but to protect human and animal health, as well as the interests of consumers and, therefore, would not, in conformity with the Canada's own test, infringe Article III:4. Although two products need not be identical in order to be "like" for the purposes of Article III, previous panel reports

[251] Panel report on "US - Restrictions on Imports of Tuna I", DS21/R (unadopted), 3 September 1991, 39S/155, 193-195, paras. 5.8-5.14.

had taken a consistently narrow approach when interpreting this term. In "EC - Measures on Animal Feed Proteins", the panel had rejected a claim by the United States to the effect that all products used for the purpose of adding proteins to animal feeds were "like". The panel noted, *inter alia*, that the products concerned had different protein contents and different origins (vegetal, animal or synthetic).[252] More recently, the panel report on "Japan - Taxes on Alcoholic Beverages", a case concerning the application of Article III:2, had concluded that:

> "... only vodka could be considered as like product to shochu since, apart from commonality of end uses, it shared with shochu *most* physical characteristics. Definitionally, the only difference is in the media used for filtration. Substantial noticeable differences in physical characteristics exist between the rest of the alcoholic beverages at dispute and shochu that would disqualify them from being regarded as like products. More specifically, the use of *additives* would disqualify liqueurs, gin and genever; the use of *ingredients* would disqualify rum; lastly, *appearance* (arising from manufacturing processes) would disqualify whisky and brandy"[253] (emphasis added).

4.338 The European Communities reaffirmed its views that meat from animals to which had been administered any of the six hormones at issue for growth promotion had substantially different properties, composition and appearance than meat from animals to which those hormones had not been administered or to which they had been administered only for therapeutic purposes. Moreover, meat from treated animals was perceived by EC consumers as a distinct product. For these reasons, animals treated with hormones for growth promotion, and meat from those animals, could not, in light of the criteria used by previous panel reports, be considered as "like" to other animals, and meat from those animals, for the purposes of Article III:4.

4.339 The European Communities added that meat from animals treated with any of the hormones at issue for growth promotion was different from meat from untreated animals or from animals treated for therapeutical purposes in several ways. First, the precise mode of action of the prohibited hormones was not yet understood. It could not be excluded, on the basis of the available scientific evidence, that they might act as genotoxic agents that induced permanent genetic mutations in those animals to which they were administered. The presence of residues which were potentially genotoxic rendered the meat unfit for human consumption. Meat which from the sanitary point of view was not allowed to be consumed and hormone-free meat could not under any circumstance be defined to be "like" for the purposes of Article III:4 of GATT. In addition, trenbolone, zeranol and MGA were not naturally produced by animals. Thus, meat from animals to which these hormones had been administered

---

[252] Panel report on "EC - Animal Feed Proteins", para. 4.2. The other Panel report dealing with a regulatory measure discriminating between non-identical products is the Panel report on "US - Measures affecting Alcoholic and Malt Beverages". In this case, the panel found that low alcohol and high alcohol beer were "similar" in terms of physical characteristics but were not "like" for the purposes of Article III:4 because the distinction was not applied so as to afford protection to domestic production, BISD 39/206, pp.93-295, paras. 5.70-5.77.

[253] Panel report on "Japan - Taxes on Alcoholic Beverages", para. 6.23.

contained residues of hormones which were not found in meat from other animals, including animals treated for therapeutic purposes, to which only natural hormones could be administered. In addition, meat from animals treated with these hormones contained metabolites from these hormones which did not appear in meat from other animals.

4.340 The European Communities further maintained that meat from animals to which any of the three natural hormones had been administered for growth promotion contained a level of residues which was in excess of the level that it would otherwise contain. Moreover, as admitted by Canada, the residues might be present in different proportions from those found in nature, for example higher levels of male hormones in female animals and vice-versa[254]. Furthermore, meat from animals treated with these hormones was more likely to contain an unusually high level of residues than meat from untreated animals, in particular where the hormones had been administered combined in "cocktails" or in disregard of good animal husbandry practices. Obviously, this risk was dominated or reduced when the hormones were administered for therapeutic purposes under veterinary control.

4.341 In addition, carcasses from animals treated with hormones might differ in fat content, fat composition, water content and connective tissue from those of untreated animals. Combinations of androgens and oestrogens, and androgens alone, decreased fat content and increased water content, whereas combinations of progestagens and oestrogens increased fat content, particularly in male animals. The use of trenbolone and oestrogen decreased the amount of connective tissue and unsaturated fatty acid in muscle. Cocktails of progestagens and oestrogens altered the relative proportions of saturated and unsaturated fat in treated carcases. In general, anabolic steroids had a "partitioning" effect, resulting in the deposition in carcasses of about 8 per cent more protein and 12 per cent less fat.[255]

4.342 The European Communities argued that even if animals treated with hormones for growth promotion, and meat thereof, and other animals, and meat thereof, were found to be "like products", its measures would still be consistent with Article III:4 because they afforded identical treatment to imported products and to domestic like products. The European Communities recalled that Canada had advanced two types of arguments in order to justify its claim that beef from animals treated with any of the sixth growth promoting hormones and other beef were "like":

(i) that residues from oestradiol, testosterone and progesterone administered to animals were indistinguishable from residues of these substances naturally produced by animals; and

(ii) that EC meat from untreated animals contained residues of antimicrobial growth promoters and other veterinary drugs.

4.343 The European Communities argued that the first of these two arguments was flawed. In the first place, it did not account for the presence of residues of the three

[254] The European Communities noted that, at para. 130 of its first submission to the Panel, Canada admitted that "for the purposes of growth promotion, animals are administered those hormones in which they are deficient. Generally, for growth promotion purposes, males are given oestrogens and gestagens, and females are given androgens".

[255] *1995 EC Scientific Conference Proceedings*, pp.74-75 and 242.

synthetic hormones in meat from treated animals. These residues were not found in meat from untreated animals and were readily distinguishable from the residues of the three natural hormones. Second, the fact that the residues from administered hormones could not be easily distinguished from the residues of those hormones naturally produced by animals did not mean that there were no differences between the two types of meat. There were substantial differences between them. The technical difficulties to identify the origin of the residues had rendered it necessary for the European Communities to require from importers a certification that animals had not been treated, instead of conducting inspection of meat at its borders, but it did not make the two types of meat "like".

4.344 The second argument was equally misguided. As the European Communities had demonstrated, hormones and antimicrobial growth promoters and other veterinary drugs were different substances and posed different risks to human health. Consequently, meat which contained residues of antimicrobial growth promoters and other veterinary drugs was not "like" meat which contained residues of administered growth promoting hormones.

4.345 The European Communities disagreed with the Canadian interpretation of Article III:4. The wording of Article III:4 called for a comparison between the treatment given to "*the products* of the territory of any contracting party imported into the territory of any other contracting party ..." and the treatment accorded to "*like products* of national origin ...", and not between the treatment given to "*any* imported product" and the treatment accorded to "*any* domestic like product". The ordinary meaning of Article III:4 did not require that a comparison be made on an import-by-import basis, but a comparison of the treatment given to all imported products as a whole vis-a-vis all domestic like products as a whole. In the EC view, the object and purpose of Article III had been made explicit in the general principle set forth in the first paragraph of that Article, which stated that internal taxes and regulations "should not be applied to imported or domestic products so as to afford protection to domestic production". Article III:4 gave effect to this principle with respect to internal regulations, other than tax regulations and mixing regulations, and should be interpreted in conformity with it. Where an internal regulation laid down different requirements for imported and domestic products, it might be assumed that domestic production was "protected" if any imported product received "less favourable treatment".[256]

4.346 The European Communities argued that the situation was different where, as in the present case, the internal regulation did not distinguish between imported and domestic products but between different types of like products, irrespective of their origin. The mere fact that an internal regulation accorded more favourable treatment to certain types of like products vis-a-vis other types of like products did not necessarily mean that domestic production of the like product as whole was protected. For that, it would be necessary that those types of like product which were accorded more

[256] Hence the "no-balancing" principle established by previous Panel reports which have dealt with formally discriminatory internal regulations. See panel report on "United States - Section 337 of the Tariff Act of 1930", adopted on 7 November 1989, 36S/345, 387, at para.5.14; and panel report on "US - Standards for Reformulated Gasoline", WT/DS2/R, paras. 6.14-6.15.

favourable treatment were inherently or at least predominantly domestic and/or that the types which received less favourable treatment were inherently or at least predominantly imported. This view was supported in the panel report on "US - Measures affecting Alcoholic and Malt Beverages", which stated that:

> "The Panel recognized that on the basis of their physical characteristics, low alcohol beer and high alcohol beer were similar. It then proceeded to examine whether, in the context of Article III, this differentiation in treatment of low alcohol beer and high alcohol beer is such "as to afford protection to domestic production". *The Panel first noted that both Canadian and United States beer manufacturers produce both high and low alcohol beer. It then noted that the laws and regulations in question in various states do not differentiate between imported and domestic beer as such*, so that where a state law limits the points of sale of high alcohol content beer or maintains different labelling requirements for such beer, that law applies to all high alcohol content, regardless of its origin. *The burdens resulting from these regulations thus do not fall more heavily on Canadian than on United States producers*"[257] (emphasis added).

4.347 Although in the EC view the panel report on "US - Measures affecting Alcoholic and Malt Beverages" erred by ascribing the analysis of the effects of a measure to the determination whether two products were "like" and not exclusively on the characteristics of the products, this panel report confirmed that Article III:4 was not infringed unless a regulatory distinction between like products had the *effect* of protecting domestic production.

4.348 With reference to the EC argument that the perception of European consumers was a relevant factor in determining the "likeness" of a product, **Canada** submitted that this factor was irrelevant. The public authorities of WTO Members had a responsibility to educate the public and to make them aware of scientific facts. If the Panel were to allow "public perception" to become a factor in a "like product" determination, it would open the door to misapprehensions concerning scientific facts becoming the basis of a justification in the WTO for the adoption of discriminatory measures. Such an interpretation would obviously remove any incentive whatsoever for public authorities in the European Communities to make their populations aware of the scientific facts in respect of the six hormones at issue.

4.349 Canada observed that the 1987 panel report in "Japan - Customs Duties, Taxes and Labelling Practices on Imported Wines and Alcoholic Beverages"[258] dealt with the issue of the relevance of consumer preferences in a "like product" determination for purposes of GATT Article III:2. The 1987 finding, which was cited with approval by the recent panel on the same subject matter[259] was that "... the traditional Japanese consumer habits with regard to shochu provided no reason for not considering vodka to be a 'like' product ... " Thus, in the context of Article III:2, two panels

---

[257] Panel report on "US - Measures affecting Alcoholic and Malt Beverages", para. 5.73 .

[258] BISD 34S/83, para. 5.7.

[259] "Japan - Taxes on Alcoholic Beverages", WT/DS8/R; WT/DS10/R; WT/DS11/R, para.6.23, footnote 103.

had expressly rejected the relevance of consumer perception in a "like product" determination. Canada submitted that consumer perception was equally irrelevant in the context of GATT Article III:4.

4.350 Canada pointed out that the issue of whether regulatory differentiation of "like products" could be justified under Article III:4 was discussed by the panel report on "United States - Standards for Reformulated and Conventional Gasoline".[260] Having found that "chemically-identical imported and domestic gasoline are like products under Article III:4"[261], the panel had to deal with the US argument "that the requirements of Article III:4 [were] met because imported gasoline [was] treated similarly to gasoline from *similarly situated* domestic parties - domestic refiners with limited 1990 operations and blenders".[262] The panel rejected this argument.[263] According to Canada, although the facts in this case were different, it was useful to quote the Panel's caution in response to the US attempt to justify regulatory differentiation:

> "Apart from being contrary to the ordinary meaning of the terms of Article III:4, any interpretation of Article III:4 in this manner would mean that the treatment of imported and domestic goods concerned could no longer be assured on the objective basis of their likeness as products. Rather, imported goods would be exposed to a highly subjective and variable treatment according to extraneous factors. This would thereby create great instability and uncertainty in the conditions of competition as between domestic and imported goods in a manner fundamentally inconsistent with the object and purpose of Article III."[264]

Thus Canada submitted that regulatory differentiation by the European Communities between beef from cattle to which the six hormones at issue had been administered for growth promoting purposes and other beef, *i.e.*, like products, placed the Canadian beef at issue at a competitive disadvantage and as such was inconsistent with Article III:4.

4.351 In any event, even *arguendo* accepting the EC reliance on the panel report in "United States - Measures Affecting Alcoholic and Malt Beverages", Canada submitted that the panel report did not support the EC proposition. The European Com-

---

[260] WT/DS2/R, 29 January 1996.

[261] *Ibid.*, para. 6.9.

[262] *Ibid.*, para. 6.11. The report explains further:

> According to the United States, the difference in treatment between imported and domestic gasoline was justified because importers, like domestic refiners with limited 1990 operations and blenders, could not reliably establish their 1990 gasoline quality, lacked consistent sources and quality of gasoline, or had the flexibility to meet a statutory baseline since they were not constrained by refinery equipment and crude supplies.

[263] *Ibid.*, see also paras. 6.13-6.16.

[264] *Ibid.*, para. 6.12. The panel report in "United States - Standards for Reformulated and Conventional Gasoline" was the subject of an appeal. The appeal, however, dealt only with issues related to Article XX and did not concern the Panel's conclusions regarding Article III:4. The report of the Appellate Body is contained in WT/DS2/AB/R, 29 April 1996.

munities ignored the following paragraph in the same report that directly contradicted their argument:

> "The Panel recognized that the treatment of imported and domestic products as like products under Article III may have significant implications for the scope of obligations under the General Agreement and for the regulatory autonomy of contracting parties with respect to their internal tax laws and regulations: *once products are designated as like products, a regulatory product differentiation, e.g. for standardization or environmental purposes becomes inconsistent with Article III even if the regulation is not "applied ... so as afford protection to domestic production"*. In the view of the Panel, therefore, it is imperative that the like product determination in the context of Article III be made in such a way that it not unnecessarily infringe upon the regulatory authority and domestic policy options of contracting parties. The Panel recalled its earlier statement that a like product determination under Article III does not prejudge like product determinations made under other Articles of the General Agreement or in other legislative contexts" (emphasis added).[265]

4.352 Canada therefore submitted that Canadian beef and EC beef were "like products" within the meaning of GATT Article III:4 and the European Communities could not, consistent with that provision, ban the importation of Canadian beef produced with the six hormones at issue.

4.353 The **European Communities** recalled its previous arguments on Article III and disagreed with Canada's contention that meat treated with hormones and hormone-free meat were like because they "contain comparable residues". It ignored the potential hazards which these residues posed to human and animal health. It was the position of the European Communities that these two types of meat were not like because hormone-treated meat might cause cancer. Indeed, meat containing residues of exogenously administered hormones was not different from meat infected with a disease. The 1987 panel report on "Japan - Customs Duties, Taxes and Labelling Practices on Imported Wines and Alcoholic Beverages" referred to "traditional Japanese consumer habits". The wish of the EC consumers to eat hormone-free meat was not a habit and was not traditional. It evolved from a number of examples reported in the European Communities and elsewhere (e.g. Puerto Rico and the United States) of the hazards arising from the use of these hormones, which had been scientifically documented.

(b) Article XI

4.354 **Canada** claimed that, in the alternative, the EC import prohibition infringed GATT Article XI, but noted that this claim should only be considered by the Panel if it decided that Article III of GATT did not apply in this case. Article XI of GATT set out the obligations of Members with respect to the general elimination of quantitative

265 Panel report on "US - Measures Affecting Alcoholic and Malt Beverages", BISD 39/206, para. 5.72.

restrictions. Article XI:2 provided for limited exceptions to the general prohibition of Article XI:1, none of which were applicable in this case. Thus the European Communities were prohibited from banning the import of beef produced with growth hormones and had infringed Article XI of the GATT.

4.355 The **European Communities** responded that the measures at issue were internal regulations within the scope of Article III of GATT. Therefore, Article XI of GATT did not apply.

(c) Article XX

4.356 **Canada** claimed that Article XX of the GATT did not justify the infringement demonstrated above of Article III or Article XI.

4.357 The **European Communities** submitted that in case the Panel were to find that measures infringed Article III:4, they satisfied the requirements of the SPS Agreement and, consequently, must be presumed to be in accordance with GATT, and in particular with the provisions of Article XX(b).

5. Nullification and Impairment

4.358 **Canada** claimed that the inconsistency of the EC measures with the SPS Agreement and the GATT, or in the alternative with the TBT Agreement, established a *prima facie* case of nullification or impairment pursuant to GATT Article XXIII:1(a) and Article 3.8 of the DSU.[266] However, even if the Panel were to decide that the EC measures were consistent with the WTO Agreement, the application of the EC measures nullified or impaired benefits accruing to Canada under the WTO Agreement, within the meaning of Article XXIII:1(b) of the GATT 1994. Article XXIII:1(b) had been interpreted in GATT 1947 practice to mean even if a measure was not inconsistent with a provision of the GATT, it might be challenged as nullifying or impairing benefits. Article 26(1) of the DSU made it clear that complaints concerning non-violation nullification and impairment could be made within the new framework of the WTO Agreement. Traditionally, three conditions were required by GATT 1947 panels for determining whether a case of "non-violation" nullification or impairment existed. These conditions were:

(i) the negotiation of a tariff concession;

(ii) the subsequent introduction of a government measure that upset the competitive relationship between the bound product with regard to like or directly competitive imported products; and

[266] Previous GATT 1947 panels had determined that a *prima facie* case of nullification and impairment is established where there is an infringement of obligations under the GATT. The DSU codifies this in Article 3.8 which provides that where obligations under an agreement such as the GATT or the TBT Agreement are infringed, the action is considered prima facie to constitute a case of nullification or impairment.

(iii) that the measure at issue could not have been reasonably anticipated at the time of the negotiation of the tariff concession.[267]

4.359 In the present case, all of the relevant tariff items were subject to tariff concessions by the European Communities.[268] These concessions included Canadian access to a tariff rate quota of 11,500 tonnes, with an in quota rate of 20 per cent, for high quality, fresh, chilled or frozen beef allocated to Canada and the United States (the "Hilton beef quota").[269]

4.360 The Hilton beef quota had originally been granted by the European Economic Community during the Tokyo Round Multilateral Trade Negotiations (contained in the European Economic Community schedule of concessions annexed to the Geneva (1979) Protocol), prior to the events which ultimately led to the EC hormone ban. The Hilton beef quota originally was a 10,000 tonne levy free tariff quota.[270] When the Hilton beef quota was established, the European Community had adopted regulations which excluded Canadian high quality beef from its scope, which had led to the establishment of a panel at the request of Canada. The panel had ruled in Canada's favour, and this report had been adopted by the GATT Council in March 1981.[271] The European Community subsequently amended its regulations to allow Canadian high quality beef access under the Hilton beef quota. As a result of the Uruguay Round Trade Negotiations, the European Communities converted the Hilton beef quota to the tariff rate quota as indicated above. Subsequently, in the Article XXIV negotiations of 1995, due to the accession of Finland, Sweden and Austria to the European Communities, the European Communities increased the Hilton beef quota to 11,500 tonnes.[272]

4.361 Thus, the first requirement of the traditional analysis of GATT 1947 panels had been met. Second, the introduction of the EC measures had upset the competitive relationship between Canadian and EC beef. Third, at the time when Canada had won access to the Hilton beef quota, it could not have reasonably foreseen the intro-

---

[267] See "EC - Payments and Subsidies Paid to Processors and Producers of Oilseeds and Related Animal-Feed Proteins", report of the panel adopted on 25 January 1990, BISD 37S/86, paras. 142-154.

[268] *Uruguay Round Schedule LXXX - European Communities*, Part I Most Favoured-Nation Tariff, Section I - Agricultural Products, Section I A Tariffs and Section I B Tariff Quotas, as subsequently modified. Tariff items covered by the EC beef and veal regime are:

02011050; 02012015; 02012035; 02012055; 02012090; 02013000; 02021000; 02022010; 02022030; 02022050; 02022090; 02023010; 02023050; 02023090; 02061010; 02061091; 02061095; 02061099; 02062100; 02062210; 02062290; 02062910; 02062991; 02062999; 02102010; 02102090; 02109041; 02109049; 16025010; 16025090; 16029061; and 16029069.

[269] *Schedule CXL - European Communities*, Part I Most-Favoured-Nation Tariff, Section I - Agricultural Products, Section I B Tariff Quotas.

[270] "European Economic Community - Imports of Beef" from Canada, BISD 28S/92.

[271] *Ibid.*

[272] Therefore, Canada maintained the increase in the Hilton beef quota did *not* amount to a rebalancing of concessions between Canada and the European Communities. See "EC - Payments and Subsidies Paid to Processors and Producers of Oilseeds and Related Animal-Feed Proteins", report of the panel adopted on 25 January 1990, *BISD 37S/86*, para. 145.

duction of the EC measures. Therefore, Canada claimed that benefits accruing to it under the WTO Agreement had been nullified or impaired.

4.362 The **European Communities** responded that Canada failed to meet the minimum requirements provided for in Article 26 of the DSU as regarded a detailed justification of any non-violation complaints. In the present case, Canada's claim of non-violation nullification and impairment was unwarranted for the following reasons:

(i) the "benefits" invoked by Canada only accrued to Canada *after* the adoption of the measures at issue;

(ii) in any event, the measures could have reasonably been anticipated by Canada at the time when, according to Canada, the benefits accrued; and

(iii) Canada had not provided any justification for its claim that the competitive relationship between domestic and imported products had been upset by the adoption of the measures. In fact, the consistency of the measures with the WTO Agreements cited by Canada presupposed that the measures were not capable of having such an effect.

4.363 The European Communities argued that the so-called "Hilton beef quota" granted by the European Economic Community during the Tokyo Round had been withdrawn during the Uruguay Round negotiations and replaced by a new package of concessions on the same product. These new concessions had become binding upon the European Communities long after the introduction of the measures at issue. Thus, Canada could not claim that these new concessions had been nullified or impaired by the measures at issue.[273]

4.364 During the Uruguay Round, the European Communities had replaced this tariff quota by an entirely new package of concessions, but it had done so in the context of the new Agreement on Agriculture. Under the Agreement on Agriculture, Members had agreed to achieve specific binding commitments in the areas of market access, domestic support and market competition. The concessions outlined below must therefore be seen as new concessions negotiated in the context of a new Agreement:

- first, variable levies on imports of beef had been eliminated as part of the "tariffication process";
- second, the European Communities had bound the rate of the ordinary customs duties applicable on all imports of beef. The initial bound rate was 20 per cent plus a specific amount ranging from 2763 ECU to 4740 ECU per tonne, depending on the type of beef. The final bound

[273] The European Communities explained that as regarded Canada, the concessions granted by the European Economic Community during the Tokyo Round negotiations with respect to imports of beef consisted of a 10,000 ton tariff quota for high quality beef with an in-quota rate of 20 per cent. In addition, imports within this quota were free from the variable levy applied at the time by the European Economic Community. No other tariff concessions had been granted by the European Economic Community with respect to imports of beef. Accordingly, imports of beef outside the quota were subject to customs duties and agricultural levies at the rate autonomously established by the European Economic Community.

rate was 12.8 per cent plus an specific amount, ranging from 1768 ECU to 2652 ECU per tonne;

- third, the European Communities had opened a 10,000 tonne tariff quota with an in-quota rate of 20 per cent allocated to Canada and the United States.

4.365 This new package of concessions on imports of beef was substantially different from, and more "valuable" than, the Tokyo Round concessions on the same product. It represented a new concession which had replaced the Tokyo Round concession on the same product and was part of a new "balance of concessions" achieved by the parties during the Uruguay Round. The additional benefits obtained by Canada must be regarded as the counterpart for Canada's own concessions, including the renouncement by Canada to any outstanding non-violation rights with respect to the Tokyo Round tariff quota, which was implicit in Canada's consent to the replacement of the old concession by the new package of concessions.

4.366 In the EC view, the present case was to be distinguished from the case considered by the panel on EC - Oilseeds. In that case, the panel had found that on the occasion of Article XXIV:6 negotiations following the successive enlargements of the Community, the concessions at issue had not been "modified" but rather "extended" to the new EC member States. For this reason, the panel had concluded that, despite the formal modification of the schedules of concessions, the original "balance of concessions" had not been altered. Hence the expectations created when the concessions had been originally granted continued to be protected.[274] However, the European Communities argued that the present case differed from the EC - Oilseeds case in two fundamental respects. Firstly, in the present case the Uruguay Round tariff concessions on beef were substantially different from the pre-existing concessions on the same product since they were market access concessions as envisaged in Article 4 of the Agreement on Agriculture, a new Agreement. Secondly, the new concessions on beef were granted as part of a negotiated exchange of concessions; in the EC - Oilseeds case, only one party was required to make concessions. The findings of the EC - Oilseeds panel were therefore inapplicable to the present case.

4.367 The European Communities argued that in any case, the measures at issue could have reasonably been anticipated by Canada already at the time of the Tokyo Round. Because there existed no international standards, guidelines or recommendations on the use of hormones as growth promoters in 1979, Canada could not reasonably assume that the European Economic Community would not take any measures in order to restrict their use to animals or meat from animals. Sanitary concerns about the use of hormones as growth promoters predated the Tokyo Round. When the Hilton beef quota had been negotiated, Canada was aware that the safety of using hormones as growth promoters was questioned in some scientific circles as well as by consumer organizations and the general public. Canada was also aware that, prompted by those concerns, a majority of EC member States, as well as other countries, had already taken steps to restrict the use of hormones.

[274] Panel report on "EC - Payments and Subsidies Paid to Processors and Producers of Oilseeds and Related Animal Feed Proteins", adopted 25 January 1990, *BISD 37S/86*.

4.368 The European Communities claimed that Canada had not advanced any justification whatsoever for its claim that the EC measures had upset the competitive relationship between domestic products and imports. In this regard, the Canadian submission failed to meet the minimum requirements provided for in Article 26 of the DSU. Unlike "violation" cases, in "non-violation" cases there was no presumption of "nullification and impairment". The burden of proving that the measures at issue had in fact upset the competitive relationship between domestic and imported products lay with Canada.

4.369 **Canada** claimed that the Hilton beef quota was not the subject of explicit negotiations between Canada and the European Communities during the Uruguay Round. In the agricultural area the Uruguay Round had made a clear distinction between tariff rate quotas that confirmed pre-existing access rights and new access rights.[275] The current tariff rate quota was listed in the Schedule of the European Communities under the heading of "Current Access Quotas".[276] Thus the Hilton beef quota clearly fell within the category of quotas under which existing market access opportunities were maintained. Canada argued that even if scientific concerns could have been anticipated in 1979, Canada could hardly have foreseen that the European Communities would adopt the most trade-restrictive measures imaginable, i.e., a total ban on the importation of beef from cattle to which any of the six hormones at issue had been administered for growth promoting purposes. Furthermore, of the EC member States that banned the use of growth promoting hormones before the EC ban came into effect, at least one, Denmark, and possibly others as well, did not prohibit the importation of beef produced with the hormones at issue. Canada had submitted detailed information on the devastating impact of the EC measures at issue on its beef exports to the European Communities (paragraph 4.28).[277] Therefore, Canada submitted that the European Communities had nullified or impaired Canada's rights within the meaning of Article XXIII:1(b) of the GATT.

4.370 The **European Communities** responded that Canada failed to meet the minimum requirements provided for in Article 26 of the DSU as regards a detailed justification in support of any non-violation complaint. No justification whatsoever was advanced for the claim that the EC measures had upset the competitive relationship between domestic production and imports. As for Canada's argument that the quota of 11,500 tonnes allocated to the United States and Canada was a current access quota and, hence, "falls under the category of quotas under which existing market opportunities were maintained", the European Communities noted that the term "current access" was a term used during the Uruguay Round negotiations for the purpose of drawing up market access commitments, in the context of the Guidelines which had been developed for agriculture negotiations. Such guidelines had become

[275] *GATT Press Release NUR 080*, 14 December 1993, on the Final Act of the Uruguay Round, p.9.

[276] Schedule CXL of the European Communities (Schedule LXXX at the end of the Uruguay Round), Section I - B Tariff Quotas.

[277] At the second meeting of the Parties with the panel, Canada produced a table which set forth eleven tariff lines of the European Communities (020610; 02061010; 02062210; 02062910; 02061091; 02062290; 02061099; 02062100; 02062999; 02109049; 16025090; 16029069) with regard to beef products which were bound prior to the Uruguay Round and the trade figures for each of these tariff lines from 1984 through 1995.

obsolete once the Uruguay Round Schedules were finalized and the Final Act was signed. In fact, the provisions of the Agreement on Agriculture contained no reference to "current access" as a specific kind of commitment, but only referred to "market access commitments" (Article 4.1). The European Communities, therefore, reiterated that the quota contained in the Uruguay Round Schedule was part of a whole new balance of concessions, in the context of a wholly new agreement, the Agreement on Agriculture. With regard to the pretended nullification or impairment of benefits accruing to Canada, the European Communities argued that previous to the Uruguay Round, the only GATT commitment that the European Communities had with respect to the tariff lines concerned was the Tokyo Round commitments on high quality beef tariff quotas, including the 10,000 quota to which Canada successively gained access. No commitment existed for any beef outside of high quality meat. Claims advanced by Canada concerning nullification or impairment of benefits as regarded commitments on the tariff lines mentioned above were, therefore, incorrect. At the time of the negotiation of these concessions, the measures at issue were already in existence.

V. THIRD PARTIES SUBMISSIONS

1. Australia

5.1 **Australia** noted that it had set out its views on the relationship between the EC ban on the importation of hormone growth promotant treated meat and its obligations under the SPS Agreement in its submission of 27 September to the panel in regard to the complaint by the United States. Australia said that its submission to the panel in regard to the complaint by Canada was intended to supplement this earlier submission by providing a summary of the key legal issues and addressing several issues raised in the EC submission of 23 December to the panel considering the Canadian complaint.

5.2 Australia indicated that as a major exporter of meat and, in recent years, the world's largest beef exporter it had a major trade interest in this matter. Stressing its specific interest in the EC beef market, Australia noted that it had managed to continue its trade with the European Communities despite the implementation of Council Directive 88/146/EEC by the development of an Hormone Growth Promotion (HGP) control system. This system had allowed Australian cattle producers who wished to continue to trade with the European Communities to do so, but, at the same time to be able to access and use hormones for growth promotion purposes for other markets that did not impose such restrictions. This had been at a cost to the Australian industry of about $A10 million a year. However, Australia had never accepted the legitimacy of the EC measures. Noting that the purpose of the three Directives was the protection of human life or health and that the prohibition on the importation from third countries of meat from animals to which hormones had been administered was a sanitary measure as defined by the SPS Agreement, Australia claimed that the consistency of the EC measures with EC obligations should be considered against the provisions of the SPS Agreement which required that SPS measures "shall be developed and applied in accordance with the provisions of this Agreement" (Article 1.1).

5.3 Australia argued that the SPS Agreement established, *inter alia*, the basic rights and obligations of Members in respect of sanitary measures necessary for the protection of human life and health which may directly or indirectly affect international trade. Notwithstanding any other WTO rights and obligations, Australia considered that if a Member were acting inconsistently with its obligations under the SPS Agreement, it stood in breach of its WTO obligations. In addition, as the SPS Agreement represented an elaboration of the GATT in respect of SPS measures and as conformity with SPS obligations gave rise to a presumption of conformity with Article XX(b) of the GATT, Australia considered that the EC measures should be examined in the first instance against the rights and obligations of the SPS Agreement as it was this agreement which established the basic rights and obligations of Members in respect of SPS measures.

5.4 Australia placed particular stress on the fact that in observing that an international standard as provided for in Article 3.1 of the SPS Agreement existed in relation to the EC hormone ban, the European Communities had failed to demonstrate its compliance with Article 3.3. In particular, Australia argued that the European Communities had failed to demonstrate either that there was a scientific justification for its adoption of measures resulting in a higher level of protection or that it had carried out an examination and evaluation of available scientific evidence, including in accordance with the relevant provisions of Article 5 to show that the international standard was not sufficient to achieve its appropriate level of protection.

5.5 Referring to the conclusions of the 1995 EC Scientific Conference (see paragraph 2.33), Australia argued that although these conclusions provided clear support to the view that the five substances considered at the Conference were safe to use within the conditions specified in Australia and within the Codex standards, the European Communities had confusingly claimed that "... The scientific evidence for the necessity to maintain our measures is the evidence from the 1995 Scientific Conference ...". The European Communities had made no attempt to substantiate its assertion or to explain the contradiction between this statement and the Conference conclusions.

5.6 Although the European Communities had asserted that for the natural hormones it was known that they have adverse effects, which combined with a lack of knowledge of their action, lack of data on the effect of combinations and the lack of definition of "good veterinary practice", permit the European Communities to adopt a different level of protection, i.e. ensure the EC consumers that there are no residues left other than the naturally produced ones by the animals themselves", Australia argued that the European Communities had failed to establish that these statements reflected the findings of a risk assessment or an examination and evaluation of available scientific information in conformity with the provisions of the SPS Agreement. The European Communities had also not established the basis for its claim that there was a lack of definition of "good veterinary practice", which was generally taken to mean using veterinary chemicals in accordance with conditions of registration, including observing intended purpose, correct dose rates and withholding periods that were determined by the technical registration process.

5.7 With regard to the EC arguments that hormones had serious adverse effects on health including cancer, Australia noted that such claims had also been made in respect of drugs containing hormonal substances which were directly administered to humans for medicinal purposes. The European Communities had not explained why it practised a zero risk policy in the issue under examination by the Panel but not in other comparable circumstances when it was known that the hormonal product would directly enter the human system. Good veterinary practice was the basis for use of the hormones at issue and to focus only on the worst case scenario as the European Communities had done could render the use of all veterinary chemicals illegal, just as the use of all chemicals used in human medicinal preparations might be banned. Furthermore, the statement that the intensive large-scale production of meat rendered effective control of hormone growth promoters technically and economically unfeasible, flew in the face of the fact that major meat exporting nations apart from the European Communities were able to effectively control inappropriate hormone use without the imposition of a total ban on the use of these substances. All agricultural and veterinary chemicals used within Australia must undergo assessment and registration prior to distribution and use. This required a thorough assessment of detailed technical data packages by the National Registration Authority. The outcome of registration was to control the use, labelling, packaging and supply of the product. This was underpinned by legislation, with penalties where these conditions were not followed. Additionally, Australia backed up the system with individual property identification of cattle to the point of slaughter, a National Residue Survey to assess compliance with MRLs, and a National Vendor Declaration system for cattle through which vendors must declare the chemicals used on cattle offered for sale and the date of treatment.

5.8 Australia argued that, despite the European Communities repeated claims to the contrary, there was no evidence that the European Communities had undertaken a risk assessment on this matter, in accordance with the provisions of Article 5. The European Communities had stated that "the European Communities has twice formed groups of scientists to examine the hormones at issue". However, it had stated itself that "the purpose of the 1995 EC scientific Conference was not to perform for it a risk assessment, but to provide a public forum for discussion of the scientific aspects of the use of growth promoters". Therefore, the European Communities had explicitly accepted that this Conference was not part of a risk assessment process. At the Canada/EC consultations on 25 July 1996, at which Australia was present as a third party, the EC representative had said that there had been no risk assessment done since the Lamming Committee and that no work had been done in this area since 1988. However, nowhere within the EC first submission in this case, had it claimed that the Lamming Committee had undertaken a risk assessment process which could be considered to have met the requirements of Articles 5.1 and 5.2.

5.9 Emphasizing that Article 5.4 required Members, when determining the appropriate level of sanitary or phytosanitary protection, to take into account the objective of minimizing negative trade effects, Australia submitted that there was no evidence to suggest that the European Communities had taken into account negative trade effects when imposing the prohibition on imports of meat treated with hormones for growth promotion purposes. This prohibition had imposed significant compliance costs on the Australian meat industry.

5.10 With regard to Article 5.5, Australia argued that the European Communities had failed to demonstrate its compliance with this provision. "Consistency" did not demand a quantified level of risk, or that Members must have the same level of risk in respect of every measure. However, the European Communities must justify why it had adopted a lower level of risk in this case than in comparable circumstances. Australia agreed that in a general sense it was true that, through risk management, each country's acceptable level of risk might reflect societal values, but, as specifically stated by Article 5.5, the acceptable level of risk determined by a country through this process must be applied in a consistent manner, and could not be applied on an arbitrary or unjustifiable case-by-case basis. For example, the European Communities choosing to accept zero risk in the case of meat from animals treated with growth promoting hormones or, as pointed out by Canada, apparent inconsistencies between the level of protection that the European Communities had applied to imports of meat to which hormones had been administered for growth promotion purposes, and the levels of protection that the European Communities applied to the use of other growth promoters and veterinary drugs. These distinctions in the levels of protection would appear to be arbitrary and unjustifiable.

5.11 Australia furthermore argued that the European Communities had failed to demonstrate its compliance with the obligation of Article 5.6 as there would appear to be less trade restrictive approaches to achieve the European Communities' appropriate level of protection. It observed that the European Communities had claimed that its measures were not provisional: they were definitive, and therefore submitted that Article 5.7 of the SPS Agreement was not relevant in this case. Noting that as the European Communities had failed to comply with the provisions of Article 3.3, by failing to demonstrate that there was a scientific justification for its level of sanitary or phytosanitary protection or that its maintenance of a level of protection higher than the relevant international standard was a consequence of the level it had determined in accordance with the provisions of Article 5, Australia concluded that there must be a presumption that the EC measures were not in conformity with the basic obligations of Articles 2.2 and 2.3 of the SPS Agreement.

2. *Norway*

5.12 **Norway** argued that this case concerned the right of every state to make its own sovereign decision on the level of protection it afforded its citizens with respect to health hazards. This principle had always been part of GATT law and several panels when deciding disputes related to Article XX(b), had reaffirmed such right.[278] The

[278] Panel report on "US - Restrictions on the Imports of Tuna":

> "The panel further noted that *Article XX(b) allows each contracting party to set its human, animal or plant life or health standard.* The conditions set out in Article XX(b) which limits the resort to this exception, namely that the measures taken must be "necessary" ... refer to the trade measure requiring justification ... not to the life or health standard chosen by the contracting party.(...)".

Furthermore, the Appellate Body in the case "US - Standards for Reformulated and Conventional Gasoline", in its concluding remarks stated:

> "WTO Members have a large measure of autonomy to determine their own policies on the environment (including its relationships with trade), their environmental objectives and the environment legislation they enact and implement. So far as concerns the WTO, the autonomy is circumscribed only by the need to respect the requirements of the *General Agreement* and the other covered agreements."

SPS Agreement, within its scope of application, might be considered an exemplification of Article XX(b). This was not a case of discrimination between like products, or discrimination between producers from different countries. The question was purely one of reaffirming the Member's right to decide, when a risk to its population was present, the limits to the risk to which it would expose its citizens, and its freedom to choose the measure to achieve this protection as long as the measure itself was consistent with WTO obligations. In an era of increasing consumer concern over the safety of food and the presence of potentially harmful residues from the use of veterinary drugs, pesticides etc., and at a time when old "scientific truths" had often been overturned by new evidence, it was of utmost importance that the WTO uphold this right of the State to protect its citizens against the risks connected with the use of such substances.

5.13 Noting that the SPS Agreement restated the right of a Member to set its health standards in its preamble and in Article 3.3, Norway argued that it was clear that a Member had the right to determine the level of protection it considered appropriate for its population, subject to general WTO requirements with respect to the existence of a risk, and requirements with respect to justification of the measure the State applied. In the determining the appropriate level of protection, Norway argued the obligation upon the Member was only to show that a risk to its population was present. As long as the existence of such a risk had been established, the WTO was only concerned with the justification of the *measure* the Member choose to apply to achieve the level of protection it had deemed appropriate. According to Article XX(b), as well as Article 5.2 of the SPS Agreement, a Member did not have to scientifically prove the extent of the risk. The Member only had to show that such a risk existed (risk identification), and thereafter it was for the Member to define the level of probability of harm it wanted to assume, be it zero or greater (risk management).

5.14 A Member must consider present day scientific evidence when making a risk assessment. Such evidence might ascertain or disprove the risk, and might be more or less complete, but this was only one of the elements to be taken into account in the risk assessment. Other relevant elements might be i.a. the existence of adequate testing methods and internationally approved production methods or control requirements. Norway argued that the SPS Agreement did not require a Member to base its levels of protection solely on suggested maximum tolerances presented in current scientific evidence. The cases referred by the European Commission in its submissions clearly showed from history how often old scientific "truths" had been disproved by new scientific evidence. It had never been the intention of the GATT/WTO, nor should it be the task of this Panel, to infringe upon the Member's right to decide to be on the safe side where current evidence did not exclude beyond doubt a potential risk to human health.

5.15 Norway stressed that once the right of the Member to determine *its* appropriate level of protection was reaffirmed, it had to be ascertained that the chosen *measure* complied with the general obligations spelled out in the GATT or the SPS Agreement. In Norway's view, the test to be applied according to GATT Article XX and Article 5 of the SPS Agreement was the following:

- the measure was not applied in a manner which would constitute a means of arbitrary or unjustifiable discrimination between countries where the same conditions prevailed;

- the measure was not applied in a manner which was a disguised restriction on international trade;
- the measure was necessary, i.e. not more trade restrictive than required to achieve the appropriate level of protection, taking into account technical and economic feasibility.

Having applied this test to the measure, its consistency with the WTO obligations should be readily ascertained.

5.16 Norway submitted that the European Communities had the right to set its own level of protection in this case, and at the chosen level. It had clearly shown the uncertainties related to the possible harmful effect of long term exposure to the substances at issue and had clearly shown that its measure did not discriminate between countries, nor had there been any disguised restriction on international trade. The measure had been applied uniformly to all products containing the substances in question, be they domestic or foreign. In selecting the measure which was necessary to minimise the potential risk (risk management) so as to ensure the appropriate level of protection (zero or other acceptable level of risk), many factors had to be taken into consideration, of which MRL was but one. The technical feasibility of ensuring adequate control of the use of the hormones, i.e. strict veterinary supervision of each implant, were of utmost importance, as well as the technical feasibility of control of the residue level in all the meat in question. Furthermore, the economic cost of the measure must be taken into account. An MRL system with extensive controls and verifications at the producer level and at point of importation might be so prohibitively expensive as to be ruled out. The European Communities had shown that other measures than the contested ban were not available to achieve the appropriate level of protection, which was consequently not more trade restrictive than necessary.

3. *New Zealand*

5.17 **New Zealand** indicated that its third party's substantial interest in this case was due to the fact that New Zealand was an agricultural exporting nation and meat exports formed a significant portion of its total exports. In the year ending December 1995, primary produce (e.g. meat and meat products, dairy, fish, fruit and vegetables etc) accounted for 72.10 per cent of New Zealand's total merchandise exports (NZ$ FOB). For the same period, meat and meat products accounted for 15.99 per cent of New Zealand's total merchandise exports (NZ$ FOB). Accordingly, the proper implementation of the SPS Agreement was a matter of fundamental importance to New Zealand and the potential for sanitary or phytosanitary measures to be used as disguised restrictions on trade a major concern. New Zealand claimed that the SPS Agreement was an elaboration of relevant GATT provisions and Articles 2.1 and 2.4 of the SPS Agreement established the primacy of that Agreement in determining the WTO legality of sanitary or phytosanitary measures. Accordingly, the legality of a measure falling within the definition of a "sanitary or phytosanitary measure" was to be determined in accordance with the provisions of the SPS Agreement.

5.18 Noting that the European Communities had justified the import ban on the basis that the importation of meat from animals treated with any of the substances might pose a risk to human health and safety[279], New Zealand concluded that the ban appeared to be a measure that fell within the definition of a "sanitary or phytosanitary measure" as defined in the SPS Agreement.[280] New Zealand noted that Article 1 of the SPS Agreement did not make provision for any Member to exclude specific sanitary or phytosanitary measures from the ambit of the Agreement. Moreover, the effect of Article XVI:4 of the Marrakesh Agreement was to require Members to ensure the conformity of all their laws, regulations and administrative practices with the SPS Agreement. Accordingly, the import ban and all other sanitary or phytosanitary measures affecting international trade in place within the jurisdiction of any Member, were subject to the requirements of the SPS Agreement.

5.19 With regard to Article 2.2, New Zealand claimed that no evidence had been produced of an appreciable risk of an adverse health effect arising from the use of any of the substances. Even if it were to be shown that there was an appreciable risk, the European Communities would be required to demonstrate that the import ban was necessary to address it. In this regard, New Zealand noted that the European Communities had expressed particular concern about the perceived risks associated with the inappropriate or illegal use of hormonal growth promotants, particularly when used in "combinations" or "cocktails". However, even if it was demonstrated that an appreciable risk existed from such inappropriate or illegal use, the European Communities would need to demonstrate that a ban on imports was in fact "necessary" to address this specific concern. Finally, from the history of the scientific investigations into the five substances, under intense scrutiny by scientists in the last two decades, New Zealand did not consider that the importation ban could be presented as being "based on scientific principles" nor sustained by "sufficient scientific evidence". Moreover, in the case of the sixth substance, MGA, New Zealand was not aware of the existence of any scientific information which would warrant the import ban in its regard.[281]

---

279 New Zealand noted that in the preamble of EC Council Directive 81/602/EEC of 31 July 1981 the banning of new licences for anabolic agents for growth promotion was characterised as being in the "interests of the consumer" and it discussed the potential "harmful effects" of the use of the substances in question. EC Council Directives 85/649/EEC of 31 December 1985 and 88/146/EEC of 7 March 1988 cited concerns relating to the effect on human health from the use of hormonal growth promotants. The preamble of the Proposal for a Council Regulation (93/C 302/06) on 14 October 1993 stated that the presence of such substances "may be dangerous for consumers and may also affect the quality of foodstuffs of animal origin". And finally, EC Council Directives 96/22/EC and 96/23/EC state in their preambles that such substances may be dangerous for consumers.

280 New Zealand argued that the import ban would also be inconsistent with Article 2.2 of the TBT Agreement were it not that Agreement explicitly noted (in Article 1.5) that it did not cover sanitary or phytosanitary measures. In the event that the import ban were determined to be neither a sanitary measure, nor a technical barrier to trade, the provisions of GATT would then need to be considered.

281 New Zealand indicated that because of differing use requirements and commercial factors, there were differences in the range of agricultural chemicals (such as MGA) registered around the world and hence differences in the standards contained in national laws. The absence of an international standard for a particular substance should not in itself be seen as justification for a particular import ban. In addition, it should be noted that Article 4 of the SPS Agreement encouraged Members to

5.20 New Zealand submitted that scientific evidence demonstrated that the level of hormones present in meat varied considerably. Meat from animals treated with the substances for growth promotion had a similar range or even lower hormonal residues than meat from some animals that had never been treated. Additionally, the European Communities allowed meat from animals that had been treated with the three naturally occurring substances for therapeutic purposes to be produced, imported and marketed within the European Communities.[282] New Zealand considered that for these reasons, EC measures contravened Article 2.3 of the SPS Agreement.

5.21 New Zealand stressed that Codex had adopted international standards, satisfying itself that there was sufficient scientific basis. It was unclear what "available scientific information" the European Communities could rely on to provide "scientific justification" for the import ban and a selective examination and evaluation of available scientific information would not be sufficient to meet the requirements of Article 3.3. Moreover, there should be a scientifically established risk to human or animal life or health before any determination could be made as to a Member's "appropriate level of protection". In this case, there did not appear to have been any scientifically defensible determination of an appreciable risk in the case of the import ban.

5.22 New Zealand claimed that the SPS Agreement did not allow for the adoption of a sanitary or phytosanitary measure that provided for a higher level of protection than an international standard in the absence of a scientific justification or a risk assessment process that had identified an appreciable risk. In the case of all six hormones, there would not appear to have been any EC assessment, meeting the requirements of Article 5, which had identified any such risk. While it was evident that consumers in the European Communities might harbour concerns about the use of these substances, consumer perceptions as to risk did not provide a basis for the adoption of measures under Article 5. Furthermore, New Zealand submitted that the usual EC risk assessment and evaluation processes for veterinary medicinal products[283], which might otherwise have ensured a consistent approach as required by Article 5.5, did not form the basis for the EC measures.[284] Equally, given that many other products freely marketed within the European Communities contained much higher levels of the hormonal residues that the European Communities was seeking to avoid through the import ban, there would appear, in the absence of evidence to

mutually recognise, for the purposes of trade, the equivalence of different sanitary or phytosanitary measures in jurisdictions other than their own.

282 New Zealand indicated that it understood that the European Communities had not set any ADIs or MRLs for meat from animals treated for therapeutic purposes.

283 New Zealand clarified that the guidelines for assessments of veterinary medicinal products were contained, at that time, in EC Council Directives 81/851/EEC and 81/852/EEC. There were also guidelines presented in a proposed draft directive entitled "Testing of medicinal products for their mutagenic potential" and this was published as Annex II in the *EC Official Journal* C 293/11 dated 5 November 1984.

284 New Zealand added that, furthermore, since that time, the European Communities has not utilised the applicable assessment and evaluation processes to assess the use of these substances for growth promotion although it has assessed and approved their use for other therapeutic purposes without stipulating any MRLs (see, for example, *Commission Regulation* (EC) 3059/94 of 15 December 1994).

the contrary, to be arbitrary and anomalous levels of protection in place. Finally, Article 5.6 made it clear that even if it could be shown that there was an appreciable risk to health, given the significant trade implications of the import ban, the European Communities would have had to consider whether there were alternative less trade restrictive measures that could be applied to address such a risk. Noting that the European Communities did not seek to rely on Article 5.7, which was a manifestation of the "precautionary principle", as the basis for its import ban, New Zealand emphasized that the present situation appeared to be one where the scientific evidence was neither insufficient nor inadequate.[285] Accordingly, this was clearly not an instance where the "sufficient evidence" standard could be substituted with the less rigorous standard of "available pertinent information". The fact that Codex had adopted an international standard would always create a strong presumption that sufficient scientific evidence existed.

4. *United States*

5.23 The **United States** indicated that it had a strong interest in the Panel's review of the EC measures at issue, as demonstrated by the submissions of the United States to the Panel established at the request of the United States.[286] The United States had suffered significant adverse economic effects from the EC measures. Furthermore, the Panel had indicated that it intended to conduct its deliberations on this dispute concurrently with its deliberations on the challenge brought by the United States. This meant that the Panel contemplated that the facts and arguments advanced in the Canadian proceeding might affect the Panel's report in the US proceeding. As a result, the arguments and facts presented in this proceeding could be expected to have a substantial effect on the interests of the United States with respect to the EC measures. Accordingly, the United States requested the Panel to provide the United States with extended third party rights in this proceeding. The United States requested:

5.24 (i) to receive all of the submissions of the parties to the dispute;

(ii) to observe the whole of the proceedings at the substantive meetings of the Panel with the parties to the dispute and with the experts; and

(iii) to make a brief statement at a suitable moment during the second substantive meeting.

5.25 The United States stated that this request would accord to the United States rights equivalent to those accorded by the Panel on European Communities - Régime for the Importation, Sale and Distribution of Bananas to Canada as a third party in the proceeding on bananas. In the EC-Bananas proceeding, the Panel had concluded that the Understanding on Rules and Procedures Governing the Settlement of Disputes (DSU) permitted such an extension of third party rights. The US interests in this proceeding were far greater than Canada's interests in the EC-Bananas proceed-

[285] New Zealand noted that even the 1995 EC Scientific Conference which was procedurally defective as a risk assessment process in that it excluded certain relevant participants and information, nonetheless, concluded that there was sufficient scientific information to determine that the five growth promotant substances could be used safely.
[286] WT/DS26/6.

ing, and thus presented an even more compelling need for access to all facts and arguments presented. The panel proceedings in the Canadian complaint on the EC hormone ban directly affected the rights of the United States under the Marrakesh Agreement Establishing the World Trade Organization. That was not the case for any of the third parties in the EC-Bananas proceeding. Neither Canada's, nor any other third party's, WTO rights were at issue in the EC-Bananas proceeding. Furthermore, the United States was the only party that would not have access to the submissions to the Panel in both proceedings. Canada had access to all the submissions in the US proceeding because both the United States and the European Communities had made their submissions public. The European Communities had access to all the documents since it was a party to both disputes.

5.26 The United States also noted that it was a fundamental principle that parties to a proceeding should know the facts or arguments that may influence the panel in preparing its report. Nowhere did the DSU provide that a panel might receive material from any source without disclosing that material to a disputing party. Accordingly, if in its deliberations in the US proceeding, the Panel considered materials submitted to it by the parties in the Canadian proceeding, and those materials were not provided to the United States, then the Panel would be basing its deliberations in the US proceeding on an *ex parte* communication prohibited by Article 18.1 of the DSU.

5.27 The United States indicated with respect to the substance of the dispute that for all the reasons provided in the proceeding of the panel established at the request of the United States, the United States agreed with Canada that the EC measures at issue in the proceedings of this Panel were inconsistent with the EC obligations under the WTO Agreement, in particular the SPS Agreement and GATT. The United States affirmed the arguments it had already made in that proceeding and indicated that they did not need to be further elucidated in this panel proceeding. For this purpose, the United States incorporated all of the facts and arguments presented by the United States in those proceedings. For a summary of those facts and arguments, see the report of the Panel in those proceedings.

5.28 With respect to the joint meeting of the Panel with the United States, Canada, and the five scientific experts selected by the Panel to provide information, advice, and their opinions on certain aspects of the matter that was the subject of the dispute, the United States stated that the advice received from the experts helped to clarify the inconsistency of the EC ban with the provisions of the SPS Agreement and the GATT.

5.29 The United States stated that it was clear that, contrary to Article 2.2 of the SPS Agreement, the European Communities did not have sufficient scientific evidence to support its ban. Numerous scientific reviews, evaluations and risk assessments had been conducted with respect to the six hormones involved in this dispute. Five of the hormones had been evaluated both by national regulatory authorities in WTO Members and by the Codex Alimentarius Commission, the entity designated by the SPS Agreement as the international standard setting body for food safety. All of those reviews concluded that the scientific evidence established that residues in meat of these hormones used for growth promotion in accordance with good practice were safe. The sixth hormone, MGA, had been reviewed by WTO Member national regulatory authorities who had also concluded that MGA residues from growth promotion in accordance with good practice were safe. While the raw data were proprietary, the results and conclusions of the relevant studies were available in the published literature as well as from the US Food and Drug Administration (FDA). A summary of all the studies were available as public documents.

5.30 The United States argued that the European Communities put all this evidence aside and offered instead some data that it claimed were sufficient to show that these hormones were genotoxic carcinogens and the European Communities claimed that this would mean that no residue of these hormones from growth promotion would be acceptable. With respect to the relevance of this data, the United States stated that first, the data from Dr. Liehr applied only to one of the six hormones involved in this dispute -oestradiol-17ß. It did not involve the other five hormones. Second, Dr. Liehr's studies were not new, they were conducted prior to the JECFA report and were referenced in that report.

5.31 The United States observed that the data presented as evidence that oestradiol-17ß was genotoxic concerned DNA adducts (these were compounds bound to DNA that were not supposed to be there). These adducts occurred in the kidney of male Syrian hamsters following treatment with high doses of oestradiol-17ß. Regulatory scientists that were responsible for protecting the health of consumers relied on tests akin to tests like these (so-called "short-term assays") as a screen to determine whether carcinogenicity studies were warranted. They were not sufficient to serve as a basis for regulatory action. Furthermore, positive results in one of these short-term assays did not mean that a compound was a genotoxic carcinogen.

5.32 The United States explained that a determination of carcinogenicity required long-term testing in live animals. The standard model for determining carcinogenicity was a test called a "two year rodent bioassay." It was conducted in male and female rats and mice. A more definitive test - a two-year rodent bioassay had already been conducted for oestradiol-17ß. The results of the bioassay together with the results of other short-term tests had been reviewed by various scientific experts and used in determining the safety of oestradiol-17ß. Based on the results of these tests and other relevant scientific data, it had been determined that oestradiol-17ß was not a genotoxic carcinogen. Since long-term *in vivo* carcinogenicity tests had already been conducted for these hormones, the results of additional short-term assays were of little value. In other words, the full scientific process necessary to make the regulatory decision that oestradiol was not a genotoxic carcinogen had already been completed. The very low levels of oestradiol-17ß present in food were not adding to the cancer risk of women, children or men. Moreover, two-year rodent bioassays had also already been conducted on trenbolone and zeranol and also established that these were not genotoxic carcinogens.

5.33 The United States also observed that if the EC data were correct, then it could not be understood why the European Communities would permit the use of the same hormones for zootechnical purposes. The United States explained that "zootechnical" referred to such matters as synchronizing the estrus cycles in a herd. This involved administering hormones to healthy animals. It had nothing to do with treating disease. It was done solely for the convenience of the farmer. It was an *economic* purpose whose objective was to produce more animals (that is, produce more meat or other animal products) more efficiently. This was why the United States had used the less technical, more accurate term "herd management" with respect to these uses.

5.34 In addition, the United States stated that in the United States each sponsor of an approved product had an ongoing burden to demonstrate the safety of that product. There was a continuing review of the scientific data related to that product. No data had arisen to alter the FDA determination that these six hormones were safe when used for growth promotion in accordance with good practice.

5.35 The United States observed that in this dispute the European Communities had largely ignored MGA. It had offered no scientific evidence in support of its ban on MGA and had essentially admitted that it had never studied MGA.

5.36 The United States further stated that the experts selected by the Panel had confirmed that:

(i) The three natural hormones administered for growth promotion purposes were chemically identical to the three natural hormones produced by the animal and by humans and to the three natural hormones permitted by the European Communities to be administered for zootechnical and therapeutic purposes. In other words, for purposes of the health of a consumer eating the meat, it did not matter why the residue was there, it was still the same chemical.

(ii) The residues in meat were within the normal physiological levels for the three natural hormones when administered for growth promotion purposes in accordance with good animal husbandry practice. Again, in other words, two consumers could be exposed to the identical level of hormones residues even though one ate only banned meat and the other ate only non-banned meat. Indeed, the consumer eating EC meat could well be exposed to substantially higher levels of hormone residues than the consumer eating only banned meat.

(iii) There would always be residues of a hormone administered to an animal, however minute, even though the residues may be below the level of detection.

(iv) There was no way to distinguish meat produced using the three natural growth hormones in accordance with good animal husbandry practice from other meat.

The United States stated that all of this demonstrated that the EC ban was unscientific. It was based neither on scientific principles nor on sufficient scientific evidence. It also demonstrated that banned and unbanned meat were "like" products and therefore that the EC ban was inconsistent with Articles III:4 and I:1 of GATT.

5.37 The United States also claimed that, contrary to the requirements in Article 5.1, the European Communities had failed to base its ban on an assessment of the risks. The European Communities had never provided a copy of any risk assessment that could serve as a basis for its ban. It was obvious that the European Communities had not relied on any of the opinions of the scientists referred to by the European Communities during the 17 and 18 February 1997 meeting with the experts when it implemented the ban that became effective in 1989, nor when it promulgated its new directives in 1996 to become effective in July of this year. Indeed, the European Communities apparently had not consulted any of these scientists until it was well into a WTO dispute settlement proceeding to review its ban. By contrast, the competent EC authorities had officially determined that, contrary to a ban, the Codex standard was correct and no MRL or ADI was necessary.

5.38 The United States observed that the various presentations of the outside scientists during the 17-18 February 1997 meeting did not in any manner constitute a risk assessment. They were simply an attempt at a *post hoc* rationalization of the EC ban and as such were irrelevant to the Panel's examination, in accordance with its terms of reference, of whether the EC ban was based on a risk assessment. If the EC ban were truly based on a risk assessment, one would expect to find a record of the competent EC regulatory authorities expressing health concerns related to each of the substances at issue, commissioning laboratory tests or other studies, reviewing the results of those studies and reaching certain conclusions, and then taking regulatory action. The European Communities had presented no such record to the Panel. The European Communities did undertake a risk assessment by the Lamming Committee, but the results of that risk assessment did not support the EC ban. One would also have expected any risk assessment to include some determinations regarding exposure of consumers to the substance. There was no evidence that the results of the residue testing described by the European Communities were reviewed to determine exposure levels.

5.39 According to the United States, contrary to Article 3.3, the European Communities had failed to show that its ban was designed to achieve a higher level of protection than the Codex standard for the hormones, which was designed to result in "no appreciable risk" from exposure to residues. The European Communities never opposed the scientific consensus on the Codex standards through seven stages of Codex review. At the last stage the European Communities opposed adoption by Codex, but even then the European Communities never raised any concerns with the scientific justification for the standards. Nor had the European Communities ever requested JECFA to review the standards.

5.40 The United States also stated that the EC professed concern over possible misuse did not justify the EC ban. Even if misused, the residues of the six hormones could well be below the Codex or FDA MRLs (in the case of the three synthetic hormones) or within normal physiological ranges (in the case of the three natural hormones). Indeed, direct injection (rather than use of an implant) of doses 100 times higher than approved doses still resulted in residues well below the established ADI. Furthermore the EC ban was not so carefully tailored so as to apply only to products derived from improperly treated animals. Finally, if the European Communities wanted to say that it was all right to use these hormones in accordance with good practice, but it was not all right to misuse them, then the United States would support the European Communities.

5.41 The United States did not condone misuse and operated a rigorous compliance programme for these hormones. The US control programme was comparable to the EC programme. The EC references to the number of samples tested in the United States presented an inaccurate picture. Residue testing was only one component of a well-designed control programme. In the United States, the FDA and the Food Safety Inspection Service of the US Department of Agriculture had extensive compliance programmes to ensure that animal drugs were used safely. Testing was just one part of this compliance programme. The philosophy of the US animal drug compliance programme was the same as that of other quality assurance programmes. That is, quality must be built into a product not tested into a product. Since the United States believed that one could not test one's way into compliance, the US compliance programme involved various activities to ensure that animal drugs were used properly. These activities included:

(i) Surveillance of sales records to determine where the drug was being sold and used.

(ii) Education, including teaching field investigators about food safety concerns that would arise following any misuse of animal drugs.

(iii) On-site inspection. Field inspectors were not only present in the slaughter plants but FDA inspectors had on-farm authority that included surveying all the drugs used on the farm and auditing records of drug use.

5.42 The United States stated that testing of the food supply for violations was part of this compliance program. When residue violations were found, an inspector followed up on this violation by visiting the farm and determining what drugs were being used. Finally, the United States utilized various legal actions including criminal prosecution of producers and veterinarians that misused animal drugs.

5.43 With respect to the 1986 report of misplaced implants referred to by the EC, the United States explained that in 1986, the FDA did indeed identify a problem with the misplacement of implants. The "misplacement" dealt largely if not exclusively with placement of the implant in the wrong part of the ear of the cattle. FDA took swift compliance action to correct this problem and the problem had not occurred since. Rather than a failure of the US system, the United States believed the incident demonstrated the effectiveness of the US regulatory compliance system.

5.44 With respect to the EC claim that the United States had established ADIs for the three natural hormones, the United States explained that it had not established ADIs for these three hormones. The numbers referenced by the European Communities were not ADIs. They were not legal limits at all. They were a benchmark that was one of several factors considered when deciding whether to approve a product. They were not legal, regulatory limits. If a shipment of meat were found that exceeded these figures, this would not itself be a basis for regulatory action.

5.45 The United States also commented on the responses of the experts to the 18 February 1997, "Additional Questions of the Panel to the Experts." The United States first noted that while one possible explanation of the mechanism of action of carbadox was that it acted as an anti-microbial to reduce the amount of flora in the intestines, this hypothesis had not been confirmed. The growth promotion effect of carbadox was clear, but carbadox was not essential for animal health. Secondly, the concept that one could separate the adverse effects on human health, if any, of residues of endogenous hormones from the same hormone supplied by an implant was without scientific support and had no basis in fact. Finally, it was the US belief that compliance was easier if an animal drug were legal. Legal use permitted the collection of sales records, patterns of use, control of manufacturing procedures, and education programs on safe conditions of use. Similar compliance mechanisms were not available for illegal products sold on the black market. The United States also observed that since the EC had explained that all six of the hormones were covered by the EC residue testing programmes, and that it tested 200,000 samples, then it was clear that residue testing was a feasible alternative to the EC ban.

5.46 The United States concluded by stating that it was important to put this whole dispute in perspective. It did not make sense to examine the issue of residues of these hormones from growth promotion in isolation as though this would be the only exposure for consumers. Humans were all constantly exposed to significant quantities of hormones, both due to endogenous production and to exposure from many food sources. Humans all had natural mechanisms in their bodies to regulate the levels and balance of hormones within a set range, rather like a thermostat in a home regulated the temperature within a range. In any given person, hormone levels varied over a wide range each day. Humans were constantly exposed not just to these hormones, but to many other hormones and other substances as well - chemicals produced endogenously in their bodies and chemicals naturally found in foods or added to foods. Indeed the amount of hormones in meat, regardless of whether the meat was from an animal which had been administered hormones for growth promotion, was small compared to the amount of hormones in some other common foods, such as milk. The residues in meat were inconsequential compared to the natural production in humans. These residue levels were nowhere near enough to disrupt hormone levels or the hormone balance in even the most sensitive members of the population.

VI. PANEL'S CONSULTATION WITH SCIENTIFIC EXPERTS

6.1 As regarded the selection procedures and criteria, the **European Communities** considered that the use of experts by the Panel for the purposes of scientific and technical advice should respect general principles of law. In particular, it should be transparent, avoid conflicts of interest, affirm the integrity of the dispute settlement process and aid public confidence in the outcome of the dispute[287]. In addition, Appendix 4 of the DSU included general rules of law relating to the use of expert advice on the part of Panels. Even though the experts would not constitute an Expert Review Group but would be consulted individually and separately, such rules should be applied by analogy whenever relevant and appropriate[288]. In order to ensure that the principles outlined above were respected, the European Communities believed that a number of general criteria should be followed in the selection of the scientific experts by the Panel.

6.2 The European Communities indicated that, first, the experts nominated by the Panel should not be nationals of the parties to the dispute nor nationals of third parties in the same dispute. This principle aimed at ensuring a fair and impartial selection of experts and appeared all the more necessary in light of the possibility given by the Panel to the parties to nominate one expert each, without any limitation of nationality. Second, the Panel, in selecting experts with different fields of expertise, should ensure that all the areas which it had identified were covered, so that all the questions of the Panel received replies to the fullest extent possible. Third, given the very small number of experts that the Panel would consult, only scientists with

287 The European Communities noted that in a letter addressed to the Panel on 21 October 1996, the United States had also agreed to these general principles.

288 The European Communities noted that this had also been acknowledged in the Panel's letter of 30 October 1996.

proven expertise in the use of hormones in general and for animal growth promotion should be selected. Fourth, the experts should not have served as members of the Codex/JECFA group which produced the 1988 JECFA report on the use of hormones for animal growth promotion. Fifth, past or present significant ties with the industry producing these hormones would not provide sufficient guarantees of lack of conflict of interest, of integrity and of aiding public confidence in the outcome of the dispute. The European Communities considered that the above comments constituted compelling reasons for the European Communities and underscored the limited pool proposed by the Codex secretariat from which the Panel would make its choice, despite the existence of a large number of scientific experts on these issues internationally. The European Communities indicated that Panel's favorable response to the EC request to add a fifth scientist with expertise in the area of carcinogenic effects of hormones in this case addressed one of the concerns of the European Communities.

6.3 As regarded the purpose of requesting information from, and the type and nature of the questions to be asked to, experts, the European Communities stated that this should be "to further the Panel's understanding of the scientific facts relevant to the dispute". In order to fulfil this objective and be in conformity with the provisions of the SPS Agreement and the DSU, the questions the Panel intended to ask must relate directly to the scientific issues of the case. These questions must be addressed to persons who on the basis of their recognized fields of expertise, could provide direct, reliable and verifiable information to the Panel. The questions should not concern legal issues or issues of interpretation of any of the WTO Agreements under consideration, because it was the sole responsibility of the Panel to interpret the legal provisions which had been invoked by the Parties and to apply them to the facts of the present case. The European Communities observed that the questions the Panel intended to ask should also not address nor request pure factual information, which was the responsibility of the parties to the dispute to provide, in accordance with the DSU rules and its provisions on burden of proof. They should not address issues of trade policy either, which were again the sole responsibility of the parties and on which scientists were not competent and could not be expected to pronounce themselves. The European Communities claimed that scientists must be asked only scientific questions directly relevant to this dispute and in the light of the scientific arguments made by the parties to this dispute. The European Communities recalled that it was the Panel's responsibility to interpret and apply the relevant legal provisions. Accordingly, the European Communities considered necessary to stress that it reserved all its rights with regard to the conformity of the Panel's approach on these issues with the relevant provisions of the SPS Agreement and the DSU.

Panel Procedures with Regard to Scientific Expertise

6.4 Following consultation with the parties, the Panel decided to seek scientific and technical advice as foreseen in paragraphs 1 and 2, first sentence, of Article 13 of the DSU, and pursuant to paragraph 2, first sentence, of Article 11 of the SPS Agreement.

6.5 Names of individuals expert in the subject matter before the Panel were provided by the Codex Commission secretariat as well as by the International Agency for Research on Cancer ("IARC"). Brief curricula vitae were solicited from all experts who were prepared to assist the Panel.

6.6 The Panel decided to seek advice from the same experts selected to advise the panel considering a separate complaint regarding the same measure, the Panel on European Communities - Measuring Concerning Meat and Meat Products (Hormones) - established at the request of the United States. The parties to that dispute had been provided the opportunity to comment on these potential experts on the basis of the curricula vitae, and in particular to state any compelling objections they might have with regard to any individual. The parties had been invited to nominate one expert each, not necessarily from the list provided by the Panel. The Panel than selected two additional individuals from the list taking into account the comments of the Parties. At the request of the European Communities, the Panel decided to select an additional expert in the area of carcinogenic effects of hormones, on the understanding that the European Communities agreed that the Panel established at the request of Canada would seek advice from the same five experts. Canada was invited to comment on the experts identified by the two parties. These experts were requested to serve, in their personal capacities, as individual advisers to the Panel. The Panel also sought information from the Codex Commission secretariat.

6.7 The Panel, in consultation with the parties, prepared specific questions which it submitted to each expert individually. The experts were requested to provide their responses, in writing, to those questions they felt qualified to address. The Parties agreed that their written submissions to the Panel, including the written versions of their oral statements, be provided to each of the selected experts. Written questions were also submitted to the Codex Commission secretariat. The written responses of the experts and of the Codex Commission secretariat were provided to the parties.

6.8 The experts were invited to meet with the Panel and the parties to discuss their written responses to the questions and to provide further information. A summary of the responses provided by the experts is presented below.

6.9 The experts selected to advise the Panel were:

Dr. Francois André, Laboratoire des dosages hormonaux, France

Dr. Dieter Arnold, Deputy Director, Federal Institute for Health Protection of Consumers and Veterinary Medecine, Germany

Dr. George Lucier, Environmental Toxicology Programme, National Institute of Environmental Health Sciences, United States

Dr. Jock McLean, University of Swinburne, Pro Vice Chancellor, Division of Science, Engineering and Design, Swinburne University of Technology, Australia

Dr. Len Ritter, Executive Director, Canadian Network of Toxocilogy Centres, University of Guelph, Canada

Dr. Alan Randell of the Codex secretariat also advised the Panel.

Views of the Scientific Experts

Question 1:

In various JECFA and Codex references the terms "good animal husbandry practice", "good veterinary practice" and "good veterinary and animal husbandry practice" are used. Can you define "good animal husbandry practice", "good veterinary practice" and "good veterinary and animal husbandry practice"? What are the implications, in terms of residue levels and potential hazards to human or animal health, of non-application of "good veterinary and animal husbandry practices" for five of the hormones in dispute?

6.10 **Dr. André** responded that these concepts related to quality assurance systems, however they were not precisely described or standardized, and the use of some of these concepts was not yet widespread. "Good animal husbandry practice" was described in various ways, such as "the stable to table approach" which took into account the use of veterinary drugs such as in a Herd Health Surveillance Programme (HHSP). In such a recording system, farmers, veterinarians and other people concerned with all aspects of primary production should cooperate to ensure good animal husbandry practice.

6.11 "Good veterinary practice" described each country's national or professional guidelines or rules which provided guarantees for professional activities. The use of veterinary drugs was controlled by means of an international code of practice of the Codex Alimentarius which described the use of veterinary drugs, from the necessity of a pertinent diagnosis to residue management (respect of withdrawal periods) in meat-producing animals. Dr. André noted that special attention should be paid to the prescription and to using the correct dosage, site and route of administration for medicines. Moreover, specific conditions for the use of particular drugs was regulated; ie., in Europe, EC Directive 96/22 described precisely the conditions of therapeutical or zootechnical use of the hormones in dispute.

6.12 Dr. André noted that "good veterinary and animal husbandry practice" did not appear to be well defined but could be considered as a combination of the two above-mentioned practices. The strict observance of "good veterinary and animal husbandry practice" was the only way to guarantee that each drug would be used according to the conditions for which it had been registered. Any disrespect of such practices, in term of dosage, injection route, withdrawal period or other conditions specified for use, would change the expected level of residues. Concerning the hormones in dispute, it could easily be demonstrated that overdosage, shorter withdrawal periods (when defined), or liquid solution injections instead of implants might lead to higher residue levels. Potential hazards to human and animal health might then appear.

6.13 Dr. André indicated that the real problem was one of control: how to ensure that these practices were really respected. There were official control services charged with this control. But now more and more veterinarians, farmers, and farmer organizations were taking the control and were ensuring that they only used registered drugs as they were officially meant to be used.

6.14 **Dr. Arnold** observed that "good animal husbandry practice" was a broad term relating to the proper management and handling of animals. Particularly intensive production methods required good management. The terms management and husbandry included, for example, efforts toward improving rate of gain and feed efficiency and management of reproduction (e.g., hormonal control of oestrus, embryo transfer, treatment of infertility, prevention of pregnancy, termination of pregnancy, induction of parturition, etc.). Veterinarians were involved in the management of several of these conditions and were *inter alia* responsible that certain drugs were only administered after thorough diagnosis and in compliance with the approved label instructions. It was also a fundamental requirement that drugs (hormones, growth promoters, parasiticides and other substances) should not be used to replace good veterinary and animal husbandry practices.

6.15 Dr. Arnold indicated that the hormones under discussions were not *per se* hazardous or innocent substances. If ingested with food, their possible biological effects depended *inter alia* on the amounts ingested. Therefore, it was important that during the approval process conditions of use were established which guaranteed that even preferential consumption of food from treated animals would not lead to the ingestion of residues causing biological effects. The essential issue was compliance with the established conditions of use which were normally laid down in the label instructions. If "good veterinary and animal husbandry practices" were not applied, in particular if "good practices in the use of veterinary drugs" were not observed when using these substances, residue levels higher than those resulting from the authorized conditions of use may occur/were likely to occur in edible portions of the treated animals. These elevated levels did not always have biological effects - because the established margins of safety were usually high.

6.16 **Dr. Lucier** indicated that he had little expertise in this area, but it seemed reasonable to assume that non-application of such guidelines or inconsistent application of them would substantially increase the chance that acceptable residue levels could be exceeded, which would likely increase the potential risk to human health.

6.17 **Dr. McLean** responded that "good practice" was the operative part of these definitions. The word "veterinary" implied that a veterinarian was involved in the process as the prescriber, advisor or administrator. "Animal husbandry" was caring for animals and might involve a veterinarian in the process. "Good practice" in relation to the use of hormones involved the use of a registered product according to the prescribed instructions for its use and employing good farming practice. It might also include the use of approved administration apparatus and the identification of treated animals.

6.18 Dr. McLean indicated that departure from "good practice" was undesirable and a breach of the registration conditions. However, in practice, it was unlikely that minor departures from good practice with registered products would cause significant increases in hormone levels in meat.

6.19 **Dr. Ritter** indicated that these terms had been elaborated in a recommended international code of practice (Codex Alimentarius, 1993) intended to foster the safe use of veterinary drugs in food producing animals and to ensure that, in accordance with the principles of this code, residues of veterinary drugs in food did not exceed permitted levels and residues did not pose a hazard to humans consuming food commodities produced with the aid of veterinary drugs. In practice, JECFA and Codex had not utilized these terms, but rather had employed the term "good practice in the use of veterinary drugs", which had been defined (Codex Alimentarius 1993) as "the official recommended or authorized usage including withdrawal periods, approved by national authorities, of veterinary drugs under practical conditions. The maximum residue limit for veterinary drugs may be reduced to be consistent with good practice in the use of veterinary drugs". The maximum permitted residue was based on the type and amount of residue considered to be without toxicological hazard for human health while taking into account other relevant public health risks. When the hormones at issue were used in accordance with the prescribed use conditions, the levels that were present were in fact indistinguishable from those which would be present in an animal which had not been treated at all.

6.20 Dr. Ritter further noted that the principle or philosophy of good veterinary and good husbandry practice also implied that all veterinary products to be utilized in food producing animals should only be administered in strict compliance with relevant product information, approved by the appropriate regulatory authority, and in strict accordance with instructions issued by qualified veterinarians. Violations of any of these principles might result in higher than expected residues or residues of unexpected drugs. The implications of such violations were proportional to the frequency with which they occurred, the magnitude of the violation and the prevalence of such violations within the food production system. Notwithstanding, given the exaggerated estimates of safety inherent in the approach to the establishment of MRLs, it was unlikely that occasional violations could increase overall residue levels to those which, on an infrequent exposure basis, could pose a risk to consumers.

Question 2:

> Can meat produced with any of the six hormones in dispute for growth promotion purposes (natural and/or synthetic) be physically differentiated, by consumers or by any particular detection methods, from meat produced without them? Are residues of the three natural hormones administered for growth promotion purposes chemically different from residues of these hormones administered for purposes permitted by the EC?

6.21 **Dr. André** noted that no physical differences were observed between meat produced with or without the use of growth-promoting hormones, but questions of meat quality could be raised as far as physicochemical or organoleptic criteria were concerned. Significant alteration of eating quality and loss of tenderness of meat produced with various implants had been reported. These changes might also stem from differences in the chemical composition of meat. According to sex and/or implant type, differences of moisture and fat rates were observed.

6.22 Furthermore, sophisticated detection methods allowed differentiation of meat produced with or without synthetic hormones, even if a long withdrawal period was respected. For natural hormones, this differentiation was possible when esters of natural hormones were still present in the meat. In some cases it is possible to distinguish the two by physical means of isotope relations, but it would be very difficult to do at very low levels, Theoretically, *quantitative* differences might be expected between the legal use of natural hormones as growth promoters (i.e. as an implant) and their use as veterinary drugs (i.e. usually as injection); from the *qualitative* point of view, chemical differences could be expected in terms of metabolites and/or conjugates, owing to the dosage, the route of administration and the length of treatment.

6.23 **Dr. Arnold** responded that it was not possible to physically differentiate meat from treated animals from meat of untreated animals. However, many studies showed that the composition of the carcass was improved upon treatment in terms of more lean meat and less fat than in untreated control animals. Residues found in the meat from treated animals for growth promotion purposes would be qualitatively the same as residues found in meat from animals treated with the same substances for purposes permitted by the European Communities, but quantitatively could be slightly different depending on the compound administered, the dose, the route of administration, etc. If the substances were used according to good veterinary practices, there was initially a slight difference but at the time of slaughter there was no means to discriminate between treated and non-treated animals, irrespective of whether for growth promotion or for therapeutic and zootechnical purposes.

6.24 Of the categories of residues of biological concern, only the residues of the parent drug administered to the animals (e.g. the hormones itself or its esters) could be analytically differentiated with currently available analytical methods. Theoretically, hormones could be labelled with stable isotopes to permit discrimination between added hormones and endogenous hormones, but this had no relevance in practice. It was possible to discriminate whether or not animals had been treated with exogenous hormones. Despite their short half-lives in circulation, it was even possible, but not normally routinely feasible, to measure the concentrations of the esters at sites distant from the injection site.

6.25 It appeared that the substances used for growth promotion in the United States were (with the possible exception of testosterone-propionate) also used in the European Union for therapeutic or zootechnical purposes. Working-Group III of the 1995 EC Scientific Conference had concluded that: "While residue analyses for natural hormones on animals treated experimentally can show differences between them and untreated animals, *it is not possible in routine use to identify treated animals on the basis of assays of edible tissue samples* and it is difficult in blood, urine or faeces. Successful identification of treated animals may be made by analysis of injection sites or detection of esters (e.g. oestradiol benzoate) in blood shortly after treatment. Identification of animals treated with natural hormones on the basis of a single time-point analysis is difficult. The situation is more complex for food-producing animals, where typically a mixture of androgen only is used. *Identification of meat from animals treated with natural hormones and imported from third countries is not at present possible*"[289]. (emphasis added)

6.26 **Dr. Lucier** indicated that the residues which occurred from the natural hormones were indistinguishable from those which occurred from the natural endogenous materials. This was not true, of course, for the synthetics. With appropriate analytical methods and appropriate residue levels one could detect residues of the synthetic materials here in question. The half life, the biological persistence, of the agents in question was for the most part rather short; they did not stick around the body very long. Half-life was the time it takes for half the material to disappear. If, for example, something had a half life of one day and, if you started out with 10 units of it, one day later you would have five, two days later you would have two and a half and so forth. So even though several months might elapse following an exposure to an agent even with a relatively short half life, a few molecules might remain. The number of molecules might be remarkably close to zero, probably not detectable by analytical methods, but a few molecules would likely remain. (See also response to question 5).

6.27 Dr. Lucier noted that it was likely that, on the average, meat from growth-promoted animals would be leaner (i.e. less fat) than meat produced without those agents. However, it was unlikely that, for a given piece of meat, one could physically

---

289 Working Group III, Detection and Surveillance, in *1995 EC Scientific Conference Proceedings*, p.31.

differentiate whether or not it was from a growth-promoted animal. Residues arising from administration of the three natural hormones would not be chemically different from those in the body of non-treated animals although the residues were likely to be slightly higher in the growth-promoted animals.

6.28 **Dr. McLean** responded that for all practical nutritional and health purposes the meat was the same regardless of how it was produced, although there might be variations in the ratio of fat to lean meat. The residues of the natural hormones were generally similar when administered for growth promotion or for other purposes. Because the mode of administration used for growth promotion resulted in lower daily dosing, there might be quantitative and qualitative variations in the composition residues.

6.29 **Dr. Ritter** observed that it was generally known that when used as growth promoters, the naturally occurring gonadal steroid hormones - oestrogen, progesterone and testosterone and the related substances MGA, zeranol and trenbolone, could increase the growth rate, the proportion of lean meat to fat and food conversion efficiency in some species. Overall the response might vary between hormones, and might be maximized by the use of certain combinations of hormones. In general, the lean meat content of the carcass was improved and the fat content was decreased. Except in the case of some veal calves, effects on meat quality were generally not significant. Thus it was most unlikely that consumers could differentiate physically between meat produced with or without these hormones. JEFCA concluded that it would be very difficult to determine residue levels attributable to the exogenous use of the naturally occurring gonadal hormones.

6.30 While it was most unlikely that consumers could physically differentiate meat produced with synthetic hormones, residues could be reliably detected well below those levels regarded as safe. However, qualitatively the residue would be indistinguishable. Quantitatively, the amount that could be detected would be a function of the amount that would have been administered either for growth promotion or therapeutic uses.

Question 3:

> If any one of the six hormones or a combination thereof is administered to the animal, will there always be a residue of that hormone in the meat of that animal, even if it is so small that it cannot be detected? Question 32: Further to question 3, could the hormone load ingested by humans from other foodstuffs (including endogenous hormones) be greater than which occurs from the consumption of beef derived from hormone-treated cattle?

6.31 **Dr. André** indicated that a specific detection limit below which a residue could not be identified and/or quantified was defined for each method. It never meant that the residue was not still present in a given matrix. The lower the detection limit of the method, the lower the level of residue which could be revealed, but the longer the time of possible identification of the residue. For some growth promoters the time during which it was possible to find residues had changed from one week to one month after substantial improvement of the method (high resolution mass spectrometry instead of low resolution mass spectrometry for instance). With the development of sophisticated new methods, it was possible to observe residues remaining much longer than was commonly known.

6.32 Other foodstuffs than meat from hormone-treated cattle contained hormones, especially oestrogens. This was the case of offals, of certain plants, of meat from specific animals (such as pregnant cows); all contained high levels of hormones. However, the consumption of these foodstuffs was always occasional and would not enhance risks for human health. This was not comparable to the systematic enhancement of the hormonal content of meat.

6.33 **Dr. Arnold** stated that he was not considering the endogenously produced hormones as "residues" in his answer. Any exogenously administered hormones present in the body of treated animals should, however, be considered as "residues", even if there was no difference in structure and biological activity compared with the endogenously produced hormones. The use of the term "residue" did not imply that these residues were potentially harmful to human health.

6.34 Whether animals were slaughtered without any withdrawal time or at the end of the legally established withdrawal time, there would always be a residue. The exogenous compound was not absent at the end of the withdrawal time; however, the sum of both the endogenous and exogenous molecules would be at or within physiological limits. If the presence of residues were to be regulated on the basis of "no-detectable-residues" (which was impossible because the endogenous hormones alone were already above the limit of detection), there would nonetheless be more than 1000 billions molecules of the administered exogenous hormone present in one kilogramme of meat at the limit of detection. In other words, the "no-detectable-residue" concept was a false-zero-residue" concept. For any of the six hormones, it was impossible to estimate the withdrawal times required to reach true "zero-residue" levels even with the aid of the most sensitive analytical methods.

6.35 Many foods of both plant and animal origin contained natural hormonal substances in such amounts that, depending on the actual diet, the dietary intake could be lower, equal or higher than the amount ingested with beef from hormone-treated cattle. If the endogenous production was taken together with the dietary intake, it would always be much higher. Given their natural presence in food, he stated that one cannot escape eating these hormonally active substances, or similar substances with related biological potential.

6.36 **Dr. Lucier** responded that biological half-life data was available for each of these hormones, so residues could be reasonably predicted at various times after exposure had ceased. In the case of zeranol the half-life was approximately one day. Thus, if a sample contained 100 ppb when exposure ceased, 50 ppb would remain after one day, 12 ppb at three days, three ppb at five days and so on. Although the levels after several months would be extraordinarily small and very likely non-detectable, a few molecules would remain.

6.37 **Dr. McLean** indicated that a minute residue, well below any present method of detection, might remain. This could be postulated from a knowledge of pharmacokinetics. This minute residue would be of no significance when compared with endogenous production of natural hormones in the human body, or the dietary intake of natural oestrogenic substances in food or contaminants which were oestrogenic.

6.38 **Dr. Ritter** observed that in the case of the natural hormones, and in accordance with appropriate use procedures, hormone levels could be expected to decline to levels that would be associated with untreated control animals. Because these hormones were normally produced endogenously, it would be essentially impossible to distinguish these low levels as originating from an exogenous source, and in any case these levels fell well within the range normally present in untreated animals. In the case of the xenobiotic hormones, and in particular trenbolone acetate and zeranol, residue levels of these hormones would not normally be expected in untreated animals and hence could be detected in monitoring programmes. It was possible that, depending on the withdrawal period selected, some residues of the xenobiotic hormones might remain, even if below the limits detectable by routine methodology.

Question 4:

> How do the residues from the three synthetic hormones in dispute differ, in general, from those of the three natural hormones in dispute if administered in accordance with good husbandry practice and good veterinary practice? And, in particular, when used for animal growth promotion in accordance with good husbandry practice and/or good veterinary practice? How do residues of hormones naturally present in animals, meat, meat products or human beings, differ from those of additional hormones administered to animals? Do these differences, if any, result in different potential risks to human health?

6.39 **Dr. André** replied that because the compounds were not the same, they led to chemically different residues. The residues also differed quantitatively according to the dosage. Levels of oestradiol, testosterone and progesterone residues increased significantly in animal tissues after treatment, when compared with corresponding untreated animals. Usually, the increase of residue levels was more pronounced in fat than in muscle and other edible tissues. Concerning trenbolone and zeranol the approximate residue levels could be considered, for both compounds, to be close to the ppb level.

6.40 Differences between natural occurring hormones at a natural occurring level and the same hormones at a higher level or synthetic hormones (whatever their level of residue) resulted systematically in different potential risks to human health, due either to the level of residue or the nature of the residue (metabolites). According to the route of administration of additional hormones, some differences in metabolites patterns might appear. Metabolites could be species-specific: metabolites not formed in cows might form in humans and result in potential risks for human health. The potential induced risk could be due to the hormonal activity of residues. The potential adverse effect could also be a carcinogenic effect.

6.41 Within the physiological range these hormones had no different biological effects on human beings. But if one ate only meat from treated animals, there would be a very small enhancement of the mean of food hormonal intake and this would not be transformed in classical biological effects for human beings. The problem was that some other biological effects had needed to be studied over a long time. Such effects included, for example, changes in human fertility or change in the sex ratio, which was currently changing in some countries. But there was no currently known relationship between these developments and the fact whether these countries banned or not these hormones.

6.42 **Dr. Arnold** responded that in chemical terms, there was no difference between endogenously produced "natural hormones" and exogenously administered "nature-identical" hormones. There were, however, clear chemical differences between the "natural" and "nature-identical" hormones on the one side and the xenobiotic hormones on the other side. The xenobiotic hormones do not naturally occur in animals, meat, meat products or human beings, so any reliably detected residue of the three synthetic (xenobiotic) hormones was indicative of a treatment of the animals. If the products were administered in accordance with the "good practices", such residues might frequently occur in concentrations too low to be detectable in meat.

6.43 In terms of biological activity, in principle, the potential biological effects of the "nature-identical" exogenous hormones were the same as for the "natural" endogenous hormones. While the concentrations of endogenous hormones were, however, regulated depending on e.g., sex, age, developmental stage etc., the exogenous hormones could, in principle, be added in such amounts as to either gradually disturb or - at high doses - even overwhelm the internal regulatory mechanism. Single high doses (e.g., resulting from the ingestion of a "full" injection site) would normally cause transient effects. Repeated high doses (not reached through ingestion of residues resulting from uses such as growth promotion, therapy, or zootechnical treatment) could significantly change the hormonal balance of the individual.

6.44 Dr. Arnold summarized that the potential risks to human health arising from the hormonal activity of the xenobiotic hormones was slightly different in quantitative terms. The potential risks arising from *other than* hormonal actions were qualitatively different. These risks were assessed during the review and approval process, and the approved conditions of use eliminated all unacceptable risks.

6.45 **Dr. Lucier** replied that the residues from the three synthetics differed in several ways from the naturally-occurring hormones. First, the chemical structure was different. Second, any metabolite or breakdown products would likely be different. Third, the synthetic hormone, although mimicking the natural hormone, might have additional biological properties not found in the natural hormone. These differences could possibly result in different potential risks to human health.

6.46 Some biological effect could occur. For example, a normal woman might have 30 per cent of her oestrogen receptors occupied at some given point in time. At that same point in time, if she was consuming meat that contained an additional burden of oestrogens because of the use of growth promoters, that receptor occupancy might be something like 30.01 or 30.001, a very very small increase. This increase would not be detectable, not even close to being detectable, by any experimental tools available today. Thus, a biological effect could be occurring; if it was occurring it would not be detectable; and finally the relationship between that biological effect (receptor occupancy) and a toxic effect, say cancer or birth defect or something like that, would be unknown. But if such an effect were occurring, it would be extraordinarily small, close to zero.

6.47 **Dr. McLean** indicated that the residues from the synthetic hormones differed from those of the natural hormones because they were chemically different compounds and therefore their metabolites would also be different. In the case of the naturally occurring hormones, the residues in meat and humans would be very similar. Any difference would not pose a potential risk to health.

6.48 In relation to the naturally occurring hormones, Dr. McLean noted that it was not possible to differentiate between the effects of meat from treated animals against meat from untreated animals because essentially they were in the same biological range. In the case of the non-naturally occurring hormones, in establishing the ADI very sensitive end points were derived from studies in non-human primates, and then the situation of sensitive members of the population was taken into account when establishing safety factors. The levels in meat were substantially below those causing any effects in primates, and there was a reasonably good correlation in effects of hormonal levels in primates against humans. Therefore the levels present in meat from animals that were treated with the two non-natural growth promotants would not cause effects in humans consuming the meat.

6.49 **Dr. Ritter** observed that when introduced exogenously as subcutaneous implants, the natural hormones were absorbed and metabolized in an identical manner to the endogenous form thereby producing a spectrum, both qualitatively and quantitatively, of residues which were indistinguishable from the normal endogenous hormones. In the case of the synthetic hormones, trenbolone acetate, zeranol and MGA used as growth promoters, tissue residues were not normally present and hence detectable residues were attributable to their use. In this case, maximum residue levels were recommended only after careful and thorough evaluation of the safety file, food consumption factors, selection of appropriate withdrawal periods and, in consideration thereof, residues remaining were not considered to pose a risk to consumers of meat or meat products containing these residues at or below internationally recommended limits.

Question 5:

> The EC has identified certain potential health hazards of concern to it (ie., carcinogenicity, synergistic effects, genotoxic effects, long-term use and exposure to combination of the hormones in question). To what extent were these hazards taken into consideration in the context of the 1988 JECFA report or in the establishment of the Codex standards for the hormones in issue? To what extent do the risk assessments referred to by the EC assess these suggested hazards? Had the six hormones in dispute been used as animal growth-promoters over a sufficient number of years for an assessment of the long-term effects of such hormones on human or animal health to be made? Question 29: Further to question 5, to what extent do the ADIs and MRLs established by Codex for any food additive, pesticide, etc., take into account the effects on human health of exposures to mixtures of veterinary drugs, or exposure to the hormones in question originated by other sources? To what extent do the ADIs and MRLs established by Codex take into account the effects on human health of exposure to mixtures of veterinary drugs, or exposure to the hormones in question originated by other sources?

6.50 **Dr. André** indicated that the potential health hazards taken into account by JECFA were based on data available in 1988. Moreover only toxicological effects of these drugs were evaluated. Synergistic effects, long term use and combination of hormones were not fully evaluated. New results concerning toxicological effects of natural and synthetic hormones had been published since 1990, most of them in 1995 and 1996. Some of these new data were taken into consideration when preparing EC 96/22 and 96/23 Directives, however they were not taken into account by the 1995 EC Scientific Conference because the bibliography for the Conference had been prepared at the beginning of 1995. Many other hazards for human health could be either scientifically proven or excluded. Owing to the nature of these hormones, the residue levels, and the way they were ingested (assuming that good veterinary practice and good animal husbandry practice were respected), a 30 to 50 year period might be necessary to obtain substantial data (as for oral contraceptives or asbestos inhalation).

6.51 When individual drugs were used in common veterinary practice for therapeutic purposes, the probability of the simultaneous use of two drugs was low; the probability of an interference between them was lower, and lower still was the probability that one could influence the elimination rate of another. For the hormones used as growth promoters, the problem was different. They were used on a very large scale. Many animals were treated so that the probability to have simultaneous administration of other drugs and of these hormones became much higher. A good risk assessment should take this into account, but he was not aware of that having been done either in the countries where these hormones were in use or at the international level.

6.52 **Dr. Arnold** replied that synergistic (and antagonistic) interactions of these hormones at all levels - from the molecular to higher organisational levels - were key elements of their normal biological functions. It was difficult to identify what theoretical hazards might arise from theoretically possible maximal changes in the order of < 0.1 per cent of internal hormone pools due to the consumption of meat from animals treated with the approved hormonal growth promoters. Long-term exposure to hormones in laboratory animals and humans was fully covered by the JECFA evaluations (e.g. in the case of zeranol and trenbolone-acetate by the chronic/carcinogenicity studies reviewed). Data not available to the 32nd JECFA were completed at the 34th meeting of the Committee.

6.53 In the Community, the competent advisory body for the safety evaluation of oestradiol-17β, progesterone and testosterone was the Committee for Veterinary Medicinal Products (CVMP), a section of the European Medicines Evaluation Agency (EMEA). EMEA was also, in principle, the competent authority for the review of applications for marketing authorization of veterinary medicinal products used for growth promotion. A centralised review process would be mandatory under the provisions laid down in Regulation 2309/93. The use of any hormonal substance for growth promotion was, however, currently prohibited.

6.54 Under the provisions of Articles 7 and 14 of Council Regulation 2377/902[290], Maximum Residue Limits (MRLs) had to be established for the therapeutic and zootechnical uses of the three "nature-identical" substances before the end of 1996. The EMEA reviewed (in accordance with regulation 2377/90) the therapeutic uses of oestradiol-17β in cattle and horses. The public summary report states:

> "3. Toxicological effects found after oestradiol administration comprise hyperplasia of the endometrium, behavioural changes and effects of metabolic processes. Oestradiol does not induce gene mutations *in vitro*, but conflicting results are found in chromosomal aberration assays. Following long term exposure the incidence of tumours in tissues with a high level of hormone receptors is increased (e.g. mammary tumours). It is concluded that the toxic effects including

[290] Council Regulation (EEC) 2377/90, *EC Official Journal* L224/1 of 18 August 1990.

> carcinogenicity occur as an extension of the physiological effects of oestradiol ...
>
> 7. The conclusion of the FAO/WHO Expert Committee on Food Additives (JECFA) that no ADI and MRLs for oestradiol need to be established is adopted. Milk and plasma residue levels after treatment with oestradiol benzoate and oestradiol valerate have shown to be at or within physiological limits. Although it is likely that tissue residue levels will also be within physiological limits, this cannot be guaranteed, given the results with oestradiol hexahydrobenzoate. Still, compared to the lowest human daily production rate of oestradiol in prepubertal boys (6 (μg/d)) and compared to the amount of oestradiol in other food stuffs that are part of the human diet, the amount of exogenous oestradiol that humans will be exposed to through ingestion of tissue from treated animals is biologically insignificant, and will be incapable of exerting a hormonal effect in human beings".

6.55 EMEA also evaluated progesterone in accordance with regulation 2377/90. The public summary report consists of 17 paragraphs and shows that the following aspects had been considered by the Committee: natural occurrence, veterinary uses, target animal safety, biological effects, endogenous production in humans, normal levels in food animals and in food of animal origin, pharmacokinetics and metabolism, acute and short-term toxicity in laboratory animals, reproductive toxicity, teratogenicity/embryotoxicity, and long-term effects including carcinogenicity. The evaluation by JECFA of this substance was also considered.

With respect to carcinogenicity it was stated:

> "9. According to the International Agency for Research on Cancer (IARC), progesterone does not exhibit mutagenic activity in most *in vitro* and *in vivo* tests performed, but is known to increase the tumour incidence in endocrine target tissues (ovaries, uterus, mammae) after continuous (parenteral) doses clearly above the physiological levels. Progesterone is not carcinogenic per se, but acts via an epigenetic mechanism associated with its endocrine activity, i.e. its ability to cause a hyperproliferative effect at cellular levels mediated by steroid-hormone receptor interaction. Hence, tumours will not result from ingestion of progesterone at levels that do not produce any hormonal effects".

The evaluation process of testosterone in accordance with regulation 2377/90 was still ongoing.

6.56 So far no complete risk assessment had been conducted in the Community; the most competent assessment was made by the Scientific Working Group on Anabolic Agents in Animal Production chaired by Professor Lamming. This Committee comprehensively reviewed the available scientific evidence, including industry data, concerning five of the substances under dispute. Its recommendations were endorsed by the Scientific Committee on Animal Nutrition, the Scientific Committee on Food and the Scientific Veterinary Committee of the EC. However, when the interim report was published, long-term toxicity data on the xenobiotic substances was available only for trenbolone acetate. The report also does not mention that "synergistic effects" and exposure to combinations had been considered. The "Pimenta Committee" did not itself perform a scientific risk assessment but rather expressed views on public perception of scientific opinion, the role of science in society, consumer preference, other socio-economic factors and various aspects of implementation and control of a ban.

6.57 The 1995 EC Scientific Conference had no legal mandate and the Steering Committee was entirely free to design the programme and to nominate invited participants. A legal notice in the report clarified that neither the European Commission nor any person acting on behalf of the Commission was responsible for the use which might be made of the information. The Conference did not assess the hazards referred to by the EC in this dispute. With regard to the Codex process, Dr. Arnold noted that it was true that the EC had objected to move these MRLs to the next step in the procedure, but without raising any health issues. The EC had opposed because it had specific legislation prohibiting the use of, and consumers did not wish to eat meat from, treated animals.

6.58 Sufficient time had elapsed to allow an assessment of the long-term potential effects on the health of the target animals. If long-term effects of these substances were to be studied, the effects of the endogenously produced amounts of these substances and of the exogenously administered human doses in therapy etc. were most relevant. Lifestyle and ingestion as normal food constituents could also be important. In the unlikely event that the minute amounts added from residues would have any effect on human health, it would not be possible to discover this effect against this background.

6.59 In response to the follow-up questions (in particular, question 29), Dr. Arnold noted that the primary mode of exposure to food additives was through ingestion of the substance in the food supply. JECFA considered, where applicable, the occurrence of the substances as normal body constituents; the natural occurrence in foods; exposure from other uses; and interactions with other food additives. For example, when canthaxanthin was evaluated, the Committee considered also the uses of this substance as feed additive in animal nutrition and as an orally administered pigmenting agent for human skin in both pharmaceutical and cosmetic applications. Early in its deliberations about safety margins the Committee had concluded that the margin of safety should allow for, *inter alia*, the possibility of synergistic action among food additives. The ADI for food additives generally included the natural occurrence and the deliberate addition to food of the substance. Testing of "mixtures" was not normally required. However, some food additives were by their very nature mixtures.

6.60 With regard to pesticides, testing of "mixtures" was also not required, neither in the framework of the activities of the FAO/WHO Joint Meeting on Pesticide Residues nor in the legislation of the European Communities as laid down in Directive 91/414/EEC Annex II, Part A (O.J. L 230 pp.15-18).

6.61 For veterinary drugs, testing of "mixtures" was not required. However, the comprehensive basic pharmacological screening required for all drugs could provide information requiring further follow-up in specifically designed tests. JECFA had evaluated a number of substances where the ADI was based on a pharmacological No Observed Effect Level. The legislation of the European Union also did not require testing of "mixtures" (see Directive 92/18/EEC amending the Annex to Directive 81/852/EEC, O.J. L 97 of 10 April 1992, pp.1-23). However, there was a difference between "mixtures" and fixed combinations. Such combinations required justification on the basis of adequate testing. Repeated dose toxicity testing could be modified (i.e. reduced) in certain instances, for example, if new combinations of known substances were proposed and no potentiating effects had been observed during initial screening.

6.62 Dr. Arnold noted that testing of "mixtures" of hormones was not normally required, unless an unknown fixed combination was administered. He noted that the experimental animals in toxicity testing (or humans, if there were uses in human therapy) were typically exposed to all hormones existing in the body. Virtually all cells were targets of one or several of the approximately 50 known hormones and their metabolites. The same hormone could have several targets; the same cell might have several responses to a single hormone. The battery of tests included exposure at all stages of development from embryonic to fetal to neonate to reproductive state until the end of the whole lifespan, and this way all situations of hormonal control were covered. This meant also that all xenobiotic hormonally active substances had been tested with respect to possible interactions with the hormone system. No specific toxicity testing had been performed with the fixed combinations authorized in the European Communities.

6.63 JECFA developed its strategies concerning the evaluation of anabolic hormones in its 25th and 26th Report. These indicated that the toxicological evaluation of residues of anabolic agents that are present in human food obtained from animals treated with these agents must take into account whether the residue was identical to a human endocrine hormone. In the latter case, the possible endocrinological effects and carcinogenic potential of the residue must be closely examined. In addition, it was noted that chemically modified hormones, hormonally active agents from plants, and synthetic anabolic agents presented the following specific problems:

(i) extreme potency and consequently the need to ensure minimal residues;

(ii) potential tumorigenic activity; and

(iii) the presence of their metabolites in animal products that might be of endocrinological or toxicological consequence.

The evaluation for acceptance of the use of xenobiotic anabolic agents in animal food production resembled in many respects the evaluation of pesticides, since the two essential elements required were:

(i) adequate, relevant toxicological data; and

(ii) comprehensive data about the kinds and levels of residues when the substances are used in accordance with good animal husbandry practice, which required evidence as to the efficacy of the anabolic agent, the amounts used to produce the effect, the residue levels based on field trials, and information about methods of analysis of residue levels that could be used for control or monitoring purposes.[291]

6.64 **Dr. Lucier** responded that the issues of carcinogenicity, synergistic effects, genotoxic effects and chronic exposure appeared to be considered in the JECFA re-

[291] Environmental Health Criteria 70, WHO, Geneva, 1987.

port, although the basis for the evaluation (ADI recommendation) was based primarily on hormonal effects in monkeys because the other effects or issues were considered of less relevance to human health risks. The hormones in question had been used long enough to get information on whether or not they posed animal health risks, provided that good records were available. However, there was no tractable approach for detecting human health risks from long-term use as the health risks, if any, would be quite small.

6.65 The number of molecules that remain following appropriate use of these agents was very small, particularly in relation to the amount of naturally occurring oestrogens or androgens. So the accompanying risk that would be associated by consuming meat containing residues would be extraordinarily small. It would be very hard on scientific grounds to say that the risk was zero, but it was likely to be very, very small. It could be zero.

6.66 In terms of the carcinogenic activity of the hormones in question, it was already known that naturally occurring physiological levels of androgens and oestrogens were carcinogenic. Therefore, the issue of threshold was irrelevant to the toxicological evaluation of these agents. If a hundred thousand molecules of something already exist in the body and some of those molecules were producing a DNA damage event, there was some possibility that the same damage event would occur if another molecule was added to it because it was the same molecule. It would not be possible to distinguish that additional event from the ones that occurred from the thousand molecules. But it would not be possible to say that none of those events were related to that additional one molecule. This would not be detectable. The chances were very very small, but it would be impossible to say that the event could not occur.

6.67 With regard to the increased incidence of some tumours occurring in various countries in the world referred to by Dr. Epstein, it was probably true that there was a real increase in testicular cancer and this increase appeared to be predominant in young men which was especially disturbing. Why this was occurring, no one really knew its cause. There was no reason to think, however, that it was associated with oestrogen. There were many other factors that could be causing that. Breast cancer was also on the rise. However, one could not necessarily attribute that increase to exposure to exogenous external oestrogens. There were many reasons why exposure to genotoxic agents could be accounting for the rise in breast cancer rates; one needed to be cognisant of other factors and not just blame the exogenous oestrogens for everything. Regarding the oral contraceptive issue, Dr. Lucier indicated that Dr. Epstein was probably right that there would be an increase in breast cancer risk for women who started taking the pill very young because that extended the period of time in which they were exposed to high levels of oestrogen and this was a known risk factor for breast cancer. The same exposures a little bit later probably would not have an increase, so when averaged out, there was no statistically significant increase in breast cancer from oral contraceptives. No one challenged the fact that oestrogens were carcinogenic.

6.68 With regard to Dr. Metzler comments, Dr. Lucier noted that the adducts that may arise from synthetic materials were likely different and of more concern, in terms of a risk assessment, than the ones that arise from the naturally occurring ones, because there already was a given body burden of the naturally occurring oestrogens.

The question of genotoxic or non-genotoxic was essentially irrelevant here since the dose response relationships for oestrogen increases in cell division (one possible mechanism of carcinogenesis) was likely to be linear because normal levels of oestrogen were causing cell replication.

6.69 **Dr. McLean** replied that the 1988 and 1989 JECFA reports addressed the issues of carcinogenicity and genotoxicity and their findings were accepted by Codex. The compounds were not genotoxic carcinogens and the responses seen were related to their hormonal effects. These hormonal effects were evaluated using sensitive end-points in non-human primates. In the case of synergistic effects, it was recognized that the levels resulting from treatment with the naturally occurring hormones were significantly less than the natural levels already present in the treated animals. In addition, it must be recognized that all three hormones occurred in male and female animals and humans. With regard to mutagenicity, data for the naturally occurring substances was reviewed and referenced in the JECFA 1988 Report. The report was not silent on the matter but it referred to mutagenicity data that was in the published literature. In the case of progesterone, testosterone and oestradiol-17β, there were a number of published documents that JECFA did look at, and they are referenced in its report.

6.70 There was also human data available from therapy with various natural and synthetic hormones. This therapy was continued in humans for many years and the risks have been evaluated. The levels found in meat after treatment are many orders of magnitude lower than therapeutic levels, are poorly absorbed orally and so do not represent a hazard. The compounds had been used in many countries for long periods of time and there was no human epidemiological data which suggests any hazard. With regard to Dr. Epstein's observations related to increasing numbers of tumours, Dr. McLean observed that the increase in tumours occurred also in those countries where the use of growth promotants was not widespread and the increase began before the hormonal growth promotants received widespread use.

6.71 **Dr. Ritter** noted that data relating to carcinogenicity and genotoxicity were indeed available to the Joint FAO/WHO Expert Committee on at least five of the six hormones under discussion (all but MGA). In all of these cases, the relevant data formed the basis of: (i) the safety evaluation, (ii) the decision by the Committee that an ADI need not be allocated for the natural hormones, and (iii) the establishment of both an ADI and MRL's for trenbolone acetate and zeranol.

6.72 With relation to oestradiol, progesterone and testosterone, JECFA concluded that the increased tumour incidence was attributed to the hormonal activity of these hormones associated with the very high doses utilized in the experiment. These effects were not considered relevant to an evaluation of the safety of food residues. The Report was silent on the results of mutagenicity studies, which were available to the Committee for review. With relation to trenbolone acetate, JECFA similarly concluded that the carcinogenic effects detected were a direct consequence of the hormonal effect associated with the high doses utilized in the study and not of direst relevance to the interpretation of the safety of the food residues. JECFA also concluded that the tumorigenic effect of zeranol was associated with its oestrogenic properties at the high doses utilized in the cancer study, and therefore a safe exposure level to humans could be determined.

6.73 The issue of potential synergy was addressed, at least in part, by JECFA through the conduct of biochemical studies directed at the effect of excretion of hormone combinations when compared to single hormones alone. Although these studies did not specifically address issues related to altered toxicity due to synergy, these limited data did provide evidence that while administration of hormone combinations could be expected to alter excretion kinetics quantitatively, there was no evidence of important qualitative changes. It was, however, clear that definitive studies relating to genotoxicity or carcinogenicity of hormone combinations had not been carried out, even though this was frequently the preferred method of use.

6.74 Dr. Ritter observed that the use of gonadal type hormones as anabolic agents had been in agricultural practice for approximately 40 years through many parts of the world. Regarding the synthetic hormones, both zeranol and MGA had been used as anabolic drugs, at least in the United States, for approximately thirty years while trenbolone acetate had been in use for approximately ten years. At least in the case of the natural hormones and both zeranol and MGA, broad scale use had now been in place for more than a generation with only few and isolated reports of potential adverse effects. The primary potential concern with regards to human health effects had been that of carcinogenicity. While the use of the growth promoting hormones for periods as long as 40 years should have been sufficient to result in an increased cancer risk in the human population, an increase which could be attributable to the use of these hormones had not become apparent. Noting that both breast cancer, particularly in post-menopausal people, and prostatic cancer had increased sharply in affluent countries. Dr. Ritter pointed out that this increase was thought to be primarily associated with genetic predisposition and significant alterations in lifestyle (Houghton and Ritter, 1995).

6.75 **Dr. A. Randell** commented on the relationship between the Acceptable Daily Intake (ADI) and the Maximum Residue Limit (MRL) and whether or not these were measures of acceptable risk. The maximum residue limit was definitely not a health-based limit. It was a limit established for the control of veterinary drugs in actual practice. The establishment of a maximum residue limit was such that the maximum residue would never lead to residues which would, in a normal ingestion of the product, cause any consumer to exceed the acceptable daily intake. Therefore there was an upper boundary to the maximum residue limit imposed by toxicology considerations. The lower limit was normally derived from residue trials in practice according to the proposed good veterinary practices in the use of these drugs. However, in the case of zeranol, this limit fell so far below not only the toxicologically derived limit but also the limit that one could determine with normal methods of analytical chemistry, that it was increased to take into account the fact that if a decent control programme were not going to be overly expensive, than the limit must be controllable by analytical procedures rather than by residue trials. The acceptable daily intake itself also was not a direct risk assessment in the sense that it provided a statement of quantitative risk. The ADI concept stated that there would be *no appreciable risk* as a result of exposure to the chemicals concerned. This was true within the JECFA and JMPR framework, for food additives, residues of veterinary drugs and pesticide residues. (Dr. Lucier's comment that the risk was probably somewhere between zero and one in a million, provided some sort of quantitative framework, but JECFA had never established a quantitative evaluation of risk in the application of the ADI.)

Question 6:

Is there any more recent scientific evidence available with respect to the effects on human or animal health of the use of any of the six hormones in dispute especially when used for growth promotion purposes, other than the evidence already taken into account by Codex? How reliable are extrapolations from animal studies to possible adverse effects in humans? Further to questions 6 and 8, are you aware of new scientific evidence showing that the carcinogenicity, synergistic effects, genotoxic effects, long-term use and/or exposure to combinations of the hormones in question and their metabolites, if any do not only depend on the hormonal activity of the dose administered? Would such evidence invalidate the ADIs and MRLs established by JECFA/Codex?

6.76 **Dr. André** noted that recent reports of the effects on *animal health* from the use of the six hormones in dispute as growth promoters confirmed and finalized previous results.[292] Based on anatomical or histopathological observations, these results demonstrated the effects of commercially available implants on animal behaviour, development and reproduction. Young bull behavioural modifications had been confirmed: young bulls treated with zeranol "spent more time idling, eating and ruminating than controls".[293] Animal libido was systematically altered. The changes in the behaviour of bulls were usually correlated with histopathological modifications, well described in the 1980s as a tool for treatment diagnosis and more recently confirmed in bulls.[294] Similar phenomenon had been recently studied in other species, as the effect of trenbolone in male pigs.[295] The influence of these hormones used as growth promoters on reproductive tract development and reproduction had been confirmed in beef heifers: "The lower pregnancy rate in zeranol implanted heifers 100 days after exposure to bulls was caused by failure to cycle early in life and, in those that were cycling, failure to conceive and abortions between 25 and 45 days of gestation".[296]

6.77 First results of recent research work with mice on the effects of hormones on animal sexual development and reproduction were published in 1995. They concluded that "DES and Zeranol administered during mid pregnancy leads to decrease fetal weight and size and lower numbers of male offspring at birth".[297] In 1996, the same authors demonstrated "that prenatal exposure to zeranol or DES induced abnormal testicular differentiation in the mouse".

6.78 Concerning *human health*, there was a discussion on the decrease of human sperm counts[298], an apparent increase of the incidence of hormonally-mediated diseases like breast cancer and endometriosis, and a decrease in the male/female ratio, which were thought to be due to oestrogens in the environment. Whether the use of

---

292 Renaville *et al.* (1987), Dehaan *et al.* (1990), Moran *et al.* (1988), (1990), Herenda (1987), Beal *et al.* (1988).

293 Legoshin *et al.* (1994).

294 Tipirdamaz 1991, Ciftci (1990).

295 Lopez-Bote *et al.* (1994).

296 King *et al.* (1995).

297 Perez-Martinez *et al.*

298 Nimrod and Benson (1996).

hormones for growth promotion was contributing to this could not be scientifically proven at the present time.

6.79 Extrapolations from animal to human was an official tool for toxicological and efficiency evaluation of drugs under development. In general, they were regarded as conservative even if they did always contain a certain level of uncertainty. Moreover, these tests on animal models did not take into account the multiple exposure to many different compounds (characteristic for human diet). Humans were sometimes more sensitive for a certain effect than animals, and they were not always in as good health as laboratory animals. The action of food processing on residues was not checked in animal experiments. For some effects of chemicals on humans, such as long term effects over generations, no animal models existed. In other cases, results on animal models have sometimes been considered as not representative. For these reasons, many drugs which had been fully validated in animal models had been banned after several years of use in humans and the discovery of an unknown hazard.

6.80 **Dr. Arnold** indicated that since the last (JECFA) evaluation, science had made further progress in several areas, including the molecular mechanisms of action and the epidemiology of cancer The newly available information did not, however, substantially change the basis for the evaluation of the five substances by the Codex/ JECFA system. Although animal studies, in general, could provide useful information on possible adverse effects on human health resulting from exposure to chemical substances, the possible health effects resulting from the oral ingestion of trace amounts of residues of the three nature-identical hormones, (oestradiol-17β progesterone and testosterone) could not be reliably and *quantitatively* predicted from the information contained in available studies.

6.81 Early studies in mice, which were conducted between 1940 and 1973, and which were referenced in the IARC Monographs, were in no way designed to assess the human cancer risk resulting from oral ingestion of low doses of oestradiol-17β. None of these studies used the oral route of exposure in any animal species. None of them was conducted under GLP-like conditions or according to contemporary test guidelines. Many of them were poorly documented. The principal aim of these studies was *to experimentally produce tumours* under a variety of condition. The test substance was usually subcutaneously administered (frequently as implant). The doses were often extremely high and not infrequently caused a high number of early deaths. Such dosing was inadequate for carcinogen testing in relation to the safety evaluation of residues. The studies demonstrated that subcutaneous injection or implantation of high doses of oestradiol-17β or of its esters alone or in the presence of other carcinogenic factors resulted in increased incidence of mammary, pituitary, uterine, cervical, vaginal, lymphoid and interstitial-cell tumours in mice. The IARC working group concluded on the basis of all animal data that there was *sufficient evidence* for the carcinogenicity of oestradiol-17β in experimental animals.

6.82 Similarly the animal studies with progesterone which were reviewed by IARC were also limited to subcutaneous and intramuscular injections and subcutaneous implantations of high doses; in rats and rabbits it was always given in combination with other sex hormones. Progesterone was administered together with carcinogenic substances such as dimethylbenzanthracene, methylcholanthrene, diethylstilboestrol or N-2-fluorenyl-diacetamide in the majority of the studies reviewed. From these studies IARC concluded: "There is *limited evidence* for the carcinogenicity of progesterone in experimental animals. In the absence of epidemiological data, no evaluation of the carcinogenicity of progesterone to humans can be made."

6.83 Similarly to the other two nature-identical steroid hormones, testosterone and its esters were tested in experimental animals by subcutaneous injection and/or implantation, and in rabbits by intramuscular injection. In this case IARC concluded: "There is *sufficient evidence* for the carcinogenicity of testosterone in experimental animals. In the absence of adequate data in humans, it is reasonable, for practical purposes, to regard testosterone as if it presented a carcinogenic risk to humans. The only related data in humans, although insufficient for an evaluation, concern the possible long-term effects of androgenic anabolic-steroids."

6.84 The contribution of information obtained from these animal studies was of little relevance for the *quantitative* assessment of the potential effects on human health of orally ingested, very low residual amounts of these substances having no effects on the physiological hormonal balance. In particular no additional human cancer risk could be deduced from these animal studies in the absence of other relevant information. With reference to studies conducted by other scientists, namely Dr. Liehr and Dr. Cavalieri regarding different types of DNA damage or genotoxicity established for oestrogen, Dr. Arnold agreed that with chemical methods all these things could be produced. The question was whether it occurred in living cells, at what concentrations, what enzymes were involved, what was the compartmentalization of these enzymes, etc. In his view, there were many gaps in the evidence. A scientist could not exclude that at the end somebody might show that oestrogens acted directly on the gene. For the moment, the evidence was not convincing and did not invalidate the basic conclusions of JECFA 1988.

6.85 In response to the follow-up questions, Dr. Arnold indicated that hormonal activity was a necessary requirement of hormonal carcinogenesis caused by the substances in dispute. He was not aware of any evidence which would invalidate the ADIs and MRLs established by JECFA/Codex.

6.86 **Dr. Lucier** indicated that animal data were usually relevant for estimating human health risks, particularly for hazard identification, and there was a substantial body of knowledge and past record to substantiate this conclusion. However, it should be kept in mind that there is considerable uncertainty in extrapolating high dose animal data to low dose human risks. Over the last 5-10 years much had been learned about (i) the mechanisms whereby hormones triggered responses in target cells including the interplay or cross talk between receptor systems, (ii) the development of credible approaches for dose-response evaluation, (iii) the spectrum of toxic effects produced by hormonally-active agents, and (iv) the role of metabolic activation of hormones. There was a growing body of knowledge that some hormones could be converted to genotoxic metabolites. However, it was not clear whether these metabolites are involved in the carcinogenic process.

6.87 **Dr. McLean** responded that he did not believe that data developed after 1989 would justify a revision of the present use of hormones for growth promotion. For example, studies of *in vitro* receptor binding assays in the presence of pesticides had not produced evidence of concern. The extrapolation in the case of the hormones was arguably more reliable than with any other class of compounds because their mode of action and their metabolism was similar in both animals and humans. Non-human primate and human data was also available in many cases. In the case of trenbolone and zeranol, the usual safety factors for inter- and intra-species variation were still applied. The extrapolations from animal studies to humans was reliable in this case. The current ADI and MRL would only be invalidated if new data established a lower NOEL. In the case of trenbolone and zeranol, the NOEL used was conservative and therefore low. In any event, if any national body or group believed that it was time for re-evaluation of some of the hormones previously evaluated by JECFA it should approach the JECFA as had been done on a number of occasions with the number of compound of varying chemical classes.

6.88 **Dr. Ritter** observed that the JECFA review, and the subsequent decisions by Codex, were based largely on reviews conducted approximately a decade ago. In respect of the three natural hormones (oestradiol, progesterone and testosterone), the 1995 EC Scientific Conference generally recognized that these substances could increase the growth rate, the properties of lean meat to fat and the feed conversion efficiency of some species of animals. The Conference re-affirmed that the resulting residues in meat were within the normal physiological range and concluded that the conditions of use of the natural growth promoting hormones provided a reasonable safeguard of public health. In respect of the synthetic hormones utilized for growth promotion (trenbolone and zeranol), the 1995 EC Conference advanced the view that at doses required for growth promotion, residue levels of these xenobiotic hormones were well below the levels regarded as safe. The Conference also noted the availability of only limited data on possible adverse effects in target animals and emphasized the need for further study of the effects of growth promoters administered in combination, as the presence of one might alter the metabolism of the other.

6.89 The validity of extrapolations from animal studies to humans was the preeminent issue in contemporary toxicological hazard and risk assessment and was the basis of the hazard evaluation for drugs, pesticides, food additives and other contaminants worldwide. Given the reliance by both national regulatory authorities and international agencies on animal studies for predicting possible adverse effects in humans, it would seem *de facto* that the international scientific community had placed a great deal of faith in the validity of these extrapolations. At the same time, however, it was also clear that the validity of animal models in predicting adverse human effects was influenced by many factors including selection of the appropriate animal model, dose selection, duration and route of exposure and selection of appropriate risk models designed to estimate human risks resulting from the use of a substance under realistic and practical use conditions.

6.90 Recognizing the inherent limitations of any predictive model, Dr. Ritter indicated that the scientific community had elaborated a hazard and risk assessment paradigm that involved evaluation of a broad range of toxicological endpoints, selection of the most sensitive for determination of a NOEL, application of an additional uncertainty factor for derivation of an ADI and models for estimation of dietary exposure which invariably substantially exaggerated intake levels. The net effect of this series of overly conservative calculations was most likely very conservative estimates of risk, intended to compensate at least in part, for the limitations inherent in the reliability of animal to human extrapolations. Indeed, in its concluding commentary, the Steering Committee of the 1995 EC Scientific Conference noted that the nature of the calculations described above was such that adherence to the ADI provided a high degree of confidence that adverse effects would not become apparent in people.

In other words the European Conference essentially reaffirmed and strengthened the earlier conclusions reached by JECFA that in accordance with operating procedures that were provided for the use of these substances, their use did not constitute a risk to consumers of food commodities produced with the hormones at question, at least for five of the six substances.

6.91 Dr. Ritter noted that Dr. Liehr's work and the work of many investigators was to produce an effect. This was to the most fundamental issue in pharmacology and in toxicology, the concept of dose response. Dr. Liehr was very interested in understanding the induction of cancer as a result of exposure to these hormones. Therefore, his protocol would necessarily be designed in such a way so as to produce the desired effect, in his case the tumour. The intent in the case of food residues, was obviously to avoid a dose level which might constitute a human risk. Therefore, the levels that were present as residues in food were thousands or hundreds of thousands or millions of times lower than they would be in an experiment which was specifically designed to induce a tumour. These two experiments were completely at cross purposes with each other; they were from their very initiation intended to produce entirely different results. To compare a protocol which had been designed to produce a tumour to a food residue the use practice of which was set up in such a way so as to minimize the presence of the residue, was a relatively meaningless comparison. Moreover, no one could reasonably assure that the presence of these residues albeit at low levels constitutes zero risk; in fact scientifically it would be impossible to ever test to a certainty. But the point was that if these low levels did constitute a risk, they constituted a risk of a magnitude which approached zero.

Question 7:

> Is there any scientific evidence available which demonstrates that a potential for adverse effects on human or animal health arises from the administration of any of the six hormones in dispute, in general, and in particular for animal growth-promotion purposes, if administered in accordance with good animal husbandry practice and/or good veterinary practice?

6.92 **Dr. André** replied that there was no published scientific evidence that the administration, in accordance with good animal husbandry practice and/or good veterinary practice, of any of the six hormones in dispute in general (i.e. for therapeutical and zootechnical purposes) and in particular for animal growth promotion purposes, induced adverse effects on human health. This only meant that during the last decades, in countries where they are in use either for growth promotion purposes or for therapeutical and zootechnical purposes, none of the heath problems which could be due to their use (such as cancers, reproduction problems ...) had been scientifically related to their use. However the questions remained whether this had been studied and whether the period of use was long enough (see response to question 5 above). Concerning animal health, see response to question 6 above.

6.93 **Dr. Arnold** indicated that he was not aware of the existence of such evidence.

6.94 **Dr. Lucier** responded that, to his knowledge, there was no piece of scientific evidence to indicate that any of the six hormones in question had unequivocally caused adverse effects in humans when administered and used properly. However, there was some information available which raised concern for a slight effect on incidence of human disease (see response to question 8).

6.95 **Dr. McLean** stated that there did not appear to be any evidence which unequivocally established that adverse effects had been caused in animals treated with hormonal growth promotants or in humans consuming meat from treated animals.

6.96 **Dr. Ritter** observed that as early as 1982, a WHO appointed Working Group concluded that when the natural sex hormones were used in accordance with instructions for their use in growth promotion, such use would not present any harmful effects to consumers of products which had been produced with the aid of these promoters. This Working Group also concluded that the levels of zeranol and trenbolone, and their major metabolites, found in edible tissue following appropriate use as growth promoters, were substantially below the hormonally effective doses in animal test systems and did not present a risk of harm to humans. Overall, the Working Group concluded that the five compounds were safe for use in target animals and in subsequent consumers when they were used as prescribed for growth promotion in meat production.

6.97 The EC 1995 Scientific Conference concluded that the effects on *animals* in terms of disease incidence, performance, general mobility and meat producing efficiency were either unchanged or improved. The effects on animal welfare were negligible in terms of health, performance and effects on behaviour, although it was noted that there might be a transient increase in sexual activity for 2-10 days in some adult steers receiving oestradiol.

Question 8:

> Is there any scientific evidence available that residues of any of the six hormones in dispute could have carcinogenic effects, even though in the case of the two synthetic hormones these residues fall within the MRL levels established by the Codex? Is there any scientific evidence concerning the biochemical and physiological mechanisms by which the hormones subject to this dispute exert their carcinogenic effects? Please describe the relationship between the hormonal effect and the toxic effect of the six hormones. Is there a threshold level below which there is no scientific evidence that residues of the hormones would have adverse health effects on humans? Are the concepts of "Acceptable Daily Intake" and "Maximum Residue Level" valid for, or applicable to, genotoxic carcinogens?

6.98 **Dr. André** indicated that previous results on the carcinogenesis of hormones had recently been confirmed. This was true for single hormones as well as for mixtures of hormones, administered *in vivo* and *in vitro*. Concerning the mechanism by which the hormones exerted their carcinogenic effects, the most important model was oestradiol-17β itself. It had been proven that oestradiol-17β, which was involved in the development of breast cancer, stimulated the development of malignant cells. Recent results showed that oestradiol-17β enhanced genomic instability in malignant cells, inducing deletions or additions in DNA. It was reported that natural oestrogens (mainly oestradiol) induced cell transformation via over expression and synthesis of oncoproteins. Some new information about the potential role and mechanism of action of progesterone in breast cancer induction and about the biochemical aspects of pituitary oestrogen induced carcinogenesis were published; however, they did not demonstrate achieved molecular induction process.

6.99 Recent data on the mechanism of the carcinogenic effects of hormones led to the conclusion that hormones or their metabolites exerted a direct effect on tumour initiation by DNA damage; for oestrogen-dependent tumours, catechol oestrogens and their quinone forms would appear to be involved. Further, hormones stimulated the growth of tumours in tissues in which they had specific receptors. They had a complex carcinogenic and genotoxic effect. The hormonal effect stemmed from receptor binding, translocation to the nucleus and gene activation. Powerful oestrogens were strongly bounded and concentrated in the nucleus. If their hydroxylation and oxidation induced potential genotoxicity and carcinogenicity, it was not surprising that the more hormonally efficient they were, the more genetoxic and carcinogen they could be.

6.100 Dr. André concluded that hormones had to be considered as genotoxic compounds and for such carcinogens, no threshold level could be defined; no ADI and consequently no MRL could be established. This was the general opinion of toxicologists (Kuiper, EC 1995 Scientific Conference). This opinion had also been adopted by the United States Environment Protection Agency (EPA) for a carcinogenic non genotoxic dioxin, TCDD.

6.101 **Dr. Arnold** responded that there was no evidence available showing that residues of any of the six hormones in dispute could have carcinogenic effects, even though in the case of the two synthetic hormones these residues fell within the MRL levels established by the Codex. It was not possible to summarise briefly all the known facts published in thousands of papers in the last decades and in particular in the past 5-20 years.

6.102 Steroid hormones primarily influence the expression of genetic information at the level of transcription by binding to, and activating, transcription factors. The activated transcription factors interact with the regulatory or promoter region of the genes. The hormone receptors are these transcription factors in the case of e.g., steroid and thyroid hormones. The complete DNA sequence of the human oestrogen receptor was cloned for the first time in 1986 using the breast cancer cell line MCF-7. In the mean time, the genomic genes for all three receptors (oestrogens (ER), progestins (PR) and androgens (AR)) had been cloned. Dr. Arnold characterized the biochemical hormone-receptor-interactions as follows: receptors were present in low concentrations; their binding sites were saturable at physiological concentrations. The binding sites exhibited high specificity and high binding affinity; binding was reversible. Specific receptor binding was the initial and necessary step in the sequence of events leading to a hormonal effect although it was not the only reaction the hormones could undergo. The effects terminated upon dissociation of the hormone-receptor complex.

6.103 The involvement of receptors in hormonal signal transduction was thus explained by the fact that in addition to the recognition domain for the hormone they possessed a second functional domain (about 70 amino acids long) through which they could bind to DNA. Steroid-hormone-regulated genes had at least two different regulatory elements, a "generic" promoter element and (a) hormone response element(s) (it was not clear how many response elements actually existed in naturally occurring genes). It bound the hormone-receptor complex more avidly than the surrounding DNA did. The hormone-receptor might also regulate several genes in the same cell and different genes in different target cells. Metabolites and related exogenous synthetic hormones might work on a different set of response elements. The details of how the interaction with DNA promoted transcription was still an area of investigation. However, the basic principle was well established.

6.104 Carcinogenesis could be operationally described as a multistage process involving at least three stages: initiation, promotion and progression. The intermediate stage of promotion did not appear to involve structural alteration of the genome of the cell but rather depended on altered gene expression. Both oestrogens and androgens had been shown to be effective promoters in their target cells as well as in liver. In contrast to initiation, promotion was a reversible stage depending on continued administration of the promoting agent. Besides tissue specificity, the general characteristics of hormonal carcinogenicity were: long induction periods and prolonged exposure at high levels with concomitant severe derangements in homeostasis. The dose-response relationship of promoting agents (as well as the receptor-hormone binding) exhibited sigmoidal curves with an observable threshold and a maximal effect.

6.105 Hormonal carcinogenesis in experimental animals had mainly been studied in rats, mice and hamsters. The promotor model of hormonal carcinogenesis had been developed through studies of a variety of tissues of these animals. The question under dispute was not whether these models were still valid but rather whether genotoxic mechanisms could additionally exist or would need to be considered in order to fully explain the carcinogenic potential of hormones. In a recent review ("Molecular Mechanisms of Oestrogen Carcinogenesis", J.D. Yager and J.G. Liehr, Annual Review of Pharmacology and Toxicology 1996, Vol. 36, pp. 203-32) it was confirmed that the hormonal effects of oestrogens were necessary but not sufficient to induce tumours. One metabolite of oestradiol (16-Hydroxyoestrone) was claimed to be capable of binding to DNA *in vitro* but this could not be confirmed *in vivo* (unpublished observations by one of the authors). It was furthermore postulated that the catechol-oestrogen formed by hydroxylation in position 4 of the A-ring of the molecule could be involved in the generation of reactive oxygen species through redox cycling. Catecholoestrogens were also able to bind to DNA *in vitro*, a finding which was not confirmed in vivo.

6.106 Dr. Arnold further responded that according to current scientific knowledge, threshold levels below which residues of the hormones had no adverse health effects did exist for a given individual. The individual threshold levels varied and this has to be considered when setting exposure limits for the entire population.

6.107 Dr. Arnold indicated that the ADI was derived from a "No Observed Effect Level" (NOEL) using appropriate safety factors. While it did not itself represent a threshold dose, it was indirectly related to a not precisely known threshold dose. Therefore, the ADI concept as defined by JECFA could not be applied in order to establish an exposure limit for direct-acting genotoxic carcinogens for which, at least theoretically, no threshold dose could exist. MRLs could be established, in principle, to regulate genotoxic carcinogens. Basically there existed two possibilities: if the residues were genotoxic carcinogens, alternative models, e.g., risk extrapolation, could be used to find an MRL; in the case of carbadox, JECFA was unable to allocate an ADI because the parent drug was considered to be a genotoxic carcinogen. In this case, however, the residues were demonstrably not carcinogenic under approved conditions of use. Thus, an MRL could be established on the basis of regulating an innocuous metabolite.

6.108 Dr. Arnold noted that MRLs primarily facilitated fair international trade and were not directly related to health effects. Only the total dietary intake of the residues of concern, taking into account all MRLs established for the same substance and all relevant commodities and their consumption by the population, could be compared with an exposure limit.

6.109 **Dr. Lucier** responded that in the case of the naturally occurring hormones, particularly oestradiol-17β and testosterone, there was very good evidence that physiological levels were carcinogenic. For example, breast cancer would strike one in nine women in the United States over their lifetime and there was compelling evidence that physiological levels of oestradiol-17β were necessary for this effect. The evidence came from both animal experiments and human studies and was derived from a large base of peer-reviewed published information. In the case of oestrogen, early menarche and late menopause increased risk whereas ovariectomy was protective. Also, endometrial cancer was dramatically increased by oestrogen replacement therapy if unopposed by progesterone. In the case of breast cancer, consumption of beef with elevated levels of oestradiol-17β could increase risk slightly if the carcinogenic risk was not already saturated by physiological levels of oestrogen. The question of threshold was irrelevant. It was known that existing levels were already carcinogenic.

6.110 However, Dr. Lucier noted that evaluation of carcinogenic risk in people consuming meat from growth-promoted animals was complex. For example, progesterone might protect against endometrial cancer. From a different perspective, one knew that diet was a critical determinant of breast cancer risk and that fat in the diet was a risk factor. Therefore, consumption of meat containing residues of growth-promoting agents might actually decrease risk because that meat contained less fat than meat from non-growth promoted animals. On balance, breast cancer and prostate cancer risk could possibly be decreased by eating meat from growth-promoted animals. Moreover, exogenous oestrogens protected against osteoporosis and cardiovascular disease.

6.111 Dr. Lucier indicated that simple categorization of agents as genotoxic or non-genotoxic, alone, had little value in determining if an ADI approach or a linear approach was more valid for risk assessment. This opinion was supported by analysis of 500 cancer bioassays conducted by the National Toxicology Programme (NTP).

6.112 **Dr. McLean** replied there was no evidence that the residues had any carcinogenic effect. In the case of the two synthetic hormones which had a MRL, this was based on a NOEL derived from a hormonal end-point in non-human primates. There was data available which gave information on the mechanism by which hormones influence the occurrence of tumours in animals and humans. This was a very active field of research because of the importance of tumours of various organs, such as the breast or the prostate. Natural and synthetic hormones exerted their effects by binding to cell receptors and causing a series of biochemical events which influenced the metabolism of the target tissues. In addition, cell proliferation and/or turnover might be influenced. If the level of hormone was below that required to cause these events, there would be no adverse effects. However, in the case of the natural hormonal growth promoters, the normal levels of hormones in the human body were already many times greater than those from residues in food. The small amount in meat would not influence the course of events and therefore would not affect human health. Indeed it was very difficult to determine exactly where our hormone burden came from. But the fact of the matter was that humans were constantly being exposed to very significant levels of hormones and that the incidence of tumours which were associated with hormones in humans such as, for example, the breast or the prostate, had not significantly increased since the surveying had been carried out.

6.113 **Dr. Ritter** noted that carcinogenicity data had been available and reviewed for the three natural hormones and for both trenbolone and zeranol (see response to question 5). The issue of increased tumour production with all five hormones was therefore more a matter of theoretical consideration than one of practical risk. As was the case with oestradiol, and indeed with the other hormones under consideration, tumour induction associated with high exposure to these substances was a manifestation of tissues with high levels of specific hormone receptors that were normally responsive to stimulation by the particular hormone (JECFA, 1988). These effects, when they occurred, were generally considered to be the expression of very high dose receptor stimulation and were not believed to have any particular relevance for the evaluation of risks associated with dietary exposure to residues at much lower levels.

6.114 It was also widely recognized that toxic effects which might typically manifest at considerably lower levels then those required for receptor stimulation and attendant tumorigenic effects were a more appropriate basis for evaluation of potential adverse effects in humans following exposure to dietary residues. Notwithstanding, some authors (Liehr, 1996, unpublished; Adlercreutz, unpublished; Arnold, et al., 1996) had recently advanced alternative hypotheses regarding metabolism and mechanism of action of the gonadal hormones.

6.115 Historically, for chemicals which displayed carcinogenic properties in laboratory animals, it was assumed that a threshold dose did not exist. This view was due, in large part, to the fact that early studies focused on very potent carcinogens which manifested their effect by direct covalent binding to DNA; agents of this type which acted through direct covalent binding to DNA had also referred to as genotoxic. The subsequent hypothesis argued that even a single molecule of a substance might cause a heritable change in the DNA structure which would ultimately lead to tumour formation. In practice, it was now recognized that such a scenario was not likely, and that in any case many carcinogens acted through a non-genotoxic mechanism and hence did not target cellular macromolecules such as DNA. This particular point had been extensively elaborated with trenbolone, which was the subject of elaborate studies which demonstrated the absence of covalent binding potential associated with this hormone (JECFA, 1988). It was now apparent that NOELs could be determined for many chemicals that may show some evidence of carcinogenicity under experimental conditions. Under conditions where the effect was clearly non-genotoxic it might be possible to derive NOELs, establish an ADI and propose an MRL. Chemicals which produced carcinogenicity through a clear genotoxic mechanism should be regulated as if a threshold dose could not be derived and hence a NOEL, ADI and MRL could not be proposed. In the case of non-genotoxic carcinogens, there was little scientific validity to the belief that these chemicals should be treated or regulated differently than chemicals which produced other adverse effects through non-genotoxic pathways.

6.116 Dr. Ritter concluded that there was no compelling evidence to suggest that these compounds should be immediately re-evaluated, on the basis not only of the historical reviews which had been carried out by JECFA and other organizations, but also on much more recent reviews, including those published as a result of the European Conference on Growth Promotion in late 1995, early 1996, and indeed on the basis of the statements presented by Dr. Liehr, Dr. Metzler and others. Dr. Liehr's recent work and the work which others recently cited suggested that there were circumstances under which adverse effects could be demonstrated in association with a multitude of these compounds. However, scientists were compelled to look at the totality of the evidence as it was available. In Dr. Ritter's view, the totality of evidence, recognizing the information presented by Dr. Liehr and other scientists, as well as the historical information, suggested that the assessments that were provided in JECFA 1988 continued to assure a reasonable degree of safety to consumers of these commodities. This was not only his opinion, he stressed, but indeed also the consensus conclusion of the 1995 EC Scientific Conference.

Question 9:

> Is there scientific evidence of particular human health effects in countries where meat produced with the use of any of the six hormones in dispute for growth promotion purposes is allowed for consumption as compared to health effects in countries where the use of such hormones is forbidden?

6.117 **Dr. André** indicated that there was no known scientific evidence of such particular health problems. Only serious, long term epidemiological studies could give informative data (see also response to question 5). Furthermore, the causal relation could be difficult to identify, i.e. if comparisons between human health disorders was between the United States population and the Community population, there were so many differences in life style between the two continents, that the probability to prove the responsibility of one causal factor (like hormones) would be very low. However, a correlation between breast cancer incidence and blood oestrogen levels in the North American and Japanese populations was demonstrated. Other markers of particular human health effects could be prostatic cancer, human fecondity or sex ratios.

6.118 **Dr. Arnold** replied that no such evidence existed. Such comparisons could probably not be made because other factors, such as genetic differences of populations, lifestyle differences, differences in therapeutic uses of some of the substances and numerous other factors, would have much greater influence on the incidence of possible health problems.

6.119 **Dr. Lucier** stated that he did not believe that geographical patterns of human disease offered an approach for determining if residues of growth-promoting agents in meat increased risk of those diseases.

6.120 **Dr. McLean** noted that he was not aware of any evidence that there was any difference between the health of humans in countries where hormonal growth promoters were used and in those countries where they were not used. The life-span of humans in countries where hormonal growth promotants were used had steadily increased for a number of years. However, the reported incidence of cancer had increased because the population was older, diagnostic capacity had improved and better nutritional status increased cancer rates.

6.121 **Dr. Ritter** indicated that he was unaware of any data or other evidence of adverse human health effects in countries where meat was produced with the aid of the hormones in question, when compared to countries where the hormones were not utilized for meat production.

Question 10:

> How do the potential adverse effects on human health from residues in food in general, and meat in particular, from pesticides administered in accordance with good agricultural practice compare with potential adverse effects from residues of the six hormones in question, when the meat is from animals to which have been administered these hormones for growth-promotion in accordance with good animal husbandry practice and/or good veterinary practice?

6.122 **Dr. André** noted that these parameters were not developed with the aim of comparing the potential health risk of compounds. Each compound with potential adverse effects on human health was submitted to individual evaluations, so as to determine specific ADIs and MRLs (in food of concern). With regards to pesticides, Dr. André pointed out that some of the pesticides might facilitate adverse effects of oestrogens on human health.

6.123 **Dr. Arnold** responded that pesticides had biocidal properties and were frequently also otherwise very potent chemicals. Certain groups of pesticides were also used as veterinary drugs, e.g. as ectoparasiticides. These substances might have a significant potential to harm human health if not used according to good agricultural practices. The MRLs established in the EU and elsewhere provided sufficient consumer protection. It appeared that the margin of safety applied when establishing Codex MRLs for residues of veterinary drugs might be somewhat higher if the food baskets used and the calculated Theoretical Maximum Daily Intakes (TMDIs) were compared. JECFA/JMPR and CRVDF/CCPR had started harmonising MRLs for substances which were used in both agriculture and animal production.

6.124 **Dr. Lucier** replied that the tools of risk assessment were not sufficiently accurate to determine if pesticide residues or residues of anti-microbial agents posed a greater risk than residues of growth promoting agents. In each case, the risk was somewhere between zero and a small number.

6.125 **Dr. McLean** observed that there have been very few documented cases of adverse effects caused by pesticide residues in food, when they were administered in accordance with "good practice". There did not appear to be any proven cases linked to hormonal growth promotants. The use of the word "potential" implied hypothetical cases. Given that hormones had effects on sexual characteristics and metabolic processes, then potentially these would change, if the changes could be perceived or detected.

6.126 **Dr. Ritter** indicated that MRLs need not be established for the natural hormones, when used in accordance with good veterinary and/or agricultural practice (see response to question 5). In the case of the synthetic hormones, the nature of the studies used to establish their safety, and the methodological approach for the establishment of MRLs, including determination of a NOEL, calculation of an ADI, establishing a withdrawal period and proposing MRLs, was virtually identical for both pesticide residues and hormone residues. As a result, one would not expect that potential adverse effects on human health would be lesser or greater for hormone residues than might be the case for pesticide residues.

Question 11:

How do the potential adverse effects on human health from residues of carbadox (used in swine production) differ from the potential adverse effects arising from residues of the six hormones in question when used for growth-promotion in accordance with good animal husbandry practice and/or good veterinary practice? Question 30: Further to question 11 and 26, would you consider that the potential adverse effects on human health and/ or animal health from residues of carbadox, monensin, olaquindox, avoparcin, benzylpenicillin, carazolol, ivermectin and organophosphorous compounds are comparable to the potential adverse effects arising from residues of the six hormones at issue when used for growth-promotion in accordance with good animal husbandry practice and/ or good veterinary practice? Are any of the above mentioned substances carcinogenic? If any one of these substances or a combination thereof is administered to the animal, would there always be a residue of that substance in the meat of that animal, even if it is so small that it cannot be detected?

6.127 **Dr. André** indicated that carbadox proved to be a genotoxic compound, and consequently no ADI value had been proposed by JECFA (see also response to question 10). Olaquindox was known to be carcinogenic. Dr. André was not familiar with the others.

6.128 **Dr. Arnold** noted that as long as the "good practices" were observed, there was no relevant difference. If the lengthy withdrawal time was not observed in the case of carbadox, potentially genotoxic carcinogenic residues of the parent drug and another carcinogenic metabolite were likely to be present in meat of treated animals. In the case of the hormones, only the frequent consumption of injection sites or implants would potentially cause effects on human health.

6.129 Olaquindox was genotoxic in a number of tests. However the parent drug was extensively metabolised and was not present as a residue if "good practices" were applied. Ivermectin was extremely potent against parasites, but it was safely used in humans for the treatment of e.g. "river blindness" at much higher than residue levels. Carazolol was a hazardous substance for humans with chronic bronchitis which was a substantial part of the general population. In addition, carazolol was administered to the target animals by injection. Benzylpenicillin was absolutely harmless for the general population but could provoke allergic reactions in some sensitized people even at the level of the MRL. Avoparcin was not registered as feed additive on the American continent; its use in the EU had recently been withdrawn. Strict adherence to the identified "good practices" was an absolute requirement for the use of some of these substances. Nearly all of these substances left detectable residues in meat of treated animals under conditions of "good practice in the use of veterinary drugs". At the oral hearing Dr. Arnold added that there is a commercially available alternative for carbadox mainly oxytetracycline.

6.130 **Dr. Lucier** indicated that it was difficult to accurately compare risks from carbadox residues to risks from residues of growth-promoting substances (see also response to question 10). However, he expressed concerns about carbadox residues and that the risks from these residues were likely greater than the risks associated with the use of growth promoters.

6.131 **Dr. McLean** replied that carbadox and its metabolite desoxycarbadox were not permitted in meat, because the latter compound was carcinogenic. In the case of carbadox, a withholding period was set to achieve the situation where there were no detectable residues in food. The three naturally occurring hormones were normally found in animals and humans. The data supporting the use of trenbolone and zeranol was extensive, with toxicological end-points related to their hormonal effects. Finite residues were permitted for trenbolone and zeranol. In this way any risk of adverse effects was managed through the MRL and safety to consumers was assured.

6.132 Dr. McLean further noted that olaquindox was considered to be genotoxic and no toxicity studies were available on its metabolites, therefore JECFA was unable to determine an ADI or MRL. Benzylpenicillin was widely used as an antimicrobial agent in animals and humans. Allergenic potential was the major toxic effect and it was recommended that the total intake be kept below 30 micrograms per day for a human. Benzylpenicillin showed no carcinogenic potential. While carazolol showed no genotoxic or carcinogenic potential, it was a potent beta-adrenoceptor blocking agent. MRLs had been established for pig tissues. However, if carazolol was used in pigs to prevent stress during transport to slaughter, there was concern that residues at the site of injection could result in consumers receiving a pharmacologically active dose of the drug. The toxicity and residue data base for ivermectin and related compounds was extensive and the drug was also used in humans. The compound did not show genotoxic or carcinogenic potential and an ADI and an MRL had been established.

6.133 The organophosphorus compounds (OP) were described by Dr. McLean as powerful neurotoxins, and most of the untoward effects were related to the direct exposure of operators and others. There was a new syndrome of organophosphate - induced delayed polyneuropathy - which was of concern when there was acute exposure.[299] The OP had been associated with carcinogenicity and there were reports of acute poisoning associated with the consumption of treated food. Very low levels of the parent compound and/or metabolites might remain, although they could not be detected by sensitive analytical techniques. Dr. McLean did not comment on monensin or avoparcin because of the limited amount of registration data available which was in public domain.

6.134 **Dr. Ritter** observed that carbadox was reviewed by the JECFA in 1990. In its review, the JECFA considered data from short-term and long-term carcinogenicity, mutagenicity and reproduction studies with carbadox, and data from mutagenicity and long term studies of its metabolites. JECFA noted that results from several long term feeding studies in rats demonstrated dose-related increases in both benign and malignant tumours at doses above 1.0 mg/kg BW/day. Positive findings were also noted in 14 of the 15 mutagenicity studies reported. JECFA concluded that carbadox appeared to be both genotoxic and carcinogenic. Results from additional studies carried out with quinoxaline-∝-carboxylic acid, an important metabolite of carbadox, indicated that there were no effects on incidence of tumours, even at doses of 100 mg/kg BW/day. In view of the carcinogenic and genotoxic nature of carbadox and desoxycarbadox, a metabolite of carbadox, JECFA was not able to establish an ADI.

---

[299] M. Lotti, *Toxicology 21*, (1992) p.465.

Notwithstanding, the JECFA recommended MRLs of 0.03 mg/kg in liver and 0.005 mg/kg in muscle of pigs, based on and expressed as quinoxaline-$\propto$-carboxylic acid.

6.135 The establishment of an ADI and recommendation of an MRL reflected scientific confidence in the expressed residue levels being essentially devoid of risk to humans exposed to dietary residues on a lifetime basis. Therefore, neither carbadox nor the growth promoting hormones should pose potential adverse human health effects as a result of exposure to dietary residues at or below the MRLs specified by JECFA. Notwithstanding, it was noteworthy that carbadox and at least one of its metabolites was both carcinogenic and mutagenic, while the hormones were not considered carcinogenic or mutagenic at biologically relevant doses. In addition, reliable residue monitoring and risk estimation of carbadox residues was somewhat complicated by the presence of bound residues, while residues of the hormones either fell within normal physiological range or could be reliably and easily measured.

Question 12:

> Are residues of the six hormones in question found in milk or milk products? If yes, how do the levels of these residues compare to those found in meat from animals to which hormones have not been administered? How do the residue levels in milk compare to those found in meat from animals which have been administered these hormones for growth-promoting purposes? For therapeutic or zootechnical purposes?

6.136 **Dr. André** replied that residues of hormones in general are found in milk. However, the comparison with meat levels was not relevant. Moreover, hormones were not supposed to be used for growth promotion purposes in lactating cows, only in culled cows. For specific therapeutic or zootechnical purposes, only individual animals were allowed to be treated with hormones. In this case, the milk was not to be delivered for human consumption, as was the case for many other drugs.

6.137 **Dr. Arnold** noted that after injection of approved products (nature-identical molecules) permitted for use in the EU to lactating cows, residues would be found in milk. Depending on the product it could take several milkings before the residue levels would have returned to physiological values. Residues found in milk could be higher, equal or lower, depending on which tissues were compared and depending on many other factors (dose, route, age, sex, withdrawal time etc.)

6.138 **Dr. Lucier** indicated that if residues of the hormones in question existed in the human body, then residues would also be present in human milk.

6.139 **Dr. McLean** replied that hormones are lipid soluble and therefore pass into the fat portion of milk. More polar metabolites would also pass into milk, but it must be stressed that the hormones should not be used for growth promotion in lactating animals. When the various hormones were used for therapeutic or zootechnical purposes, the doses were much higher, therefore the levels in the tissues were higher. It had to be expected that the levels in milk would also be higher.

6.140 **Dr. Ritter** observed that growth promoting hormones were generally only permitted for use in beef cattle and veal calves, and not in lactating dairy cattle. Foxcroft and Hess (1986) reported that, at least in the case of the natural hormones, the residue levels of the administered compound or it metabolites in animal products were insignificant in comparison to the levels of the same steroids to which human subjects might normally be exposed. This could occur either (i) as a consequence of the endogenous production rate of sex steroids in human subjects or (ii) as a consequence of the steroids in meat and/or milk products derived from untreated animals.

Question 13:

> What factors and procedures should scientists consider in establishing an appropriate assessment of the potential adverse effects on human health from the use of the hormones in question?

6.141 **Dr. André** responded that an appropriate assessment of the potential adverse effects on human health stemming from the use of the hormones in dispute "should be more rigorous than common veterinary drugs because of the duration of their use and the very limited, if any, health benefits to the target species".[300] Scientists should consider all data available at the present time in dealing with the adverse effects of each compound (see response to question 8), their metabolites and their mechanisms of action, including their action at the level of exposure. Species-specific metabolite patterns should be compared, using (as far as possible) a combination of *in vivo* and *in vitro* experiments. Studies should include long-term feeding trials to address life time exposure. All studies should be performed with combinations of the hormones in dispute prior to registration, to obtain valuable data. The effects of the treatment on the kinetics of other common drugs had to be assayed. Epidemiological studies in humans concerning cancer incidence and other hormone related diseases had to be initiated.

6.142 **Dr. Arnold** indicated the following should be considered: pharmacokinetic data including metabolism in test animals and target animals, where available in humans; data (preferably quantitative data) from adequately designed toxicity studies in suitable animal species, including information on genotoxicity/carcinogenicity, and no hormonal effect levels; target animal safety studies; efficacy trials; epidemiological studies and other relevant observations in humans; kinetic residue studies; natural occurrence and human exposure from all sources, including endogenous production of the same or similarly acting substances; experience from the history of use in human and veterinary medicine (if applicable); and known or proposed conditions of use. A marketing authorization should only be given to strictly formulated products (not to the active substances). Conditions of use should be fixed in a binding manner in the approval process.

6.143 **Dr. Lucier** replied that there were several factors that should be systematically studied or evaluated if information was not available for assessment of risks from the hormones in question. Of special concern were potential risks for cancer and non-cancer effects (reproduction, development, cardiovascular disease, etc.). Additionally, information on effects in sensitive sub-population should be considered. Sensitivity could be conferred by genetic predisposition (presence or absence of cancer susceptibility genes), age (fetus, children or the aged), gender, existing disease status, nutrition, and co-exposure to other chemicals. These factors needed to be considered, although it was unlikely that information on them would ever be complete for any given substance.

---

[300] Bridges, *1995 EC Scientific Conference Proceedings*, p.250.

6.144 **Dr. McLean** noted that the testing protocols used in countries such as the United States, Canada, the United Kingdom, Australia and by JECFA were adequate to assess the effects of the use of hormones on human health. In addition, there was a need for residue monitoring programmes to ensure that residues in meat were less than any MRL which had been established.

6.145 **Dr. Ritter** observed that scientists considered a wide array of toxicological endpoints and risk assessment procedures in estimating potential adverse effects on human health from residues of all chemicals, including anabolic hormones, other veterinary drugs and pesticides. The issue of factors and procedures which were appropriate to the assessment of the potential adverse effects on human health included toxicity studies which established the following: which organs and/or systems were most vulnerable to the toxic effects and under what exposure conditions; the nature of any damage and/or disease produced, and the dose response relationship; the time course for the onset and any progression of the adverse effect; the mechanism responsible for the adverse effect; the relevance of the adverse effect observed in experimental animals to humans; the potential impact of biological mechanisms which led to the adverse effect but which, by virtue of the dose utilized, were not relevant to the assessment of the biological effect in humans (this was particularly important for the hormones in question which were only associated with adverse effects at doses which were not considered to be of relevance to the assessment of human health effects arising from food residues); whether it was appropriate to consider the adverse effects observed as a function of a threshold mechanism, or rather if a genotoxic mechanism was more likely and hence a threshold mechanism would be an inappropriate risk model.

6.146 In addition, Dr. Ritter noted that it might also be relevant to establish if the nature of the residue was distinguishable from normal endogenous levels - this was particularly relevant for the use of the natural gonadal hormones which resulted in residue levels typically in the range of untreated animals; whether appropriate and reliable methods existed for the estimation and monitoring of residues of the hormones following their use as growth promoting substances; and knowledge of the uncertainty inherent in the hazard and risk assessment paradigm.

Question 14:

> What are the potential hazards, if any, to human or animal health of the use of large quantities, or doses higher than those recommended, of any of the six hormones in dispute? And from the administration of these hormones contrary to good animal husbandry practice and/or veterinary practice? Can you think of any incentives or disincentives for farmers to use quantities larger than those specified in the label of the manufacturers or to administer these hormones contrary to good animal husbandry practice and/or veterinary practice? Are you aware of any evidence of such use by farmers?

6.147 **Dr. André** indicated that a higher dosage, another route of administration than those recommended for delivery (other location for implants, injectable solutions of hormones, etc.), shorter withdrawal periods, etc., in short, any disrespect of good animal husbandry and/or good veterinary practices, might induce higher levels of residues or changes in metabolite patterns. The first consequence would probably be a modification in animal behaviour and/or health. It was reasonable to think that a higher residue content in meat would enhance the risk of hazards to human health.

6.148 The anabolic effect of the hormones in question was proportional to the dosage, with a maximum effect. Farmers tried to obtain larger effects through administration of more implants than recommended, although it was not evident that a double dose, even at one time, gave a better response. In some cases, a parenteral administration (e.g. intramuscular injection) produced a more rapid effect than implants, and farmers tried by this mean to obtain faster effects. Disincentives for farmers to use larger quantities would be a decrease of the benefit/cost ratio, but implants were usually cheap. In countries where they were in use for growth promotion purposes, penalties due to higher residue levels detected in meat products compared to the MRLs might also have dissuasive effects on farmers. When five out of the six hormones in dispute were allowed in France, the experience was that farmers tried to give a second dose later. They did not respect the withdrawal period and they injected another dose at half way through the theoretical withdrawal period. Clearly they saw benefit to do this because the effect was longer at the time. Dr. André further reported that during the four to five years when these hormones were allowed as growth promotants in France, the misuse of other hormones continued and the black market was also present.

6.149 **Dr. Arnold** noted that there were considerable safety margins built into the established MRLs for the synthetic residues. As long as "good practices" were observed, the calculated theoretical maximum daily intakes of residues would range around 5 per cent of the ADI for both zeranol and trenbolone acetate. It had been shown that the implantation of approximately five times the recommended dose of zeranol would have almost no effect on maximum residue levels in the muscle and liver of steers slaughtered only five days after implantation. When a total dose more than 100-times higher than the recommended dose was intravenously administered as 6 split doses over three days to steers and the animals were slaughtered on the third day after the last dose, consumption of the meat of these animals would still not have caused an above-ADI intake of residues of zeranol.[301] The studies available to the 32nd and 34th JECFA showed that residues of trenbolone were highest if heifers were implanted shortly (15 days) before slaughter. With respect to the calculated theoretical maximum intakes, there was no difference whether this implant was the first or the second which the animal had received. From these data, it seemed unlikely that even the frequent use of higher doses, or repeat doses or slaughtering the animals at earlier than recommended times after implantation, could result in residue intakes in excess of the ADI by the consumer. For the three nature-identical hormones, the safety margins (theoretical residue intakes compared with endogenous production rates of the most sensitive sub-population) were much higher than for the synthetic substances.

6.150 Dr. Arnold had no information with regard to melengestrol acetate, nor regarding incentives or disincentives for farmers to use combinations or illegal "cocktails" of these hormones. Although these pellets and another devices had been developed to give optimum results when the dose was respected, this did not necessarily prevent some farmers using more implants. But this did not necessarily cause higher residue levels in the carcass. On the other side, it was clear that if twice the amount

[301] *Food and Nutrition Paper 41*, pp.44-45, FAO (1988).

was injected directly, all levels increased in plasma and in tissues, not necessarily in a linear way, but significantly. That was the difference between a slow release device (like ear implant) and a direct injection. On the other hand, the long term release of high doses might influence the pattern of hormone excretion in the animal's body and this was the intention of using such compounds.

6.151 **Dr. Lucier** indicated that any increase in the magnitude of exposure would likely increase any potential risks, but he did not consider himself qualified to answer the rest of this question.

6.152 **Dr. McLean** responded that the hormones in question, with the exception of MGA, were not well absorbed when administered orally. Grossly excessive doses might have an effect on consumers of meat, but these effects were likely to be mild and transient and could pass without being noticed. The dose prescribed under "good practice" was sufficient to exert a commercially satisfactory response, and there was no advantage in exceeding this dose. The dose suggested by the sponsor gave the optimum response and therefore, within limits, there was no need or benefit in administering more than was suggested. The regulatory authorities also examined the effects of overdosing during the registration process. Most regulatory authorities, including JECFA, required that data for residues setting did take into account dose rates that were in excess of what was normally used (generally at least twice and sometimes more) so that the effect of overdosing or variations in uptake could be seen. In countries where the use of these compounds was permitted, there were good educational campaigns for farmers as to the correct use and the reasons why the prescribed dose should not be exceeded, and the penalties that existed if one did. The results from residues surveys showed that, by and large, there was no exceeding of the MRL. In Australia, trenbolone and zeranol had been targeted in residue surveys very specifically looking for violations, and to all intents and purposes violations did not occur. Even if there was misuse, and that was difficult to prove, there were still no residues that exceeded the MRL. A similar situation existed with the naturally occurring hormones, where it was not possible to determine whether or not a violation had occurred because the levels that were found in the carcass fall within the normal range.

6.153 Dr. McLean observed, however, that in countries where the use was not controlled and there was no farmer education campaign and where it was difficult to apply a penalty, then the MRL was significantly exceeded. One of the important factors of legalizing these compounds was to conduct an education campaign and to put in place monitoring procedures to ensure that the MRL is not exceeded. What was important with the maximum residue limit is to understand that it was a legal limit and not a health limit. In other words, exceeding of the MRL did not represent a hazard to health but rather a limit at which the authorities took action. However, to exceed the MRL would not be considered to be good practice.

6.154 **Dr. Ritter** noted that it was very difficult, if not impossible, to estimate potential hazards which might be associated with the administration of the hormones contrary to good practice, as the magnitude of the potential hazard would be related to the nature, extent, frequency and magnitude of the inappropriate administration. It had been reported that in the case of the anabolic hormones and using commercially available implants, repetitive implantation had only little influence on the residue profile.[302] Similarly, full and half-dosages led to similar hormone levels in edible tissues which, in the case of the endogenous hormones, were within the physiological range. Further, unlawful and improper use of oestradiol might result in residue levels some 300-fold in excess of established tolerance limits, and yet it was virtually impossible to visualize any hazard to humans ingesting meat from animals treated with zeranol.[303] Similarly, when steer calves were implanted with zeranol in accordance with recommended procedures, the margin of safety for consumption of edible products was greater than 25,000 and 150,000 for liver and muscle, respectively. While this work did not specifically address the issue of potential abuse, the large margins of safety postulated by the authors suggested that even under limited circumstances of abuse, it was unlikely that consumers would be exposed to unacceptable risks.[304] In countries where use of these hormones, the six hormones in particular, had been permitted for a very extended period of time, most notably Canada and the United States, monitoring and compliance programmes which had been conducted for many years consistently demonstrated that residue levels were entirely within recommended limits and that instances of violative residues, that was residues which would indicate abuses taking place, had almost never been reported. It seemed that at least in those jurisdictions where use was lawful, the practicality of abuse had never become a reality. There were few and isolated examples of violative residues in those countries where use had been permitted.

Question 15:

> What are the consequences in terms of potential hazards to human or animal health from the use of legally marketed combinations, if they exist, or illegal "cocktails" of the six hormones in dispute for animal growth promotion? Have legally marketed combinations been subject to the same testing regime as each of their individual components? Is there any evidence of synergistic effects of combinations of hormones? Can you think of any incentives or disincentives for farmers to use combinations or illegal "cocktails" of these hormones?

6.155 **Dr. André** replied that specific consequences stemming from the use of legally marketed combinations were not known. If they existed potential hazards could be due to synergistic and/or additive effects of the residues. This answer was also valid for illegal "cocktails" of the six hormones in which more than two components could be present. However there was another important potential hazard from the systematic use of these combinations: their use could result in modifications of kinetic parameters of other drugs. For example, trenbolone and testosterone were shown to dramatically decrease the elimination rate of sulfamethazine, trimethoprim and antipyrine in goats, with opposite experimental results in rats. As a consequence, residue levels could be higher than the MRLs at slaughter, even when legal with-

302 Hoffman and Evers (1986).

303 Truhaut *et al*. (1985).

304 Sundlof and Stickland (1986).

drawal periods were respected.[305] Recently, the increase of the level of beta agonist residues in liver owing to concomitant oestradiol treatment had been demonstrated in calves.[306]

6.156 Dr. André was aware of only one combination (TBA + oestradiol) having been assayed by the JECFA in the context of residue determination in steers. No other combinations had been tested whereas individual components had been tested for toxicological effects. Evidence of synergistic effects of combinations of hormones existed and were well studied mechanisms. For example, concerning endocrinological therapy in humans, combinations of oestrogen and progestin hormones were used; oestrogens induced the synthesis of specific receptors for progestins, which could then exert their specific action. Legally marketed combinations had been developed on the basis of synergistic effects of their components on growth promotion.

6.157 Incentives for farmers to use combinations (legally marketed) or illegal "cocktails" of these hormones were frequently reported by official control bodies, since farmers tended to think that the more hormones used, the better the anabolic effect. Moreover, interactions between these hormones and other endogenous biochemical parameters (e.g. corticoids, IGF, etc.) were of great importance for human health and could be documented.

6.158 **Dr. Arnold** noted that fixed combinations were registered in the form of strictly formulated veterinary medicinal products and were different from illegal mixtures for which the term "cocktail" had been coined in Europe. Fixed combinations were not only used for growth promotion but also for the purposes permitted in the European Union. These combinations were approved and registered by the competent authorities under the respective rules governing veterinary medicinal products. The applicant had to justify the combination and had to demonstrate the quality, efficacy, target animal safety and consumer safety of these products before they could be marketed. For these types of registered products, there was no evidence of a hazard to human health.

6.159 Dr. Arnold reported that the pharmacodynamic and toxic effects of practically all possible combinations of oestrogens, progestins and androgens had been studied in whole animals, organs, tissue and cell cultures, and other *in vitro* systems under a great variety of conditions. There was ample evidence of both synergistic and antagonistic effects. Such effects physiologically played important roles in endocrinology and metabolism. The current understanding of these phenomena clearly indicated that concerns over human health hazards arising from combinations of minute amounts of residues in meat were not justified.

6.160 The flourishing grey market in other veterinary medicines within, for example, Germany showed that farmers tried bypassing official distribution channels when purchasing otherwise licensed high quality products, mainly in order to save costs and prevent having to pay the veterinarian. To what extent "good practices" in the use were otherwise followed remained subject to speculation. It seemed, how-

[305] Van Miert (1988).

[306] Kuiper, *1995 EC Scientific Conference Proceedings*, p.377.

ever, that not all rules were violated at one time. The situation with prohibited substances (e.g. hormones, chloramphenicol) and with abused substances (e.g., clenbuterol) was completely different. There was clearly a black-market where the "dirty products" prevailed. The availability of reasonably priced legal alternative products could be an incentive for many farmers to legalise their practices. Whether this would eliminate illegal cocktails now that the black-market has been well established, remained entirely speculative.

6.161 **Dr. Lucier** indicated that there was a definite research need in area of synergistic and/or antagonistic responses to combinations of endogenous or exogenous hormones. Based on current knowledge, it was likely that interactions existed but it was impossible to say with any degree of confidence for a given combination whether the interaction would be synergistic, additive or antagonistic. There was limited evidence to suggest that synergistic responses were occurring although the relevance of these findings to human risks had not been shown. Dr. Lucier noted that the same combinations of hormones, at certain levels, could have both some adverse health effects and some positive ones.

6.162 **Dr. McLean** replied that the legally marketed combinations had been examined by regulatory authorities to ensure that residues did not exceed levels seen in normal animals or the prescribed MRL. There were synergistic growth promoting effects seen in treated animals. Illegal "cocktails" were mostly found in countries where the use of hormones was prohibited, resulting in the establishment of an illegal market. They were not normally used where the full range of drugs was available because there was no advantage in the use of illegal drugs, and registered products were usually cheaper and of consistent quality.

6.163 **Dr. Ritter** noted that when growth promoting hormones were used as combinations, this use did not alter existing MRLs which had been either recommended internationally or established by national regulatory authorities, and hence the use of hormone combinations was not likely to have any direct adverse consequences in terms of human health. In the case of "illegal" cocktails, it was impossible to speculate on the potential for adverse effects in either humans or animals, as this potential would be a function of the nature of the cocktail, the species of use, the dose, frequency and duration of use, and a range of other factors which could not be assumed.

6.164 In general, safety (toxicology) evaluations of drugs, pesticides and other food contaminants were carried out on single compounds only, rather than as combinations. There were several reasons for this approach which included prior pharmacological and biochemical knowledge that toxicity associated with combinations was not likely to produce effects greater than the sum of the individual components. On a more practical level, it was difficult to contemplate the broad range of possible combinations which would be the subject of testing. Finally, as different commercial interests might be involved in the production and sale of various growth promoting hormones, proprietary interests would make it unlikely that combinations could be evaluated toxicologically. In some cases, the efficacy of hormone combinations had been evaluated. In the case of combinations of trenbolone with zeranol or oestradiol, for example, it was found that (i) the combinations were equivalent in young bulls and steers, (ii) anabolics containing oestradiol were more effective in veal calves, and (iii) the composition and quality of the meat was not modified by the use of combinations when compared to single use.[307] As with any drug or unlawful drug combination, farmers sometimes were under the incorrect impression that combinations which had not been evaluated might provide significantly enhanced efficacy over those which had been approved for use. Such improper use of illegal cocktails could affect withdrawal times and residue limits and might, in some jurisdictions, result in compliance and enforcement as disincentives to the unlawful use of non-approved cocktails. Dr. Ritter noted that it must also be recognized that the quest for ever improved yield could lead some producers to the use of unapproved drug combinations.

6.165 **Dr. Randell** indicated that the monographs which were prepared by JECFA at the 32nd session clearly indicated that trials were done on mixed implants as well as on single substance implants. JECFA had considered such mixtures as oestradiol together with testosterone, oestradiol together with progesterone, oestradiol benzoate together with testosterone propionate and also oestradiol with trenbolone acetate under the oestradiol evaluations. These were known to JECFA at the time, and the pharma-kcenetics of these substances as they were gradually metabolized and excreted by the animals were studied by the experts at that time. Moreover, the information which was available to JECFA included carcinogenicity studies for all of the substances concerned.

Question 16:

> Which substances in addition to the hormone compounds at issue are present in the commercially available products marketed for animal growth promotion? Are there any potential adverse effects on human or animal health? Question 33: Further to question 16, are there other substances in human implants potentially dangerous to human health?

6.166 **Dr. André** noted that if the question referred to the excipient or to potential sub-products of synthesis, these data, as property of manufacturers, remained confidential. Concerning the simultaneous use of other drugs marketed for growth promotion (e.g. antibiotics), their residue levels could be modified by the use of the hormones (see response to question 15), so that a potential adverse effect on human health could appear.

6.167 **Dr. Arnold** indicated that other growth promoters (antibacterials) were used under the feed additives legislation of the European Communities (e.g., flavomycin, virginiamycin, zinc bacitracin, salinomycin, monensin, lasalocid). The review process was centralised. There were no known potential adverse effects on human or animal health if these additives are properly used. The use of glycopeptide avoparcin was recently withdrawn as a precautionary measure because of some suspicion that glycopeptid-resistance selected by the use in animal production could be transferred to human-pathogenic enterococci.

6.168 **Dr. Lucier** responded that there are many known cases of the presence of oestrogenic substances arising from plant products, pesticides and industrial con-

[307] Bouffault and Willemart (1983).

taminants. It was likely that the oestrogenic potency of these substances, taken together, exceeded that from meat residues of the six hormones in question.

6.169 **Dr. McLean** stated that there were a number of non-active components used in the implants to ensure that the drug was delivered over the life of the implant. These included a carrier for the drug and an inert matrix which made up the implant. The formulation was approved by the regulatory authorities in each country. The components were often used in human and other animal drug formulations and their safety had been established.

6.170 **Dr. Ritter** replied that the composition of commercially available products was generally regarded as proprietary information. Consequently, he had no direct knowledge of the identity of the substances other than the hormones which might be present in commercially available hormone preparations.

Question 17:

> What are the implications for human or animal health of residues from misplaced implants or improper administration, i.e. when administered differently than indicated in the label of the manufacturer, of any of the six hormones in dispute ?

6.171 **Dr. André** indicated that the consumption of meat (or of any meat-containing food preparation) containing a misplaced implant could be a hazard for human health, in particular for children, fetuses, pregnant women or immunodeficient people. Misadministration of any of the six hormones in dispute could change the kinetics of elimination of these hormones and induce a subsequent higher level of residues. This could become a real health hazard if there was systematical misuse.

6.172 **Dr. Arnold** observed that there might be a concern only where misplacement (growth promotion) or improper administration (therapy, zootechnical treatment) lead to consumption of a whole implant or injection site. Otherwise, residues remaining in the carcass of the respective animal would have no effects, even if they were higher than would be expected if "good practices" had been applied. The worst case assumption was that a whole fresh implant containing oestradiol or an ester of this hormone is consumed, because the implanted dose was higher than the doses injected for the other purposes and orally active oestradiol-doses were lower than the required doses of the other hormones. If this entire dose was ingested at once, only transient effects on hormonal feedback mechanisms would be expected. Clear hormonal effects would occur if an entire injection site was processed, e.g., into a meat containing product and the same person would eat the whole product in divided portions over a couple of days.

6.173 **Dr. Lucier** stated that improper or misplaced implants could very well increase residues, thereby increasing the potential risk of the hormones in question. Preventive strategies for misuse needed to involve veterinary supervision, educational programmes, monitoring and stiff penalties for abuse.

6.174 **Dr. McLean** replied that the implants would likely be detected if they were eaten because the matrix could not be chewed. If swallowed, they would not be digested but would pass through the human gastrointestinal tract largely unchanged. The implications of misplaced implants may not be of great concern because they were often placed under the skin and removed at slaughter or during processing. In order to facilitate correct and easy administration, applicators were generally available from the pharmaceutical companies. One of the features of injections subcutaneously in the ear was that there was no massive reaction at the site. It was specifically designed, and all the residue studies were carried out, with the implant injected in the ear. The aim of injecting it there was to get prolonged and slow release at low levels over a period of time. It was specifically designed to be that way. Moreover, the injections were usually implanted in the ear because it was very easy to palpate a pellet or an implant under the skin of the ear which was a second way of identifying treated animals.

6.175 **Dr. Ritter** responded that the growth promoting hormones were generally administered as feed additives or as implants. In the event that implants were implanted at sites other than those recommended, it was possible that these sites contain unacceptably high residue levels if utilized as a source of human food. The selection of the ear as a site of implantation rather than other sites was because it was a tissue which normally did not enter the food chain and it made identification of the source of the material very easy. Injection site residues, which could be much higher than normal tissue residue levels, were thus extremely unlikely to enter the food supply. The extent to which acceptable residue levels might be exceeded would depend on the exact site of implantation and the withdrawal period involved. The implication for human health would in turn be related to these two variables.

6.176 Dr. Ritter indicated that illegal injection of oestradiol preparation could produce injection site residues which largely exceeded tolerances. In the case of feed additives, improper use might imply use of approved drugs in non-approved species, improper dose, improper combinations, improper duration of use and improper withdrawal periods. However, the provision of human safety was assured through the establishment of maximum residue levels, levels considered to be safe if consumed by humans in the diet for an entire lifespan. In the event that any of the improper use conditions noted above occurred, and to the extent that such improper use would impact on final residue levels, human safety was assured through appropriate monitoring of the food supply for compliance with approved MRLs.

Question 18:

> What are the effects on growth promotion of the use of female hormones on male animals and vice-versa? Are there any potential adverse effects on human or animal health from such use?

6.177 **Dr. André** said that the effects of hormones on growth promotion was sex-dependent. The use of male hormones associated with female hormones (ratio 10:1) in heifers had the best anabolic effect without sexual behaviour problems and vice-versa. Concerning the human health, the level of residues had to be taken into account, whatever the gender of the meat producing animals. Concerning animal health, the use of oestrogenic compounds in male animals was shown to result in squamous metaplasia, hyperplasia of the collecting ducts and fibromuscular hypertrophy in the prostate and bulbo-urethral gland, fibromuscular hypertrophy and hypoplasia of the epithelium in the seminal vesicles and epididymis and impaired testicular development. In female animals, oestrogen treatment resulted in squamous metaplasia and fibromuscular hypertrophy in the Bartholin's gland, hyperplasia and secretory activity in the vagina and cervix, and impaired follicular developments in the ovaries. The latter could also be observed when females were treated with androgens, impaired follicular developments in the ovaries sometimes resulted in cystic ovaries.

6.178 **Dr. Arnold** indicated that supplemental oestrogens in castrated males increased growth rate, presumably through an increase of endogenous levels of growth hormone, improved feed efficiency and reduced aggressive behaviour. Testosterone was mainly used to slow down the release rate of oestradiol because blood levels required for anabolic effects could not be reached with implants. No adverse effects were known on humans. The use in animals of hormonally active growth promoters might have behavioural side-effects in individual animals.

6.179 **Dr. Lucier** observed that some effects, possibly adverse, could occur in the animals receiving the growth-promoted substances. These effects could include feminization of male animals and masculinization of female animals based on both molecular and biological endpoints. These effects should not occur in people eating meat containing residues at the MRL of the hormones in question.

6.180 **Dr. McLean** commented that there was a wide range of combinations and doses available for a range of types of cattle. The combinations were designed to ensure maximum dose response in the target animals. These combinations had been subjected to studies to ensure that the residue levels did not exceed prescribed values.

6.181 **Dr. Ritter** indicated he had no expertise in this area.

Question 19:

> What differences exist between the therapeutic or zootechnical use of hormones permitted by the EC and the use of hormones for growth promotion purposes, as permitted in the US and in accordance with good animal husbandry practice and/or good veterinary practice, in terms of administered quantities, residue levels and potential adverse effects on human or animal health? Do common therapeutic or zootechnical uses of the hormones in question in the EC involve large scale (ie.,whole herd) or repetitive treatments?

6.182 **Dr. André** observed that the use of the hormones for therapeutic or zootechnical purposes and for growth promotion purposes was not comparable for many reasons. The number of animals treated was different, as for therapeutic use very few animals were treated. For zootechnical purposes, the number was higher but remained limited. There were no systematic, repetitive treatments. For growth promotion purposes, the number of animals seemed to be large.

6.183 In addition, Dr. André stressed that the future of the animals treated either for therapeutic or zootechnical purposes or for growth promotion purposes was very different. In the first case the animals usually remained on the farm for months or years after treatment and the problem of residues was not of concern. The only comparable situation was for oestradiol benzoate, for which, in case of unsuccessful treatment in a cow, a withdrawal period of two months had to be observed. In the second case, the animals were slaughtered weeks or months after the treatment. Furthermore, the delivery conditions differed. In the EC, the therapeutic use of these hormones was particularly regulated. Finally, Dr. André noted that none of these therapeutic/zootechnical uses would change the level of residues of hormones in meat on large scale as occurred from growth promotion use. No scientist had said that it was a bad thing to use these hormones for therapeutical use; their use on a large scale for growth promotion was not the same thing.

6.184 **Dr. Arnold** replied that the total dose contained in an implant of oestradiol-17β was much higher than the dose injected for therapeutic purposes because the implant contained the quantity needed over a long time (e.g., 200 days). On a daily basis, however, the dose injected was much higher, and therefore, tissue residues (excluding the injection site) after treatment were much higher if compared with the residues measured at any time after implantation. No representative data were available for progesterone or testosterone that would permit comparisons. With the exception of oestrus synchronisation, individual identified animals were treated.

6.185 **Dr. Lucier** indicated that it was possible that extraordinarily low residues (likely non-detectable) of the hormones could be present at slaughter if the animals had received the hormones for therapeutic use (see response to question 3).

6.186 **Dr. McLean** replied that the therapeutic use of hormones generally required the administration of a larger dose, which in turn resulted in greater levels of residues. The persistence of these residues depended on the dose, formulation and site of administration. Individual animals or groups of animals were often treated at one time, but rarely the whole herd. Treatments may be repeated. Treated animals should be identified so that they were not slaughtered for human food until a suitable withdrawal period had elapsed. It was often necessary to withhold milk. When hormones were used for growth promotion, the implants slowly released the active ingredients and there was never a high peak of hormones in the tissues. In the case of therapeutic use, there often was a significant peak.

6.187 **Dr. Ritter** responded that the primary difference between the therapeutic and/or zootechnical uses of the hormones permitted by the Community when compared to growth promoting uses related primarily to the frequency of use, dose, and the potential number of animals to be treated. In all cases, therapeutic and/or zootechnical uses would generally involve lower doses at less frequent intervals in fewer animals, and, in the case of the Community, was restricted to administration by a licensed veterinarian. Notwithstanding, at least in the case of the natural hormones, the approach adopted by the Community for therapeutic/zootechnical uses provided for residue levels which fell within the range of levels normally found in untreated animals. While the basis for use of these hormones for growth promotion purposes was fundamentally different, the resulting residues appeared, nevertheless, to also fall well within the normal physiological range.

Question 20:

> Do you consider that the conditions imposed by the EC for the therapeutic or zootechnical use of these hormones can achieve its aim of avoiding any potential adverse effects on human health resulting from residues in meat from animals treated for such purposes?

6.188 **Dr. André** commented that this question was not related to a scientific expertise, and as a consequence, he could only give a personal opinion. When used for therapeutic or zootechnical purposes, these hormones were used by (or under the control of) veterinarians. This guaranteed that they were used according to the indications for which they had been registered (i.e. dosage, route of administration, withdrawal period). Moreover these hormones were used either on individual animals or in well defined herds, usually in order to synchronize oestrus. In this case, the animals were reproducting animals, they had a high value and would be slaughtered only several years after the treatment. The problem of residues was not of concern for these animals. It could not be compared with the use of these hormones for growth promotion. When used for therapeutic purposes, these drugs were needed to restore health and the benefit/cost ratio was very high. When used for zootechnical purposes, the consequence for a great majority of the animals was to become pregnant and, exceptionally, to be slaughtered.

6.189 **Dr. Arnold** indicated that the products which could be used were reviewed according to the criteria established for the approval process of veterinary medicinal products, including established withdrawal times. If the approved conditions of use were observed, any potential adverse effects on human health resulting from residues in animals treated for such purposes could be avoided.

6.190 **Dr. Lucier** replied that the EC measures for the therapeutic or zootechnical use of these hormones could not guarantee "zero risk", although the potential risks were likely lower than risks from their use as growth promoter.

6.191 **Dr. McLean** responded that he was not fully familiar with practices in the Community. However, studies on antibiotic residues have shown that the involvement of veterinarians in the control and prescribing of antibiotics on farms did not always guarantee that residues would be controlled. The same situation would probably exist with hormones.

6.192 **Dr. Ritter** recalled that the Community allowed the administration of oestradiol, testosterone and progesterone to animals for therapeutic and zootechnical purposes only under conditions which restricted administration to a veterinarian, required registration of treatments and a sufficient withdrawal period. Given the nature of conditions imposed for such use, it was unlikely that residues resulting from exogenous application of the gonadol hormones would be present as residues. Notwithstanding, growth promotion uses of the natural hormones similarly would not result in residue levels in excess of those expected in untreated animals.

Question 21:

> Is there a difference in terms of potential adverse effects on human or animal health between residues of these hormones administered as feed additives, compared to residues of these hormones which are implanted or injected?

6.193 **Dr. André** indicated that as far as he knew, the metabolism of these hormones administered as feed additives had not been studied. To produce residues meant that they were absorbed, and that they are efficient and metabolised. Nevertheless, their use as feed additives could induce a risk for people potentially in contact with these hormones (factories, farmers, children etc.), and a risk for the environment.

6.194 **Dr. Arnold** responded that melengestrol acetate was only used as a feed additive. Zeranol and trenbolone acetate were used as implants only. Oestradiol-17β, progesterone and testosterone were administered by different routes including injection and implantation. It was difficult to make comparisons about potential effects due to means of administration because there were too many variables in the equation (chemical nature, dose, route, formulation, target species). If all uses were carried out in compliance with the established conditions of use, the remaining residues could be regarded as safe. The safety margins might vary from one condition to the other and the consequences of non-compliance might also be different.

6.195 **Dr. Lucier** commented that the residues would be the same in terms of chemical structure, although the residue levels could be different quantitatively.

6.196 **Dr. McLean** observed that the control of the administration of hormones to animals as feed additives was by removing them from feed at a given time. In practice, because of carry-over in feed mixing plants and residues in storage silos and feeding stalls, there was not a sharply defined cut-off point. In the case of antibiotics, it was often necessary to use a dedicated mixing plant to avoid carry-over from treated to untreated feed. The dose absorbed could also vary depending on food intake and absorption from the gut. There was also the problem of accurately mixing small amounts of potent active ingredients through the feed. Injection was more accurate and reliable, and on balance the method of choice.

6.197 **Dr. Ritter** replied that potential adverse effects on human health invariably related to residues which exceeded acceptable limits. Proper use of growth promoting hormones as either implants or feed additives might result in residues which, if used in accordance with recommended and approved practice, should not exceed acceptable levels regardless of the method or means of administration. He noted that improperly placed implants could result in failure to properly identify implantation sites at slaughter and could thereby result in excessively high residues in those tissues which would otherwise be identified and removed. Properly located implants, when implanted in accordance with approved practice, should not result in unacceptable residues and hence there should be little impact on potential adverse human health effects regardless of the method or route of administration.

Question 22:

> With respect to Zeranol, Trenbolone and MGA, what are currently the technological limits of detection and/or quantitation of residues? Ie., what is the lowest level of residue which can be detected?

6.198 **Dr. André** observed that these hormones were considered as classical banned compounds (within the EC). They were controlled with methods whose limits of detection (LD) were equal or better than 2 ppb. However, most methods in use for screening purposes of these hormones were immunological ones. Their real limits of detection were usually lower than 0.5 ppb. Mass spectrometric methods allowed confirmation of results at this level. Furthermore, using techniques with high performance output such as high resolution mass spectrometry or MS-MS, the level of 10 ppt. or so could be reached.

6.199 **Dr. Arnold** replied that the technological limitations would allow the quantification of certain residues in certain tissues at concentrations below 1 ng/kg. This could not, however, be achieved in routine monitoring. Moreover, the limits of detection of current routinely applied methods may vary from country to country (within certain limits). Only few methods had been internationally collaboratively studied according to internationally harmonised protocols. Only few methods were fully validated in accordance with the criteria first defined by the Codex Alimentarius and later adopted by the EEC in Directive 85/592.

6.200 **Dr. McLean** explained that there were two basic types of assays used. *Screening methods* were used to detect drugs for metabolites at the level of interest.

These had high sample throughput and aimed to avoid false negative results. *Confirmatory methods* provided unequivocal identification of the drug and/or metabolites at the level of interest. The cost of analysis was considerably greater than for screening methods. These methods were constantly being reappraised.

6.201 **Dr. Ritter** responded that methodology for MGA had been reported[308] with a limit of detection of 5 ppb. and a limit of quantitation of 10 ppb., both in fat, the target tissue for this residue. LC methodology for the trenbolone acetate had been reported[309] with a limit of detection of 2 ppb in muscle and liver for β-trenbolone, and a limit of quantitation of 2 ppb in muscle and 4 ppb in liver for α-trenbolone in liver and kidney. GC/MS methodology for zeranol had been reported by Covey *et al* (1988) with a limit of detection of 0.1 ppb. and a limit of quantitation of 0.2 ppb. in liver or muscle. The Joint FAO/WHO Expert Committee on Food Additives (WHO, 1988) reported that radioimmunoassays could detect free and conjugated α- and β-trenbolone at levels of 75ng/kg in tissues. Radioimmunoassays were generally regarded as appropriate screening methods only, while conventional analytical procedures such as gas chromatography/liquid chromatography/mass spectrometry are generally regarded as suitable for confirmatory analysis.

Question 23:

> Can you describe how the EC ban is enforced in the EC's internal market both formally and in practice? How is the EC ban enforced at the EC's borders both formally and in practice? How are the conditions linked to the exceptions to the ban (i.e. administration of hormones for therapeutic and zootechnical purposes) enforced, both formally and in practice, in the EC's internal market and at the EC's borders? What is the formal content and practical effect of the EC's control programme which ensures that imported products do not receive treatment more favourable than domestic products?

6.202 **Dr. André** noted that this question was not related to scientific expertise. From a personal point of view he believed that the important number of workshops, international congresses (e.g. Congress on Anabolizing Agents in Gent : 1992, 1993, 1994; Euroresidue I in 1990, Euroresidue II in 1993, Euroresidue III in 1996), laboratory networks system, European research programmes, as well as the development of Quality Assurance Systems in Europe had to be considered.

6.203 **Dr. Arnold** replied that since its entry into force Council Directive 86/469/EEC had essentially harmonised the control of residues in live animals and meat. Starting from 1987, EC member States presented an annual updated national residue control plan for approval by the Commission. The results of residue controls were also reported to the Commission. The Directive was very clear and relatively inflexible in what concerned the identification of the substances and the species of animals to be checked and the number of samples to be taken. Unfortunately, a major part of the analytical capacities of the laboratories of the EC member States had to be used regularly to monitor substances which did not necessarily present the real problem areas (e.g., the stilbene oestrogens).

---

[308] Anderson and Fesser (1996).

[309] Shih-Hsien Hsu *et al* . (1988).

6.204 The scientific concept behind sampling, however, was not clear and was subject to different interpretations. It seemingly mixed elements of a statistically based monitoring system with other concepts. The reporting format was only semi-quantitative with respect to the reported residue contents of positive samples. In consequence, the results could not be used to compare the situation in the EC member States or, for example, to conduct a crude assessment of exposure of European consumers to residues of anabolic substances.

6.205 Dr. Arnold further explained that a network of reference laboratories had recently been set up with an outstanding European reference laboratory on top. However, the moderate financial contribution to the European reference laboratories from the Commission was given only on an annual basis, leading to difficulties in ensuring experienced permanent staff in these institutes. The quality of the national reference laboratories co-ordinating the activities of the routine laboratories carrying out the daily work could not be judged. Although it was not known how many routine laboratories were accredited nationally, it was obvious that systems of quality management had not yet been established everywhere in the Community.

6.206 The endogenous production in the animals of oestradiol-17β, testosterone and progesterone causes difficulties in the control of their use. MRLs have not been set, and cannot be set, for the therapeutic and zootechnical uses, because the distribution of the three natural hormones in the three categories of animals (untreated animals, animals illegally treated for growth promotion, and animals legally treated for the permitted purposes) largely overlap. Because withdrawal times could not be enforced on a broad scale and distribution chains were insufficiently controlled, only limited attempts - requiring a lot of man-power and other resources - could be made to enforce compliance. If there was a suspicion, of course, the animal involved can be traced back and the producer questioned about, e.g., the prescription of the drug, the veterinarian involved etc. The main difficulty was to identify suspect animals in order to start further investigations and measures. Only the discovery of an injection site or an implant containing illegal substances could provide proof of a treatment. Decision limits for the levels of oestradiol-17β had provisionally been established in order to identify suspect animals.

6.207 Enforcement was difficult if people did not want to comply with the legal rules - which otherwise would perfectly guarantee consumer protection. It appeared that illegal anabolic hormones were readily available. The expectation of extra profits was an incentive for the continued the use of these substances including beta agonists, not only for farmers but also for participants in the illegal network of distribution.

6.208 **Dr. Arnold** recalled that the requirements of Directive 86/469/EEC also applied to third countries exporting live animals and meat to the Community. Missions were regularly sent to these countries to evaluate their systems of residue monitoring and surveillance. At the border, enforcement relied entirely on the discriminating power of analytical methods. This was not possible in the case of meat from animals treated for therapeutic or zootechnical purposes, because this meat was not different from meat obtained from animals never treated or treated with the same substances for growth promotion. Although domestically produced and imported products were formally treated equally, the possibility of detecting illegal practices of growth promotion (illegal referring to non-compliance with EU legislation, not to uses which were also prohibited in the country of origin) was probably significantly greater for domestically produced meat because of the possibilities to inspect production plants with a history of non-compliance, to take samples from live animals, etc.

6.209 **Dr. Ritter** indicated that he had no expertise with regard to EC enforcement, in relation to a discussion about the number of animals checked per year in the European Communities and other countries. However, he noted that the number of samples taken could be misleading. The intent of any monitoring programme was the development of a programme that had the statistical confidence necessary to detect violations to the extent that the compound was used, to identify residue levels which were out of compliance. The relevant question was whether the monitoring programme was statistically confident and able to detect compliance. Most monitoring programmes were intended to detect a 5 per cent violation rate 95 per cent of the time. The number of samples that were required to do that varied from country to country and from commodity to commodity because it was a function of the use practices for the substances involved.

Question 24:

> What analytical methods, or other technical means, of residue detection exist to control the use of the six hormones in dispute for growth promotion purposes in accordance with good animal husbandry practice and/or good veterinary practice. What means exist to control the use by farmers of the six hormones in dispute for growth promotion purposes in accordance with good animal husbandry practice and/or good veterinary practice? What are their respective cost implications?

6.210 **Dr. André** replied that since these hormones were prohibited within Europe, their control was included in national plans, the aim of which was to survey their misuse. Analytical methods were available both for screening purposes and confirmatory purposes. For screening purposes, several methods had been developed. Research was also carried out to prove the exogenous origin of natural hormones, when detected in urine samples, based on methods used in human for doping control. For confirmatory purposes, different methods existed, with most of the available methods being based on GC-MS detection and identification. These techniques had been developed for matrices like urine, fat, tissue, faeces or injection sites.

6.211 **Dr. Arnold** noted that the analytical community of the European Communities was very active. To provide the appropriate methodology to detect illegal practices of growth promotion - particularly the potentially hazardous practices involving black market drugs - was a great challenge for the scientists working in both academic and official laboratories. As a result, a large number of probably valid - although not always validated - methods relying on different principles was available. Furthermore, in the European Communities it was possible to inspect farms and sample live animals, with the consequence of fines or legal prosecution in case of violations.

6.212 **Dr. McLean** indicated that descriptions of analytical methods use were published by the regulatory authorities of many countries. Control of use by farmers was done through legislation which detailed restrictions on the sale, possession and use of the various hormonal preparations. The cost of these measures varied from country to country and the cost of analysis depends on the drug in question and whether screening or confirmatory methods were employed.

6.213 **Dr. Ritter** responded that the residue detection methodology utilized to control the use of the six growth promoting hormones generally followed those procedures described in question 22. Detection methodologies for veterinary drug residues were largely described by two main types of analysis (Blanchflower, 1995). Screening methods generally had a high sample throughout, permitting analysis of large numbers of samples in a relatively short period of time, and at minimal cost. They generally had a low probability of false negatives and could detect, but not accurately quantify, potentially positive samples. Screening methods for the growth promoters were typically represented by the radio immunoassays. In contrast, confirmatory methods were used to confirm unequivocally, and to quantitate, the presence of a drug residue. They were characterized by relatively low throughput and high cost both in terms of equipment and supplies, and a low probability of false positives.

6.214 Control of veterinary drugs used in food production by farmers was generally achieved by national authorities through imposition of regulations requiring that drugs of this type be dispensed only on the written authority of a properly qualified veterinarian and in compliance with relevant use information established by appropriate national regulatory authorities. Compliance was further assured through rigorous monitoring and, where appropriate, through enforcement activity. Cost implications generally related to the increased cost associated with the requirement that such drugs only be administered under the authority of a properly qualified veterinarian. Costs would also be proportional to the rigour with which a monitoring and compliance programme was designed and implemented.

Question 25:

> What analytical methods, or other technical means, exist to control the use of the six hormones in dispute according to the conditions set out in the proposal of the EC Commission in 1984 (COM(84)295 final) and what are their respective cost implications?

6.215 **Dr. André** noted that this twelve year old proposal had been rejected by the European Parliament.

6.216 **Dr. Arnold** recalled that this proposal had envisaged the controlled use of the three natural hormones for growth promotion and proposed re-visiting the prohibitions of trenbolone acetate and zeranol after a scientific evaluation of these substances. In analytical terms, the enforcement problems would have been similar to those of today because residues in meat remaining after the (proposed) legalised uses for growth promotion would not have differed significantly from residues found after illegal uses in most cases. The pharmaceutical industry could have applied for marketing authorization of strictly formulated products, which would have been evaluated and approved under the veterinary medicines directives. There would have been competition between high-quality, efficacious and safe products and products of the black-market. However, Dr. Arnold could not judge whether this would have limited the growth of the now existing black market, thereby reducing the costs of enforcement.

6.217 **Dr. McLean** noted that the methods proposed in that Directive were similar to the methods now used in other countries. However, the passage of time had permitted better analytical technology and techniques and increased automation, often resulting in increased laboratory throughput at decreased cost per sample. Farmers were also much better educated about the need to avoid residues which exceeded the

MRL. The Community would now be in a much better position to screen for residues in meat products than it was in 1984.

Question 26:

> Are there other products (including veterinary drugs) commonly used in the production of meat and animal products which have comparable potential adverse effects on human or animal health as the six hormones in question? If so, what analytical methods, or other technical means, of residue detection exist to control their use in accordance with good animal husbandry practice and/or good veterinary practices. What technical means exist to control their use by farmers in accordance with good animal husbandry practice and/or good veterinary practice? How do the cost implications for controlling the use of these other products differ from those used to control the use of the six hormones in question?

6.218 **Dr. André** responded that to the extent a compound was active as a drug, it could exert toxic effects. Drugs were submitted to regulation and were registered for precise indications, under precise conditions, including data on MRLs and definition of withdrawal periods (see also response to question 10). Several methods for control were available. Drugs could only be registered for use when a method designed for residue control existed. Networks of laboratories and control plans were set up for drugs according to the same scheme as the one used for illegal drugs.

6.219 For products for which particular conditions of use were indicated, the control was usually in the hands of practitioners. New recording systems were under development (see response to question 1). Controls by official bodies (e.g. Veterinary Inspection Services) were effective in some countries. In other countries regulations were changing in order to apply EC Directive 96/23, allowing for more controls to be performed on the farm itself. This was particularly true for the hormones in dispute, as for other banned compounds (chloramphenicol, rhonidazol, etc.).

6.220 **Dr. Arnold** indicated that a rather large number of active principles (probably a few hundred) were used as veterinary drugs in one or all countries involved in this dispute. Some substances were so active that their therapeutic doses were as low as micrograms per kilogramme of body weight of the animal. Other substances were used in both veterinary medicine and in crop protection, with some transfer of residues from animal feed via products of animal origin to the human consumer. Considerable progress had been made to regulate these substances on the basis of "tolerances" for residues or MRLs. Many of the underlying ADIs had been proposed by JECFA. More JECFA evaluations had indirectly been appreciated and found acceptance (e.g., in the MRL setting process within the European Union) as one would conclude from the list of substances which had formally passed the elaboration process of the Codex Alimentarius Commission.

6.221 In the European Communities, no new active principle had been placed on the market since 1992 unless a Community MRL had been established under the provisions of regulation 2377/90. New animal drug applications had to be accompanied by a proposed regulatory method suitable to enforce tolerances/MRLs. The main performance characteristics (accuracy, precision, limit of detection, limit of quantification, specificity) and the ruggedness, practicability, applicability, susceptibility to interference of the methods were reviewed together with the other documentation relating to the quality, safety and efficacy of the drug.

6.222 The review of the old substances, however, was still ongoing. The evaluation of the old substances had also begun in the pesticides sector. The majority of these substances had a long history of uses. Although they had never been evaluated according to contemporary safety requirements, they could probably be regarded as safe in the light of the experience with these substances. Should new evidence indicate that human health hazards could arise from the permitted uses of these substances, the competent authorities would withdraw the respective products until the problems were clarified. There were some examples, however, where highly efficacious substances with a long history of use had to be withdrawn from the market of veterinary drugs for food animals when more contemporary standards were applied in their re-evaluation (e.g., chloramphenicol, nitrofuranes, nitroimidazoles).

6.223 When old substances were reviewed in the Community to establish MRLs, the Committee for Veterinary Medicinal Products always considered the available analytical methodology. An MRL was not proposed if no analytical method was available. The review of the methods and international harmonisation of methods suitable for the enforcement of Codex Standards was conducted by the FAO/WHO Codex Committee for Residues of Veterinary Drugs in Foods.

6.224 The more difficult problem was to monitor so many substances in all foods of animal origin. The chemical properties of these substances were so different that it was impossible to include all residues in a few multi-residue methods. There were substances requiring special equipment for their detection. It was not practically feasible to monitor all potential residues in all food commodities every year. The most reasonable approach was to categorise compounds according to potential hazard and the likely exposure of consumers to the residues. Some compounds required inclusion in residue-monitoring programmes every year; others might be selected for longer cycles. For a few compounds, perhaps no monitoring was necessary. Directive 86/469/EEC covered veterinary drug residues in meat. Starting in 1988, EC member States and countries exporting meat to the Community had to submit residue control plans also for these substances. EC member States had more flexibility to adapt the plans to the actual needs (e.g., areas of risk). The new legislation adopted in 1996 enlarged the scope to cover other foods than meat. An increasing number of screening tests were now available which were based, e.g. on microbiological inhibition or immunochemistry. These methods were suitable to identify suspect "positives" (samples violating MRLs) and exhibit a low rate of "false-negative" results. However, an important aspect of the control of "good practices" was the control of distribution; distribution of veterinary drugs was not harmonised in the Community.

6.225 **Dr. McLean** replied that many products used in animal production had the potential to cause adverse effects on human or animal health. The hazard was identified and managed through the use of "good practice", the application of an MRL, residue surveys and legal sanctions for violations (see also responses to questions 11, 22 and 24). There was no significant difference in the cost implications for controlling the use of other veterinary drugs when compared with the hormones.

6.226 **Dr. Ritter** replied that there were a variety of products, including veterinary drugs and pesticides, which were utilized in the production of meat and animal products. Establishment of MRLs for other production aids, including both veterinary drugs and pesticides, implied that these chemicals could also be used essentially free of potential adverse effects in the human population, provided that appropriate conditions had been followed in the use of the production aid. Simply stated, once MRLs had been established, adherence to internationally accepted maximum limits implied that all products carry similar risks, or more appropriately stated, a similar lack of risk, as did the hormones at issue in this dispute.

6.227 Control of use was generally accommodated through appropriate control of sale (restriction of use generally associated with "prescription" drugs) and rigorous monitoring and compliance programmes, further supported by appropriate enforcement action. In regard to analytical methodology available for detection and monitoring purposes, both screening and confirmatory methods were utilized. Availability of appropriate and reliable analytical methodology for other production aids, such as veterinary drugs, varied somewhat with the specific agent and might range from difficulties of bound residues with carbadox and nitrofuran, to the special and important considerations which were necessary when assessing the microbiological risk due to residues of antimicrobial drugs in food.

Question 27:

> What potential adverse effects on human health arise from the occasional consumption of meat containing residues in excess of the Codex MRL in the case of Zeranol and Trenbolone?

6.228 **Dr. André** noted that all of the previously described potential adverse effects on human health may arise. With regard to their hormonal effects, the lower the frequency and the level of residue, the smaller is the risk of health hazards. With regard to their potential carcinogenic effects, the frequency of consumption and the level of residue was not of concern.

6.229 **Dr. Arnold** indicated that if the residues were due to treatment of the animals and not to contamination of the meat and the meat was not an injection site so that the causes of the violation of the MRLs were limited to biological variability of the animals response to treatment; he did not know of any specific adverse effect on human health which could arise from the occasional consumption of such meat because of non-compliance with the established conditions of use, and if this was a single, rare or occasional event Any such event would, however, require regulatory action and - where indicated - legal prosecution in order to guarantee the integrity of the margin of safety which had been found to be required to ensure the medium and long-term protection of the consumers' health.

6.230 **Dr. Lucier** responded that it would be necessary to conduct formal risk assessments to estimate exposure-effect relationships following different levels of exposure for the six hormones. In order to be useful, endpoints of concern needed to be determined (i.e., cancer, hormonal effects, etc.) and dose response models applied and/or developed that made use of all available and relevant information. It might be necessary to conduct additional research to put the risk assessments on a credible scientific foundation. It should be noted, however, that one would never have all the scientific information needed to remove all uncertainty in risk assessments. Priorities had to be agreed upon regarding which pieces of information are most critical. It was also important to note that selection of the risk assessment. model could influence the result. Threshold or linear models might give different results although if "mimicking of hormone effects" were determinative, then the issue of threshold was not relevant since physiological levels of the natural hormone exceeded any threshold that might exist (see response to question 8). The synthetic hormones could exert toxic effects not only related to their hormone action but also because of other structural/functional properties.

6.231 **Dr. McLean** observed that the occasional consumption of meat containing levels in excess of the Codex MRL was of no health concern. The degree of excess would need to be defined, but the type of toxic response and NOEL would give some guidance. It must be remembered that the NOEL was derived taking into account studies involving administration for a lifetime, with the lowest effect level based on a response which could be as minor as a body weight change.

6.232 **Dr. Ritter** replied that in view of several assumptions inherent in the models utilized to develop MRLs, which overestimated safety (NOEL, application of safety factors, assumption that MRL was always present and that dietary exposure to residues would occur daily for an entire lifespan), it is most unlikely that significant potential adverse effects on human health would arise from the occasional consumption of meat containing residues in excess of the Codex MRL for zeranol and trenbolone. It was, however, important to note that the potential for adverse effects increased as a function of both the frequency and exposure level regarding consumption of residues in meat in excess of the Codex MRL for both trenbolone and zeranol.

Question 28:

> How would you assess the feasibility of labelling with respect to meat products from animals treated with growth-promoting hormones? How does this compare with the feasibility of labelling in other food safety contexts?

6.233 **Dr. André** indicated that this question was not related to scientific expertise, but to political decision. However, such labelling would be consistent with the traceability concept which was rapidly being improved in European countries (ready to be implemented in France). However, this implied that an adequate control to qualify products would have to be established; in the case of residues of hormones, detection in meat did not stand in the way of feasible labelling.

6.234 **Dr. Arnold** said that in his view it was not feasible to control labelling, since it could not be confirmed through laboratory testing whether an animal had ever been treated with growth promoters. If the objective was to verify that something had never been used, e.g., a pesticide, the situation was similar. The chances to detect food-irradiation, on the other hand, were much better. Also, if genetically modified organisms were involved in food production, it was sometimes possible to routinely detect the altered genetic material. There seemed to be no generally valid answer to this question.

6.235 **Dr. Lucier** replied that meat products could be labelled to indicate that they were from animals treated with growth-promoting agents so that consumers would have as much information as possible to decide which meat to buy. If growth-promoting agents produced meat with lower fat content, a consumer with cardiovascular disease might specifically want to buy meat from a growth-promoted animal.

6.236 **Dr. McLean** observed that the effective labelling of treated meat would necessitate identification of the animal at birth, the farm, sale, slaughter, processing and on to the consumer. The logistics of the process would be complex and make it difficult to regulate, especially in the case of processed meat products. The cost would far outweigh any perceived benefit. The same problem arose with the feasibility of labelling other foods, but because of the complex process for meat processing, it was much more expensive. In his view, the money spent on such a labelling process would be better spent on ensuring microbiological safety of food. Food contaminated with microbes and their toxins disabled or killed many people every year. The adverse effects of veterinary drugs or agricultural chemicals were rarely reported, but reports of food poisoning from microbial contamination were very common. For example, a recent outbreak of *Escherichia coli* food poisoning in Scotland made 400 people seriously ill and killed 17, while a similar outbreak in Japan infected 10,000 and killed 11 (Coghlan, A (1997) New Scientist *153* (2066)7).

6.237 **Dr. Ritter** replied that the issue of labelling of food products was the subject of intense public debate, to which there was no easy resolution. The issue with regard to the feasibility of labelling in the case of the hormones could therefore relate as much to the objective of such a strategy as to its feasibility. Use of the natural gonadal hormones in meat production produced residue levels consistent with those which might typically be expected in meat products from untreated animals. Other than to fulfil a "right to know" objective, labelling in this case would not appear to provide information of value to consumers in a health related context. Particularly noteworthy was that as residue levels are comparable in both treated and untreated animals, and as exogenous hormones are, in any case, quantitatively and qualitatively indistinguishable from those endogenously present, it was unlikely that a labelling programme could be implemented at any practical level.

6.238 In the case of the synthetic hormones utilized in growth promotion, at least two had been subjected to international review and safe residue levels had been recommended. The purpose of such a labelling programme would be unclear given that an international review had already concluded that residues at or below proposed levels did not constitute a risk to consumers, even under the exaggerated calculations and assumptions utilized in the development of MRLs.

Questions 29-34 were follow-up questions to those presented earlier, and the responses to the follow-up questions have been included with the responses to the earlier questions.

Question 35:

> With reference to therapeutic and zootechnical use of the natural hormones at issue, do you believe that the EC Directive 88/299 „ensures that there are no residues left in meat for human consumption" (para 19, EC first submission in the Canadian complaint)?

6.239 **Dr. Arnold** replied that no such insurance can be given. The meat would always contain residues even if withdrawal times were observed. The concept of "no residue" had been largely abandoned some 20 years ago when it became evident that "no residue" was a function of the limit of detection of the analytical method. All *permitted* substances, including the hormones, were regulated on the basis of an "acceptable residue" in the EEC. The "no residue" concept still applied to banned substances, but this was trivial. In the case of hormones it was acceptable if the sum of endogenous plus exogenous hormones was at or within physiological limits.

6.240 The response of **Dr. Ritter** to this question is contained in his response to question 20 above.

VII. INTERIM REVIEW

7.1 On 21 May 1997, the European Communities and Canada requested the Panel to review, in accordance with Article 15.2 of the Understanding on Rules and Procedures Governing the Settlement of Disputes ("DSU"), the interim report that had been issued to the parties on 7 May 1997. The European Communities also requested the Panel to hold a further meeting with the parties to discuss the points raised in its written comments and other points which they would develop during that meeting.

7.2 We decided to hold concurrent interim review meetings with the parties for both this dispute and the parallel panel requested by the United States. This decision was, *inter alia*, based on the similarities of both cases and the fact that the interim reports in both cases only differ in the description of the arguments of the parties, whereas the sections dealing with the scientific experts and the legal findings in the two cases are almost identical. In light of that decision, and after consultations with the parties involved, we also decided to make a copy of the sections of our interim report dealing with our consultation with scientific experts and our findings, together with the comments submitted in that regard by the European Communities and Canada, available to the United States. By letter of 3 June 1997, the European Communities objected to both decisions, arguing that they affected due process and its rights of defense and, consequently, its rights and obligations under the WTO Agreement. It made, however, no specific claims of prejudice. Since we could not see how the European Communities could be prejudiced by these decisions, we rejected this objection.

7.3 In a letter dated 23 May 1997, Canada requested us to rule that, on the basis of Article 15.2 of the DSU, the discussion at the interim review meeting should be limited to only those issues identified in the parties written comments of 21 May 1991. By indicating that it intended to submit its specific comments on the Panel's findings and conclusions at some time in the future, Canada submitted that the European Communities had failed to state the precise aspects of the findings and conclusions it wished the Panel to review in its written comments of 21 May 1997. Canada argued that the intent of Article 15.2 of the DSU is that the panel and parties are fully aware of issues to be raised at the interim review meeting so they may prepare and make reasoned responses.

7.4 Article 15.2 of the DSU provides the following:

> "... Within a period of time set by the panel, a party may submit a written request for the panel to review *precise aspects* of the interim report prior to circulation of the final report to the Members. At the request of a party, the panel shall hold a further meeting with the parties *on the issues identified in the written comments...*" (emphasis added).

It appeared to us that the European Communities, by only enumerating the numbers of the paragraphs of the findings section of our interim report in relation to which it has concerns and not stating in its written comments the precise aspects it wishes the Panel to review, did not respect the wording of Article 15.2 of the DSU. We considered, however, that the main object and purpose of Article 15.2 is to make sure that the other party is aware of the issues which will be raised at the interim review meeting in order to allow it to prepare its rebuttal. In light of the fact that the EC's written request for review of the findings section only related to factual aspects, *i.e.*, the correct reflection of the EC arguments and the names of and references to individual scientific experts, we considered that Canada would not be unduly prejudiced by allowing the European Communities to present these factual points at the interim review meeting. We, therefore, decided that the European Communities could raise these points on the conditions that it would limit itself to factual issues and to the paragraph numbers it had enumerated in its written comments. We note that this decision corresponds to what Canada requested in its letter of 23 May 1997.

7.5 The Panel met with the parties on 4 June 1997 in order to hear their arguments concerning the interim report. We carefully reviewed the arguments presented by the European Communities and Canada and the responses offered by both sides.

7.6 The European Communities requested us to find that Articles 15.2 and 15.3 of the DSU and the general principle of due process prevent the Panel from modifying aspects of the interim report on which the parties did not submit comments. However, at the end of the interim review meeting the European Communities appeared to modify this request by asking the Panel to review its findings in light of the factual comments made. Canada submitted that at the interim review stage a panel should only correct factual aspects and arguments made by the parties and, as the case may be, expand on its reasoning or findings. According to Canada, it is inappropriate to change, at the interim review stage, in any fundamental way any of the major findings of fact and law which informed the Panel's conclusion. We considered that no provision in the DSU limits us to only modify those paragraphs commented upon by the parties or to only correct or slightly change factual elements or arguments. Article 15.3 of the DSU only provides that "[t]he findings of the final panel report shall include a discussion of the arguments made at the interim review stage...".

7.7 The European Communities made two types of comments on the findings section of the interim report. The first concerned 20 paragraphs in which the European Communities is stated to have argued or agreed to something which, according to the European Communities, does not or not completely reflect the EC's position taken during the proceedings. These comments related to the following paragraphs: 8.105, 8.109, 8.111, 8.112, 8.115, 8.131, 8.175, 8.176, 8.187, 8.190, 8.193, 8.204, 8.205, 8.213, 8.220, 8.224, 8.228, 8.232, 8.243 and 8.274. Since these proposed changes concerned the representation of the EC's own legal or factual arguments, we accepted most of them.

7.8 The second type of comments made by the European Communities related to paragraphs where the phrase "the scientific experts advising the Panel" is used without, according to the European Communities, citing the names of the scientists nor the place where they have made the statements the Panel is invoking. It also argued that frequently the reference provided does not reflect the views of all the scientists. Canada recalled that during the meeting on 17 and 18 February 1997, the scientists had a full opportunity to comment on and qualify each other's opinions and that, therefore, silence may be taken to indicate acceptance or lack of relevant knowledge on the particular issue. The European Communities also requested us to review the accuracy of the factual information contained in several paragraphs. We carefully considered all the factual comments thus made and, where we agreed with them, modified those paragraphs accordingly.

7.9 The European Communities and Canada also requested us to include in the final report the procedural decisions taken by the Panel during the course of its work. We added these decisions in a new Section B on organizational issues.

7.10 Canada submitted corrections of its own arguments and factual elements and suggested several drafting changes, most of which have been taken into account in our final report. It argued, for example, that it never limited its claim under Article 5.5 of the SPS Agreement to the substances carbadox and olaquindox. This remark is reflected and dealt with in paragraph 8.174.

7.11 Both parties also suggested further changes or additions in respect of the interim reports' descriptive sections which we took into account in re-examining that part of the report. In this context, the European Communities requested us to append the transcripts of the joint meeting with the experts advising the Panel to the descriptive part of the report, arguing that many important statements made by the experts in these meetings are not reflected in Section 6 of the interim report. In order to increase the transparency of our work and to take into account most of the comments made by the European Communities on the descriptive part of the interim report, we decided to annex the transcripts of the joint meeting with the experts of 17-18 February 1997 to our final report.

VIII. FINDINGS

A. *Claims of the Parties*

8.1 This dispute arises essentially from the following facts. In 1981 the Council of the European Communities ("EC Council") adopted Directive 81/602/EEC[310], *inter alia*, requiring the EC member States of the European Communities to prohibit the administration to farm animals of substances having a thyrostatic, oestrogenic, androgenic or gestagenic action. Directive 81/602/EEC further provided that pending adoption of a decision of the EC Council on the administration to farm animals for growth promotion purposes[311] of oestradiol-17β, testosterone, progesterone, zeranol and trenbolone[312] EC member States could continue to apply the national regulations in force concerning those substances.[313] In 1988 the EC Council adopted Directive 88/146/EEC[314] which brought the administration to farm animals for growth promotion purposes of these five hormones within the general prohibition imposed by Directive 81/602/EEC. The 1988 Directive also required the prohibition of importation from third countries of animals and of meat from animals to which substances with thyrostatic, oestrogenic, androgenic or gestagenic action have been administered.[315]

---

[310] *EC Official Journal*, L 222, 7 August 1981, p.32.

[311] Article 5 of Directive 81/602/EEC uses the term "for fattening purposes". However, during the Panel proceedings and in this report the term "for growth promotion purposes" is used.

[312] The five hormones are the subject of this dispute. A sixth hormone in dispute, melengestrol acetate or MGA, falls under the general prohibition of Directive 81/602/EEC and is addressed in paragraph 8.4.

[313] See para. 2.2.

[314] *EC Official Journal*, L 70, 16 March 1988, p.16.

[315] See para. 2.3.

Two exceptions to this general ban are provided in Directive 88/299/EEC[316]: (i) the administration for therapeutic treatment[317] of oestradiol-17β, testosterone, progesterone and some of their derivatives; and (ii) the administration for zootechnical treatment[318] of substances having an oestrogenic, androgenic or gestagenic action which are authorized in accordance with EC Directives on veterinary medicinal products.[319] On 29 April 1996, the EC Council adopted Directive 96/22/EC[320] (repealing and replacing Directives 81/602/EEC, 88/146/EEC and 88/299/EEC) which confirms and extends the above-mentioned prohibitions. This 1996 Directive will enter into force on 1 July 1997.[321]

8.2 Canada claims that the European Communities, by banning the importation of meat and meat products from animals to which any of six specific hormones have been administered for purposes of promoting the growth of the animals, has acted inconsistently with the Agreement on the Application of Sanitary and Phytosanitary Measures ("SPS Agreement"), in particular Articles 2, 3 and 5; the Agreement on Technical Barriers to Trade ("TBT Agreement"); and the General Agreement on Tariffs and Trade 1994 ("GATT"), in particular Articles III and XI. Canada also claims that, even if the EC measures in dispute are consistent with all of these agreements, the application of the EC measures at issue in any event nullifies or impairs benefits accruing to Canada under the Marrakesh Agreement establishing the World Trade Organization ("WTO Agreement") within the meaning of Article XXIII:1(b) of GATT.

8.3 The European Communities rejects these claims.

8.4 The six hormones in dispute are: oestradiol-17β, testosterone, progesterone, zeranol and trenbolone (the five hormones mentioned above which were brought within the general prohibition required by Directive 81/602/EEC by Directive 88/146/EEC) and melengestrol acetate ("MGA"; a sixth hormone falling under the general prohibition of Directive 81/602/EEC). Oestradiol-17β is a natural hormone with oestrogenic action (*i.e.*, responsible for female characteristics); testosterone is a natural hormone with androgenic action (*i.e.*, responsible for male characteristics); progesterone is a natural hormone with gestagenic action (*i.e.*, responsible for maintaining pregnancy); zeranol is a synthetic hormone with oestrogenic action (which mimics the action of oestradiol-17β); trenbolone is a synthetic hormone with androgenic action (which mimics the action of testosterone); and MGA is a synthetic hormone with gestagenic action (which mimics the action of progesterone).[322] Natural hormones are hormones which are produced endogenously in animals and humans. Synthetic hormones are hormones which are artificially produced. Oestradiol-17β,

---

316 *EC Official Journal*, L 128, 21 May 1988, p.36.

317 *Therapeutic* treatment means treatment of a disease or other health problem.

318 *Zootechnical* treatment for the purposes of the EC measures in dispute means, *inter alia,* treatment for the synchronization of oestrus, termination of unwanted gestation, the improvement of fertility and the preparation of donors and recipients for the implantation of embryos (Article 2, paragraph 1(b) of EC Directive 88/299/EEC).

319 See para. 2.4.

320 *EC Official Journal*, L 1125, 23 May 1996, p.3.

321 See para. 2.5.

322 See paras. 2.8-2.9.

testosterone and progesterone are hereafter also referred to as the three natural hormones; zeranol, trenbolone and MGA are hereafter also referred to as the three synthetic hormones.

B. Organizational Issues

1. Scientific Evidence

8.5 In the course of these proceedings, we considered several issues related to the gathering and submission of scientific evidence. These concerned the appointment of scientific experts to advise the Panel, the deadline for submission of scientific evidence by the parties to the dispute and a request by the European Communities to ask specific national and international authorities to provide the Panel with scientific studies and data.

8.6 Article 11.2 of the SPS Agreement provides the following:

> "In a dispute under this Agreement involving scientific or technical issues, *a panel should seek advice from experts* chosen by the panel in consultation with the parties to the dispute. To this end, *the panel may, when it deems it appropriate, establish an advisory technical experts group*, or consult the relevant international organizations, at the request of either party to the dispute or on its own initiative" (emphasis added).

Article 13 of the DSU reads as follows:

> "1. Each panel shall have the right to seek information and technical advice *from any individual or body which it deems appropriate* ...
>
> 2. Panels may seek information *from any relevant source* and may consult experts to obtain their opinion on certain aspects of the matter. With respect to a factual issue concerning a scientific or other technical matter raised by a party to a dispute, *a panel may request an advisory report in writing from an expert review group*. Rules for the establishment of such a group and its procedures are set forth in Appendix 4" (emphasis added).

8.7 As outlined above[323], we decided to request the opinion of experts on certain scientific and other technical matters raised by the parties to this dispute. For our examination of this dispute, we considered it more useful to leave open the possibility of receiving a range of opinions from individual experts on specific scientific and technical questions, rather than to establish an expert review group which would have been required to reach a consensus view on the basis of general terms of reference given to it by the Panel. We considered that neither Article 11.2 of the SPS Agreement nor Article 13.2 of the DSU limits our right to seek information from *individual* experts as provided for in Article 11.2, first sentence, of the SPS Agreement and Articles 13.1 and 13.2, first sentence, of the DSU. The procedures we adopted in this respect and the views expressed by the experts are set out in paragraphs 6.1 and following.

---

[323] See paras. 6.1 ff.

8.8 After consultation with the parties to the dispute (in accordance with Article 11.2 of the SPS Agreement), we decided to seek advice from the same experts selected to advise the panel requested by the United States.[324] We considered this to be in line with the object and purpose of Article 9.3 of the DSU which provides the following: "[i]f more than one panel is established to examine the complaints related to the same matter, to the greatest extent possible the same persons shall serve as panelists on each of the separate panels and the timetable for the panel process in such disputes shall be harmonized".

8.9 The procedures we adopted for our consultation with the experts and the views they expressed are set out in paragraphs 6.1 and following. It is of particular importance that we made clear to the experts advising the Panel that we were not seeking a consensus position among the experts but wanted to hear all views.[325] However, we also pointed out at the meeting with experts that, in order to gain time, where an expert agreed with a statement made or answer provided by another expert, the former expert did not have to take the floor.[326] Any reference made in our findings to "scientific experts advising the Panel" (or "experts" or "scientific experts") refers to one or more of the five individual experts we thus appointed and, as the case may be, the expert sent by the Codex Commission secretariat. This phrase does not refer to nor includes the scientists who were part of the delegations of the parties to this dispute. These are referred to in this report by name, followed by the name of the delegation of which they were part.

8.10 With respect to the submission of scientific evidence by the parties to this dispute, we decided that they could submit written material on new scientific evidence to support their arguments by no later than 8 February 1997. We took this decision in order to ensure that both the parties and the scientific experts advising the Panel would get an opportunity to examine the scientific evidence before the 17-18 February meeting with the experts.

8.11 The European Communities also requested that Canada provide the Panel the originals of the studies and other relevant data on which its competent authorities based the decision to authorize the use of the hormones at issue. It also considered that the originals of the studies and other data on which the 1988 JECFA Report based its recommendations should be provided to the Panel. As far as the studies and data used by Canadian authorities is concerned, we did not consider this information to be relevant to address the EC measures in dispute. Similarly, we did not consider it necessary to request the studies and data on which the 1988 JECFA Report is based since it was our understanding that both parties involved in this dispute participated in the elaboration of this report.

---

[324] The procedures followed for the appointment of these experts in the panel requested by the United States as well as the parties' arguments in respect of the appointment of the experts in this Panel are set out in paras. 6.3 ff.

[325] See Transcripts of the joint meeting with experts of 17 February 1997, p.14.

[326] *Ibid.*, p.20.

2. *Third Party Rights*

8.12 In the course of our work, we considered several issues related to the parallel existence of this Panel, requested by Canada, and the panel requested by the United States. Although different panels, both panels relate to the same EC measures, were dealt with by the same panel members and were assisted by the same scientific experts. These issues relate to a request by the United States for extended third party rights, the organization of joint meetings and the access by parties in one of these panels to materials submitted to the other panel.

8.13 In this respect we note, as a general guideline, Article 9.3 of the DSU, which reads as follows:

> "If more than one panel is established to examine the complaints related to the same matter, to the greatest extent possible the same persons shall serve as panelists on each of the separate panels and *the timetable for the panel process in such disputes shall be harmonized*" (emphasis added).

8.14 In its third party submission to this Panel, the United States requested to be allowed to participate more fully in our work, *i.e.*, to receive all the submissions of the parties to this dispute, to observe the whole of the proceedings at the substantive meetings of the Panel with the parties to the dispute and with the scientific experts and to make a brief statement at a suitable moment during the second substantive meeting. The United States based this request on the strong interest it has in this Panel's review of the EC ban, as demonstrated by the submissions of the United States to the panel in the separate proceedings requested by the United States. It further argued that since both panels will decide on their report in each of the two disputes concurrently, the arguments and facts presented in this proceeding can be expected to have a substantial effect on the interests of the United States in the separate proceeding it requested. In support of this request, the United States also invoked the (as of today unadopted) Panel Report on "European Communities - Régime for the Importation, Sale and Distribution of Bananas" where Canada and other third parties to that dispute were accorded extended third party rights.[327]

8.15 The rights of third parties are dealt with in Article 10 and Appendix 3 of the DSU. Article 10 provides that third parties "shall have an opportunity to be heard by the panel and to make written submissions to the panel". It also provides that third parties are entitled to receive the submissions of the parties made to the first substantive panel meeting. Paragraph 6 of Appendix 3 specifies that third parties shall be invited "to present their views during a session of the first substantive meeting of the panel set aside for that purpose. All such third parties may be present during the entirety of this session". Under prior GATT practice, more expansive rights were granted to third parties in several disputes.[328] In these cases, however, and contrary to

[327] Panel Report on "European Communities - Régime for the Importation, Sale and Distribution of Bananas", circulated on 22 May 1997, WT/DS27/R/USA, paras. 7.4-7.9.

[328] See, for example, Panel Report on "Japan - Trade in Semiconductors", adopted on 4 May 1988, BISD 35S/116, pp.116-117, para. 5; Panel Report on "EEC - Import Regime for Bananas", issued on 11 February 1994 (not adopted), DS38/R, p.4, para. 8; Panel Report on "EEC - Member States' Import Regimes for Bananas", issued on 3 June 1993 (not adopted), DS32/R, p.2, para. 9.

the situation in the present dispute, parties agreed to the extension of such rights. In the Panel Report on "European Communities - Régime for the Importation, Sale and Distribution of Bananas", where no agreement between the parties on the issue existed, the panel granted the following extended third party rights: it invited third parties to observe the whole of the first substantive meeting and the second substantive meeting of the panel with the parties and gave third parties the opportunity to make a brief statement at a suitable moment during the second meeting.[329] The panel did not expect third parties to submit additional written material beyond the responses to the questions already posed during the first meeting and refused to grant further participatory rights to third parties following the second substantive meeting, including participation in the interim review process.[330]

8.16 Having considered representations by the United States, Canada and the European Communities relating to the US request for extended third party rights, we decided, prior to our first substantive meeting with the parties, not to invite the United States to observe that part of the first meeting normally restricted to parties to the dispute. This decision was, *inter alia*, based on the fact that the US request was only made one day before the first meeting and that the third party rights of the United States with respect to our first meeting seemed to be sufficiently safeguarded by the normal procedures as set out in Article 10 of the DSU and paragraph 6 of Appendix 3.

8.17 However, considering the special status of the United States in this case, as demonstrated by the fact that it is the sole complainant in the parallel panel proceeding concerning the same EC measures and dealt with by the same panel members in accordance with Article 9.3 of the DSU, we decided as follows with respect to the third party rights of the United States at our meeting with scientific experts and our second substantive meeting:

"(i) the United States will be invited to participate in the meeting with scientific experts to be held by the Panel requested by Canada;

(ii) the Panel reserves the right to invite the United States to attend the second substantive meeting with the parties".

8.18 Prior to our meeting with scientific experts, we decided to hold that meeting jointly for both this Panel, requested by Canada, and the parallel panel requested by the United States. This decision stemmed from the similarities of the two cases (the same EC measures are at issue and both cases are dealt with by the same panel members), our decision to use the same scientific experts in both cases and the fact that we had already decided to invite Canada and the United States to participate in the meeting with scientific experts in each of the two cases. In addition, we considered that, from a practical perspective there was a need to avoid repetition of arguments and/or questions at our meetings with the scientific experts. The European Communities objected to this decision arguing that one joint meeting with the experts, instead of two separate meetings, was likely to affect its procedural rights of defence.

[329] Panel Report on "European Communities - Régime for the Importation, Sale and Distribution of Bananas", *op. cit.*, paras. 7.7 and 7.8.

[330] *Ibid.*, paras 7.8 and 7.9.

Where it made precise claims of prejudice to its rights of defence, we took corrective action.[331]

8.19 In view of that decision, we also decided to give access to all of the information submitted under each panel proceeding to the parties in the other panel proceeding, including the parties' second written submissions, written versions of oral statements and questions raised by the Panel and the parties, and answers thereto, in each case, as well as all scientific documentation submitted by the parties. By doing so, we understood that, in this Panel, we could also consider, where appropriate, the materials submitted before the panel requested by the United States.[332] The European Communities objected to this decision arguing that it was most likely going to affect its substantive and procedural rights of defence. It made, however, no specific claims of prejudice. We considered that providing all information to all parties involved in both panels would increase the transparency of our work, without depriving parties of their substantive or procedural rights, and is in line with the object and purpose of Article 9.3 of the DSU calling for a harmonization of timetables of both panels. On these grounds we rejected the EC's objection.

8.20 Prior to our second substantive meeting, we decided to invite the United States to observe that meeting with the parties and to grant it the opportunity to make a brief statement at the end of the meeting. This decision was, *inter alia*, based on the fact that our second meeting was held the day after our joint meeting with the scientific experts and that the parties to this dispute would, therefore, most likely comment on, and draw conclusions from, the evidence submitted by these experts to be considered in both cases. Since in the panel requested by the United States the second meeting was held before the joint meeting with scientific experts, we considered it appropriate, in order to safeguard the rights of the United States in the proceeding it requested, to grant the United States the opportunity to observe our second meeting in this case and to make a brief statement at the end of that meeting.

C. *General Interpretative Issues*

1. *Scope of the Measures in Dispute*

8.21 Canada contests the EC ban on imports of *meat* and *meat products* from *cattle*, treated with any of *six specific hormones* (oestradiol-17β, testosterone, proges-

[331] The European Communities argued that a joint meeting with experts deprived it of its right to present its legal and scientific positions twice (a first time before this Panel and a second time before the panel requested by the United States). In light of this objection we decided that the European Communities would be allowed to address the joint meeting twice (a first time after the United States and a second time after Canada). See Transcripts of the joint meeting with experts of 17 February 1997, paras. 1-2.

[332] This does, of course, not mean that, in this Panel, Canada has incorporated or agreed with the arguments submitted by the United States in the parallel panel it requested or that we have to deal, in this Panel, with the arguments and claims submitted by the United States in the other panel. It only means that, where we considered it appropriate, we would be able to invoke or address, in this Panel, factual elements, scientific evidence or arguments submitted by the European Communities or the United States to the parallel panel requested by the United States.

terone, zeranol, trenbolone and MGA) for *growth promotion* purposes.[333] Canada does *not* challenge the EC ban on imports of *live animals*, of meat and meat products from animals *other* than cattle, from cattle treated with hormones *other* than the six specified or treated with *any* hormones for purposes *other* than growth promotion.

8.22 We further note that the European Communities argues that its import ban on *live animals* to which any of the six hormones have been administered, is necessary for the protection of both human and animal health.[334] However, the European Communities does not make this argument with respect to its import ban on *meat* or *meat products*. Specifically, the European Communities has not argued that its import ban on meat or meat products is necessary for the protection of animal health either inside or outside the EC territory. Since the animal health arguments invoked by the European Communities exclusively relate to its import ban on *live animals* and considering that the EC ban on imports of live animals treated with hormones has not been challenged by Canada, and thus falls outside the scope of this dispute, we find that within the scope of this dispute we need not take into account the arguments made by the European Communities which relate to animal health.[335]

2. *Application of the SPS Agreement, the TBT Agreement and GATT*

8.23 Canada invokes arguments relating to three different agreements: the SPS Agreement, the TBT Agreement and GATT. The European Communities, in turn, invokes the same three agreements in its defense. We next examine which of these agreements apply to the present dispute.

8.24 With respect to the SPS Agreement, both parties agree that the EC measures in dispute are sanitary measures in the sense of Paragraph 1(b) of Annex A of the SPS Agreement.[336] Paragraph 1(b) of Annex A defines a sanitary measure as

> "any measure applied to protect human or animal life or health within the territory of the Member from risks arising from additives, contaminants, toxins or disease-causing organisms in foods, beverages or feedstuffs".

Footnote 4 to Annex A specifies that "contaminants" include, for the purposes of Annex A, "pesticide and veterinary drug residues and extraneous matter". Since the six hormones in dispute are veterinary drugs, the parties agree that the alleged risks at issue arise from contaminants.

8.25 We agree with the parties that the EC measures in dispute are "applied to protect human ... life or health" within the territory of the European Communities from risks arising from "contaminants", namely residues of six specific hormones, in foods (according to paragraph 1(b) of Annex A). That the contested EC measures

---

333 See para. 3.1.

334 See para. 3.6.

335 Our finding that animal health does not fall within the scope of this dispute does, of course, not mean that we cannot take into account scientific evidence relevant for risks to human life or health which is derived from studies or tests applied to animals.

336 See paras. 3.1 and 3.7.

are, *inter alia*, "applied to protect human ... life or health" can be inferred from the preambles to, and legislative history of, Directives 81/602/EEC and 88/146/EEC.[337] Since both parties agree that the contested EC measures are "sanitary measures", we see no need to further examine in this dispute the definition of measures "applied to protect human ... life or health".

8.26 Both parties also agree that, according to Article 1.1 of the SPS Agreement, the SPS Agreement is applicable to this dispute.[338] Article 1.1 provides that the SPS Agreement

> "applies to all sanitary and phytosanitary measures which may, directly or indirectly, affect international trade"

We agree with the parties that the EC measures "may, directly or indirectly, affect international trade". It cannot be contested that an import ban affects international trade.

8.27 With respect to the application *ratione temporis* of the SPS Agreement to the EC measures in dispute, we note that the SPS Agreement entered into force on 1 January 1995 (the date of entry into force of the WTO Agreement of which, according to Article II:2 of that Agreement, the SPS Agreement is an integral part). The EC measures in dispute, however, were enacted *before* 1 January 1995 (namely 31 July 1981 and 7 March 1988), thus raising the issue of whether the SPS Agreement applies to these measures.

8.28 Article 3.2 of the DSU directs us to clarify the provisions of the SPS Agreement "in accordance with customary rules of interpretation of public international law". According to established practice, the fundamental rules of treaty interpretation set out in the Vienna Convention on the Law of Treaties ("Vienna Convention") form part of these customary rules of interpretation.[339] The general principle in international law, as embodied in Article 28 of the Vienna Convention, is that "[u]nless a different intention appears from the treaty or is otherwise established, its provisions do *not* bind a party in relation to ... any *situation* which *ceased to exist before* the date of the entry into force of the treaty ..." (emphasis added). The EC measures can, in this context, be considered as continuing "situations" which were enacted *before* the entry into force of the SPS Agreement but which did *not* cease to exist *after* that date (contrary to the situation envisaged in Article 28). In line with Article 28 of the Vienna Convention, the SPS Agreement should, therefore, in principle apply to these EC measures, unless an intention to the contrary can be established.[340]

---

[337] See paras. 2.2-2.3.

[338] See paras. 4.23-4.25.

[339] See Appellate Body Reports on "United States - Standards for Reformulated and Conventional Gasoline", adopted on 20 May 1996, WT/DS2/AB/R, DSR 1996:I, 3 at 14-15 and "Japan - Taxes on Alcoholic Beverages", adopted on 1 November 1996, WT/DS8/AB/R, DSR 1996:I, 97 at 104-106.

[340] We refer, in this respect, to the Reports of the Panel and Appellate Body on "Japan - Taxes on Alcoholic Beverages", adopted on 1 November 1996 (WT/DS8/R and WT/DS8/AB/R), where both the Panel and the Appellate Body applied GATT (which entered into force on 1 January 1995) to the Japanese Liquor Tax Law (of 1953 and last amended on 1 May 1994), even though that Japanese measure had been enacted and most recently been amended *before* the entry into force of GATT, on the implicit ground that the Japanese measure remained in force *after* that date. The same reasoning

8.29 An examination of the SPS Agreement reveals no intention to the contrary. Indeed, several provisions of the SPS Agreement confirm the general principle that the SPS Agreement should also apply to sanitary measures which were enacted before its entry into force but which remain in force thereafter. Except for Article 14 which authorizes delays in the application of some or all of the provisions of the SPS Agreement for least-developed and other developing countries, no transition periods are provided for. The fact that Article 14 explicitly provides for a two-year transition period for developing countries with respect to some of their *existing* sanitary and phytosanitary measures, confirms that the SPS Agreement generally applies to measures enacted before the entry into force of the SPS Agreement but which are maintained in force after that date. This is also confirmed in several provisions of the SPS Agreement which explicitly address situations where Members "maintain" a sanitary or phytosanitary measure, such as Article 2.2 ("Members shall ensure that any sanitary ... measure ... is based on scientific principles and is not *maintained* without sufficient scientific evidence ..."), Article 3.3 ("Members may introduce or *maintain* sanitary ... measures ... if ..."), Article 5.6 ("... when establishing or *maintaining* sanitary ... measures ... Members shall ensure that ...") and Article 5.8 ("... a specific sanitary ... measure introduced or *maintained* by another Member ...").

8.30 We finally note that according to Article XVI:4 of the WTO Agreement, each Member "shall ensure the conformity of its laws, regulations and administrative procedures with its obligations as provided in the annexed Agreements [including the SPS Agreement]". This provision confirms that measures which already existed as of the date of entry into force of the SPS Agreement also need to be consistent with the requirements imposed by that Agreement.

8.31 Thus, we find that the SPS Agreement is applicable to this dispute.

8.32 In respect of the applicability of the TBT Agreement to this dispute, we note that Article 1.5 of the TBT Agreement reads as follows:

> "The provisions of this Agreement do not apply to sanitary and phytosanitary measures as defined in Annex A of the Agreement on the Application of Sanitary and Phytosanitary Measures".[341]

Since the measures in dispute are sanitary measures, we find that the TBT Agreement is not applicable to this dispute.

8.33 We finally note that this dispute relates to trade in goods (*in casu* imports of meat and meat products) and that on its face GATT applies.[342] In this context, we note that Canada only invokes GATT after having addressed the SPS Agreement and that the European Communities does not invoke any GATT provision other than Article XX(b) as a justification for the EC measures in dispute.

---

was applied in the Reports of the Panel and Appellate Body on "United States - Standards for Reformulated and Conventional Gasoline", *op. cit.*

[341] Similarly, but less explicitly, Article 1.4 of the SPS Agreement provides that "[n]othing in this Agreement shall affect the rights of Members under the Agreement on Technical Barriers to Trade with respect to measures not within the scope of this Agreement".

[342] With respect to the application *ratione temporis* of GATT to this particular case, the same reasoning and findings apply as those developed for the application *ratione temporis* of the SPS Agreement in paragraphs 8.27 and 8.28.

3. *Relationship Between the SPS Agreement and GATT*

8.34 Since both the SPS Agreement and GATT apply to this dispute, we next examine the relationship between these two agreements.

8.35 The parties to the dispute present diverging views with respect to whether we should first address GATT or the SPS Agreement. However, neither of the parties claims that the relevant provisions of the SPS Agreement and GATT are in conflict. Therefore, we do not need, as a preliminary matter, to address the General Interpretative Note to the Multilateral Agreements on Trade in Goods which only applies "[i]n the event of conflict between a provision of [GATT] and a provision of another Agreement in Annex 1A [*inter alia*, the SPS Agreement]".

8.36 The European Communities makes a distinction between the "substantive" and "procedural" provisions of the SPS Agreement. According to the European Communities, the substantive provisions only interpret Article XX(b) of GATT[343], without adding any new obligations, while the procedural provisions contain requirements additional to GATT. Therefore, the European Communities concludes, the "substantive" provisions of the SPS Agreement can only be addressed if recourse is made to GATT Article XX(b), *i.e.*, if, and only if, a violation of another provision of GATT is first established. The additional "procedural" provisions, on the other hand, can be examined directly and independently of a prior GATT violation.[344]

8.37 Canada argues that the SPS Agreement is the *lex specialis* for a review of sanitary measures and should, therefore, be addressed first. Canada claims that the application of the SPS Agreement does not require a prior violation of GATT since the SPS Agreement is a "free-standing" agreement which applies to all sanitary measures and imposes requirements additional to those in GATT.[345]

8.38 In examining the relationship between GATT and the SPS Agreement, we recall the fundamental rules of treaty interpretation set out in the Vienna Convention.[346] Article 31 of the Vienna Convention prescribes that a treaty has to be interpreted "in good faith in accordance with the ordinary meaning to be given to the terms of the treaty in their context and in the light of its object and purpose".[347]

8.39 We first consider the wording of Article 1.1 of the SPS Agreement which reads as follows:

> "This Agreement applies to all sanitary and phytosanitary measures which may, directly or indirectly, affect international trade. Such

---

343 Article XX(b) of GATT reads as follows: "Subject to the requirement that such measures are not applied in a manner which constitute a means of arbitrary or unjustifiable discrimination between countries where the same conditions prevail, or a disguised restriction on international trade, nothing in this Agreement shall be construed to prevent the adoption or enforcement by any contracting party of measures: ... (b) necessary to protect human, animal or plant life or health".

344 See para. 4.3.

345 See paras. 4.1 and 4.4.

346 The legal basis for the Panel to invoke the Vienna Convention is outlined above in paragraph 8.28 and footnote 339.

347 According to Article 32 of the Vienna Convention, recourse may only be had to supplementary means of interpretation "in order to confirm the meaning resulting from the application of Article 31" or in case Article 31 leaves the meaning "ambiguous or obscure" or leads to "a result which is manifestly absurd or unreasonable".

measures shall be developed and applied in accordance with the provisions of this Agreement".

According to Article 1.1 of the SPS Agreement, two requirements need to be fulfilled for the SPS Agreement to apply: (i) the measure in dispute is a sanitary or phytosanitary measure[348]; and (ii) the measure in dispute may, directly or indirectly, affect international trade.[349] There are no additional requirements. The SPS Agreement contains, in particular, no explicit requirement of a prior violation of a provision of GATT which would govern the applicability of the SPS Agreement, as asserted by the European Communities.

8.40 We further note that the distinction proposed by the European Communities between "substantive" and "procedural" provisions of the SPS Agreement has no basis in the text of that Agreement and would, in any event, seem to be difficult to apply to most provisions contained therein. For example, the obligation to base a sanitary measure on a risk assessment in accordance with Article 5 of the SPS Agreement includes both substantive and procedural elements.[350]

8.41 Moreover, we find the EC claim that the SPS Agreement does not impose "substantive" obligations additional to those already contained in Article XX(b) of GATT not to be persuasive. It is clear that some provisions of the SPS Agreement elaborate on provisions already contained in GATT, in particular Article XX(b). The final preambular paragraph of the SPS Agreement provides, indeed, that the Members desired "to elaborate rules for the application of the provisions of GATT 1994 which relate to the use of sanitary or phytosanitary measures, in particular the provisions of Article XX(b)". Examples of such rules are, arguably, some of the obligations contained in Article 2 of the SPS Agreement. However, on this basis alone we cannot conclude that the SPS Agreement only applies, as Article XX(b) of GATT does, if, and only if, a prior violation of a GATT provision has been established. Many provisions of the SPS Agreement impose "substantive" obligations which go significantly beyond and are additional to the requirements for invocation of Article XX(b).[351] These obligations are, *inter alia,* imposed to "further the use of harmonized sanitary and phytosanitary measures between Members"[352] and to "improve the human health, animal health and phytosanitary situation in all Members".[353] They are not imposed, as is the case of the obligations imposed by Article XX(b) of GATT, to justify a violation of another GATT obligation (such as a violation of the non-discrimination obligations of Articles I or III).

8.42 We note in this respect that the general approach adopted in Article XX(b) of GATT is fundamentally different from the approach adopted in the SPS Agreement.

[348] As defined in Paragraph 1 of Annex A of the SPS Agreement, quoted and discussed in paras. 8.24 and 8.25.

[349] See para. 8.26.

[350] See paras. 8.115 ff.

[351] One example is the obligation contained in Article 3.1 of the SPS Agreement which provides that "[t]o harmonize sanitary and phytosanitary measures on as wide a basis as possible, Members shall base their sanitary and phytosanitary measures on international standards, guidelines or recommendations, where they exist ...".

[352] Preambular para. 6 of the SPS Agreement.

[353] Preambular para. 2 of the SPS Agreement.

Article XX(b), which is not limited to sanitary or phytosanitary measures, provides for a general *exception* which can be invoked to justify any violation of another GATT provision. The SPS Agreement, on the other hand, provides for specific *obligations* to be met in order for a Member to enact or maintain specific types of measures, namely sanitary and phytosanitary measures.

8.43 The conclusion that the SPS Agreement contains obligations which are not already imposed by GATT is confirmed in Article 2.4 of the SPS Agreement which provides that "[s]anitary or phytosanitary measures which conform to the relevant provisions of this Agreement shall be presumed to be in accordance with the obligations of the Members under the provisions of GATT 1994 which relate to the use of sanitary or phytosanitary measures, in particular the provisions of Article XX(b)". Indeed, to presume that one set of obligations (*in casu* GATT) is met because another set of obligations (*in casu* the SPS Agreement) has been fulfilled, seems to imply that the latter set of obligations imposes at least as many as, and probably more obligations than, the former. Support for this conclusion is also found in Article 3.2 of the SPS Agreement which provides that "[s]anitary or phytosanitary measures which conform to international standards, guidelines or recommendations shall be deemed to be necessary to protect human, animal or plant life or health, and presumed to be consistent with the relevant provisions of this Agreement *and* of GATT 1994" (emphasis added). While both agreements may apply in a given factual situation, the foregoing provision nonetheless establishes the SPS Agreement as an agreement which imposes obligations which are different from those imposed by GATT.

8.44 We therefore find that, in accordance with the ordinary meaning to be given to the terms of the SPS Agreement in their context and in the light of its object and purpose (in conformity with Article 31 of the Vienna Convention), there is no requirement, in any of the provisions of the SPS Agreement, that a prior violation of a GATT provision need be established before the SPS Agreement applies.

8.45 Having reached the conclusion that we are not *per se* required to address GATT claims prior to those raised under the SPS Agreement, we must then decide which of the two agreements we should examine first in this particular dispute. The SPS Agreement specifically addresses the type of measure in dispute. If we were to examine GATT first, we would in any event need to revert to the SPS Agreement: if a violation of GATT were found, we would need to consider whether Article XX(b) could be invoked and would then necessarily need to examine the SPS Agreement; if, on the other hand, no GATT violation were found, we would still need to examine the consistency of the measure with the SPS Agreement since nowhere is consistency with GATT presumed to be consistency with the SPS Agreement. For these reasons, and in order to conduct our consideration of this dispute in the most efficient manner, we shall first examine the claims raised under the SPS Agreement.

D. The SPS Agreement

1. Overview of the Provisions in Dispute

8.46 Canada claims violations of Articles 2, 3 and 5 of the SPS Agreement. Article 2 elaborates on the basic rights and obligations of Members under the SPS Agreement. Article 3 deals, more specifically, with the objective of harmonization of sanitary measures on the basis of international standards, guidelines or recommendations.

Article 5 deals, in turn, with the obligation of risk assessment and the determination and application by Members of their appropriate level of sanitary protection.

8.47 Article 3.1 requires Members to base their sanitary measures on international standards, guidelines or recommendations except as otherwise provided for in the SPS Agreement, and in particular in Article 3.3. We note, therefore, that even if international standards may not, in their own right, be binding on Members, Article 3.1 requires Members to base their sanitary measures on these standards.

8.48 According to Article 3.2 sanitary measures which conform to international standards, guidelines or recommendations are presumed to be consistent with both the SPS Agreement and GATT. We shall therefore, as a first step, examine whether there are international standards, guidelines or recommendations with respect to the EC measures in dispute and, if so, whether the EC measures are *based on* these standards, guidelines or recommendations in accordance with Article 3.1.

8.49 If there are international standards, guidelines or recommendations and the European Communities has *not* based its measures thereon, we will need, as a second step, to examine whether the European Communities can justify its measures under Article 3.3 since Article 3.1, which imposes the requirement to base sanitary measures on international standards explicitly refers to Article 3.3 as providing for an exception to this requirement.

8.50 Finally, if there are no international standards, guidelines or recommendations with respect to the EC measures in dispute, or to some of them, there would be no standards, guidelines or recommendations for these measures to be based on in line with Article 3.1. However, even in that case the consistency of the EC measures in dispute with Articles 2 and 5 of the SPS Agreement would still need to be examined.

2. *Burden of Proof*

8.51 Given the nature of disputes under the SPS Agreement, which imposes substantive and procedural requirements raising various, and in this case complex, issues of fact, the allocation of the burden of proof is of particular importance. It involves consideration of the wording, general outline and object and purpose of the SPS Agreement as a whole. We, therefore, first examine this issue in general before addressing the specific burden of proof for each of the provisions in dispute in more detail below.

8.52 With respect to burden of proof, Canada submits that under Article 3.8 of the DSU it is up to the European Communities to rebut Canada's *prima facie* case.

8.53 The European Communities argues that the burden of proof should rest on the party challenging the consistency of sanitary measures with the SPS Agreement (*in casu* Canada). The European Communities claims, *inter alia*, that it is up to Canada to provide evidence that the use of the hormones in dispute for growth promotion is safe and without risk.[354]

8.54 In addressing the burden of proof under the SPS Agreement, we consider that, as is the case in most legal proceedings, the initial burden of proof rests on the

---

354 See para. 4.65.

complaining party in the sense that it bears the burden of presenting a *prima facie* case of inconsistency with the SPS Agreement. It is, indeed, for the party that initiated the dispute settlement proceedings to put forward factual and legal arguments in order to substantiate its claim that a sanitary measure is inconsistent with the SPS Agreement. In other words, it is for Canada to present factual and legal arguments that, if unrebutted, would demonstrate a violation of the SPS Agreement. Once such a *prima facie* case is made, however, we consider that, at least with respect to the obligations imposed by the SPS Agreement that are relevant to this case, the burden of proof shifts to the responding party.[355]

8.55 In our view, the allocation of evidentiary burden under the SPS Agreement to the Member imposing a sanitary or phytosanitary measure flows directly from the wording of many of the provisions contained in that Agreement and in particular the first three words thereof:

> "*Members shall ensure* that..." (*e.g.* Articles 2.2, 2.3, 5.1 and 5.6 of the SPS Agreement; emphasis added).

8.56 Moreover, the wording of Article 5.8 (although this provision relates more to transparency than to any requirement of legal justification) further supports our reading of this assignment of burden of proof to the party imposing the measure:

> "When a Member has reason to believe that a specific sanitary or phytosanitary measure introduced or maintained by another Member is constraining, or has the potential to constrain, its exports and the measure is not based on the relevant international standards, guidelines or recommendations, or such standards, guidelines or recommendations do not exist, *an explanation of the reasons for such sanitary or phytosanitary measure may be requested and shall be provided by the Member maintaining the measure*" (emphasis added).

[355] Two provisions of the SPS Agreement do, however, explicitly confer the burden of proof upon the exporting Member (*i.e.*, the Member contesting the sanitary or phytosanitary measure), namely Article 4.1 on equivalence and Article 6.3 on pest- or disease-free areas or areas of low pest or disease prevalence. The fact that in these instances the burden of proof is explicitly conferred upon the exporting Member confirms that under other SPS provisions the burden of proof may shift to the Member imposing the sanitary or phytosanitary measure. We note, in this respect, the Report of the Appellate Body on "United States - Measures Affecting Imports of Woven Wool Shirts and Blouses from India" (adopted on 23 May 1997, WT/DS33/AB/R) which addressed the issue of burden of proof under the Agreement on Textiles and Clothing (the "ATC") as follows:

> "... a party claiming a violation of a provision of the *WTO Agreement* by another Member must assert and prove its claim. In this case, India claimed a violation by the United States of Article 6 of the *ATC*. We agree with the Panel that it, therefore, was up to India to put forward evidence and legal argument sufficient to demonstrate that the transitional safeguard action by the United States was inconsistent with the obligations assumed by the United States under Articles 2 and 6 of the *ATC*. India did so in this case. And, with India having done so, the onus then shifted to the United States to bring forward evidence and argument to disprove the claim. This, the United States was not able to do and, therefore, the Panel found that the transitional safeguard action by the United States "violated the provisions of Articles 2 and 6 of the ATC", DSR 1997:I, 323 at 337-338.

8.57 Finally, we note that this assignment of burden of proof to the party imposing the measure is also supported by Article 3.2 which introduces a presumption of consistency with the SPS Agreement for sanitary measures which conform to international standards, guidelines or recommendations. Article 3.2 states the following:

> "Sanitary or phytosanitary measures which conform to international standards, guidelines or recommendations shall be deemed to be necessary to protect human, animal or plant life or health, and presumed to be consistent with the relevant provisions of this Agreement and of GATT 1994".

Introducing a general presumption of consistency with an agreement in favour of a party (*in casu* the party imposing the measure) in the event that certain conditions are met, seems, indeed, to presuppose that the burden of proof under that agreement in principle (*i.e.,* in cases where these specific conditions are *not* met) rests on that party.

8.58 We thus find that, for the purposes of this dispute, Canada bears the burden of presenting a *prima facie* case of inconsistency with the SPS Agreement, after which the burden of proof shifts to the European Communities to demonstrate that its measures in dispute meet the requirements imposed by the SPS Agreement.

3. *Article 3.1: Sanitary Measures Based on International Standards*

8.59 Article 3.1 of the SPS Agreement reads as follows:

> "To harmonize sanitary and phytosanitary measures on as wide a basis as possible, Members shall base their sanitary and phytosanitary measures on international standards, guidelines or recommendations, where they exist, except as otherwise provided for in this Agreement, and in particular in paragraph 3".

The first question we must address is whether there exist any "international standards, guidelines or recommendations" with respect to the administration of any of the six hormones in dispute for growth promotion purposes. For food safety, the health concern at issue in this dispute, paragraph 3(a) of Annex A of the SPS Agreement defines "international standards, guidelines or recommendations" as

> "the standards, guidelines and recommendations established by the *Codex Alimentarius Commission* relating to food additives, *veterinary drug* and pesticide *residues*, contaminants, methods of analysis and sampling, and codes and guidelines of hygienic practice" (emphasis added).

8.60 In line with Article 3.1, we consider that if such Codex Alimentarius Commission standards, guidelines or recommendations ("Codex standards") exist with respect to the administration of any of the six hormones in dispute for growth promotion purposes, a sanitary measure taken by a Member should either be based on these standards or be justified under Article 3.3 of the SPS Agreement.

(a) Codex Standards

8.61 Within the scope of the measures in dispute, we note that Codex standards exist for five of the six hormones at issue (*i.e.*, for all hormones at issue other than MGA).[356] We will accordingly examine the definition and scope of application of these Codex standards and determine whether they apply to the EC measures in dispute.

8.62 The Codex Alimentarius Commission ("Codex"), an international body of which most WTO Members (including Canada and the member States of the European Communities) are members, establishes, *inter alia*, Acceptable Daily Intakes ("ADIs"), Maximum Residue Limits ("MRLs") and other recommendations for veterinary drugs. It does so on the basis of the advice of the Codex Committee on Residues of Veterinary Drugs in Foods and the recommendations of the Joint FAO/WHO Expert Committee on Food Additives ("JECFA"). While Codex is composed of government representatives of member States, JECFA is composed of independent scientists. JECFA makes scientific evaluations and recommendations; Codex takes the decision whether or not to adopt these recommendations. However, once adopted Codex recommendations are, according to the General Principles of Codex, *not* binding upon Codex members. They are only of an advisory nature. The procedures to be followed to adopt a Codex recommendation have been outlined above.[357]

8.63 The goal of JECFA's evaluation of veterinary drugs is

> "*to establish safe levels* of intake by setting Acceptable Daily Intakes (ADIs) and to develop maximum residue limits when veterinary drugs are used in accordance with good veterinary practice" (emphasis added).[358]

The term "good veterinary practice" (as well as the term "good animal husbandry practice" often used in JECFA Reports) is for Codex purposes, according to the Codex expert advising the Panel[359], a synonym for what is known in Codex terminology as "Good Practice in the Use of Veterinary Drugs" ("GPVD"; hereafter also referred to as "good practice"), in turn defined as

> "the official recommended or authorized usage including withdrawal periods, approved by national authorities, of veterinary drugs under practical conditions".[360]

8.64 An ADI set by Codex is "an estimate by JECFA of the amount of a veterinary drug, expressed on a body weight basis, that can be ingested daily over a lifetime *without appreciable health risk* (standard man = 60 kg)" (emphasis added).[361] This ADI is derived from the experimental no observable effect level in the most appropriate animal species, by applying an appropriate safety factor. A Codex MRL, on the other hand, if implemented in national law, determines the amount of residues which is legally permitted or recognized as acceptable in food and is primarily a regulatory

---

356 See para. 2.20, 2.21 and 2.23.

357 See paras. 2.15-2.16.

358 See para. 2.14.

359 See para. 2.19.

360 *Ibid.*

361 See para. 2.17.

tool to ensure that intake does not exceed the ADI and that good practice is observed. A Codex MRL is frequently set at levels below (even far below) the theoretical safe levels determined from an ADI. Codex MRLs for veterinary drugs are normally expressed in µg/kg on a fresh weight basis in meat.[362]

8.65 With respect to the three natural hormones in dispute, *oestradiol-17β*, *progesterone* and *testosterone* (classified by Codex as "veterinary drugs"), similar Codex standards apply. For all three hormones, when used for growth promotion purposes, it was considered "unnecessary" to establish an ADI or MRL. For all three hormones the following footnote explained the word "unnecessary":

> "Establishing an ADI and an [MRL] for a hormone that is produced endogenously at variable levels in human beings was considered unnecessary by the Committee. Residues resulting from the use of this substance as a growth promoter in accordance with good animal husbandry practice are unlikely to pose a hazard to human health".[363]

The 32nd JECFA Report of 1988, on which the Codex standards are based, concluded for all three natural hormones administered for growth promotion purposes that the residue levels of each of these hormones when found in meat from animals treated with implants according to good animal husbandry practice are extremely low when compared with the amounts endogenously produced daily in human beings or normally present in the dairy products or tissues of untreated animals or other foods. According to JECFA, the potential toxic effect of residues of these hormones is directly related to their hormonal effect. Since the additional residue levels in treated animals have no hormonal effect, the Report concluded that these residue levels are not capable of exerting any toxic effect. JECFA further noted that the total residue levels in treated animals fall well within the normal range of levels found in untreated animals of different types and ages. On the basis of this safety assessment and in view of the difficulty of determining the levels of residues attributable to the use of this hormone as a growth promoter in cattle (residues of endogenous natural hormones in meat cannot, according to JECFA, be practically distinguished from those exogenously administered), JECFA concluded that it was "unnecessary" to establish an ADI or MRL for these hormones.[364]

8.66 With respect to two of the three synthetic hormones at issue, *zeranol* and *trenbolone* (classified by Codex as "veterinary drugs"), the following Codex standards apply: an ADI of 0-0.5 and 0-0.02 µg/kg body weight, respectively, and an MRL of 2 µg/kg β-trenbolone in bovine muscle and 10 µg/kg α-trenbolone in bovine liver.[365]

8.67 The 32nd JECFA Report of 1988, on which the Codex standard for *zeranol* is based, noted that zeranol was shown to be a weak oestrogen which mimics the action of oestradiol-17β. The Report concluded that the toxic (*in casu* tumorigenic) effect of zeranol is associated with its hormonal (*i.e.,* oestrogenic) properties and that an

---

[362] See para. 2.18.
[363] See para. 2.21.
[364] See para. 2.22.
[365] See para. 2.23.

ADI could thus be established on the basis of a no-hormonal-effect level. Adopting what it considered to be a conservative approach by using as a basis studies on ovariectomized female cynomolgus monkeys (highly sensitive to oestrogenic substances) and using a safety factor of 100, JECFA set an ADI for human beings of 0-0.5 μg/kg of body weight. For a 70 kg person consuming 500 g of meat daily over an entire lifetime, the maximum permissible or safe level of zeranol residues in meat would then, according to JECFA, be 70 μg/kg of edible tissue. However, the Report noted that when zeranol is administered to cattle according to the proposed good practice, the maximum mean residue levels would not exceed 0.2 μg/kg in muscle and 10 μg/kg in liver *at any time after implantation* (irrespective of the withdrawal period respected). These residue levels obtained on the basis of good practice are thus far below what JECFA determined to be the safety level of 70 μg/kg. However, in order to set a level which is detectable by using methods available for routine residue analysis, the official Codex MRL was increased to 2 μg/kg in muscle and set at 10 μg/kg in liver.[366]

8.68 Trenbolone acetate is the chemical form or ester used for the administration of *trenbolone*. Trenbolone, or trenbolone acetate ("TBA"), an androgen which mimics the action of testosterone, is rapidly hydrolysed after administration to cattle, the major metabolites (*i.e.,* compound into which TBA breaks down by chemical activity when entering the body) being α-trenbolone, occurring, *inter alia*, in liver, and β-trenbolone, present in muscle.[367] With respect to TBA, the 32nd JECFA Report of 1988 concluded that its potential toxic effects only arise as a consequence of its hormonal activity and concluded that, therefore, an ADI could be established on the basis of a no-hormonal-effect level.[368] Adopting what it considered to be a conservative approach by using as a basis studies on castrated male rhesus macaque monkeys which are highly sensitive to compounds with antigonadotropic activity and pigs which are a sensitive model for assessing hormonal effects of TBA and using a safety factor of 100, JECFA later set an ADI for human beings of 0-0.02 μg/kg of body weight (34th JECFA Report of 1989).[369] The maximum ADI for a 60 kg person would thus be 1.2 μg of TBA residues. JECFA then set MRLs for β-trenbolone in muscle and α-trenbolone in liver of 2 μg/kg and 10 μg/kg respectively, based on average residue levels in heifers at 15-30 days after implantation of 300 mg TBA, noting that concentrations would even be lower at the proposed good practice. According to JECFA, the MRLs thus obtained on the basis of conservative estimates would not exceed the Codex ADI or safe level *at any time after implantation of the drug* (irrespective of the withdrawal period respected).

8.69 The European Communities argues that the Codex standards outlined above are not relevant to this dispute. It argues that there are no Codex standards for the *use* of hormone growth promoters, only Codex standards for *maximum residue levels* and that since the EC measures in dispute do not set maximum residue levels, there exist no Codex standards on which the EC measures need to be based. Moreover, the

366 See para. 2.24.
367 See para. 2.25.
368 *Ibid.*
369 *Ibid.*

European Communities argues, the Codex standards invoked are *levels* of protection, not *measures*, and since there is no obligation in the SPS Agreement to adopt Codex recommended levels of protection, the standards invoked are irrelevant for the EC measures in dispute.[370]

8.70 The European Communities also notes that the decision by Codex (of July 1995) to formally adopt the five Codex standards at issue was taken by a majority of only 33 votes in favour, 29 votes against and 7 abstentions; a very close vote which is unusual in Codex practice where proposals are normally adopted by consensus, indicating that the issue of hormone growth promoters has been and continues to be very controversial.[371]

8.71 The European Communities finally argues that the process which led to the adoption of the Codex standards started long before the entry into force of the SPS Agreement and was only completed six months after that date. At the time the standards were discussed, Codex members were, therefore, according to the European Communities, unaware of the fact that the Codex standards, which within the Codex system are only of an advisory nature, would in the future become "binding" by virtue of the SPS Agreement.[372] The European Communities seems to consider this element as a reason to disregard these Codex standards in this dispute.

8.72 In considering these EC arguments, we note that Article 3.1 unambiguously prescribes that "... Members shall base their sanitary ... measures on international standards ... *where they exist* ...' (emphasis added). Paragraph 3 of Annex A of the SPS Agreement states equally clearly that the international standards mentioned in Article 3:1 are "for food safety the standards ... *established by the Codex Alimentarius Commission* relating to ... *veterinary drug ... residues* ..." (emphasis added). No other conditions are imposed in the SPS Agreement on the relevance of international standards for the purposes of Article 3. Therefore, as a panel making a finding on whether or not a Member has an obligation to base its sanitary measure on international standards in accordance with Article 3.1, we only need to determine whether such international standards exist. For these purposes, we need not consider (i) whether the standards reflect *levels* of protection or sanitary *measures* or the *type* of sanitary measure they recommend, or (ii) whether these standards have been adopted by consensus or by a wide or narrow majority, or (iii) whether the period during which they have been discussed or the date of their adoption was before or after the entry into force of the SPS Agreement.[373]

8.73 We note that the five Codex standards outlined above are standards relating to veterinary drug residues as required in paragraph 3(a) of Annex A[374] and apply exclusively with respect to cattle and meat and meat products of bovine origin and with

[370] See para. 4.66.

[371] See para. 4.209.

[372] See para. 4.92 and EC submissions to the panel considering the US complaint on the same measures.

[373] We recall in this respect that the Codex standards in dispute have in any event been adopted in July 1995, *i.e., subsequent* to the entry into force of the SPS Agreement on 1 January 1995. With respect to the timeframe for the application of the SPS Agreement in general, we refer to paragraphs 8.27-8.30.

[374] See para. 8.59.

respect to five of the six hormones in dispute when these hormones are used for growth promotion purposes.[375] We recall the scope of the EC measures in dispute, in particular that they are limited to the EC ban on imports of meat and meat products of bovine origin from cattle treated with any of six specific hormones if the treatment with any of these substances is carried out for growth promotion purposes.[376] We find, therefore, that international standards exist with respect to the EC measures in dispute, to the extent they relate to five of the six hormones at issue (all but MGA), in the sense of Article 3.1 and paragraph 3(a) of Annex A. We must next determine whether the EC measures are *based on* these international standards in terms of Article 3.1.

(b) Sanitary Measures *Based On* Codex Standards

8.74 Canada argues that the EC measures for zeranol and trenbolone are based on MRLs of zero and are, therefore, not based on the Codex MRLs. Canada further claims that full acceptance of the Codex MRLs for residues of veterinary drugs in food dictates that distribution of food conforming with the MRLs will not be hindered by legal provisions. Since the EC measures in dispute prohibit the distribution of beef treated with any of the five hormones for which Codex standards exist for growth promotion purposes, Canada concludes that the European Communities has not accepted the Codex MRLs and has thus not based its measures on them.[377] The European Communities does not submit that its measures are based on the Codex standards, but rather argues that, as discussed above[378], there are no relevant Codex standards on which its measures in dispute need to be based.

(i) The Meaning of *Based On*

8.75 The SPS Agreement does not explicitly define the words *based on* as used in Article 3.1. However, Article 3.2, which introduces a presumption of consistency with both the SPS Agreement and GATT for sanitary measures which *conform to* international standards, equates measures *based on* international standards with measures which *conform to* such standards. Article 3.3, in turn, explicitly relates the definition of sanitary measures *based on* international standards to the level of sanitary protection achieved by these measures. Article 3.3 stipulates the conditions to be met for a Member to enact or maintain certain sanitary measures which are *not* based on international standards.[379] It applies more specifically to measures "which result in a *higher level* of sanitary ... protection than would be achieved by measures based on the relevant international standards" or measures "which result in a *level* of sanitary ... protection *different* from that which would be achieved by measures based on in-

[375] See para. 2.20.

[376] See para. 8.21.

[377] See para. 4.64.

[378] See paras. 8.69-8.72.

[379] Article 3.1 explicitly refers to Article 3.3 as providing for exceptions to the general obligation to base sanitary measures on international standards: "... Members shall base their sanitary ... measures on international standards ..., except as otherwise provided for in this Agreement, and *in particular in paragraph 3*" (emphasis added).

ternational standards". One of the determining factors in deciding whether a measure is *based on* an international standard is, therefore, the level of protection that measure achieves. According to Article 3.3 all measures which *are* based on a given international standard should in principle achieve the *same* level of sanitary protection. Therefore, if an international standard reflects a specific level of sanitary protection and a sanitary measure implies a *different* level, that measure cannot be considered to be *based on* the international standard.

8.76 We find, therefore, that for a sanitary measure to be *based on* an international standard in accordance with Article 3.1, that *measure* needs to reflect the same level of sanitary protection as the *standard*.[380] In this dispute a comparison thus needs to be made between the level of protection reflected in the EC measures in dispute and that reflected in the Codex standards for each of the five hormones at issue.

8.77 Without limiting the possibilities of how a *level of protection* may be expressed for a particular substance, we consider that in the specific field of veterinary drugs (including the six hormones at issue), a level of protection can be directly linked to the *amount of residues* of that drug allowed either to be ingested by humans on a daily basis or to be present in a particular food.[381] A level of protection can thus, *inter alia*, be expressed by way of setting a maximum amount of residues allowed for daily intake by humans over a lifetime (often defined as acceptable daily intake or ADI[382]) and (or) by way of adopting a maximum amount of residues allowed to be present in a particular food (often defined as maximum residue limit or MRL[383]). However, the fact that an ADI or MRL can *reflect* a *level* of protection (without *stricto sensu* itself *being* a level of protection), does not exclude, as the European Communities has argued, that an ADI or MRL can also be a sanitary *measure* in the sense of the SPS Agreement.

(ii) Comparison of Levels of Sanitary Protection

8.78 In this dispute, two of the international standards applicable, namely the Codex standards with respect to *zeranol* and *trenbolone* (two synthetic hormones), provide for an ADI of 0-0.5 and 0-0.02 μg/kg of body weight, respectively, and an MRL of 10 μg/kg for bovine liver and 2 μg/kg for bovine muscle for zeranol and an MRL of 10 μg/kg α-trenbolone for bovine liver and 2 μg/kg of β-trenbolone for bovine muscle.[384] These ADIs and MRLs reflect the level of protection set by the Codex standards.[385] To determine whether the EC measures in dispute with respect to zeranol and trenbolone are based on these Codex standards, we need to examine whether the level of protection reflected in the EC measures is the same as the level of pro-

---

380 We recall, however, that, given the exceptions provided for in Article 3.3, the requirement that a sanitary measure reflects the same level of protection as the relevant international standard is in no way absolute. This requirement is only imposed for a measure to be *based on* such international standard in accordance with Article 3.1.

381 The concept of "appropriate" level of protection is examined in paragraph 8.82.

382 See paras. 8.62 ff.

383 *Ibid.*

384 See paras. 2.23-2.25.

385 See para. 8.77.

tection expressed by the Codex standards.[386] Since the EC measures in dispute do not allow the presence of any residues of these two hormones in any meat or meat product or any of these residues to be ingested by humans (imposing what it calls a "no residue" level), the level of protection reflected in the EC measures is significantly *different* from the level of protection set by the Codex standards (a "no residue" level as opposed to an ADI of maximum 0.5 and 0.02 μg/kg of body weight and an MRL of 2 and 10 μg/kg for, respectively, bovine muscle and bovine liver). The EC measures in dispute, in as far as they relate to zeranol and trenbolone, are, therefore, not *based on* existing international standards as specified in Article 3.1.

8.79 When establishing the other three Codex standards applicable to the EC measures in dispute, Codex considered it "unnecessary" to set an ADI or MRL for residues of *oestradiol-17β, testosterone* and *progesterone* (the three natural hormones).[387] The amount of residues of these hormones administered for growth promotion purposes allowed by these Codex standards is, therefore, in any event higher than zero (a maximum level of such residues has not even been prescribed; this level is hereafter referred to as an "unlimited residue level"). The EC measures in dispute, on the other hand, do not allow the presence of any residues of these three hormones administered for growth promotion purposes (again imposing what the European Communities calls a "no residue" level). The level of protection reflected in the EC measures is, therefore, significantly *different* from the level of protection reflected in the Codex standards (a "no residue" level as opposed to an unlimited residue level). The EC measures in dispute, in so far as they relate to oestradiol-17β, testosterone and progesterone, are, therefore, not *based on* existing international standards as specified in Article 3.1.

8.80 We thus find that the EC measures in dispute (except to the extent they relate to the hormone MGA) result in a different level of sanitary protection than would be achieved by measures based on the relevant Codex standards and are, therefore, not *based on* existing international standards as specified in Article 3.1.

8.81 We next examine whether the EC measures with respect to five of the six hormones in dispute, which are not based on existing international standards, otherwise are consistent with the requirements of the SPS Agreement (sections 4 and 5). We then address the EC measures which relate to the sixth hormone, MGA, for which no international standard exists (section 6).

4. *Article 3.3: Sanitary Measures not Based On International Standards*

8.82 The fact that the EC measures for oestradiol-17β, testosterone, progesterone, zeranol and trenbolone are not based on existing international standards does not necessarily mean that those measures are inconsistent with the requirements of the SPS Agreement. Article 3.3 reads as follows:

---

386 See para. 8.76.

387 See para. 8.65.

> "Members may introduce or maintain sanitary or phytosanitary measures which result in a higher level of sanitary protection than would be achieved by measures based on the relevant international standards, guidelines or recommendations, if there is a scientific justification, or as a consequence of the level of sanitary or phytosanitary protection a Member determines to be appropriate in accordance with the relevant provisions of paragraphs 1 through 8 of Article 5. Notwithstanding the above, all measures which result in a level of sanitary or phytosanitary protection different from that which would be achieved by measures based on international standards, guidelines or recommendations shall not be inconsistent with any other provision of this Agreement".

A footnote to Article 3.3, first sentence, then specifies:

> "For the purposes of paragraph 3 of Article 3, there is a scientific justification if, on the basis of an examination and evaluation of available scientific information in conformity with the relevant provisions of this Agreement, a Member determines that the relevant international standards, guidelines or recommendations are not sufficient to achieve its appropriate level of sanitary or phytosanitary protection".

The concept of an "appropriate level of sanitary protection" is defined in paragraph 5 of Annex A of the SPS Agreement as:

> "The level of protection deemed appropriate by the Member establishing a sanitary ... measure to protect human, animal or plant life or health within its territory".

A Note to this paragraph adds the following:

> "Many Members otherwise refer to this concept as the 'acceptable level of risk' ".

(a) Requirements for Justification

8.83 For a sanitary measure to be justified under Article 3.3 the measure needs, first of all, to "result in a higher level of sanitary protection than would be achieved by measures based on the relevant international standards, guidelines or recommendations". We recall the comparison made above between the level of protection reflected in the EC measures and that implied in the Codex standards for each of the hormones at issue, in particular that the level reflected in the EC measures is *different* from that implied in the Codex standards.[388] For purposes of our analysis under Article 3.3, we assume that the former level is *higher* than the latter, in line with the first sentence of Article 3.3. In addition, the sanitary measure needs to fulfil one of the following two conditions:

- there is a "scientific justification" for imposing the measure, i.e., the Member imposing the measure has determined "on the basis of an examination and evaluation of available scientific information in conformity with the relevant provisions of [the SPS] Agreement, ... that the relevant international standards, guidelines or recommendations

[388] See para. 8.80.

are not sufficient to achieve its appropriate level of sanitary ... protection" ("the first exception"); *or*

- the measure is "a consequence of the level of sanitary ... protection a Member determines to be appropriate in accordance with the relevant provisions of paragraphs 1 through 8 of Article 5" ("the second exception").

However, according to the second sentence of Article 3.3, even if one of these conditions is fulfilled, the party imposing the measure must still comply with the other provisions of the SPS Agreement.

8.84 We will consider first whether either the first or the second exception outlined above is met. In doing so, we first address the relationship and difference between these two exceptions. Canada argues that the two exceptions are similar and complementary: the first exception deals with situations where an international standard is outdated in such a way that it does not provide the level of protection it was thought to have provided; the second exception deals with situations where an international standard is valid but where the Member's level of protection is different from the level of protection provided by the international standard.[389] The European Communities argues that the first exception is fulfilled when the international standard is inadequate, faulty or obsolete from a scientific point of view and that, according to the second exception, a Member is in any case entitled to introduce or maintain measures which aim at achieving its appropriate level of protection, to be determined in accordance with Article 5 of the SPS Agreement.[390]

8.85 We note that both exceptions explicitly refer to other provisions of the SPS Agreement. The first exception contains the following reference: "... on the basis of an examination and evaluation of available scientific information *in conformity with the relevant provisions of [the SPS] Agreement* ..." (emphasis added). The second exception refers to "... the relevant provisions of *paragraphs 1 through 8 of Article 5*" (emphasis added). Article 3.3, second sentence, in turn, explicitly states that even if the sanitary measure at issue falls under one of the two exceptions of Article 3.3, first sentence, the sanitary measure in question still needs to be consistent with all provisions of the SPS Agreement other than Article 3.

8.86 We find, therefore, that, whatever the difference might be between the two exceptions, a sanitary measure can only be justified under Article 3.3 if it is consistent with the requirements contained in Article 5. If we were to find that the EC measures in dispute are inconsistent with the requirements imposed by Article 5, these measures cannot be justified under Article 3.3. However, even if we find that the EC measures at issue are consistent with the requirements imposed by Article 5, this will still not be sufficient for these measures to be justified under Article 3.3 since to reach that conclusion we also need to find that the EC measures in dispute fulfil all provisions of the SPS Agreement other than Articles 3 and 5 (*in casu* Article 2).

---

389 See para. 4.78.

390 See paras. 4.86-4.89.

(b) Burden of Proof

8.87 We recall the findings made above on the burden of proof under the SPS Agreement[391], in particular that for the obligations imposed by the SPS Agreement that are relevant to this case, the party contesting a sanitary measure (*in casu* Canada) bears the initial burden of proof in that it has to present a *prima facie* case of inconsistency with the SPS Agreement, after which the burden of proof shifts to the party imposing the measure (*in casu* the European Communities).

8.88 We consider that this allocation of burden to the party imposing a sanitary measure is, for the reasons set out above[392], applicable to Article 3.3 and particularly justified under the first sentence thereof which contains specific requirements to be fulfilled for a Member to justify a sanitary measure which is *not* based on an international standard.

8.89 One purpose of the SPS Agreement, as explicitly recognized in the preamble, is to promote the use of international standards, guidelines and recommendations. To that end, Article 3.1 imposes an obligation on all Members to base their sanitary measures on international standards except as otherwise provided for in the SPS Agreement, and in particular in Article 3.3 thereof. In this sense, Article 3.3 provides an *exception* to the general obligation contained in Article 3.1. Article 3.2, in turn, specifies that the complaining party has the burden of overcoming a presumption of consistency with the SPS Agreement in the case of a measure based on international standards. It thereby suggests by implication that when a measure is not so based, the burden is on the respondent to show that the measure is justified under the exceptions provided for in Article 3.3.

8.90 We find, therefore, that once the complaining party provides a *prima facie* case (i) that there is an international standard with respect to the measure in dispute, and (ii) that the measure in dispute is *not* based on this standard, the burden of proof under Article 3.3 shifts to the defending party.[393]

8.91 Since in this dispute we have already found that there exist international standards[394] and that the EC measures at issue are not based on these standards[395], we

[391] See paras. 8.51-8.58.

[392] See paras. 8.54-8.57.

[393] This approach is in line with established practice under GATT 1947 and GATT 1994 where, for example, the burden of proof to justify an inconsistency with another GATT provision under Article XX also rests on the defending party. See Panel Report on "Canada - Administration of the Foreign Investment Review Act", adopted on 7 February 1984, BISD 30S/140, p.164, para. 5.20; on "United States - Section 337 of the Tariff Act of 1930", adopted on 7 November 1989, BISD 36S/345, p.393, para.5.27 and on "United States - Standards for Reformulated and Conventional Gasoline", op. cit., p.38, para. 6.20. In this respect, we also note that the Report of the Appellate Body on "United States - Measures Affecting Imports of Woven Wool Shirts and Blouses from India" stated the following with respect to the burden of proof under Articles XX and XI:2(c)(i) of GATT: "Articles XX and XI:(2)(c)(i) are limited exceptions from obligations under certain other provisions of the GATT 1994, not positive rules establishing obligations in themselves. They are in the nature of affirmative defences. It is only reasonable that the burden of establishing such a defence should rest on the party asserting it" (*op. cit.*, DSR 1997:I, 323 at 337).

[394] See para. 8.73.

[395] See para. 8.80.

find that the burden of justifying the measures in dispute under Article 3.3, and in particular under the first sentence thereof, rests on the European Communities.

8.92 *In summary*, in sections 3 and 4 we have found that: (i) there exist international standards, as defined in Article 3.1 and paragraph 3(a) of Annex A of the SPS Agreement, with respect to the EC measures in dispute to the extent they relate to five of the six hormones at issue (all but MGA); (ii) the EC measures in dispute, in as far as they relate to these five hormones, are *not based on* these international standards, as required in Article 3.1; and (iii) the EC measures, to the extent they are *not* based on these international standards, can only be justified under Article 3.3 if these measures meet, *inter alia,* the requirements imposed by Article 5.

8.93 In the next section we will, therefore, examine whether the EC measures in dispute *with respect to the five hormones at issue for which international standards exist* are consistent with the requirements imposed by Article 5.

5. *Article 5: "Assessment of Risk and Determination of the Appropriate Level of Sanitary or Phytosanitary Protection"*

(a) Risk Assessment and Risk Management

8.94 Article 5 of the SPS Agreement deals mainly[396] with two separate aspects of a Member's decision to enact or maintain a sanitary measure. These two aspects are separated in the SPS Agreement, which provides for specific rights and obligations in respect of each of them.

8.95 The *first aspect* relates to the exercise of assessing the risks to human, animal or plant life or health against which a sanitary measure is intended to protect. This is referred to in the SPS Agreement as *risk assessment.*[397] With respect to food safety, the potential adverse effects (if any) related to a specific substance are established together with the probability of occurrence of any such effects.[398]

8.96 According to Article 5.1, a Member needs to ensure that its sanitary measures are *based on* an assessment of risks. The obligation to base a sanitary measure on a risk assessment may be viewed as a specific application of the basic obligations contained in Article 2.2 of the SPS Agreement which provides that "Members shall ensure that any sanitary ... measure is *applied only to the extent necessary to protect* human, animal or plant life or health, is *based on scientific principles* and is *not maintained without sufficient scientific evidence* ..." (emphasis added). Articles 5.1 to 5.3 sum up factors a Member needs to take into account in making this assessment of risks.[399]

[396] Except for Article 5.8 which has not been invoked in this dispute.

[397] See the title of Article 5 of the SPS Agreement ("Assessment of risk ...") and Annex A of the SPS Agreement providing a definition for "risk assessment".

[398] See the definition of "risk assessment" contained in paragraph 4 of Annex A of the SPS Agreement, discussed below in para. 8.101.

[399] Article 5.7 deals with cases where relevant scientific evidence is insufficient at which point a Member may, under certain conditions, take provisional sanitary measures. The European Communities has explicitly stated that this provision does not apply to the EC measures in dispute.

8.97 As will be outlined below[400], an assessment of risks is, at least for risks to human life or health, a *scientific* examination of data and factual studies; it is not a policy exercise involving social value judgments made by political bodies.

8.98 The *second aspect* of a Member's decision to enact or maintain a sanitary measure relates, *inter alia*, to the determination and application of the *appropriate level of sanitary protection* by that Member against the risks to human, animal or plant life or health which have been assessed in accordance with Articles 5.1 to 5.3. This aspect is commonly referred to by the parties to this dispute as an essential part of *risk management*.[401] The Member wishing to impose a sanitary measure must decide the extent to which it can accept the potential adverse effects related to a specific substance which have been identified in the risk assessment.

8.99 Articles 5.4 to 5.6 are particularly relevant to the risk management decision. Article 5.4 establishes the objective of minimizing negative trade effects in the *determination* by a Member of its appropriate level of protection. Article 5.5 aims at achieving consistency in the *application* of the concept of appropriate level of protection. Article 5.6, in turn, provides that the sanitary *measure* which is finally adopted shall not be more trade-restrictive than required to achieve the appropriate level of protection of the Member concerned. Articles 5.4 to 5.6 may be viewed as specific applications of the basic obligations provided for in Article 2.2 which, *inter alia*, states that "Members shall ensure that any sanitary or phytosanitary measure is *applied only to the extent necessary to protect* human, animal or plant life or health" (emphasis added) and Article 2.3 which provides that "Members shall ensure that their sanitary and phytosanitary measures do *not arbitrarily or unjustifiably discriminate between Members* where identical or similar conditions prevail ..." and that "Sanitary and phytosanitary measures *shall not be applied in a manner which would constitute a disguised restriction* on international trade" (emphasis added).

8.100 As will be outlined below[402], the risk management phase involves *non-scientific* considerations, such as social value judgments.

(b) Articles 5.1 to 5.3: Risk Assessment

8.101 According to Article 5.1

> "Members shall ensure that their sanitary or phytosanitary measures are based on an assessment, as appropriate to the circumstances, of the risks to human, animal or plant life or health, taking into account risk assessment techniques developed by the relevant international organizations".

Paragraph 4 of Annex A of the SPS Agreement defines "risk assessment" with respect to contaminants (including residues of the hormones at issue) as

> "the *evaluation* of the *potential* for *adverse effects* on human or animal health arising from the presence of ... contaminants ... in food, beverages or feedstuffs" (emphasis added).

[400] See paras. 8.101 and 8.107-8.110.

[401] See paras. 4.97, 4.106 and 4.124.

[402] See paras. 8.163 ff.

Guided by the wording of these provisions, we consider that, in this dispute, a risk assessment carried out in accordance with the SPS Agreement should (i) *identify* the *adverse effects* on human health (if any) arising from the presence of the hormones at issue when used as growth promoters *in meat or meat products*, and (ii) if any such adverse effects exist, *evaluate* the *potential* or probability of occurrence of these effects.

8.102 Article 5.1 provides in general terms, without any limitation in time, that "Members shall ensure that their sanitary or phytosanitary measures are based on an assessment, as appropriate to the circumstances, of the risks ...". It does not prevent that with respect to a sanitary measure enacted *before* the entry into force of the SPS Agreement, the risk assessment is carried out or invoked *after* the entry into force of that Agreement (and thus *after* the enactment of the sanitary measure in question). However, the fact that a sanitary measure may be enacted *before* the entry into force of the SPS Agreement does not mean that, once the SPS Agreement entered into force, there is no obligation for the Member in question to base that measure on a risk assessment.[403] Moreover, the more general obligation contained in Article 2.2 of the SPS Agreement explicitly provides that "Members shall ensure that any sanitary or phytosanitary measure ... is based on scientific principles and is not *maintained* without sufficient scientific evidence ..." (emphasis added).

8.103 We also recall our finding reached above on the specific burden of proof under Article 3.3[404], in particular that the burden of proving that the requirements imposed by Article 3.3 (*inter alia*, consistency with Article 5) are met, rests with the Member imposing a sanitary measure which deviates from an international standard. Since the EC measures examined in this section (relating to all hormones in dispute other than MGA) are not based on existing international standards and need to be justified under the exceptions provided for in Article 3.3, the European Communities has the burden of proving that its measures are based on a risk assessment in accordance with Article 5.

8.104 In this respect we consider at the outset that it is for the European Communities to submit evidence before the Panel that its measures are based on a risk assessment; it is not for the Panel itself to conduct its own risk assessment on the basis of scientific evidence gathered by the Panel or submitted by the parties during the Panel proceedings.

8.105 We next examine: (i) the techniques and factors to be taken into account in a risk assessment in accordance with Article 5; (ii) whether the European Communities has demonstrated the existence of such a risk assessment; and (iii) assuming that such risk assessment exists, whether the European Communities has demonstrated that its measures at issue are based on this risk assessment.

---

[403] Our reasoning and general finding with respect to the application *ratione temporis* of the SPS Agreement developed in paragraphs 8.27-8.30 also applies to Article 5.1 of that Agreement.

[404] See paras. 8.87-8.91.

(i) Techniques and Factors to be Taken into Account

8.106 None of the parties suggest that there are "risk assessment techniques developed by the relevant international organizations" in the sense of Article 5.1 which have to be taken into account in a risk assessment for the hormones at issue.[405] We note, however, that, even though no formal decision has as yet been taken by Codex with respect to risk assessment techniques, Codex, and more particularly JECFA, has a long-standing practice with respect to the assessment of risks related to veterinary drug residues (including hormone residues). The techniques thus developed have been outlined above.[406] We also note the Report of the Joint FAO/WHO Expert Consultation on the Application of Risk Analysis to Food Standards Issues convened at the request of Codex in March 1995. In this Report "risk assessment" is defined as follows:

> "The scientific evaluation of known or potential adverse health effects resulting from human exposure to foodborne hazards. The process consists of the following steps: (i) hazard identification, (ii) hazard characterization, (iii) exposure assessment, and (iv) risk characterization. The definition includes quantitative risk assessment, which emphasizes reliance on numerical expressions of risk, and also qualitative expressions of risk, as well as an indication of the attendant uncertainties" (p.6).[407]

8.107 Article 5.2 provides for the factors which a Member has to take into account in the assessment of risks:

> "In the assessment of risks, Members shall take into account available scientific evidence; relevant processes and production methods; relevant inspection, sampling and testing methods; prevalence of specific diseases or pests; existence of pest- or disease-free areas; relevant ecological and environmental conditions; and quarantine or other treatment".

8.108 None of the parties involved in this dispute has argued that any factors listed in Article 5.2 other than the following three are relevant for an assessment of risks related to the hormones at issue in this case:

(i) available scientific evidence;

(ii) relevant processes and production methods;

(ii) relevant inspection, sampling and testing methods.

In particular, we note that none of the parties has argued that factors not listed in Article 5.2, such as consumer preferences, can be taken into account in a risk assessment in accordance with Article 5.

[405] See paras. 4.122-4.123.

[406] See paras. 8.62 ff.

[407] A revised version of this definition has been accepted at the 12th session of the Codex Committee on General Principles held in November 1996 and reads as follows: "A scientifically based process consisting of the following steps: (i) hazard identification, (ii) hazard characterization; (iii) exposure assessment, and (iv) risk characterization" (Codex Alimentarius Commission, CX/GP96/3).

8.109 Article 5.3 sums up relevant economic factors to be taken into account in assessing risks to *animal* or *plant* life or health. Since the scope of this dispute is limited to issues of *human* life or health[408], Article 5.3 has no application to the matter under consideration.

8.110 We finally note that the parties agree that, for the purposes of the EC measures in dispute, a risk assessment in accordance with Article 5 is a *scientific* process aimed at establishing the *scientific* basis for the sanitary measure a Member intends to take.[409]

(ii) The Existence of a Risk Assessment

8.111 The European Communities has referred to the following scientific evidence concerning the five hormones at issue:[410]

- the 1982 Report of the EC Scientific Veterinary Committee, Scientific Committee for Animal Nutrition and the Scientific Committee for Food on the basis of the Report of the Scientific Group on Anabolic Agents in Animal Production[411] ("Lamming Report");
- the 1983 Symposium on Anabolics in Animal Production of the *Office international des epizooties* ("OIE")[412] ("1983 OIE Symposium");
- the 1987 Monographs of the International Agency for Research on Cancer ("IARC") on the Evaluation of Carcinogenic Risks to Humans. Supplement 7[413] ("1987 IARC Monographs");
- the 1988 and 1989 JECFA Reports[414];
- the 1995 European Communities Scientific Conference on Growth Promotion in Meat Production[415] ("1995 EC Scientific Conference");
- articles and opinions by individual scientists relevant to the use of hormones (three articles in the journal Science, one article in the International Journal of Health Service, one report in The Veterinary Record and separate scientific opinions of Dr. H. Adlercreutz, Dr. E. Cavalieri, Dr. S.S. Epstein, Dr. J.G. Liehr, Dr. M. Metzler, Dr. Perez-Comas and Dr. A. Pinter, all of whom were part of the EC delegation at our joint meeting with experts).[416]

---

408 See para. 8.22.

409 See paras. 4.98 and 4.124.

410 See para. 4.125.

411 See para. 2.28.

412 See para. 4.17.

413 See paras. 4.153-4.155.

414 See paras. 2.22-2.25.

415 See para. 2.33.

416 With respect to the scientific evidence referred to by the European Communities in relation to the potential adverse effects of the hormones at issue on the health or life of *live animals*, we recall our findings reached in paragraph 8.22 that the animal health arguments invoked by the European Communities exclusively relate to the EC import ban of *live animals* (which does not fall within the scope of the EC measures in dispute) and that these arguments need, therefore, not to be taken into account within the scope of this dispute.

8.112 The European Communities also referred to several reports of the European Parliament (the Nielsen Report of 1981, the first Collins Report of 1985, the second Collins Report of 1989 and the Pimenta Report of 1989)[417] and opinions of the EC Economic and Social Committee (of 1981 and 1984).[418] However, we recall the findings we reached above, in particular that risk assessment is a scientific process. Thus, we consider that the non-scientific reports and opinions of the European Parliament and the EC Economic and Social Committee, which *evaluate* the scientific and other reports submitted to them, are not part of the *risk assessment* process, but of the *risk management* process, further elaborated below.[419]

8.113 We next consider whether the scientific evidence and attendant evaluation referred to by the European Communities constitutes a risk assessment in the sense of Article 5. We recall that under the SPS Agreement a risk assessment should, for the purposes of this dispute, identify the adverse effects on human health arising from the presence of the specific hormones at issue when used as growth promoters in meat or meat products and, if any such adverse effects exist, evaluate the potential or probability of occurrence of these effects.[420] We further recall that a risk assessment should be a scientific examination of data and studies[421] and that the SPS Agreement sets out factors which need to be taken into account in a risk assessment.[422] We finally recall that no risk assessment techniques, as referred to in Article 5.1, have as yet been formally adopted by Codex.[423] The Agreement does not further specify the requirements of what constitutes a risk assessment in accordance with Article 5.

8.114 We note that the European Communities has invoked several scientific reports which appear to meet these minimum requirements of a risk assessment (in particular the Lamming Report and the 1988 and 1989 JECFA Reports) and that the scientists advising the Panel seemed to consider these reports, from a scientific and technical point of view, to be risk assessments.[424] We shall, therefore, for the purposes of this dispute, assume that the European Communities has met its burden of demonstrating the existence of a risk assessment carried out in accordance with Article 5.

(iii) Sanitary Measures to be Based on a Risk Assessment

8.115 Article 5.1 requires Members to "ensure that their sanitary ... measures ... are *based on* an assessment ... of the risks to human ... life or health". It does not, however, specify how to determine whether a measure is *based on* a risk assessment. In our view, this determination has both a procedural and a substantive aspect.

---

[417] See paras. 2.31 and 4.19.

[418] See para. 4.18.

[419] See paras. 8.163 ff.

[420] See para. 8.101.

[421] See para. 8.110.

[422] See paras. 8.107 and 8.108.

[423] See para. 8.106.

[424] See, in general, answers by experts to Panel Questions 5 and 13, paras. 6.50 ff. and 6.141-6.146 and, in particular, Dr. Arnold at para. 6.56, Dr. McLean at para. 6.144 and opinion of Dr. Ritter, Transcripts of the joint meeting with experts of 17 February 1997, paras. 20 and 352.

Procedural Requirements

8.116 Notwithstanding the fact that Article 5 does not contain specific procedural requirements for a Member to *base* its sanitary measures *on* a risk assessment, we consider that, according to the ordinary meaning of the words *based on* put in their context and in light of the object and purpose of Article 5[425], there is a minimum procedural requirement contained in Article 5.1. In our view, the Member imposing a sanitary measure needs to submit evidence that at least it actually *took into account* a risk assessment when it enacted or maintained its sanitary measure in order for that measure to be considered as *based on* a risk assessment.

8.117 We note that in this dispute the European Communities, which has the burden of proving that it based its measures on a risk assessment, has not provided any evidence that the studies it referred to (in so far as they can be considered as part of a risk assessment) or the scientific conclusions reached therein, have actually been taken into account by the competent EC institutions either when it enacted these measures (in 1981 and 1988) or at any later point in time. We note, in this respect, that none of the preambles to the EC measures at issue mention any of the scientific studies referred to by the European Communities. These preambles only refer to the non-scientific reports and opinions of the European Parliament and the EC Economic and Social Committee, which cannot be considered as part of a risk assessment.[426]

8.118 In particular with respect to the *articles and opinions of individual scientists* on which the European Communities focused our attention, we note that the European Communities has argued that some of these articles and opinions (in particular those published in 1995 and 1996) are what it called "new evidence" of which it was only informed during the Panel process.[427] In so far as that is the case, these articles and opinions cannot for the purposes of this dispute be considered as part of a risk assessment on which the European Communities based its measures unless there would be some evidence that the competent EC institutions actually considered these articles and opinions or reexamined the potential risks related to the specific substances at issue in light of these articles and opinions. In that event, the European Communities would then have confirmed or changed its earlier conclusions on the basis of such consideration or reexamination. According to the terms of reference given to us as a dispute settlement panel, we have no mandate to reexamine the risk assessment referred to by the European Communities in light of this "new evidence", nor to make our own risk assessment. These articles and opinions, in so far as they constitute "new evidence" gathered by the European Communities during the Panel process can, therefore, from a procedural point of view, not be considered as part of

425 In accordance with the rules of treaty interpretation contained in Article 31 of the Vienna Convention.

426 See para. 8.112.

427 See paras. 4.160-4.169. However, later on in the Panel process, the European Communities confirmed that many of these articles and opinions constitute evidence which was already taken into account in the other studies referred to by the European Communities. In so far as this is correct, see paras. 8.135 ff.

a risk assessment on which the European Communities based its measures in dispute.[428]

8.119 For these reasons, we find that the European Communities has not met its burden of proving that it met the minimal procedural requirement contained in Article 5.1 and that, therefore, the EC measures in dispute are inconsistent with the requirements of Article 5.1.

Substantive Requirements

8.120 Even if the European Communities would have fulfilled these minimum procedural requirements, there would still be a need to examine the substantive requirements contained in Article 5.1 From a substantive point of view, we consider that in this dispute we should, in accordance with the ordinary meaning of the words *based on* put in their context and in light of the object and purpose of Article 5[429], proceed as follows to determine whether the EC measures at issue are *based on* a risk assessment: (i) we need to identify the scientific conclusions reached in each of the studies referred to by the European Communities; (ii) we need to identify the scientific conclusion reflected in the EC measures in dispute; and (iii) we need to determine whether the scientific conclusion reflected in the EC measures can be considered as being in conformity with any of those reached in the studies referred to by the European Communities.

8.121 For purposes of this analysis, we first address the studies referred to by the European Communities which *specifically* address one or more of the hormones in dispute when used for growth promotion purposes before examining the studies which *generally* relate to one or more of these hormones.

1. *Scientific conclusions reached in the studies referred to by the European Communities which specifically address one or more of the hormones in dispute when used for growth promotion purposes*

8.122 The *Lamming Report* came to the following conclusions with respect to the potential for adverse effects on human health arising from the presence in meat of residues of the hormones in dispute administered for growth promotion purposes:

> "5.1. The Scientific Working Group is of the opinion that the use of oestradiol-17β, testosterone and progesterone [the three natural hormones in dispute] and those derivatives which readily yield the parent compound on hydrolysis after absorption from the site of application, *would not present any harmful effects to the health of the consumer when used under the appropriate conditions as growth promoters in farm animals.*
>
> 5.2. Evaluation of the data on 'trenbolone' and 'zeranol' [two of the three synthetic hormones in dispute] revealed that some data on the

[428] These articles and opinions are, from a substantive point of view, further addressed in paras. 8.133 ff.

[429] In accordance with the rules of treaty interpretation contained in Article 31 of the Vienna Convention.

> hormonal no-effect-level and the toxicology of these compounds and their metabolites are still missing.
>
> 5.3. The Scientific Working Group considers it necessary that additional information be provided before a final conclusion can be given on trenbolone and zeranol" (emphasis added).[430]

The Scientific Working Group continued its review of trenbolone and zeranol up to 1985 but was dismantled by the EC Commission just before it was to submit its final report.

8.123 Some of the members of the group published, in their personal capacity, the unofficial report in "The Veterinary Record". The conclusions reached with respect to the potential for adverse effects on human health arising from the presence in meat of residues of *trenbolone* and *zeranol* administered for growth promotion purposes, were the following:

> "(1) We have examined the extensive data available concerning the toxicology of trenbolone and zeranol.
>
> (2) We believe there is adequate evidence from both short term and long term tests that these compounds and their metabolites found as residues do not show significant genotoxic potential.
>
> ...
>
> (5) *The levels of trenbolone and zeranol and their major metabolites found in edible tissue, following accepted husbandry practices, are substantially below the hormonally effective doses in animal test systems and therefore do not present a harmful effect to health*" (emphasis added).[431]

8.124 With respect to the *1983 OIE Symposium*, we note that the report of the symposium consists of a book with a series of articles by individual scientists or groups of scientists. No formal scientific conclusion was agreed by all participants or by the OIE itself. The book contains, however, a foreword to the articles which includes the following statement with respect to the potential for adverse effects on human health arising from the presence in meat of residues of the three natural hormones in dispute administered for growth promotion purposes:

> "The myth that all anabolics are dangerous to human health is still very much alive in many countries. It must be discredited. *There is common agreement with the proof presented at this meeting that the endogenous anabolics (natural hormones) such as 17β-estradiol, progesterone, and testosterone, when administered as implants in animals, are not hazardous to man*" (emphasis added).

The European Communities invokes two specific quotes from individual articles submitted at the OIE Symposium in support of its measures.[432] However, these quotes, which only stress the inherent uncertainties of scientific evidence and the

[430] See para. 2.28.

[431] See para. 4.12.

[432] See paras. 4.157, 4.159.

evolving character of science, do not seem to invalidate the "common agreement" outlined in the foreword quoted above.

8.125 The *1988 JECFA Report* came to the following conclusion with respect to the potential for adverse effects on human health arising from the presence in meat of residues of all three natural hormones in dispute administered for growth promotion purposes:

> "The Committee therefore concluded that the amount of exogenous [oestradiol-17β, testosterone and progesterone] ingested in meat from treated animals would be *incapable of exerting a hormonal effect, and therefore any toxic effect, in human subjects.*
>
> The Committee considered an ADI unnecessary for a hormone that is produced endogenously in human beings and shows great variation in levels according to age and sex. *The Committee concluded that residues arising from the use of [any of the three natural hormones in dispute] as a growth promoter in accordance with good animal husbandry practice are unlikely to pose a hazard to human health ...*
>
> On the basis of its safety assessment of residues of [any of the three natural hormones in dispute], and in view of the difficulty of determining the levels of this hormone as a growth promoter in cattle, the Committee concluded that it was unnecessary to establish an Acceptable Residue Level" (emphasis added).[433]

As outlined above[434], the *1988 and 1989 JECFA Reports* set ADIs and MRLs for zeranol and trenbolone (two of the three synthetic hormones in dispute). JECFA reached the conclusion that their toxic effects are linked to their hormonal effects and that, therefore, a no-hormonal-effect level could be established which would ensure that residues up to such level are safe. JECFA also concluded that the safety level or ADI it thus adopted would not be exceeded at any time after proper implantation (irrespective of the withdrawal period respected).

8.126 The Steering Committee of the *1995 EC Scientific Conference* came to the following conclusions with respect to the potential for adverse effects on human health arising from the presence in meat of residues of the hormones in dispute administered for growth promotion purposes:

> "When used as growth promoters, the naturally occurring gonadal steroid hormones (oestrogen, testosterone and progesterone) can increase the growth rate, the proportion of lean meat to fat and the food-conversion efficiency of some species of animals ... while the residues of hormone in the resulting meat are within the normal physiological range ... To the extent that improved food-conversion efficiency reduces excretion of nitrogen and phosphorus per unit of meat production, the environmental benefits (while small) are likely to be positive. That is the basis on which the *Steering Group endorses the conclusions of Working Group II that the conditions defined in countries*

433 See para. 2.22.

434 See paras. 8.66-8.68.

where the use of these hormones as growth promoters is permitted are a reasonable safeguard of public health.

Several materials similar in their physiological effects to the natural sex hormones (such as trenbolone and zeranol) are also used as growth promoters in meat production ... *The Steering Committee endorses the opinion of Working Group II that the definition of the MRL for trenbolone and its metabolites reached by various international committees* [*inter alia,* JECFA] *provide reasonable protection of public health*" (emphasis added).[435]

The relevant conclusions of Working Group II of the Conference on "Assessment of Health Risk", which specifically address the safety of the hormones at issue when used as growth promoters, read as follows:

"Natural sex hormones

At present, there is no evidence for possible health risks to the consumer due to the use of natural sex hormones for growth promotion, since:

- Residue levels of these substances measured in meat of treated animals fall within the physiological range observed in meat of comparable untreated animals.
- The daily production of sex hormones by humans is much higher than the amounts possibly consumed from meat, even in the most sensitive humans (prepubertal children and menopausal women).
- Due to an extensive first-pass metabolism, the bioactivity of ingested hormones is low, thus providing a further safety margin.

Zeranol and trenbolone

...

At the doses needed for growth promotion, residue levels are well below the levels regarded as safe (the MRLs). There are, at present, no indications of a possible human health risk from the low levels of covalently-bound residues of trenbolone" (emphasis added).[436]

8.127 As can be deduced from all conclusions outlined above, none of the scientific evidence referred to by the European Communities which specifically addresses the safety of some or all of the hormones in dispute when used for growth promotion, indicates that an identifiable risk arises for human health from such use of these hormones if good practice is followed. All of the scientific studies outlined above came to the conclusion that the use of the hormones at issue (all but MGA, for which no evidence was submitted) for growth promotion purposes is safe; most of these studies adding that this conclusion assumes that good practice is followed. We note

[435] See para. 2.33.

[436] *Ibid.*

that this conclusion has also been confirmed by the scientific experts advising the Panel.[437]

2. *Scientific conclusions reached in the studies referred to by the European Communities which generally relate to one or more of the hormones in dispute*

8.128 The European Communities puts particular emphasis on the 1987 IARC Monographs and the articles and opinions of individual scientists outlined above.[438]

8.129 The *1987 IARC Monographs*, in so far as they relate to human health[439], contain evidence with respect to three general categories of hormones, namely oestrogens, androgens and progestins, without distinguishing the specific hormones falling within each of these categories or the natural hormones from the synthetic hormones.[440] The Monographs classify oestrogens as agents which are carcinogenic (meaning that there is sufficient evidence of carcinogenicity in humans); androgens as agents which are probably carcinogenic; and progestins as agents which are possibly carcinogenic.[441]

8.130 We note that the scientific evidence included in these Monographs relates to the carcinogenic potential of entire *categories* of hormones or the hormones at issue *in general*. The Monographs do not consider the carcinogenic potential of these hormones when used specifically for growth promotion purposes or with respect to residue levels comparable to those present after such use.[442] Moreover, the Monographs do not specifically evaluate, as is required on the basis of paragraph 4 of Annex A of

[437] See answers by experts to Panel Question 7, paras. 6.92 ff, including the answers by Dr. André (at para. 6.92) and, albeit slightly qualified, Dr. Lucier (at para. 6.94: "Dr. Lucier responded that, to his knowledge, there was no piece of scientific evidence to indicate that any of the six hormones in question had unequivocally caused adverse effects in humans when administered and used properly. However, there was some information available which raised concern for a slight effect on the incidence of human disease"). In this respect, we note Dr. Lucier's statement that, according to his tentative estimates, between zero and one person in a million who eat 500 grams of meat, treated with oestrogens for growth promotion purposes in accordance with good practice, per day over their lifetimes, get cancer (see Transcripts of the joint meeting with experts of 18 February 1997, paras.742 and 819). This 0-1 in a million risk is caused by the *total* amount of oestrogens in treated meat (the amount of endogenous oestrogens being highly variable and, according to Dr. Lucier, already being carcinogenic), not by the small fraction thereof which is added for growth promotion purposes and which is relevant for the purposes of this dispute. Moreover, this estimate only represents a statistical range of 0 to 1 in a million, not a scientifically identified risk. The concept of "zero risk", to which this statement is closely related, is further dealt with in paras. 8.152 ff. We note, finally, that all experts confirmed that there is no evidence that particular or more significant health problems exist in countries where the hormones at issue are allowed for administration as growth promoters as compared to countries where such use is prohibited (see answers by experts to Panel Question 9, paras. 6.117-6.121).

[438] See paras. 4.151-4.174.

[439] In this respect, we recall our finding that within the scope of this dispute we need not to take into account thearguments made by the European Communities which relate to animal health (see para. 8.22).

[440] As outlined in para.2.8, oestradiol-17β and zeranol are oestrogens; testosterone and trenbolone are androgens and progesterone is a progestin.

[441] See para. 4.155.

[442] See para. 4.154. See also answer by Dr. Arnold to Panel Question 6, paras. 6.82 ff.

the SPS Agreement[443], the potential for adverse effects arising from the presence *in food* (*in casu* meat or meat products) of residues of the hormones in dispute or from residue levels comparable to those present in food.

8.131 We further note that, according to the scientific experts advising the Panel[444], the data and studies contained in these Monographs with respect to the carcinogenic potential of the hormones in dispute have been fully taken into account in the 1988 and 1989 JECFA Reports which, at several occasions, explicitly refer to these Monographs. Nowhere do the 1988 and 1989 JECFA Reports reject the conclusions reached in the 1987 IARC Monographs. On the contrary, the Monographs constitute part of the evidence on which the JECFA Reports are based. JECFA recognized that all five hormones at issue have a carcinogenic potential but concluded that this potential was linked to the hormonal effect of these hormones.[445] Since JECFA considered that the additional residues of the three natural hormones present in treated meat are not capable of exerting any toxic effect, it decided that it was unnecessary to set ADIs or MRLs for these hormones.[446] With respect to zeranol and trenbolone, JECFA identified a no-hormonal-effect level and adopted, on that basis, ADIs and MRLs which, if respected, would ensure the safe use of these hormones.[447] The IARC Monographs and JECFA Reports did not, therefore, reach contradictory but rather complementary scientific conclusions.

8.132 For these reasons, we consider that the 1987 IARC Monographs, in so far as they can be regarded as part of a risk assessment for the specific hormones at issue when used as growth promoters in the sense of Article 5.1, have been taken into account in, and do not contradict, the other studies referred to by the European Communities (in particular the 1988 and 1989 JECFA Reports) which explicitly conclude that the specific use of these hormones as growth promoters in accordance with good practice is safe.

8.133 The European Communities finally invokes several *articles and opinions of individual scientists*. These articles and opinions deal with the carcinogenic or genotoxic potential of hormones and criticize the scientific methodology or conclusions of the other studies referred to by the European Communities. A summary of the content of some of these articles and opinions is contained in paragraphs 4.154-4.166. The scientific evidence included in these articles and opinions relates to the

---

443 See para. 8.101.

444 See answers by experts to Panel Question 5 (paras. 6.50 ff.) where all experts confirm that the JECFA Reports took into account cancer risks. See, in particular, statements made by Dr. Randell, the Codex expert, at the joint meeting with experts of 17 February 1997 (Transcripts, paras. 239, 297 and 436) and by Dr. McLean at the joint meeting with experts of 18 February 1997 (Transcripts, para. 823).

445 The link made by JECFA between hormonal and toxic effect does not contradict the conclusions in the IARC Monographs; on the contrary, since the latter state the following: "There is a basic incongruity between the human data and the animal carcinogenicity data. As noted earlier, however, *the effects of these chemicals* [*inter alia*, the general categories to which the hormones in dispute belong] *in humans appear, at least in most cases, to be linked to the hormonal milieu*" (emphasis added; see para. 4.154).

446 See para. 8.65.

447 See paras. 8.66-8.68.

carcinogenic or genotoxic potential of entire *categories* of hormones or the hormones at issue *in general*; not when used specifically for growth promotion purposes or with respect to residue levels comparable to those present after such use.[448] Moreover, these articles and opinions do not specifically evaluate, as is required on the basis of paragraph 4 of Annex A of the SPS Agreement, the potential for adverse effects arising from the presence *in food* (*in casu* meat or meat products) of residues of the hormones in dispute or from residue levels comparable to those present in food.

8.134 Of the articles and opinions invoked, the European Communities has put much emphasis on the opinion of Dr. Liehr, a scientist with the EC delegation, on "Potential Genotoxicity of Hormones". We note the statement by Dr. Liehr himself that the evidence he submitted is only based on tests carried out at elevated doses of oestrogens and that the relevance of these high dose effects to potential risks related to the low levels of oestrogens in meat from growth promoted animals has not yet been evaluated.[449] Moreover, we recall that this opinion only applies to one of the hormones in dispute, namely, oestradiol-17β and does not address the use of this hormone as a growth promoter.

8.135 We further note that, according to the Codex expert advising the Panel, most of the evidence contained in these articles and opinions and the potential risks addressed therein were already evaluated and taken into account in the 1988 and 1989 JECFA Reports.[450] Indeed, in the event these articles and opinions should be considered as evidence which was, as the European Communities itself argued at the end of the Panel proceedings, not "new" but was already taken into account in the 1988 or 1989 JECFA Reports, the Lamming Report or the 1995 EC Scientific Conference, these articles and opinions would then not invalidate or contradict the scientific conclusions reached in these other studies, which specifically address the use of the hormones in dispute for growth promotion purposes, but rather constitute part of the evidence on which these studies are based.

8.136 We also note that, even if these articles and opinions could be considered as scientific evidence which is part of a risk assessment for the specific hormones at issue when used as growth promoters in the sense of Article 5.1 and which was not yet considered in the other studies invoked by the European Communities, the scientific experts advising the Panel were of the view that this evidence, *as it stands today*, does not invalidate or contradict the scientific conclusions reached in the other studies invoked by the European Communities which specifically relate to the safety of the hormones at issue when used for growth promotion purposes:

---

[448] See para. 2.22.

[449] See para. 4.160-4.161. In this respect, we also note the following statements by Dr. Liehr: "...we have no genotoxicity data at low levels" and "... I agree ... that at the moment this is an interesting hypothesis and I have never labelled it more than a hypothesis and I also agree ... that many pieces are missing ..." (Transcripts of the joint meeting with experts of 17 February 1997, para. 330). The fact that Dr. Liehr repeatedly called for a more thorough scientific examination of the risks related to oestrogens and for more data, reveals that the studies he provided to us do not yet contain conclusive evidence of an identifiable risk.

[450] See para. 6.162 and Transcripts of the joint meeting with experts of 17 February 1997, para. 297. See also answers by experts to Panel Question 5, paras. 6.50 ff.

Dr. McLean:

"Some of the new data that has been submitted particularly relies upon *in vivo* and *in vitro* carcinogenicity testing and also some of the mutagenicity testing but I do not believe that it is any more significant than the sort of data that was available at the time the original appraisal was made [in the 1988 and 1989 JECFA Reports]".[451]

Dr. Arnold:

"... from my point of view, the significant new evidence which has been produced since that Committee [the 32nd and 34th meetings of JECFA] did not invalidate the basic conclusions and therefore I still am feeling very comfortable with the conclusions although I admit that a lot of new evidence has been produced by the scientific community".[452]

Dr. Ritter:

"The nature of scientific interpretation is that legitimate *bona fide* knowledgeable scientists may reach different conclusions from the same set of data. But I think the consensus opinion of that Conference [the 1995 EC Scientific Conference] was that the weight of evidence used then continues to prevail now, and that the assessments and conclusions drawn then are still consistent with the available information now".[453]

"I agree that there is further work that is indicated. I agree that statements made by scientists, such as Dr. Liehr, will continue to contribute to our understanding, but I also agree that the totality of evidence, re-evaluated as recently as December 1995 [by the 1995 EC Scientific Conference], suggests that the way in which these substances are used and the residues which they produce, do not constitute a risk to human health".[454]

Dr. Lucier:

"There is a group of scientists [including Dr. Liehr, a scientist with the EC delegation] who are looking at the role of oxidated damage and genotoxicity of oestrogens ... But for this narrow purpose that we are talking about today, about the influence of this on additional risk from oestrogens from eating, consuming meat containing oestrogens from growth promoted animals, it doesn't have too much consequence. ... I would come up with the same answer either case; there would be no difference in the risk. So I think in that respect whether or not oestro-

[451] Transcripts of the joint meeting with experts of 17 February 1997, para. 4.
[452] *Ibid.*, para. 356.
[453] *Ibid.*, para. 352.
[454] *Ibid.*, para. 424.

gen is genotoxic, has less consequence then what we talked about up to this point in time".[455]

8.137 For these reasons, we find that the European Communities has not demonstrated that the scientific evidence it referred to, which generally addresses the safety of some or all of the hormones in dispute, would indicate that an identifiable risk arises for human health from the use of these hormones for growth promotion purposes if good practice is followed. In this respect we recall that all scientific experts advising the Panel confirmed this conclusion and stated that, as of today, no scientific evidence is available which concludes that an identifiable risk arises from the use of any of the hormones at issue for growth promotion purposes in accordance with good practice.[456]

8.138 The finding we thus make does, of course, not exclude that future scientific developments could require modifications to the scientific conclusions reached in the studies referred to by the European Communities.

3. *Scientific conclusion reflected in the EC measures*

8.139 The European Communities bans the use for growth promotion purposes of any of the hormones in dispute, including the use of these hormones in accordance with good practice. During the Panel proceedings it has made clear that it considers *any* residue level of these hormones to be unsafe for human health, setting its level of protection at a "zero residue" level. The scientific conclusion reflected in the EC measures in dispute is thus that the use of the hormones in dispute for growth promotion purposes, *even in accordance with good practice*[457], poses an identifiable risk to human health.

4. *The conformity of the scientific conclusion reflected in the EC measures with the scientific conclusions reached in the studies referred to*

8.140 In our view, the scientific conclusion reflected in the EC measures in dispute, *i.e.*, that the use of the hormones in dispute for growth promotion purposes, even in accordance with good practice, is *not* safe, does not conform to any of the scientific conclusions reached in the evidence referred to by the European Communities. All the evidence referred to by the European Communities which specifically relates to the use of the hormones at issue for growth promotion purposes concludes that the use of these hormones as growth promoters in accordance with good practice *is* safe.[458] Moreover, none of the evidence referred to by the European Communities which generally deals with one or more of the hormones in dispute contradicts this

[455] The other scientist advising the Panel, Dr. André did not explicitly express his views on this issue but did not contest the statements made by the other scientists. Dr. McLean has furthermore answered in the affirmative when asked whether he believed that the Codex standards are fully adequate to address the problem (Transcripts of the joint meeting with experts of 17 February 1997, para. 9).

[456] See footnote 437.

[457] Since, according to the experts advising the Panel (answers by experts to Panel Question 3, paras. 6.31 ff.), any use of the hormones in dispute will always leave some residue level, albeit a very small one, the administration of these hormones in accordance with good practice will also leave some residue and thus not achieve the EC "zero residue" level of protection.

[458] See para. 8.127.

conclusion.[459] The EC import ban of meat and meat products from animals treated with any of the five hormones at issue for growth promotion purposes, allegedly necessary to protect human health, in so far as it also applies to meat and meat products from animals treated with any of these hormones *in accordance with good practice*, is, therefore, not based on the scientific evidence submitted to the Panel.

8.141 The European Communities, however, submits the following additional arguments (sections 5 and 6). We note that these arguments have not been supported by scientific evidence other than the evidence examined above. We consider it nonetheless appropriate to examine whether these arguments demonstrate that the EC measures in dispute are, from a substantive point of view, based on a risk assessment in accordance with Article 5.1.

5. *General categories of risks invoked by the European Communities*

8.142 The European Communities argues that it has based its ban on the existence of the following categories of risks related to the hormones at issue: (i) risks arising from the nature and mode of action of the hormones; (ii) risks arising from the action of metabolites; (iii) risks arising from the action of combinations (or cocktails) of hormones and from multiple exposure of humans; (iv) risks arising from problems related to detection and control of hormones; (v) risks arising from the administration and use of hormones; and (vi) risks arising from various other parameters, in particular the inherent limits to science.[460]

8.143 Canada argues that the European Communities has never performed an appropriate assessment of these alleged risks and has, in any event, not relied on, nor put forward, any assessment of these risks that could serve as a basis for the EC ban.[461]

8.144 We recall that the European Communities has not referred to any scientific evidence, other than that examined above[462], in which the categories of risks put forward by the European Communities have been assessed and that none of the scientific evidence referred to by the European Communities reached the conclusion that any of the hormones in dispute when administered for growth promotion purposes in accordance with good practice has an adverse effect on human health.[463]

8.145 Moreover, with respect to the alleged risks related to the *nature and mode of action of the hormones* in dispute (including carcinogenicity and long-term effects) and the action of *metabolites or combinations of and multiple exposure to these hormones* (*i.e.*, the first three categories of risks invoked by the European Communities), we note the statements of the scientific experts advising the Panel that the available data relating to these risks have all been taken into account by the JECFA Reports and/or the Lamming Report and/or the 1995 EC Scientific Conference.[464] All

[459] See para. 8.137.

[460] See para. 4.150.

[461] See para. 4.122.

[462] See paras. 8.122 ff.

[463] See para. 8.140.

[464] See answers by experts to Panel Question 5, paras. 6.50 ff., in particular the answers by Dr. Arnold, Dr. McLean and Dr. Ritter and the opinions of Dr. Randell, para. 6.165 (see also Tran-

three reports concluded that these risks do not materialize if the hormones in dispute are used as growth promoters in accordance with good practice. The European Communities has not provided any evidence to the contrary. The EC import ban of meat and meat products from animals treated with any of the five hormones at issue for growth promotion purposes, in so far as it also applies to meat and meat products from animals treated with any of these hormones *in accordance with good practice*, is, therefore, not *based on* an assessment of these categories of risks.

8.146 In addition, with respect to the alleged risks arising from problems related to the *detection, control, administration and use* of the hormones in dispute (*i.e.*, the fourth and fifth category of risks invoked by the European Communities), we note that the European Communities has not referred to evidence, other than that outlined above[465], in which an assessment is made of the possible adverse health effects related to the potential abuse of these specific hormones when used for growth promotion purposes. The European Communities has restricted itself to pointing out the condition contained in many of the scientific conclusions mentioned above, namely that the safety of the hormones is to a certain extent conditional upon their administration in accordance with good practice[466], without further providing an assessment of the potential adverse effects related to non compliance with such practice.

8.147 We further note that the European Communities argues that if it were to allow the use of the three *natural* hormones at issue it would encounter special problems in *inspecting, sampling or testing* for residues of these hormones in meat. These problems relate, according to the European Communities, to the inherent characteristics of the natural hormones which make them indistinguishable from natural hormones present endogenously in meat or present in meat subsequent to therapeutic or zootechnical use of these hormones.[467]

8.148 We recall that, in this dispute, the factors which can be taken into account in a risk assessment under Articles 5.1 and 5.2 are limited to "available scientific evidence" and "relevant inspection, sampling and testing methods".[468] To the extent that the problems in inspecting (sampling and testing) natural hormones would actually pose a risk and could thus, arguably, be taken into account as a risk arising from "relevant inspection, sampling and testing methods" in the sense of Article 5.1, we consider that the European Communities encounters the same problems in inspecting for natural hormones under its current regime. The EC ban of natural hormones used

scripts of the joint meeting with experts of 17 February 1997, paras. 239, 374 and 436 and of 18 February 1997, paras. 730 and 823).

465 See paras. 8.122 ff.

466 However, we note, in this respect, the statements made by some of the scientific experts advising the Panel that even if good practice is not followed the use of the five hormones at issue will in many cases still be safe (see answers by experts to Panel Question 17, paras. 6.171-176, in particular the answers by Dr. Arnold, Dr. McLean and Dr. Ritter and opinions of Dr. McLean, Dr. Randell and Dr. Arnold, Transcripts of joint meeting with experts of 17 February 1997, respectively at paras. 3, 26 and 166). We also recall the conclusions reached by JECFA that the MRLs (*i.e.*, the levels which are set on the basis of good practice) it established for zeranol and trenbolone are far higher than the safety levels for these hormones.

467 See para. 4.186.

468 See para. 8.108.

for growth promotion purposes, combined with its tolerance for these hormones when used for therapeutic or zootechnical purposes or when present endogenously in meat and other foods, would seem to cause more problems in inspecting for banned natural hormones than a regime where the use of all natural hormones would be allowed in combination with, for example, a maximum residue or tolerance level for all natural hormones in any meat regardless of the origin and use of these hormones. Indeed, only under the EC current regime does the problem of how to distinguish between endogenous and added natural hormones arise; under a regime with an MRL or tolerance level for all natural hormones there would be no need to distinguish endogenous from added natural hormones.

8.149 With respect to the alleged risks related to the *control* (or, in other words, the abuse) of the hormones at issue (both natural and synthetic), we further note that even though a Member would seem to be able to take into account risks arising from difficulties of inspecting, sampling or testing which are specific to a particular substance in a particular food, the "relevant inspection, sampling and testing methods" referred to in Article 5.2, do not seem to cover the general problem of control (such as the problem of ensuring the observance of good practice) which can exist for any substance. The risks related to the general problem of control do not seem to be specific to the substance at issue but to the economic or social incidence related to a substance or its particular use (such as economic incentives for abuse). These non-scientific factors should, therefore, not be taken into account in risk assessment but in *risk management*. Moreover, even if these factors could be taken into account in a risk assessment, we note that the European Communities has not provided convincing evidence that the control (or the prevention of abuse) of the hormones in dispute is more difficult than the control of other veterinary drugs the use of which it allows. It has neither provided evidence that control would be more difficult under a regime where the hormones in dispute were allowed under specific conditions than under the current EC regime where the hormones in dispute when used as growth promoters are banned. The experts advising the Panel made clear that the potential for abuse under both regimes would be comparable, some noting that abuse would probably occur more frequently under a regime where the hormones are banned compared to one allowing the controlled use of prescribed products in predetermined dosages with well-defined educational programmes, good communication between the different actors involved and appropriate penalties for misuse.[469] In this context, we note, therefore, that banning the use of a substance does not necessarily offer better protection of human health than other means of regulating its use.

8.150 In this respect, we finally note that for the three natural hormones in dispute, the European Communities has, for control purposes, adopted MRLs and thereby accepted tolerance levels which are higher than the "zero residue" level reflected in the measures in dispute.[470] In so doing, the European Communities itself seemingly confirms the scientific conclusions reached in all the scientific evidence examined

[469] See, for example, answers by Dr. André and Dr. Ritter to Panel Question 14, paras. 6.148 and 6.154 and opinions of Dr. Arnold, Dr. Lucier and Dr. André, Transcripts of the joint meeting with experts of 17 February 1997, paras. 269 and 274 and of 18 February 1997, para. 4.68.

[470] See para. 4.68.

above, namely that residues of these hormones, including when used as growth promoters, are safe below a certain level, and contradicts the conclusion reflected in the EC measures in dispute, namely that only a "zero residue" level ensures the protection of EC consumers.

8.151 For all the reasons outlined above[471], we find that the EC import ban of meat and meat products from animals treated with any of the five hormones at issue for growth promotion purposes, in so far as it also applies to meat and meat products from animals treated with any of these hormones *in accordance with good practice*, is not *based on* an assessment of the fourth or fifth category of risks invoked by the European Communities.

8.152 In the sixth general category of risks invoked by the European Communities (risks arising from various other parameters), the European Communities argues that none of the studies it referred to as part of a risk assessment proves beyond doubt or concludes in an unqualified manner that the presence of residues of the hormones in dispute in meat or meat products present *no risk whatsoever*. The European Communities refers, *inter alia*, to the conclusions of the 1988 JECFA Report which state that residues arising from the hormones at issue used as growth promoters are only *unlikely* to pose a hazard to human health and to the basic premise of JECFA recommendations which aim at establishing standards which correspond to a *no appreciable* or *no significant* risk increase due to the exposure to the substances in question and not to a *zero* risk increase. The European Communities apparently considers, therefore, that this residual risk, albeit minute and not appreciable, constitutes the risk (derived from a *risk assessment*) on which the EC ban is based in accordance with Article 5.1, arguing that, according to EC *risk management*, risk other than zero is not acceptable.[472]

8.153 Canada contests the notion of "zero risk" and argues that the European Communities has set an unattainable goal in demanding absolute proof that there is zero risk associated with the hormones in dispute.

8.154 We recall the conclusions we reached above on burden of proof, in particular that the European Communities has, with respect to its measures which deviate from international standards, the burden of proving the existence of a risk assessment (and, derived therefrom, an identifiable risk) on which the EC measures in dispute are based. It is not, in this dispute, for Canada to prove that there is *no* risk.

8.155 We further note that, according to scientists advising the Panel, science can never provide a certainty, *i.e.* exclude once and for all that a specific substance can ever have adverse health effects.[473]

8.156 In this respect we also note that the sixth category of risks invoked by the European Communities is, as stated by the scientific experts advising the Panel[474]

---

471 See paras. 8.146-8.150.

472 See paras. 4.82 and 4.201.

473 See, for example, opinions of Dr. Arnold, para. 6.81 and Dr. Ritter, para. 6.88. In this respect, we note that the SPS Agreement explicitly deals with situations where there is scientific uncertainty regarding risks related to a substance, in Article 5.7 (discussed in paras. 8.251 ff.), but that the European Communities has not invoked this provision in this case.

474 *Ibid.*

and admitted by the European Communities[475], not identifiable and that, therefore, these risks can *a priori* not be *assessed* by scientists (as required in Article 5.1). In this sense, these potential risks, which are present for any substance (also for substances or uses of substances allowed in the European Communities), are only the consequence of science not being capable of assuring that no risks will ever arise from a substance.

8.157 We finally note that the EC objective of "zero risk" cannot be achieved in practice; not even under the EC ban itself since the European Communities cannot guarantee that there is a zero probability that illegal use of the hormones at issue will occur. Moreover, this "zero risk" objective cannot, as further examined below[476], in any case be achieved for the three natural hormones in dispute since the European Communities allows the ingestion of these same hormones occurring endogenously in meat and other foods as well as the use of these hormones for therapeutic or zootechnical purposes.

8.158 The EC ban on the use of the hormones in dispute for growth promotion purposes is, therefore, not *based on* an assessment of the sixth and final category of risks invoked by the European Communities.

8.159 For these reasons, we find that the EC import ban of meat and meat products from animals treated with any of the five hormones at issue for growth promotion purposes, in so far as it also applies to meat and meat products from animals treated with any of these hormones *in accordance with good practice*, is not *based on* an assessment of any of the six general categories of risks invoked by the European Communities.

6. *The precautionary principle*

8.160 The European Communities also invokes the precautionary principle in support of its claim that its measures in dispute are based on a risk assessment. To the extent that this principle could be considered as part of customary international law *and* be used to interpret Articles 5.1 and 5.2 on the assessment of risks as a customary rule of interpretation of public international law (as that phrase is used in Article 3.2 of the DSU), we consider that this principle would not override the explicit wording of Articles 5.1 and 5.2 outlined above, in particular since the precautionary principle has been incorporated and given a specific meaning in Article 5.7 of the SPS Agreement. We note, however, that the European Communities has explicitly stated in this case that it is not invoking Article 5.7.

8.161 We thus find that the precautionary principle cannot override our findings made above, namely that the EC import ban of meat and meat products from animals treated with any of the five hormones at issue for growth promotion purposes, in so far as it also applies to meat and meat products from animals treated with any of these hormones *in accordance with good practice*, is, from a substantive point of view, not *based on* a risk assessment.

8.162 *In summary*, in this section we have found that, even assuming that the European Communities has demonstrated the existence of a risk assessment in accordance

---

[475] See para. 4.208.

[476] See paras. 8.189 ff.

with Article 5, it has not fulfilled the minimal procedural requirements contained in Article 5.1 to base its sanitary measures on a risk assessment. We have also found that, even if it would have fulfilled these minimal procedural requirements, the European Communities has not met its burden of proving that its measures in dispute, in so far as they also ban the import of meat and meat products from animals treated with any of the five hormones at issue for growth promotion purposes in accordance with good practice, are, from a substantive point of view, based on a risk assessment. The EC measures in dispute, in so far as they relate to five of the six hormones at issue for which international standards exist, are, therefore, inconsistent with the requirements of Article 5.1. The fact that these measures are not based on existing international standards (contrary to Article 3.1)[477] cannot, therefore, be justified under Article 3.3 which includes as one of the requirements for justification, consistency with Article 5.1. The EC measures, in so far as they relate to five of the six hormones at issue for which international standards exist, are, therefore, also inconsistent with the requirements of Article 3.1.

(c) Articles 5.4 to 5.6: Risk Management

8.163 We recall that there is a distinction between *risk assessment* which is a *scientific* examination and *risk management* which involves social value judgments.[478] Once the risks have been assessed, *i.e.*, once the risks and their probability of occurrence identified, a Member will need to decide, on the basis of its own value judgments, whether it can accept these risks. In so doing a Member sets its "appropriate level of sanitary protection". The determination and application of the appropriate level of protection by a Member is part of risk management.

8.164 We recall the definition of "appropriate level of sanitary protection", namely:

> "The level of protection deemed appropriate by the Member establishing a sanitary ... measure *to protect human, animal or plant life or health* ..." (paragraph 5 of Annex A of the SPS Agreement; emphasis added).

We also note the wording of Article 5.5, further examined below:

> "... in the application of the concept of appropriate level of sanitary ... *protection against risks* to human life or health, or to animal and plant life or health, each Member shall avoid ..."

Guided by the wording of these provisions and the object and purposes of the SPS Agreement, we consider that if there is no scientific evidence of an identifiable risk, there is no basis on which to adopt a measure to achieve a level of sanitary protection under the SPS Agreement, except as provided in Article 5.7. If this were not the case, *i.e.,* if a Member could adopt a level of protection and implementing sanitary measures even if it did not provide scientific evidence of an identifiable risk, no effect would be given to the obligation contained in Article 5 to base sanitary measures on an assessment of risks. This approach would undermine the wording and object and purpose of the SPS Agreement.

---

[477] See para. 8.80.

[478] See paras. 8.94 ff.

8.165 We have found above[479] that the European Communities has not provided evidence of an identifiable risk related to the presence of five of the six hormones at issue for which international standards exist when these hormones are used for growth promotion purposes in accordance with good practice. Accordingly, the European Communities has not established the existence of any identifiable risk against which the EC measures at issue, in so far as they also ban the use of the five hormones when used as growth promoters in accordance with good practice, can protect human life or health. Since we considered above[480] that the adoption of a sanitary measure presupposes the existence of an identifiable risk (except as provided in Article 5.7), it is not possible for the European Communities to ban the use of these hormones as growth promoters in accordance with good practice .

8.166 However, even if we would have found that the European Communities met its burden of proving that its measures are based on an assessment of risks in accordance with Articles 5.1 and 5.2 and even if, for that reason, the European Communities could have adopted a measure to achieve its appropriate level of protection against these risks, there would still be a need to examine whether the determination and application of this level of protection is consistent with Articles 5.4 to 5.6. We will, therefore, next examine these provisions.

8.167 The parties to this dispute seem to agree that the establishment of an "appropriate level of sanitary protection" by a Member is a sovereign act, namely, as the definition in paragraph 5 of Annex A of the SPS Agreement provides, the level of protection "*deemed appropriate by the Member* establishing a sanitary ... measure" (emphasis added). As outlined above[481], we note, however, that Members have agreed, in exercising their sovereign right to set their appropriate levels of protection, to observe the provisions of the SPS Agreement, in particular Articles 5.4 and 5.5 thereof. Furthermore, in choosing a measure to achieve that appropriate level of protection Members have agreed to observe the provisions of Articles 2, 5.1 to 5.3 and 5.6.

8.168 We finally recall our findings reached above on the specific burden of proof under Article 3.3.[482] In particular, we found that the burden of proving that the requirements imposed by Article 3.3 (*inter alia*, consistency with Article 5) are met, in order to justify a sanitary measure which deviates from an international standard, rests with the Member imposing that measure. Since the EC measures examined in this section (relating to all hormones in dispute other than MGA) are not based on existing international standards and need to be justified under the exceptions provided for in Article 3.3, the European Communities bears the burden of proving that the determination and application of its level of protection is consistent with Articles 5.4 to 5.6.

(i) Article 5.4: Minimizing Trade Effects

8.169 Article 5.4 provides the following:

[479] See para. 8.140.
[480] See para. 8.164.
[481] See paras. 8.164 ff.
[482] See paras. 8.88 ff.

> "Members *should*, when determining the appropriate level of sanitary or phytosanitary protection, take into account the *objective* of minimizing negative trade effects" (emphasis added).

Guided by the wording of Article 5.4, in particular the words "should" (not "shall") and "objective", we consider that this provision of the SPS Agreement does not impose an obligation. However, this objective of minimizing negative trade effects has nonetheless to be taken into account in the interpretation of other provisions of the SPS Agreement.

(ii) Article 5.5: Distinctions in Levels of Protection

8.170 Article 5.5 provides the following:

> "With the objective of achieving consistency in the application of the concept of appropriate level of sanitary or phytosanitary protection against risks to human life or health, or to animal and plant life or health, *each Member shall avoid arbitrary or unjustifiable distinctions in the levels it considers to be appropriate in different situations, if such distinctions result in discrimination or a disguised restriction on international trade*. Members shall cooperate in the Committee, in accordance with paragraphs 1, 2 and 3 of Article 12, to develop guidelines to further the practical implementation of this provision. In developing the guidelines, the Committee shall take into account all relevant factors, including the exceptional character of human health risks to which people voluntarily expose themselves" (emphasis added).

8.171 We note, in this respect, the basic obligations contained in Article 2.3:

> "Members shall ensure that their sanitary and phytosanitary measures *do not arbitrarily or unjustifiably discriminate between Members where identical or similar conditions prevail*, including between their own territory and that of other Members. Sanitary and phytosanitary measures *shall not be applied in a manner which would constitute a disguised restriction on international trade*" (emphasis added).

Article 2.3 deals, in general terms, with *sanitary measures* which discriminate between Members or which are applied in a manner which would constitute a disguised restriction on international trade. Article 5.5, on the other hand, deals more specifically with *distinctions in levels of protection* (which will normally be reflected in one or more sanitary measures) which result in discrimination or a disguised restriction on international trade.

8.172 We consider that the first part of the first sentence of Article 5.5 ("*With the objective of achieving consistency* in the application of the concept of appropriate level of sanitary or phytosanitary protection against risks to human life or health, or to animal and plant life or health ..."; emphasis added), unlike the second part, does not impose an obligation upon Members. Consistency is not imposed as an obligation but as an objective which nonetheless has to be taken into account in the interpretation of Article 5.5.

8.173 We further note that the Committee on Sanitary and Phytosanitary Measures, established by Article 12 of the SPS Agreement to "provide a regular forum for consultations", has been given a mandate by Article 5.5, second sentence, to "develop guidelines to further the practical implementation of this provision" and, in so doing, needs to "take into account all relevant factors, including the exceptional character of human health risks to which people voluntarily expose themselves". No such guidelines have to date been developed. However, considering the mandatory wording of the second part of the first sentence of Article 5.5 ("each Member *shall avoid* arbitrary or unjustifiable distinctions in the levels it considers to be appropriate in different situations ..."; emphasis added) and the existence of the basic obligations contained in Article 2.3[483], we find that the lack of guidelines by the Committee in no way limits the legally binding nature of the second part of the first sentence of Article 5.5.

8.174 Canada argues that the European Communities fails to justify the following differences in regulatory treatment: (i) a ban on natural and synthetic hormones when used for growth promotion purposes as opposed to not setting any limit for residues of the natural hormones present endogenously in untreated meat and other foods (such as milk, cabbage, broccoli or eggs) and residues of these hormones when used for therapeutic or zootechnical purposes; and (ii) a ban on the hormones in dispute when used for growth promotion purposes as opposed to allowing the use of antimicrobial growth promoters as feed additives to livestock (in particular the substances carbadox, olaquindox and avoparcin)[484] and other veterinary drugs as therapeutic agents (*e.g.*, benzylpenicillin, carazolol, ivermectin and organophosphourus compounds).[485] During the Panel proceedings Canada focused the discussion of its claim under Article 5.5 to the difference in treatment between the six hormones in dispute and two of the three antimicrobial growth promoters, namely carbadox and olaquindox.[486]

8.175 The European Communities rejects these claims, arguing that it does not make distinctions in its levels of protection for different situations and that, even if it were to make such distinctions, these distinctions are justified and do not result in discrimination or a disguised restriction on international trade.[487]

The Three Elements Contained in Article 5.5

8.176 We next examine the elements that must be assessed to determine if a Member's sanitary measure does not conform to the requirements of the second part of the first sentence of Article 5.5. The relevant part of Article 5.5 reads as follows:

> "each Member shall avoid arbitrary or unjustifiable distinctions in the levels it considers to be appropriate in different situations, if such distinctions result in discrimination or a disguised restriction on international trade".

---

483 See para. 8.171.

484 See paras. 4.245, 4.246 and 4.249.

485 See paras. 4.250, 4.252, 4.255 and 4.256.

486 The European Communities informed the Panel that avoparcin, the third antimicrobial agent mentioned by Canada, has been withdrawn from the EC market following a decision of the EC Council of 26 February 1996 (see para. 4.266).

487 See para. 4.282.

8.177 The *first element* contained in Article 5.5 is that the Member concerned adopts different appropriate levels of sanitary protection in "different situations". The *second element* is that the distinction in levels of protection for the different situations is "arbitrary or unjustifiable". The *third element* is that the distinction in levels of protection results in "discrimination or a disguised restriction on international trade". In order to find a sanitary measure to be inconsistent with Article 5.5 all three elements need to be present.

8.178 As to the *first element*, the words "different situations" have been interpreted by the parties as follows. The European Communities argues that "different situations" only covers different situations for the *same residue* or for different residues where the *adverse health effect is the same.*[488] According to the European Communities, "different situations" cannot mean that the same level of protection must be applied to similar health hazards, whatever their nature or severity, coming from similar substances. Canada submits that "different situations" captures *all* the different sanitary risks posed to *human* health contemplated by the SPS Agreement. In the alternative, Canada argues that at the very least the scope of "different situations" encompasses *similar risks* and *similar products*.[489]

8.179 We note that both parties in dispute agree that the scope of "different situations" contained in Article 5.5 includes situations which deal with the *same substance* as well as situations which involve the *same adverse health effect*. For this reason, considering the lack of guidelines by the Committee on Sanitary and Phytosanitary Measures and without further defining or limiting the scope of "different situations", we find that, for the purposes of this dispute, we can compare situations where the same substance or the same adverse health effect is involved as "different situations" in the sense of Article 5.5. For the sake of clarity in this particular case, we will hereafter refer to such "different situations" as "comparable situations" since these situations need to be compared for the purposes of Article 5.5 and are, therefore, "comparable".

8.180 The *second element* contained in Article 5.5 is that the distinction in levels of protection for comparable situations is "arbitrary or unjustifiable".

8.181 Canada argues that the phrase "each Member shall avoid *arbitrary or unjustifiable* distinctions in the levels it considers to be appropriate" (emphasis added) indicates that only some distinctions are to be avoided, *i.e.*, those that are arbitrary or unjustifiable. Canada submits that distinctions may be justified when the severity of the adverse health effects posed by dissimilar risks are significantly different. However, according to Canada, such a distinction would be arbitrary and unjustifiable if the risks compared involve adverse health effects of comparable severity.[490] The European Communities argues that Article 5.5 clearly states that "arbitrary or unjustifiable" distinctions are to be avoided if, and only if, they result in discrimination or a disguised restriction on trade. If they do not result in discrimination or a disguised

488 See para. 4.179.

489 See para. 4.272.

490 See para. 4.274.

restriction on trade, the European Communities concludes, they are not prohibited by Article 5.5.[491]

8.182 The *third element* contained in Article 5.5 is that the distinction in level of protection results in "discrimination or a disguised restriction on international trade".

8.183 Canada submits that a disguised restriction can be found when additional factors not relevant to the protection of health lead to the introduction of measures that are more restrictive than necessary to meet legitimate sanitary concerns, albeit presented in the guise of a sanitary measure. Without this discipline of Article 5.5 there would, according to Canada, be ample scope for governments to succumb to political pressures to protect certain domestic interests, without regard to their impact on international trade, through their decisions regarding acceptable levels of sanitary protection.[492] The European Communities argues that the measures in dispute do not result in discrimination and that the fact that sanitary measures affect imports is not a sufficient reason to claim that they restrict trade, or even less, that they discriminate.[493]

8.184 We note, first of all, the relation between this third element of "discrimination or a disguised restriction on international trade" in Article 5.5 and the basic obligations contained in Article 2.3 of the SPS Agreement providing that:

> "Members shall ensure that their sanitary and phytosanitary measures *do not arbitrarily or unjustifiably discriminate* between Members where identical or similar conditions prevail, including between their own territory and that of other Members. Sanitary and phytosanitary measures *shall not be applied in a manner which would constitute a disguised restriction on international trade*" (emphasis added).

We also note the relation between these two provisions and the language of the chapeau of Article XX of GATT which reads as follows:

> "Subject to the requirement that such measures are *not applied in a manner which would constitute a means of arbitrary or unjustifiable discrimination* between the countries where the same conditions prevail, *or a disguised restriction on international trade*, nothing in this Agreement shall be construed to prevent the adoption or enforcement by any contracting party of measures: ...." (emphasis added).

8.185 With respect to the meaning of "discrimination" and "a disguised restriction on international trade" we recall the conclusions reached by the Appellate Body in its Report on "United States - Standards for Reformulated and Conventional Gasoline" where the terms "arbitrary or unjustifiable discrimination" and "a disguised restriction on international trade", contained in the chapeau of Article XX of GATT, were examined as follows:

> " 'Arbitrary discrimination', 'unjustifiable discrimination' and 'disguised restriction' on international trade may, accordingly, be read side-by-side; they impart meaning to one another. It is clear to us that

---

[491] See para. 4.282.

[492] See para. 4.275.

[493] See paras. 4.39 and 4.305.

> 'disguised restriction' includes disguised *discrimination* in international trade. It is equally clear that *concealed* or *unannounced* restriction or discrimination in international trade does *not* exhaust the meaning of 'disguised restriction'. We consider that 'disguised restriction', whatever else it covers, may properly be read as embracing restrictions amounting to arbitrary or unjustifiable discrimination in international trade taken under the guise of a measure formally within the terms of an exception listed in Article XX. Put in a somewhat different manner, the kinds of considerations pertinent in deciding whether the application of a particular measure amounts to 'arbitrary or unjustifiable discrimination', may also be taken into account in determining the presence of a 'disguised restriction' on international trade. The fundamental theme is to be found in the purpose and object of avoiding abuse or illegitimate use of the exceptions to substantive rules available in Article XX" (original emphasis).[494]

8.186 We further recall the Appellate Body Report on "Japan - Taxes on Alcoholic Beverages" where the Appellate Body found that for an internal tax measure to be inconsistent with the second sentence of Article III:2 of GATT, three separate issues must be addressed so as to give full meaning to the text and context of this provision: (i) the products need to be "directly competitive or substitutable"; (ii) they need to be "not similarly taxed"; and (iii) the dissimilar taxation needs to be "applied ... so as to afford protection to domestic production".[495] The Appellate Body found that the panel had erred in blurring the distinction between the second and third issue by equating dissimilar taxation (*i.e.*, tax difference above a *de minimis* level) with the separate and distinct requirement of demonstrating that the tax measure "affords protection to domestic production".[496] The Appellate Body then concluded the following:

> "As previously stated, a finding that 'directly competitive or substitutable products' are 'not similarly taxed' is necessary to find a violation of Article III:2, second sentence. Yet this is not enough. The dissimilar taxation must be more than *de minimis*. *It may be so much more that it will be clear from that very differential that the dissimilar taxation was applied "so as to afford protection". In some cases, that may be enough to show a violation*. In this case, the Panel concluded that it was enough. Yet in other cases, *there may be other factors that will be just as relevant or more relevant to demonstrating that the dissimilar taxation at issue was applied 'so as to afford protection'* ... And, in every case, a careful, objective analysis, must be done of each and all relevant facts and all relevant circumstances to determine 'the existence of protective taxation'. Although the Panel blurred its legal

[494] Appellate Body Report on "United States - Standards for Reformulated and Conventional Gasoline", adopted on 20 May 1996, WT/DS2/AB/R, DSR 1996:I, 3 at 23.

[495] Appellate Body Report on "Japan - Taxes on Alcoholic Beverages", adopted on 1 November 1996, WT/DS8/AB/R, DSR 1996:I, 97 at 116.

[496] Panel Report on "Japan - Taxes on Alcoholic Beverages", adopted on 1 November 1996, WT/DS8/R, paras. 6.33-34 and 7.1(ii).

reasoning in this respect, nevertheless we conclude that it reasoned correctly that in this case, the Liquor Tax Law is not in compliance with Article III:2" (emphasis added).[497]

8.187 We consider the reasoning in both Appellate Body Reports to be equally relevant to the relationship between the three elements contained in Article 5.5. All three elements impart meaning to one another. Nevertheless, in order to give effect to all three elements contained in Article 5.5 and giving full meaning to the text and context of this provision, we consider that all three elements need to be distinguished and addressed separately. However, we also agree that in some cases where a Member enacts, for comparable situations, sanitary measures which reflect different levels of protection, the significance of the difference in levels of protection combined with the arbitrariness thereof may be sufficient to conclude that this difference in levels of protection "result[s] in discrimination or a disguised restriction on international trade" in the sense of Article 5.5 (in line with the argument that the magnitude of the very differential of a dissimilar taxation may be enough to conclude that a dissimilar taxation is applied so as to afford protection, as provided for in the second sentence of Article III:2 of GATT).

8.188 We next examine, in light of the three elements of Article 5.5 outlined above, the distinctions in levels of sanitary protection allegedly made by the European Communities which have been invoked by Canada. In order to conduct our consideration of this dispute under Article 5.5 in the most efficient manner, we first address the alleged differences in treatment provided by the European Communities for the *natural hormones in dispute*. In this examination we compare the treatment of these hormones when used as growth promoters with both the treatment of these hormones occurring endogenously in meat and other foods (such as milk, cabbage, broccoli or eggs) and when used for therapeutic or zootechnical purposes. In a second step, we address the alleged differences in treatment provided by the European Communities for the *natural hormones in dispute as opposed to that of the synthetic hormones at issue*. In a third step, we address the alleged differences in treatment provided by the European Communities for *all hormones in dispute* (other than MGA) when used as growth promoters as opposed to that for some antimicrobial growth promoters, namely *carbadox and olaquindox*.

Natural Hormones for Growth Promotion Compared to (i) those Occurring Endogenously in Meat and Other Foods, and (ii) those for Therapeutic or Zootechnical Purposes

1. *Comparable Situations with Different Levels of Sanitary Protection*

8.189 This examination involves a comparison of the levels of protection for the *same substance*, namely, respectively, oestradiol-17β, testosterone and progesterone, in different situations depending on the origin or use of that substance. Since we have found above that we can compare situations where the *same substance* is in-

[497] Appellate Body Report on Japan - "Taxes on Alcoholic Beverages", adopted on 1 November 1996, WT/DS8/AB/R, DSR 1996:I, 97 at 121.

volved as "different" situations (which we refer to as "comparable" situations for the purposes of this dispute) in the sense of Article 5.5[498], we find that the treatment of the three natural hormones in dispute when used for growth promotion purposes as opposed to the treatment of these hormones which (i) occur endogenously in meat and other foods and (ii) which have been administered for therapeutic or zootechnical purposes, constitute comparable situations in the sense of Article 5.5.

8.190 The European Communities argues that the origin of these hormones (whether endogenously produced or exogenously administered) causes these hormones to be different, claiming that the hormones present endogenously in meat and other foods have formed part of the human diet for centuries.[499] We note, however, that the European Communities did not submit any evidence in support of its claim that these hormones have different effects. Moreover, all scientific experts advising the Panel have concluded that residues of the three natural hormones present endogenously in meat and other foods or administered for therapeutic or zootechnical purposes are qualitatively the same as the residues of these hormones administered for growth promotion and that if any differences between these hormones could exist (e.g., differences in pathways taken or metabolites), these differences would in any event not have consequences for the potential adverse effects of these hormones.[500] Therefore, even if these hormones would not be totally identical substances, they pose, in any event, the *same adverse health effect* and can, therefore, according to our finding made above[501], be considered as comparable situations for the purposes of Article 5.5.

8.191 We next examine whether the European Communities has adopted a different level of protection for these comparable situations.

8.192 With respect to the three natural hormones administered *for growth promotion purposes*, the European Communities argues that its level of sanitary protection is concerned only with *added* hormones; in other words, the European Communities does not consider that it is acceptable to expose consumers to any hormones in their food over and above the levels which occur in nature, as any such additional exposure could be a hazard to health.[502]

8.193 The appropriate level of protection set by the European Communities for natural hormones present *endogenously* in meat and other foods or administered *for therapeutic or zootechnical purposes* is an unlimited residue level.[503] In other words, the European Communities has not adopted any maximum residue level for these categories of natural hormones.[504] With respect to oestradiol-17β when used *for*

---

[498] See para. 8.179.

[499] See para. 4.84.

[500] See answers by experts to Panel Questions 2 and 4, paras. 6.21-6.30 and 6.39-6.49 and opinions of all experts advising the Panel to an oral question asked by the US representative at the joint meeting with experts of 17 February 1997, Transcripts, paras. 77, 79, 84, 95 and 87.

[501] See para. 8.179.

[502] *Ibid.*

[503] See para. 4.242.

[504] With respect to hormones administered for therapeutic treatment, the European Communities argues that in practice the residues of these hormones will not be ingested by consumers because animals undergoing such treatment are not allowed to be slaughtered. However, the fact is that the

therapeutic or zootechnical purposes, this unlimited residue level of protection has recently been confirmed by the European Communities when it adopted the conclusions reached in the 1988 JECFA Report and classified this hormone, when used for therapeutic or zootechnical purposes, as a substance for which MRLs are unnecessary.[505] With respect to the two other natural hormones in dispute, progesterone and testosterone, when used for therapeutic or zootechnical purposes, no final decision has as yet been taken by the competent EC authorities.[506]

8.194 We thus find that the level of protection adopted by the European Communities for the three natural hormones in dispute when used for growth promotion and that adopted for the same hormones (i) occurring endogenously in meat and other foods and (ii) used for therapeutic or zootechnical purposes, is *different* ("no residue" level as opposed to an unlimited residue level) and that, therefore, distinctions in levels of protection for these comparable situations exist in the sense of the first element of Article 5.5.

2. *"Arbitrary or Unjustifiable" Difference in Levels of Sanitary Protection*

8.195 We next examine whether these two distinctions in levels of protection are "arbitrary or unjustifiable". We first address the distinction made between the three natural hormones when used as growth promoters and the same hormones occurring endogenously in meat and other foods. We then examine the distinction made between the three natural hormones when used as growth promoters and the same hormones when used for therapeutic or zootechnical purposes.

8.196 *Natural hormones used as growth promoters as opposed to those occurring endogenously in meat and other foods*. The European Communities has not provided any reasons, other than those addressed above, why it has adopted a different level of protection for the residues of these two categories of natural hormones. The European Communities has, in particular, not provided any evidence that the risk related to the natural hormones used as growth promoters is in any way higher than the risk related to natural endogenous hormones. We also recall that the experts advising the Panel concluded that both categories of hormones (either exogenously administered to animals or endogenously present in animals, meat, other foods or human beings) pose the same potential adverse effects.[507]

8.197 In this respect we further recall the conclusion reached in the 1988 JECFA Report that the total residue level of natural hormones in meat from *treated* animals (*i.e.*, the combination of natural hormones endogenously present and those added for growth promotion) falls well within the physiological range of levels found in meat from *untreated* animals, which levels vary according to the sex and age of the ani-

European Communities has decided that for residues of these hormones the adoption of MRLs is unnecessary and has thus not set any residue limit (see para. 8.193 *in fine*).

[505] See answer by Dr. Arnold to Panel Question 5, para. 6.54.

[506] *Ibid.*, para. 6.53.

[507] See para. 8.190 and, in particular, the footnote thereto.

mal.[508] We also note that, according to data submitted to the Panel, the residue level of natural hormones in many natural products (such as eggs and soya oil) is much higher than the level of residues of these hormones administered for growth promotion as well as the total residue level of these hormones in treated meat.[509] In this respect, we further note that Codex has also established MRLs for substances which endogenously occur in natural products.[510]

8.198 With respect to the potential difficulties in detecting the presence of *natural* hormones used as growth promoters, we refer to our conclusions reached above[511], namely that only under the current EC regime (a ban) does the problem arise of how to distinguish between endogenous and added natural hormones whereas under a regime where one would allow the use of these hormones (with, for example, an MRL or tolerance level for all natural hormones) there would be no need to distinguish endogenous from added natural hormones. We also note that, in any event, the problem of detection would be the same for both natural hormones used as growth promoters and those occurring endogenously in meat and other foods (since the scientific experts stated that both are qualitatively the same[512]) and can, therefore, not justify a different treatment.

8.199 We finally note that even if some form of justification could be deduced from the arguments submitted by the European Communities, such could not, in any event, justify so significant a difference in levels of protection between a "no residue" level for natural hormones administered for growth promotion and an unlimited residue level for natural hormones endogenously present in meat and other foods.

8.200 We thus find that the European Communities has not met its burden of proving that the distinction it makes in levels of protection for residues of the three natural hormones in dispute when administered *for growth promotion purposes* and residues of the same natural hormones present *endogenously* in meat and other foods is justifiable and that, therefore, this particular distinction in levels of protection is "arbitrary or unjustifiable" in the sense of the second element contained in Article 5.5.

8.201 *Natural hormones used as growth promoters as opposed to those used for therapeutic or zootechnical purposes*. The European Communities argues that the

[508] See para. 8.65. This conclusion has not been contested by either the parties or experts advising the Panel. For example, according to data submitted to the Panel (the accuracy of which has not been disputed by the parties), the residue level of testosterone in 500 grams of *untreated* bull meat is 1,560 nanograms as opposed to 35 nanograms in 500 grams of meat from a heifer implanted with testosterone.

[509] For example, according to data submitted to the Panel (the accuracy of which has not been disputed by the parties), the residue level of oestradiol-17β equivalents in a 50 to 60 grams hen's egg is 1,750 nanograms (in 10 ml of soybean oil, 20,000 nanograms) as opposed to 11.4 nanograms in 500 grams of steer meat implanted with oestradiol-17β and 75 nanograms in 500 grams of untreated cow meat. In other words, the oestrogen content of 1 hen's egg is equivalent to 76.5 kg of implanted steer beef. In this respect, we also note that a pre-puberty male child naturally produces 41,000 nanograms of oestrogens in 24 hours, an adult man 136,000 nanograms and a pregnant women 20,000,000 nanograms.

[510] For example, MRLs have been adopted by Codex for (naturally occurring) cyanide in cassava flour and in Gari (a cassava product).

[511] See para. 8.148.

[512] See para. 8.190.

use of the natural hormones for therapeutic and zootechnical purposes occurs on a small scale, is subject to very strict conditions (such as administration by a veterinarian and strict withdrawal periods) and normally only involves cattle intended for breeding, not for slaughter; whereas the use of these hormones as growth promoters occurs on a much larger scale and is more difficult and costly to control. These differences in use and control, the European Communities argues, ensure that any risk related to the therapeutic or zootechnical use of these hormones is prevented and that in practice a level of "no residue" is achieved, as is the case for the use of these hormones as growth promoters. For these reasons, the European Communities concludes, the distinction in levels of protection is justified.[513]

8.202 We note that, according to scientific experts advising the Panel, zootechnical use of these hormones can occur on a large scale and at regular intervals, namely each year for oestrus synchronization of entire herds.[514] Moreover, even when these hormones are used for therapeutic or zootechnical purposes, all parties and scientific experts advising the Panel agree that some residue level, albeit a very small one, will always remain in the meat when the treated animal is eventually slaughtered.[515] Therefore, a "no residue" level cannot in practice be achieved when these hormones are used for therapeutic or zootechnical purposes.

8.203 However, since we have already concluded that the difference in levels of protection imposed in the European Communities for the three natural hormones when used *for growth promotion purposes* as opposed to those present *endogenously* in meat and other foods cannot be justified, we consider it unnecessary to decide whether or not the distinction made by the European Communities between natural hormones used as growth promoters and those used for therapeutic or zootechnical purposes is justified.

3. *Difference which Results in "Discrimination or a Disguised Restriction on International Trade"*

8.204 We next examine whether the difference in levels of protection between residues of the three natural hormones in dispute when administered *for growth promotion purposes* and residues of the same natural hormones present *endogenously* in meat and other foods, results in discrimination or a disguised restriction on international trade within the meaning of the third element of Article 5.5.[516]

8.205 We recall the considerations made above on the relationship between the three elements contained in Article 5.5.[517] We recall, in particular, that in some cases

513 See para. 4.242.

514 See answers by experts to Panel Questions 19 and 20, paras. 6.182-6.192.

515 *Ibid.* See also opinions of all experts advising the Panel on a question by the US representative at the joint meeting with experts of 17 February 1997, Transcripts, paras. 90, 91, 93 and 95 and answers by experts to Panel Question 3, paras. 6.31-6.38.

516 Since we made no finding on the justifiability of the difference in levels of protection for the natural hormones in dispute when administered as growth promoters and those administered for therapeutic or zootechnical purposes, we do not address, for that additional difference in levels of protection, the third element of Article 5.5.

517 See paras. 8.185-8.187.

the significance of the difference in levels of protection for comparable situations combined with the arbitrariness thereof may be sufficient to conclude that this difference in levels of protection results in "discrimination or a disguised restriction on international trade".

8.206 In this case, we note, firstly, the significance of the difference in levels of protection for the three natural hormones in dispute when administered *for growth promotion purposes* and residues of the same hormones present *endogenously* in meat and other foods, namely a "no residue" level as opposed to an unlimited residue level. We recall, secondly, that the European Communities has not provided any plausible justification for this significant difference. We note, finally, that this difference in levels of protection results in an import ban (on meat and meat products treated with any of the three natural hormones in dispute for growth promotion purposes) which restricts international trade. For these reasons, we find that the difference in levels of protection imposed by the European Communities for the three natural hormones in dispute when administered for growth promotion purposes and those present endogenously in meat and other foods, results in "discrimination or a disguised restriction on international trade" in the sense of Article 5.5.

8.207 We consider that this finding is further supported by two additional factors. Firstly, we recall some of the objectives (other than the protection of human health) that the European Communities had in mind when enacting or maintaining the EC ban on the use of the natural hormones for growth promotion purposes, as stated in the preambles of the EC measures in dispute[518] and in the reports of the European Parliament and the opinions of the EC Economic and Social Committee referred to by the European Communities[519], namely harmonizing the regulatory schemes of the different EC Member States, thereby removing competitive distortions and barriers to intra-Community trade in beef, and bringing about an increase in the consumption of

---

[518] Such as preambles 5 and 6 to Directive 88/146/EEC which state, *inter alia*, the following:

> "Whereas the administration to farm animals of certain substances having a hormonal action is at present regulated in different ways in the Member States; ... whereas this divergence distorts the conditions of competition in products that are the subject of common market organizations and is a serious barrier to intra-Community trade;
>
> Whereas these distortions of competition and barriers to trade must therefore be removed by ensuring that all consumers are able to buy the products in question under largely identical conditions of supply and that these products correspond to their anxieties and expectations in the best possible manner; whereas such a course of action is bound to bring about an increase in consumption of the product in question".

[519] Such as the Nielsen Report of 1981, the Collins Reports of 1985 and 1989 and the Pimenta Report of 1989 of the European Parliament and the opinions of the EC Economic and Social Committee of 1981 and 1984, outlined in paras. 4.14, 4.19 and 4.20. See also Judgment of the Court of Justice of the European Communities in the case C-331/88, "The Queen v. The Minister for Agriculture, Fisheries and Food and the Secretary of State for Health, ex parte: Fedesa and Others", 1990, ECR I-4023, at p. I-4065, para. 25: "... the material made available to the Court ... shows that the possibility of a reduction in surpluses was indeed taken into consideration during the process leading to the adoption of the directive [*in casu*, Directive 88/146/EEC]...".

beef, thereby reducing the internal beef surpluses and providing more favourable treatment to domestic producers.

8.208 Secondly, we note that before the EC ban came into force, the percentage of animals treated with any of the hormones in dispute was significantly lower in the European Communities than in Canada. At that time, according to the European Communities, only four or five EC member States allowed the use of some of these hormones. One member State (the United Kingdom) which has replied to the EC's request for information on this issue, indicated that "anecdotal evidence suggests that growth promoting hormones may have been used [in] up to 40% of UK cattle prior to the ban".[520] On the other hand, according to a table provided by Canada, based on a five year average, the number of animals treated with any of these growth promoting hormones in Canada was approximately 76.8 percent of those entering the food chain. By banning the internal sale and import of meat treated with natural hormones for growth promotion purposes (which represents a significantly higher proportion of the total Canadian meat supply than of the total European Communities meat supply) but continuing to allow any level of residues of these natural hormones present endogenously in meat, the European Communities favoured the consumption of domestic meat and, therefore, *de facto* discriminates against Canadian meat in favour of EC meat. In this sense, the difference in levels of protection in the European Communities for residues of hormones present *endogenously* in meat and other foods and residues of the same natural hormones when administered *for growth promotion purposes* could be said to result in "discrimination or a disguised restriction on international trade".

8.209 We thus find that the European Communities has not met its burden of justifying the distinction it makes in levels of protection for residues of the three natural hormones in dispute administered for growth promotion purposes and residues of the same natural hormones present endogenously in meat and other foods, in light of the three elements contained in Article 5.5, and that, therefore, the EC measures in dispute, in so far as they relate to the three natural hormones at issue, are inconsistent with the requirements imposed in Article 5.5.

Synthetic Hormones for Growth Promotion Compared to Natural Hormones

8.210 We next examine the alleged different treatment provided by the European Communities for, on the one hand, two of the three *synthetic hormones* in dispute for which international standards exist (zeranol and trenbolone)[521] and, on the other hand, the *natural hormones* in dispute occurring *endogenously* in meat and other foods.[522]

---

[520] See para. 4.16, footnote 30.

[521] As mentioned above, the hormone MGA, for which no international standard exists, will be dealt with in a separate section in paragraphs 8.253 ff.

[522] Since we made no finding on the difference in levels of protection for natural hormones administered as growth promoters and those administered for therapeutic or zootechnical purposes (see para. 8.203), we do not address the alleged difference in levels of protection for synthetic hormones

1. *Comparable Situations with Different Levels of Sanitary Protection*

8.211 In this examination we compare *different substances*, namely, respectively, zeranol and oestradiol-17β and trenbolone and testosterone. As outlined above[523], both synthetic hormones at issue are produced to mimic one of the natural hormones in dispute (zeranol mimics oestradiol-17β and trenbolone mimics testosterone). However, both parties in this dispute and the experts advising the Panel agree that the situations thus compared involve at least the *same adverse health effect*, namely carcinogenicity.[524]

8.212 Since we decided above that we can compare situations where the *same adverse health effect* is involved as "different" situations (which we refer to as "comparable" situations for the purposes of this dispute) in the sense of Article 5.5[525], we find that the treatment of zeranol and trenbolone and the treatment of the natural hormones in dispute which occur endogenously in meat and other foods, are comparable situations in the sense of the first element of Article 5.5.

8.213 We next examine whether the European Communities has adopted different levels of protection for these comparable situations.

8.214 With respect to zeranol and trenbolone, the European Communities adopted a "no residue" level as its appropriate level of protection.[526] As outlined above[527], the level of protection in the European Communities for the natural hormones present endogenously in meat and other foods is an unlimited residue level.

8.215 We thus find that the levels of protection adopted by the European Communities for residues of zeranol and trenbolone and that for residues of the natural hormones in dispute which occur endogenously in meat and other foods are different ("no residue" level as opposed to an unlimited residue level) and that, therefore, a distinction in levels of protection for these comparable situations exists in the sense of the first element of Article 5.5.

2. *"Arbitrary or Unjustifiable" Difference in Levels of Sanitary Protection*

8.216 We next examine whether this difference in levels of protection is "arbitrary or unjustifiable". The European Communities has not provided convincing evidence that the synthetic hormones (which mimic the natural hormones) are inherently more dangerous than the natural hormones.[528] Most of the evidence referred to by the

---

administered as growth promoters and natural hormones administered for therapeutic or zootechnical purposes.

523 See para. 8.4.

524 See answers by experts to Panel Question 4, paras. 6.36-6.46. See also Transcripts of joint meeting with experts of 17 February 1997, pp.62-63.

525 See para.8.179.

526 See para. 4.56.

527 See para. 8.193.

528 See also answers by experts to Panel Question 4, paras. 6.39-6.49 and Transcripts of the joint meeting with experts of 17 February 1997, para. 348, where Dr. Lucier stated that in his opinion residues of synthetic hormones are of more concern than those of natural hormones because the risks

European Communities to prove potential risks relates to the natural hormones, in particular oestradiol-17β.[529] According to the scientists advising the Panel, synthetic hormones can also be better detected and controlled than natural hormones.[530] Moreover, the fact that ADIs and MRLs exist for zeranol and trenbolone and not for the natural hormones does not, according to the experts advising the Panel, *per se* mean that the latter are inherently safer than the former since the international standards for both synthetic and natural hormones reflect essentially the same level of protection, namely a "no appreciable risk" level.[531] Therefore, even if there could be valid reasons to subject the natural hormones to a treatment different from the synthetic hormones[532], the European Communities has not provided justification for so significant a difference in levels of protection as between a "no residue" level (for the synthetic hormones at issue) and an unlimited residue level (for the natural hormones endogenously present in meat and other foods). We recall, in particular, that the European Communities has not provided evidence that the use of zeranol or trenbolone for growth promotion purposes in accordance with good practice (for example, the Codex MRLs) is unsafe.[533] In other words, it has not submitted any justification for adopting a "no residue" level, instead of the Codex MRLs.

8.217 We thus find that the European Communities has not met its burden of justifying the distinction it makes in levels of protection for zeranol and trenbolone and the natural hormones in dispute which occur endogenously in meat and other foods. For these reasons, we find that the difference in levels of protection thus made by the European Communities is "arbitrary or unjustifiable" in the sense of the second element contained in Article 5.5.

3. *Difference which Results in "Discrimination or a Disguised Restriction on International Trade"*

8.218 We recall the considerations made above on the relationship between the three elements contained in Article 5.5.[534] We recall, in particular, that in some cases the significance of the difference in levels of protection for comparable situations combined with the arbitrariness thereof may be sufficient to conclude that this difference in levels of protection results in "discrimination or a disguised restriction on international trade".

---

related to the natural hormones are already there due to those occurring endogenously in the body, whereas residues of the synthetic hormones are new to the body. This difference does not, however, relate to the inherent characteristics of both categories of hormones, but to the fact that one category occurs endogenously in humans, whereas the other does not.

[529] See paras. 4.160-4.163.

[530] See answers by experts to Panel Question 22, paras. 6.198-6.201.

[531] See, for example, opinion of Dr. Randell, para. 6.75. We also note, in this respect, the opinion of Dr. Arnold, para. 6.44: "The potential risks arising from *other than* hormonal actions [related to the synthetic hormones] were qualitatively different. These risks were assessed during the review and approval process, and the approved conditions of use eliminated all unacceptable risks".

[532] See, for example, the Codex standards which have adopted MRLs for the synthetic hormones and not for the natural hormones.

[533] See para. 8.140.

[534] See paras. 8.185-8.187.

8.219 In this case, we note, firstly, the significance of the difference in levels of protection for zeranol and trenbolone and that for the natural hormones in dispute which occur endogenously in meat and other foods, namely a "no residue" level as opposed to an unlimited residue level. We recall, secondly, that the European Communities has not provided any plausible justification for this significant difference. We note, finally, that this difference in levels of protection results in an import ban (on meat and meat products treated with zeranol or trenbolone) which restricts international trade. For these reasons, we find that the difference in levels of protection imposed by the European Communities for zeranol and trenbolone and that for the natural hormones in dispute which occur endogenously in meat and other foods, results in "discrimination or a disguised restriction on international trade" in the sense of Article 5.5.

8.220 We consider that this finding is further supported by the two additional factors outlined above[535], which are equally valid for the distinction in levels of protection made by the European Communities for zeranol and trenbolone and the natural hormones in dispute which occur endogenously in meat and other foods.

8.221 We thus find that the European Communities has not met its burden of justifying the distinction it makes in levels of protection for zeranol and trenbolone and the natural hormones in dispute which occur endogenously in meat and other foods, in light of the three elements contained in Article 5.5, and that, therefore, the EC measures in dispute, in so far as they relate to zeranol and trenbolone, are inconsistent with the requirements imposed in Article 5.5.

The Hormones in Dispute Compared to Carbadox and Olaquindox

8.222 We next examine the alleged different treatment provided by the European Communities for five of the six hormones in dispute (all but MGA) when used for growth promotion purposes and carbadox and olaquindox. We recall that these agents are antimicrobial growth promoters used as feed additives in swine production.[536]

1. *Comparable Situations with Different Levels of Sanitary Protection*

8.223 In this examination we compare *different substances*. However, both parties in this dispute and the experts advising the Panel agree that the situations thus compared involve the *same adverse health effect*, namely carcinogenicity.[537]

8.224 Since we have found above that we can compare situations where the *same adverse health effect* is involved as "different" situations (which we refer to as "comparable" situations for the purposes of this dispute) in the sense of Article 5.5[538], we find that the treatment of the five hormones at issue when used as growth promoters

[535] See paras. 8.207 and 8.208.

[536] See paras. 4.245-4.246.

[537] See answers by experts to Panel Question 11, paras. 6.127-6.135.

[538] See para. 8.179.

as opposed to that of carbadox and olaquindox are comparable situations in the sense of the first element of Article 5.5.

8.225 We next examine whether the European Communities has adopted a different level of protection for these comparable situations.

8.226 Canada argues that the EC level of protection for the hormones at issue when used for growth promotion is different from that for carbadox and olaquindox: in the former situation, the substances are banned and the level is "zero residue"; in the latter, the substance is allowed for use in the European Communities without the imposition of an MRL.[539]

8.227 With respect to the hormones in dispute when used for growth promotion purposes, the European Communities adopted a "no residue" level as its appropriate level of protection.[540] With respect to carbadox and olaquindox, the European Communities argues that, even though these substances are allowed, strict controls, specific characteristics of these substances and the way they are administered, ensure that no residue levels will remain in treated pigs when slaughtered and that, therefore, in the European Communities in practice the same level of protection applies to carbadox and olaquindox as the level adopted for the hormones in dispute, namely a "no residue" level.[541]

8.228 We note that the European Communities allows the use of carbadox and olaquindox as growth promoters in pigs and has not set any MRL for these substances. The European Communities thus, in principle, accepts an unlimited residue level of these substances in pork meat. Moreover, we recall that, contrary to what the European Communities argues, a "no residue" level cannot be achieved in practice when use of the substance concerned is allowed (even under strict conditions) since there will always be some residue level of the substance or a metabolite, albeit a very small one, left in the meat, even after a long period of time.[542] We consider, for these reasons, that the European Communities cannot reasonably claim that its level of protection for carbadox or olaquindox is a "no residue" level.

8.229 We thus find that the level of protection adopted by the European Communities for the hormones at issue when used for growth promotion purposes as opposed to that adopted for carbadox and olaquindox is different (a "no residue" level as opposed to an unlimited residue level) and that, therefore, a distinction in the levels of protection for these comparable situations exists in the sense of the first element of Article 5.5.

2. *"Arbitrary or Unjustifiable" Difference in Levels of Sanitary Protection*

8.230 We next examine whether this distinction in levels of protection is "arbitrary or unjustifiable" in the sense of the second element of Article 5.5.

---

539 See para. 4.245.

540 See para. 4.56.

541 See para. 4.284.

542 See opinions of all experts advising the Panel in Transcripts of the joint meeting with experts of 17 February 1997, paras. 90, 91, 93 and 95 and answers to Panel Question 3, paras. 6.31-6.38.

8.231 Canada argues that the risks related to carbadox and olaquindox are at least as serious as those related to the use of the hormones in dispute as growth promoters.[543] It refers to the 36th JECFA Report of 1991 which could not set an ADI for carbadox but did adopt MRLs for one of its metabolites and was unable to allocate an ADI for olaquindox, as opposed to the 32nd and 34th JECFA Reports of 1988 and 1989 which only adopted ADIs and MRLs for zeranol and trenbolone and considered MRLs for the three natural hormones to be unnecessary. Canada submits that none of the arguments put forward by the European Communities justifies a stricter level of protection for the hormones in dispute (which, according to Canada, are safe) than the level of protection for carbadox or olaquindox (substances which, according to Canada, may pose serious risks).[544]

8.232 The European Communities claims that the distinction in levels of protection is justified on the following grounds: (i) carbadox and olaquindox are not hormones; (ii) carbadox and olaquindox only indirectly act as growth promoters by combating the development of bacteria and by aiding the intestinal flora of piglets, thereby also exerting preventive therapeutic effects (whereas the hormones directly act as growth promoters and have no preventive therapeutic action when used as growth promoters); (iii) carbadox and olaquindox are only commercially available in prepared feedstuffs (not as injections or implants) in predetermined dosages; (iv) there are no alternatives to carbadox or olaquindox available which have the same therapeutic action; (v) carbadox cannot be abused since it only has growth promotion effects in piglets up to four months old and a withdrawal period of at least 28 days is fixed; and (vi) carbadox is used in such small quantities and is hardly absorbed that it leaves practically no residues at all in meat destined for human consumption.[545]

8.233 We note, first of all, that the European Communities has not submitted scientific evidence in support of these alleged justifications. We next examine the six arguments put forward by the European Communities in light of the opinions of the experts advising the Panel and the arguments submitted by Canada.

8.234 With respect to the first EC argument, *i.e.*, the fact that carbadox and olaquindox are antimicrobial agents and not hormones, the European Communities has not submitted any reason why this difference could in itself justify a different regulatory treatment in the light of their potential carcinogenic effect. We thus find that this argument does not justify the distinction in levels of protection for the five hormones at issue when used as growth promoters and carbadox or olaquindox.

8.235 The European Communities next argues that the five hormones at issue when used as growth promoters have no therapeutic effect on animals as opposed to carbadox and olaquindox which combat the development of bacteria and aid the intestinal flora of piglets.[546] In this respect, Canada submits that there is no reason to subject consumers to higher risk from residues of veterinary drugs used for therapeutic purposes as opposed to those used for other purposes, such as growth promotion.[547] We

543 See para. 4.273.
544 See para. 4.275.
545 See para. 4.284(i).
546 See para. 4.284(ii).
547 See para. 4.274.

note, moreover, that, according to scientific experts advising the Panel, the hormones at issue when administered as growth promoters may also have beneficial effects (such as improved composition of the carcass upon treatment in terms of more lean meat and less fat).[548] Finally, we recall that the hormones at issue are, effectively, used for therapeutic purposes and that such use of the three natural hormones in dispute is allowed in the European Communities. For these reasons, we consider that both the hormones in dispute and carbadox and olaquindox may have therapeutic effects and thus find that the second EC argument does not justify the distinction in levels of protection for the five hormones at issue when used as growth promoters and carbadox or olaquindox.

8.236 With respect to the third EC argument, *i.e.*, the fact that carbadox and olaquindox are only commercially available in prepared feedstuffs (not as injections or implants) in predetermined dosages and are, therefore, allegedly less open for abuse[549], we note that one of the scientific experts advising the Panel stated that injections or implants are more accurate and reliable methods to administer growth promoters than additives in feedstuffs (because of carry-over risks from treated to untreated feed).[550] The experts also stated that additives in feedstuffs pose additional risks in that they may harm the persons handling the feedstuff.[551] We also recall that, according to the experts advising the Panel, the commercially available products containing any of the five hormones at issue for implantation or injection also contain predetermined dosages of these hormones.[552] We thus find that the third EC argument does not justify the distinction in levels of protection for the five hormones at issue when used as growth promoters and carbadox or olaquindox.

8.237 Addressing the fourth EC argument that there are no alternatives to carbadox or olaquindox available which have the same therapeutic action, we note that one of the experts advising the Panel stated that there are readily available alternatives, such as oxytetracycline.[553] We thus find that this EC argument does not justify the distinction in levels of protection for the five hormones at issue when used as growth promoters and carbadox or olaquindox.

8.238 We recall the fifth EC argument, *i.e.*, that the potential for abuse is allegedly smaller for carbadox than for the hormones at issue since the former only exert growth promotion effects in piglets up to four months and are subject to a strict withdrawal period.[554] We note that, according to the experts advising the Panel, there is no guarantee that the piglets treated with carbadox will not be slaughtered. Resi-

[548] See answers by experts to Panel Question 2, paras. 6.21-6.31, in particular answers by Dr. Arnold, Dr. McLean and Dr. Ritter. See also opinion of Dr. Lucier, Transcripts of the joint meeting with experts of 18 February 1997, para. 742, where he feels unable, as a scientist, to compare the risks related to the hormones with their potential benefits.

[549] See para. 6.26.

[550] See answers by experts to Panel Question 21, paras. 6.193-6.197, in particular answer by Dr. McLean at para. 6.196.

[551] See answers by experts to Panel Question 21, paras. 6.130-6.197, in particular answers by Dr. André and Dr. McLean at paras. 6.193 and 6.196.

[552] See answers by experts to Panel Question 15, paras. 6.155-6.165.

[553] See opinion of Dr. Arnold, para. 6.129.

[554] See para. 4.284.

dues of this substance or its metabolites may thus enter the food chain. We also note that, as is the case for the use of carbadox in the European Communities, the use of the hormones at issue as growth promoters may also be made subject to strict conditions. We thus consider that the European Communities has not submitted evidence proving that carbadox can be more easily controlled than the five hormones at issue and find, therefore, that the fifth EC argument does not justify the distinction in levels of protection for the five hormones at issue when used as growth promoters and carbadox.

8.239 The European Communities further argues that carbadox is used in such small quantities and is hardly absorbed so that it leaves practically no residues at all in meat destined for human consumption.[555] We recall that, according to the experts advising the Panel, once a substance has been administered to an animal there will always be some residue level of this substance or a metabolite left, albeit a very small one, in the meat of that animal.[556] We further note that, according to the 36th JECFA Report of 1991 which assessed the risks related to carbadox and olaquindox, not only carbadox itself (for which no ADIs could be established) but also one of its metabolites, quinoxaline-2-carboxylic acid (for which an MRL was adopted) may present a health risk. We finally note that, according to the scientific experts[557], residue levels of the hormones at issue will also rapidly decline after administration to an animal or ingestion by humans. For these reasons, we find that the sixth EC argument does not justify the distinction in levels of protection for the five hormones at issue when used as growth promoters and carbadox or olaquindox.

8.240 The European Communities finally submits that it authorizes the use of about 10,000 to 15,000 veterinary medicinal products and that the fact that Canada limits its claim under Article 5.5 to only one [two] substances, proves that the European Communities has already achieved a remarkable degree of consistency in its levels of sanitary protection. The European Communities also informed the Panel that the EC Council, by decision of 26 February 1996, already took action on its own initiative to review both carbadox and olaquindox. We consider that these arguments do not justify the distinction which is currently still made by the European Communities in levels of protection for the five hormones at issue when used as growth promoters and carbadox or olaquindox. On the contrary, these arguments suggest an acknowledgment by the European Communities that the distinction in levels of protection it currently makes may not be justified and will be reviewed.

8.241 For the above reasons, we find that the European Communities has not met its burden of justifying the distinction it makes in levels of protection for the five hormones at issue when used as growth promoters and carbadox or olaquindox and that the European Communities has, *a priori*, not met its burden of justifying so significant a distinction between a "no residue" level for the hormones at issue when used as growth promoters and an unlimited residue level for carbadox and olaquindox. We

555 See para. 4.240.

556 See para. 8.202 and, particularly with respect to carbadox, opinion of Dr. Lucier, Transcripts of the joint meeting with experts of 18 February 1997, para. 575.

557 See, for example, opinion of Dr. Lucier, para. 6.36 and Dr. Arnold, Transcripts of the joint meeting with experts of 17 February 1997, para. 79.

find, therefore, that the distinction in levels of protection thus made by the European Communities is "arbitrary or unjustifiable" in the sense of the second element contained in Article 5.5.

3. *Difference which Results in "Discrimination or a Disguised Restriction on International Trade"*

8.242 Canada submits that the distinction made by the European Communities in levels of protection for the hormones at issue when used as growth promoters and carbadox and olaquindox constitutes discrimination and a disguised restriction on international trade in the sense of the third element contained in Article 5.5 for the following reasons: (i) Canadian beef from cattle treated with the growth promoting hormones at issue poses no greater risk to EC consumers than EC meat treated with carbadox or olaquindox and (ii) the EC ban causing the distinction in levels of protection is based on additional factors not relevant to the protection of health (such as harmonizing the regulatory schemes of the EC member States thereby removing competitive distortions and barriers to intra-Community trade, meeting consumer anxieties and expectations and bringing about an increase in the consumption of meat products). According to Canada, the European Communities succumbed to political pressures to protect certain domestic interests without regard to their impact on international trade.[558]

8.243 We recall that the three elements contained in Article 5.5 all impart meaning to one another and that in some cases the significance of the difference in levels of sanitary protection for comparable situations combined with the arbitrariness of thereof, may be sufficient to conclude that this difference in levels of protection results in "discrimination or a disguised restriction on international trade".[559]

8.244 In this case, we note, firstly, the significance of the difference in levels of protection for the five hormones at issue when used as growth promoters and carbadox and olaquindox, namely a "no residue" level as opposed to an unlimited residue level. We recall, secondly, that the European Communities has not provided any plausible justification for this significant difference. We note, finally, that this difference in levels of protection results in an import ban (on meat and meat products treated with any of these five hormones at issue) which restricts international trade. For these reasons, we find that the difference in levels of protection imposed by the European Communities for the five hormones at issue when used as growth promoters and carbadox and olaquindox, results in "discrimination or a disguised restriction on international trade" in the sense of Article 5.5.

8.245 We consider that this finding is further supported by the two additional factors outlined above[560], which are equally valid for the distinction in levels of protection made by the European Communities for the five hormones at issue when used as growth promoters and carbadox and olaquindox.

---

558 See para. 4.183.

559 See paras. 8.185-8.187.

560 See paras. 8.207 and 8.208.

8.246 We finally note that there is another factor which indicates that the distinction in treatment made by the European Communities for the hormones at issue when used as growth promoters and carbadox and olaquindox results in "discrimination or a disguised restriction on international trade". That is the fact that the hormones at issue, which are *banned* in the European Communities, are used for growth promotion in the *bovine* meat sector where the European Communities seemingly wants to limit supplies[561] and is arguably less concerned with international competitiveness, whereas carbadox and olaquindox, which are *allowed* in the European Communities, are used for growth promotion in the *pork* meat sector where the European Communities has no domestic surpluses and where international competitiveness is a higher priority.[562]

8.247 We thus find that the European Communities has not met its burden of justifying the distinction it makes in levels of protection for five of the six hormones at issue (all but MGA) when used as growth promoters and carbadox or olaquindox, in light of the three elements contained in Article 5.5, and that, therefore, the EC measures in dispute, in so far as they relate to these five hormones in dispute, are inconsistent with the requirements imposed in Article 5.5.

8.248 *In summary,* in this section we have found that the EC measures in dispute, both in so far as they relate to the two synthetic hormones (zeranol and trenbolone) and the three natural hormones at issue for which international standards exist, are inconsistent with the requirements contained in Article 5.5. The fact that the EC measures in dispute are not based on existing international standards (contrary to Article 3.1) can, for that reason, not be justified on the basis of Article 3.3. The EC measures, in so far as they relate to five of the six hormones at issue for which international standards exist, are, therefore, also inconsistent with the requirements of Article 3.1.

(iii) Article 5.6: Measures not More Trade Restrictive than Required to Achieve the Appropriate Level of Protection

8.249 Article 5.6 reads as follows:

> "Without prejudice to paragraph 2 of Article 3, when establishing or maintaining sanitary or phytosanitary measures to achieve the appropriate level of sanitary or phytosanitary protection, Members shall ensure that such measures are not more trade-restrictive than required to achieve their appropriate level of sanitary or phytosanitary protection, taking into account technical and economic feasibility".

A footnote to Article 5.6 states the following:

> "For purposes of paragraph 6 of Article 5, a measure is not more trade-restrictive than required unless there is another measure, rea-

561 See also para. 8.207.

562 These factual considerations were provided to the parallel panel requested by the United States. However, we considered it appropriate to mention them in this Panel report as well (see our reasoning in para. 8.19).

sonably available taking into account technical and economic feasibility, that achieves the appropriate level of sanitary or phytosanitary protection and is significantly less restrictive to trade".

8.250 Since we found above that the EC level of protection reflected in the EC measures in dispute has been adopted in violation of Article 5.5, we do not consider it necessary to further examine whether these measures are also more trade restrictive than required to achieve that level in the sense of Article 5.6.

(d) Article 5.7: Provisional Sanitary Measures

8.251 Article 5.7 reads as follows:

"In cases where relevant scientific evidence is insufficient, a Member may provisionally adopt sanitary or phytosanitary measures on the basis of available pertinent information, including that from the relevant international organizations as well as from sanitary or phytosanitary measures applied by other Members. In such circumstances, Members shall seek to obtain the additional information necessary for a more objective assessment of risk and review the sanitary or phytosanitary measure accordingly within a reasonable period of time".

8.252 We recall our finding reached above on the role of the precautionary principle in the SPS Agreement, in particular that this principle would not override the explicit wording of that Agreement, *inter alia*, because it has been incorporated in a specific form in Article 5.7.[563] In this dispute, the European Communities has explicitly stated that its measures are not provisional measures in the sense of Article 5.7. We do, therefore, not need to further examine this provision.

6. Sanitary Measures where no International Standards Exist: Melengestrol Acetate ("MGA")

8.253 We recall that with respect to the third synthetic hormone in dispute, MGA, no international standard exists.[564] As outlined above, the European Communities is, therefore, not under an obligation to base its sanitary measure in respect of this hormone on an international standard in accordance with Article 3.1.[565]

8.254 However, even though no international standard exists for MGA, the EC measures in dispute relating to MGA still need to comply with the other provisions of the SPS Agreement. Canada has invoked violations of Articles 2 and 5. Since Article 2 provides for basic rights and obligations which are further specified in Article 5, we first examine the consistency of the EC measures in dispute relating to MGA with the requirements of Article 5.[566] The consistency of the EC measures relating to

[563] See para. 8.161.

[564] See para. 8.73.

[565] See paras. 8.59 ff.

[566] We only examine the consistency of the EC measures relating to MGA with the requirements contained in Articles 5.1 to 5.3 and 5.5. With respect to the other provisions of Article 5 we refer to our considerations set out in section 5 which equally apply to the EC measures relating to MGA.

all hormones in dispute (including MGA) with the requirements of Article 2 will be dealt with below.[567]

(a) Burden of Proof

8.255 We recall our finding reached above on the general burden of proof under the SPS Agreement[568], in particular that for the obligations imposed by the SPS Agreement that are relevant to this case, the party contesting a sanitary measure (*in casu* Canada) bears the burden of presenting a *prima facie* case of inconsistency with the SPS Agreement, after which the burden of proof shifts to the party imposing the measure (*in casu* the European Communities). We consider that, for the reasons mentioned above[569], this allocation of evidentiary burden is applicable to the obligations imposed on Members under Article 5. We recall, in particular, the wording of Article 5.1, especially the first three words thereof:

> "*Members shall ensure* that their sanitary ... measures are based on an assessment ... of the risks ..." (emphasis added)

and the wording of the second part of the first sentence of Article 5.5 :

> "... each *Member shall avoid* arbitrary or unjustifiable distinctions in the levels it considers to be appropriate in different situations, if ..." (emphasis added).

Therefore, in this dispute Canada has to present a *prima facie* case that the EC measures in dispute relating to MGA are *inconsistent* with the requirements of Article 5, after which the burden shifts to the European Communities to prove that it *has* complied with these requirements.

(b) Articles 5.1 to 5.3: Risk Assessment

8.256 With respect to Articles 5.1 to 5.3 dealing with the requirement of a *risk assessment*, Canada argues that the European Communities has not submitted any scientific evidence which could constitute a risk assessment for the hormone MGA and that the European Communities has, therefore, *a priori*, not based its measures with respect to MGA on any risk assessment as required by Article 5.1.[570] We find that Canada thus meets its burden of presenting a *prima facie* case of inconsistency with Article 5.1.

8.257 We recall our reasoning outlined above on the requirement of the *existence* of a risk assessment in accordance with Articles 5.1 to 5.3[571], in particular that with respect to the five other hormones in dispute we assumed that the European Communities met its burden of demonstrating the existence of a risk assessment since it referred to several scientific reports which appear to meet the minimum requirements of a risk assessment.

---

567 See para. 8.274.

568 See paras. 8.51 ff.

569 See paras. 8.55-8.57.

570 See para. 4.122.

571 See paras. 8.111-8.114.

8.258 With respect to MGA, we note, however, that the European Communities has not submitted any scientific evidence in which the potential for adverse effects on human health of MGA residues is evaluated. Moreover, the scientists advising the Panel have at several occasions stated that they are not aware of any publicly available scientific study which evaluates the safety of MGA[572]; the studies carried out by Canada are proprietary studies which remain confidential.

8.259 The European Communities argues that the EC measures in dispute regulate hormones on the basis of their physiological action, not on the basis of individual substances and that the administration of any substance having an oestrogenic, androgenic or gestagenic action is covered by the EC ban, including MGA which has a gestagenic action.[573]

8.260 We note, however, that with respect to all five other hormones in dispute, JECFA, Codex and the European Communities itself have conducted or invoked risk assessments for each individual substance. We further note that one of the basic principles of a risk assessment appears to be that it needs to be carried out for each individual substance.[574] As was stated in the 1995 EC Scientific Conference:

> "It must be emphasised that a separate risk assessment must be conducted on each growth promoting substance. It is not appropriate to attempt to produce a detailed generic risk assessment for a class of growth promoters".[575]

8.261 We thus find that the European Communities has not met its burden of demonstrating the existence of a risk assessment with respect to MGA and that, therefore, the EC measures in dispute, in so far as they relate to the hormone MGA, are not based on an assessment of risks in accordance with Article 5.

8.262 We recall, in this respect, that the European Communities has explicitly stated that Article 5.7, which deals with cases where relevant scientific evidence is insufficient and allows a Member to take provisional sanitary measures, does not apply to the measures in dispute, including those relating to MGA.[576]

8.263 We further recall our reasoning and findings reached above (with respect to the five other hormones in dispute) on the procedural and substantive requirements a Member must satisfy in order to *base* its sanitary measures *on* a risk assessment in

572 See, for example, statements by Dr. Ritter and Dr. McLean, Transcripts of the joint meeting with experts of 17 February 1997, paras. 352 and 354.

573 See para. 4.56.

574 See, for example, answer by Dr. André to Panel Question 13 (para. 6.141) and the practice in JECFA which only examines specific substances and this, mostly, when these substances are used for specific purposes. In particular, the Joint FAO/WHO Expert Consultation on Residues of Veterinary Drugs in Foods (29 October - 5 November 1984; FAO Food and Nutrition Paper No. 32) recommended that a " ... scientific body should rely on the advice of experts in veterinary medicine, animal science, toxicology, microbiology, immunology, analytical chemistry and related sciences, and establish criteria for the safety of *individual* veterinary drug residues as appropriate, taking into account their public health significance, good animal husbandry and drug use practices, the likelihood of residues and the availability of adequate analytical methodology" (add p.15, emphasis added).

575 *1995 EC Scientific Conference Proceedings*, p.250.

576 See para. 8.252.

accordance with Articles 5.1[577]. We recall, in particular, that the European Communities has, from a procedural point of view, not provided any evidence that the studies it referred to have actually been taken into account by the competent EC institutions or are reflected in the EC measures in such a way that these measures could be said to be *based on* these studies. We further recall that the European Communities has not met its burden of proving that its measures in dispute, in so far as they also ban the use of the five hormones at issue for growth promotion purposes in accordance with good practice, are, from a substantive point of view, based on a risk assessment.

8.264 The same reasoning applies *a priori* to the EC measures with respect to MGA since the European Communities has not submitted any study in which the risks related to MGA are assessed. We thus find that the European Communities has not met its burden of providing evidence to the Panel that its measures in dispute, in so far as they relate to the hormone MGA, are, either from a procedural or a substantial point of view, *based on* a risk assessment and that, therefore, these measures are inconsistent with the requirements of Article 5.1.

(c) Article 5.5: Distinctions in Levels of Protection

8.265 Even if we had found that the European Communities met its burden of proving that its measures relating to MGA are based on an assessment of risks in accordance with Articles 5.1 and 5.2 and even if, for that reason, the European Communities could have adopted an appropriate level of protection against these risks, there would still be a need to examine whether the determination and application of this level of protection is consistent with Article 5.5.[578] In this respect, Canada argues that the European Communities fails to justify the following differences in regulatory treatment: (i) a ban on MGA when used for growth promotion purposes as opposed to not setting any limit for residues of the natural hormones present endogenously in untreated meat and other foods (such as milk, cabbage, broccoli or eggs) or used for therapeutic or zootechnical purposes; and (ii) a ban on MGA when used for growth promotion purposes as opposed to allowing the use of antimicrobial growth promoters as feed additives for livestock (in particular carbadox and olaquindox)[579]. Only with respect to the last mentioned difference in treatment does Canada explicitly invoke Article 5.5.

8.266 We refer to paragraphs 4.280-4.285 for the arguments submitted by Canada with respect to these distinctions in light of the three elements contained in Article 5.5 and find that Canada meets its burden of presenting a *prima facie* case of inconsistency with Article 5.5.

---

577 See paras. 8.115 ff.

578 See para. 8.166.

579 See paras. 4.199 and 4.275.

(i) MGA for Growth Promotion Compared to the Natural Hormones Occurring Endogenously in Meat and Other Foods

8.267 We recall our reasoning and findings reached above with respect to the EC measures in dispute relating to the hormones at issue other than MGA, in particular our finding that the European Communities has not met its burden of justifying the distinction it makes in levels of protection for residues of zeranol and trenbolone (two of the synthetic hormones in dispute) and residues of the natural hormones in dispute which occur endogenously in meat and other foods, in light of the three elements contained in Article 5.5, and that, therefore, the EC measures in dispute, in so far as they relate to zeranol and trenbolone, are inconsistent with the requirements imposed in Article 5.5.[580]

8.268 We consider that this reasoning and these findings equally apply to the EC measures in dispute relating to MGA (the third synthetic hormone in dispute). Firstly, the European Communities has adopted different levels of protection (a "no residue" limit[581] as opposed to an unlimited residue level) for comparable situations, *in casu* situations posing the same adverse health effect (*i.e.*, carcinogenicity), namely for MGA used as a growth promoter and the natural hormones in dispute which occur endogenously in meat and other foods in the sense of the first element of Article 5.5. Secondly, the European Communities has not submitted evidence that this difference in levels of protection is justified and has thus not met its burden of proving that this difference is not "arbitrary or unjustifiable" in the sense of the second element of Article 5.5. Thirdly, the European Communities has not met its burden of rebutting the arguments and evidence submitted by Canada that this difference in levels of protection results in "discrimination or a disguised restriction on international trade" in the sense of the third element of Article 5.5.

8.269 We thus find that the European Communities has not met its burden of justifying the distinction it makes in levels of protection for MGA used as a growth promoter and the natural hormones in dispute which occur endogenously in meat and other foods, in light of the three elements contained in Article 5.5, and that, therefore, the EC measures in dispute, also in so far as they relate to MGA, are inconsistent with the requirements imposed by Article 5.5.

(ii) MGA for Growth Promotion Compared to Carbadox and Olaquindox

8.270 We further recall our reasoning and findings reached above with respect to the EC measures in dispute relating to the hormones at issue other than MGA, in particular our finding that the European Communities has not met its burden of justifying the distinction it makes in levels of protection for residues of the hormones at issue (other than MGA) when used for growth promotion purposes and residues of carbadox and olaquindox in light of the three elements contained in Article 5.5 and that, therefore, the EC measures in dispute, in so far as they relate to the hormones in

580 See para. 8.221.

581 See para. 4.56.

dispute (other than MGA), are inconsistent with the requirements imposed by Article 5.5.[582]

8.271 We consider that this reasoning and these findings equally apply to the EC measures in dispute relating to MGA. Firstly, the European Communities has adopted different levels of protection (a "no residue" limit[583] as opposed to an unlimited residue level) for comparable situations, *in casu* situations posing the same adverse health effect (*i.e.*, carcinogenicity)[584], namely for MGA used as a growth promoter and carbadox and olaquindox in the sense of the first element of Article 5.5. Secondly, the European Communities has not submitted any evidence that this difference in levels of protection is justified and has thus not met its burden of proving that this difference is not "arbitrary or unjustifiable" in the sense of the second element of Article 5.5. Thirdly, the European Communities has not met its burden of rebutting the arguments and evidence submitted by Canada that this difference in levels of protection results in "discrimination or a disguised restriction on international trade" in the sense of the third element of Article 5.5.

8.272 We thus find that the European Communities has not met its burden of justifying the distinction it makes in levels of protection for MGA used as a growth promoter and carbadox or olaquindox, in light of the three elements contained in Article 5.5, and that, for this reason, also the EC measures in dispute which relate to MGA are inconsistent with the requirements imposed by Article 5.5.

8.273 *In summary*, in this section we have found that the EC measures in dispute relating to MGA are inconsistent with the requirements contained in Articles 5.1 and 5.5.

7. *Article 2: "Basic Rights and Obligations"*

8.274 Since we have found that the EC measures in dispute are inconsistent with the requirements of Articles 3 and 5 of the SPS Agreement and considering that Articles 3 and 5 provide for more specific rights and obligations than the "basic rights and obligations" set out in Article 2, we see no need to further examine whether the EC measures in dispute also violate Article 2.

E. *Articles III and XI of GATT*

8.275 Since we have found that the EC measures in dispute are inconsistent with the requirements of the SPS Agreement, we see no need to further examine whether the EC measures in dispute are also inconsistent with Articles III or XI of GATT.

8.276 As noted above in paragraph 8.45, if we were to find an inconsistency with Article I or III of GATT, we would then need to examine whether this inconsistency could be justified, as argued by the European Communities, under Article XX(b) of GATT and would thus necessarily need to revert to the SPS Agreement under which we have already found inconsistencies. Since the European Communities has not

582 See para. 8.247.
583 See para. 4.56.
584 See para. 4.284.

invoked any defence under GATT other than Article XX(b), an inconsistency with Article I or XI of GATT would, therefore, in any event, not be justifiable.

F. *Claim of Nullification and Impairment under Article XXIII:1(b) of GATT*

8.277 Since we have found that the EC measures in dispute are inconsistent with specific provisions of the SPS Agreement, we see no need to further examine whether the EC measures in dispute also constitute a case of nullification or impairment of a benefit accruing to Canada under the WTO Agreement pursuant to Article XXIII:1(b) of GATT.

G. *Concluding Remarks*

8.278 In order to avoid any misunderstanding as to the scope and implications of the findings above, we would like to stress that it was not our task to examine generally the desirability or necessity of the EC Council Directives in dispute. The ability of any Member to take sanitary measures which do not affect international trade was not at issue in the present case. Our examination was confined to those aspects of the EC measures that have been raised by Canada, namely the EC import ban on meat and meat products of bovine origin treated with any of six specific hormones for growth promotion purposes. It was further limited to the specific provisions of GATT and the SPS Agreement which have been invoked by the European Communities in support of this import ban. That is the necessity of the import ban, which the European Communities strictly construed as a sanitary measure, for the protection of human life or health. Likewise, the ability of any Member to enact measures which are intended to protect not consumer health but other consumer concerns was not addressed. In this regard, we are aware that in some countries where the use of growth promoting hormones is permitted in beef production, voluntary labelling schemes operate whereby beef from animals which have not received such treatment may be so labelled.

IX. CONCLUSIONS

9.1 In light of the findings above, we reach the following conclusions:

(i) The European Communities, by maintaining sanitary measures which are not based on a risk assessment, has acted inconsistently with the requirements contained in Article 5.1 of the Agreement on the Application of Sanitary and Phytosanitary Measures.

(ii) The European Communities, by adopting arbitrary or unjustifiable distinctions in the levels of sanitary protection it considers to be appropriate in different situations which result in discrimination or a disguised restriction on international trade, has acted inconsistently with the requirements contained in Article 5.5 of the Agreement on the Application of Sanitary and Phytosanitary Measures.

(iii) The European Communities, by maintaining sanitary measures which are not based on existing international standards without justification under Article 3.3 of the Agreement on the Application of Sanitary and Phytosanitary Measures, has acted inconsistently with the requirements contained in Article 3.1 of that Agreement.

9.2 We *recommend* that the Dispute Settlement Body requests the European Communities to bring its measures in dispute into conformity with its obligations under the Agreement on the Application of Sanitary and Phytosanitary Measures.

ANNEX

PANEL ON EUROPEAN COMMUNITIES - MEASURES CONCERNING MEAT AND MEAT PRODUCTS (HORMONES) - PANEL ESTABLISHED AT THE REQUEST OF THE UNITED STATES

PANEL ON EUROPEAN COMMUNITIES - MEASURES CONCERNING MEAT AND MEAT PRODUCTS (HORMONES) - PANEL ESTABLISHED AT THE REQUEST OF CANADA

Transcript of the Joint Meeting with Experts, held on 17 and 18 February 1997

First day - 17 February 1997

Chairman

1. I would like to welcome the scientific experts and the parties to this expert meeting. Let me start by informing you that the proceedings of this meeting are being recorded, therefore, when taking the floor, representatives and experts should please use their microphones. As indicated in my letter of 7th of February 1997 the Panel decision to join the two meetings with scientific experts stems from the similarities of the two cases, as does the Panel's decision to use the same scientific experts in both cases and to invite Canada and the United States to participate on equal footing in the meetings in both cases. In addition, there is the consideration that from a practical perspective there will be a need to avoid the repetition of arguments and of questions. I recall that as to the proceedings in legal terms, the cases are not formally joined. They are joined for this session today and tomorrow as a hearing of the experts and the debate with the experts. I tend to say that there can only be one truth in this matter; we cannot have two truths. That is the philosophy we should address at this meeting and take advantage of full mutual information here. The purpose of this meeting is that the experts can expand on their written briefs and that our questions can be put to them, views can be challenged. I would like to take the opportunity at this stage to thank the experts very deeply that they responded in such a short period of time to the request of the panel. As you know, we are operating under very stringent time constraints, we have to produce reports with certain delays and this puts an enormous pressure not only on us but also on you. And I very much would like to thank you at the outset that you agreed mostly to work on this, I assume, over Christmas holidays to produce your substantive reports. These reports are very substantive and it is not a matter of repeating them line by line but really to highlight the main points and the focus and also to put the Panel into a position to be fully informed about controversial issues which may exist here which would allow us to make a legal assessment here.

2. I also would like to stress that the proceedings are confidential. Everything which is being said in this room is subject to the rules of dispute settlement. So it's confidential unless release is permitted by one of the parties. We had a request this morning from the European Community at an informal meeting to grant the opportu-

nity to have the parties' experts from EC side making upfront statements in order to fully inform the parties and the Panel in these proceedings on their views. The Panel has discussed this request and has come to the conclusion that we would deny this opportunity for the following reasons. This meeting of two days was set up as a hearing of experts and the purpose is to hear the experts and put questions to the experts by making use of scientific experts within the delegations. It is not the purpose of this meeting to hear new evidence which has not been submitted by February 8th. And it is not the purpose of this meeting to have formal statements by the parties, but just from the experts. Now, this will not exclude that the experts which are on the delegations of the parties can speak to the point, that they would do so when time is given to the delegations and they are in a position to expand on their views during these interventions. These interventions will then again give the experts the opportunity to react to what was said from the delegations. In the light of this, I would like to explain how we would like to proceed today. We would first have statements by the experts and I would like to invite you to focus on your main points, your main arguments, your main areas where you see the issues, the main areas of contention and also where you see the problems in your colleagues' reports. After the statements, followed by the expert of the Codex, there will be discussion within the panel of experts. When this is concluded, the United States will have the opportunity to put questions and to comment on the experts' views. This will be followed by the intervention of the European Community, with the possibility, as I said, to have statements by your own experts and it will then go to Canada for the same proceeding. And since we have two proceedings here mixed, the EC will again have an opportunity to take the floor in the very end. After this process, we would intend to give the experts again individually the floor for a final statement where they could stress their views again and their conclusions. The Panel would then sit in the evening and we would then try to focus on more specific questions which from a legal point of view may still not be clear and in the meeting of tomorrow afternoon we as a Panel would then come in with very specific questions to the experts which we still may have to clarify. So we have a general debate which in the beginning hopefully that which will allow us to focus on the main issues and tomorrow there might be very specific questions here. This does not exclude that today the parties may raise specific questions to the experts based on their written submissions, based on the answers to the questions here. And I assume that delegations are prepared to do so. My last point is please try to be short and to the point in all your interventions. Please try to avoid repetitions, repetitious statements, so that we can go along with the time. This is, I think, the end of my introduction. I would now like to declare open the hearings. I repeat that all that is said in this room remains confidential under the rules of Panel proceedings and I would propose the following order: Professor McLean, Dr. Arnold, Professor André, Dr. Ritter, Dr. Lucier and then Dr. Randell as the Codex expert. I am informed that the slide machine has not been installed, so if somebody would like to show slides it would have to be done in the afternoon. I apologize for this. So may I then give the floor to Professor McLean.

Dr. McLean

3. Thank you Mr. Chairman. I will be brief and highlight the parts of my submission that I think are most germane. In relation to good practice and good veterinary and good animal husbandry practice, I think it is important to realize that this

good practice is the practice that is negotiated between the sponsor of the product and the registering authorities to define the conditions under which the compound will be used. And once those conditions are defined, then they make up part of the registration approval and in that way the maximum residue limit can be established. The other thing that is important with the maximum residue limit is to understand that it is a legal limit and not a health limit. In other words, the exceeding of the MRL does not represent a hazard to health but is rather a limit at which the authorities take action. However, I must say that to exceed the MRL would not be seen to be good practice. In relation to the meat that is produced, to all intents and purposes, the meat is similar. In fact it may not be possible to tell the difference between meat produced using growth-promoting agents and meat that is produced without them. That when we look at those two hormones for which there is a maximum residue limit, then a minute residue may remain that cannot be detected by commonly-used regulatory methods. I think it is important to realize that the methods used are regulatory methods rather than some of the more sophisticated methods that can go to orders of magnitude below the regulatory method. If we were relying upon those sorts of methods then the surveillance process would be cumbersome and costly and actually preclude satisfactory surveillance. One of the keys to the use of these sorts of compounds is to combine the use of the compounds with surveillance to ensure that good practice is followed and the MRL is not exceeded.

4. JECFA has looked at these compounds particularly in its 1988 meeting and again in 1989 and it was at that point that the ADI and MRL was established, or in the cases of three naturally-occurring hormones it was deemed that an MRL was not necessary. These two meetings were particularly important, because it was determined for the three naturally-occurring hormones that there was no way of showing that meat treated with the hormones or untreated meat were substantially different and so therefore to regulate them by an analytical technique would not be possible or practical and indeed in many cases the levels that were seen after treatment were extremely small in relation to the naturally-occurring substances. It is interesting to note that JECFA since 1988 and 1989 has reviewed a number of compounds on a second occasion. These compounds have been referred to the JECFA meetings by sponsors or by regulatory authorities and governments. But on no occasion has the matter of the determination the '88 and '89 JECFA meetings in relation to the five hormones that it approved been, on no occasion has any organization sought to revisit the matter of oestradiol 17 beta, progesterone, testosterone, trenbolone and zeranol. I think it is very important because on a very significant number of occasions JECFA has at the request of various groups revisited the matter of the toxicology and/or the residues of products or compounds that it set MRL and ADIs for. And that the opportunity exists and has existed since 1988 and 1989 to revisit the matters of the five hormones under consideration and that opportunity has not been taken. It is interesting to see at this stage the amount of material that is alleged to show that the compounds should be revisited, that is being produced for this particular meeting yet no one has taken the opportunity to refer to JECFA. Yet on number of occasions, as I said, the opportunity to do that is being taken with other compounds. When JECFA approved the use of the three naturally-occurring hormones it accepted the fact that indeed we live virtually in a sea of hormones. These hormones came from endogenous levels produced in humans, and it came in material that we take in in the diet either from eating meat naturally or from eating other material that contains hormon-

ally active substances; things that are commonly found in the diet including eggs, soya products, a number of plant materials and fungal products such as those from Fusarium from which zeranol is derived. Indeed it is very difficult to determine exactly where our hormone burden comes from but the facts of the matter are that humans are constantly being exposed to very significant levels of hormones and that the incidence of tumours associated which are with hormones in humans such as, for example, the breast or the prostate, have not significantly increased since the surveying has been carried out. When I say that we must take into account that the diagnostic technology available for diagnosing some of these tumours and also the level of education of the public has substantially increased but, if you correct for that sort of data and correct it for age, then there has been very little change. Some of the new data that has been submitted particularly relies upon *in vivo* and *in vitro* carcinogenicity testing and also some of the mutagenicity testing but I do not believe that it is any more significant than the sort of data that was available at the time the original appraisal was made.

5. The hormones in question are used in a number of countries and have been used for many years and epidemiological data do not suggest that this has had an untoward effect on human health. There are a number of compounds that have been used in veterinary medicine or in association with crops from which we have seen untoward effects in humans, but the residues present in the five hormones in question have not shown any deleterious effects in humans that have been accurately documented. Many of the hormones are lipid soluble and therefore pass into the fat portion of milk and that is a significant intake for humans, particularly for young children and also for adults in the intake of butter and cheese; I'm referring to the three naturally-occurring hormones. The hormones in question are not well absorbed orally, and indeed the uptake there is extremely small with the exception of course of melengestrol acetate. As well, there is data that shows that anything up to approaching 80 per cent of some of the hormones are actually destroyed upon cooking.

6. In relation to the illegal cocktails, in the countries where the compounds are registered then the use of the illegal cocktails is virtually non-existent. There are registered products which are combinations of zeranol and trenbolone, oestradiol and progesterone or trenbolone or testosterone and combinations like that and the registration of the products permits control of use. In relation to the use of the compounds, they are packaged in such a way that they are in an inert matrix and that matrix is injected into the animal, in the ear, by specially developed injection apparatus, and that therefore does control the injection into the animal. In countries where the drugs are not registered and used illegally then the administration by an acceptable technique that controls the release and is removed on slaughter, is not available.

7. Coming back again to the MRL, I stress that it is a legal limit based on daily consumption of a product for a lifetime corresponding to the uptake of the ADI, however, it is not a health limit and occasional consumption is of no concern and I think I will stop there Mr. Chairman.

Chairman

8. Thank you very much, Professor. Could your statement be summarized that you believe that the current standards we have are fully adequate to address the problem?

Dr. McLean

9. Yes, Mr. Chairman, I do believe on having examined countries where the compounds have had a long history of use, having examined the packages of data submitted to JECFA and I think it is particularly important that people that are talking about these hormones see the full packages of data submitted to JECFA by the sponsors. These packages of material contain the individual animal data and are much more satisfactory if one is going to pass judgement than some of the material in the open literature. Where these compounds have been used, then I believe that evidence shows that they are used responsibly as compared with countries where the use is not permitted but they are still used, and under those circumstances I believe that there should be some concern but used in accordance with the agreed protocols, then I believe that they are safe.

Chairman

10. Thank you very much for your statement. I give the floor to Dr. Arnold.

Dr. Arnold

11. Thank you Mr. Chairman. Since I share many views expressed by Professor McLean I will not repeat arguments put forward by him. I will also not try to summarize my written answers which I have submitted in due time. I will try to be very brief and only make a few very general statements at this time.

12. My general view of the problem is very similar to what has been expressed most recently by the Steering Committee and a specialist working party of a scientific conference on growth promotion in meat production organized by the European Community. The experts which had been invited by Commissioner Fischler have summarized, and this is also my view, concerning the natural sex hormones and I read from their summary: "At present there is no evidence for possible health risks to the consumer due to the use of natural sex hormones for growth promotion since residue levels of the substances measured in meat of treated animals fall within the physiological range observed in meat of comparable untreated animals. The daily production of sex hormones by humans is much higher than the amounts possibly consumed from meat. Even in the most sensitive humans, pre-pubertal children and menopausal women, due to an extensive first pass metabolism, the bio-availability of ingested hormones is low, thus providing a further safety margin." And on zeranol and trenbolone this conference has stated, and I share these views: "At the doses needed for growth promotion, residue levels are well below the levels regarded as safe, the MRLs. There are at present no indications of a possible human health risk from the low level of covalently-bound residues of trenbolone."

13. This is my first very general statement. Concerning the not-disputed carcinogenic properties of these substances, my personal views very similar to what has most recently been expressed by Professor Jonathan Li, who is a leading expert in the field of kidney carcinogenesis. He has summarized on the basis of the evidence we have today: "The inescapable conclusion is that hormones, particularly oestrogens, are non-genotoxic carcinogens. This latter term, however, is somewhat misleading since non-genotoxic carcinogens by definition ultimately affect permanent genetic changes leading to neoplastic transformation. Perhaps a more appropriate term would be epigenotoxic, defined as referring to an agent that is not involved in direct covalent or indirect interactions with genetic material, but nevertheless is able to elicit

heritable changes by alternative mechanisms." I am inclined to share these views. I think a lot of confusion has emerged in recent years because at the time when the policies towards genotoxic carcinogens have been established, genotoxicity has meant clear mutagenicity. In the meantime, over the past decades, many tests have been developed which picked up very early end points of damage to the genome. Just to mention one, single-strand breaks, I could mention many others, in the DNA. Now the problem is, it is clearly a genotoxic effect a single-strand break observed, for example, *in vitro*. However this Panel should know that typically in a cell this event occurs some 5,000 times per hour and the capacity to repair such a damage is in the order of 200,000 such events per hour. Now for example, I give only one example, Dr. Liehr was able to demonstrate such breaks at extremely high doses and he was able to demonstrate a ten per cent increase it remains to be confirmed that such an event is of any significance *in vivo*. I have similar problems with Dr. Metzler's paper who reports about genotoxic potential. For example, in his paper on page 12, he says with respect to agents causing numerical chromosomal abberations (aneuploidy) a biochemical threshold can be expected on theoretical grounds and can be measured in *in vitro* systems such as culture cells. However, it is impossible to determine this threshold in an intact organism *in vivo*, because it is not known which tissue is most susceptible at which stage of development and in different individuals. For residues in food, exposure occurs for people of all ages and values of susceptibilities. I agree, first of all, that on theoretical grounds there should be a threshold. I also agree that we do not know where this threshold exactly lies but what we perfectly know is that the doses which have provoked such effects are many orders of magnitude above the concentrations we are talking about today, a minimum of 1,000, sometimes 10,000 or 100,000 times. There exist many papers and literature which have demonstrated that the no-effect levels for such effects are in the order of one micro-molar or slightly below and there we are still far above the concentrations we are talking about today. So, my conclusion is a lot of evidence has been put together about genotoxicity of the substances, mostly *in vitro*, but the relevance to the *in vivo* situation still remains unclear. Particular activities have been focused on the metabolism of the so-called catechol oestrogens. This is a category of compounds which is known since several decades. I had already to learn these structures when I was a student and also more than 20 years ago their metabolic activation has already been proposed. However, the real relevant work has been done in the past years and the idea is that these substances could be activated in metabolism to act as carcinogens. The problem which I have with the papers written by Dr. Liehr, not only on the occasion of this Panel but I have very carefully examined, a review article he has published last year in Annual Review of Pharmacology and Toxicology, that sometimes I have the idea that he does not clearly discriminate between what has been done as pure chemical synthesis or in tests in *in vitro* and what has been shown in *in vivo* situations. I cannot find any evidence supporting the view that the metabolic pathways elucidated to sometime by *in vitro* studies are of relevance in *in vivo*. So, I think a lot of misunderstanding is created by the different uses of the term "genotoxic carcinogen" as it has evolved in history and as it is used nowadays. I think I would not like to add much more at this moment, but I will be open to answer questions.

Chairman

14. Thank you very much Dr. Arnold. Do you have from the Panel any questions at the moment? Not now? Okay. Thank you very much for your statement. Now I give the floor to Professor André, please.

Dr. André

15. Thank you, Mr. Chairman. I will be a very short for the moment because I did not prepare a specific assessment. You don't ask before, but maybe you don't know how to manage this meeting today.

Chairman

16. Yes, and I didn't ask you, so that the speeches will be short indeed.

Dr. André

17. Okay, thank you. So it's a nice surprise. But I think also that many things have been said before and written in the answers to the questions. I would just like to add some comments, personal comments. As an expert I am here as a veterinarian first, I am a biochemist secondly. But I am now working more in the analytical field of residue control of these hormones in dispute. And when I received the questions it looked that many of these questions more or less outside my field of strict competence, because I am more concerned with toxicology as well as with some veterinary or animal husbandry practices. However, I accept to answer and I decided at the beginning to work as a student would do, which means looking at first at recent scientific available data and synthesizing them. I was very impressed to discover the number of recent publications, between 1990 and now, about these topics of hormones and specifically on hormone's action in animal health or about their toxicology. I also try always to stay outside the political debate and to be strictly an honest scientific. About some points here, I just comment. For example, about good animal husbandry practices as well as good veterinary practices, it has been said just before my talk that when drugs in general are registered, this registration is with some withdrawal periods and rules of impairment. In fact problems, the real problem, I think, is the problem of control, how to be sure that these practices are really respected and what we can say now is that official control services are in charge to control these. But also that now more and more people themselves, I would like to say, people as veterinarians, as farmers, as farmer organizations, are taking the control and are ensuring that they will only use registered drugs as it is possible to officially use them. About residues and remaining residues, there is a question about the persistence of residues in meat and animals. It is clear that this depends of any drug but it sometimes very surprising to discover that when you develop new sophisticated methods, you observe that residues are still remaining a very very very longer time than it is commonly known. And we have personal experiences for certain drugs, near hormones in this field. About toxicity of these compounds, and more precisely carcinogenicity or genotoxicity, I was very impressed to read many papers about these compounds, recent scientific papers (and I sent you the original papers) and just looking fast on summaries, conclusions of these papers, it seems for everybody now clear that they have very dramatic toxicity and that most of the natural as well as synthetic hormones have an action on DNA as said by Dr. Arnold. The problem is just the problem of dose response and the problem of threshold. I think that when a compound is

usually recognized now as genotoxic, the problem of threshold is not of concern. And I would like to compare in simple words as if, Mr. Chairman, you were student, and I am sorry for the comparison. If you drive, for example, 30,000 miles a year, you have a probability, a risk, to have an accident. If you drive only 1 kilometre a year, you have also a probability to have an accident. You cannot say that under one thousand kilometres or under a thousand miles a year, you will never have an accident. And that is, I think, the same thing for these kind of compounds. The more you use, the more you have risk to have an accident. But you have no limit under which it is possible to be sure that you will never have an accident. Sorry for the comparison, if you think it is too simple, but I think it is sometimes useful. Concerning the very first problem of JECFA and Codex and these institutions, it is clear that the jobs they do is very useful for everybody and that nobody, no scientist, will think that it is a bad assessment done by these organizations. I just have a personal problem about the definition of drugs as published by the Codex, for the reason that drugs in these definitions involve all familiar known drugs but also physiological modifiers, as these hormones are when they are used for growth promotion. And to my personal opinion, there is very big difference between a drug, I mean zootechnical and therapeutical purposes of these hormones, and the use as growth promoter, for the reason that you may admit that you have a small risk when use a drug because in this case, you cannot avoid to use it and it is very more difficult to admit that you take a risk when using just to modify. Maybe also the consequence is that a risk assessment for such modifiers must be done with other rules than the classical rules for drugs. This has been said in the previous conference in Brussels in 1995. Coming back to the comparison, you can admit that you could have an accident going to the hospital. So for the moment I think I will stop the speech. I apologize too for my English, which is bad, it is not my mother tongue. But we can later come back on many points, if you wish.

Chairman

18. Thank you very much for your excellent introduction to your paper and assessment. May I now turn to Dr. Ritter.

Dr. Ritter

19. Thank you, Mr. Chairman. This communication system, I must comment, is a wonderful device in itself for arbitration as it only permits one person to speak at a time. I should say that coming fourth following three distinguished scientists leaves me little opportunity to add anything of any consequence additionally. But having said that of course I will take the opportunity to say a few things. I should begin by really thanking the Panel for the opportunity to contribute to the debate. This is a debate which has gone on for sometime now and I suspect one which may continue for sometime yet, and it is of course an extraordinary privilege to be given the opportunity to contribute to the debate with my understanding of the issue. So, I am grateful for that understanding, for that opportunity.

20. I will attempt to very quickly add a few points to those that have already been made by those who came before me. You know of course, Mr. Chairman, that myself and my three colleagues were provided with a very limited period of time in which to provide comments and so at least in my case I have attempted to do so to the best of my ability within the time constraints that were provided. There will be unquestiona-

bly information that some may cite that I omitted in my comments and that is a matter, I think of practical necessity rather than an error, if you wish. In formulating my opinions I have, to the extent available to me, attempted to use as large an international database as possible. That is why I have made extensive use of ... [data](?) [cassette side finished] ... by WHO, by JECFA, by Codex and in the published scientific literature. I have not referred to proprietary data, even to the extent to which I may have had it available to me. I have, of course, made extensive reference to the proceedings of the European Conference on Growth Promotion for two reasons. First and foremost, because I believe that that Conference which was held in Brussels in late 1995, represented the views of an outstanding group of scientists from the international community and brought some considerable expertise to the debate. And secondly, because I believe that this 1995-96 Conference was a very important and very recent updating of information which had already been reviewed internationally by organizations such as JECFA in 1988 and in 1989. So certainly it is my opinion that this whole issue has been re-evaluated as recently as early 1996. And it is my view that the European Conference has essentially reaffirmed, and indeed I'll go as far as to say strengthened, the earlier conclusions which were reached by JECFA, and that is that in accordance with operating procedures that are provided for the use of these substances, that their use does not constitute a risk to consumers of food commodities produced with the hormones at question, at least for five of the six. The Panel would be aware that MGA has not had the benefit of an international review. My colleague Professor McLean has already articulated the fact that an MRL is not a health limit, but rather a regulatory limit and that the limit may well be different in different jurisdictions for different operational reasons, because of climate, because of geography, because of use practice and otherwise. But the ADI is an international value. And I would draw the attention of the Panel particularly to the point that for the three natural hormones, it was the opinion of JECFA, and indeed the view re-enforced by the international conference in December of 1995, that these natural hormones do not require the establishment of an acceptable daily intake, because in fact their use reflects levels which are entirely within the range that one might expect in animals that had not been treated at all. That is, their use would result in a residue which would be indistinguishable from animals which had never been treated. In the case of xenobiotic hormones it goes without saying of course that these hormones are not natural by definition, and hence any level which can be detected is outside of what one might expect in an animal which has not have been treated. But even in that case, the conclusion that has been drawn internationally, is that again in accordance with the recommended use procedures that these levels which do remain constitute no risk whatsoever for consumers of the product.

21. I should say, Mr. Chairman, that there has been some considerable debate as to the potential for abuse of these products and the health risks that this abuse may constitute. I would add my personal conviction that I do not believe that the potential for abuse in any way speaks to the safety of appropriate use. I make that point because the juxtaposition that is created often in the debate is that because there is potential for abuse of anything, whether we are talking about these hormones or whether we are talking about motor vehicles or whether we are talking about alcohol, I think we need to remember that that potential has no impact whatsoever on the appropriate use. I would also suggest to the Panel that because the potential for abuse exists, in my view, is not a reason to impute the safety of appropriate use. And if I

may be permitted to draw a very simplistic example, not unlike the one that my colleague Professor André drew a moment ago, I hardly think that we would be considering the banning of the automobile because some people speed. It is a question of risk management and not risk assessment. And the issue that I think we have to deal with is how do we control those people who speed so that we can all enjoy the benefit of the automobile and similarly how do we appropriately manage the potential for abuse with these hormones rather than imply that this abuse somehow or another makes the appropriate use unsafe. I should add perhaps before I leave the issue of abuse just very quickly that it is noteworthy that in countries where use of these hormones, the six hormones in particular, has been permitted for a very extended period of time, and I refer most notably to Canada and the United States, monitoring and compliance programmes which have been ongoing now from many many years have consistently demonstrated that residue levels are entirely within recommended limits and that instances of violative residues, that is residues which would indicate abuses taking place, have almost never been reported. So that it seems that at least in those jurisdictions where use is lawful, the practicality of abuse has never become a reality. There are, as I say, few and isolated examples of violative residues in those countries where use has in fact been permitted.

22. It is perhaps important, I think, to bring to the attention of the Panel the fact that we have an enormously rich experience in the human case with these hormones, and I draw the Panel's attention specifically to the use of oestrogen, and most notably oestrogen in combination with progesterone, as an oral contraceptive which has now been in practice in the human population for perhaps 35 to 40 years and that there have been tens of millions if not hundreds of millions of women who have taken these steroids on a daily basis, in many instances for their entire reproductive life, periods of time that may have ranged from 30 to 50 years. And that these levels have typically reflected an intake and exposure that ranges somewhere between 20 and 100 micrograms, depending on the pharmaceutical preparation, on a daily basis for the entire reproductive cycle of the hundreds of millions of women in question. It is interesting to note that these levels are thousands, if not hundreds of thousands, of times greater than the levels, Mr. Chairman, to which you or I might be exposed in consuming meat which results from the use of these hormones in production. And although the issue of breast cancer most notably is certainly one of considerable interest these days, I think it is fair to say that to date, there is no compelling evidence whatsoever to demonstrate that the use of oral contraceptives containing two of the very hormones at issue before this panel, over at least an entire generation in hundreds of millions of patients, has not resulted in any compelling evidence to suggest that the use of these drugs in fact constitutes any increased risk to these women of cancer whatsoever. Finally, Mr. Chairman, I would only conclude by saying that certainly in the case of the natural hormones, and as I have already indicated at least in the case of trenbolone and zeranol for the xenobiotic hormones, I think the five have all been subjected to both national and international reviews which have been re-reviewed, if you like, as recently as December 1995. It would certainly be my view, I would certainly share the views expressed both by JECFA and by this international forum that the use of these compounds, in accordance with provisions provided on a regulatory level for their use in countries that in fact permit the use of these products, does not constitute an increased risk or harm to those consumers who consume food commodities produced with the aid of these hormones. Thank you, Mr. Chairman.

Chairman

23. Thank you very much for your statement. May I turn now to Dr. Lucier.

Dr. Lucier

24. Thank you, Mr. Chairman and I also thank the Panel for inviting me to participate in this review. My comments really evolve from my research activities in the field of receptor biology. I have had a laboratory activity in the area of receptor biology for over 20 years now, and more recently I have been involved in coordinating a national toxicology programme within the Department of Health and Human Services of the United States, that is responsible for providing a toxicological evaluation on agents of public health concerned whether they be in the environment, in the workplace, in foodstuffs, physical agents and so forth. I have also been involved over the years working with the International Agency on Research on Cancer on a number of their efforts in their hazard identification, their risk identification, chemical carcinogens and in particular those in which hormonal activity seems to be at the root of the potential carcinogenic activity. Having come last, I probably won't say too many things that haven't been said before, but let me go through some of the key issues at least from my perspective and those that I feel comfortable in commenting on. One is that the residues that occur from the natural hormones are certainly going to be indistinguishable from those which occur from the natural endogenous materials. This is not true, of course, for the synthetics. With appropriate analytical methods and appropriate residue levels one is capable of detecting residues of the synthetic materials here in question. I should also point out that the half-life, the biological persistence, of the agents in question is for the most part rather short. They do not stick around the body very long. But having said that, half life being just what it says is the time in which it takes for half the material to disappear. So, if something has a half life of one day if you start out with ten units of it, one day later you have five, two days later you have two and a half and so forth. So even though several months may elapse following an exposure to an agent even with a relatively short half life, a few molecules may remain. The number of molecules may be remarkably close to zero, probably not detectable by analytical methods, but a few molecules will likely remain. I should also point out in terms of the carcinogenic activity of the hormones in question, we already know that physiological levels, naturally-occurring levels of androgens and oestrogens are carcinogenic. One out of ten women in the industrialized world gets breast cancer. There is compelling mechanistic biological information, human studies and toxicological studies to show that oestrogens are at the root of this. That their cancer is a multi-step process but that oestrogens appear to be responsible for the majority of the carcinogens that are seen in the site. So we already know that physiological levels are carcinogenic. We already know that early menarche increases risk, late menopause increases risk. We know that when a woman loses her ovaries and her oestrogen production diminishes, the risk to breast cancer also diminishes. Charles Huggins in his noteworthy work back in the early sixties show that ovariectomy (removal of the ovaries) prevented breast cancer in experimental animals. The same is true of endometrial cancer. We know from human studies that endometrial cancer is elevated significantly by exposure to oestrogen replacement therapy when this is unopposed by progesterone. Conjugated oestrogens have been called a known human carcinogen by the International Agency for Research on Cancer. DES of course has, but DES is not a question here and the mecha-

nism by which DES produces cancer may not be relevant to the issues here. Tamoxifen, an anti-oestrogen in breasts produces cancer in the endometrium because it acts like an oestrogen in the endometrium, the uterus. It acts like an anti-oestrogen in the breast so it blocks ... chemotherapeutic agent in women who have breast cancer and the size of the tumours frequently diminish after this exposure. Oral contraceptives are also a known human carcinogen but not because of breast cancer. They are a known human carcinogen because of increased risk of liver cancer. The increased risk is quite small, but nevertheless there has been a consistent risk shown across studies. After having said that, I need to add that the number of molecules that remain following appropriate use of these agents is very small. They are very small in relation to the amount of naturally-occurring oestrogens or androgens. So the accompanying risk that would be associated by consuming meat containing residues would be extraordinarily small. It would be very hard on scientific grounds to say that the risk was zero. But it is likely to be very, very small. It could be zero. It could be as high as by estimates as one cancer in a million people exposed to them over their lifetime. So the risk, to sum up those comments, is somewhere between zero and somewhere around one in a million. And that one in a million is a very difficult number to pin down. A lot of assumptions go into it. What I would say would be a conservative estimate, an upper bound estimate, and I can go through as to how I came up with that number if those details are required. A couple of other points that I would like make. One is that the issue of threshold really is not relevant here. As I already said, the amount of material that is added to the existing burden is very very small. The amount of naturally-occurring oestrogens and likely androgens are already carcinogenic, so you are already adding to a carcinogenic burden. So the issue of threshold is totally irrelevant to the toxicological evaluation of these agents. It may also be irrelevant to distinguish between genotoxic and genotoxicity, when one gets right down to it. I would say that there is a great deal of evidence to support the notion that receptor mediated events, i.e. normal hormone pathways, are the main reason why hormones and hormonal agents are carcinogenic. However, there is a body of knowledge that suggests that they do genotoxic activity, this genotoxic activity could possibly contribute to the carcinogenicity I mean there are examples of some *in vivo* experiments that have shown this in whole animals, and I can go over those if requested. But my bottom line is an extensive discussion of genotoxicity versus non-genotoxicity really isn't relevant to the discussion and to the outcome because we already know that the existing levels of hormone are carcinogenic. The only reason for distinguishing genotoxicity from non-genotoxicity in my understanding, and it may be a naive understanding, is to determine whether or not to apply a linear or a threshold model for risk assessment. A threshold model would assume that there is a dose below which no effect could occur. Since we are already into the effect region, again we are adding an existing burden by adding an existing number of chemicals to that burden, again keeping in mind that this is a very small addition and may be remarkably close to zero. We also, in the course of the national toxicology programme, done carcinogenicity evaluations on approximately 500 agents. Many of these agents are carcinogenic by virtue of their genotoxic activity, many are carcinogenic by virtue of their non-genotoxic activity. When we looked at those response relationships for genotoxic and non-genotoxic carcinogens, we couldn't distinguish one from the other. In other words, non-genotoxic carcinogens were no more likely to exhibit linear behaviour than genotoxic ones. So again that goes back to my point that the genotoxic versus non-genotoxic issue, I don't think that is a real one. A couple of other points to make. One is, when one looks at the natural versus the synthetic compounds, the synthetic compounds clearly have hormonal activities, that's why they are used in the situation. They may also have other kinds of activity in addition to that because molecular structure is different than that for the naturally-occurring oestrogens so there may be different metabolites, possibly a different spectrum of adverse effects. I assume that when one looks at the toxicological data that is available on these, and not all of it was available to me because some of it is proprietary, that the appropriate studies would be done to determine that other effects are not occurring. Effects that could be detected by sub-chronic 90 days studies or three year studies and by appropriate molecular screening techniques. Another point regarding the cocktails, the synergy. There was a recent paper indicating possible synergy of oestrogens in science, using yeast. At this point, the relevance of that system to even risk has not been shown, and those results have not been repeated in human cells. So I think the issue of synergy, more than you might expect from adding two weak oestrogens together, the issue of additivity or antagonism, of one inhibiting the other, really is an open question. In my mind, additivity is the appropriate way to establish risk. I should also reiterate again that cancer is a multi-step process. We can define the different steps operationally, in some cases, somewhat mechanistically. It involves DNA damaging steps, creation of mutation, the ability of cells that harbour this mutation to proliferate more rapidly than normal cells. It is generally thought that oestrogens act primarily at that step that stimulates the growth rate of genetically altered cells, cells that already harbour mutation, and there is a wealth of scientific information and literature to show that. The work by Dr. Liehr, Dr. Metzler, Dr. Cavalieri and other folks indicate that there may be some genotoxic activity for these agents, suggesting that they may act to some extent on that first step, which would be the creation of that mutation. So it appears possible that within the framework of a multi-step model for cancer, that hormones and these hormones in question by act on more than one step. And the last point that I want to make is we talk a lot about the toxicology of these agents, however, it is important to point out that oestrogens have been used in therapy for a long time for many purposes. Certainly oestrogen replacement therapy is one. There is a convincing body of knowledge to show that oestrogens can prevent bone loss in women who are susceptible to that, so it can reduce the risk of osteoporosis. There are also studies to show that oestrogens can decrease heart disease. So when one starts looking at an overall risk assessment, the small amount of oestrogens that are added by the consumption of meat containing these residues, it seems appropriate also to look at the whole balance of effects, what are the benefits versus risks. And I think that is going to be a hard question to answer. There may be a very very small risk from adding these smaller molecules , but there may also be a small benefit. I don't think we have the tools in which to adequately determine that risk benefit ratio, and I think that is going to be one of the difficulties that the Panel has in coming to grips with what recommendations, what decision that they make. Let me stop there, and again I will be glad to add more details to my comments or respond to questions as the meeting is on.

Chairman

25. Thank you very much for your introduction. May I give the floor to Dr. Randell, the Codex expert.

Dr. Randell (Codex)

26. Thank you, Mr. Chairman. And thank you for the opportunity of meeting with you and your fellow Panel members. And also for the opportunity of meeting so many old colleagues from my JECFA days; I haven't seen some of them for quite a number of years. JECFA is the FAO-WHO Joint Expert Committee on Food Additives. It was founded in 1955 by FAO and WHO with the intention of giving guidance to these organizations and their member governments on the matter of chemical substances added to food, essentially for whatever reason. In its early days, JECFA established what was known as the ADI (Acceptable Daily Intake) concept, initiated in fact by Professor Rene Truhaut, who is no longer with us. The ADI concept is built around a concept of adding no appreciable risk when you add chemicals to food. That concept has been with us, as I say, since the late 1950s and with very minor modifications it stands as it stands today. Chemicals that have been given an ADI by JECFA, or by national authorities because the same concept has been adopted by many national authorities, an intake less than that ADI, over a lifetime, produce no appreciable risk to the person consuming it. In 1960-61, FAO and WHO then turned their attention to pesticide residues and the joint meetings on pesticide residues formulated the concept of the Maximum Residue Level. This is different to the ADI. Maximum Residue Limit was established to ensure that pesticides used in field conditions under good agricultural practice did what they were supposed to do and did it within a framework of safety. If I could use a relatively simple explanation of the MRL in the pesticide context. If we apply a pesticide to a field we do it for certain reasons, we do it to kill a pest. If you apply more than that then you have exceeded what you need to do and you have surplus residue, which is thought to be an unwise thing. If you spray less pesticide on the field you get the worst of both worlds: you get the pest and you get residues which you didn't want to have in the first place. So to a certain extent the maximum residue level is a measure of how much of the chemical is needed to achieve the objective of pest control and at the same time falls within the framework of the safety analysis. JECFA and JMPR were expert committees and they still are expert committees. And it was in 1962 that FAO and WHO formed the intergovernmental Codex Alimentarius Commission, which was established to protect the health of consumers and to facilitate, to remove unnecessary barriers to trade in food products. The work of Codex, the work of JECFA and the work of JMPR went on, and still goes on, with increased interest from many parties and certainly a lot of increased interest since the Marrakesh Agreement. In the early 1980s, a number of Codex committees began to raise questions, governments at these committee meetings, began to raise questions about how do we deal with the residues of the substances used for growth promotion. It is of interest to note that these were brought up in the Pesticide Residues Committee, Committee on Food Additives, Committee on Meat Hygiene, Committee on Poultry Products. There was in fact some sort of competition between the Codex committees as to who was going to handle this hot potato. In 1984, FAO and WHO convened an expert consultation to advise the two organizations on how to handle this particular problem. It was an expert consultation on process rather than on scientific detail. However, the consultation did come to the conclusion that it was an appropriate area for Codex to work in; that the most significant problem in the field was not the legitimate use of growth promoters or any other veterinary drugs, under good veterinary practice conditions, but rather the abuse or uncontrolled use; that it would be appropriate for the Codex

Commission to establish a separate committee to handle these matters. And the expert consultation also had the first stab at providing a definition of what was meant by veterinary drugs. It was the intention of the experts of this consultation, and I was privileged to be the secretary of that consultation, to make the definition as broad as one could possibly imagine and this is why we even get references in the definition to apiculture and bee growing. The expert consultation resulted in the establishment of a committee by the Codex Alimentarius for residues of veterinary drugs in food, and it also gave the stimulus for JECFA to begin work in this area in earnest and to obtain the first really comprehensive data packages on the substances about which we are speaking today. They were evaluated in 1987, and a follow-up evaluation for trenbolone acetate in 1989. The recommendations of the JECFA were in the form of maximum residue limits (MRLs) although of course for the endogenous hormones the rather peculiar statement that the MRL was that an MRL not necessary, an internal tautology which I think we are going to have to live with for sometime. These MRLs were processed through the Codex system and were first discussed at the 19th Codex Alimentarius Commission session in 1991, when it was decided not to adopt the MRLs as they currently stood. When the complementary information on trenbolone acetate had passed through the system, the MRLs were re-presented for adoption at 21st session of the Codex Alimentarius Commission, and were adopted. That is the historical level.

27. On the scientific side, I would like to come back to questions which you asked the Codex and I assume JECFA Secretariat in your written questions, particularly about the relationship between the acceptable daily intake and the maximum residue limit and whether or not these are measures of the acceptable risk. The maximum residue limit is definitely not a health-based limit. It is a limit established for the control of veterinary drugs in actual practice. The thinking which goes into the establishment of a maximum residue limit is such that the maximum residue limit will never lead to residues which would, in a normal ingestion of the product, cause any consumer to exceed the acceptable daily intake. Therefore there is an upper boundary to the maximum residue limit imposed by toxicology considerations. The lower limit is normally derived from residue trials in practice according to the proposed good veterinary practices in the use of these drugs. However, in certainly one case, in the case of zeranol, this limit falls so far below not only the toxicologically derived limit but it even falls well below the limit that one can determine with normal methods of analytical chemistry, and therefore has been increased to take into account the fact that if you are going to operate a decent control programme, that is not going to be overly expensive, than you have a limit which is controlled by the analytical procedure rather than by the residue trials. The acceptable daily intake itself also is not a direct risk assessment in the sense that it provides a statement of quantitative risk. The ADI concept states that there will be *no* appreciable risk as a result of exposure to the chemicals concerned. This is true of within the JECFA and JMPR framework. This is true of food additives, residues of veterinary drugs and pesticide residues. I appreciate very much your comment Dr. Lucier that the risk is probably somewhere between zero and one in a million (one in ten to the minus six), because this does put some sort of quantitative framework on that. But JECFA has never established a quantitative evaluation of risk in the application of the ADI. I think I will leave my introductory comments there if that is satisfactory to you, but I would be very pleased to answer additional questions on the evaluations. Thank you.

Chairman

28. Thank you very much, Mr. Randell. According to our procedures, I would now like to give the floor to the United States delegation for comments or questions to the experts. May I give you the floor, Mr. Brinza?

Mr. Brinza (US)

29. Thank you, Mr. Chairman. First with respect to comments on the responses that we received from the experts, we do have some written comments that we would like to make available to you all now that would facilitate us getting through what I suspect would be a lengthy exercise - it would not be very fruitful to just read them. So let me provide those to you. I think we should have enough copies for the Panel and the experts as well as for the other delegations. We thought it would be useful to ask some questions that would go to all five of the experts. The representative from Codex of course is welcome to respond as well, but we assume that you are serving more in your ex-officio capacity with respect to the Codex institutional issues. What we would like to do would be to ask some questions of all five, that I think would be fairly simple questions, just to make sure that we understood the areas of the responses where there was consensus since there were different responses - there were in some cases different wordings - so we just want to make sure we understood correctly all the responses and the foundations for some of those responses.

30. For example, with respect to the three natural hormones - oestradiol 17 beta, progesterone and testosterone - we assumed that all five would agree that these three compounds are all present in the meat-producing animals as well as in humans naturally (endogenously produced, I think, would be the better way of explaining that).

31. Secondly, assuming that is true, do they also agree that these three hormones are all naturally present in the meat and the milk from those animals? I believe we have heard some of the experts already refer to that but it could be useful to make sure that all the five of them agree with that. Assuming there is agreement on that, when food products containing the natural levels of these hormones, in other words levels within the normal physiological range, do these hormones have a biological effect on consumers? We have a few more like this and I will defer to you on whether it is appropriate to get responses now on those and then we go on from there or whether you prefer to do them all at once in this particular series and then have the responses. It may be difficult for them to keep track of the different questions.

Chairman

32. I would propose that you directly put the questions to the Panel and enter into a dialogue and then go on through your programme.

Mr. Brinza (US)

33. Thank you, Mr. Chairman. If that is the instance then, if I could ask the five experts with respect to each of those first three questions, I just want to make sure we understood correctly your responses, firstly are these three hormones naturally present in the meat-producing animals and in humans? It may be useful to just go around the table starting with Dr. Ritter.

Dr. Ritter

34. The extent to which they are presented of course as you will know is a function to some extent of the status of the human in question and the age, but to provide a general answer, I think, in my view the general answer is "yes", noting that there will be some exceptions in variance on the degree. I understand that the levels are different but that they are all present to some extent.

Dr. McLean

35. Yes. There will be variations in levels but the three naturally-occurring hormones are found in both animals and humans.

Dr. Arnold

36. I agree, Mr. Chairman, and we perfectly know the levels occurring from fetal life to until very late age.

Dr. André

37. Yes. The hormones are the same but it is not clear if the metabolites sometimes could be different. For example, if you give a natural hormone as (.?.) to calves or to any meat producing animals, they can metabolize and transform the hormone and in these conditions the food intake for human is not the same. You see animals have been treated as if they are not treated, qualitatively.

Dr. Arnold

38. If I could just clarify with Professor André, are we talking about levels of that magnitude with respect to the administration of any of these three for growth promotion purposes in accordance with good animal husbandry practice?

Dr. André

39. The metabolic transformation, the biological transformation, is totally independent of the level. It is not a problem of level. Maybe I don't understand well your question.

Dr. Arnold

40. I thought your earlier answer had been that there is a possibility that these could be administered at such a level that they cannot be metabolized by the animal. And my question was, are the doses we are talking about for growth promotion so high that they would be at a level that the animal cannot metabolize them.

Chairman

41. There will be no answer to this.

Dr. Lucier

42. Yes, these materials would be present at all stages of life, in both males and females, as my colleagues have said, in varying amounts.

Mr. Brinza (US)

43. Then, the next question was, would the hormones also be present in the meat of the animals and milk from those animals? Again recognizing that the levels will vary.

Dr. Arnold

44. Mr. Chairman, I think there are different pathways of metabolism for these substances. And certainly at high levels, it depends somewhat on the dose which pathway is used, but essentially metabolism is similar in animal and in man. For example, in cattle the 17 alpha oestradiol plays a certain greater role than in human beings, but this metabolite is less active as an oestrogen or practically not active as an oestrogen. So there are slight differences.

Chairman

45. This goes to the first question. I am very glad I could understand this. So let's go to the second question, then. Just as a matter of procedure, we don't go for consensus. We just take and record what the experts say, but we are not trying to assess some consensus here.

Mr. Brinza (US)

46. I understand, Mr. Chairman. It is just that to the extent that we are all talking from a common understanding of the facts, then it is useful for us to perceive that. Yes, the second question is then will each of these three hormones be present in the meat and the milk from these animals - the oestradiol 17 beta, testosterone and progesterone.

Dr. Ritter

47. Subject to the same variances that I indicated a moment ago, the answer is yes.

Chairman

48. They will be in the milk?

Dr. Ritter

49. Yes, again subject to the same variances that we discussed a moment ago, although the levels and the extent to which they are present and the ratios and so on and so forth will be a function of the particular status of the animal in question, but to avoid going into a lengthier response, than is really necessary in the general case the answer Mr. Chairman, I think would be yes. They would be present.

Mr. Brinza (US)

50. Mr. Chairman, it may be useful as part of these questions, to save some time, we are also asking whether the levels that we are talking about would be within the normal physiological range with respect to these hormones when they are administered for growth promotion purposes.

Dr. Ritter

51. To answer that question, again the answer is yes. The position, certainly that the that I have offered, Mr. Chairman, is at least that when these substances are used in accordance with the prescribed use conditions, the levels that are present are in fact indistinguishable from those which would be present in an animal which had not been treated at all. I should say, to clarify that just a little bit further, there is a range of concentrations which is what I have been attempting to allude to that one might normally detect in untreated animals. It's not a finite number, but rather there is a distribution of values over which one typically might find these hormones in an un-

treated animal. The levels in animals that have been treated falls within the range of those numbers that might be detected in animals that have otherwise [cassette ended ...]

52. I don't want to impart the impression that there is a precise number for testosterone levels, there is a range of values that one finds. As one might expect, these are biological living systems and there is a distribution of values, but treatment results in a residue level which falls within that range.

Dr. McLean

53. Mr. Chairman, the answer is yes and to facilitate an explanation, I suggest that if you look at Attachment 1 of my submission, then there are a number of figures in there that relate to progesterone to oestradiol 17 beta, and to testosterone in various tissues and in particular the excretion in the milk, and when you come to the other than naturally-occurring hormones, for the other hormones trenbolone and zeranol, because they are lipid soluble, one would expect them to appear in the tissues and in the milk.

Dr. Arnold

54. Chairman, we have a rather complete data base showing us, as the previous speakers have already said, there is a large variability according to physiological status and there can be a factor for certain hormones up to 1,000 and I have presented the data in my written responses. Therefore I agree that if the substances are used according to good veterinary practices, either for growth, promotion or for the therapeutic uses authorized in the EC, you have initially a slight difference but at the time of slaughter there is no means to discriminate between treated and non-treated animals, irrespective of whether for growth promotion or for therapeutic and zootechnical purposes.

Dr. André

55. Yes, both hormones are present in meat and milk, it's clear, and the level is a very variable level is clear also. I don't agree with Professor Arnold just on the last point, when he says that it is impossible to distinguish between hormones, injected hormones and natural produced hormones. In some cases it is possible to distinguish the two by physical means of isotope relations, but maybe not at a very low levels, it is very difficult to do.

Chairman

56. Thank you.

Dr. Lucier

57. Yes, these materials are present in milk at varying levels. Progesterone is much higher than the other two, as much as a 100 to 1,000 times higher, but they all are present.

Chairman

58. Thank you. You wanted to reply.

Dr. Arnold

59. A broad comment on Professor André, I totally agree this is a theoretical possibility, if you label the hormones with stable isotopes, you can discriminate between

added hormones and endogenous hormones, but this has absolutely no relevance in practice.

Dr. André

60. No, I totally disagree. I was speaking about natural occurring isotopes, C-12, C-13 and its possible to distinguish in this case, some hormones naturally-occurring or injected, as they do in sportsmen. They do this currently in sportsmen now for doping in sport and they can distinguish endogenous testosterone and injected testosterone, even if the compound is really the same, but the isotopic composition is not really the same.

Chairman

61. Thank you, Sir. We take note of the two views.

Dr. McLean

62. I just want to add another thing. I think it is important when one looks at milk, that because these hormones are fat soluble, then the concentration in the two commonly used or common articles of commerce, which are cream and milk, is very substantially greater. It is something of the order of three to four times into cream and about 40 times into butter, and so I think one must take that into account as well.

Chairman

63. Thank you. Then the next question was at the levels we are talking about, within the normal physiological range, would these residue hormones have a biological effect on the consumer?

Dr. Ritter

64. I think that to attempt to answer that question would really be to pre-empt the outcome of this Panel. I think that is the question which the Panel will endeavour to answer. So Mr. Chairman, with respect, I think the issue that you face at the end of these proceedings is to answer exactly that question. At the levels that are present after the use, does this constitute a level which may result in a biological activity? I am going to, if I may Mr. Chairman, modify your question a little bit to the one I would like to answer, rather than the one you asked. I must say I feel somewhat restrained to make an attempt to answer your question directly for the reasons that I have said. Because as I have indicated, at least in my view, that in the case of the natural hormones these levels that are present in the meat of treated animals is essentially within the range that it would be present in the meat of untreated animals, I would suggest that the question becomes moot as to whether or not there is biological activity associated with these levels of the hormone. I think it is a moot point because the level is no greater or lesser than it would be in the meat of an untreated animal. That is a consumer would be exposed to no lesser or greater biological activity as a result of this level from either a treated animal or from an untreated animal because both levels are essentially in the same range. Thank you.

Dr. McLean

65. Mr. Chairman, in relation to the naturally-occurring hormones, then it is not possible to differentiate between the effects of produce from treated animals against produce from untreated animals because essentially they sit in the same biological range. In the case of the non-naturally occurring hormones, in establishing the ADI,

then there were very sensitive end points derived from studies in non-human primates, and then the situation of sensitive members of the population was taken into account when establishing safety factors. So the levels that one would get in meat are substantially below those causing any effects in primates, and there is a reasonably good correlation in hormonal levels in, or effects of hormonal levels in primates against humans. So therefore the levels that you would see in meat from animals that were treated with the two non-natural growth promotants would not be causing effects in humans if they consume the meat.

Dr. Arnold

66. Mr. Chairman, the three natural hormones as they endogenously occur at physiological levels certainly have biological effects of human beings. This is their role and their function. These steroids are amongst the most successful molecules which have evolved and you find them already in very low species. So it is quite clear that at physiological levels they have important functions and they interact with many other hormones and they act almost on every cell in the body. Now, the additional amount you could ingest with meat, either from untreated or from treated animals according to what veterinary practices, cannot modulate this endogenous activity of these hormones because the amounts are too small.

Chairman

67. I take that this is all subject to the application of good veterinary practices. It is always the big "if", as I read it in your paper too, that is the assumption.

Dr. André

68. I agree with that fact and I believe with my colleagues that within the physiological range as these hormones have no acute difference biological effects on human beings. But in the physiological range the problem and the question is to know if when you treat animals or whether you don't treat animals you have the same mean in the physiological range. I mean I believe that if you only eat meat from treated animals, you will have as Dieter Arnold said, a very small enhancement of the mean of your food hormonal intake and this will not be transformed in classical biological effects for human beings. You don't see anything, but the problem is that some other biological effects have not been studied and need a very very very long time to be studied. I think for example, as changes in human fertility or change in sex ratio as we know this sex ratio for example is now changing in some countries. But we have no relation between these countries and the fact that they banned or not these hormones, that is not the problem now. But what I only say is that this change in human reproduction for example, has not been studied nor related to hormonal change or not, and I have personally some doubt on this.

Chairman

69. Thank you, Dr. Lucier.

Dr. Lucier

70. The short answer is yes, some biological effect could occur. If you think about in terms of a normal condition, say a normal woman would have 30 per cent of her oestrogen receptors occupied at some given point in time. At that same point in time, if she is consuming meat that contains an additional burden of oestrogens be-

cause of the use of growth promoters, that receptor occupancy may be something like 30.01 or 30.001, a very very small increase. This increase would not be detectable, not even close to being detectable, by any experimental tools that we have today. So the answer is that a biological effect could be occurring, if it is occurring it would not be detectable, and finally the relationship between that biological effect and a toxic effect, say cancer or birth defect or something like this, would be unknown. But if such an effect was occurring it would be extraordinarily small, remarkably close to zero.

Chairman

71. Thank you. Dr. Randell would you like to take the floor. Now? A procedural question or? OK.

Mr. Christoforou (EC)

72. Mr. Chairman, thank you. During the organizational meeting we had this morning, you said that we would review how the procedure is going after a while and now it is our feeling that it would probably be appropriate, after the United States has posed the three or four or five questions, so probably we can stay here, and then Canada will come up with the follow-up questions in this same area, and then we take up the floor ourselves, because that is going too long and we would like if possible to intervene in this area of residue levels and distinctions between the three natural and the three synthetic. I think that it would be more appropriate and will probably improve the quality of the debate and the discussion we are having here. If the United States can continue with one or two more questions and Canada, and then we can come in at this stage with similar questions in this area which you are discussing now.

Chairman

73. Well my personal feeling is that we are in a good process. To me it is very educational the way we proceed and I would prefer to stick to the modes we set out and you can come in with a question when it's your time. You can then also focus on the points you want being less reactive than when you have to follow up to what they are doing. I think, it's my assessment that it's efficient and of course as time goes by, less and more specialized question will become necessary and we will focus and target more down and you will bring in other aspects than the other parties. I would have a preference to continue the way we are doing. I give you the floor.

Mr. Brinza (US)

74. Thank you Mr. Chairman. The next question is related to the one we were just asking. I just want to make sure I understood the response correctly which is, would the residues found in the meat be chemically identical whether it came from application for growth-promotion purposes versus endogenously produced versus applied for zootechnical or therapeutic purposes? Would it be the same chemical residue, recognizing the levels again would be variable?

Dr. Ritter

75. I presume that your question is directed of course to the natural hormone?

Mr. Brinza (US)

76. Yes.

Dr. Ritter

77. In the interest of expediency Mr. Chairman, I will say essentially yes. Essentially yes.

Dr. McLean

78. Mr. Chairman, the residues will be similar for zootechnical uses where quite high levels are used, you can get spill-over or inhibition of certain of the metabolic pathways, and in that way you might get qualitatively similar but quantitatively quite different residue profiles.

Dr. Arnold

79. This is also my answer, Mr. Chairman, qualitatively the same but quantitatively could be slightly different depending on the compound administered, the dose, the route of administration, etc. There are some differences.

Chairman

80. Thank you, yes Dr. Ritter.

Dr. Ritter

81. I am sorry Mr. Chairman, just to clarify, perhaps I misunderstood the question, but was the question directed at for the same use, that is what ...

Chairman

82. Could you restate?

Mr. Brinza (US)

83. Yes, the question was would the residue be chemically the same whether it was endogenously produced, for example, pick testosterone. Whether it was endogenously produced testosterone, testosterone administered for growth promotion purposes or testosterone administered for zootechnical or therapeutic purposes.

Dr. Ritter

84. Then of course I certainly agree with the answer provided by my colleagues. Qualitatively the residue in my view would be indistinguishable. Quantitatively, of course, the amount that could be detected would be a function of the amount that would have been administered either for growth promotion or therapeutic uses.

Dr. André

85. I think that the residues are for the greatest part of the residues the same, when used for growth promotion natural hormones and for use as therapeutic zootechnical. If differences appear it can be in metabolic profiles, I mean that with the long term effect you induce some different enzyme panels and this enzyme, after a long time, can produce small amounts of different metabolites as when you are just using these hormones one time. But to my knowledge, this is known for other compounds but not for hormones, but to my knowledge also it has not been studied.

Chairman

86. Thank you, Dr. Lucier.

Dr. Lucier

87. Yes.

Chairman

88. Thank you. Well, if you agree you don't have to take the floor, in order to win time that is fine.

Mr. Brinza (US)

89. The next question I think Dr. Lucier will find it an easier time to agree with because I believe I understood a statement he made that given the concept of half-life, that if you administer one of these hormones to an animal, in this case I am talking of all six of them, you administer a hormone to an animal there will be a residue, even far out into the future, even though it may be only so few molecules it could not be detected by any available means that we have at our disposal currently. I just wanted to make sure I had understood that and whether that was the view or what I had understood from the responses of the other experts as well. Please correct me if I have misstated.

Dr. Lucier

90. Are you asking me specifically? That is correct a few molecules would likely remain, not detectable certainly, but there is every likelihood there would be a few of them left around.

Dr. Arnold

91. Mr. Chairman, hormones administered from exogenous sources have very short half-lives initially after administration, in the range of minutes. But then the half-lives becomes longer and longer because these hormones go to different compartments in the body and after a few hours, the half-life is already in the order of some 50, 100 minutes, initially it is in the order of some 10-15 minutes. So it is very difficult to predict for how long the last molecule will persist in the body, but certainly for a very long time.

Chairman

92. Thank you.

Dr. McLean

93. For the sake of the record Mr. Chairman, I agree with Dr. Arnold.

Chairman

94. You nod as well?

Dr. Ritter

95. If you would like a complete record, Yes.

Chairman

96. Well it is not necessary, thank you. Can we go on?

Mr. Brinza (US)

97. I would like to turn now to questions that have been raised in some of the documents that have been provided to you all and make sure that I had understood correctly the responses in some of these instances. With respect to the studies that

Dr. Liehr had performed, I want to make sure that we are all understanding that the dose comparisons of the studies, the doses that he was using in his study versus the doses that we are talking about for growth promotion purposes. I just want to make sure that we all understood this the same way, that the dosage used in Dr. Liehr's study was 61 micrograms per day in the male Syrian hamster, which weighs approximately 100 grams. Let me just run through these, then we can discuss this a little bit. That would be approximately 610 micrograms per kilogram per day, if we are doing our math correctly, and for a 60 kilogram adult male human that would be equivalent to about 36.6 milligrams per day and that adult male humans produce about 48 micrograms of oestradiol 17 beta per day. Given that math then, what Dr. Liehr was delivering to the hamsters in question was 36,360/48 times more than the comparable average daily production rate in adult men, and that in turn is 15,000 times more than the residue of oestradiol in meat from treated animals. I just wanted to make sure that we had the numbers there correctly, because then that would lead to result of a difference between the dose used in the treatment of the hamsters and the residue in 500 grams of meat, of a significant difference, it would be equivalent to the oestradiol from 11.5 million 500 gram portions of meat being injected into a human male every day to be comparable. I can run through those numbers again, I recognize that was rather fast.

Chairman

98. Yes, the Community, Mr. Christoforou.

Mr. Christoforou (EC)

99. I think it would be probably more useful, if we can get the written version of these statements and the numbers.

Chairman

100. Well, I understood its about hamsterizing humans.

Mr. Christoforou (EC)

101. Yes, indeed, but there was some other references to other animals, so we would like really to see some other products, so we would appreciate it if we can get the written version with the exact figures for us to have a look, thank you.

Chairman

102. Yes, I assume you want to come back to this comparison later on. But are you in a position to answer or would you postpone this need of figures? Dr. Arnold.

Dr. Arnold

103. Provided that I correctly understood the question, I can perhaps give a preliminary answer. If a pellet is administered to hamsters in the order of several milligrams 20, 50 or more, you can think about 100, 150 micrograms which are released per day. Therefore some authors in some studies have simulated this situation by constantly infusing similar amounts to the animals. So these are in fact very high doses which are released from such implants.

Chairman

104. Professor Mc Lean.

Dr. McLean

105. If it's helpful Mr. Chairman, I would take the same line as Dr. Arnold. It is quite clear that the dose administered to the hamster in a pellet was a number of milligrams, a hamster weighs a few hundred grams and to extrapolate from the work in the hamster to the human situation I think is fairly dangerous.

Dr. Ritter

106. Mr. Chairman, without double checking all of the calculations that were just given to us *vis-à-vis* the comparisons, I think the point of my colleagues Professor McLean and Dr. Arnold make is the correct one. That is that there is orders of magnitude difference here, between the dose levels that were used by Professor Liehr and those that might result as residues for exposure in the question of meat. I think we need to remind ourselves that the fundamental intent here is different. That is Professor Liehr's work and the work of many investigators is to produce an effect. This speaks to the most fundamental issue in pharmacology and in toxicology and that is the concept of dose response. Professor Liehr is very interested in understanding the induction of cancer as a result of exposure to these hormones, so of course his protocol would necessarily be designed in such a way, so as to produce the desired effect, in his case the tumour. The intent obviously in the case of food residues, Mr. Chairman, is to avoid a dose level which may constitute a human risk, so it will come as small surprise that the levels that are present as residues in food are thousands or hundreds of thousands or millions of times lower than they would be in an experiment which is specifically designed to induce a tumour. These two experiments, if you like, are completely at cross purposes with each other. They are from their very initiation intended to produce entirely different results. So to compare a protocol which has been designed to produce a tumour to a food residue the used practice of which is set up in such a way so as to minimize the presence of the residue, is in my view a relatively meaningless comparison. Thank you.

Dr. Lucier

107. I am not in fundamental disagreement with what has been said, but I think it is important to point out one thing, that physiological levels of oestrogen do result in oxidative damage to DNA and this has been shown in the rat and so this type of damage does occur in physiological situations in experimental animals and this is a particular form of damage to DNA that's been quantified. So the levels that are normally circulating in the body are producing some of these DNA damaging metabolites. Exactly how it does it, is open to question and with the work of Dr. Liehr which would suggest one way, other works may suggest other ways, but I think it is clear that that amount of damage is occurring and would occur following a small dose because it is already added to an additional body burden in which this is already occurring. But again that additional DNA damage would extraordinary small, again remarkably close to zero.

Chairman

108. Thank you. When you talk about physiological levels, may I take it that means naturally-occurring levels?

Dr. Lucier

109. That is right. Of course these change during the normal cycling phases of people as well as experimental animals, so there is a range of values that occur, but within that normal range of values that you see in experimental animals, which is similar to what is seen in people as well.

Chairman

110. Thank you. Any further remarks on this point?

Mr. Brinza (US)

111. Sorry, I just had a follow up to the last intervention. I just want to make sure I understood. Is there evidence that at the levels we are talking about of residue in meat from the use of these hormones for growth-promotion purposes in accordance with good animal husbandry practice, is there evidence being put forward of DNA damage from those levels of residue?

Dr. Lucier

112. Let me answer the question in another way, perhaps I have caused some confusion. Say you already have a hundred or thousand molecules of something in the body, and that some of those molecules are producing a DNA damage event. If you add another molecule to it there is some possibility that that same event will occur because it is the same molecule. You will not be able to distinguish certainly that additional event from the ones that occurred from the thousand molecules, but you won't be able to say, no none of those events are related to that additional one molecule. That is what I meant that it would not be detectable, very very small, but it would be impossible to say that that event could not occur.

Chairman

113. Can I just follow up for my understanding. The comparison between Dr. Liehr's protocols, inducing cancer on the one hand using very high doses and on the other hand using very very limited doses here. Is it your view that despite one uses very very small doses, there still might be some effects?

Dr. Lucier

114. Yes, because you are already adding to an existing very large number of same molecules, so just instead of 1,000 molecules you have 1,001 is irrelevant here.

Chairman

115. And that is why you basically challenge, if I am correct, that the concept of thresholds...

Dr. Lucier

116. That is exactly right. I should also point out though, to make it clear from my view, that I do not think it has been demonstrated that this particular mechanism is related or proven to be related to the carcinogenicity of oestrogens. It is at this point an interesting hypothesis, there some plausibility to it, but it has not been proven to be associated or a cause of tumours produced by oestrogen.

Chairman

117. Yes ....

Mr. Palecka

118. Thank you very much, sorry perhaps to interfere into the discussion. Just one precision: by adding one molecule, does it mean that there is a linear increase in probability of DNA damage or you think that its progressive? Does it mean that it will perhaps put something more or it is just a very linear function?

Dr. Lucier

119. It is already adding to an existing burden, if that burden that already exists is on a linear part of a dose response curve, then adding an additional molecule would create a small amount of additional damage. It is possible that that mechanism is already saturated maximal at the physiological concentrations, if that is the case, then that damage would not occur, this is the opposite situation of the threshold.

Chairman

120. Thank you. Any further comments on this? No, ok. One more.

Mr. Brinza (US)

121. I said one moment please.

Chairman

122. Oh one moment, I see.

Mr. Brinza (US)

123. Mr. Chairman, a few more questions. I just did want to follow up on this last point. This might get a bit technical so I may have to impose on the experts to help translate this into terms that are easily understood by people like myself, who are more lay person than toxicologist or scientist.

124. Let's make sure I understood. I believe I understood reference to DNA damage. I just want to make clear. Is DNA damage, in other words DNA adducts, always indicative of a genotoxic effect?

Dr. Lucier

125. No. Do you want a longer answer? There is a wealth of scientific evidence to show that for many carcinogens a DNA adduct step is essential. For many of the polycyclic aromatic hydrocarbons for example, that occur as contaminants and many industrial processes at present in our air, there is a specific DNA adduct that's been identified that has been shown to be related as close as you can come in a causal sense to the tumours that result. In other cases, some DNA adducts have no mutating capability, so there is a wide variation. Not all adducts are alike, some have very strong mutating potential, some have weak mutating potential, others have no mutating potential at all.

Chairman

126. Sorry, would you like to take the floor on this point?

Dr. Arnold

127. I think it could be interesting to the Panel to note that a very large number of adducts to DNA exists at all times in all cells of the body.

Mr. Brinza (US)

128. Thank you, I was about to invoke Dr. Arnold's name. I understood earlier that we heard that a single strand break in DNA actually occurs something in the order of 5,000 times per hour, I may not have gotten all this correctly, and that the human ability to repair is about 200,000 events per hour. I just was going to ask Dr. Lucier whether the DNA damage that he was referring to would fall within the range that we are referring to here, that Dr. Arnold had referred to as normally occurring.

Dr. Lucier

129. I think that the kind of damage that would result from oxidation, catechol oestrogen formation of 17 beta oestradiol, would result, and I am not a hundred per cent sure of that and, I am sure I will be corrected when the other folks start asking questions, but I believe that would be something called 8-hydroxyguanosine would be the primary oxidative damage step. You don't remember that, we will not give you a quiz later, but this occurs in very high frequency. I do not have the exact numbers, but it does occur in very high frequency in the human body.

Chairman

130. Thank you.

Dr. Arnold

131. Mr. Chairman, I did not want to suggest to the Panel that we should not take such effects seriously. This is the value of these indicator tests, of these early events, that we get conscious that something is happening to DNA and that we further investigate. The only thing I wanted to say is that single-stranded breaks are *per se* insufficient evidence, particularly if observed *in vitro* and you need to do follow up studies.

Chairman

132. Thank you.

Dr. Lucier

133. I would like to add one comment to that. I think that that is a very good point. There are a lot of different ways of looking at genetic damage and the science of chemical carcinogenesis evolves or progresses in itty bitty little steps and each piece of evidence adds to the total degree of evidence that a chemical is acting through that pathway. But simply having a positive DNA adduct test or a positive cell-transformation test in itself is not convincing. What becomes convincing when you have a whole body of knowledge from cell systems, from experimental systems, *in vivo*, from limited studies you may obtain from human samples, and start putting it all together and that adds to the degree of compelling nature of the evidence. So it is not like now we do not have it, now we have it, it sort of goes in a step wise fashion.

Chairman

134. Thank you. Would you like to continue Mr. Brinza?

Mr. Brinza (US)

135. If there are no other comments. I wanted to ask a couple of questions with respect to the concept of an acceptable daily intake level, which was explained I thought quite well by Dr. Randell earlier. I just would like to make sure that I under-

stood, and from the experts' responses that they were using the concept of an ADI in the same way, which is that it is the amount of a substance that can be consumed daily by humans over a lifetime without an adverse effect.

Dr. Ritter

136. Yes.

Mr. Brinza (US)

137. The silence means the others were doing it in the same manner, using the same manner? In that case conceptually would it be possible to establish an ADI for the three synthetic hormones involved in this dispute, trenbolone, zeranol and MGA?

Dr. Ritter

138. Certainly in my view the answer is yes.

Dr. McLean

139. The answer from my point of view is yes. I would just like to reiterate that the end points for both of them took into account sensitive subpopulations, sensitive human subpopulations, such as pre-pubertal children and menopausal women and also that they were supported by data generated from studies or administrations to non-human primates.

Dr. Arnold

140. I agree with the previous speakers.

Chairman

141. Could perhaps Dr. Randell explain why we do not have ADIs on these hormones. Why were they not established?

Dr. Randell (Codex)

142. The difference between the three natural hormones and the xenobiotic hormones I think has been discussed earlier today. Firstly, for the xenobiotic hormones it is relatively simple application of the ADI concept and the ADI paradigm if you wish to establish ADIs for these substances. For the endogenous hormones, the JECFA looked at the available information, found that because these were produced in man and that the levels of ingestion were several magnitudes less than endogenous production, then it was unnecessary to set an ADI. On the basis that the end point would achieve the same result, that there would be no additional risk to the humans.

Chairman

143. On the necessity, is that view shared by the other experts? Dr. Arnold?

Dr. Arnold

144. Mr. Chairman, it might be interesting to the Panel that in the EC we have reviewed the three natural hormones independently from JECFA. At least a result of one such evaluation has been published in the Official Journal. We have set an MRL not necessary for oestradiol two years ago for the therapeutic uses and the whole evidence has been reviewed by the Committee for Veterinary Medicinal Products and the European Medicine Evaluation Agency. Since these are just nine lines, maybe I can read the conclusions of the EC Committees and its legally binding now, pub-

lished in the Official Journal. "The conclusions of the FAO/WHO Expert Committee on Food Additives, JECFA, that no ADI and MRLs for oestradiol will need to be established, is adopted. Neck and plasma residue levels after treatment with oestradiol benzoate and oestradiol valerate have shown to be within physiological limits. Although it is likely that tissue residues levels will also be within physiological limits, this cannot be guaranteed given the results with oestradiol-hexahydrobenzoate. Still compared to the lowest human production rate of oestradiol pre-pubertal boys, 6 micrograms per day, and compared to the amount of oestradiol in other foodstuffs that are part of the human diet, the amount of exogenous oestradiol that humans will be exposed through ingestion of tissue from treated animals is biologically insignificant and will be incapable of exerting hormonal effect in human beings." So it is about the same line of evidence and of arguments put together by the EC Committee, than has been previously done by JECFA.

Chairman

145. Thank you. Is this reference in your paper.?

Dr. Arnold

146. Yes, it is.

Chairman

147. Thank you.

Dr. Arnold

148. And if you want I can give you a copy of that Council Regulation.

Chairman

149. Please Dr. Randell.

Dr. Randell (Codex)

150. I would just like to state that an acceptable daily intake is a numerical estimate of what might be called a no effect level in humans, with built in safety factors. However, in the broad range of substances that JECFA has evaluated over a number of years, it has on many occasions not allocated a numerical ADI. The reason for doing this is that certain substances are essentially safe to ingest at any level and in these cases JECFA will give an ADI which it calls "not specified". It does not specify the acceptable daily intake. Very common safe food additives such as ascorbic acid, vitamin C, fall into this group. On these three substances were the only three substances in which JECFA has used the expression "not necessary". In this particular case JECFA felt that it was not necessary because of the overwhelming endogenous production by humans of these substances and that to set an ADI would not achieve any additional improvement in understanding of the safety of these substances in humans. So "not necessary" was basically an evaluation of what JECFA was trying to achieve in general in terms of trying to protect health of consumers.

Chairman

151. Thank you. Further comments on this or would you like to go on?

Mr. Brinza (US)

152. Thank you Mr. Chairman. I believe that I have understood previously Dr. Randell and would like to make sure and confirm, that in the instance of the two synthetics that were reviewed by JECFA, on trenbolone and zeranol, that the ADI was set using the methodology that you described in general for an ADI. That ADI has the same meaning for those two as it does for other substances.

Dr. Randell (Codex)

153. The ADI for the zeranol and the trenbolone was established on the basis of a no-effect level being identified in test animals. In these two particular cases, the no-effect level which JECFA selected was the no hormonal effect level for both substances.

Mr. Brinza (US)

154. Thank you. If I could turn to a subject that was touched on by one of the experts earlier today, I will just make sure I understood correctly. With respect to the particular implantation of five of these hormones under discussion, what factors, if any, make the ear as a site of implantation favourable for use over other sites of implantation?

Chairman

155. Would you like to take the floor?

Dr. Ritter

156. I suppose, following the order that we now seem to have set, Mr. Chairman.

Chairman

157. Well it is unfair that you have to take it, just feel free when you want to answer.

Dr. Ritter

158. I think the primary impetus, Mr. Chairman, for the selection of the ear is because it is a tissue which is not normally used to enter the food supply, so it makes identification of the source of the material very easy. I do not want to say ensures, but it goes some very considerable distance to ensuring, that injection site residues, which understandably could be much higher than normal tissue residue levels, are extremely unlikely to enter the food supply. It is my understanding that that is the primary motivation for selecting a site which will never enter the food supply.

Dr. McLean

159. And one additional advantage of using the ear, it is very easy to palpate a pellet or an implant under the skin of the ear, whereas if it is subcutaneously on the body then you would never find it. So that is a second way of identifying treated animals. In fact for some other treatments with hormones, but not these ones, it is actually possible to remove the implant from the ear.

Mr. Brinza (US)

160. If I could just follow up on that, I understood a reference earlier that in fact the implants come with a device which is specially designed to implant the pellet in the ear. I believe I have understood the reference that that device would not be suit-

able for implanting it through the hide, for example. I just want to make sure I have understood that correctly.

Dr. McLean

161. I would be a little bit unwilling to extend it that far. It is just that the "gun" used to administer the implants is such that it makes administration convenient, easy and accurate, in that the pellets or the implants are generally in a cartridge and it rotates around a little bit like a six shooter and so it is a convenient, easy and accurate way to administer the prescribed dose.

Mr. Brinza (US)

162. Thank you. If I could then ask whether there is any specific evidence that the experts are aware of evidence that using a dose of hormone greater than that approved for growth promotion would lead to a proportionately greater response in feed efficiency.

Dr. McLean

163. Generally not. When the sponsor suggests the dose, then the dose that they suggest will give the optimum response and so therefore, within limits, there is no need, no return in administering more than is suggested. The second thing is, however, most regulatory authorities, including JECFA, require that data setting residues does take into account dose rates that are in excess of what is normally used, generally twice at least and sometimes more, so that the effect of overdosing, if you like, or variations in uptake, can be seen.

Mr. Brinza (US)

164. Thank you and then if I could just follow on, I am sorry did you ...?

Dr. Ritter

165. I was only going to add, Mr. Chairman, that I think Dr. Randell in his opening comments articulated in my view very very clearly, the nature of the balance that one tries to strike in establishing an ADI and an acceptable use practice. I think, in my view, he made the point very very well, that to use too little achieves nothing. That is one does not obtain the desired effect but at the same time results in a residue. To do too much, to use too much, goes beyond what one can anticipate in terms of an effect. So that the correct is the one which is ultimately recommended and that is a value which will optimize the balance between the return, the benefit if you and the residue. That is the level to which we are referring.

Dr. Arnold

166. Mr. Chairman, in the development by industry of these pellets and another devices, they have been optimized with respect to the dose. However this does not necessarily prevent some farmers to use more implants, for example. But this again does not necessarily cause higher residue levels in the carcass. There are some examples that I have shown in my written response, where the use of up to six implants did not necessarily have the effect that the residue levels in the remaining carcass were significantly higher. So it is a question you cannot easily answer, you have to answer on a case-by-case basis. On the other side, it is quite clear that if you inject twice the amount directly, that then all levels increase in plasma and in tissues, not necessarily in a linear way, but they increase significantly, if you double the dose, for

example by injection. That is the difference between a slow release device and a direct injection. On the other hand the long term release of high doses may have influences on the pattern of hormone excretion in the animal's body and this is the intention of using such compounds.

Chairman

167. Thank you very much. May I just make, oh sorry, yes, please.

Dr. André

168. Just one comment on this point. It is not so evident that a double dose, even at the same time, will give a better response. But what we observed a lot of years ago in our country, when these hormones were allowed by implants in the ear, is that farmers tried to put another of the same doses but later. They do not wait the withdrawal period and they inject another one maybe at the half of the theoretical withdrawal period, and they had benefit to do this, clearly, because the effect was more longer at the time. Consequently it is clear also that respecting the strict withdrawal period at the end, the residue level was higher. Do you understand?

Chairman

169. Yes. My question would be, do you think this was typical for European situation or is that a phenomenon which is observed world-wide?

Dr. André

170. It is not a scientific question, but then, well I think really it is not typical for any countries. It is a problem of farmer, of respect with regulation and of benefits that they have. I can return through the same question, do you think people drive faster than allowed in any country or in another one? It is a problem of respect of regulation, only. But it is clear that it was the same situation at that time in France as it is now in US, for example. Because one implant was allowed in the ear with a withdrawal period, it is quite the same situation it was just 10 years ago. That situation seems to be the same, I think.

Chairman

171. Thank you. Would you like to comment on this point?

Dr. McLean

172. I just would like to make a comment. Generally, of course, for zeranol and trenbolone the use of excess would be or could be picked up if the MRL was exceeded, and so therefore there would be a penalty if the MRL was exceeded. And so therefore, farmers knowing that you can analyze for quite accurately, or screen for and confirm, the presence of zeranol or trenbolone are not going to do that. And the other interesting thing is that in countries where the use of these compounds is permitted and there are good educational campaigns for farmers as to the correct use and the reasons why you should not exceed the prescribed dose, and the penalties that exist if you do, the results from residues surveys show that by and large there is no exceeding of the MRL. However in those countries where the use is not controlled and that is no farmer education campaign and difficult to apply a penalty, then we know that the MRL is significantly exceeded. So one of the important factors of legalizing these compounds is to be able to conduct an education campaign and to be able to put in place monitoring campaigns to see that the MRL is not exceeded.

Chairman

173. Thank you. Dr. Arnold.

Dr. Arnold

174. Mr. Chairman, in JECFA we use a term called theoretical maximum daily intake. That means we multiply arbitrarily high consumption figures with MRL figures, to calculate what could happen in the worse case scenario. If you assume all animals are treated, all are at the MRL and under these conditions about five per cent of the ADI is used with zeranol and trenbolone. It was very interesting for me to see that in the documentation of the 32nd JECFA there was an example of very big abuse. It was intentionally done this study, and I tell you what people had done. They had administered a dose more than 100 times higher than the recommended dose. They have administered it intravenously, in six doses over three days, so really it is a scenario you cannot more exaggerate. Under these conditions the theoretic maximum daily intake was increased by a factor of three, so that we were in the order of 15-16 per cent of the ADI. This is my comment, to show the potential consequences of misuse or abuse of these substances. We have some data, and this data had been available to this 32nd JECFA.

Chairman

175. Thank you very much. We are past one o'clock and I wonder, do you intend to continue with the questions for some time, I suppose.

Mr. Brinza (US)

176. Well, Mr. Chairman, actually I was about to say, looking at the clock, that it might be of some relief to you and the Panel and others that we only have one or two more questions, relatively short ones ...

Chairman

177. If we could finish the US questions and then we would break. Would you agree to that or would you need a break? Well, yes. If you agree why don't we finish your questions and then break.

Thank you.

Mr. Brinza (US)

178. Just a quick follow up I believe to the answer we received earlier. Is there any evidence that implantation of the approved implants at a site other than the ear would lead to greater feed efficiency? In other words, is there any reason to implant it somewhere else to get a better effect?

Dr. McLean

179. I think the general consensus would be that providing it subcutaneously, probably not.

Mr. Brinza (US)

180. One further question, there are several hormonal compounds that are used for as oestrus control in the European Union and among these are medroxy progesterone acetate and allyltrenbolone and another compound methyl testosterone is also used for sex reversal in aquaculture, we understand. The question, though, is whether

these compounds are chemically related to the synthetic hormones used for growth promotion in animals.

Dr. Ritter

181. Mr. Chairman, I like the use of the word related because it provides one with enormous scope. Of course they are related. They are structure-related and they have activity and function which is similar to the hormones that we are discussing here at issue. But of course there are notable differences as well, so they are "related", I think is a good word to use.

Dr. Lucier

182. Yes, I would agree with that comment that chemically they are different. In total, but they very have conserved parts of the molecule and they perform or stimulate cells in much the same way. Nevertheless, since their parts are a little bit different, they will be metabolised different so you will have some different breakdown products, you will have different, they may go to different parts of the body, preferentially because of those differences in the molecule. So they will act pretty much the same way once they get into a tissue, but the amount that gets into a tissue might be quite a bit different, or its biological persistence in a tissue or cell might be quite a bit different.

Chairman

183. Thank you. Dr. Arnold.

Dr. Arnold

184. Two substances named by the US delegation are certainly chemically related and also what concerns the mechanism of action, there are great similarities. Nevertheless, allyltrenbolone is not useful for growth promotion, it has no anabolic properties and therefore there is an exemption in the EC directives concerning this substance.

Chairman

185. Thank you.

Dr. McLean

186. Generally I am in agreement, except I think we also should note that methyl testosterone is more active orally than testosterone and I think allyltrenbolone is active orally as well. But I think we should note that the oral activity of those two compounds is higher than the oral activity of the chemically related compounds. That is the only point I make.

Chairman

187. Thank you. Yes, Professor Arnold.

Dr. Arnold

188. I agree with what has been said about the relation between hormones they are related. It is a good word. But we have just to compare what is comparable. When we speak about these hormones we have to speak only about the therapeutic and zootechnical uses of the hormone in question and not about growth promotion. It is

very different, because they are used punctually (?) on any individual or groups, well defined, of animals so it is very different. It is not the same use.

Mr. Brinza (US)

189. Thank you Mr. Chairman. I just want to thank all of the experts for their assistance and thank the Panel for their patience.

Chairman

190. Thank you very much. This brings us to the end of this morning's session. I have the impression that the learning rate this morning was much higher than it usually is in these rooms and I was very impressed. About timing, could we continue at three o'clock with the questions by the European Community? Could we do it three o'clock sharp, otherwise we may run into night. Do you have a procedural point, Mr. Christoforou?

Mr. Christoforou (EC)

191. When would we expect the document by the US on these quantities of micrograms?

Chairman

192. Could you arrange to hand them over

Mr. Brinza (US)

193. Mr. Chairman, we do not have copies with us but we can certainly provide that to you when we reconvene.

Chairman

194. Thank you very much. The meeting is adjourned.

Mr. Christoforou (EC)

Mr. Chairman and Members of the Panel, Ladies and Gentlemen, Experts advising the Panel

195. I think it is the normal practice to allow this delegation to present itself, if you please excuse me, because there are so many scientists from so many places. I think five minutes or three minutes presentation by all the delegation might be helpful as these scientists will be intervening in this debate. Since the EC delegation is known to the Panel, it is the normal composition of the delegation, I would only request scientists which are advising the European Community in this case to present themselves very briefly towards on what they have been until now.

196. I will start then with Doctor Liehr on my left-hand side please.

Dr. Joachim Liehr (EC)

197. Mr. Chairman, my name is Dr. Joachim Liehr and I am a chemist and have worked for the last 17 years on the mechanism of oestrogen-induced tumours. This mechanism I have concentrated on, the genotoxicity studies, because everybody knew at the time when I started these studies that oestrogens are hormones and many people accepted the fact that hormonal agents act as hormones and it was at the same time clear that oestrogens are complete carcinogens. There are quite a number of animal model systems where oestrogens are complete carcinogens without any other agents. So in order to examine this carcinogenicity effect, complete carcinogenicity

effect, I wanted to know can oestrogens also act as genotoxins in addition to, not separate of, but in addition to, the hormonal effects that they normally exert. This has resulted in a number of positive genotoxicity effects not just *in vitro* but also many of them *in vivo* and quite a different class, many different classes of genotoxicity, so that we can talk in the words of Dr. Lucier of compelling evidence that there is genotoxicity by oestrogens.

Dr. Ercole Cavalieri (EC) of the Cancer Institute University of Nebraska Medical School

198. I am here because also I have done from a different approach what Dr. Liehr has tried to attempt. When I started my research in chemical carcinogenicity I have a strong feeling that oestrogen is the origin of many human cancers, and it took more than 25 years to resolve the problem. Mr. Chairman, that happened because in order to understand how oestrogen induced cancer, could initiate cancer, we have studied a large class of moderate compounds called polycyclic aromatic hydrocarbons which induce cancers and are present, many of them, in our environment, from the combustion of organic material like gasoline, etc. These compounds have been an excellent model for understanding how oestrogen induced cancer and we are now at the point in which we can say that oestrogens are initiating cancer and by the so-called receptor-mediated process in cancer and produce cancer. Therefore my point in contention is that since they initiate cancer for people that they do not have the protective mechanism that normally everybody should have, even a minimal dose that can imbalance our equilibrium could be a factor in inducing cancer to humans. I would be very glad to express this in a more visual way with the slides later during these procedures if I can.

Dr. Jim Bridges (EC) from the University of Surrey in Guildford

199. I am professor of toxicology and I sit on the Scientific Committee on Animal Nutrition for the EU and the UK Veterinary Products Committee. My interest is mechanisms of toxicity and their use in risk assessment.

Dr. Manfred Metzler (EC) - Professor of Food Chemistry and Toxicology at the University of Karlsruhe in Germany

200. I have been trained as a chemist and worked in field of biochemical toxicology for more than 20 years. My major interests over the years have been the biochemical mechanisms of oestrogen and hormonal carcinogenicity and more recently we have focused on the chromosomal effect of oestrogens as carcinogens, which we think is an important aspect of hormonal carcinogenesis.

Dr. Alan Pinter (EC)

201. I am a pathologist by training and I have been involved in mutagenesis oestrogen and carcinogenesis for the last 15 to 20 years. Now I am at the National Institute of Public Health in Budapest, Hungary. Thank you.

Dr. Samuel Epstein (EC)

202. I am a pathologist by background. I have worked for some three to four decades in problems of carcinogenesis and to a lesser extent in mutagenesis. My major interests are in public health and preventive medicine. Of relevance in this connection I was a key advisor to the United States Congress in the early 70s in relation to a

series of actions leading to the eventual banning of DES, having analysed DES residue data which we obtained from a variety of sources including FDA and USDA. My testimony was critical to the banning of the use of DES as an anabolic.

Dr. Reiner Stephany (EC)

203. I am a chemist and 25 years involved in residue analysis of anabolic agents, all types of analysis, research, development, regulatory, forensic, whatsoever. The last years I am focused on the question of the reliability of analysis, for what purpose and for what price. I am employed with the Dutch National Institute of Public Health and the Environment and involved in EC groups and Codex groups and so on.

Dr. Adolfo Pérez-Comas (EC)

204. I am a pediatric endocrinologist, Associate Professor of Pediatrics Endocrinology in the University of Ponce in Puerto Rico and prior with the University of Puerto Rico Medical Science Campus. I am also an advisor for the Centre for Disease Control and for NIA, National Institute of Health, on the area of diabetes. I am an advisor on diabetes and technology for HEW in the United States.

Mr. Christoforou (EC)

205. As you see there is one scientist missing and this is Dr. Adlercreutz, who unfortunately could not join us today but he will be with us tomorrow. He informed me that he would only like to make a very short statement, less than five minutes, when he is in the room and be willing to reply to statements and questions since his paper has been reviewed and criticized both by the United States and Canada. Mr. Chairman, while I have the floor one more procedural issue is that the United States has argued against the submission of any evidence, new evidence in this case. We have heard that this morning in the Preparatory Meeting, and yet we have seen today a fairly long document circulating commenting on the replies of the scientists. According to the rules of the DSU, this document should not circulate unless it is read out. The Community would agree that it is circulated if we are given the chance to provide a similar document within a very short time-limit. This document is circulated so I do not know the status of this document. If it is to remain, I have no objection, but it stays with the files of the Panel, but we are given the chance of three days maximum or four to provide similar documents in this respect. I think that would be according to the rules of the Dispute Settlement Understanding.

Chairman

206. Mr. Christoforou, would you give us the rule which prescribes that every document has to be read out?

Mr. Christoforou (EC)

207. Mr. Chairman, the rule is that every time we meet you say please give the written version of your oral statement otherwise you cannot file documents with the Panel. If you provide a limited interpretation to that practice I can provide documents without reading them. But I remember the argument was made by the United States in our second substantive meeting where they would like that we read literally the documents that we were submitting. This is the rule and a standard practice, and it is the submissions in the annex giving the table of the dispute settlement, it is the writ-

ten version of the oral statements will be provided. It is in the annex of the DSU. I can provide you with the exact provision.

Chairman

208. We do invite, we have invited you in fact, to submit your comments in writing, but this would not mean that you have to read them out because I usually encourage people to summarize what they hand in in writing instead of reading it out. I think it should not be a problem of you having such a document submitted within a short period of time - three days - okay.

Mr. Christoforou (EC)

209. Thank you. Mr. Chairman, we have heard carefully the summarizing that was made by the distinguished experts advising of the Panel in this case and we would like to tackle a number of responses that were given to first their initial presentation and then the way the United States and a number of the questions posed by the United States.

210. The first question would relate to what we discussed this morning in this room. Physiological levels of residues of these hormones in the human body. Of course this relates to the three natural hormones only which occur naturally, it does not relate to the discussion on the synthetic xenobiotic hormones. It is also frequently referred to in the JEFCA report of 1988, where sometimes reference is made that the residues, for example, of oestradiol, would be increased from two to five-fold but this was still considered to be within the physiological normal physiological levels. In this case and in this respect I have Dr. Epstein who would like to make a two-minute explanation then ask a particular question and I think, I understand from the Secretariat, a paper is circulating that gives the exact calculations of those so-called physiological levels. This is important in our view because we later link this to the most sensitive part of the population - the so-called pre-pubertal boys, and the values that they have given for daily 24-hours concentration of oestradiol, because this is an important issue in our view. So I will give the floor to Dr. Epstein please.

Dr. Epstein (EC)

211. Thank you. I first of all would like to thank the Chairman of the Panel for allowing me this opportunity to address you briefly. Before I commence my brief statement I have just been reminded that I neglected to give you my professional affiliations, which is Professor of Environmental and Occupational Medicine at the School of Public Health in Chicago.

212. The JEFCA document and preceding documents clearly give the impression that residues of natural anabolics fall within the normal physiological ranges as indicated previously. There is also a clear statement that levels in muscle are normal. There is also the statement that levels in pre-pubertal boys are about six micrograms a day, which is roughly a thousand times the residue levels of oestradiol.

213. I would now like to comment on these statements and point out that they appear to be inconsistent with industry data which I believe are available and have been available to JEFCA and other bodies. Let us look first of all at the data for Synovex S which is oestradiol and progesterone and when you examine levels of oestradiol in liver you find they increase six-fold, in kidney nine-fold, in muscle twelve-fold and in fat twenty-three fold. So that doesn't appear to be entirely consistent with what we

heard this morning: namely that muscle levels are not increased when in fact they increased twelve-fold and a twenty-three fold excess for fat hardly appears to be trivial. Now these relate of course just to the levels of the parent oestradiol, and not of course its metabolites, so therefore this represents an underestimate of the true hormonal residues in the meat.

214. Turning now to the question of the factor of six micrograms a day being a thousand times the residue levels of oestradiol for pre-pubertal boys: this pre-pubertal data, however, does not relate to children and enfants from the age of 0 to 8. Now based on IARC documentation, volume 21, 1979, page 42 to 46, you can make the very simple calculations showing what are the levels of oestradiol production daily for children of this age and it turns out that the levels range from 0.16 to 0.8 micrograms a day. So we are now shifting the levels in pre-pubertal boys from six micrograms to 0.16. This is important for two reasons: first of all the figure of six is clearly misleading and secondly our level of concern is very much greater for infants and young children and children under the age of eight, because there is abundant data on the much higher level of sensitivity to carcinogens of young children than to adults. So for these two reasons, I think it is important to focus on this. In fact the mathematics clearly show that the margin of safety, the so-called margin of safety or the excess over background levels, is not a thousand-fold but say for fat it is eight-fold, less than an order of magnitude. It ranges from eight to 40, less than an order of magnitude at the lower level. So these are some very fundamental distinctions and misapprehensions on these conceptions which I would like to focus on.

215. All this relates purely to the legal application. The application conformance with standard recommended good husbandry practice. If I may turn for the moment to the illegal, I should like to preface my comments on the illegal by quoting from a reference that Dr. Ritter kindly provided us with; namely the reference to Truhaut in 1985 who stated that the unlawful use of the anabolics can result in residues 300-fold in excess of the established tolerances. I repeat, the unlawful use can result in residues 300-fold in excess of the established tolerances. I have not reviewed the original paper of Dr. Truhaut but I rely on Dr. Ritter's reference to it and the statement - the quotation - he makes from it.

216. The second point in this connection I should make is when we are talking about illegal or misplaced implants, we are not talking about an occasional liberation by an irresponsible farmer. We are talking about two things: first of all about common practice as I will prove in a moment. Secondly we are talking about a situation in which to all intents and purposes there is no reasonable or practicable way of monitoring whether or not illegal practice is common or not. I refer you to a 1986 USDA survey of some 32 major feedlots in the United States where half the cattle were found to have misplaced implants. I repeat, we are not dealing with an occasional abberation of an irresponsible farmer. We are dealing with a common place situation in which there is no way of monitoring, of residue analysis, of practical residue analysis, so how can we even begin to discuss concepts of ADI if we do not have the slightest level, slightest idea, of the kind of residues. We already know that when administered, when the hormones are administered in accordance with recommended practice, the levels are way in excess of what you gentlemen have been led to believe. But when it comes to the misplaced implants we have two sets of problems. One you have the problem at the implant site in which it could be argued that

in fact inspectors regularly check every piece of the meat and if they find an implant they would cut out that affected piece of meat and discard it. It is questionable whether in fact that happens and our friends from USDA may perhaps be willing to give us the assurance that every portion of every animal slaughtered is inspected for misplaced implants. But far more to the point the fact is when you implant, put an implant in the avascular, the non-vascular subcutaneous tissue under the skin of the ear, the rate of absorption is extremely low, but when you implant it in muscle which is highly vascular, you can have a much higher rate of absorption. Now I have searched the literature as thoroughly as I could and cannot find any reference or any data at all levels of hormones of oestradiol at sites at a distance from the implant site. The basic knowledge of pharmacology could make it very clear that when you implant a hormone or any agent in a highly vascular tissue then its rates of absorption would be many-fold higher, whether it's one order of magnitude, two orders of magnitude, three orders of magnitude - I do not have the slightest idea, but I do know that misplaced implants are not uncommon and I do know from the industry data that the levels of the residues, are way in excess of what you have been led to believe.

Mr. Christoforou (EC)

217. I would like now to raise two questions, after the statement of Dr. Epstein, and to all our scientists advising the Panel. If it is correct as we have been making the calculations, and the document is circulating, about the level of oestradiol in prepubertal boys, which is not six micrograms per 24 hours but it is eight-fold less than the physiological levels, then I would request the scientists to give us their view: Is this really a risk, an additional or an increased risk of these residues causing the risks we have been discussing here among other things carcinogenicity, to this type of sensitive part of human population? This is the first question, thank you.

Chairman

218. Thank you. May I invite you just to comment generally on Doctor Epstein's thesis, because we would like to have your reaction on this? Who would like to take the floor? Doctor Ritter, please.

Dr. Ritter

219. Thank you Mr. Chairman. I offer to, I foolishly offer to lead only because I think I would like to clarify for the Panel a specific reference that Dr. Epstein made to my submission with regard to the Truhaut reference. It is correct indeed that I cited this reference, but I would submit to the Panel that the reference has been somewhat misquoted. As a point of clarity, Dr. Epstein did correctly note that I refer to the possibility of the 300-fold excess in residues with oestradiol.

220. But if I may, Mr. Chairman, and I will provide specific reference to the Panel and to the EU, I have brought it along will me. But to put into proper context what the authors have said exactly is that "when 50 milligrams of oestradiol in an oil-injectable preparation is administered intra-muscularly in the neck of a veal calf three weeks prior to slaughter" and then they go on to talk about this illegal practice, "the levels of residues in the vicinity of the injection site may be 300-times greater".

221. This is a pivotal issue, Mr. Chairman, because in fact there is not an injection at issue for the proper use. So this particular three-fold increase in residues refers to a multiple of abuses, if you like. It would be at the wrong site and using the wrong

method of administration. The 300-fold increase in potential residue does not refer to the normal use. This refers to an extraordinarily abnormal use. The same authors in referring to that very conclusion that they have drawn then go on to say in their conclusion: "It is our belief that neither 17 beta oestradiol nor zeranol, poses any toxicity problem when used as an anabolic in animal production. It is widely agreed that in the instance of hormonally mediated toxicological effects including carcinogenesis, a tolerance level can be set". They finally conclude "even in the instances in which misuse may have occurred, it is virtually impossible to visualize any hazard to humans ingesting meat from animals treated with zeranol". These are their words, not mine.

222. I make this point of clarity because I did not want the Panel left with the impression that this 300-fold increase to which I referred is something that could be anticipated, if you like, under normal circumstances, and indeed as the authors suggest it is not likely that one could anticipate it even under abnormal conditions of abuse. It simply demonstrates than one can create a scenario where at the injection site, which would not be applicable in normal growth promoting uses, it can be in excess.

Chairman

223. Who would like to speak to the question submitted by the Community?

Dr. McLean

224. Just to make a comment about the reaction to the implant if it is placed in the ear compared with in the muscle. Of course in those vascular tissues like the muscle then you get quite an active tissue reaction and indeed you get the implant walled off. One of the features of injections subcutaneously in the ear is that you do not get the massive reaction at the site and it is specifically designed, and all the residue studies are carried out, with the implant injected in the ear. The aim of injecting it there is to get prolonged and slow release at low levels over a period of time; so that is specifically designed to be that way.

Chairman

225. Thank you. Could you offer any comments on the table we were given and in particular the impact on the pre-pubertal situation? You do not have to speak. Let me know. Yes please Doctor.

Dr. Arnold

226. Chairman, there is one problem when this information comes so quickly, it takes some time to look at the evidence. The only thing I can do at the moment is to confirm that these figures really stand in the IARC report in volume 21. It is important to note that these values differ tremendously according to the source. So I can't say from where this level of six micrograms came. This I do not know currently, but I have some tables from some text books of endocrinology with me showing that there is a tremendous range and if you read carefully the text in which IARC explains the way how they have estimated, they make quite clear that this is an estimate and that the variability can be enormous and they give examples of individual goods where there was a very large range of data. So the figures are okay, but you cannot insist and say this is the one.

Dr. Ritter

227. Thank you Mr. Chairman. I offer only two points for consideration by the Panel. I think as Dr. Arnold has already noted we are responding somewhat on the fly, even though you suggested that we need not feel any obligations to do so.

228. In the table we have been provided, Mr. Chairman, the intake factors that have been calculated are based on approximate level of exposure to 500 grams of meat. This table has been calculated on the basis of pre-pubertal boys under eight years of age. I would suggest to you Mr. Chairman that it is not likely that a child of two or three will consume 500 grams of meat a day. This calculation is based on daily intake in a 500 gram sample of food, every day for his entire life. I would submit to you Mr. Chairman that as a member of the JEFCA process now for some years, I feel that the 500 gram estimate is an over-exaggeration even in the case of adults. But I think to presume in calculating the risks that a child under eight years of age will consume 500 grams of meat every day, respectfully Sir, I think it is somewhat of an exaggeration.

229. The other point that I would bring to your attention and again I apologize for responding on the fly, is I think the point that Dr. Arnold has already elaborated on and that is that the numbers that you see before you are presented as, how shall I put this, as if they were rigid when in fact hormone levels, either present as residues or normally circulating endogenous levels, you would normally be accustomed to seeing them as a range. These do not have rigid values. If you look, for example, at the, let us take the most extreme example of the table before you, if you take a look at fat, the 23-fold excess factor is of course assuming that the five-year old or the four-year old or the two-year old has consumed 500 grams of meat. I think if that calculation were redone with a more realistic figure the 23-fold excess might in fact be reduced to a two-fold excess. But in addition to that, I would suggest to you Mr. Chairman that the test value of 41.4 microgram is a value from a range if you like and that the range is very broadly distributed Similarly the 1.82 in the untreated control is extracted from a range. Depending on where in the range these two values fall, respectively, may impart the impression that it is high or low, when in fact what we should be doing when talking about ranges is just that, we should be expressing a range rather than a rigid point estimate.

Dr. Lucier

230. Thank you. Many of the numbers are similar to the numbers that I put together in preparation for the meeting - certainly the range of oestrogen production per day in young boys and girls is about what is reported here from that IARC publication, the range of 0.4 to 0.2 micrograms per day. This is about 140 times, from my estimates, higher than the amount obtained from eating if one of these young boys or girls ate 500 grams of meat containing the maximum level permissible. In addition, if you looked at a pre-menopausal woman in terms of oestrogen that would be about 200 times that is what is normally seen in a young boy or girl, so that ratio instead of one over 140 becomes one in 28,000. So eating that amount of meat per day for a pre-menopausal woman would add one molecule for every 28,000 she would normally have in her body, and I take the point that this is a point estimate and of course that is an average estimate for the women, not encompassing the range that Dr. Ritter just described which is in fact true. But at least a point estimate it would be one molecule per every 28,000 normally present in a woman's body. In addition, probably

only about ten per cent of that is going to be absorbed because it is degraded in the stomach, so you can add another factor of ten on that so it becomes one over 1,400 or one over 280,000 for the young boys or girls and the pre-menopausal woman, respectively. But some of these numbers are very consistent with the numbers that I have had - just used differently.

Dr. McLean

231. Mr. Chairman, if I could make two comments following on from my colleague. The other thing is that depending on the mode of cooking we can lose up to 80 per cent of these steroid hormones in the cooking process and not terribly many people eat raw meat.

232. The main point I would like to make was to address the matter of misplaced implants and violations of administration. In my country and in the United States, but particularly in my country, we have targeted in residue surveys trenbolone and zeranol, very specifically looking for violations, and in fact to all intents and purposes violations do not occur. Now this means that even if there is misuse, and that is difficult to prove, we are still not getting residues that exceed the MRL. I would suggest that a similar situation exists with the naturally-occurring hormones, where it is not possible to determine whether a violation has occurred or not because the levels that you find in the carcass sit within the normal range. But I think that you can take some comfort in the residue surveys of zeranol and trenbolone which show to all intents and purposes violative residues not present.

Chairman

233. Are there any further comments from the Panel? May I ask Professor Epstein to comment briefly on what was said?

Dr. Epstein (EC)

234. Unfortunately American (you may gather from my accent that I am not American) but one of the things that has impressed about American boys is their appetite for "Whoppers" and for hamburgers. It is not at all uncommon for a child of seven or eight to have a hamburger at lunch and a "Whopper" at lunch and another one in the evening, and that is roughly 500 grams. That is the first point.

235. The second point is we are really dealing with a situation in which we have provided the Panel with data which are entirely inconsistent with data provided to them previously by JECFA. One can try to explain this away in various ways and means but the data are fundamentally different and the pre-pubertal levels in pre-pubertal boys are clearly the margin of safety is less than one order of magnitude. Again, let me also emphasize that influence has been made that misplaced implants are the exception rather than the rule. I repeat, in 1986 a survey of USDA feedlots showed that some 32 major feedlots or feedlots by the USDA, showed misplaced implants in half of them.

236. My final point is that in the absence of routine monitoring chemical analysis we do not have the slightest idea, we have no information at all, as to whether we have 100 per cent misplaced implants, ten per cent misplaced implants or any number at all.

Mr. Christoforou (EC)

237. I meant to ask a specific question, this question of potential misuse, for the scientists' reply, but if they want to come in earlier that is fine with us as well. Because in our view the question about the pre-pubertal boys has nothing to do with misuse. We are talking about proper use of these implants and in that case the JECFA Report said, and the calculation was based on the 6 micrograms per 24 hours and they said the residue that would result is 1,000-fold whereas in this case we see it is eight-fold less than is the physiological level. This issue has to be disconnected from the potential increased risks from misuse on which I will come to later. We are talking about proper use of these implants and what is the sensitive part of the population which may be affected by this. Thank you.

Chairman

238. As I understood there were two lines of argument but the scientific data was for regular use. I give you the floor. I am sorry I have to give the floor first to Doctor Randell, I think he was first.

Dr. Randell (Codex)

239. Thank you Mr. Chairman. I would just like to dispel the impression given that the data in the table just presented to us, which is entitled Symtex NADA 9-576 1983 Synovex Steers, was not available to JECFA. Those data are in fact abbreviated data from Table 6 of the JECFA evaluation of 1987 published in 1988. It is one line in one table of the data which JECFA considered and I would point out that the JECFA also examined the variations in the data, that is the JECFA data contains the ranges of each of these data points as well. So the data which have been presented here are taken in isolation from a larger set of data which JECFA considered. Thank you.

Dr. Arnold

240. Mr. Chairman, in the meantime I have found the tables I have produced in preparation of today's meeting. I used a brand new text book of endocrinology and metabolism published in 1995. What you can easily see from these tables that in fact there is a tremendous range of values. So first of all, whether it is two or six, it is the same order of magnitude. Then one needs to know whether it is an average, a mean or a medium; there can be a tremendous difference because the range and I have all the figures from foetal life, all stages of puberty and adult life, the range sometimes is a 250-fold or even greater and therefore you can fully explain the difference if two people take the same data and one scientist takes the mean and the other takes the medium and therefore what I did - I put together the mean, the minimum and the maximum and here you can see that for some of these hormones there is just a 500-fold range. This has been put together from all sources available in a most recent 2,500 page text book on this subject. If you want the full reference is given and I can leave it for you. It was my personal preparation but if it is of value to the Panel, you may have it. It is not included in my statement. I did it after.

Chairman

241. Could it be given to the Panel and we would hand it also to the parties.

Mr. Christoforou (EC)

242. Mr. Chairman, we would be grateful of course to have a look into those. At least I can explain our sources. Our sources, and I think there might have been again a misunderstanding, it is on page 19 of the JECFA Report, where it is stated and I quote "even in pre-pubertal boys the amount of oestradiol 17 beta produced daily (6.5 micrograms) is a 1,000 times the amount derived from ingestion of 5 grams of treated meat." We did not look into the tables referred to by Dr. Randell, we looked into the text where this is a citation. Then we tried to find out what the citation was and it turned out that it was an article published in 1974.

243. Our data, which you see from this paper we circulated, came from the IARC volume and they are based on a more recent article by Brown and Tolle, 1987. So this is our basis of calculation and we would of course appreciate that there are other calculations made that would show a different calculation. But we also take the points that may be arranged and there may be variations but we all based ourselves on what it is in the publication of the International Agency for Research of Cancer.

244. Mr. Chairman, I can now proceed with posing the other questions. I would like to request because some of my scientists would like to have a precise, if possible, reference on what Dr. McLean is saying, that upon cooking about half of these are destroyed and we do not know of any such reference in any academic reviews. I think it will be useful if we can get the reference so that we can control this but we do not have this type of information and I would appreciate a reference to that.

245. My next question is linked to the misuse because this is a slightly different issue. Dr. Epstein has made the reference to the misuse that this has been reported in the United States. We have also made the reference to this misuse in our submissions. I will remind only with a number of figures here and our exports and then I will raise the question.

246. For example, we have examined the national plans, the annual control plans in the United States and it would appear that between 1972 and 1994 there was no control on trenbolone. There was never any control on progesterone. There was never any control on testosterone. On oestradiol it was checked only for the years 1987 to 1990. MGA was checked only for the years 1978 to 1983. then it was discontinued, and started again in 1987 to 1990 and then discontinued and then in 1993 only.

247. For zeranol it was tested for the years 1973 to 1974. Again then in 1977 and in 1985 to 1989. This has been referred to the Panel it is paragraph 57 of our second written submission of the United States Panel. We have also calculated on the basis of the samples that are examined annually in the United States that, for example, in the year 1993 there were checked only 39,128 samples. On making the calculations what does this number represent in terms of total livestock production the United States tells us this is only 0.005 per cent. I link then these factual statements and I also note that in the year 1993 there were only 22 samples of MGA for MGA tested, 22 samples only and there was one violation. If we extrapolate this for the further amount of livestock that enter the food chain, that can amount to 4.5 per cent of tests positive.

248. The question is because Dr. McLean also said there is no incentive for the farmers to misuse because there will be penalties if they are caught. In light of this, and I can cite similar numbers for Canada, they are in paragraph 11 of our second

written submission, if you would like I can make similar references. In light of this 0.005 per cent - check - do you really think it is? - the threat of penalties it is a real dissuasive instrument so that farmers will not misuse those implants, because those implants are very cheap apparently and they may speed the growth rate and we have heard this morning that they may be an additional injection of an implant before the withdrawal period has expired. So how credible really is this disincentive on farmers to misuse in view of the potential advantages of either misusing or adding more implants. Thank you.

Chairman

249. Would you like to comment this?

Dr. McLean

250. As far as I can Mr. Chairman. The residue surveys that are carried out in the United States, I cannot comment precisely on the numbers, but the violation rate of five per cent is significantly less than the violation rate that was being quoted before of 50 per cent, so there is a variation and I think that the United States delegation could throw light on the levels of violation.

251. The second thing is that the residue misuse that we were talking about was in 1986. I would suggest now that with the advent of pellets and pelleting administration devices then it is my impression that the implant administration to the ear have improved quite dramatically.

252. In answer to the question about cooking, I was fairly careful to say that steroids in general there could be destruction of up to 80 per cent. My figures come from a submission made on another steroid for registration and as I said I was very careful to say it was up to 80 per cent and I would suspect that the destruction of steroids by cooking would be similar across the range.

Chairman

253. Thank you very much. Any other comments on this question? Doctor Arnold?

Dr. Arnold

254. Mr. Chairman, I cannot speak on the details of American residue surveillance plans. What could perhaps help, maybe other people have that information, what is the result of European residue control on imports. I have seen that, for example, France does a lot of work in this field, but as far as I know, I saw more than 1,000 samples in 1995 but no positive.

Chairman

255. Thank you. I would like to stay with this residue controls and ask what is the situation in the European Community operating under the ban? You need to have controls as much as when you allow it, but how is it done, do you have figures on this? Does any other delegation have figures on this?

Mr. Christoforou (EC)

256. Mr. Chairman, it is in our submission brought for the United States and Canada and this has not been disputed as far as I know and I should know because I am always in all meetings present. There are samples tested every year, there are about

200,000 samples of animals tested in the European Community. This is what is the level of testing in the European Community.

257. We also have provided the reply to the question by Canada concerning the natural hormones and we said we test annually 59,000 of blood to verify the levels for the natural hormones. These are the figures we have already given to the Panel and I have so far no comments on this. But this is our official figures.

Dr. Arnold

258. Mr. Chairman, since I am also from the European Community I may slightly correct this figure. This is the total number of samples for all residues and not for hormones. For hormones the number with all food animals and all substances altogether is in the order of 20,000 and almost half of that figure comes from one country.

Mr. Christoforou (EC)

259. Mr. Chairman, for the natural hormones we have verified each individual check done in response to the question by Canada for that we are sure. For the natural hormones the blood samples tested are 59,000. For the total number of checks done it is indeed 200,000 samples of animals tested. We are not going to verify how much of this, our understanding is very much higher than 20,000 mentioned by Dr. Arnold. I will clarify this for the total hormones, but for the blood residues, for the natural hormones checked last year, it was 59,000.

Chairman

260. Do you have any indications of percentage in herds? What that would mean?

Mr. Christoforou (EC)

261. Mr. Chairman, we need to understand also that the natural hormones are not allowed to be used in the EC for growth promotion. The checks are done because only one of those natural hormone, oestradiol, is allowed to be used for therapeutic or zootechnical reasons. So the information is there is no excess but I do not have the exact figure if there was any violation or if there is any physiological level for the natural hormones. We do not have any figure of violation in the Community because they are not used and they cannot detect high violations in those 59,000 we checked last year.

Dr. Ritter

262. Thank you Mr. Chairman. I offer just a brief commentary. I of course will not endeavour to speak for the United States or for Canada with regard to how many samples they have sampled but I think it is important to recognize that the number of samples that one takes and measures can be somewhat misleading. 20,000 may appear to be larger than 5,000 for example, but the intent of any monitoring programme is the development of a programme that has the statistical confidence necessary to detect violations to the extent that the compound is used, if in fact residue levels which are out of compliance are present. I would be surprised that either the Canadian or the US scheme has not considered that statistical design in the monitoring programme.

263. I think the issue of how many samples were measured can really be somewhat misleading. I think the more relevant question is - is the monitoring programme sta-

tistically confident and is it able to detect in either country, or in the European Community for that matter, is it able to do what it is intended to do? And generally speaking most monitoring programmes are intended to detect a five per cent violation rate 95 per cent of the time. The number of samples that are required to do that will vary from country to country and from commodity to commodity because it is a function of the use practice. I make this point only because I think it would be relatively fruitless to get into a debate as to whether or not 20,000 is larger than 5,000. It clearly is. But that quite frankly, I do not think, is the relevant issue.

264. I would just add one other commentary perhaps on that. The Council for the European Community has just made reference to the fact that there may be somewhat less than a rigorous programme for some of the anabolics because the compounds are not used and hence of course, one would not expect to detect them. But the international experience with clenbuterol, for example, which is not permitted for use as an anabolic, is that it is widely used and abused particularly in Europe, with very real cases of adverse effects in humans, in some cases I think death, resulting from the use of a anabolic, clenbuterol, in this case, which most certainly is prohibited for use. So the fact that it is not permitted, I think as you referenced yourself a moment ago Mr. Chairman, certainly is not evidence that it is not used. To draw some confidence from the fact that it may not be approved for that use and therefore should not be present I think is euphoria.

Dr. André

265. I do not wish to go on in these disputes of a number of samples because it is a regulatory problem, it is not a real scientific one. But I just would like to invite you to observe what is done with the sample, because you can manage a lot of samples for one or two hormones and you can have samples for 30 or more hormones, and in these cases the efficiency of the control is very different.

266. To my knowledge, in France as well as in most countries in Europe now, we developed very nice multi-residue control programmes. It means that for one sample we check sometimes for 30 anabolics, different anabolic steroids, and in this case it shows that we discover sometimes black-market compounds. It is not that everybody knows it.

267. But my question is to know when our colleagues say that in their country they do not observe misuse of hormones, my question would be what hormones are you checking for? If it is only trenbolone zeranol they can be sure that there is no misuse of these hormones - these two or three hormones - in that they have no higher residue levels than allowed as MRL. But to my knowledge I do not think that all these hormones are assayed in these countries as well as we do up to now, so they cannot say that they have no misuse of other xenobiotics.

Chairman

268. Thank you. May I just follow up one question. I know this is not a strictly scientific question but you have extensive experience in this. Do you consider the control to be more efficient, more feasible, under a system which allows and restricts or under a system which at the outset prohibits and tries to find those who step over the law. Just from your assessment, from your background and experience: I know you have not extensively discussed this in your papers because it is not a scientific

question, but I think from the legal point of view it has some relevance. Would you like to speak on that?

Dr. Arnold

269. I am a little bit reluctant because this is certainly subject to speculation. I would assume, and I expressed this in my paper, I would assume a certain competition between legal products and illegal substances. I would assume that a significant number of farmers would use legal products because they are efficient and not too expensive, but to say this would result in no misuse I think would be pure speculation.

270. If I may just add one more sentence to the sampling and residue control. It is in fact very important to consider the importance of multi-residue methods and also whether the programme is based on random sampling, statistically-based sampling or on suspicion. In the EC, for example, we have at least these two aspects: random sampling and sampling of suspected animals, plus control of imports.

271. If we look at the random sampling, then the situation is not so bad except for certain substances in certain countries. But if we look at the suspect sampling, then we find all substances including zeranol and trenbolone from our domestic production. The only area where I feel that even under conditions of random sampling we have some problems is with veal calves and the natural hormones. If we look at the plasma levels, there we have sometimes in some countries some problems with a high incidence of violating levels. But here as a scientist, I must say, distribution of physiological levels and of levels resulting from misuse are overlapping to such an extent that this may just be a course because the decision limits have been inappropriately defined to separate the two populations.

Dr. André

272. May I add something to Dieter Arnold's presentation? We have also the opportunity, more than random samples and suspected samples, to go on farm and to check for misuse during breeding of animals and not only at slaughter house and this is sometimes very efficient tool.

273. As I said this morning, in France we, concerning the operation, we had four years, or five years, I do not remember, during when these hormones were allowed and after this long period during which these hormones were banned and really I was in charge of control during this two different periods I can confirm that even if in my country hormones were allowed, the misuse of other hormones, the black market was also present based on the idea that when you allow something you have an official label and people have an official label and can have treated animals, but then try always to give more and more and to give different compounds to have more results and we never observed differences in the black market when the hormones were allowed or after. It was so important.

Dr. Lucier

274. If I can offer my speculation on this. My feeling would be that the violations probably would occur more frequently in cases where it was banned if you are comparing it to a controlled use in which there was well-defined educational programmes, very good communication efforts and appropriately stiff penalties for misuse. If all of those things were in place with the control programme, my guess is that

you would have fewer violations in that case - if it was a very systematic approach for controlling them that adequately addressed those and also very stiff penalties for violations.

Chairman

275. Can we go on with your questions and comments?

Mr. Christoforou (EC)

276. Mr. Chairman, I think one of our experts would like to make a very short statement on the issue of cooking - the percentage of the natural hormones destroyed during cooking - I think he might have a couple of words to say, then I will proceed to the next question. Thank you.

Dr. Stephany (EC)

277. First of all I assume that we are talking about cooking and I do not have to add anything to that. I only have questions. I very recently did a literature research on behaviour of veterinary drugs in general during the preparation in the kitchen - so that is what I call cooking: frying, braising, etc. I could not find any data on steroids but what I found on other types of veterinary drugs in general, ranging from very old work with diethylstilboestrol to more recent work.

278. The general pattern is that most of these residues are quite stable. Some are lost, not because they are destroyed, but they are cooked out of the tissue when they are fat soluble and so on, so if you do not use the drippings you will lose something. That is the general pattern. So I am very much surprised about the statement of Dr. McLean (sic) that up to 80 per cent or 80 per cent of these residues will be destroyed. I would be very interested in having a reference or the data of that. That is my remark, so it is more of a question.

Chairman

279. Thank you very much. Would the Panel like to comment on the effects of cooking?

Dr. McLean

280. Mr. Chairman, I made the comment and it was in relation to a submission that was made about a steroid that is commercial in confidence and before I left I approached the manufacturer or the sponsor and at this stage they are still trying to get clearance for me to release the information. I can say no more and very carefully I must say that the cooking methods vary - they involve braising, boiling and the figures varied quite considerably. I can say no more.

Chairman

281. Are there any other data on cooking available or not now?

Mr. Christoforou (EC)

282. Mr. Chairman, since we have such a wide range of expertise present here, I think, Dr. Liehr has done some research himself and would like to say a few words on this particular point on cooking.

Dr. Liehr (EC)

283. Not on cooking itself, but the process of heating. I have done chemistry, chemical work, chemical preparations of oestrogens which involved heating these oestrogens to 120-140 degrees and we found no evidence for decomposition in various organic solvents. Oestrogens are quite stable products and I cannot imagine an 80 per cent destruction of these compounds under cooking procedures. Thank you Mr. Chairman.

Dr. Randell (Codex)

284. Thank you Mr. Chairman. The discussion puzzles me because there is nothing in the JECFA or Codex evaluation that takes into account possible reduction factors as a result of cooking. In fact the JECFA Codex figures would be applicable to those people, who for some reason of their own, ate raw meat, raw kidneys, raw liver and raw eggs.

Chairman

285. So you are saying that basically you would assume that 100 per cent is still in the food which is being prepared and eaten by people.

Dr. McLean

286. It was me that introduced it and I think that the important thing to realize is that the evaluations that normally occur through, say for example, the JECFA process, do look at the worst case and the worst case is that you get the full load and it is a benefit if processing removes some of it.

Dr. Arnold

287. I think that what Dr. Liehr has said is absolutely correct. The steroid hormones are so stable you find them in petrol, in mineral oil, they survive even the conditions under which these products have been formed. Mr. McLean was not speaking about steroids, he was meaning another substance.

Dr. Lucier

288. Yes, I think that is absolutely correct. There is no reason to think that they would be extensively destroyed. The only way you would get rid of them, I think was mentioned earlier, is in getting rid of the drippings which would contain many of the steroids just by extracting them out because they are so fat soluble.

Chairman

289. When the artificial hormones are used and added to what is naturally there on stock are they going to stay in that way in the environmental situation given their stability?

Dr. Lucier

290. Yes, they should stay in the same form. Through the cooking process you mean?

Chairman

291. No, just when they are released and they are not destroyed by cooking or other ways and you said they would even be found in petrol. My question is whether

the amount of hormones on the globe are just increasing by adding artificial hormones.

Dr. Lucier

292. Most of the steroids themselves once in the biota and subjected to living organisms on the planet, those organisms would tend to degrade most of the steroids. They have some of the same abilities to deactivate them as people have so the biota itself is capable of degrading them, so you would not get a gradual accumulation of these in the environment as you would for say some of the more persistent organochlorine compounds such as the PCBs and DDEs and these kind of things which are much more resistant to this kind of degradation. You would not get that same kind of bio-accumulation with the steroids.

Dr. McLean

293. If I could add to it cholesterol, which is the basic nucleus upon which the steroids are based, is extensively oxidized on cooking, and in fact it is thought that it is oxidized cholesterol which is the contributing factor to heart disease rather than cholesterol *per se*. I would suggest that to compare an environment where a steroid is an inorganic solvent, which we know protects the non-extraction compared with the cooking environment which contains water, oxygen and a number of other salts and other compounds would be indeed the ideal environment for destroying compounds. So I do not want to explore it any further - I think the jury is still out, but I am not sure that the steroid hormones in the cooking environment are quite as stable as people would believe.

Dr. Ritter

294. Mr. Chairman, I do not know if you wish any further comment on this table that was recently circulated but I have just taken a moment now. I am a little slower perhaps than most and I need a moment to absorb the information and try to come to terms with it, but as I look at these numbers now and under No. 2 - this Syntex data - I am not entirely sure what this is intended to represent. I am left with the impression that these numbers are derived from use data which has no withdrawal period whatsoever, because when I look at the food standards programme - the residue levels - which I think we all referenced in our submissions, and I look on page 9 of that, I note that, for example, with withdrawal periods of as little as 24 hours, following implantation with 24 milligrams of oestradiol 17 beta control-released implants and withdrawal periods as little as 24 hours, residue levels were in fact identical to the control - they were not higher at all. If one increases that withdrawal period, in fact the scenario continues - withdrawal periods in this particular study were measured up to 72 hours, which is still a very short withdrawal period and certainly much shorter than what is recommended in the actual use practice, the residue levels for the E_2 are identical for all tissues to their respective control. They are not 23-fold higher, they are precisely the same number. So I am not sure I know what the basis for these numbers are at all, or what the experimental conditions are, which are represented in this table.

295. Would I be correct in assuming that this table does not represent or reflect any withdrawal period whatsoever?

Chairman

296. Can I give the floor to Doctor Randell and then Professor Epstein.

Dr. Randell (Codex)

297. If you take the volume of Nutrition Paper 41 which is the residue studies or the evaluation of the residue studies done by JECFA at its 32nd Session, you will find on page 11 in Table 6 the numbers that are in this piece of paper just handed to us. They are the numbers associated with the study done at 15-day withdrawal period. The JECFA table, as I said earlier, puts these numbers in context by giving ranges of the data that were presented. I might point out that of all of the studies, and of all of the withdrawal periods looked at by JECFA and reported in this particular volume, I think this is about the highest set of numbers that you could select out of this group of data. However, they have to be seen within the overall context, Mr. Chairman, of all of the studies that JECFA looked at when it did its evaluation and these data presented to us today are not new data; they were data that was part of the package evaluated by JECFA.

Dr. Epstein (EC)

298. I am glad to have the opportunity of explaining this table further. If you refer to Table 2 under the column marked "test" it says 15D - this is for 15 days. As you know when it comes to implants in the US, there are implants relied on two occasions: one on entry into the feedlot and the other half-way through the feedlot period, but this is a sample taken at 15 days and I should simply say that I simply picked this out of a wide range of NADAs which I have and this is by no means atypical. For instance I have another NADA for Synovex H referring to testosterone where levels in fact were 30-fold times. So if you really would like to have a detailed analysis of all the NADAs of which I have a fair sample, I am sure you could get them all from Syntex, Upjohn and all the other companies and do comparable simple calculations. This is by no means a selected sample, but just one I happened to pick out and I can assure you that there are many others that show similar high ranges and the one on Synovex H is another example: 30-fold increase in fat.

Dr. Ritter

299. Mr. Chairman, forgive me, I do not really want to take up a great deal more time with this residue issue but it is perhaps an important one. If I refer to the same page, page 11, of the same document, the residue document that Dr. Randell referred to a moment ago, we should perhaps make this specific table available to anyone so that we are all speaking from the same piece of paper.

300. Table 5 specifically refers to residue results in muscle, liver, kidney and fat from both treated and controlled animals following a 63-day withdrawal period after the administration of a 24 milligram implant of oestradiol 17 beta in 12 bulls weighing approximately 850 lbs. In that particular study and reported here in Table 5, the fat values by way of example are barely twice what they are in the control - not 23 times as is reported in Table 2 that Dr. Epstein has presented.

301. I think the point that Dr. Randell was attempting to make is a very important one. That is that these values represented in Table 2, while they are of course taken from data that has been presented in some context, they are, in my view, at one extreme. That is I refer to Table 5, for example, on page 11, these values are barely

twice, and in fact when one looks at the statistical range of the values reported here, one might even argue that there is some significant degree of overlap between the control and the treated values.

302. I have of course made the point because it refers specifically to my submission with regard to Table 3 in the footnote - Truhaut et al 1985 states that unlawful use can result in residue levels from 300-fold in excess of established tolerance limits. I have of course made the point, Mr. Chairman, but I think this misrepresents somewhat the context of the remark made by these authors.

Chairman

303. Are you saying Dr. Ritter that taking a test after 15 days is unusual? That would never be the normal ordinary slaughter date from which it would come into the food chain?

Dr. Ritter

304. The withdrawal period is more typically in the range of 60 days and what I am saying is that with a 63-day withdrawal period reported here in Table 5 the residue levels, utilizing withdrawal periods which is more consistent with typical use practice, the comparison between the treated and the controlled is very much narrower than a 23-fold range as is reported here. It is barely twice.

Dr. Epstein (EC)

305. I think the situation has been for some time the FDA allows a separate implant half-way through the feedlot period. So 63 days in fact would represent the time when the initial pellet for the initial implant is tailing off. So 15 days is a much clearer indication of levels in the animal than 63 days at which time levels have tailed off and furthermore, as I said before, you have second implants. So at 63 days now you would have the initial residue from the initial implant when the animal enters the feedlot, plus a second round of extra hormone added at 50 days. So in fact your 63-day period would be equivalent to 13 days after the second implant.

Mr. Christoforou (EC)

306. Mr. Chairman, the table that has been circulated and discussed contains two elements: one is the one we are discussing now, the other element was the level in pre-pubertal boys and since we are now all looking at the JECFA Report in page 15 for pre-pubertal boys the value 5 micrograms per 24 hours a day is given. That is what also what we contest strongly because this is based on data of 1974 and our calculations are on the basis of the Institute for Research of Cancer which are more recent, but this value is incorrect. There are a number of things on this page as well which I hope will be clarified in this case.

Dr. Lucier

307. Are you saying that the numbers that you believe are correct are 0.4 to two micrograms per day as opposed to the six. I believe that the 0.4 to two probably is more in line with reality. I believe you are correct on that.

Chairman

308. Could you repeat that again and just elaborate on the impact?

Dr. Lucier

309. The impact is if you use a number - say one microgram per day that the young boys or girls produce - and if you compare that number to the amount that is ingested from 500 grams of beef you will have a ratio of about 140 above that. In other words, the boys are making 140 times more than what they are ingesting, just from their natural bodies. If you use a number of six, then that will be six times higher than that, and they would be making 840 times what they are ingesting in that meat. So it means that the safety factor would change from 140 to 840. Is that correct?

Mr. Christoforou (EC)

310. If there is no argument I can continue ..

Dr. McLean

311. Can I just raise the point, Mr. Chairman, I think it might be important - I am not absolutely sure that the figures in Table 6 for the controls are actually correct. I suspect that they are out by one order of magnitude all the way through because we are talking, for example, of muscle at .84 whereas most of the other control muscles in all of the other tables are somewhere around the six, seven, eight mark. Liver is .91 whereas most of the others are 8, 10, 16. I would draw it to your attention, without being able to go any further, I suspect that the control values in that first bit of the table for oestradiol are in fact out by a factor of ten. They differ very significantly from all of the other controlled data and that would not be beyond the realms of possibility.

Chairman

312. I think we should go on with remarks and questions.

Mr. Christoforou (EC)

313. First this information to Dr. Arnold. It seems that the number of samples tested is very close to 2,000,000 samples per year for the hormones. But this is our own figures. For example in Germany 205,000 checks were made for inhibitor substances for the year 1995. The number is really very high. For the year 1995 we checked, as I said, 69,000 for blood for the natural hormones. That shows that the total number of the checks made for the other hormones is much higher and it is confirmed that it is this figure that was cited at 200,000 samples for hormones is correct.

314. The next question relates to since now has been clarified what is the level of what we would consider to be normal physiological levels, especially in the area of the sensitive population that is pre-pubertal boys. Then we would intervene in the area of threshold and whether it is really appropriate in that case and indeed it seems in the JECFA Report, that the 1,000 fold as it said higher than what it is in the normal so-called, but is now contested. In that case by fixing the DAI and by suggesting and recommending the maximum residue limit, in this case, they did not recommend because they thought the JECFA Report may fall within the physiological level, but that is not correct; the second reason was that they cannot control and check. In that case, and also this is linked with the argument made about the existing physiological levels are already dangerous; that was suggested by one of the five experts here. Dr. Liehr would like to intervene in that case with respect to threshold and genotoxicity and he will have three questions to ask in that respect.

Dr. Liehr (EC)

315. I would like to start out with genotoxicity since this was already earlier brought up by several of the experts because, as you remember Mr. Chairman, it was said that the genotoxicity was tested largely only *in vitro* at too high doses and that the data were irrelevant. When I started out the studies in the early 80s, the general consensus was that oestrogens, which had been known at that time already to be carcinogenic in several animal models, that oestrogens were carcinogens by a mechanism involving solely receptor mediator pathways. In other words that oestrogens acted only the way hormones act as we understand it.

316. I started out with these genotoxicity tests at higher doses because indeed, as pointed out by Dr. Ritter, the aim was to establish whether any genotoxicity could be found in the meantime many other laboratories and many other researchers participated and contributed in this and there are several or multiple classes of genotoxicity established for oestradiol - the natural hormone. And just to ... [tape ends]

317. Single strand breaks, Dr. Arnold, has been determined by us *in vivo* and not *in vitro* as you asserted this morning. It has been determined by Dr. Nater and Abul Haj in Minnesota in cells in culture, in breast cancer cells in culture, 8-hydroxy radical DNA damage to guanine bases(?) has been established by us *in vitro* and *in vivo* chromosomal abberations have been established by Dr. Karl Barret *in vitro* and also *in vivo*, by Dr. Jonathan Li whom you cited this morning Dr. Arnold. Furthermore, DNA adducts have been determined and established *in vitro* by Dr. Cavalieri, who can certainly elaborate on this later on than, *in vivo*. We have also determined *in vivo* DNA adducts by lipid pro-oxidation products that are generated by oestrogen administration. So there is a whole variety of different types of DNA damage of genotoxicity established for oestrogen and I would submit to you Mr. Chairman that this whole variety of DNA damage constitutes what Dr. Lucier this morning called compelling evidence for genotoxicity of oestrogens. Now the JECFA report in 1988 considered for genotoxicity tests mainly bacterial assays. This is an assay test called the Ames Test and it is well known and well established that oestrogens are not mutagenic in the Ames test. This is a bacterial test system where many carcinogens have been tested for mutagenic activity. Now when Dr. Ames introduced this test in the 70s, a number of carcinogens were tested and a high correlation between mutagenicity and carcinogenicity was established. And so when oestrogens were tested and were found not to be mutagenic it was generally assumed there is no mutagenicity and there is no genotoxicity. However, as we have been testing in the Ames test thousands and thousands of compounds, carcinogens, it has been determined that the Ames test is actually a very poor predictor for carcinogenic activity. The mutagenicity test that I reported to you for oestrogen by myself and by other laboratories have all been done in mammalian systems and I submit to you, Mr. Chairman, that these mammalian genotoxicity tests are much more important than the Ames test that has been done in bacterial test systems, we are quite different from bacteria. Now there is another point that I would like to bring up that is very important. This DNA damage by itself might or might not be highly significant. These tests were done at elevated doses and the impression was given to you this morning that testing genotoxicity at elevated doses was highly unusual and was a skewing of the scientific evidence and Mr. Chairman this is not the case. Because carcinogens are routinely tested, initially at elevated doses and when carcinogenicity is found then people test at lower and

lower doses to find out whether this is still the case. The same is true for genotoxicity initially as it is tested at higher doses and then later on lower and lower doses are tested. And these tests have only begun, we have determined genotoxicity at elevated doses, I agree. They need to be tested at much lower doses to determine if at the levels that are found in beef, genotoxicity exists and I submit to you that the parties that discuss this case might want to fund such studies because it is difficult to obtain funding for this type of work.

318. One additional point I would like to make, we have demonstrated earlier on or postulated earlier on, that oestrogens are carcinogens by a combined pathway - both their hormonal action which is stimulating cell division and genotoxicity. Now this is an important fact that oestrogens can have both these qualities or both these characteristics, because a cell which has been damaged genetically can then at the same time be stimulated to divide and this represents a fixation of the mutation mechanism. And these things need to be explored in the future further, but the preliminary evidence exists that such possibilities exist. At the moment all we have is the genotoxicity data at elevated doses, yet how can we establish that at "physiological levels" these carcinogens present no risk when oestrogens in line with many other carcinogens are genotoxic at elevated doses and we have not determined how low a level is safe. So I would like to end with a quote. Dr. Arnold has quoted Dr. Jonathan Li and I would like to end with a quote from Dr. Karl Barrett, a colleague of Dr. Lucier at the National Institute of Health in North Carolina and that quote comes from the Journal of Environmental Health Perspective's review article of Dr. Barrett's in volume 100, pages 9-20 1993. Dr. Barrett states that "It can be concluded that there is significant evidence that certain oestrogens can also cause genetic alterations by a mechanism not involving the classical oestrogen receptor, [in other words, the physiological hormonal pathway] and that hormonal carcinogenesis is most likely a result of the interplay of both genetic and epigenetic factors", exactly what I have been arguing. So based on this, I would like to conclude that it is difficult to establish that low doses are not genotoxic when these experiments have not been done.

Chairman

319. Thank you very much. May I ask the Panel to comment on what was said and to tell us whether they believe this is somewhat far-fetched or whether there is reason to believe that there is a potential that such effects could occur within the ADI levels which have been defined. Dr. Ritter?

Dr. Ritter

320. Thank you Mr. Chairman. I will attempt to begin perhaps. I think Dr. Liehr makes the point that when referring to the studies at the elevated concentrations and he quite correctly points out that these are high concentration compared to what one might expect in terms of exposure to food residues. I think he is quite correctly in order that the relevance of these high dose effects to actual human risk remains to be evaluated.

Chairman

321. But he is not talking about high doses now. He submits that future trials have to take them down and that there is reason to believe that the risk exists and now I would like to know what your reaction is on the potential of having the risk within the accepted levels because this seems to be a new series of trials.

Dr. Ritter

322. I would offer only two very simplistic views, Mr. Chairman, in that regard. The first is to refer to the arguments that were advanced this morning by Dr. Lucier, and that is that at the very low levels that we are talking about in terms of food residue exposure, the contribution of that residue to the already existing biological load that we normally carry in our bodies, I think that the example that Dr. Lucier used was as if we are adding one additional molecule, in one instance he referred to every 28,000 that are present. I do not think anybody can reasonably assure you that the presence of these residues albeit at low levels constitutes zero risk, in fact I am not even sure that is a fair question to ask, scientifically it would be impossible to ever test to a certainty. But I think the point that Dr. Lucier attempted to make is that if these low levels do constitute a risk, they constitute a risk of a magnitude which approaches zero. This is the order of the magnitude of risk that we are talking about for these very low levels and the example that he referred to as I say is that it may constitute one additional putative molecule in the presence of 28,000 others. Additionally though, I would remind the panel and in fact I think the argument is made in one of the Canadian submissions, that particularly in the case of oestradiol, we have what I believe are some very relevant human experience, never mind trying to model from bacterial or mammalian genotoxic systems or from animal studies for that matter. We have a population literally of hundreds of millions of women who have taken these compounds, as I mentioned this morning, in many cases for periods of 25 to 35 years. In spite of that exposure study if you like which has now gone on for a period in excess of a generation and populations which would certainly be large enough to detect an increase in cancer risk if it were associated with these compounds, I think that it is fair to say that while there has been reports in literature reporting or purporting to report such an increase from time to time, that the weight of evidence with regard to increased cancer risk in association with the use of steroid oral contraceptives is that they do not constitute an increased risk. The best testimony of that conclusion which I have just drawn is the fact that their use continues largely unabated, in spite of the fact that all of this work has gone on now for, I'll say 35 years with regard to the risk of the use of oral contraceptives in women throughout the entire world. There has certainly not been any restriction on prescribing this medication for women, there certainly has not been a reduction in use, in fact if anything, and I don't have the numbers in front of me, but I think use in general has somewhat increased over a period of years. And this is an experiment conducted in the ultimate species. Thank you

Chairman

323. Thank you, Dr. Arnold.

Dr. Arnold

324. Mr. Chairman, this morning and obviously this afternoon I will not make any attempt to challenge the excellent quality of Dr. Liehr's work, this is not my problem, he is doing excellent work and he should continue doing this work because these are interesting possible pathways he is trying to elucidate. What my problem was this morning and still is that I feel that there are still too many missing links. For example, if you would say catechol oestrogens or the 16-hydroxyestrone whatever they bind *in vivo* to DNA, OK that would be strong evidence. But in your very excellent

review article in Annual Review of Pharmacology and Toxicology of last year, you write, yourself, you write that you were unable to confirm these data *in vivo*. You say you that it could not be demonstrate *in vivo* using the post-labelling techniques. So for the moment at least, I think we exclude this. I am also not at all opposing the idea to further investigate the probable pathway of creating reactive oxygen species, but since you were referring to the work of Nater, I have seen there that they for example say in one of their publications in Chemical Research and Toxicology, while the reactive oxygen theory in oestrogen induced DNA damage is a reasonable one, there is no direct evidence utilizing oestrogen quinones and the physiological conditions that support this hypothesis and so on. So I see there are still some missing links or gaps in the evidence. Also if I have correctly understood Dr. Cavalieri's work, but we will later hear from himself, he has synthesized these quinones and he has synthesized with more or less chemical methods the possible adducts and this is quite an interesting piece of information because now we have reference substances for further research. And I see in your paper which you have for example published in Chemical Research and Toxicology last year, that you were saying in conclusion the adducts described here provide insight into the type of DNA damage possible when catechol oestrogen quinones are generated *in vitro* and *in vivo* and will be used in studies designed to elucidate the structure of oestrogen adducts in biological systems. So again I have the feeling that it is quite attractive and if I look at these substances with the eyes of the chemist, I would immediately agree with chemical methods you can produce all these things. The question to me is does it occur in living cells, at what concentrations, what are the enzymes involved, what is the compartmentalization of these enzymes, etc. etc. In some of your papers, Dr. Liehr, you were talking about indirect DNA adducts, I am not sure whether I have correctly understood these papers, but might it be that these were adducts of malondialdehyde resulting from stimulation of lipid peroxidation? What do you think of the mechanism of stimulation of lipid peroxidation by oestrogens? So this is just a small number of questions I have and I reiterate it is not the purpose of my statement to criticize in any way the quality of Dr. Liehr's excellent work, but I feel there are many gaps in the evidence. I can't exclude as a scientist that at the end somebody you will show that oestrogens can act directly on the gene, nobody can exclude. For the moment I don't see that the evidence, the convincing evidence. Thank you, Mr. Chairman.

Chairman

325. Dr. Lucier.

Dr. Lucier

326. Yes just a few comments on Dr. Liehr's comments. One is on the ability of non-genotoxic materials to cause cancer. We have analyzed at a national toxicology programme 500 bioassays and approximately one third of them that turn out to be positive are negative in the salmonella test for mutagenicity. So that statement is correct. There are many carcinogens in animals systems that do not cause mutations, so this statement is correct, and that is about one-third of the ones that we have tested, the 500. The other points that I want to make, one relates to the receptor mediated response versus the genotoxic response. The receptor mediated response being the one in which an oestrogen binds the oestrogen receptor and stimulates the growth, the division of cells that already contain a mutation. There is a great deal of evidence

in the scientific literature that supports that as a critical event in the ability of hormones to cause cancer. So I think that, and Dr. Liehr says that that is clearly an important aspect of hormonal carcinogenesis. In addition he is proposing that genotoxic events may also be facilitating the carcinogenic process of hormones. I would say the evidence, although not weak is not as strong in that case as it is to the receptor mediated pathway. That does not mean that it is not occurring and not playing a role, but is not as compelling at this point in time as the evidence is for the receptor mediated pathways. But if say if it is an important event, I think Dr. Ritter gave my example, 28,000 molecules of oestrogen being naturally produced to the body for every one that was introduced by meat containing the growth promoting agents. Once the body sees those molecules, it doesn't differentiate, it isn't that there is the one from the growth promoted animals, it treats all 28,001 as identical so the chance of that one molecule being converted to a genotoxic molecule is equal to that of any other molecule of oestrogen that the body produced. So it just gets thrown into the mix and I think that may be an important point to consider. So even though it would be unusual for an event to occur in that one molecule, it is possible, and we said earlier we can't rule out that not occurring, even though it wouldn't contribute much because the number of molecules are so small relative to what is naturally occurring. The other point with breast cancer and oral contraceptives that was made, there has been a number of studies looking at breast cancer, I don't know how many maybe 15 or so and some of them show an increase, some of them don't show an increase. If you add them all up you don't know what to make of it. If you add them all up you get about a 15 to 20 per cent increase in breast cancer in women who use oral contraceptives but this not statistically significant. So that may just be occurring by chance. Epidemiology studies are very insensitive in picking up the changes in tumour incidence especially when the tumour incidence occurs in very high frequency. Since one out of ten women get breast cancer, a ten per cent increase or five per cent increase or two per cent increase is significant in terms of the number of cases, but this could never be picked up by epidemiology studies, they are simply not sensitive enough. It is not like the case with diethylstilboestrol, we had a very rare tumour so it was very easy to pick it up. The vaginal adenocarcinoma in female offspring who had been exposed at that age and during their gestations, so that generally occurred in low frequency and was very easy to pick up. Changes and incidences of breast cancer are very very hard to pick up from epidemiology studies.

Chairman

327. Thank you very much. We would propose maybe we close the debate at this point and we would briefly have a break maybe for 10, 15 minutes. I was informed that the coffee bar closes at 5:30, so ... you make it and then we will continue perhaps until 7:00 which is the usual time. .... Well, during the Uruguay Round it was even later! But how shall we proceed, would you like to comment on this question?

Mr. Christoforou (EC)

328. Somehow I think Dr. Liehr would like to make a comment and then Dr. Cavalieri and Dr. Epstein would like to intervene on this particular point.

Chairman

329. OK, so we have three interventions briefly. Thank you.

Dr. Liehr (EC)

330. First of all Mr. Chairman, considering the comments of Dr. Ritter, you said that you quoted this case of one additional molecule over 28,000 and that this constitutes a very low risk and that the risk is approaching zero at these low levels. I would like to submit to you Mr. Chairman this is pure speculation, we have no genotoxicity data at low doses. This is exactly the point that I am making. The experts make statements that they cannot back up with data, and until we have data I would like to first see this carcinogen oestrogen tested fully before large populations are being exposed to this. Secondly, I agree concerning Dr. Arnold, I agree with you that at the moment this is an interesting hypothesis and I have never labelled it more than a hypothesis and I also agree with you that many pieces are missing but this is exactly our point. I think that in face of a substance which where there are many troubling aspects, we should proceed carefully and we should proceed in a very measured way before we storm in and permit the exposure of wide populations until these troubling questions have been clarified. Concerning the indirect DNA adducts and the stimulation of lipid peroxidation, Mr. Chairman is one aspect, a non-genotoxic aspect of action of free radicals in cells induced by oestrogen metabolites. The stimulation of lipid peroxidation nevertheless is very important because it reroutes or alters metabolism, including metabolism of oestrogen, and permits the formation of reactive metabolites at much much higher levels. So they are processes that are set into motion and then feed on themselves which have really insufficiently been examined and we have really only started to scratch at the surface. I agree with you but nevertheless they are troubling aspects that really need to be examined in more detail. Concerning Dr. Lucier's comments, that in the debate of receptor mediated responses versus genotoxic responses, the genotoxic hypothesis may not be as compelling at the moment, again in the absence of data I don't know whether we can make such a judgement or statement at the moment. It is possible that genotoxicity is elicited only in the relatively rare instances, but let's please not forget at this point we are dealing also with a hormone and so when a hormone stimulates cell proliferation and a mutation gets fixed, Mr. Chairman, I agree with Dr. Lucier that because we breath oxygen and because we are exposed to a wide range of genotoxic substances this is a process that is occurring on a daily basis within all of us. However, and Dr. Lucier made an argument that these oestrogens would provide an incremental increase that is so small that it is negligible however, since oestrogens are also hormones, the hormonal stimulation of cell division then may well fix the mutation and induce tumours. So at the moment in the absence of more data I don't see how we can arrive at a safe passage for oestrogens.

Dr. Cavalieri (EC)

331. I would like to comment in answering Dr. Arnold that, I thank him for having acknowledged just the tip of the iceberg of all of the problem. So practically what he has recognized is that these metabolites of the oestrogen can react with part of the nucleic acid and this has been very vital in creating the standard compounds that now we have demonstrated *in vitro* and *in vivo*, as you can see in my report that I have submitted to you. The basic principle, Dr. Arnold, on which that it is very difficult to demonstrate the genotoxicity of oestrogens has been there because we didn't know what a chemical carcinogen is. That has been the big problem and we know now what a chemical carcinogen is since two years and this is the basic paper that now

has been published in 1995 in the Proceedings of the National Academy of Science. A chemical carcinogen is a compound, and we have demonstrated that for the polycyclical aromatic hydrocarbon that is huge class of carcinogen and can be extended to compounds like aflatoxin etc., is a compound that produces in excess what we call apurinicides. It means that it takes out of the DNA two bases. One is called adenine and the other one is called guanine and this process is so rich in the sense that it is so high compared to the normal depurination that we have everyday. You know that a carcinogen becomes carcinogenic, it initiates cancer, when these processes of repair of these apurinicides is not any more longer possible. By adding this basic knowledge on aromatic hydra-carbon, we have found out the same formation of apurinicide by a specific metabolite of the oestrogen that is called 4-catechol oestrogen quinone. These they bind to the DNA forming an amount of apurinicide. These we have demonstrated that *in vitro* and you can see from the report and *in vivo* by injecting the catechol on the mammary gland of the rat and finding out this kind of atom. We think as Dr. Lucier has mentioned in the morning that the adducts that they form apurinicide inside they are the most mutagenic adducts, that they are consistent with the definition of a chemical carcinogen. This is the initiating event is cancer and I think and I not only think, I am sure because of uniqueness of these phenomena of forming these depurinating carbons that oestrogen they are the origin of breast cancer as Dr. Liehr and other they already have very strong compelling evidence for prostrate cancer and for other human cancers. Therefore, I really think the major problem that we have in our lifetime is that we have the oestrogen. When the oestrogens are placed correctly, you know in the normal human being they are placed correctly, they are very well controlled, they are all beneficial, but if something goes wrong in the control because we have all protective mechanisms in order not to go on the wrong place. But if this protective mechanism for some or for some reasons or for complex they don't work, these oestrogens can become chemical carcinogens and initiating the series of events that lead to cancer. What in hormonal carcinogen is being studied and what the data that here are based the same data as you call it, ADI etc., is based only on the hormonal effect of the receptor mediated process. The initiating defect can occur in a non-protected person, in a person very likely that when he is 30 has breast cancer because this protective mechanism they don't work, and this can come with a very minute amount of oestrogen. You know because the protective mechanism they are not there to impede that the wrong pathway occurs. This wrong pathway is the metabolism of oestradiol to catechol oestrogens. These two exist, two kinds of catechol oestrogens. The most abundant in general is called 2-catechol oestrogen is not dangerous, it doesn't produce cancer. The other one that is called 4-catechol oestrogen if oxidized further to quinone can induce cancer and that is the thing that we have to take into account. Unfortunately, or fortunately, this research is on the making now but is going to be any moment out and the reason that we worked on a different paradigm of other people creates the problem in communicating here today and communicating in general with the scientific community. But you know, I think that all human endeavours work on different paradigm and at a certain moment the one that they count they have to be considered. Thank you for the possibility.

Chairman

332. Thank you very much, Professor Epstein please.

Dr. Epstein (EC)

333. Apart from the fascinating technical details of the genotoxicity, I think that mammalian genotoxicity data which we have been talking about for the last half hour, I think that the importance is, really relates to the fundamental fact that in the FAO/WHO and JECFA documents the basis for classification of oestradiol as epigenetic was largely derived on the negative Ames test, negative bacterial tester and because of this ADIs, the concept of ADI and thresholds crept into the whole of the documentation because you can have thresholds for epigenetic carcinogens. Now I would submit that the evidence for that is to say the least shaky and it's high time that the FAO/WHO documents reflected the growing body of data on mammalian genotoxicity. Even at the time of the JECFA document, there was a body of data on this which was in no way reflected, I think that's the first point I would make. Secondly, let me mention three of the most potent known human carcinogens: benzene, asbestos and arsenic, for a long time these were classified as epigenetic because they were negative in the Ames test, but subsequent work over the last decade or so has shown the mammalian genotoxins. In fact in one of them, a Dr. Legator, a colleague of Dr. Liehr has titrated the levels with mammalian genotoxicity tests and shown genotoxic effects at the lowest level possible, 40 parts per B, which isn't very much higher than when you go to a garage and fill your car with gasoline and stand next to it and sniff it, you'll get it. So in fact, in the one or two instances where genotoxicity has been titrated down, we find no effect levels similarly to what we know from our vast knowledge of radiation biology on linear dose responses. Over and above that, in view of the fact that the negative Ames test was used to establish the concept of thresholds, I should point out that there are various other issues that have to be taken into account when you want to consider setting thresholds. One is the question in this context of the interrelationship of the fact that you give two different anabolics together, two different hormones together, like oestrogen and progesterone which we know have additive or synergistic effects. It ignores the synergism between the hormones and between pesticide residues, which some of which are carcinogenic and some of which oestrogenic. It also ignores the high fact of the sensitivity of children. Nowhere in the JECFA document is there any reference to the high sensitivity of infants and children. Furthermore, to say that a compound has a threshold it puts the onus on those that say it to produce bioassay data to confirm that. In the absence of bioassay data you can't say there is a threshold if you haven't titrated it down and found a no effect level. Let me move very briefly on to two other issues, namely, the differentiation between the hormonal and the proliferate effects of oestrogens and the carcinogenic effect. A great deal has been made of the fact that the carcinogenic effects of the oestradiol is directly related to the hormonal things. I would suggest that we should re-think that. For instance, oestrogens increase the incidence of salivary cancer, thyroid cancer and melanin cells cancer or melanotic cells in humans and in fact other oestrogen receptors, I don't know. Are these tissues reproductive? Certainly not. Are they proliferative? No. So the whole concept of hormonal, of carcinogenesis being due to hormonal proliferative effect needs very very careful re-examination. Coming back to the oral contraceptive, I would agree with Dr. Lucier that it is difficult to do epidemiological studies when you are dealing with a relatively common cancer. However, I should point out to him, that in the October issue of Contraception, there was an analysis of every single study done on the carcinogenic effects of contraceptives, oral contraceptives, in relation to breast cancer. Over 60

studies were analyzed and metoanalysis and detail every single possible permutation and combination was studied. And with due respect and contrary to Dr. Lucier, what was found was as follows: that when you focus on adolescents or women starting to take oral contraceptives at 15, 15, 17 which is not uncommon now, and taking it for prolonged periods of times, there was a highly significant increase in rates of breast cancer, a very highly significant increase, this is the largest compilation of studies ever analyzed. Let me end up by making one comment on reproductive cancers. Dr. McLean this morning made some comment to the effect that there hasn't been any increase in reproductive cancers. With due respect Sir, this is quite contrary to the fact. Let's take first what testicular cancer. Testicular cancer in the United States based on National Cancer Institute and SEER data show somewhere in the region of about 150 per cent excess than age standardized data from 1950 to now, and when you concentrate on an age group of 28 to 35, the figure comes 280 per cent, nearly a threefold increase in testicular cancer in that period of time, number one. Number two, breast cancer. To suggest that the increase in breast cancer rate is due to improved detection mammography is largely incorrect and the evidence for this is as follows: in the United Kingdom, large scale mammography has only relatively recently started. We've seen the same rate of increase in the United Kingdom as we see in the United States. In the United States large scale mammograph started in about 1981 and 82. If you look at the data from 1950 to 1981, you find that the rate of increase in breast cancer is perhaps the same or a little bit greater then that from 1982 onwards. As far as prostate cancer, so in other words, to suggest that there hasn't been any major increase in reproductive cancers is entirely contrary to an established database from the National Cancer Institute and Surveillance Epidemiology and End Result Programme. As far as prostrate is concerned, there is no question that there has been a significant increase in prostrate cancer. However, I would agree that a certain amount of this is due to over-diagnosis and particularly with the PSA test and other things, so one cannot exclude that there is an element in the increased incidence of prostrate cancer due to over-detection. However, there is also an increase in mortality rate and mortality rate can't be an expression of improved early diagnosis. So the points that have been made, that there are no data whatsoever relating oestrogens and human cancer, exogenous oestrogens and human cancer, is contrary to a very substantial body of epidemiological data, which in the time available to me and I've had to summarize terribly briefly and terribly hardly. Thank you Sir.

Chairman

334. Thank you very much. Well I think we will briefly break here so you can still make it and we would inform the cafeteria that there will be a queue. Could we resume at 5:45, 6:00 please, the meeting is adjourned.

Chairman

335. Over to Dr. Lucier to comment briefly on what was said before the break. I'd just like to indicate the intention of the Panel. We intend to conclude with the part of the European Communities as a response to the United States for this session, because tomorrow we cannot have a meeting in the morning, because the experts are not available due to other commitments. But I would like to assure that we start at 2:00 with the statements and questions by the Canadian delegation so that we have enough time for this round and then the final comments by the EC and then the ex-

perts. So I would like to urge the experts on the EC delegation to have in mind that we should finish by tonight with their presentations which is now being scheduled in this first block here and I hope this can be done by 7:00-7:15 so please keep this in mind. Okay thank you. Dr. Lucier, can I give you the floor in response to the statements by the EC experts before the break.

Dr. Lucier

336. Thank you, Mr. Chairman. I just wanted to make a few comments regarding Dr. Epstein's presentation. One regarding the presence of the oestrogen receptor in various tissues of the body. He had made the point that there were oestrogen caused tumours in numerous sites. It is also true that oestrogen receptors are found in every tissue of the body, so there is no reason to think that oestrogen action isn't occurring through a normal receptor mediated pathway. That doesn't mean genotoxic events aren't also occurring, but it's clear that classical receptor mediated events would be occurring as well. The other point relates to the increased incidences of some tumours occurring in various countries in the world. Regarding testicular cancer, I think that it's probably true that there is a real increase in testicular cancer and this increase appears to be predominant in young men which is especially disturbing. Why this is occurring, no one really knows, but as a public health person it is very disturbing. There is no reason however to think that this has to be associated with oestrogen, there are a lot of other kinds of things that could be causing that, so there is not a direct link to it, although that increase is in fact a real one. Regarding breast cancer, that is also likely increasing. However, one can't necessarily attribute that to exposure to exogenous external oestrogens. There are several studies in the literature which suggest that or demonstrate that exposure to genotoxic agents during the time that a woman is a teenager causes a dramatic increase in breast cancer. This was shown in atomic bomb survivors from Japan. Those women who survived the atomic bomb, who were teenagers at the time, had very elevated risk of breast cancer later in life, women who survived who were in their 20s or 30s had no increase in risk and there is very plausible biology for this which I won't go into. It's also been shown now in three publications that women who start smoking as teenagers have a higher increase in breast cancer later in life, whereas if they start smoking later, they do not. So there are a lot of reasons why exposure to genotoxic agents could be accounting for the rise in breast cancer rates that are seen throughout the world. So we need to be cognisant of other factors and not just blame the exogenous oestrogens for everything. Regarding the oral contraceptive issue, I think Dr. Epstein is probably right that there would be an increase in breast cancer risk for women who start taking the pill very young because that extends the period of time in which they are exposed to high levels of oestrogen and this is a known risk factor for breast cancer. The same exposures a little bit later probably wouldn't have an increase, so when you average everything out together you don't get a statistically significant increase in breast cancer from oral contraceptives. I don't think that anyone is challenging the fact that oestrogens are carcinogenic, IARC is classified conjugated oestrogens as a known human carcinogen, they have classified oral contraceptives as an ... [tape ends]

... carcinogen based on an increase of liver cancer not on the increase in breast cancer. They have also classified tamoxifen as a known human carcinogen because of its oestrogenic activity in the uterus. I don't think that anyone is disputing that fact that oestrogens do cause cancer.

Chairman

337. Thank you.

Dr. McLean

338. Just by way of explanation, I did not mean to mislead and I can see how that appeared. I was talking in the context of tumours relating to the use of hormones as growth promotants, and I just make one observation that the increase in tumours occurs in those countries where the use of growth promotant is not widespread and the increase began before the hormonal growth promotants received widespread use. But it was in the context of the hormonal growth promotants rather than an increase in cancer *per se* that I meant to convey, and if I misled then I apologise.

Chairman

339. Thank you. Mr. Christoforou can I come back to you. Oh Dr. Arnold, you wanted to speak as well, sorry.

Dr. Arnold

340. Just a short remark, Mr. Chairman. Dr. Liehr and Dr. Cavalieri have proposed interesting mechanisms how oestrogens could induce cancer by genotoxic mechanisms. The Panel should know that other well-known people working with other models came to different views. For example, I mentioned Dr. Schulte-Hermann who is a well-known expert in rodent liver carcinogenesis. He says for the hormones to exert their action, there must be some pre-neoplastic lesions already present in the animals, and although his evidence is also not complete, he has quite a lot of data supporting his ideas. He for example has shown that the incidence of tumours after oestrogen treatment depends on the age of the animals at the time they start the treatment. And he has developed experimental techniques to reduce the number of pre-neoplastic lesions by restricting the diet, and he could show that under these conditions the incidence of tumour formation was lower when he started with old animals he kept on the restricted diet and then administered oestrogens. So there is some evidence in other models that perhaps there is no need that oestrogens are complete carcinogens but the first step could be an unknown initiation, the formation of pre-neoplastic lesions and then in addition the hormone promotes the further development. Thank you.

Chairman

341. Thank you very much. Can we go to your next comment and question?

Mr. Christoforou (EC)

342. We have been addressing until now, the potential at least genotoxic effects of the natural hormones. But three of the hormones in dispute in this case also are synthetic. They don't occur naturally by the other animals. So we would like also to address the potential genotoxic and carcinogenic effects of the synthetic hormones. I would give the floor with your permission to Dr. Metzler who has produced a paper and who will after this short presentation conclude by framing a question to the scientists. Thank you.

Dr. Metzler (EC)

343. Thank you Mr. Chairman. Although the synthetic oestrogens or I would rather call them xenobiotic oestrogens and androgens, trenbolone and zeranol have been far less thoroughly studied in terms of their genotoxicity, they have most been subject to routine toxicological testing which is difficult to pick up the genotoxicity of hormonal carcinogens. Nevertheless, there is some evidence that these xenobiotic hormones also are genotoxic and I'd just briefly summarize the evidence. There are data from three different laboratories showing that there is DNA binding at a low but significant amount or degree with a covalent index of about 10. There is induction of chromosomal damage in mammalian cells by trenbolone and other by the non-hormonally active isomer diethyl trenbolone and there is evidence for cell transformation *in vitro* in different laboratories. For zeranol there is also evidence for DNA binding with a similar covalent binding index and for closely related compounds, zeralenone there is recent evidence of DNA adducts *in vivo* in mice in different organs. So although there are not many studies available, the few studies indicate that there is also genotoxic potential for these xenobiotic hormones and I would like to finish this brief presentation by addressing a question to Dr. Lucier. Dr. Lucier has indicated that for the natural hormones it does not make much sense or he called it irrelevant to discriminate between genotoxic and non-genotoxic compounds. How would you view this issue for the xenobiotic compounds?

Dr. Lucier

344. Before I answer, you have to answer one of mine before I answer your question Manfred. What is, at the risk of getting too technical, what is the evidence for the DNA adduct formation for zeralenone or zeranol? Is this simple binding of radioactivity to a DNA fraction or has altered nucleoside isolated and characterized?

Dr. Metzler (EC)

345. For zeralenone or the microtoxin, or the micro-oestrogen I should probably say, there has been a recent study with the post-labelling assay indicating *in vivo* in mice both in the kidney and in the liver a level of adducts, of various adducts as shown by the post-labelling assay at the level of about 1,000 nucleitides, modified nucleitides per 10(?) nucleitides. So it's such a spining of discrete adducts that shown for zeralenone. No such study has been done for zeranol to my knowledge, for the growth promotant.

Dr. Lucier

346. One other quick question. Is it possible that P-30 post-labelling which doesn't characterize an individual adduct, is it possible that that is just arising because a change in self-proliferation rates because when a cell divides, of course, it loses its DNA adduct, or if it doesn't divide it keeps its adducts. So a measurement of the endogenously occurring adducts could lead to an alteration in the apparent number but not be related to the zeranol itself. In other words, so that adduct hasn't been characterized it's just been seen as a spot on a TLC plate?

Dr. Metzler (EC)

347. Well these adducts have been seen as spots but there were controls on untreated animals of course and there were also species differences like in rats. None of

these adducts were seen with zeralenone, they were only seen in mice. So there is a species difference which also is in favour of real adduct.

Dr. Lucier

348. Sorry Mr. Chairman for that digression, but I needed that information to answer Dr. Metzler's question. The adducts that may arise from synthetic materials are likely different and of more concern than the ones, in terms of a risk assessment, than the ones that arise from the naturally-occurring ones, because we already know that there is a given body burden of the naturally-occurring oestrogens. So whether DNA adduct formation is occurring or whether its cell replication you are just adding a very small amount to an existing burden, whether it be genotoxic or whether it be non-genotoxic so that mechanism is irrelevant as Manfred said for the naturally-occurring oestrogens. That is not necessarily true for the synthetic materials and in fact an adduct or DNA damage has been characterized and identified this may be starting out from ground zero. We have no kind of damage like that is currently in the body, so there the issue of a threshold versus linear models becomes much more important in terms of a hazard identification. So that in fact an adduct has been characterized and I would probably say at this point the data is suggestive of that. That a DNA adduct is occurring that's related to the zeranol itself or zeralenone, but not convincing because that adduct has not been identified in terms of the altered nucleoside. In other words it could be just be altering the occurrence of naturally-occurring adducts is a possibility. Although the date the Dr. Metzler has briefly presented is suggestive that such an adduct independent of the naturally-occurring adducts is in fact being formed.

Chairman

349. Thank you very much.

Mr. Christoforou (EC)

350. Mr. Chairman, I think we have reviewed the potential to toxic and carcinogenic effects of now all the substances in question. The next question is related to the response the distinguished experts gave to the question whether the JECFA report of 1987 and 1988 is taken into account this type of evidence which you have been hearing this afternoon. As you already noticed, this evidence has started appearing quite late, I would rather put it roughly, mid 1980s and it is growing very fast in this area. The scientists have replied that all these aspects of genotoxicity, synergistic effect, long-term exposure to these substances have indeed been taken into account in the JECFA report. But there were very strong differences in my views. For example Dr. Ritter would say that they have not addressed mutagenicity for all hormones, they have not addressed definitive studies for genotoxicity or carcinogenicity of combinations although this is the preferred method for use. The other scientist, Dr. Arnold for example, would say that genotoxicity and carcinogenicity have been examined and Dr. André would say that synergistic effects have not been taken into account. I would appreciate if all the scientists could summarize once again whether this synergistic effect, the long-term exposure and the potential effects or increased effect from the use of combinations have indeed been taken into account in the JECFA report. And if they have not been taken into effect what is the consequences of that? Do we have to review that report now in view of that evidence? Dr. Ritter has said there is no compelling evidence that we need to review it today. In his writ-

ten reply he said the weight of evidence would not appear to suggest that there is no, that they are genotoxic and carcinogenic. So there are some variations and slight nuances in the expression. So I would appreciate if we can come back on this issue by hearing the five experts on this.

Chairman

351. Did you get the question and could you, who would like to start? Dr. Ritter.

Dr. Ritter

352. Thank you Mr. Chairman. In the written comments which I offered with regard to the xenobiotic hormones, I think that it will be evident to all that MGA for example, has not been subjected to a JECFA evaluation. As I indicated earlier on in the day, my assessments were drawn primarily, let me go further, they were drawn entirely from information which was published in the open literature and obviously dominated by JECFA reports and other ones. It is clear that MGA has not been subjected to such an evaluation and consequently, I have no information other than of a proprietary nature which I did not use, from these evaluations to offer any public opinion on MGA. In so far as the carcinogenicity testing of the combinations are concerned it will also be evident to any reader of the JECFA reports, that the assessments and conclusions offered therein are based on the single compound that were evaluated by the Committee and it was in that context that I offered those views. When I concluded that there is no compelling evidence to suggest that these compounds should be immediately re-evaluated, it was on the basis again of my understanding not only of the historical reviews which have been carried out by JECFA and other organizations, but indeed how much more recent reviews, including those published as a result of the European Conference on Growth Promotion in late 1995, early 1996, and indeed on the basis of the statements presented by our colleagues here today, Dr. Liehr, Dr. Metzler and others. I think as Dr. Liehr indicated, the work which he has carried out recently the work which others made out recently, the work which others have presented recently, suggest that there are circumstances under which adverse effects may be demonstrated in association with the multitude of these compounds. But I think the scientists in my view have quite correctly noted that their relevance to the doses at which this debate focuses is unknown, and I'm simply suggesting that that is not in my view necessarily a reason to argue that it should therefore be immediately redone. In other words, let me put it another way, if Mr. Chairman, an organization like JECFA or indeed a national regulatory authority, were to immediately conclude that every evaluation that it had carried out should always be subject to an immediate re-evaluation at any time that a report indicating that there are circumstances under which an adverse condition can be demonstrated with a particular compound, then I would respectfully submit we will always be re-evaluating everything that we had ever done. Because work goes on, not only on these hormones but indeed on every substance that we can think of. But as scientists, I think we are compelled to look at the totality of the evidence as it's available. I think that totality of evidence, certainly recognizing the information that has been presented here today as well as the historical information, suggest to me that the assessments that were provided then continue to assure a reasonable degree of safety to consumers of these commodities. As I say this is not only my opinion but in fact it was the conclusion of a conference held very recently and sponsored by the European Com-

mission on exactly this issue. That these compound when used in accordance with accepted practice, I should perhaps use a phrase that we have all been using, good veterinary practice, good practice in the use of veterinary drugs, whichever acronym you would like to use. I think this has been the consensus view of this Conference if you like. I use the word consensus because clearly in any scientific endeavour of this sort one can quite properly and realistically anticipate that there will be a divergence of opinion. The nature of scientific interpretation is that legitimate *bona fide* knowledgeable scientists may reach different conclusions from the same set of data. But I think the consensus opinion of that Conference Mr. Chairman, was that the weight of evidence used then continues to prevail now, and that the assessments and conclusions drawn then are still consistent with the available information now. I think as Dr. Arnold has indicated, this in no way is intended to cast any doubt or validity on the work which others such as Dr. Liehr have performed. And certainly this sort of work should continue, and I don't think anybody can assure you that in some time down the road, that it will not require or dictate that there be a re-evaluation. But as we sit here in this room today, I continue to be of a view that those assessments served the community well then, the international community, and they continue to do so now. And that there has not been compelling evidence that has been provided to suggest that those assessments have been in serious error.

Chairman

353. Thank you very much. Professor McLean.

Dr. McLean

354. Thank Mr. Chairman. I'll be brief. I'd like to highlight the fact that in my submission I made no comment about melengestrol acetate because there hasn't been a large amount of data package available for evaluation and so I restricted my comments to the other five hormones. The only other comment I would make that if any national body or group believe that the time for re-evaluation of some of the hormones previously evaluated by JECFA was upon us, then I would invite them to make an approach to JECFA as has been done on a number of occasions with the number of compound of varying chemical classes. It is interesting that if this information that has concerned some has been so compelling, to ask why an approach to JECFA has not been made.

Chairman

355. Thank you very much. Dr. Arnold.

Dr. Arnold

356. Thank you Chairman. Concerning the table I have presented in my written contribution, I just wanted to facilitate the work of this Panel so that you don't need to read all these documents and so I summarize the kind of information, I was saying information pertaining to the effects have been considered by the study, it's on page 9. I have not stated that I felt that all this evidence was complete at that time, I explicitly mentioned that some data had been completed only at the 34th meeting of the Committee. This was only to facilitate the discussion. What concerns the six substances, I made no statement on melengestrol acetate because I haven't seen the data. The only statement I made was on the availability of analytical methods because this is something I know, but otherwise I have limited my statements on the five endoge-

nous hormones. I did however say that from my point of view, the significant new evidence which has been produced since that Committee did not invalidate the basic conclusions and therefore I still am feeling very comfortable with the conclusions although I admit that a lot of new evidence has been produced by the scientific community. Coming to the question of combinations the synergistic and antagonistic effects of whatever, I had some difficulties to understand this question because every time if we administer fixed combination to animals or humans, it's quite clear and in all countries participating in this dispute there are mechanisms that these fixed combinations are evaluated. But I didn't understand the significance of these questions when we are talking about the residue levels because at those concentrations, all these substances occur simultaneously in human beings of all sexes all ages and it's quite obvious that these substances have both synergistic or antagonistic effects in living animals including human beings. This is their normal physiological function and they can synergize in one tissue in one cell with respect to one effect and they can antagonize each other. Therefore I had difficulties if these substances enter the internal pools of the hormones they are immediately confronted with all kinds of hormones, so I didn't understand what the question meant at the residue level. At pharmacological levels of course they are tested in all states if they are administered as fixed combinations.

Chairman

357. Could you Professor Epstein precise the question?

Dr. Epstein (EC)

358. I am sorry that my point that I raised was so obscure. I would have thought that if you add two carcinogens to an animal or to a human, you stand the risk of interactions of one kind or another. There are data showing that are positive interactive effects whether they be additive or synergistic such as those between oestrogen and progesterone. With oestrogen and progesterone together, produce a far greater increase in mammary cancers in rodents than do either separately. So that is clear what one means by synergism. I'm unaware of any evidence of antagonistic, any experimental evidence of antagonistic effects of any anabolics and would be happy if you could refer me to the appropriate citations.

Dr. Arnold

359. I agree with Dr. Epstein that there are examples of synergistic effects but I could list a number of situations where these hormones counteract. I'm not prepared at the moment to give you such references but I'm sure I can do it tomorrow.

Chairman

360. Dr. Lucier.

Dr. Lucier

361. Probably the best example is the one that you just cited; oestrogen and progesterone in which oestrogen unopposed by progesterone causes an increase in uterine cancer. If progesterone is given at the same time then that effect is blocked. So where as oestrogen and progesterone seem to synergize each other in terms of breast cancer risk, they actually antagonize each other for uterine cancer risk. So it just points to the fact that's very difficult to fully appreciate the complexity of trying to

estimate synergistic responses, additive responses or antagonistic responses. Even the same two hormones in different tissues will do exactly the opposite, one synergize, the other antagonize.

Chairman

362. Thank you very much. Can I give you the floor?

Dr. André

363. We will speak about the six hormones and not of MGA, it is clear we are just speaking about the other ones. I think that concerning this question when JECFA has considered these hormones, they have been considered as drugs, as classical drugs and for this reason, all the data concerning toxicological assays has been asked to companies and evaluated by very well scientific expert groups. But I think they have not been evaluated as for the reviews for growth promoters, I mean with a very large scale use. I think interference between this large scale use of hormones and the other drugs used also in animal breeding has never been studied, and its clear that the use of hormones has been demonstrated to longer some withdrawal period and elimination rates of other drugs. The probability to have interference between two drugs when they are used for therapeutic use is very small because you have no opportunity to have at the same time two different illnesses and two drugs at the same time. But when you are using such compounds in large scale as hormones, then you have a higher probability to see on the same animal at the same time the use of these hormones and use of another drug. And I think in this particular case of growth promoting substances, the assay has to be done. And concerning the new scientific evidence we are speaking about very recent data from this morning altogether and I would just make two remarks that many of these data concerning mode of mechanism of action carcinogenicity and other are recent data from '90 to now and most of them have been published during 1995 and 1996, the two last years. So this could also explain in some ways that many of these data, recent data have not been taken into by the EC Conference in '95 because the bibliography and the investigation has been done for this Conference up to the beginning of '95 and not more recently.

Chairman

364. Can I give you the floor?

Mr. Christoforou (EC)

365. Mr. Chairman, Dr. Liehr would like to make a comment on the synergistic effects and then Dr. Bridges would like to intervene on the so-called 1995 EC Scientific Conference what was .... during that Conference. Then if you allow me I will summarize once again what was said I may be making probably slightly legal but directly related question to what is the JECFA standards in this case and what is the legal context in which we are litigating in this case. I think that will be important for our scientists. Thank you.

Dr. Liehr (EC)

366. Mr. Chairman, concerning the synergism of hormones, I agree with Dr. Lucier who stated that the combination of oestrogen plus progestin inhibits uterine tumour formation whereas it appears to enhance mammary tumour formation. It certainly does so in animals and the epidemiological evidence in humans is also quite

strong. In this context, I think it is very important for all of us to realise that when several hormones are combined and given as a combination that the balance of hormones within the body, the regulation by various hormones appears to be altered or influenced in ways that we have not sufficiently taken into account. If for instance progestin inhibits uterine tumour formation then and enhances mammary tumour formation, then it is obvious that circulating within all of us are hormones in a quite well-defined balance and as humans proceed through life, through stages, the endocrine regulation is quite well balanced. Once combinations of hormones are added this balance is being destroyed and I think an obvious example of how this, effects, synergistic effects can arise, is the fact that the metabolism of oestrogen is clearly or has clearly been shown to be inhibited by progestins. So combinations of hormones they easily alter the balance between these, between endogenous hormone levels and for the many synthetic progestins, I don't know to what extent this is known. A number of synthetic progestins have been examined but certainly not all of them. Thank you Mr. Chairman.

Chairman

367. Thank you very much.

Mr. Christoforou (EC)

368. Mr. Chairman before giving the floor to Dr. Bridges, I would like to clarify one point and Dr. Stephany will intervene just afterwards. Dr. Ritter has said, JECFA evaluated only single compounds, single substances. From what we know in the market, the implants, there is only one implant that is one substance only marketed. All the others are implant of compounds of similar substances and I think Dr. Stephany would like to say a couple of words about this. So in fact, what it is administered to the animals in this case, they are no single substances except one. The majority of all the rest of the implants are several compounds together. That I think Dr. Stephany would like to say a couple of words on this.

Chairman

369. Yes? Dr. Ritter please.

Dr. Ritter

370. I don't want to pre-empt the comments, but in addressing the issue of combinations, I'm not sure if you are dealing with the issue of animal safety, who presumably would be at greatest risk from the combination, if the combination was to produce synergistic effects? Because I'm left with the impression, perhaps these comments will be addressed, that in terms of human safety, the issue is the exposure to the levels which are present as food residues, which indeed are present in combination with hundreds of other substances, not only these two alone. So I'm not sure if the comments are intended to be more relevant to the issue of safety in the cow, or to the issue of safety to humans who consume commodities from which the residues may indeed be present in combination but at very much reduced levels and again in present in combination not only for the two steroids in question, but indeed present in combination with hundreds of other residues of both natural and exogenous origin.

Mr. Christoforou (EC)

371. Thank you, thank you very much indeed. Because there is one aspect which is not practically discussed in this room but has been argued in the submissions of the parties, especially in submissions of the European Community. This case concerns both the facts on human beings of course, but also on animals, and we did not elaborate because the effects on the animals are even more obvious than what the effects are of this residue for human beings. But Dr. Stephany will also given you some information on animal health also in this case, that is the prostate of animals that are affected. Our question is not only the potential effects of the animals but also the potential effects of those combinations for human beings. And the link that was made, has been explained, is since the implants which are used on the market, apart from one the others are compounds of several substances, this is linked to our question, what are the possible synergistic effects of this combination? Has this been studied by the JECFA Report? That was the aim or the point that we were trying to make. But I give the floor first to Dr. Stephany then will come back to Dr. Bridges. Thank you.

Dr. Stephany (EC)

372. Thank you Mr. Chairman. First of all I have to make one very small correction, of the implants that are on the market, there are two having a single active component but only one having oestradiol and the other one is zeranol. So there are two, one is oestradiol the brand name is Compudose and the other one contains zeranol, xenobiotic and the name is Ralgro. All others as far as I am aware are combinations of having at least one xenobiotic hormonal active compound in it. What surprises me a little is that we always talk about, that the implants contain compounds that are identical to the natural ones. That's simply not true because the implants contain either the natural ones in chemical different form like an ester like oestradiol benzoate and or the testosterone as a testosterone propionate. And at least testosterone propionate what is xenobiotic circulates freely in the body as is known from clinical chemical studies, and I'm not aware of any residue studies of testosterone propionate as such and it is certainly not true that all testosterone propionate or all oestradiol benzoate only will hydrolyse and will yield the natural identical hormones. So I think that's one thing and coming or responding to the remarks of Dr. Ritter, if you have two hormonal active components in your implants you will have two at least two hormonal active residues. So the consumer will in his food have, in between a wealth of other things, I fully agree, the probability of being served with two hormonal active hormones or residues at the same time, at least two different ones. Well what's next? Oh the remark on animal health, it's only a small remark. Some recent research in the Netherlands with, picking up old research, we know that if you treat bull-calves with oestrogenic compounds then at least a few organs will change like the prostate and with some new technology based on histo-chemical its a new thing, we found that at least this effect is much more extended than we have found previously. Whether that will effect the health of the animal as such, I can hardly say especially for calves only having a full life of half a year. But at least it's another signal that a lot of things change in the body of the animal, besides that more meat is produced. And also that's an item that is touched in the European Conference, ranging from animal health to animal welfare, but that's completely another thing. I think that's it

for the moment, and once again I think the most important thing is that the implants do not contain in most cases natural identical compounds.

Chairman

373. Thank you could. I'm sorry I missed before Dr. Randell he wanted to intervene. May I give you the floor?

Dr. Randell (Codex)

374. Thank you Mr. Chairman. I would not like the Panel to go away with the idea that JECFA did not evaluate the residues present in animals from these mixed implants. The monographs which were prepared by JECFA at the 32nd session clearly indicate that trials were done on mixed implants as well as on single substances implants and exactly the sort of mixtures that we have just heard, that is, oestradiol together with testosterone; oestradiol together with progesterone; oestradiol benzoate together with testosterone propionate and also oestradiol with trenbolone acetate under the oestradiol evaluations. These were known to JECFA at the time and the pharmacokinetics of these substances as they were gradually metabolized and excreted by the animals were studied by the experts at that time. Thank you.

Chairman

375. Sorry, Dr. Arnold.

Dr. Arnold

376. Thank you Mr. Chairman. Dr. Stephany is absolutely right that the esters are administered. However, this is also the case in the European Union. If these substances are legally used for therapeutic purposes because, and I think here the rules are entirely right, it is recognized that the esters are readily hydrolyzed to yield the substances. Therefore it doesn't make a great difference if we have talked about oestradiol, testosterone and progesterone because these esters are in fact readily hydrolyzed. The reason why the esters are used is that the free substances are more slowly released because we discussed this earlier today. The plasma half-life is so short. However, in order to give you an idea how ineffective these substances still are, when testosterone propionate was used in earlier times as androgen substitution therapy, it was necessary to inject 25 mg. every day intra-muscularly, so although he is from an academic viewpoint entirely right, I think we can continue discussing the effects of the free substances. Thank you.

Chairman

377. Thank you very much. I give the floor back to the Community.

Dr. Bridges (EC)

378. Chairman, I'd just like to clarify the nature of the December 1995 Conference because several speakers have referred to it as if it was an up-to-date comprehensive risk assessment on steroids. It wasn't really of that nature at all, it had nearly 400 participants, which is a pretty difficult way of going about risk assessment. It was covering three areas, development of new growth promoters generally, risk assessment across a range of growth promoters and then monitoring and surveillance. So there wasn't and the way the papers were identified was that we had a small organizing committee who chose the speakers. Now in their wisdom or otherwise, they chose not to have any body who was involved in genotoxicity and so as a conse-

quence, and I was a plenary speaker for risk assessment so I remember the brief well, as a consequence this issue of genotoxicity was not addressed at all by the conference and therefore the conclusions of the Conference did not take it into account. So it isn't and was never intended to be a comprehensive risk assessment and it didn't really consider any other mechanism because of the way the speakers were selected other than just to look at the hormonal mechanism and how that may be related to cancer.

Chairman

379. Can I ask you, the fact that you did not invite speakers, was that an indication that this was not part of the mainstream thinking at the time, or?

Dr. Bridges (EC)

380. Chairman, I wasn't a member of the organizing committee but they were clearly very wise because they chose me as a plenary speaker so I couldn't argue with them. I think really the thinking was that they wanted to follow up to the so-called Lamming Report, and the Lamming Report had concentrated very much on hormones acting as hormones or hormonal mechanism. So I think the natural assumption was that they would get an update on those sort of issues rather than look at broader issues and I've taken the opportunity to talk to members of the organizing committee recently to confirm that that was their view.

Chairman

381. But could it be said that if this would be organized today they would probably take a different approach? Is that, I mean these issues we're discussing have they moved into the debate?

Dr. Bridges (EC)

382. I'm sure Chairman that if we were organizing the same conference today, genotoxicity issues would loom very large in the discussion and I'm sure I would have had to refer to it particularly in my paper.

Chairman

383. Thank you very much. Dr. Arnold.

Dr. Arnold

384. Thank you Mr. Chairman I totally agree with you that this Conference has not produced the slightest element of risk assessment, I totally agree with you. But I have recognized that some important information has been disseminated including your own very important key lecture, but I wanted to underline this Conference has not produced the slightest element of risk assessment.

Chairman

385. Thank you very much. Dr. Ritter please.

Dr. Ritter

386. Thank you Mr. Chairman. I think it may be useful, a number of us have referred to the report, I have the report with me which I brought at the risk of great personal injury to transport it ... [tape ends]

Mr. Christoforou (EC)

387. It is addressed, particularly for Dr. Ritter, Dr McLean, Dr. Arnold and of course, Dr. Randell.

Chairman

388. Thank you very much. Could I start with you Dr. Randell because the procedural questions are addressed to JECFA.

Dr. Randell (Codex)

389. Thank you, Mr. Chairman.

390. First I'd like to say that the JECFA Secretariat, of which I had the honour to be a part for a period of my career, would feel very disturbed if they were aware that data were available to the scientific community that were not available to JECFA, or were not being proposed to be available to JECFA, in a manner that would render JECFA's advice to FAO and WHO member countries, either obsolete or inappropriate.

391. Therefore, my comment earlier, was really to maintain, what I believe to be the standing excellence of JECFA's evaluations in all of the fields that JECFA deals with, in order that, we could perhaps encourage those scientists that have these data to assemble them and bring them to JECFA for review. It was meant as a positive, not a negative, statement.

392. A few minor corrections to the history which we've just heard. The vote which took place, in which the hormones were failed to be adopted by the Codex Commission, was in 1991, not 1992.

393. The four principles concerning the role of science in Codex decision-making, and the extent to which other factors are taken into account, was never discussed, as far as I am aware, by JECFA. It was not processed through the JECFA system. It is entirely a Codex matter and, therefore, entirely operated by the member governments of Codex and not by the experts in JECFA.

394. Let me put the JECFA material into perspective. JECFA provides advice to FAO and WHO and through them to the members of those two organizations and also to the Codex Alimentarius Commission.

395. The Codex Alimentarius Commission has, as a matter of procedure, taken the JECFA recommendations in a variety of areas and plugged them into the eight-step elaboration system and the result of this, in most cases, is a consensus adoption of these points of view which are then available for countries to apply, if they feel that they wish to. They are not obliged to under the Codex rules.

396. There have been any number of emergency re-evaluations in JECFA which have been initiated in Codex and which have found themselves reflected in Codex opinion.

397. As to the direct question if there is one that has occurred in the nine-month period since the entry into force of the Uruguay Round Agreements, I'd have to check that in but I can't think of one. The most recent one which has similar import would be the decision of JECFA to withdraw previous evaluation in regard to potassium bromate, as a flour-treatment agent, and the subsequent withdrawal by Codex of all approved uses of potassium bromate in flour, primarily because potassium bromate

residues remain in the flour at the time of ingestion by the human consumer, and potassium bromate is a carcinogen.

398. The maximum residue limits are not exclusively concerned with trade. They are concerned with the control of good agricultural or good veterinary practice and they are applied in trade. To be quite practical about it, it's definitely beneficial to trade if countries have the same numerical values for maximum residue limits, or at least if you are exporting a product, the level at which you are exporting is lower than the limit applied by your importer.

399. However, the maximum residue level should reflect the good agricultural, or good veterinary practice, on your territory and not be linked exclusively to trade considerations.

400. I would take umbrage at the point that the MRL is a trade-derived figure. It is, in fact, a figure derived from good veterinary or good agricultural practice.

Chairman

401. Can I ask you to go into the question which was put forward?

Dr. Ritter

402. Very quickly, I think the principle that was being elaborated, the philosophy is more popularly referred to as the precautionary principle.

403. As to what is the most appropriate action in the face of the kind of information, for example, that has been presented today, I take that really to be the work of the Panel, and so I will make no attempt to answer that question.

404. I think it goes well beyond the jurisdiction that I've been provided here to comment.

405. I will, very quickly, comment on, if you like, the age of the assessment and I've already made comments on this a number of times, but it perhaps bears repeating.

406. I think it is incorrect and I would respectfully submit that it is misleading to suggest that 1988/1989 is the last time that this issue on the safety of the hormones, in question, has been examined.

407. I've already mentioned that certainly in my view, this issue, without going into a lengthy debate as to whether or not the strict definition of risk assessment was made by the European Conference, I think it goes without question that the issue of the safety of the hormones, in the general sense, was most certainly re-evaluated in December 1995, which is a little more than one year ago.

408. Indeed, a number of people who are here today were active participants at that conference.

409. I must say that I disagree with the view that 1989 is the last time that this issue was formally evaluated on an international level. I think that's incorrect and I think it's misleading.

410. More specifically, on the issue of risk assessment, whatever that means. We could spend the rest of the evening debating whether or not risk assessment have, or have not, formally been discussed by the Conference.

411. I would refer the Panel to a specific section entitled, Risk Assessment, on page 3 of the Conference Report, and it falls under the general section of the Report

entitled Report and Conclusions of the Steering Committee, specific section entitled, Risk Assessment.

412. Although the Conference was concerned with many technical matters, it is inevitable that general interest should have centred on the risk assessment of different classes of both promoting substances, the subject of discussions of Working Group 2.

413. Then I would refer, Mr. Chairman, the Panel to a number of specific papers which I would respectfully submit, dealt with very much with the issue of risk assessment. I refer to Workshop No. 2 on pages 245-401 and I would refer specifically to a number of papers, including the one presented by Professor Bridges, but also including papers presented by Dr. Miller from the United States, Dr. Hoffmann from Germany, and so on and so forth.

414. If I refer, just by way of example, not to give particular preference to any one of these papers, to the paper presented by Dr. Miller from the USFDA at that Conference, she concluded, at that time, "hormonal growth promoting agents include a variety of compound which very markedly in pharmacology and biochemistry" so on and so forth.

415. "When these animal drug products are used according to label directions, the edible tissues from treated animals, are safe for all consumers."

416. I would respectfully submit, Mr. Chairman, that that is very much an assessment of risk, regardless of whether or not we can come to a formal definition of what constitutes a risk assessment. It's certainly my view that this is most definitely the element of risk assessment. It strikes the heart of what a risk assessment is, because after all the product of a risk assessment, is the statement of safety to the target population. That's why we carry out risk assessments. It's not merely a mathematical exercise.

417. I would suggest to the Panel that there are a number of papers here that deal very much with the issue of risk to human populations, resulting from the use of these compounds, and that the consensus of this Workshop was that the use of these compounds, as recently reviewed as December of 1995, does not constitute any risk.

Dr. André

418. May I add some comments for the Panel? It can also see in the same paper, page 378, conference.

419. I will read what it says:

"New quantitative risk assessment models are needed for the safety evaluation of chemicals with toxic actions, like general carcinogen."

420. It's in the same paper so it's not possible to extract something when you don't extract all the information.

Dr. Ritter

421. I didn't intend to mislead. I mean obviously I'm not going to read into the record the entire Conference Report it is available.

422. There is no question that a number of deficiencies, in terms of our state of knowledge, as identified throughout the report, but those efficiencies, those deficiencies were weighed in the conclusion which the Panel has reached. They weren't weighed by me. But the conclusions of the Working Group was that the present state

of knowledge is sufficient to demonstrate the safety, in their view, of the use of these chemicals in contemporary times.

423. I think it would be silly for any scientist to presume that the day will ever come, on this issue or on any other, where we could say we know enough and that there is no need to do any further work. I have never been associated with a scientific issue where I have ever heard a scientist say, there is no need to do any further work on this topic, we know all that we need to know.

424. I agree that there is further work that is indicated. I agree that statements made by scientists, such as Dr. Liehr will continue to contribute to our understanding, but I also agree that the totality of evidence re-evaluated, as recently as December 1995, suggests that the way in which these substances are used and the residues which they produce, do not constitute a risk to human health.

425. I don't find those statements to be contradictory at all.

Chairman

426. Dr. Lucier.

Dr. Lucier

427. My question may show a certain amount of naivety but did JECFA document or the 1995 meeting address the issue of carcinogen risk assessment, in any kind of way?

428. It seemed to me like the risk was based on the hormonal activity of the agents, in primates.

Chairman

429. We discussed that briefly before. Would you like to give your views on this.

Dr. Ritter

430. I think only to say that unless we were to spend a great deal of time strictly defining what we mean by the phrase "risk assessment" we could continue to go around this circle, I think, all night. The point that I was trying to make that, in the opinion of the scientists that were gathered at the Conference, it was their collective wisdom, for whatever reasons they considered. I think, as Professor Bridges has already quite correctly indicated that it did not include extensive examination of some of the evidence which was presented today. But for all the totality of reasons that they considered, at that time, they came to conclusions which have already been made clear. One may raise the question if they were redoing it tomorrow, would they come to the same conclusion? I think this is speculation. One could raise the question, if they were doing it again a year from now, would they come to a different conclusion? I don't know.

Dr. Lucier

431. Were the acceptable levels, or the acceptable daily intakes, were they derived, primarily, from the tests of hormonal activity in non-human primates? Is that correct?

Dr. Ritter

432. No, I don't think that's correct. I think there were extensive carcinogenicity data that were available to the JECFA Committee. These data have been described,

the assessments provided, at least in the case of two of the xenobiotic hormones. To the best of my recollection, monographs on the three natural hormones are not available, but they are available for the two synthetics, and certainly they were based on chronic toxicity carcinogenicity studies that had been conducted in a very classical, NTP kind of methodology.

433. No, the naturals were evaluated, what I indicated, to the best of my knowledge, monographs are not available on the naturals. But data was evaluated by the Committee, on which they drew their conclusions, I have not been privy to that data. But then again, I have to be candid, I have not re-evaluated the carcinogenicity data for any of these compounds, in order to prepare this session. This would have been neither practical or arguably even necessary. I would never pretend to suggest that I have greater wisdom in this area than the collective wisdom of the JECFA Panel.

Chairman

434. Dr. Randell, please.

Dr. Randell (Codex)

435. Mr. Chairman, just perhaps to clarify that point.

436. In the case of zeranol, for example, the JECFA Committee did evaluate carcinogenicity studies, in rats and in mice, and so forth, but the conclusion that JECFA came to in this substance and in the other substances, that the carcinogenicity was linked with the hormonal effect, and therefore the establishment of the "no hormonal effect" level was the point at which the evaluation hinged, it hinged around that point.

437. This is why the new data, which we're hearing about today, is of interest because it would supplement that evaluation and help us considerably. However, the information which was available to JECFA definitely did include carcinogenicity studies for all of the substances concerned.

Chairman

438. I'm looking at my watch. It's about 7.30. Could you come to a close for today?

Mr. Christoforou (EC)

439. Mr. Chairman, I will come to a close on this particular point, if you allow me.

440. I will read from what the response of Dr. Ritter was to Question No. 5, because that is what we are discussing now.

441. I quote page 12 of his reply to Question 5, at the end of the first big paragraph:

442. For progesterone:

> "The report was silent on the results of mutagenicity studies which were available to the Committee for review."
>
> For testosterone:
>
> "Results from mutagenicity studies, although available to the Committee, were not described in the report."
>
> For the synergy:

"The issue of potential synergy has been addressed, at least in part, through the context of biochemical studies, directed at the effect of excretion of hormone combinations when compared to single hormones alone."

This is on page 14.

"It is, however, clear, that definitive studies relating to genotoxicity or carcinogenicity of hormone combinations have not been carried out even though this is frequently the preferred method of use."

443. I'm slightly puzzled by the positive terms in which Dr. Ritter is now phrasing his replies for the review of the, in the JECFA report. All issues we have been discussing here now about the genotoxicity, not only due to the hormonal effects, as has been rightly pointed by Dr. Lucier but all the other possible sources of risks we have identified.

444. At least the way I understand his replies is that these studies have not been carried out. They might have been available but they have not been reported in the report. We don't know if they were real studies.

445. He was not part of the JECFA committee, in that particular case. So I don't know where he has got this information. Whereas Dr. McLean was part of this report and also he might have an interest to explain to us whether this has been done. From the reports we have in front of us, Dr. Arnold has provided a table, where there are some black holes where things which have not been examined. I see there is, at least some, contradiction between what our scientists are saying on this particular issue. If one reads the entire report of JECFA, it is clear that only the hormonal effects of those substances have been studied for the potential carcinogenic effect. So what is the exact scientific basis on which Dr. Ritter is making these comments?

446. One more comment.

447. I think Dr. André, because he was part of the Organizing Committee of the 1995 Conference, he has, in my view, direct inside information on how this conference was organized. The Community only funded the Conference and left the scientists entirely to address some issues.

448. In the report of Dr. Ritter, it is frequently referred to as the EC Conference. It is not the EC Conference. It is a conference funded, but no more than that. It was entirely left to the Steering Committee who to invite and what to discuss in this conference.

Chairman

449. I would propose that we have a final round on this question and then we will close the meeting for today, and I would give the opportunity to respond to the scientific experts.

450. Maybe Dr. Ritter would speak at the end.

451. I'll start with Dr. McLean.

Dr. McLean

452. I thoroughly concur with the comments of Dr. Randell. We were trying to put a positive view on the availability of JECFA, if people wanted to take that opportunity, rather than forcing people to do it.

453. In relation to the mutagenicity data for the naturally-occurring substances, the mutagenicity data that was reviewed is referenced in the report, in each case, and so therefore, not so much that is was silent but it referred to mutagenicity data that was in the open literature. So, in the case of progesterone, testosterone and oestradiol 17 beta, there were a number of published documents that the Committee did look at, and they are referenced in the report.

Chairman

454. Dr. Arnold.

Dr. Arnold

455. Mr. Chairman, I have two points.

456. The first point is I have difficulty understanding how it could happen, but the legally competent authorities of the EEC, on the advice of the competent advisory scientific body, have established no MRL for oestradiol and this happened two years ago.

457. The public summary report states, *inter alia*, "The conclusion of the FAO/WHO Expert Committee on Food Additives, JECFA, that no ADI and MRL for oestradiol need to be established, as adopted." And then all the other things I mentioned this morning, this is what I have difficulty in understanding, this happened in 1994. And this Regulation has been implemented, it has passed all the EC institutions and the result has been published in the Official Journal. I refer to this in my answers to the question of the Panel.

458. My second point is I was rapporteur of the Codex for five consecutive years. That means I had jointly, with the secretaries of the two agencies of the United Nations and with the US Secretariat of the Committee, to prepare the report. I was in a really difficult situation because it's true that the EC objected to move these MRLs to the next step in the procedure, but without raising any health issues. So, I was really in trouble and you can find the result in the report. I finally got a written statement and the arguments you will find there are, *inter alia*, the EC is opposing because they have specific legislation prohibiting the use and the EC consumer doesn't wish to receive meat from animals treated.

459. These were the arguments, so I'm a little disappointed that these questions have not been raised earlier, first of all, in earlier years during the Codex discussions. It could have happened, for example, to refer the whole matter back to JECFA with new health arguments for re-evaluation, at that time, but this proposal was not made.

460. And that secondly, two years ago it happened that we came to the same conclusions by the competent authorities of the EC regarding oestradiol. Progesterone has also been finished but not yet published in the Official Journal, and testosterone is still under evaluation.

Chairman

461. I think we will reserve this for tomorrow.

462. I'd like to conclude and if anybody of you would like to speak?

Dr. André

463. Just to say a little more about this Conference because I have been asked to do so.

464. It's clear that the EC has just asked four experts to organize this Conference: Sir John Maddocks is the Head Director of the Nature Review, a scientific paper, an Irish colleague, Bergen colleagues and myself.

465. I can witness that we were very, very free of our to our choices, in terms of selecting scientific people. And we organized this with a first group of two people for the three Work Shops, and they proposed that we invite scientific people and we agreed, on the basis of the publication and the famous of these people.

466. But, I think, and I personally regret now that we didn't take enough care with the scientific publication. I discovered this morning a lot of publications on this topic and some of them were available and the scientific were also available, and maybe we have not done our best. We have done our best but maybe it was not good enough, and that will explain also the missing of some information in this Conference.

467. On the last point, I would like to say that the conclusions are a reflection of a common discussion, and it is not a complete reflection of the majority of people. It is not a total opinion of the members of the Committee and it cannot be taken into account as something coming from an official body. Our objective was just to put some light, some knowledge, on these hormones in order to inform politicians preparing new regulations and no more. It is not the same thing as to establish an official MRL. The responsibility was not exactly the same order.

Chairman

468. Dr. Lucier.

Dr. Lucier

469. I'm just surprised in reading through this report that, given the fact that oestradiol is a known human carcinogen, that an ADI was considered unnecessary for it. There is a tolerance but not an ADI, if I'm reading the report correctly.

Chairman

470. What page?

Dr. Lucier

471. 19.

Chairman

472. The JECFA Report. This was the 1988 JECFA Report. Is that correct?

Dr. Lucier

473. In the middle of page 19 it said the Committee considered an ADI unnecessary for a hormone that is produced endogenously in human beings and shows great variation and level according to age and sex.

Dr. McLean

474. The difficulty that JECFA had of setting any ADI was the problem of the increase that one saw upon treatment, against a background of very large levels that occurred naturally. And so therefore it meant that the setting of the ADI really wasn't possible, because the treatment altered the levels by such a small amount when com-

pared with the endogenous levels in cattle to make any ADI meaningless, and that was the difficulty we had.

475. I would suggest, today, that is not possible to regulate the use of the three naturally-occurring hormones by the setting of an ADI because you can't tell the difference between treated animals and untreated animals, by a method that is suitable for regulatory purposes.

476. It's a practical consideration, a real and practical consideration. I don't quarrel with what you say, but in practise there's no way of regulating it.

Dr. Lucier

477. But if one knew, which we do know, what are given body burden in the cattle would be produced by the use of growth promoters, we can certainly estimate various eating habits of people, what they would take in their body from those agents that were exogenously administered.

478. One could come up with reasonable estimates on that and establish an ADI. In my mind, that could be done. From my comments this morning, I don't argue with your point that it's a very small number of molecules, one in 28,000 I came up with in my calculations, not taking into account the fact that it is poorly absorbed and that would make it one in 280,000.

479. But nevertheless, some sort of an assessment should have been made, in my mind, of what that risk was, as low as it is. I'm not saying that the risk is high but I believe the risk is extraordinarily low or zero. That's not my point. I am just surprised that that exercise was not done.

Chairman

480. If more points on this are to be discussed, I would like to discuss them tomorrow because I think we are a little tired.

481. Would you like to make statements tonight?

482. I apologise for the length of the meeting but it has been, in my view, very informative and I would like to thank the experts and also the delegations for their support.

483. As agreed, we will meet tomorrow at 2 o'clock, hopefully sharp, and we will open discussions with the statements and questions by the Canadian Delegation.

484. Thank you very much and good night.

485. The meeting is closed.

Second day - 18 February 1997

Chairman

486. As announced yesterday, we shall proceed in the following manner. We will go first to Canada for their comments and questions to the experts. We will then turn again to the European Communities and I would urge the Community to limit their interventions to the utmost necessary in order to save time. We will see how much time can be allocated when the Canadians have made their statements and questions and then there will be final questions from the Panel to the experts and then the final statements by the experts in the end. I have to be able to conclude this meeting by around 6 o'clock. I am not able to say whether we will be able to do so. It depends on you and I am in your hands to a large extent.

Mr. Christoforou (EC)

487. We would really do our best to respect what you have indicated, but our delegation has a serious problem in the sense that the planes of two of our scientists are leaving at 6 o'clock and we consider their testimony and their presentation very important. It is just a request and we hope we have the understanding of the Panel in this room. If it is possible by 4 o'clock, Canada does not finish, I do not know how many questions they have, if we can stop for a while they can make their presentations and if there are any questions or answers and then they could probably be able to take their taxis and get to the airport in time. That is the request.

Chairman

488. Thank you very much. I think we will see where we are with Canada at 4 o'clock.

Mr. Brinza (US)

489. Mr. Chairman, a procedural question. Last night we had left that the Panel was going to deliberate on our question about the follow-up submission. That was requested by the Europeans and I wondered if the Panel had come to a conclusion with respect to the matter we had raised last night. It is important, in part, because as we understand, the procedure that was just described, there would be no more opportunity for comments by either Canada or the United States after the Canadians have finished their questions today (and obviously we finished our questions yesterday), and there are a number of points that have been made that I think it would be appropriate to give us an opportunity to respond to.

Chairman

490. Thank you very much. I intended to take this up at the end of the meeting but since you raise it I can give the answer of the Panel. We have looked into the question and based upon the text which was communicated on 3 February by the Secretariat to the Parties, which I will read in a second, we reviewed the decision I made yesterday and we will not accept any ex-post submissions from the Parties. The United States has submitted some materials, you have submitted some materials yesterday which we took on the file, but we will not take on any more written materials after this day. The text reads "Please find attached the responses of four of the five scientific experts responses to Panel questions. Professor Arnold requested a few more days to submit these responses. [They came later on.] The Parties are informed that their comments to these questions at the 17-18 February meeting with scientific experts should be made available, as is customary with the Parties' oral statements at panel meetings, in the written form and if possible on diskette to the Secretariat". So this means that we expected these comments by today and I think we will conclude the proceedings based on this letter. So if you have additional materials, please hand them in by the end of this meeting.

Mr. Christoforou (EC)

491. Mr. Chairman, the practice though is that we are allowed to submit a document at least the next day after the oral presentation. This has always been the case. We are adjusting the text while we are speaking and I have been doing that for so many years and it is always the next day we are allowed to submit in writing the oral

presentation. It is very restricted this time-limit of today. I would appreciate it if tomorrow there is also a chance for us to submit a document. Thank you.

Chairman

492. I think the problem is that then we need to have another go on rebuttals. And I think we stick to this here for the moment because this has been a hearing of experts by a panel and we do record on tape and will transcribe everything which is being said at this meeting so I do not think that we would need another written statement on the side of your part.

Mr. Christoforou (EC)

493. Mr. Chairman, if you apply this rule then the entire text which is in the text that the United States has circulated has not been read out orally. Then I would have unfortunately to request you to exclude all those parts of the documents which have not been read out. I really regret that in this part of the document there are so many things which have not been said yesterday.

Chairman

494. I think it was not required that this be read out because it says that the comments on these questions should be made available to the Secretariat. It is not exactly the same proceeding in my view as in the ordinary first and second substantive meetings here. I do hope that you are able to provide some of the materials as it was done yesterday, today - the statements by the experts and so on.

Mr. Thompson (Canada)

495. Thank you Mr. Chairman. If I am going to get started before my 4 o'clock deadline then I had best get quicker with the finger on the button.

496. It had been Canada's original intention to comment quite briefly on the experts' answers to the Panel's questions. Primarily by noting in point form some seven areas where the experts were in general consensus and then to put what we hoped were a few focused questions. We still intend to do that, however some of the events of yesterday require some broader comments on Canada's understanding of the purpose of this meeting and the rulings that you made on how we were to proceed.

497. We came here prepared to comment on and explore the Panel of Experts' answers to your questions and abide by your ruling that no new evidence would be introduced after 8 February. I believe, Mr. Chairman, that you will recall the purpose of that ruling was intended to provide all participants with an equal opportunity to review relevant material in advance so that informed commentary could be made.

498. Yesterday we all had the privilege to hear some of the world's leading experts comment and debate the properties and characteristics of the substances in issue. Some highly technical and complex issues were discussed with clarity and precision. Unfortunately and unfairly, in Canada's submission, we were sometimes deflected from that very high level of debate by the introduction of new material, some of which was apparently presented out of context and in a selective way. The Panel's experts were asked to make extemporaneous replies on matters they had not had an opportunity to consider in advance. This sometimes led to prolonged discussion

clarifying facts on matters of marginal importance to the issues this Panel must decide.

499. An example, no better or worse than many I could choose, is Dr. Epstein's table on oestradiol residues in eight-year olds, which ultimately led to the somewhat surprising assertion that two quarter-pounders or 110 gram whoppers were the equivalent of 500 grams of meat. If I could be permitted a pun, that was a real whopper! With respect, it is important to refocus the issues these experts are here to help elucidate.

500. The complaint before this Panel concerns a measure of the EC which bans the importation of beef or any of the six hormones, alone or in combination, that have been used for growth promotion purposes in the face of properly established international standards of safe use.

501. One goal of the SPS Agreement is to further the use of harmonized sanitary measures between Members so as to protect health but not unnecessarily interfere with trade. The Agreement permits a Member to depart from these standards for certain prescribed circumstances. The relevant one for the issue concerning the Panel's experts, and the only one in my submission, is a scientific justification. Dr. Randell has spoken eloquently of the high standards of JECFA and Codex and the subject matter that was taken into account in establishing the standards of both the natural and synthetic hormones and the very conservative assumptions adopted to ensure safety through the use of ADIs and MRLs where required. It is clear that these organizations are to be commended for their work and nurtured rather than criticized.

502. We have learned that studies have been conducted for more than 12 years to try and prove a hypothesis that oestrogen is genotoxic. Many of these studies were known to and considered by JECFA. Dr. Liehr, in one of his studies, has injected comparatively massive doses of oestrogen in a male Syrian hamster in an experiment designed to produce tumours. The quantities are about twice the dose given to cattle. Dr. Lucier, as I understood him, agreed that in light of this evidence there was a risk, but he puts that risk at a level somewhere between zero, a concept which cannot be achieved in absolute terms, and a factor so small that it cannot be measured.

503. The question for this Panel is this in my submission: is that a risk that justifies departing from an international standard in light of its impact on trade and the objects of the Agreement. One way of testing that, Mr. Chairman, is by comparing other EC sanitary measures where there are similar or greater risks. Canada will pose some questions on the issues of consistency or lack of it in the EC's handling of these and other veterinary drugs.

504. Before turning to those questions I would like to review what Canada submits are the points of consensus between the Panel's experts: (1) good animal husbandry practice is a broad term encompassing good herd health, management practices and includes good practice in the use of veterinary drugs; (2) in the event that good practice in the use of veterinary drugs is not followed, higher residue levels may result.

505. However, given the fact that the MRL was derived from an ADI where a large safety margin has been applied, such an event is unlikely to cause an adverse health effect; (3) consumers are not able to distinguish the meat of an animal treated with growth-promoting hormones and the meat of an untreated animal; (4) observing withdrawal times for the hormones does not guarantee zero residues in meat. No residues detected does not imply that there are no residues present in meat as they

may be present at levels that are below detection; (5) following treatment with the natural hormones, for either therapeutic, zootechnical or growth-promoting reasons, hormone levels will fall to those normally associated with untreated animals. There are no differences between the residues of natural hormones that are endogenous to the animal and the residues of the same hormones administered exogenously to the animal. Extensive data relating to genotoxicity and carcinogenicity were available to the JECFA and were considered by the Committee. The Committee concluded that the five compounds evaluated are not genotoxic carcinogens; and (6) growth hormones have been used in animal husbandry for many years; in some cases up to 40 years and there are no human epidemiological data that suggests a hazard. Adverse health effects have not been observed in those countries using growth hormones.

506. I have just one other point I wanted to raise briefly, not for purpose of resolution but rather to alert the Panel to an additional concern that Canada has. It has become apparent that the European Communities intend to present a slide demonstration at some time this afternoon. I have not seen that demonstration and I do not know the contents of it, but I am concerned that it may well be fresh evidence which would be introduced after the February deadline the Panel has set and I am also advised by some people who claim to have seen these slides that it is of little scientific assistance and may well be inflammatory. If and when the EC chooses to present that slideshow I would hopefully have an opportunity to discuss whether it is appropriate or not.

507. If I may I would like to turn to my questions.

508. Dr. Arnold, on pages 10 to 12 of your written answers you described the evaluations conducted by the EC for oestradiol and progesterone pursuant to Regulation 2377/90. As a result of the evaluation oestradiol has been put into Annex 2 of that Regulation and progesterone is pending I understand. Could you describe the significance of putting these substances in Annex 2 and could you contrast it with the significance of putting a substance in the accompanying Annex 4 and perhaps describe some of the substances that are in Annex 4?

Dr. Arnold

509. I should perhaps spend the first minute describing the working relationships between JECFA Codex and the competent bodies of the Community because I think then you would better understand how this happened.

510. We have set up in the Community a working party obliged to propose maximum residue limits for residues of veterinary drugs in 1984. We started at the beginning without having a true legal basis so it was a big advantage when Regulation 2377/90 became effective on 1 January 1992. If you look, for example, at the Official Journal, or maybe at Volume 6 of the Rules Governing Medicinal Products in the European Community, you will see a whole volume devoted to this issue. You will see the regulation, you will see guidelines, what the requirements are for the evaluation and you will see an annex to that regulation with a list of studies required in order to scientifically evaluate the substances. This list is absolutely identical with the list of JECFA requirements because it has practically been copied from JECFA.

511. I was the Chairman of this Safety Group at this critical time for more than three years and was helping drafting these rules and regulations at that time. This was

also an interesting time because JECFA had just started doing reviews and we quickly realized that this could be of great help to us in the European Community.

512. If I look back at the time between 1984 and 1988-90 we had not achieved to set any MRL because it is really a tedious procedure, and as soon as we were able to cooperate with JECFA and Codex and harmonized our procedures with a system, we also harmonized with the Food and Drug Administration we had regular meetings the EC Commission and various experts with the Food and Drug Administration, there was an exponential growth. If you check the list of MRLs we have so far adopted it is quite a considerable list. But you will find the exposure limits, the ADI, are almost every time identical, those proposed by JECFA with those used in the EC. There are slight differences in the MRLs and this can be readily explained because veterinary practices are not the same in all countries.

513. Coming to the hormones, when JECFA has proposed MRLs and ADIs for hormones it was impossible to discuss this issue in this Safety Group and in the Committee of Veterinary Medicinal Products because it is well known that we have had already at that time the specific agricultural policies and the specific rules. Therefore it was surprising to me, and I told you yesterday, that six years after JECFA had discussed these substances, a Committee of the EC came to the same conclusions that the JECFA position is adopted and they also felt it was unnecessary to set an amount in ADI for oestradiol and was unnecessary to set an MRL and this has been signed by the competent authorities of DGIII, of DGVI, it has been published in the Official Journal. And this demonstrates that, scientifically spoken, what JECFA produces, what the JECFA Codex system produces, even if the results have not been officially accepted in the Codex procedure they are used everyday and to the benefit of the consumer protection in Europe.

514. I wanted to say this at length because otherwise you could have the impression that we feel very uncomfortable with JECFA. In fact the opposite is true.

515. Coming back more specifically to your question Annex 2 is meant for substances which no MRL is needed. I give you maybe two examples. If you use sometimes a local anaesthetic on a horse it might be necessary to set a withdrawal time but this is a ridiculous problem in view of setting MRLs for consumer safety in a community like the EC. This could be a candidate for such a substance, or if the substance absolutely harmless after the evaluation had been done. The usual procedure is that the company has to apply for inclusion in Annex 2 and they have to submit scientific evidence. Harmless substances, mainly harmless substances, for which there is no need to set an MRL, for example, elements which endogenously occur in the body. It is a rather long list and they are put into Annex 2.

516. In Annex 4 it is a little bit more difficult. Originally this Annex had been developed to include substances for which it is impossible to develop any conditions of safe use. This means for real hazardous substances, this was the original meaning. But what then occurred that later we had substances for which there were indications that they could be hazardous and gaps in our knowledge missing information. Since these were all out of patent substances and since no sponsor applied to prolong the presence of these substances on the market in order to be able to develop the missing data, some of these substances have also been included in Annex 4. That means we find there substances for which it is quite sure that they are hazardous under all circumstances and other substances for which there is a strong indication that they

might be hazardous and no sponsor could be identified who is willing to produce the missing data. Maybe this is enough for the moment from my point of view.

Mr. Thompson (Canada)

517. My second question is also drawn from some of the material in Dr. Arnold's answers. By way of prelude I can let you know it is a compound question and there will be some follow-ups that come with it.

518. In your answer to question 2.2 on page 5 of your written answers there is a table that describes the uses of nature identical hormones and their esters in the European Communities. My first series of compound questions are: How are these substances used? Why are they used for oestrus-synchronization and when used for synchronizing oestrus, are the animals treated because they are sick or for a zootechnical purpose? This question may also venture into the expertise of Professor McLean.

Dr. Arnold

519. I cannot satisfactorily answer all your questions and sub-questions. I wanted to show only a few examples of substances for which I absolutely know that they are used. The list might be longer because a list of substances which are in compliance with our rules in the EC has been set up early on the advice by the Committee for Veterinary Medicinal Products, there are more substances on the market. I am not a veterinarian so I cannot really tell you whether this is justified to use these substances for this purpose. What I wanted to show you was how similar some of these substances are which are used on the one side for growth promotion and on the other side for therapeutic and zootechnical purposes, but there are also differences in the esters, and based on this table I developed my answer so these were just examples and I can as a non-veterinarian not justify their use but I am sure they are used in accordance with the directives in the EC.

Mr. Thompson (Canada)

520. I wonder if Professor McLean or one of the other experts can assist me with that information?

Dr. McLean

521. Thank you Mr. Chairman. Oestrus-synchronization is a commonly-used animal husbandry practice. You synchronize the reproductive activity of your herd for a variety of purposes; it may relate to the availability of feed, it might relate to the availability of markets, etc. It is a relatively common animal husbandry practice.

Mr. Thompson (Canada)

522. After use would residues of these administered substances be present in meat and milk of the treated animal?

Chairman

523. I would suggest that all of the experts may take the floor if they wish to do so. Who would like to go first?

Dr. McLean

524. Yes, the residues would be in meat or milk if the animal was slaughtered. It is interesting that oestrus-synchronization that is often used in dairy cattle in a variety of production circumstances and the residues would be in milk.

Mr. Thompson (Canada)

525. If I could continue with that table and some of the information on it. I wonder if any of the experts who feel confident could help me with the use of these various esters in the EC formulations. What are the chemical differences between the esters and why are different esters used and is there any comparison of persistence in the body of these various esters?

Dr. McLean

526. The esters are generally used to alter the rate of uptake of the drug from either the injection site or if it is in some sort of intravaginal device for example, although generally not there, it alters the rate of uptake. But what generally happens is that the oestradiol ester is actually metabolized either at the site of injection in the blood or in the tissue and the bond between the active substance, the oestradiol, and the side chain to which it is bound is readily broken and the active constituent oestradiol 17 beta, or testosterone in its various forms, is the active constituent.

527. There can be under some circumstances small quantities of the ester appearing in the blood and that is picked up by analysis. But those levels are small and no consideration when it comes to looking at the toxicity because, for example, if there were esters in the meat and someone ingested that meat then the enzymes of the gastrointestinal tract of humans that digests normal food readily cleave the ester bond.

Chairman

528. Mr. Thompson, just for the benefit of the Panel, would you anticipate to draw some conclusions from these statements? I am not in a position to do so myself.

Mr. Thompson (Canada)

529. I thought that was the purpose of tomorrow's meeting when I would be presenting oral argument. But the general purpose of these lines of questions and a few others that I have is to try and demonstrate that the European Communities use some of these hormones either alone or in combination for zootechnical purposes such as in increasing the rate of production in sheep and cattle. Notwithstanding that other alternative means may be available they continue to use these substances for these purposes. What I would be arguing tomorrow in a like manner is that North America and other places use growth hormones.

Dr. André

530. Mr. Chairman, I think there is a very big difference between the use of such drugs for therapeutical or zootechnical purposes. In very precisely defined animals, as Professor McLean said, and the use of the same hormones or similar hormones in large scale for growth promotion. No scientist has said that it is a bad thing to use these hormones for therapeutical use. The problem is for growth promotion on large scales on all the animals, it is not the same thing as is being discussed now.

Chairman

531. Is it true that for therapeutical reasons this is done under prescription by assistance of the veterinarian, while the growth promotion is not done so? Can I ask this just for my clarification to one of the experts?

Dr. André

532. In Europe it is done under veterinarian control. Directly by veterinarians in some countries or under veterinarian control by prescription in other countries. For growth promotion we have no experience.

Mr. Thompson (Canada)

533. Perhaps I could continue with some of the other parts of my question and it may become clearer as to the reasons I am asking this. My understanding is that it is not so much therapeutic uses as zootechnical uses in order to increase the production of sheep and cattle so that their gestation periods are reduced and happen more frequently.

534. Can the experts help me with whether there are any synthetic hormones used in the European Communities for synchronization of oestrus such as medroxy progesterone acetate or allyltrenbolone, or whether oestradiol is combined with progesterone in some of these proceedings?

Dr. Arnold

535. I would like to ask my colleagues to assist me. What concerns allyltrenbolone there is an exemption in the directives. This substance can be used because, as I said yesterday, it is not suited for growth promotion. Although the name is suggestive, it does not have the properties of trenbolone. Allyltrenbolone is totally different from trenbolone with respect to the biological facts. So this is the first part of my question.

536. The next part I am not so sure. I know that the European Medicines Evaluation Agency and the CVMP has just finished an evaluation of medroxy progesterone acetate under my recommendation and this does not fit into my picture of what is legal in the EC. Maybe you, François, you know?

Dr. André

537. No, I have no information of this regulatory point but in any case this compound is used for zootechnical purposes and not for growth promotion. It will never be evaluated by EC Organization as growth promoters. It is a very different thing. We are speaking about things that are not of concern with growth promotion here.

Dr. Arnold

538. My problem is that it is synthetic and it doesn't yield the natural hormone upon hydrolysis. That is my point. It is certainly not suitable for growth promotion.

Dr. McLean

539. Medroxy progesterone acetate is sometimes included into an intravaginal device along the lines of the second line on table 2.2 of Dr. Arnold's submission. It is used in a number of countries.

540. If I might just add for the sake of clarification, whilst these substances for zootechnical purposes are used in individual animals, it is not unusual in some prac-

tices for a significant portion of the herd to be treated over the life of a reproductive season, if I could put it that way.

541. In other words, whilst individual animals are treated you might get 10 or 15 or 20, I am not fully familiar with the production procedures of EU, of the herd treated over one part of the year that is associated with the breeding season.

Dr. André

542. Mr. Chairman, may be you are not very familiar with the reproduction control in farm animals. In this case, may I explain to you that the medroxy progesterone acetate is included in a sponge and the sponge is put into the vagina of the sheep with a small cord. During a period between 10 days, 15 days, two weeks or maybe a little more but it is not a problem. Then the sponge is pulled out with a small cord and then after this treatment the animal comes into oestrus and is then inseminated and becoming pregnant in most cases. Only one per cent fail to be pregnant and this maybe could be a problem for these animals, but usually people try again and it is not really a problem. It is not a problem of residue of synthetic hormones because these animals are bred to have sheep and they will stay a long time in the farm. They will not be slaughtered after such treatment. It is not the objective. It is very different to treating animals for growth promotion and to slaughter them at the end. It should be very clear in your mind.

Chairman

543. Is this a step of preventive medicine or is this a treatment for animals who have difficulties to conceive?

Dr. André

544. It is just a so-called zootechnical practice. That means it is more easy for the farmer to have all the females at the same date on oestrus and to inseminate them at the same time and then to have products at the same time. It is more convenient for management of animals. No more

Chairman

545. But it is a standard procedure which is applied to healthy animals?

Dr. André

546. It is familiar procedure. It is applied in sheep mainly. More in sheep I think than in cows.

Mr. Thompson (Canada)

547. Can I understand you to say, Professor André, that farmers did it to their whole herds at a single time in order to assist conception occurring at the same time?

Dr. André

548. If your question is to know if they can buy this product freely, the answer is no. This product is always under veterinary control.

Mr. Thompson (Canada)

549. I had not asked that question. May I proceed with my next question Mr. Chairman?

550. Again I have a somewhat compound question. In answer to question 30 of the Panel concerning the potential adverse effects on human health from residues of carbadox, monesin, olaquindox, avoparcin, benzylpenicillin and carazolol, ivermectin and organophosphorus compounds, some of the experts noted that when used correctly, the residues from approved veterinary drugs should not produce adverse effects in the human population.

551. In question 17 of the Panel the experts were asked to consider the implications for human health of residues from the misplaced implants or improper administration of the six hormones in dispute. And I wonder if the experts could extend their analysis and comment in respect to the residues of the veterinary drugs I read out and listed in question 30, as to what are some of the implications for human health when they are misused in a similar way described in question 17? For example, could the experts explain what adverse health effects may result if a hypersensitive person ingests meat or milk from an animal that was treated with benzylpenicillin, when the required withdrawal period has not been observed and the residues from benzylpenicillin in such meat or milk exceeds prescribed MRLs, as an example.

Dr. Arnold

552. Maybe I can partly cover this question. I am a little bit reluctant to compare the hormones with carbadox because both substances have been regulated, or proposals have been made by JECFA concerning these substances, that in both cases if good practises are observed there is no appreciable risk. So I could say they are equally safe if good veterinary practices are observed. Because although carbadox itself is a genotoxic carcinogen, it is so quickly metabolized that if good practices are observed neither carbadox nor its main carcinogenic metabolite is present as a residue. Only an innocent metabolite quinoxaline carboxylic acid, which has been extensively tested including carcinogenicity, and this is the compound on which the MRL has been proposed.

553. If somebody does not respect the withdrawal time there might be an increase in this innocent metabolite, but the closer you come to the administration there is an increasing risk that the carcinogenic compound itself or its metabolite is present. For example, at zero time of withdrawal it is obvious that it would be present and that now you have a different quality of risk and how do you compare this? If I am a little bit reluctant and I must insist that it is the aim of our procedures, to check whether conditions of use can be proposed which if followed guarantee that there is no appreciable risk. And if the possible risk is qualitative in nature how do you prepare this? This is the first part of my lengthy answer.

554. Concerning benzylpenicillin, I had looked carefully at benzylpenicillin, I was consultant to WHO at the time benzylpenicillin had been evaluated. What is interesting to see is that about 15 per cent of the world population, some figures are higher, other figures are lower, are sensitized against benzylpenicillin. But we have carefully looked at all the reported cases. Only a very small number of cases one can discuss between five and ten but in no way more than ten, have been observed over the many years of use. Billions of doses administered of benzylpenicillin to human individuals causing sensitization but few cases where residues were the cause of an allergic reaction. The levels proposed by JECFA of benzyl penicillin are so low that

in the whole literature you find only three cases where a lower level has caused an effect in a human being. The dairy industry needs these low levels too because the most sensitive population in this case are the starter cultures used for yogurt production, for example. They are much more sensitive than human beings. So the human consumer benefits from this that the mix cannot be used for food processing purposes if it contains high levels of penicillin.

Chairman

555. Thank you Dr. Lucier.

Dr. Lucier

556. I have a couple of questions, before I attempt to answer the question. So carbadox does produce tumours in the long term bioassays in rodents, is that correct? And are there multi-sites more than one site of cancer in the animals?

Mr. Thompson (Canada)

557. I don't know if I'm qualified to answer that question. I understand that it's 11 out of 12 sites; perhaps Man Sen Yong can answer the question for us?

Dr. Man Sen Yong (Canada)

558. Well, actually I think the JECFA has done the concrete evaluation of the toxicology of carbadox, including the genotoxicity and carcinogenicity. So maybe I would have the JECFA persons to answer for that.

Dr. Lucier

559. Let me ask one other question while you are looking that up. How are, in relation to Dr. Arnold's answer, carbadox residues ever found in products consumed by people? And if so are the MRLs exceeded from time to time?

Dr. McLean

560. An MRL was not set for carbadox and nor was ADI specified. And it's permitted for use providing with a sensitive regulatory method you cannot detect residues. It's a metabolite desoxycarbadox that's carcinogenic. It's a short-term intermediate metabolite between carbadox and quinoxaline compound. And also quinoxaline-2-carboxylic acid, the end-metabolite, there were carcinogenicity studies on that as well as the intermediate desoxycarbadox. So you have the parent compound desoxycarbadox and the final metabolite. It's a compound that's used widely in some countries including the EU and the recommendation of JECFA was that they could not on the evidence presented state an ADI or an MRL for genotoxic carcinogenic.

Dr. Lucier

561. So residues are never detected I guess of carbadox?

Dr. Arnold

562. If the withdrawal time is observed we will not even find it quinoxalinic acid with routine methods. However, with more sophisticated methods you can show that up to 70 days after treatment this metabolite persists.

Chairman

563. Can I briefly just for my clarification now ask the Panel whether they consider it possible to compare the use of the hormones we are talking about and the substances we were just discussing, you were reluctant to do so. Could I have the views of the others whether this is coming into a category where we could really start comparing the use.

Dr. McLean

564. I will try and shed some light on it Mr. Chairman. When an ADI set for a compound, providing that ADI is not exceeded, then the risk associated with consumption of produce containing the compound in question up to the ADI is essentially zero. Now I use the word essentially to putting emphasis on the fact that zero risk is not an obtainable figure. However, if you exceed the ADI, then the nature of the risk varies from compound to compound. For example, if you seriously exceeded the intake of certain compounds, then depending on this toxicological profile, you may cause some quite serious effects. However, many of the ADIs are set on a relatively minor change such as a body weight change and change in an organ weight, some minor variations in some constituents of blood. So therefore to exceed the ADI in that case would not be as serious. And so what we do is we determine a level where there is no observed effect in the test animal systems, then we apply a safety factor and by doing that you essentially reduce the risk of consuming an amount equal to the ADI on a daily basis for lifetime to zero. However, once you begin to exceed that ADI you introduce risk. The rate at which that risk comes in, if I can put it that way, and the intensity of that risk varies from compound to compound, depending on that toxicological end point which made the no effect level upon which you derived the ADI. You've got a further question I guess?

Chairman

565. Dr. Lucier, on this comparison question.

Dr. Lucier

566. That's where I was trying to get some information so that I could determine whether or not such a comparison could be made, in terms of at least carcinogenic risk. I think that what Dr. McLean was talking about was not essentially a carcinogenic risk that was a hormonal activity risk. So they are two different things, two different methods to establish risk, but I was just trying to determine with the information available if it would be possible to compare the carcinogenic risk at residues that might be normally encountered versus the residues that might be normally encountered from the six hormones in question.

Dr. Ritter

567. But the issue Mr. Chairman, I think as a number of people have already attempted to explain, is that at permitted residue levels, none of these compounds constitute a risk. That's the nature of the process of establishing an ADI and subsequently a MRL. It presumes that there can be lifetime dietary exposure, every day of your life, and that continuous dietary consumption will pose, for lack of a better term I'll say essentially no risk at all. The question that you are asking in fact is what if that residue level is exceeded? It goes beyond what's been specified in the regulation, or internationally, and I think the attempt that's being made by way of explanation is

that it would be potentially misleading to suggest to you that these risks can be compared, because the ADIs that we've referred to repeatedly are based on entirely different end points. They can range from something relatively innocuous, in which case if an ADI is exceeded the consequence would be relatively trivial. And they can on the other hand extend to such issues as carcinogenicity, in which case it would be potentially a very serious consequence. So to compare the two, simply because they both have an ADI, presumes that that ADI has been established on a similar end point. Which is almost never the case.

Chairman

568. Would you think that the fact that the use above the ADI levels varies greatly also induces the possibility to have them regulated differently?

Dr. Ritter

569. I think the nature, having been involved in the process of setting ADIs both nationally in my own jurisdiction and participating in the process on an international scale, one is left with the impression that the nature of the process is such that there is a significant margin built into the process, that in fact will have the effect of compensating for that in any case. I briefly alluded to some of those yesterday. For example the assumption is, one of the assumptions we discussed yesterday, is the consumption of 500 grams of meat per day. I mean I think we can all probably agree that in first principles that's an overestimate. And so the risk has probably been exaggerated in the calculation. That you will consume that risk every day of your life and so on and so forth. So I think collectively as toxicologists involved in that kind of a process, we have the impression that MRLs that are temporarily exceeded, occasionally exceeded, infrequently exceeded, are not likely to result in a significant health consequence, because the calculation has already built in so much overcompensation, that these occasional transgressions are not likely to produce an adverse effect. That's the inherent nature of the calculation itself.

Chairman

570. Is this a view shared by the Panel?

Dr. Lucier

571. I'm still searching for an answer to help me. I recognize that the carcinogenic risk of these agents is very low. Within that range of zero to very low, if I could get information I could say whether or not the risks were comparable for cancer. Now this is the genotoxic carcinogen, one accepts an ADI is established not on the basis of carcinogenicity for genotoxic carcinogens its on the basis of something else.

Dr. Ritter

572. In the case of carbadox I think Dr. Lucier, what has been explained is that there is no ADI and there is no MRL, because it was the consensus of the Panel that reviewed the material that as a genotoxic carcinogen we were unable to establish what would popularly be referred to as an acceptable intake. The acceptable intake is nothing.

Dr. McLean

573. We would not normally set even an end point based on carcinogenicity, because generally carcinogenicity occurs at much higher doses than we would set a no-

effect level. If the no-effect level was based on carcinogenicity, we would look at the compound and alter safety factors and other things, or again we might not permit it. And so in this process, in managing the risks through the ADI, the aim is really to make sure that you don't end up with carcinogens, as a result at least of animal toxicity studies, in the food chain.

Chairman

574. Perhaps, Dr. Lucier, you mentioned two different methods of determining risks. One would be for hormonal action and the other for carcinogenic effect. It seems to me that we have an established method for the first one and the second one is somewhat new to the field here. Could you elaborate a little bit on the second method and how you see the implications in that particular field here, in particular when we talk about whether these substances can be compared or be treated alike and so on.

Dr. Lucier

575. If I saw the tumour data for carbadox, I could establish a level at which a certain proportion of the animals got tumours, and as best I could, I could extrapolate down into the very low level risks what people might be exposed to. There would have to be some residues left of carbadox, just maybe not detectable, there have to be some residues left. And I could compare that carcinogenic risk to that from oestradiol or any of these other hormones in question. Now, that's a comparative risk of carcinogenicity the comparative potency in what people ingest from 500 grams of meat a day. So that would be a direct comparison. I would have to assume what carbadox levels exist and that was why I was wondering how often they are detected in fact in meat samples, if ever, and what the limits of detection would be. Then I could take, you know, something below the limits of detection of what people are exposed to and do the calculation on a rough estimate with considerable uncertainty but at least to see if the carcinogenic potency is in the same ball park or not. That's all that I'm after.

Chairman

576. Is such data available or not? May I ask the experts?

Dr. Arnold

577. I have never seen positive results and I see residue monitoring data since many years. But it has not been intensively monitored on the other side, that is the other difficulty. But I could perhaps say that at least in the Community it is only used in piglets up to a maximum age of 4 months, so it's quite realistic that the withdrawal times are observed and then there is no carcinogenic residue in the tissues, just maybe a trace of this innocent metabolite.

Dr. Lucier

578. I won't belabour this any more after this one point. If apparently there is tumour data that is summarized, if I could look at that sometime during the afternoon I'll do my little calculations. My intuition tells me that the risks are going to be similar, carcinogenic risks.

Mr. Thompson (Canada)

579. I'm advised that there may be residue data for desoxycarbadox, but perhaps if I could restate the question. I think we are not coming directly with what I was getting at, we have heard statements and, I think Dr. Ritter was drawing attention to the fact that when JECFA and Codex review and approve things and set standards it is assumed that there is no risk associated with any of these substances, any of the six hormones at issue, or carbadox, or carazolol or the benzylpenicillin. The experts had been asked to speculate if the standard administration procedures are abused in respect to hormones and proper procedures are not followed, is there a possibility of a carcinogenic effect. And we have heard that in respect of some of the hormones the answer was, while close to zero risk, yes. And I've been asking in respect to something like carbadox, which has also been described as genotoxic carcinogenic, where an MRL and an ADI cannot be set because of it, if we take the hypothetical situation where it has been abused, administration has not been properly followed, can we draw the same conclusions? Or to put the matter another way, is there a rational reason to distinguish between permitting substances which are genotoxic carcinogenic is like carbadox and permit their use, while imposing a total ban on hormones which are said to have no risk, verging on zero as well?

Chairman

580. Who would like the floor?

Dr. Arnold

581. Since you are asking for data, maybe for the record I could tell you what we have seen at JECFA when pigs were treated with carbadox. The residue level of this, I call it innocent metabolite, quinoxaline carboxylic acid was 18.9 micrograms per kilogram at 30 days withdrawal; was 5.5 micrograms per kilogram at 45 days, 1.3 microgram per kilogram at 70 days withdrawal.

Chairman

582. This goes to the previous question. Would you come back on the figures here?

Dr. Lucier

583. I actually do have the tumour data. Carbadox is a pretty potent carcinogen in terms of multisites. So the answer to your question is yes if improperly used and there were residues it would pose a carcinogenic risk.

Mr. Thompson (Canada)

584. And just before we leave that perhaps I could ask Dr. McLean to expand on his answer to question 11 where he discusses organophosphorus compounds and the health effects there. Perhaps I could ask him to comment on carazolol which I understand is used for transporting pigs immediately prior to slaughter and the comparative withdrawal periods, and whether there are any risks associated with the use of that drug.

Dr. McLean

585. In relation to the organophosphorus compounds, they are quite powerful neurotoxins in humans and in animals, and are used generally to kill insects although

there are other uses for them such as removing foliage from certain crops. There are two problems with them, one is delayed nerve damage and that is generally a result of direct exposure of operators and the like. However, under some circumstances residues in crops in excess of the no-effect level have caused problems, acute problems of organophosphorus poisoning. And some of them are carcinogenic and so therefore safety factors to remove the carcinogenic hazard in the appraisal, that's been taken into account although, generally, the safety limits are based on acute effects that the poisoning effects that you see. But they have been associated with poisoning associated with exceeding the MRL. In relation to carazolol, carazolol does have an effect of lowering blood pressure and heart rate, it's related to the drugs commonly used in human to control blood pressure and heart rate. It is also used to prevent a specific form of stress in pigs during slaughter. And of course pigs are sent from the farm directly to slaughter generally and if you are going to have an effective treatment for the stress associated with transport, then you have to treat them just before transport so that the drug is effective during the transport process. And there has been concern that if people were to ingest carazolol at the site of injection then they may get a dose which could have effects on heart rate and blood pressure. The sensitive human population that was taken into account in this assessment are those people already under treatment with this group of agents for the control of blood pressure and associated cardiovascular disorders, and if one was to superimpose a dose of carazolol on top of the existing medication then there could be a problem. So these two compounds in various ways, if the ADI is exceeded can cause difficulties.

Mr. Thompson (Canada)

586. Just a quick follow up. Are the organic phosphates ever used in animal production?

Dr. McLean

587. They are commonly used in animal production to keep under control insects on animals, relatively widely used.

Mr. Thompson (Canada)

588. Yesterday the European Communities quoted fingers, sorry figures, on the number of tests they do for residues of hormonal substances. We understand that Professor André's expertise is in the residue testing. He noted that the EC has developed multi-residue tests. And I wonder, Professor André, could you describe what substances the European Communities test for and comment on how many of these tests come back positive and for what substances?

Dr. André

589. I can give you some comments in the field of my competence, that means on hormones, on thyrostatic compounds and on beta agonist compounds. Concerning the first part of your question I cannot give you a complete list, so today of all the xenobiotic compounds which are looked for in a real multi-residue analysis, but you can imagine that they include progesterone, nandrolone, oestradiol and many others, usually 30 different compounds are looked systematically for. Concerning the thyrostat they are just about 6 compounds usually, small compounds, and they are all of the same groups and derivatives of uroside compounds, true - uroside compounds. And concerning beta agonists the classical research includes now something as ten

different compounds from clenbuterol and its group, I mean manbuterol and others and salbuterol as well as ractopamine and many others. All these compounds have been banned in EC and we are looking for potential misuse of these compounds. The level of detection of this research is very important to consider and its always below 2 ppb. and sometimes reach more sensitive levels as some 10 or 20 ppb's. for looking at residues in meat specifically. Concerning the second part of your question, in terms of percentage of positive results I cannot answer this question as a scientific people and the numbers I can give to you would be wrong numbers for different reasons. The reason is personally I am in charge of an official national laboratory and I have more positive than usual because I confirm results of other laboratories. This question has to be asked to official bodies or maybe to our representative of official Community reference laboratories but not to me.

Mr. Thompson (Canada)

590. I understand Dr. Arnold might be aware of results of testing of residues of hormonal substances in the EC and in particular a study or testing done in Belgium. Could you help us with that Dr. Arnold?

Dr. Arnold

591. I think François André made a good suggestion since the results of the residue testing in the EU are given to all reference laboratories. It's a good suggestion that maybe someone from these laboratories answer the question. On the other hand I also see these results on a regular basis and I, what I can say is something that I have already said yesterday, we have to discriminate between random sampling which gives you a more relevant picture and sampling of suspect animals. And I said yesterday already and I would like to confirm this, if we take the results of random sampling it's not so bad the picture. In the majority of the member States you find nothing. There are some member States, I would not name the member States, but there are some member States where in veal calf there seem to exist problems, mainly with the natural hormones. If we go to suspect sampling then the picture is totally different, then we have member States where we find trenbolone, zeranol, where we find protestosterone, sometimes just a few samples, sometimes a higher amount. But this higher figure is not representative for the situation because this then sometimes are follow up analysis, so I hope I made clear what my point is. Based on random sampling the situation seems to be relatively okay, with the exception of veal calves in some countries. Based on suspect sampling, we find all 30 things sometimes in some samples.

Dr. André

592. May I add just a short complement to these two communications. First of all, its clear that all the compounds I speak about are not looked for in any other countries as in EC. And when we discover some misuse of such compounds, usually and quite systematically I think, the meat is not delivered to human consumption.

Mr. Thompson (Canada)

593. Yesterday we heard quite a bit of discussion concerning hormone levels and I would like to clarify with the experts what is a physiological range and how that range is determined and what controls that range. In particular I believe Dr. Liehr cautioned us that permitting the use of growth-promoting hormones in meat might

upset the balance of hormones in a human ingesting the meat. Can the experts describe what the balance of hormones in the body is; is it fixed or does it change on a daily or weekly basis? And if hormones are added directly to a human, what effect does this have on that hormonal balance? Perhaps some comparisons between the ubiquitous 500 grams of meat and a couple of eggs or a glass of milk which are also ingested on a regular basis would be a useful comparison.

Dr. André

594. Concerning the balance of hormones we need to maybe a week for discussion to explain what is now known about the inter-relations between hormones and the complex feed-backs phenomena and so on. Just to have an idea of the effect of injection of hormones to human beings, it's well known I think that body-builders or sportsmen who are using hormones as anabolizing agents, with higher doses as usually used in growth promotion it's clear, but these people have always later very many problems in terms of reproduction and sterility its clear. That is one idea to illustrate what can a hormone do in human beings.

Dr. Lucier

595. I agree with what Dr. André said. The hormonal situation in your body is changing as we speak. It's changing in my body, you get nervous your glucocorticoids go up, that does other things to you, so they are constantly changing, in constant state of flux. How each of the hormones regulate each other is not an entirely known fact, in fact its not really known at all, except that that type of balance does occur. There's tremendous inter-actions, cross talk as we call it, between different hormonal systems. When this is disrupted there can be a whole cascade of events which could result in changes in biology and potentially adverse effects. After having said that, the amount that one would take in from say if we come back to the example of 17 beta oestradiol in eating 500 grams of meat a day, you basically take in one molecule of oestrogen if you were a women to every 280,000 in your body. So the chances that that would cause an endocrine disruption is probably very very slight, remarkably close to zero. If you are a man your levels would be one-fifth that so it would be one molecule to every 50,000 molecules or something like this, so the chance that that would cause in itself an endocrine disrupting event is of course highly unlikely. There's no doubt that it's causing endocrine disruption in the animals that are receiving it, that's why they grow because their hormone system is disrupted and modified and the balance is changed. It's a question of amount.

Dr. McLean

596. Just by way of illustration of the variation, if people want to turn to the attachment of my submission, you will see the enormous ranges in pregnant cattle, or in cattle of progesterone, oestradiol and testosterone; the ranges and the variations e.g. in pregnant cattle in muscle for example, the levels are 10,000 nanograms per kilogram plus or minus 6,600. Enormous variations. And I think that just reflects the individual animals and so it's terribly difficult to tie this down absolutely and precisely.

Chairman

597. I mean a very popular comparison alluded to, the egg, the amount of hormones you eat with an egg and then it's compared to what you eat when you have an

intake of hormone treated meat. Is that a comparison which can be done and could you elaborate on this?

Dr. Ritter

598. Well I'm thinking we could and in fact a number of responses contain that direct comparison. The steroid levels would be contained in a glass of milk, for example. The steroid levels that would be contained in a feeding of breast milk to a new-born infant would be thousands of times higher than what one might expect in a steak or a hamburger. But if you would like a more precise number I'm just going to.

Chairman

599. It is just whether one can make these comparisons, whether they are sound.

Dr. Ritter

600. I think what I'm intimating Mr. Chairman, is that one really can't because they are in different worlds...

Chairman

601. ... You can't ...

Dr. Ritter

602. Let me put it another way. One can physically make those comparisons, the numbers are available. But there is no basis for comparison. The steroid levels associated with a glass of milk or human breast milk or any number of foods would be many many many times greater...

Chairman

603. ... Yes, but these are the same steroids?

Dr. Ritter

604. Exactly the same. We are talking orders of magnitude difference in terms of the dimension vis-a-vis the levels of exposure from a hamburger resulting from an animal that has been treated, when compared to a glass of milk that you might have from an animal that's never been treated at all.

Dr. Arnold

605. My colleagues have limited their statements to the identical molecules. If we would add to those identical molecules other naturally-occurring hormones in food which have a different potency maybe less potent, but have oestrogenic action for example, then we would discover that in many kinds of natural food including plant origin we find such activity. The steroids and their derivatives, as I said yesterday, were very successful in evolution. So, even if you go down to molluscs to sea urchins, you find these substances, you can't escape eating these substances, or similar substances with related biological potential every day. So, there is no way even if you decide to castrate yourself, in addition to starve to death, to escape these hormones.

Dr. Ritter

606. My colleague Professor McLean points out that in the second submission of the United States (28 October 1995) that sort of comparative table, I have personally not verified each one of these numbers, but that sort of comparative table is in fact is

presented on page 4. The intake of oestrogen or oestrogenic equivalents ranges from tens of thousands in the case of soya beans; the case of in an egg, you referred to an egg as 17,015 nanograms, and when we are looking at an oestradiol implanted steer, levels that have been estimated are somewhere in the order of 11 nanograms. A glass of milk might represent 75 nanograms in this table, cabbage 24,000 nanograms. I emphasize that these are oestrogen equivalents because in some cases it is oestrogen directly, in other cases these will be what is sometimes referred to as phyto-oestrogen which are compounds which are not quite oestradiol but are known to have an activity that is what we sometimes refer to as an oestrogen mimic, it's an oestrogen want-to-be. Zeranol is in fact produced for exactly that purpose. It is not oestradiol directly, but it is clearly, it is produced as a result of a fungus, but it has an action which is so similar to oestradiol although the potency is somewhat different, that we call it an oestrogen.

Mr. Thompson (Canada)

607. Just to follow up on that a little bit, as is obvious to every one I'm not a scientist and simple examples help me. Someone has suggested an example for dealing with physiology is to compare it to a thermostat in a house where there is a range of temperature that is contained and within that range are normal things that occur, and the temperature may vary up and down but that's a normal occurrence. And when one drinks milk or eats eggs or consumes cabbage there will be an increase within that normal physiological range. One of the things I wanted to follow up on, and perhaps Dr. Lucier can help, as he drew the comparison with the 500 grams of treated beef of one molecule from 28,000, by comparison are you able to help us with how many molecules per 28,000 we might find with a glass of milk in a pre-pubertal boy, the glass of milk for breakfast?

Dr. Lucier

608. Just say young boy! to save further embarrassment!

609. Now the numbers for milk I have are a little bit different. I have them for 17 beta oestradiol and they are a little bit higher than what you see in muscle tissue, I have no way to know, since I haven't done the measurement myself, which numbers are accurate. These things as has been stated before, are present in milk and virtually everything we eat, oestrogen. So, you get an oestrogen load in addition to your endogenous oestrogen from a number of different sources. Not only the natural 17 beta oestradiol from what you eat but also from the phyto-oestrogens and the fungal oestrogens that were already talked about. There's a considerable amount of phyto-oestrogens in soya products especially soya oil. So we are exposed to a lot of different kinds of oestrogens just from day-to-day living that are exogenous, not produced by our own body. It would be very difficult for me to total them all up and that's one of my actual research interests to try and do that to see what the body burden oestrogen that we encounter from day-to-day living from exogenous sources, to get some idea what the risk of various kinds of disease might be because of those exogenous sources. So I cannot give you a very good answer except to say this would only be, the amount one received from eating 500 grams of meat, would be relatively small compared to the other sources of exogenous oestrogen one receives.

Dr. André

610. Mr. Chairman may I give you another example of hormone interactions, in relation to the quantity of hormones in order just to illustrate what has been said previously. We have known hormone the name is cortisone which has various properties and anti-inflammation properties. And we have always a secretion inside of these compounds. When you have, for example, an acute inflammatory process the physician will give you a high dosage of exogenous or similar compounds as cortisone, for example. And then your own secretion will decrease dramatically in place of the exogenous compound but after this maybe a week later you will no more need the .... [tape ends]

611. For a chronic skin disease you will take very, very small doses of the same compound, cortisol or cortisone or another one, and your own secretions will decrease very, very slowly. But if you take these very small compounds as drugs during months, and then when you will stop, you will never recover your own secretions. It will have stopped definitely.

612. That's the difference between an occasional use and a permanent use.

Chairman

613. What will be the conclusion?

Dr. André

614. We cannot compare the food intake of drugs or hormones in meat occasionally, or the consumption of a pregnant cow, beef for example, which can give you a lot of hormones and the small amount of hormone food intake for all the population during months and years. It is two very different things.

Dr. McLean

615. If I could give you another example, as a male contraceptive agent, male humans are given testosterone, which by feedback mechanism, inhibits the production of sperm. This form of contraception in human males is being trialed at the moment. In other words, you are giving extra testosterone and the pituitary gland sends a message down that there is too much testosterone and shuts off the natural production, but at the same time, it shuts off some of the hormones associated with sperm production, and renders the individual temporarily sterile. And of course once you remove the testosterone being administered to the male, then it all comes back to normal. That is therapy that is undergoing trial, at the moment, in a number of countries of the world.

Chairman

616. Could I just come in with one question which puzzles me? When we see these naturally-occurring high exposures in milk or eggs, how does that relate to the cancer research we heard yesterday? Is the risk that is being assessed today where we have seen some thesis on it, is that equally valid for this naturally-occurring intakes every day or is there something special when we talk about growth promoters? Could Dr. Lucier perhaps elaborate?

Dr. Lucier

617. Let me do the best I can on that. If you start out with a pre-menopausal woman and her oestrogen level which of course is very high, this results by a tu-

mour-promoting mechanism, and I don't think I need to go into that at this point, in about one woman getting cancer in every ten. So, out of every ten women in their lifetimes, one of them will get cancer. And that's primarily the consequence of her naturally-occurring oestrogens. And that's the point, and I've made a lot of comparisons throughout this meeting.

618. If you look at the beef, eating 500 grams of beef, you would get one molecule for every 28,000, the pre-menopausal woman normally has, and one could estimate a cancer risk based on that.

619. If one says then from other sources, besides beef, there is a hundred molecules, and I'm just pulling that number out of the air, but say it's a hundred, and that's probably a conservative estimate. Then, that would contribute a hundred molecules and so the cancer risk from all other sources of exogenous oestrogens would be a hundred times that what it is in beef, from a growth promoted animal.

620. So the risk would be very, very small. Eating meat from a growth promoted animal would only represent a small fraction of the total cancer burden caused by exogenous oestrogens, not normally produced by the body. Again, it's impossible to give a precise number for the reasons I said, because there is a vast number of environmental oestrogens out in the environment and we only know about a few of them. We certainly don't know about all of them.

621. I think my conclusion would be based on the assumption that all the oestrogens are acting alike, that they all interact with the oestrogen receptor and stimulate the same battery of genes as a naturally-occurring 17 beta oestradiol. That's certainly true for the more potent oestrogens, some of the fungal oestrogens, some of the phyto-oestrogens, these kinds of things. They activate the same kind of genes so there is a reasonable scientific foundation, for my conclusion, although there is some uncertainty in it.

Chairman

622. Mr. Thompson.

Mr. Thompson (Canada)

623. Professor André, there are a couple of questions I have concerning some of your answers to the Panel and I am hoping you can clarify them for me, in particular, your answer to Question 2. You state in part:

> "On the other hand, if the physico-chemical or organoleptic criteria are concerned by this question, and the question of meat quality can be discussed, significant alteration of eating quality, Lowman et al, and significant loss of tenderness, Gerkin 1995, of meat produced with various implants have actually been reported."

624. When we go to the source of Lowman, the statement does not seem to be supported. I could read from page 48 of the Lowman Report. It says:

> "With regard to the composition of the carcass and the meat, it was apparent that the use of the hormone implants affected a reduction in the percentage of carcass fat, an increase in the percentage lean and a marginal decrease in eating quality..."

as opposed to a significant alteration, as mentioned in your quote. It goes on:

> "... and an increase in the proportion of saleable meat for both heifers and steers."

625. In respect of the Gerkin Article, where you have indicated the Gerkin article identifies a significant loss of tenderness, at page 3323 of the Gerkin Article, the author states:

> "Results of the present study suggest that the use of single implants containing oestradiol, TBA or the combination of oestradiol and TBA, had little appreciable effect on deposition of intramuscular fat or on beef tenderness."

626. Can you help me with how these articles support your statement?

Dr. André

627. It's clear that I have not invented this assertion and that they are also inside. When you see only Lowman abstract, in the last sentence. It says:

> "...with marginal reduced eating quality."

> That means that there is a small reduction of eating quality but there is one.

628. If you discuss about the difference between significant and marginally, marginally can be significant, statistically! Sorry, but statistically, it can be small, but significant!

Mr. Thompson (Canada)

629. I also had a question about Question 6A.

630. This is dealing with whether there is any more recent scientific evidence available with respect to the effects on human or animal health of the use of the six hormones in dispute, especially when used for growth promotion purposes, other than the evidence already taken into account by Codex. And you state as follows:

> "Concerning human health, there is a discussion on the decrease of human sperm counts"

and you cite Nimrod and Benson:

> "An apparent increase of the incidences of hormonally mediated diseases like breast cancer and endometriosis and the decrease in the male/female ratio which are thought to be due to oestrogens in the environment. Whether the use of hormones for growth promotion is contributing to this or not, cannot be scientifically proven, at the present time."

631. When I look at the source, namely Nimrod and Benson, it appears that the conclusion that sperm counts have declined, is in fact controversial. And the only reported decrease in human sperm count refers to counts of men in Paris, over the past 20 years, which is within the European Community and unlikely to be directly related to eating hormone-treated beef.

632. Can you help me with the correlation between the decrease in sperm and the sex hormones at issue for growth promotion here? This question is addressed to Dr. André.

Dr. Lucier

633. The sperm count issue is controversial. Some people feel that sperm counts in the industrialized world are going down, other people feel that they are not. And there is a lot of methodological issues, without going into the details, that are creating the controversy.

634. The decreased sperm count has been reported in more than one publication, however, but that has not removed the controversy in this legitimate scientific debate. It is not only men in Paris. For example, men in California only have half the sperm as men in New York. I'm not sure why! The men in New York are very proud.

635. It is a very a controversial issue. There are data from experimental animals that show that neonatal exposure to oestrogenically active agents does cause a decrease in sperm count, later in life, in the male offspring, and there are plausible biological mechanisms for that.

636. But again, the question of whether or not, the amount received, I think it is highly questionable that the amount received in eating beef from hormone treated animals would be necessary to produce that.

Dr. Ritter

637. To contribute something perhaps to the debate here, I think my colleague, Dr. Lucier puts it quite accurately. The French data that was referred to a moment ago, was published by Pierre Roget, I believe in 1992, in the British Medical Journal. It was the first of subsequent reports that were to come popularizing the issue of declining sperm counts. There were subsequently significant methodological issues identified in that report, not the least of which were that many of these subjects originated from infertility clinics or sperm banks! Consequently, I think it was widely recognized that this may have been an inappropriate sample to use to examine declining sperm counts, or for that matter, anything related to sperm.

638. I think Dr. Lucier puts it quite accurately, when he says that this is very much an emerging area and I think the best thing or the most accurate thing that one can say, is nothing at all, because one can find as many reports in favour of a declining sperm story, as one can find opposed to it. As a matter of fact, the New York data that Dr. Lucier referred to a moment ago, was recently reported by Harry Fish, who declared New York men to have the highest sperm counts in the United States, but no higher than New York men have been for the last 25 years.

639. The point that Dr. Fish was attempting to make is that it would be inappropriate to compare New York men with Californian men, but rather you have to compare New York men with New York men, California men with California men, because there can be many variables that affect sperm count within a geographic region. I think that the point that he was trying to make is that it is inappropriate to compare across wide geographic regions, the bottom line being that it is certainly an emerging area, but one about which the only certainty is complete uncertainty!

Chairman

640. Would you like to take the floor?

Dr. André

641. I read this paper one month ago and I cannot find exactly the sentence but I am sure to find before this evening something so in this paper. I think you read it also, so we can agree at the end of this session that there is something.

642. You cannot say that the sperm elaboration is not under hormonal control, that's clear. And you cannot also say that some alkylphenol ethoxylates have a very dramatic effect on sperm elaboration in men and that these compounds have also some oestrogenic effects. That's clear or not?

Dr. Ritter

643. With respect, I'm not sure it is quite as clear as perhaps you feel it is. The nonyphenol and other ethoxylated compounds, I don't want to get into a side debate here, but there are a number of authors who have published reports indicating that when compared to E_2, in terms of their oestrogenic potency, they are 10,000 times less potent. That order of magnitude. In fact, one author suggested that if we were to call nonyphenol oestrogenic, there would be few substances that would not be considered oestrogenic, on the same scale.

644. But I think to put it more correctly, into perspective, I think as Dr. Lucier indicated, there have been dramatic increases in breast cancer which appear to go beyond those increases that can simply be attributed to the introduction of mammography, particularly in the industrialized world. There have been increases in prostatic cancer, the origin of which seems to be at least in the first instance, related in some significant measure to the introduction of prostatic specific anogen. For those men in the room who are over 40, you'll know the experience very well.

645. The interest in a potential role of the environment in breast cancer, I think, stems from the fact, that when we add up all of the known risk factors for breast cancer, we include the age of first pregnancy, the number of successful pregnancies, the number of lactations, the duration of those lactations, all of those things that we know are important risk factors in breast cancer. We can't account for all of it, and consequently there has been an interest in the scientific community to look for other things that may be influencing the disease.

646. I think it will be some time. Certainly, I doubt very much in my lifetime, where we will be able to demonstrate a clear definitive role for a specific environmental substance. The work is justified because it is the disease that has such enormous proportions that a small contribution has an enormous impact. In the United States and Canada, to put it into perspective for you, there is a new case diagnosed approximately every 29 minutes. So you don't need to make a big dent to have a huge impact. I think the work is entirely justified, but for those who are looking for quick fixes, it's going to be relatively unrewarding. The answer isn't around the corner.

Chairman

647. It's around 4 o'clock. How long are you planning to proceed or shall we make an inception with the Community presentation. What would you suggest?

Mr. Thompson (Canada)

648. Mr. Chairman, notwithstanding the slow start, if you'll permit me, I'll take 30 seconds to thank the scientists for their very helpful and concise answers and turn the phone over to Mr. Christoforou by 4 o'clock, as he wished.

Chairman

649. Thank you very much for your understanding.

650. May I give the floor to the European Communities, Mr. Christoforou.

Mr. Christoforou (EC)

651. I would like to thank the Delegate of Canada for his understanding, in this particular case.

652. Before proceeding, I would like to remind you that we have formally requested through the Panel, Dr. Ritter, the paper of Dr. Truhaut and we would appreciate if we can receive a copy of this paper for our scientists to have a look at this.

653. The speaker who will be leaving very shortly is Dr. Adolfo Pérez-Comas from Puerto Rico, who has been investigating the possibility or the explanation of a wide-scale premature sexual development in Puerto Rico for more than about 20-25 years.

654. I understood there were some problems raised by the Delegate of Canada whether these projections will be made. I can only announce there are, I think, 11 or 12 slides. Some of them are graphs showing the increase or decrease according to which diet is followed, and they are only slides which show what exactly we are talking about. I have viewed myself these slides and what they are. Most of them are documents and charts of estimations and there are only two slides with the effects on children, pre-pubertal girls, what it is about.

655. I would give the floor if our colleague from Canada or probably the United States, would like to make a comment.

Chairman

656. Mr. Brinza.

Mr. Brinza (US)

657. As my colleague from Canada had indicated earlier, we share similar concerns with the proposed presentation. It sounded from the description I just heard, that we are talking about a presentation of new scientific evidence, not a presentation designed to fall within the purpose of this meeting, today, which is to talk about the responses to the 28 questions of the five experts, and therefore we don't see how this is appropriate, at this point in time.

Chairman

658. It's hard to talk about something you don't know. The question is whether this comes in as new evidence or whether it supports what has been submitted by the date. As a practical matter, this material can be introduced tomorrow, at any rate. You could do this in the second substantive meeting. And from that perspective, just a very pragmatic point of view, I think it's simpler if it's done here.

Mr. Thompson (Canada)

659. Are you saying it's possible to introduce evidence of the second oral meeting tomorrow?

Chairman

660. I'm afraid I erred. Lawyers are often known as being champions for procedures. But the very good lawyers are interested in the truth and so sometimes they subject procedures to the finding of the truth, but this does not alter the fact that, yes, we can not introduce new evidence.

661. Whether it's done today or tomorrow. It would really depend on whether it's within the realm of what has been submitted by 8 February.

Mr. Christoforou (EC)

662. The United States has circulated previously a document which was not submitted by the 8 February. The issue about the incidence in Puerto Rico has been argued by the European Communities, both in the submissions concerning the United States extensively, and in the first and second submission for Canada.

663. The issue has been touched. It was within the time-limits. It is not new evidence. It is an elaboration of what is already in the submissions.

664. I could not have the slides so I could send them before the 7th. That is what so-called the new evidence, the slides, but I have here also the documents which I would request their circulation. If you don't allow the slides, so we can circulate the documents and have a look at them, but you will miss the "nice" pictures of girls under the age of 8 with exactly what we are talking about. This is not a new document. They are well aware of the issue. We have debated this during the second substantive meeting. The United States has submitted documents about this case. They are also annexed here so we don't really take just one view. The documents submitted by the United States, are in this document. I can circulate the document if you wish and the slides are there. There's no new evidence in this case.

665. Both of the delegations were aware when we discussed for the first time on 7 January.

Chairman

666. Yes, Mr. Thompson.

Mr. Thompson (Canada)

667. If I could respond, I am not, nor is the Canadian Delegation afraid of the truth. But as an experienced lawyer I know that, just as in science, there are a great many truths. And what I am concerned about, Mr. Christoforou has raised what occurred on 7 January. You will recall that I specifically asked Mr. Christoforou to identify the experts he proposed to call so that we would have an opportunity of preparing ourselves to deal with whatever evidence they had to present. He has never, until yesterday, indicated that this evidence was going to be called or who this person was.

668. As a matter of substantive fairness, irrespective of procedure, it is unfair to permit someone to present one side of an issue that may be controversial and inflammatory without a proper opportunity of having evidence that may go to another point of view.

Chairman

669. Mr. Brinza.

Mr. Brinza (US)

670. I would also point out that whether they are slides or documents, if the point is to go back to issues or points that were raised in previous submissions and making another presentation here, that is not the purpose of today's meeting. That would make this another substantive Panel meeting. That is not what we are here for. The Community had plenty of opportunities in our Panel process to present this and they said that they already have. There is no reason to go through this again today. We are not talking about being afraid of the truth, but as lawyers, those procedures, I like to

think are designed to help to make sure that the truth is brought out and having breaches in those procedures is not a way to ensure a fairness and a fair airing of the facts.

Chairman

671. Mr. Christoforou.

Mr. Christoforou (EC)

672. Mr. Chairman, from what I heard, they both don't deny that the issue of the incidence in Puerto Rico has been discussed extensively in the submissions. This is true. I see Question No. 7 of the Panel to the Experts saying is there any evidence and scientific evidence available which demonstrates that the potential for adverse effects on human health arise and whether there is any evidence to that effect.

673. As we did yesterday, I could have Dr. Pérez explain orally, as the other scientists did, since the issue has already been touched before. If you indeed insist that these slides are not projected, at least, there is a question to the experts and we are allowed to make comments.

674. As we did yesterday, we can elaborate five minutes and then answer the question. Is that really outside what is the understanding of today's meeting? You have been circulating documents yesterday and we can circulate those documents, as well. There is a specific question of the Panel on this issue. So as we agreed yesterday, he may make this presentation ten minutes orally and have no projections.

675. Mr. Chairman, I would forcefully really object to that type of procedure which is applied only unilaterally, in this case, I'm afraid. These issues and facts should be explained in the presentations and there is a question which we would like to comment on and provide a reply and ask a question.

Chairman

676. As I said, it is difficult to talk about something you haven't seen, so logically we have to see it before we can make a ruling. But I don't want to spend too much time on these procedural questions and I would invite you to make the presentation. Then the parties would have an opportunity to comment on this, if they want to, the United States and Canada. So the fairness is preserved.

677. The Panel would perhaps reserve it's right to submit one or the other question to the experts. So may I ask you to go ahead with the presentation?

Mr. Christoforou (EC)

678. What should I understand by presentation. Should I make it myself?

Chairman

679. No, no. Your expert, please.

Dr. Adolfo Pérez-Comas (EC)

680. Thank you Mr. Chairman. Good afternoon ladies and gentlemen, members of the Panel.

681. My name is Adolfo Pérez-Comas. I am a pediatric endocrinologist and clinical geneticist, fully trained under United States' standards and certified in endocrinology and medical genetics under United States' standards and an advisor to the Centre for Disease Control and the National Institute of Health in the United States

in the area of my specialty, participating at different ongoing steering committees, both at the CDC and NIH. I am also an associate professor of pediatrics at the Ponce Medical School and previously at the Mayaguez Medical Centre and the University of Puerto Rico Medical Science campus.

682. We are going to present to you today accurately documented data collected in Puerto Rico that has been published in prime medical journals, such as the Lancet, the New England Journal of Medicine, the Journal of Pediatrics and the American Journal of the Diseases of Children, as well as in the Puerto Rican Medical Association Medical Bulletin that is a certified journal in index medicals, and all of these journals are peer-reviewed by leading scientists in the field, in the United States and in the world.

683. I will condense here the 50-year history of Puerto Rican exposure to hormones with 28 years in the practice of pediatric endocrinology with 14 slides presenting anomalous sexual development in my country.

684. I might also add that Puerto Rico is the second-largest producer, at the moment, of oral contraceptives and has been exposed for over 40 years to oral anticonceptives because they were tested in Puerto Rico prior to its commercial disposition in the world.

685. Original studies were carried out in the island of Puerto Rico in the late 50s.

686. The aspect considered today has been presented at guest lectures in the United States, Canada, Spain, Cuba, Venezuela and the Dominican Republic. This is a summary of the patients we have seen under our care, dating back to 1969, up to the year 1985 and part of 1986, where most of the studies carried out by the CDC were done at the same time. We are not including recent data. We are just going back to the date when the data collected by the CDC was taken on.

687. This is a year-and-a-half old female child that presents anomalous sexual development, categorized as premature telarche, because she has isolated breast development, that is not normal for a child eighteen months old. Breast development should appear normally in our population after eight years of age. If you have pubic hair or laxial hair, that should not appear before the age of nine years, and if you have premature menses or menarche, it should not be present in anybody before ten years of age. Anyone of those conditions that appear before those ages, is not normal. It may be secondary to these different processes or tumours in the organism or it may be secondary to exogenous hormones in different areas that can be present.

688. This is a ten-year old girl who presented breast tissue at seven years, who presented pubic hair at a normal age, at ten years, who presented menarche at a normal age of ten years, but who also presented polycystic ovaries, a highly elevated serum total oestrogen for her age and extremely developed breasts, that I classify as virginal hyperphacial of the breast, a condition that was not previously associated with premature telarche or with increased serum total oestrogen.

689. This is another aspect of the problem we are seeing in Puerto Rico. We have severe cases and we have mild cases and it affects children of any age and it affects males, it affects females and it doesn't affect only Puerto Ricans. It affects continentals, North Americans living in the island, German people living in the island, people from Latin America living in the island. Once they get there, some of them suffer from these problems.

690. In the patients we have studied up to that date, we measured, in a significant number of them, the level of oestrogen. And we measured specifically that serum total oestrogen that were carried on under the same standards of Dr. Arnold presented yesterday, in the table with the normal value as specified and this procedure was carried on in different United States' research and commercial laboratories, Biosign, Intersign, Project Clinical Laboratory in mainland United States and not in Puerto Rico.

691. Approximately 85 per cent of those male patients who were tested and 86 per cent of the females that were tested, presented high oestrogen levels. I am speaking of 522 patients here and I am speaking here of 146 males with a high oestrogen level. I am not speaking of 30 patients, of nine patients or of 15 patients. These are a significant number of patients who presented high oestrogen levels.

692. When we started studying these clinical cases in the early 70s we found an increased size of the uteri. At that moment we didn't have available sonographic studies, laparoptomies in some children we have to investigate what happened in the ovaries. The uterus was found enlarged in some of them with the present ovarian cysts. When we started having available pelvic sonogram, this study was also done in a significant number of patients who can afford to pay for it. Out of 447 pelvic sonogram studies, in females with anomalous sexual development, 276 of them presented abnormal pelvic sonograms, enlarged uteri, polycystic ovaries, the same that can be seen in oestrus, in animal husbandry.

693. 62 per cent of those girls presented ovarian stimulation syndrome. When we studied the bone cage, we found that in 26 per cent of our patients, the bone age was accelerated. This implicates that the excess of hormones that was present in these children have been of more prolonged duration because it was accelerating the bone age of our children. This data has been published in the New England Journal of Medicine, has been published in the journals I have mentioned previously, and can be corroborated by anyone.

694. We were searching for the possible cause of this in our island. We looked for exogenous causes because the condition didn't fit what it should be in a normal endocrine situation.

695. As a pediatric endocrinologist, I should see one, two or three patients with abnormal sexual development in a year. Once upon a time I was seeing four or five a week and some days I was seeing three or four, in the same day, new cases.

696. We found in 1982 that the diethylstilboestrol was being sold over the counter in Puerto Rico, this was done in one local agricultural store in Puerto Rico. That Ralgro or Zeranol was also being sold over the counter at that time. DES was banned in the United States at that time and Puerto Rico has the same rules and regulations as the United States, and due to that, we started suspecting that something was in the feeding our children were getting and we started a group of our patients on a diet. We modified the diet with limited ingestion of meat, poultry, milk and eggs. In a period of four to six months, the males that were on a diet, 60 out of 103, 58 per cent of them presented a partial remission of the condition. The abnormal hormones in the blood started going down, the breast tissue that was present started to diminish, those that had pubic hair showed no difference, it did not increase, but it didn't disappear.

697. In the females, we observed more at the same period of time, 51 per cent reduction with the diet and a partial remission and even a total remission of the symp-

toms we have observed before. As I pointed out previously they have been published by that date. 11 per cent of the females and six per cent of the males on no diet, also had a remission, but the remission presented in a year and a half to two years. In an obvious period during which the diet may have changed by itself in growing children. This confirmed indirectly that we were dealing with some kind of exogenous contamination. There were not cases of true precocious puberty by endogenous origin.

698. This remission is presented here regarding the different ages in 1969, 1970, 1972, 1973. There was very small remission because we had not introduced the diet. When we introduced the diet modifications and after there was a big public awareness in the island when this situation appeared in one patient in the Time magazine of the United States, the remission started increasing. Not everybody remitted but a significant number of them did so with the modification in diet.

699. The FDA did some screening studies and this is a copy of one of those studies, where a poultry from Bonito Puerto Rico and a poultry from Royal Brothers Processing in Mississippi were found in this screening study as positive for oestrogenic substances. Posteriorly it had been reported that these were negative in the next studies that were performed by the Federal agencies.

700. Dr. Carmen Saenz who has been working in this area with me, who at the same time presented a publication in the same bulletin of Lancet as I did, I presented a 272 page and he presented 350 of the same condition. She measured percentage of zeranol through a laboratory in Paris by Dr. Morfine where five out of six patients that were so tested revealed levels of what appeared to be zeranol, by that time or a zeranol-like substance, confirming indirectly the suspect we had.

701. We have now a screening test positive for oestrogens and a test, possibly positive, for zeranol.

702. In 1986, Dr. Fred E. Titulowel(?), another collaborator from the CDC, published an article on an epidemiological study done in our patients in Puerto Rico. 50 of my patients, 60 of the patients of Dr. Saenz and approximately 20 more patients from the University Pediatric hospital in St. Juan.

703. Initially, we were told that this study didn't reveal any relation to what we were seeing related to exogenous hormones, but if you look in detail in the conclusions of this study, this study reflects a positive and statistical association between premature telarche and the consumption of soya-based formula, which has been widely known for a long time, various meat products and a maternal history of ovarian cysts.

704. Obviously the mother is eating the same food as the child and the family. With the clinical experience we have with the diet and with the presumption of the laboratory study, we must conclude that we are strongly thinking that an exogenous thing is happening in Puerto Rico and is strongly suggestive of an exogenous contamination by these substances.

705. Last week, on 2 February, the governor of Puerto Rico under the programme of telarche, that is the only one that exists in the world made some declaration to the San Juan Star, that is the local press. The number of children with signs of early sexual development nearly doubled in the past six years according to figures released by a survey by one of the island's top experts on this condition. The statistics adds fuel

to conjecture that Puerto Rico has the highest incidence of premature sexual development in the world. There is no other place in the world with a similar situation said Carlos Bourdony who runs the Health Department's Premature Telarche and Sexual Development Programme.

706. A study to be published in the April issue of Pediatrics, the Official Journal of the American Association of Pediatrics suggests that girls seen in pediatric office practice are developing pubertal characteristics at younger ages than suggested in standard pediatric text books and by earlier United States' studies. Early sexual development has been monitored in Puerto Rico since 1988 when the local health department set up a register, the only one of this kind in the world, according to Dr. Bourdony. To date, 6,115 cases of children with premature sexual development have been documented by the Puerto Rican Department of Health.

Chairman

707. Could I ask you to come to a close. You have one more minute.

Dr. Adolfo Pérez-Comas (EC)

708. This figure is nearly double. The 3,162 cases documented between 1969 and 1991 and do not include the 4,500 patients evaluated by Dr. Saenz and myself. This includes the patients evaluated by the other 11 endocrinologists. [Tape ends]

... studies ..... performed by the USDA Department of Agriculture found no significant or trace level of growth and enhancing hormone in the livestock specimen, according to Bourdony. But in the absence of conclusive research, we can't say this factor has been completely eliminated, as is stated by Dr. Carlos Bourdony, the Head of this Telarche Programme of the Department of Health in Puerto Rico. Thank you very much, Mr. Chairman.

Chairman

709. Thank you very much Professor for your very interesting presentation. The matter was raised, reference was made in earlier proceedings to the Costa Rica studies. We will assess to what extent new evidence was submitted here, in particular, I refer to an April study which seems to be new to us and the Panel will reserve its rights to regard or disregard the evidence submitted in the light of this test here. I would nevertheless as I indicated briefly, give the opportunities to Canada and the United States to comment on this. And I can summarize of course my impression that nothing has been said about the real causes which may have led this situation and it would take very elaborate discussions to go into this here.

Mr. Thompson (Canada)

710. Thank you Mr. Chairman. That would be my immediate reaction as well, as I am unsure how any of this material relates to the issues that the Panel must decide. If I was to be putting questions, I would be interested to know what tests methodology was used for zeranol, were the results confirmed, and what is meant by a zeranol-like substance?

Chairman

711. Thank you very much, Mr. Brinza.

Mr. Brinza (US)

712. Thank you, Mr. Chairman, one moment please. I would like to have some of our experts comment on this very briefly. Dr. Miller who is here with us is familiar with this situation, as are some of our other experts as well.

Chairman

713. Thank you very much.

Dr. Margaret Miller (US)

714. I am Dr. Margaret Miller, Centre for Veterinary Medicine, FDA, and I would like to say that these types of health effects are very disturbing to the Agency and we expended a large amount of research dollars and energy, as did our colleagues at the USDA, investigating this situation. And as a result of that activity we concluded that this situation is not due to the hormones present in meat from animals treated with approved products used for growth promotion.

Mr. Brinza (US)

715. And this is Dr. Richard Ellis who is also familiar with this situation.

Dr. Richard Ellis (US)

716. Thank you, Mr. Chairman. I had a responsibility for coordinating our sampling programme during that special study. In fact we actually conducted three studies, over the periods of which were referenced by this presentation. The third study which we conducted was by far the most extensive one and we looked at approximately 700 samples that were collected from beef animals, pig animals and poultry. We looked at both domestic production from slaughter plants, from imported product at inspection sites, and also product collected at local markets. And as Dr. Miller said, in all of our studies, we did not find the presence of any zeranol, DES or related products in our study. But in as much as we did not have methodologies for all the products that we would have liked to have looked at, we even submitted a portion of those samples for bioassays by FDA. And we had negative results on those bioassays of samples submitted to FDA for that purpose. If it would be worthwhile to the Chairman, when we go back to Washington I would be glad to send you copies of those documents to support my statements. Thank you Mr. Chairman.

Chairman

717. Thank you very much. May I ask whether one of the members of the experts would like to take the floor on this presentation here? Yes, Professor Mc Lean.

Dr. McLean

718. I just would like to make two comments. First of all, I really do not see what this has to do with the issue of using hormonal growth promoters in accordance with good animal husbandry practice. And just a comment, the use of the word "zeranol-like" would suggest to me that there is widespread contamination of food material with Fusarium fungi, for the Fusarium fungus which produces zeranol and its related compounds, so that might give some indication as to what one might look for if one is looking at a contaminant. And I would draw attention to the Panel that zeranol was actually discovered because Fusarium contamination of pig feed, as I remember it, produced signs of oestrogen responses in pigs, as I remember it. It was from there

that the research work identified that it was a product of fungal metabolism by the Fusarium species and on it went there. So I would suggest that the Puerto Ricans might like to invest some money on widespread looking of where the Fusarium is, what species it is and what it is producing. But I do not believe that this has any relevance to today's hearing.

Dr. Lucier

719. Excuse me, if I could add a bit to that. It is known that zeralenone and zeranol-like substances produced from Fusarium do produce hyper-oestrogenism in swine and in cattle, which it fed mouldy corn that contains high levels of this, and likewise it can cause neonatal problems, but these are usually massive amounts. But then I think there have been some Indian tribes in the US who have eaten large amounts of mouldy corn in which there was oestrogenic responses which are adverse as well. So there is information in the literature as to suggest that high levels of these, can cause adverse effects, in a number of different ways. The amounts that are present in growth promoted animals, however, have been very, very much lower than this and would not produce those kinds of changes that they were reported here. Although it is possible zeralenone substances from mouldy corn and other products could do it.

Chairman

720. Thank you very much. Can we close the discussion on this presentation. Mr. Christoforou?

Mr. Christoforou (EC)

721. Mr. Chairman, if you will allow us we would suggest that this presentation is about 90 per cent a reproduction of the document that the United States has circulated during the second oral meeting we had here on 11 November. As rightly Dr. Pérez has said, there are some uncertainties about the actual cause, but he has provided some insights, some information on the potential possible explanations. In the article which the United States has amended to their submission during the second meeting of the Panel, that was the official explanation given by the United States and what we did is that Dr. Stephany has gone today through the article provided by the United States as an explanation of the situation in Puerto Rico. He would like to make a two-minute statement about the analytical methods used, in that article provided by the United States in this case.

Chairman

722. Is it absolutely necessary? Because we still have a list here of questions which are very much to the point here and we do not want to, but I do appeal to you and urge you to self restraint just to really submit issues which are pertinent. Thank you.

Dr. Stephany (EC)

723. Thank you Mr. Chairman. Some material has been disclosed to me yesterday and tonight. I am not quite sure whether that is the document Dr. Christoforou spoke about, so have I to make that restriction, but basically it is not essential. I had the pleasure in 1983 according to my recollection, that Dr. Alice came to my laboratory and we discussed the whole case. At that time we had superior technologies available

for handling these problems, unfortunately samples never showed up and for me the case was closed and only yesterday I saw some details. I will not go into any details but summarizing what I have seen, I was very much surprised about the small amount of potential substances that have been checked or could be seen by the techniques used at that time. That what especially in the field of the zeranol-like compounds, I do not think that I have any criticism basically, but some of the so-called bioassays and receptor-assays I think I have severe criticism that potentially strong oestrogens have slipped through the system, not being detected. So stating it very shortly that nothing has been seen so it could not come from xenobiotic oestrogens, maybe that is a little bit too strong. But Dr. Miller summarized that this did not come from the compounds that are in the regular implants or those implants that once have been regular, like diethylstilboestrol. So I don't want to go into any details, I only offer once again after all those years to cooperate, to clarify this very intriguing affair in Puerto Rico. But whatever the cause is, it is a very serious problem, and I learned from my colleague that the problem has not stopped, elsewhere in the world also similar problems are showing up. That is what I have to say.

Chairman

724. Thank you very much. Mr. Christoforou you may continue.

Mr. Christoforou (EC)

725. Thank you Mr. Chairman and thank you very much indeed. Both the US and the Canadian delegation of this particular issue, which was of serious concern to the Community because we have been making this argument since the very beginning. With your permission then, our next scientist who will be leaving is Dr. Adlercreutz. He has already provided the paper within the time-limits. For this paper the United States have already made comments and I would state that Dr. Adlercreutz will touch only upon one which we think important and relevant issue in this case. I will give the floor to Dr. Adlercreutz.

Dr. Adlercreutz (EC)

726. I was asked to say something about the possibility of carrying over anabolic steroids to humans after eating meat. I have brought with me one of the articles, and the other because I came yesterday from the USA, I could not recover the second one. But in essence it is so that we can never be sure that the farmers really use the substances they are legally asked to use. In this article written by Demetrios Esgotas and Tom Tuten from the Department of Pathology and Laboratory Medicine Emory University School of Medicine in Atlanta. No excuse me. It was Debruyckere, Sagher and Van Peteghem and this is from the Netherlands, in Ghent, Belgium, excuse me yes [passage unclear]. I received this yesterday. In any case they state here, in this country I know that they are very careful with their testing of the meat and they tested in 1990-1991 608 injection sites. And they found that over 60 per cent contain at least one illegal anabolic agent. And I have a very long experience in the

doping field and I would say that I am of the opinion that it is impossible that good veterinary practice is used because there is some big economical benefits of getting a high gross. So I would like to ask the American delegates and Canadians also, whether any such study has been done in the United States, testing really how much illegal anabolic steroids are used. In fact there are two articles, one which I couldn't yet get but I was present at the meeting when it was presented, and they found in people who were not sportsmen and not taking part in any such activities which would need anabolic steroids, they had found one case with nandrolone metabolized in urine which must have come from the food, because there was no other possibilities. And then they did this study here and found in the control group one subject who had clostebol which is anabolic steroid in the urine, despite that there was no possibility that this person had taken any drugs. Then they added a little bit of this drug to meat and fed it to some people and found that they could detect by doping tests these compounds. And we know from the doping field that for example, nandrolone injected into humans can be detected four to six months after they have been given. So, in my opinion it is a very serious thing if sportsmen are caught and getting doping positive samples, if they eat meat. And the risk as well is relatively high, because now it is necessary for every doping laboratory to have high resolution apparatus, so it might be that they can detect even after six months, so very small residues in meat. I mean I'm sure that if you test things in meat and you get negative results you can still find these compounds in urine, absolutely sure, because the urine methods are extremely sensitive and the meat methods are not so sensitive because it is difficult to extract these compounds. So I would like to ask whether this is taken into consideration, that the farmers don't follow the rules and that this is in fact very comparable to the sports field?

Chairman

727. Thank you very much. According to our rules these questions may be submitted to the Members of the Panel and may I invite you to comment on what Dr. Adlercreutz. said and I also refer to the paper which was circulated, the evaluation of the 32nd report of Joint FAO/WHO Expert Committee in Food Additives and the discussion of Professors Liehr's report. Have you been able to read this? But if not, could you comment on the thesis that Dr. Adlercreutz is submitting.

Dr. McLean

728. Pigs and horses naturally produce 19 nortestosterone and we find that derivative of testosterone in their tissues and in urine. They can also, using the same enzymic pathway, produce 19 norsteroid derivatives of anabolic steroids, which is permitted in normal therapy in horses for certain disorders. And so it may well be possible that the human athletes have eaten pig or horse meat which could be the source of 19 nortestosterone, or even may have eaten horse meat from horses which have been treated 19 norsteroids. And so therefore it does not surprise me the sorts of results that Dr. Adlercreutz has reported are so.

Dr. Arnold

729. It seems to confirm what I have said yesterday and today and what I have also said in my written answers. There is a significant black market in Europe and in some countries it is more important than in others. So I perfectly know that, specifically in Belgium, a long list of illegal substances are regularly found. The authorities spend a lot of time and money to analyze many samples. But I do not see what the relevance is either the legal use for growth promotion or for therapeutic purposes. I mean, on both sides of the ocean, we have strict rules and we see an example that on one side of the ocean these rules are violated.

Dr. Randell (Codex)

730. The 1984 FAO/WHO expert consultation certainly pointed out the opinion of the experts at that time that the illegal use of veterinary drugs created a far greater potential public health problem than the regulated use for growth promotion. I think that that finding in 1984 probably still stands. I would like to point out two texts adopted by the Codex Alimentarius Commission, and I might add adopted on the basis of consensus, by the Codex Alimentarius Commission. The recommended International Code of Practice for the Control and use of Veterinary Drugs and the Codex Guidelines for the Establishment of a Regulatory Programme for the Control of Veterinary Drug Residues in Food. Both of these texts exist to guide governments in establishing control practices and in controlling veterinary drug residues. To go deeply into the second one of those texts, it does get into a lot of sampling statistics and unfortunately sampling statistics tend to show that unless you are willing to essentially send all of your food supply to the test laboratory, and therefore starve to death, you are not really going to find what it is you want to find at very, very low levels. So sporadic cases such as we have heard could probably exist even within the framework of a properly regulated control programme.

Mr. Christoforou (EC)

731. Before I give the floor again to Dr. Adlercreutz I would like to say something, something which probably might have escaped the point which we were trying to make. The point we are trying to make is not only from illegal use, it is also as we have heard yesterday from Dr. Lucier, that there is a probability even from the use according to the good agricultural veterinary practice. It may be an increase at what we could call, but we do not know what exactly it is the normal physiological levels. If they are allowed to be used, as it is in the United States and Canada, there is a possibility they may be, more possibility that these increases may be found. And the point Dr. Adlercreutz was trying to make is it may have repercussions not only on trade issues, these questions, but may affect legitimate sports activities because suddenly people by simply eating meat may be discovered to have increased quantities of those residues which they will disqualify them from the games without them having done anything wrong. That is the point Dr. Adlercreutz was trying to make.

Dr. Adlercreutz (EC)

732. This is in fact one of the points. In the other paper, I am well aware that 19 nor steroid metabolites occur in certain animals and so it would be possible naturally and theoretically that these people have been eating, I do not think horse meat as horse meat is not eaten much in Europe, it may be pig meat. But in fact there has not been shown that eating this kind of meat you can get these metabolites in human urine. But here in this paper in fact the clostebol is not found in any animal and here they found one case with clostebol in the control group so there is very little chance that it came from any other source than the diet. But what I would also like to point out is that which I also pointed out in my report, is that we know very little about the effects of this steroid in the brain. And I have personal experience also with regard to the behaviour of athletes both before and after taking anabolic steroids. And we know now because this neuro steroids in the brain occur in very very low concentrations and you need very small things to change the levels of normal steroids in the brain. They are really at very low levels active. So if you think that you consume

meat containing low levels of anabolic steroids every day, they will be transferred via the blood brain barrier and theoretically could interfere in the brain. And I have been involved in police cases and in severe depression cases after taking anabolic steroids and naturally the doses have been high. But now knowing the work by Etienne Emile Beaulieu in France which shows that these are very low amounts which are needed to change, for example, an impression of animal of another animal, can change their levels very little, but significantly. So it is possible that low levels of synthetic steroids can affect our brain long term and very little is known about that and I have not been able to find any studies showing how high the concentrations of, for example, anabolic steroids, are in the brain after intake. I do not have any such material, but I am a little bit reluctant because of this physiological observations made recently in recent years.

Chairman

733. Mr. Christoforou, how long would you intend to go? We want to reserve some time for final questions by the Panel which are important to us.

Mr. Christoforou (EC)

734. Mr. Chairman, I think it may take me probably until quarter to six. It will depend on the replies I will be getting from the questions of course, but about quarter to six or six o'clock, but I have a number of questions and I will cut a lot of them, but it will take me really some time.

Chairman

735. I have a feeling that a break would do good to this meeting. We would resume, if you agree, in quarter of an hour, but try to cut it down to the essentials. Thank you.

Chairman

736. I would like to give the floor to the European Community for continued intervention.

Mr. Christoforou (EC)

737. Mr. Chairman, yesterday we left the discussion at the point where we were discussing the issue why JECFA has not fixed an acceptable daily intake for the three natural hormones. And there was an argument going between, as I understood, Dr. Lucier and Dr. McLean, whether that was first of all feasible to be done and then if it was feasible, why it was not done in that case. This is already with the record of the Panel at this point, but I would like to recall and then come back with the precise question.

738. We have already explained in our second written submission to the Panel that the European Community does apply maximum residue limits and tests, as I said yesterday, 59,000 in serum for the three natural hormones. They are the values given here on page 16 of our second written submission. Exactly the same, the United States has already said in the letter that was sent to the European Community in 1987, and we have quoted these values in the footnote that we have submitted in the second written submission to the United States Panel.

739. For example, the United States has fixed for oestradiol 120 ppt, for progesterone 3 ppb and for testosterone 640 ppt. These are publicly known and have been

communicated to the European Community as being the values that should not be exceeded: the tolerances, the thresholds. But then the United States has replied that although reliable research methods are available for distinguishing these levels from background, a regulatory method is not required because under conditions of use the actual increases in the endogenous steroids are far, far below permitted concentrations. So for that reason they do not include them in their annual control plan.

740. Mr. Chairman, linked to that issue is the explanations were given by Dr. Lucier on the fact that probably the already existing physiological levels are carcinogenic of the three natural hormones, in this case it was oestrogens. The Community has submitted evidence, which was not discredited as far as I know, showing that the increase of the risk was probably two-fold from those residues and not two to five-fold as it is stated for oestradiol in the JECFA Report of 1988. We have also submitted evidence about the increased risks for the pre-pubertal boys - the calculation was wrong.

741. The two issues then linked together and my indirect question to Dr. Lucier would be, according to his own estimation that it may be one in one million the risk of additional risk from the residues of those natural hormones which, for example, if we take the total population of the European Community may lead to about 300-350 potential cancers in the European Community. And on the other side we put, this is also in the record, that the maximum economic potential benefit for the farmers of the use of these hormones ranges between minimum 30 and maximum 80 dollars - that is what it is in the literature. How would you reevaluate the response that is it really from the risk assessment, the risk management point of view, is it really worth while taking into account the potential benefits of the use of that hormone in view of the risks that are already there, as you said for the existing levels, and if you would take our levels that it is even higher. Would you really, as a scientist who is involved in the issue of risk assessment and probably management of that risk, how would you like to express yourself on the regulatory authority and how you would take that into account when legislating?

Dr. Lucier

742. Risk assessment is hard enough, now you are going to ask me about risk management too? I am really not in a position to evaluate benefits versus risk. What I know is how hormones and other agents cause cancer and how to translate that information into as good a science-based risk assessment as is possible. I really have essentially no expertise in terms of quantifying benefits in terms of what the benefit might be economically or what it might be socially, politically, whatever. I have no experience in that so I am reluctant to do that. I appreciate your point and I think it is not a trivial point, but I am really not in a position to give an informed answer to the question. My estimates are, and there is a lot of variability in these kinds of estimates, but generally an upperbound estimate of the risk of breast cancer, and I narrowed it to that particular area because I should think that is where the data is strongest, would be about one cancer in close to a million of people exposed to that by eating 500 grams of meat per day over their lifetimes. So I feel relatively comfortable with that number, recognizing all the uncertainties that are associated with any kind of extrapolated risk assessment and I wish I could give you an answer in terms of how that relates to potential benefits, I don't know. One in a million is not a very high number of course - it is a very low number, but for that one person who does get

cancer it is a significant risk to them, so one can never underestimate that, but as much as I would like to answer your question about the benefits part I really do not have a basis on which to do it.

Dr. Ritter

743. I cannot offer anything with regard to benefit, but I think there is an important point of clarification here. In the estimates that Dr. Lucier presented yesterday, I think what you have done is taken the one in a million that he talked about and multiplied it by the population in Europe and from that projected an anticipated increase of 350 cancers. I think you should note that one in a million is the upperbound. The number could be zero too. The one in a million represents, in Dr. Lucier's opinion, the highest probable risk, not the likely probably risk. But in risk assessment we talk about an upperbound, that is, the highest risk that we can contemplate from a mathematically derived model is somewhere in that range. But it would be incorrect and certainly misleading, and we see this all the time in risk assessment, to use a single number because the nature of mathematically derived risk assessment is that they provide a range of values rather than a single value. I think that was the point that Doctor Lucier was trying to make; that the risk probably falls somewhere between zero and one, and it would be incorrect to cite either zero or one because the methodology simply does not have the degree of certainty that allows you to cite a number, whichever one it is, with that degree of precision - it is a range.

Dr. Arnold

744. I wanted to make two comments on what you have just said in your recent contribution. One thing is important, I think, for the Panel to know. If you design the statistical sampling plan, it is very important what is the population to be sampled, what is the area and I know at least the American delegation can correct me if I am wrong, but I spent many hours with their experts at the Food and Drug Administration. At that year, USDA, the basis is a national residue plan. It covers all of the United States and you cannot directly compare this figure with the figure of the European Community because the plans of the European Community have to comply with certain concepts, but these are plans for the individual member States. So the minimum number required to have a certain statistical certainty, if you take a figure from the United States, and want to compare it to the EC, you have to multiply with the number of member States; so you cannot directly compare these figures. At least for Germany I know that your figures are wrong, but I would also be willing to provide you with the EC document showing that your figure is wrong. I have no explanation, maybe you combine all residue testing, but for the hormones definitely your figure is wrong. I have the paper with me and I am willing either to give you the document or the reference number: they are wrong. So in the EC, I did not have the time to sum up all samples, but it seems to be in the range of 20,000 to 25,000. And as I said yesterday, half of the samples are taken in one country so there are remaining maybe 15,000 or 12,000 for the rest of the member States. And if you then prepare this with the figures of the United States, it is roughly an equivalent programme. That is my conclusion.

745. The second point I wanted to make: I agreed that in the IARC Report the range of this production, daily production, is between 0.4 and 2. It stands in that Report. But nobody has said that the figure used by JECFA comes from this Report. I

was able to trace it back to a paper given by Doctor Farber and Doctor Arcos from the Food and Drug Administration in 1983 at the OIE meeting. I could not go further back, so I am not sure from where the data comes, but I can say they definitely do not come from the IARC Report. I tried to explain how such small differences could happen if you have a very big range and one group decides to use the mean and the other decides to use the median, then you have already this discrepancy. From my point of view, it is in the same order of magnitude and we should not spend a lot of time to say who is right or who is wrong. This figure definitely does not come from the IARC Report.

Mr. Christoforou (EC)

746. Mr. Chairman, I am afraid I will need to insist on this and I will take the time from other valuable questions but we did go back, Dr. Arnold, ourselves on this issue. As you rightly to say in the Report of the International Office for Epizootics, the article by Fabre and Arkas, they cite the article by Argus Engler(?) of 1974. And if you look at footnote 39 of the JECFA Report they cite exactly the same article. So both the Fabre and the OIE Report, both the JECFA Report, relies on the same reference which is 6 micrograms per 24 hours. Whereas the IARC Report of 1987 is based on the values of Brown which are more recent and which we have discussed yesterday - they are not 6 micrograms per 24 hours. We did that research so I can show you the documents if you wish. It is wrong the conclusions you draw.

Dr. Arnold

747. I have said the figure doesn't come from IARC and you have confirmed. Which is the better figure?

Mr. Christoforou (EC)

748. Well, in our view, we use the figures the IARC which are more recent. These figures are also discussed in the issues of Brown and they are not approved. That is the conclusion we can draw. They were coinciding with the figures of which Dr. Lucier was aware as well. But I would also, if we had the time Mr. Chairman, like to go into the comparison of the number of samples because we definitely disagree on this issue with Dr. Arnold, but that will deprive me again of valuable time which I would not like to do. We formally disagree, we have the protocols here, for serum we have checked 59,000 only for the three natural hormones of the European Community and for the total number of hormones checked in the European Community the total amount is just about 200,000 samples.

749. Mr. Chairman, I would like to come back again on this issue of the risk that was discussed between Dr. Lucier and version in the place of Dr. Ritter. The reason for which I pose this question is because the delegate of Canada has made the short statement starting the discussion and he said "Is this little risk enough to justify the departure from the restrictions on international trade" and of course this is related both to risk assessment and risk management and the effects of that. We have probably different views what the magnitude of the risk is. But these are the values we are comparing here. This risk is involuntary for the consumers. We are, of course, aware that maybe zero to one thousand, one million, but it is an involuntary risk for millions of people. The question as a scientist, if you were, you probably don't want to continue the discussion, but I was simply trying to link this to the ADI which JECFA refused to set in this case, although Dr. Lucier would say it is feasible to fix one, we

do it, the United States does it, but they do not apply it, whereas we do apply it, even if the three natural hormones of the Community are only allowed for therapeutic use. The natural hormones are not allowed to be used for growth promotion, still we check for the levels of those 59,000, as I said, in the European Community. This is an involuntary risk. Why should the consumers take such a risk, probably its low, but it is there a risk.

750. The second question of course and I will link this to what I said to Dr. Arnold that relates to therapeutic use. He has mentioned twice the evaluation made by the Institute, the agency in London of oestradiol which is already published as a regulation and of progesterone which is on its way. But Dr. Arnold did not mention probably all the conditions which are imposed for the use of these oestradiol as therapeutic instrument. We know that they have to be administered by a veterinary if it is therapeutic use, we know the animal has to be registered and identified and we know these animals do not go into the food chain because they are not slaughtered. We have provided evidence to the Panel that this percentage is not more than one, and we have more evidence which will provide to the Panel from other member States which have not replied by the end of January which indeed demonstrates that the rate is not over one per cent. These animals might have been treated, as was said by Dr. André, once for therapeutic or zootechnical treatment. But there is in a time-lapse between the treatment and when we decide for that one per cent to slaughter it and to send it to the food chain.

Chairman

751. May I ask you just to submit succinct questions to the experts and not to plead. I think this is not the hour to plead. You have another go on pleading tomorrow, but just please do submit questions and make the best use of this very, very little time we still have available this day. The experts are flying home and then they are gone and we only have correspondence, and I have a whole list of questions which are sustained and I will come in with these questions at 6 o'clock and that is my decision.

Mr. Christoforou (EC)

752. The precise question is, therapeutic treatment, we know what it is - the word explains it - would you think because of the need to have the animals treated for therapeutic purposes, an extrapolation can be made of that and allow the use of these hormones for growth promotion. Is this a comparable example? Is it comparable to say that because they are used for therapeutic purposes they should also be allowed to use for. Is, in other words, the potential risk to consumers the same from one and the other situation if you take into account the conditions under which the therapeutic use is allowed to the Community? This is in particular to Dr. McLean and to Dr. André.

Dr. McLean

753. The only reply that I can make is that you have made much of the illegal use of hormones or the abuse of the use of hormones and so, therefore, one would suggest that veterinarians are going to be no better or no worse than the rest of the population. I would remind you that it is often the case where the veterinarian leaves the material behind for administration by the farmer for later treatment and so that is a possibility - I can say no more.

Mr. Christoforou (EC)

754. We are all sometimes in our life ill and we may need treatment by a doctor. Are you suggesting that even that type of treatment should not be made because I sometimes have to be treated for therapeutic or zootechnical reasons. Either way, what we call zootechnical for the animals, if a woman cannot get pregnant she would have to go to a doctor for that treatment to be made. It is comparable, it is just once, as we said, it is done. Do you really think this is a reason enough in itself to extrapolate and allow the use of the hormones as growth promoters? That is the issue. We all get ill, but from that what is the conclusion one should draw?

Dr. McLean

755. It is very difficult to answer that question if you are asking me to extrapolate I would suggest to you that given the potential for misuse and the small amount of meat that might be eaten by the average person in the EU from imported meat then the risk would be just about the same.

Mr. Christoforou (EC)

756. The second question relates to the argument we have been discussing about. We get increased values of all these natural hormones from a number of sources. One of our experts has called the sea of oestrogens which are existing in our daily life and I would like to give the floor to Dr. Liehr to make a couple of comments and then probably ask one precise question.

Dr. Liehr (EC)

757. Mr. Chairman, yesterday we heard Dr. McLean talk about and I quote him "We live in a sea of hormones and that hormones are in our diet" and he also said that it is difficult to determine where our hormone burden comes from. Also today there were references early on in discussion about the various hormones that we are exposed to.

758. I would like to bring to your attention an important distinction here. Oestradiol, testosterone and progesterone are hormones that are circulating within all of us and carefully controlling endocrine functions within all of us. The production of these hormones within mammalian systems, including humans, are very carefully controlled, the disposition is very carefully controlled because these hormones very carefully controlled reproductive function and a variety of other functions that I cannot go and do not want to go into here. At elevated levels such hormones may be harmful - we are talking about breast cancer risk and also Dr. McLean this morning talked about extra testosterone shutting off sperm production and lowering male fertility. Many compounds, including phyto-oestrogens for instance, in soya products, have oestrogenic activity but there is a vast difference between hormones in mammalian systems and compounds with oestrogenic activity such as for instance in phyto-oestrogens. Differences are that they are different compounds with different activities - oestrogenic activities of many of these compounds are 1,000 to 10,000-fold lower than that of the mammalian hormones. There is really a vast difference between a compound that has oestrogenic activity and the actual hormone. Some of these compounds have also been shown to be oestrogenic and others are anti-oestrogenic. As Dr. Lucier said a little bit earlier on, this is a very active area of research and I know he is involved in this, nevertheless, it is obvious also that on bal-

ance between oestrogenic and anti-oestrogenic activity it may be beneficial and much of this is not known at this point. What is clear though is that a compound with much, much lower oestrogenic activity than a natural hormone introduced into a system with oestradiol in such a system, such a phyto-oestrogen may actually be anti-oestrogenic, or act in an anti-oestrogenic manner, because it competes for the oestrogen receptor. An indication of this is the low breast cancer risk in populations where high soya bean diets are consumed. So to imply that the administration of the mammalian hormone at low levels is like applying an antibiotic or a phyto-oestrogen is really inadmissible. These are different compounds, they have different spectrums of activities and they should be weighed on their own benefits.

Mr. Christoforou (EC)

759. Is there not a difference between the hormones in mammals and phyto-oestrogens in diet, in physical, chemical and health effects? Is there a difference between these three?

Dr. Ritter

760. I may be able to make this short. This answer is yes. There are differences.

Chairman

761. Could you perhaps say why?

Dr. Ritter

762. Well, I think, as has been quite correctly pointed out, there are differences in binding capacity, there are differences in structure, there are differences in function. Clearly a phyto-oestrogen was never invented to have a physiological function in a mammal. So I agree with everything you've said except that they do not contribute much to the overall risk. That part I am less certain about than you. That they are different in their structure, that they were clearly developed through evolution to have a fundamentally different purpose, I think it is an inescapable truth. But that they do not contribute to risk, I will not engage you in a debate now, about breast cancer statistics in countries where soya bean intake for example is high, except to say that it is not quite as clear as you present it. But I think the short answer, without labouring it in the limited time available, is of course there are differences in these different categories of oestrogens.

Dr. Lucier

763. I will quickly add to that. I agree with what you have said as well. There are different binding proteins and different receptors that are now being discovered for different agents. There is a beta-receptor that has just been discovered and so forth and this is a different binding spectra than the receptor that we've all come to know and love. The interaction issue is a very complex one. Nevertheless there is a lot of information in the published literature on cell systems and in-vivo systems that certain mixtures of exogenous hormones do produce stimulatory responses that are characteristically oestrogenic. So in total these things are producing an oestrogenic response. Exactly the magnitude of the oestrogenic response is highly uncertain.

Mr. Christoforou (EC)

764. The next question relates to what the lawyers among ourselves call the issue of consistency and in that case it was discussed by referring to a number of sub-

stances. I will touch only the substance of carbadox. The discussion was lively but we did not explain the conditions under which carbadox is allowed to be administered in the European Community. Carbadox does not act as a direct growth promoter as the normal hormones we are thinking about. These growth-promoting effects are only because it combats the bacteria and it helps the intestinal flora and in doing that it helps the growth of the animal. The hormone does not exert any other action apart helping the growth promotion of the animal. And there are no other readily available substances on the market which can do the same thing. It is administered only to piglets and there is a 28-day obligatory withdrawal period. From that discussion and because the Community allows the use of carbadox under the conditions and even stricter conditions than those recommended by Codex. I was left with the impression that probably because the Community allows the use of carbadox, should it allow also the use of hormones, because at the end the two types of substances for the same risk to human health, that is carcinogenicity. What should be the paradigm? Because we prohibit the hormones should we also prohibit carbadox or because we allow carbadox we also should allow the hormones? This is an important question. And as I said, we do respect exactly the conditions of JECFA as they are recommended. There is no risk because we have been doing all the samples and the checking and there is no reported case of excess. So do you think, and I address this to Doctor Lucier because at the end the question of what are we exactly comparing was critical. Do you think this comparison is really meaningful and should it be taken into account in the global risk assessment of the hormones in this case?

Chairman

765. I think the question should be limited to the scientific distinction of the agents and not the policy options which you invoked as well, if you agree?

Dr. Lucier

766. I hadn't heard that part of the question anyway, Mr. Chairman. I understand what you are saying that carbadox is not used as a growth promoter, it is used as an anti-microbial agent, so its purpose, its use, is much different than for the hormones in question. On the other hand, it is, and I only saw the carcinogenicity data on it today and my next-door-neighbour has gone and left with it, so I cannot refer to it again, but it was a fairly potent carcinogen - it was a carcinogen at multi-sites, at doses well below the maximum tolerated dose and it is genotoxic, so it is not an agent that you want to expose a lot of people to. That is my only point. So I think strict attention needs to be given to the avoidance of residue levels of carbadox given the availability of that cancer data.

Chairman

767. If I am correct, the agent works assisting the flora and it is not really having hormonal effect. Would you consider this to be a critical distinction between the two agents or not?

Dr. Lucier

768. It depends, it is a distinction, they are used for differences purposes. I do not know how to say it beyond that. The purposes are vastly different. Nevertheless, they are both present and both may have their own risk. The risk of carbadox, if residues are present, are likely greater than that of some of the hormones in question.

Dr. McLean

769. I think it would be useful for the Panel to know that there is another drug related to carbadox - olaquindox, and whilst JECFA has reviewed it, it has not set MRLs and ADIs because the data package is incomplete. But notwithstanding I believe it is used in the EU and it is just as effective, it has a mode of action that is similar, in other words, interfering or modifying the microbial population and so therefore it is an alternative and it is just as effective and of course there are other anti-microbial agents that are used in a number of other countries as growth promotants that are substitutes for both olaquindox and carbadox, such as the tetracyclines as an example.

Chairman

770. But can the agent be compared with the hormonal agents or is it ...

Dr. Ritter

771. Are you asking the question that you are asking when you ask about the difference being important between carbadox, for example, are you asking the difference in risks to human health?

Chairman

772. The problem is that legally the agreement requires consistent policies. One argument goes that you allow this agent but you do not allow the other one and of course you can make this argument if these are comparable agents. It is important for us to know whether from the scientific point of view you can compare these agents and put them on the same level, knowing that the one affects the hormonal household and the other one the microbiological situation in the stomach. So can we compare the two and put them on the same level and ask for the same policy under the agreement or is that a completely different story. Carbadox and the other one is olaquindox.

Dr. Ritter

773. The hour is late and I am going to go out on a limb and even though a number of us have consistently said during the day that we feel uncomfortable with drawing comparisons, if it would assist the Panel, carbadox is a genotoxic carcinogen. I think there are few people in this room who would disagree with that conclusion. There is very much debate, some of which you have heard in the last day or two, as to whether or not the hormones are indeed genotoxic carcinogens. To put this into perspective, within the toxicological community, we would attach greater concern to a compound which was a genotoxic carcinogen than we would to one that has been referred to in the last couple of days as epigenetic. Carbadox is such a genotoxic carcinogen. I personally would be inclined to say that the evidence for oestradiol, for example, being a genotoxic carcinogen, is weak, whereas in the case of carbadox it is definitive and if one had to put on a ranking scale where you would attach greater concern or greater importance, I think most of us in the scientific community would argue that we would probably have a heightened level of concern for genotoxic carcinogens than we would for some other class. I do not know if that assists.

Chairman

774. Yes, it does. Would you like to speak on that point?

Dr. Arnold

775. Dr. McLean mentioned olaquindox - it is also used in the EC. It is in the same annex to the feed additives directives. It is chemically similar to carbadox but there are interesting differences. Olaquindox is genotoxic in a very large number of tests, but in the carcinogenic studies, which were available to JECFA, it did not show carcinogenicity. There was no increase in either benign or malign tumours. That is a strange finding, but it is really genotoxic and I would say in more than ten test systems. The substances used in the EC as growth promoters could replace carbadox theoretically, unfortunately the residue situation is not clear. We have no marker residue, we are not able to set an MRL, so we have no means to control the use of this substance. But theoretically it could replace carbadox and it is in the same annex to the directive.

Dr. Lucier

776. In relation to that point and the point that Dr. Ritter made, I do not get so concerned about the distinction between genotoxic and non-genotoxic. There are genotoxic non-carcinogens and there are non-genotoxic carcinogens. What I prefer to look at is the strength of the carcinogenic response - what sites are affected, what number of sites, whether it occurs in multiple species, or in multiple organs. So I looked at the carbadox carcinogenicity data I was impressed for the number of sites that were affected where tumours appeared, the magnitude of the response, they were very high over a background and they occurred in more than one dose; suggesting this might be a sensitive effect. On top of that is genotoxic. But my concern was not so much for the genotoxicity, it was the fact that the tumour response was a very strong one for carbadox.

Dr. McLean

777. One point that is germane, in my country carbadox is banned and is banned on occupational health and safety grounds - in other words, we have more concern with those that have to mix it in with the feed and feed to the pigs, than we do to the consumers of the product and so it is an occupational health hazard.

Dr. André

778. I am not a specialist of carbadox but I am happy to hear this, because I understood this morning or this afternoon, that carbadox is a carcinogenic compound, but it is not a problem to use it because it is immediately and very fast transformed in an innocent metabolite. The real risk is for farmers and for manufacturers - it is not for meat or for pigs or meat containing carbadox, meat cannot contain carbadox residue, it is okay. Just to clarify.

Mr. Christoforou (EC)

779. It is unfortunate that this is going to be the final and probably your final decision on this issue. If it is indeed final question it is regrettable because we do have many questions. Then I would only comment on that Dr. Ritter said oestrogens are weak carcinogens - that is the statement I heard - weak genotoxic, could you please restate?

Dr. Ritter

780. What I said was that the available evidence in the case of carbadox in the example I was drawing is that carbadox was genotoxic in a variety of test systems. The data is outlined in the 1989 JECFA Report. What I said was that the genotoxicity of oestrogens is still open to some speculation. That is what I said.

Mr. Christoforou (EC)

781. I thought we heard the word "weak". But if it is so, we have already, and it is published, that the IARC, the Institute on Cancer Research, has classified oestrogens in group 1, which is genotoxic and carcinogenic.

Dr. Ritter

782. I am going to presume that you are directing that question to me. I think we are confusing apples and oranges. That oestrogens have the potential to be human carcinogens is absolutely true. I do not think there is anybody who would argue with that who is all familiar with the discipline. I think Dr. Lucier explained that yesterday. There is no question that we know that circulating oestrogens in a woman's body have a profound impact on her risk for breast cancer. This is of no question whatsoever. What we have been discussing here for the last couple of days is whether the levels that are present as a result of the use of these products in growth promotion are sufficient to constitute a meaningful risk, and we define meaningful as being somewhere in the range of one in a million. This has been the nature of the discussion for the last day or two. Not that at some dose oestrogens are capable of causing cancer. If I have imparted the impression that somehow or another I doubted that, let me correct it. To be clear, oestrogens are human carcinogens. I never meant to impart any other impression. But I have also indicated that in my view the oestrogens present at the levels that would be present as residues as a result of their use as growth promotion constitute, in my opinion, no significant risk at all to the human population.

Chairman

783. This now brings us to the last stage of this hearing and I am sorry we have to advance and I would really just like to get us through these questions as rapidly as possible. We have prepared a number of so-called additional questions which were circulated with the Panel and also with delegations. What I would intend to do is to touch upon them orally and then see in the end whether it might be feasible to maybe have them done in writing in order to be fully accurate. But I would like to have the opportunity of discussing them orally since you are here.

784. The first question really addresses a point we have not touched upon, which is the difference in health risks of the natural and artificial hormones. Is there a difference in the risk of using natural hormones or the artificial hormones? In other words, can they legally be classified in the same group or do you see there ground for distinguishing these agents?

Chairman

785. Just to take the floor as it comes and then we have a good debate.

Dr. Lucier

786. Let give me a stab at that. Not that we have an answer to all the questions, but for the natural hormones we have a great wealth of information about how they work

in different cells and tissues of the body. This is in the published literature. We know a lot about, as you have heard, about how they go about producing cancer as well as other adverse health effects. We know less about the synthetic materials. Now the synthetic materials are designed to mimic the natural hormones. So they will have one set of their biological properties, will be very similar to those for the naturally-occurring hormones, that is the ability to interact with the receptor system and stimulate the same kind of, say oestrogen or testosterone responsive systems that the naturally-occurring ones do. But in addition, the complicating factor is that their structure is different. So they may potentially have biological properties in addition to the hormonal properties. And that is where any level of concern would come in. Now to get any of these synthetic materials registered for use, they have to go through the significant testing protocol to determine whether not they cause cancer or produce other kinds of effects. That information is not available from the regulatory agencies because it is proprietary. So much less of it is in the peer-reviewed published literatures. You don't have as much information in peer-reviewed published literature for the synthetics as you do for the naturally-occurring ones.

Chairman

787. Thank you very much. Any other views? Addition? I take it if there is silence that you agree? Otherwise you would just oppose or clarify.

Dr. Arnold

788. It is a difficult question. I largely agree, but if for example, I take the molecular structure and look at things, Dr. Liehr has already described and Dr. Cavalieri and I must say this potential is not associated to such extent with zeranol. So depending on what you are looking, you could come to the idea that synthetic hormones are safer than the natural and if you look at other things you could come to another conclusion and that is the problem.

Chairman

789. So you would agree we know less, you know about them than the normal ...

Dr. Arnold

790. We know less about the synthetic but they might be safer than the natural.

Dr. André

791. A short point. I think the fact that Codex did not establish MRLs for the three naturals in comparison with the others is never mind that they are safer or not. The problem is that Codex establish no MRL for these natural hormones on the basis first, that they are natural, and a priori, that if they are natural, they are less toxic, I think, may be. And they are thought so. And the second reason is that the residue level has been demonstrated to be within the physiological range. And taking account these two facts, they decided not to fix MRL but not on safety basis.

Chairman

792. Thank you very much. Yes

Dr. McLean

793. Very quickly, the evaluation process, the formal evaluation process of veterinary drugs is designed to reach a point where you effectively reduce the risk to zero.

Now in the case of the naturally-occurring hormones, it was believed that the additional amount that would come from ingested food would not contribute to the overall burden in a significant way and so that risk was zero. In the case of zeranol and trenbolone, then an acceptable daily intake was set, and again, providing that wasn't exceeded, the risk was essentially zero. And the second point I would like to add that the two synthetic hormones have been subjected to a formal toxicological evaluation process designed to bring out the toxicity. And so therefore, in some ways, those processes, which are complete for zeranol and for trenbolone, are identifying the toxic hazard and bringing it out. And whilst I accept the fact the studies are not published in the open literature. The monographs that JECFA prepares are open literature and there are a hundred or so pages of material relating not to each of them, to both of them, and that is available for perusal and scrutiny. They are also included in that material, it is from the open literature, although that is not large. And so, that is the couple of additional points I would like to make, Mr. Chairman.

Chairman

794. Thank you very much. I think we don't have to address questions 2 and 3 because, we had an extensive discussion here on carbadox and olaquindox, just a minute ago. I like to turn to question 4. Are there any qualitative chemical or other differences between the three natural hormones in dispute in the human being, depending on whether these hormones are being endogenously produced by that human being; secondly are added to the human being because of consumption of food endogenously containing these hormones, or three, of meat treated with these hormones for growth promotion purposes or four, of meat treated with these hormones for therapeutic purposes? Do any of these chemicals, or other differences, if any, pose an additional risk to human health? And if Professor André could elaborate on his thesis on the natural hormones added to human beings having different metabolites.

Dr. André

795. Very quickly. When natural hormones are administered to animals first as esters, as implants or by injection, they don't follow in the body same route as the endogenous ones. Because the endogenous ones are secreted in one gland, circulate and are metabolized in another part of the body. So they cannot be exactly compared. There are small differences in the animal. So that these animals might produce different metabolites with same hormones injected as they could do with their own hormones. For example, they could produce various proportions in conjugate forms. As sulphosteroids instead of glucurono steroids, for example. After this, in the meat, you may have different varieties of metabolites. When human beings are eating these metabolites, they are eating different compounds from natural hormones as their own endogenous natural hormones. Following my example, it could be that human beings absorb some sulphosteroids and it has been said this after that a new information appear now on the role of sulphosteroids in the human brain. So that you cannot exactly assimilate the natural oestradiol, progesterone and testosterone of human beings with hormones they are consuming in food. I hope to be clear enough.

Chairman

796. Would you like to talk on this question?

Dr. Ritter

797. Not to precipitate a lengthy debate, but to simply present an alternative, if you like. To the best of my knowledge and again that information was published in the European Conference on Growth Promotion, as well. To the best of my knowledge, if the structure of the hormone that is if we are talking about the same hormone which is produced endogenously or exogenously, if introduced exogenously, they enter the identical pathway. And from that moment in time they are indistinguishable to the body. And I say I can provide the Panel with published references which support that view.

Chairman

798. But is it fair to say that there are two different views in science?

Dr. Ritter

799. I think it is fair to say that there are probably 30. As many...

Chairman

800. As authors?

Dr. Ritter

801. You know the story of the two-handed scientists: on the one hand and on the other. Lawyers are often looking for one-handed scientists.

Dr. Lucier

802. There is probably some small differences in the exact pattern of metabolites or break down products resulting from a slightly different route of exposure. This might be expected because of the way they move through the body. I don't think there would be qualitative differences in the metabolites.

There might be small differences in the pattern of metabolites. So I think that's what Dr. André was saying. I don't believe that this difference in pattern of metabolites would be toxicologically significant.

Chairman

803. Thank you. Would you...

Dr. McLean

804. I just want to concur with that view. There could be small qualitative and quantitative differences but there would be no effect on human health due to those small differences, within the biological variations, so to speak.

Dr. André

805. On the opposite, you cannot be sure that they have not.

Chairman

806. That's not an appropriate scientific method!

Dr. McLean

807. Just all I am really saying is that I accept the fact that there are qualitative and quantitative differences. I believe that demonstrate any significant effect would not be possible and it is unlikely that it would be there.

Chairman

808. I just want to say, you don't have to agree. I am not putting a deal together. The question 5 is basically just a question of clarification about the notion of normal physiological range. If you could comment on this question, whether it does relate to the range in human beings or in animals? Then the latter part of the question, the impact on the threshold approach really goes over into question 6, which then I would like to address to Dr. Lucier.

Dr. Lucier

809. The point that I was trying to make is, and this has been said now, I think, many times and no one seems to disagree with it, that the amount of hormones naturally circulating in the body are in fact carcinogenic. There is a wealth of information in the scientific literature, both experimental as well as human studies, to document this. Now when an additional molecule comes into the body adding to that burden, it will not be distinguished from those other hundred thousand molecules you put here in the question. Instead of one hundred thousand molecules of 17 beta oestradiol circulating there will be 100,001 and the biological systems won't distinguish that one from the other hundred thousand. So in that sense the issue of threshold is irrelevant, since we are already dealing with the carcinogenic dose. We know that if a threshold exists, it has already been exceeded. So adding that additional molecule would add a small increment to risk. A very small increment of risk, because the body won't distinguish that molecule from any of the other naturally-occurring ones. And the risk assessment that I talked about is really based on these relative proportions of molecules, recognizing that the threshold if one exists, it has already been exceeded. And that was the basis of my argument that the threshold issue was irrelevant here. Because even if it did exist, it has already been exceeded, by the woman's naturally-occurring hormones.

Chairman

810. What is of interest to the Panel is really what does this mean for the entire concept of the threshold under which the maximum residue levels and the ADI. From your point of view, if you take this to the end, would this make this approach redundant? This is contained in question 6 and I think it is a conceptually very interesting point. You know, is this a challenge to the thesis that if we can define these levels what we do below is safe and even what we do above it is probably safe for a long time.

Dr. Lucier

811. Any acceptable daily intake will not guarantee zero risk.

Chairman

812. So you would challenge that below it we can talk about a safety ...

Dr. Lucier

813. In other words any additional incremental increase beyond we already have, it would be reasonable to assume that an additional risk is created. So an acceptable daily intake could not be established that would guarantee zero risk for the oestrogens. Because we already know, again, that we are at the carcinogenic levels, so the

assumption is that an additional molecule add up very, very small incremental increase in risk to that.

Chairman

814. But I am correct to understand that the mainstream, the traditional understanding, is that if we operate within these limits, we are safe.

Dr. Lucier

815. Well, what that concept was developed for was looking at molecules which we normally do not have present in our bodies. So for some types of carcinogenicity you can establish a dose below which you are reasonably confident that no effect can occur. And that's what a threshold is. In cases you have in addition to an already endogenously acting mechanism and we know we have it here, the issue of threshold is really an irrelevant one. One may set an acceptable daily intake as a policy. But that policy does not guarantee zero risk.

Dr. McLean

816. The difficulty with the hormones in meat, the naturally-occurring ones is that they are already there in meat. And so the very act of eating meat adds more hormones. And so therefore that is a risk. And perhaps one would therefore, if you want to eliminate that risk, you wouldn't eat meat. But the argument I think is whether the extra amount produced or taken in by what is already there normally plus the small increment due to the treatment, is a significant extra risk. And with normal chemicals when we set an ADI, they are not normally in produce. And so therefore, you can say well it's not there and you can have that small increase and they are not naturally occurring. So it's easy to set an ADI. But with the case of the hormones, they are naturally there already and it's difficult to measure what the ADI is, because the levels of increase are quite small in relation to what is already there in many cases. I mean if you look at progesterone in the normal cycling cow and the amount that you add is very, very small in relation to the total. So it's not a practical consideration and I think that's where we are having the difficulty. Not between the colleagues, but the concept of managing risk.

Mr. Palecka

817. Thank you very much, Mr. Chairman. Perhaps just to be one hundred per cent sure ... It means that looking at this problem quite likely. If there are cabbage eaters or eggs eaters, who may perhaps add some more molecules than one in case of eating the hormone meat, it means that they may theoretically through a linear increase be exposed ... more to say dangerous or threats, then for example, those who eat hormone containing meat. There are different diets, for example, you know. Such as "cabbage eaters" or "eggs eaters", that's what I had mind.

Dr. McLean

818. Or those that drink milk ... You are just adding to the oestrogen burden. And whether you take it in meat with that little bit extra added from growth promotion which is difficult to detect because it sits in a rising and falling normal level and if you take a sample of meat out there, from the butcher and bring it in, you cannot really say whether that meat has been treated or not. Because the difference that you add is buried in the normal range. Therefore, when you eat it, you add that little bit.

Now in case of eggs or particularly, butter and cheese, for example, that have got a lot of fat in them, then you take those hormones in any way and they are quite high when you compare them on a weight basis with meat, particularly with treated meat.

Dr. Lucier

819. Put it a different way. For every million women alive in the United States, Canada, Europe today, about a 110,000 of those women will get breast cancer. This is obviously a tremendous public health issue. Of those 110,000 women get breast cancer, maybe several thousand of them are related to the total intake of exogenous oestrogens from every source, including eggs, meat, phyto-oestrogens, fungal oestrogens, the whole body burden of exogenous oestrogens. And by my estimates one of those 110,000 would come from eating meat containing oestrogens as a growth promoter, if used as prescribed. Does that help?

Chairman

820. Thank you. Could I follow up on this. In the light of this, do you consider the MRLs for the synthetic hormones adequate?

Dr. Lucier

821. From my reading of the information that I have seen the MRLs are derived by looking at hormonal responses in monkeys. And there is a series of measurements the one goes about to determine those hormonal responses. I think in any case that we are talking about carcinogenicity data has not been used except the MRL. I think that has been basically a hormone derived response. I think in the case of trenbolone, there was weak carcinogenic response. And again correct me if I am wrong, and that was essentially disregarded in establishing the ADI. In the case of zeranol, it thinks it wasn't really considered at all, there was a weak carcinogenic response that to be due to the hormonal activity of the agent. After having said that, we heard from Dr. Metzler yesterday that there is a DNA adduct which is of zeralenone, which is a structural analogue of zeranol in the metabolic chain of it. Now that DNA adduct is part of the zeralenone bound covalently to DNA, and for some chemicals this is an early step in the carcinogenic response and an early step in a genotoxic response that initial binding covalently to DNA, so when the cell replicates that adduct is fixed into the [?] or cellular mutation. If the mutation occurs in a critical target gene, it could go on to produce cancer. And that's the whole concept behind the idea that genotoxic carcinogens need to be closely regulated. Now zeranol is negative in test for genetic activity that look at the ability to produce mutations. Yet this adduct has been discovered, apparently, and there is some questions about exactly what it is an adduct of. It hasn't shown to be clearly related to the zeralenone. So I don't know, with a 100 per cent certainty of these acceptable MRLs are correct. But I see no reason to strongly dispute them at this point in terms of the zeranol. The one with trenbolone causes me a little bit more concern. Trenbolone is positive in cell transformation as says, in other words, it is capable of transforming cells. I think there are couple of studies that have shown that. And that's indicative of, it is a way that people screen for potential carcinogens, when they see this response it raises a sort of a red flag to go on and look for the carcinogenic activity of a compound that does this. So that raises an issue with the carcinogenicity studies that I guess were conducted by the company who requested that this be used. Now as I understand, the carcinogenic studies were essentially negative. That there were small increases in liver tumours. Is

that correct? I think there were small increases in liver tumours that were seen. I think the issue of trenbolone should be looked at perhaps a little more closely for the MRL, in my mind. I am more comfortable with the one for zeranol. It's a long-winded answer without being much of an answer, but it tries to give my basis for some concern on one part and little concern on the other.

Chairman

822. Thank you very much. Can I ask a question which actually comes into the first question, but it is related here. Do the studies considered by JECFA evaluate carcinogenic effect of the hormones at issue? Was this taken into account by the studies which JECFA considered?

Dr. McLean

823. Yes, they were. JECFA actually looked at trenbolone acetate on two occasions because it requested additional information. I will say that the cell transformation assays under some circumstances were equivocal, they weren't accepted by all as being positive. Of course the carcinogenicity was investigated thoroughly and on balance I feel that this compound, this compound is being pretty much looked at as well as any compound and indeed for some of studies we ask for electron microscopy rather than normal microscopy to determine certain end points. And of course the no effect levels are based on fairly innocuous changes in monkeys and they are very low, and then on top of that there are further safety factors for species, inter- and intra-species variation. So you have got that chain built in.

824. If I could add just one thing, when we were talking about the increased incidence of breast cancer of one, I think, it was in 150,000. That's I think, according to your calculations, a maximum of one. [Yes.] So it could be anywhere between essentially zero and one and I think it's important to appreciate that difference. And that comes back to the point that my colleague, Dr. Ritter made that when we are looking at risk assessment, because it's a mathematical consideration, we have a range and it lies somewhere between essentially zero and one.

Chairman

825. Thank you very much. Would you like to talk to this point.

Dr. Lucier

826. That's correct, between zero and one and I should also remember to say that, when I say one, I was just trying to make the point to put in comparison with the other oestrogens. I have looked at some of that data, though with the cell transformation assays and I don't find it equivocal. It's associated with increased production of oncogenes in the Syrian hamster embryo cells, the ras and myconcogenes, which are an expression of those critical target genes in carcinogenesis. And the result seems to be real one.

Dr. McLean

827. I was making the point that some of the studies were equivocal and some are not.

Chairman

828. I'd like to leave question 7 to the end and move on to question 8. We have the situation of a ban or prohibition with qualifications and if I am correct that Dr. André contended that the abuse will occur in similar degrees in situations where one bans the hormones in dispute as opposed to situations where allows these hormones under certain conditions. Is there any data available in this respect which could support your thesis?

Dr. André

829. The result, as I said yesterday I think, in France we knew the two situations and the same hormones were allowed between 84 and 89. So I don't know really if the data are available. They are in my Government and official bodies and maybe it is possible to get real data in archive from that date. But I can just give some witnesses on this. For example, during the authorization of these hormones, five years of authorization, we found some positive results, positive results is misuse, of the DES. And the DES misuse had disappeared in the early seventies. So it was a coming back of DES misuse during this period. A second fact is that it has been said. I speak for France, not for other countries, okay?, that in France, the ban has been followed by the misuse of new class of hormones, so-called beta agonist. And it's clear that we discovered the misuse of beta agonist just after the official ban. But in fact when now, with the methods we have, when we look in feed samples taken during the period where the hormones were authorized, we find also clenbuterol or beta agonists. So my idea is that the authorization, legalization, of these compounds had no effect, real effect on some black market and the misuse of hormones.

830. The second part of your question is concerned with the control. And to know if the control is easier under regime, with a ban or not, I would just answer that it's clearly easier technically for all the xenobiotics. Because if you have not any xenobiotics allowed each time you find one it's clearly a misuse. And it's also technically more easy because you have just to have qualitative survey, I mean, you have to check in your sample meat, urine, feeds, whatsoever, you have just to look if the compound is present. And then you say, yes it's present. So you have a qualitative analysis. When hormones are allowed, then it's the same thing for drugs, and so you are obliged to do a quantitative analysis, more complicated analysis to compare with the tolerance, with the MRL and so technically it's more easy. But it's small differences, any laboratory know how to do the two jobs.

Chairman

831. Thank you very much. My next question related to this to all the Panel members. Is there a fundamental difference ... [I am sorry.]

Dr. Arnold

832. Mr. Chairman, I would like to add few sentences. Sometimes a ban makes life of analytical chemists easier. But not always and there is no easy answer to that question. I give you two examples. Oestradiol 17-B. is used as benzoate illegally and according to legal authorizations for therapeutic purposes. On a routine basis, the only way to detect the substance, currently, is to detect an injection site. Although I know that many people are starting being able to detect the ester. But even if you detect the ester somewhere, not at the injection site, then it's still the question, was it

illegal or has it been legally used? So it's not so easy. And most results have been obtained if people had found the injection site and if they were able then to go back to the farm and look. If somebody misuses these substances, then he never uses it on an individual animal basis. Then you trace back and you see, there are many animals treated the same way and then you are sure, it was illegal. So, it's a lot of effort and costs a lot of money to control this.

Chairman

833. Can I follow up. As a layman, I assume that if the practice is illegal and you want to apply the drug, you can't use the earmark, because it is too obvious. So what you do is, you make massive injections in the muscle. And if we take the evidence that there has been about, was it 20,000 cattle controlled, this is a small percentage of all cattle controlled. And if you happen to be the consumer of getting that muscle, isn't there a risk that you have enormous intake? I mean, is the risk greater under a ban than when it's controlled? This is the main argument and I would like to just add this one and I have two more elements which should go with it. We should also consider the control of imports under the two things. And the final point is, is there a fundamental difference between controlling hormones than from other veterinary drugs and substances used Does it allow a fundamentally different approach than what we have in other areas?

Dr. Arnold

834. Mr. Chairman, the use for therapeutic uses is by injection. This is the only way which is permitted. So the illegal people, they do it by injection and try to hide the injection site. So you have injection in both the cases. This makes the thing so difficult.

Chairman

835. But you can trace it, because it is used by the veterinarian on the therapeutic side.

Dr. Arnold

836. You can ask the farmer to show his prescription, for example. So you have to do a lot of effort. Simply by analytical means it's very difficult to answer the question whether it has been used legally or illegally.

Dr. André

837. Yes, in short, concerning the control of hormones and other drugs, I think the problem is the same. Because we have also to check for banned compounds as chloramphenicol and the problem is the same to control for chloramphenicol as for trenbolone or nandrolone. It's not really different, I think. The control of imported meat, the problem is that it is imported meat. It is not a live animal and it's clear also, everybody, every scientist, analytical man can say that it's more easy to work on feed, to work on urine, as to work on meat So it's more difficult. It's not impossible. But it's more difficult. And concerning your third short question, the occasional consumption of the meat with an injection site. This is highly improbable. Because, for many reasons: first of all, these injected solutions are mainly oil solutions of benzoate, oestradiol and other compounds. So the butcher is looking for what it is. He is cutting and it is very improbable that an injection site can be eaten. Even if it is, let me remind

you that it is an occasional consumption. It will never be, you have no opportunity to eat each day an injection site. It would be an exceptional thing and maybe you will be informed by the news of that very strange thing.

Chairman

838. The next point is relating to the labelling. You had a written question on labelling, the answers were fairly short in most cases. And we would like to back up on this one. There are two approaches. You could have voluntary labelling basically of meat which has not been treated, what we call green labels, and you can have mandatory labelling of treated meat, which has to be enforced. Reading this question, do you think labelling would be a feasible approach? If not, in what ways would this labelling procedure differ from the controls already carried out by the EC to ensure that imported meat has not been treated with hormones at all? Is the fact that one cannot distinguish between treated and untreated meat sufficient reason not to label meat? What is the difference between labelling already carried out today, even with respect to meat, such as this meat is BSE-free or American meat, or French meat, and labelling for purposes as to whether meat is or is not treated with hormones? I mean the labelling is a major policy today in making or leaving decision to consumers. Most reactions were negative except yours, Dr. Lucier. And we need to know little bit more why you think this is not a doable way. Now, but well that's an answer yes. But maybe, you have scientific reasons too which it is not doable.

Dr. McLean

839. I mean, anything is possible, Mr. Chairman. It's just the cost. But if you look at the realities of labelling meat, especially when the live animal is a commodity, it's bought and sold and traded. Then what you mean by untreated, if you mean never ever treated in the lifetime, then you go to look at the calf, you got to look at as it changes hands, once or twice it moves into a feedlot. So you have got a chain of identification, you really need a passport with each animal, to which each owner attests that has never treated and their passport goes on with ...

Chairman

840. It could be another earmark.

Dr. Lucier

841. It's a practical problem. The other difficulty is with the naturally-occurring substances, how do you really determine whether it has been treated or not, except for the presence of the pellet in the ear. Because analytically you can't tell whether it has been treated. And there is another problem with zeranol. In some countries, Fusarium which produces the zeranol-like components contaminates pasture and feed. And there are countries in the EC, I believe, where when it comes to taking the farmer to court for example, it is impossible really to prove beyond all reasonable doubts that particular animal didn't take in a fair burden of the zeranol-like substances that have left some residue. So there are practical problems across the board. And I made the point, and I know that it's unrelated but one has to look at the cost of this against the benefit. And the benefit is largely psychological, but the cost is enormous. And when you look for example, there's the example that I gave with the outbreaks of *E. coli* food poisoning that is occurring all around the world, where there are hundreds of people getting ill and a number of them dying, one wonders

whether one is better to spend the dollar on rectifying this problem than putting it into something that can confers a psychological advantage to the person eating the meat. A simple practical problem.

Chairman

842. Thank you.

Dr. Lucier

843. My written comment was probably a naive one in many respects. But I think one ought nevertheless to consider whether the primary source can in fact be labelled. Obviously there is a lot of spin-off meat products that will be developed and it will be very difficult to trace those and label each of those. But I think it needs to be looked at as to whether the primary source can be labelled such as this animal has been treated with a growth promoting agent for the purpose of growth promotion. I think it could be narrowed down to that and perhaps be not quite so costly as if full-blown labelling procedures were put into effect. I think if that's all possible and it is not going to break the bank, I think it really needs to be considered. I mean, after all if the public is concerned about these issues, the public has a right to know, if at all possible.

Chairman

844. Thank you very much.

Dr. Ritter

845. In trying to prepare a written response to this, Mr. Chairman, in fact I cited in a number of references who understand this topic much better than I. But I suppose the question that I ask myself is what would be the objective of the labelling. Because I think that helps to define the strategy. We're accustomed around the world to labelling products where an informed decision is a useful thing to offer. If you want to smoke, these are the potential consequences. Or there are many therapeutic drugs, not necessarily veterinary medicines, but human medicine, which may raise the risk of birth defects, and we label them, because they may confer enormous benefits to patients. But I was unclear when the question was raised. To turn it around, if it were the view of the Panel that the use of these agents does not constitute a risk that has to be dealt with, then I ask myself what's the objective.

Chairman

846. Well, I am recalling a submission which was in the EC's submission to high US Government officials explaining the hormone treatment and when he was asked privately what type of meat do you prefer, he said, if I can afford it I buy non-hormone treated beef. And I think that's the sort of choice people would want to make. I think we make these choices every time, particularly now at the age of BSE. You find on the card in a restaurant, US beef, beef imported from the United States and that's another label, and that's a label in the meat sector, and so that label somehow works, I hope it does.

Dr. Ritter

847. Well, then, I would be inclined to think, if that's the case to provide those who wish to make a choice, the opportunity to make one. And if it's not a matter of helping a consumer decide on the basis of ....[cassette ended.]

848. I think of some of the supermarkets particularly in the United States, South West in California where there has been a whole culture of franchises that's developed around assuring the consumer that it's pesticide free or this residue free, and my view on that is all power to them, if you can create a market niche for yourself by offering a consumer something which they want but which may not provide any direct benefit. But I understood the question to asked in the context of a regulatory imposition, and in that context I asked myself what's the objective. Because if it doesn't help the consumer make an "informed" decision, and I use the word informed to imply not the knowledge that has been treated, but rather information which can materially affect the decision, then I have to ask myself if one can justify the cost and everything else that goes with it when one could simply allow the market-place to accommodate it. I don't have that view if it's a question of risk, if we're talking about a drug that may induce a birth defect and a physician has to make a decision on behalf of his patient, than I think labelling is very appropriate. Very appropriate for tobacco, although I have other views about tobacco. I think there is a more appropriate way to deal with tobacco than labelling. So I'm not in any way trying to suggest that consumers should not be given the choice. But if the choice as I say is based on preference and not science, then my position would be that I let the market prevail. And we know from worldwide experience, I cite the US as an example but there are many others, that indeed there will be entrepreneurs who will grow up to fill that niche. And I think that if they can do that and take advantage of that sort of a situation, it is the hallmark of free enterprise.

Chairman

849. Thank you very much. I'm trying to wrap up, there is one question I still have to address, a technical one. The experts have not addressed (this is No. 10). The experts have not addressed the hormone MGA. Has any risk assessment been carried out with respect to this hormone? Does this hormone pose different health risk than the other two synthetic hormones? Do you have any evidence on this? It's question 10 here on the paper, the last question.

Dr. McLean

850. I guess all I can say Mr. Chairman is that I have not had the opportunity to look at a package of data, contemporary data, that is complete, and so therefore I'm unable to comment and I made that comment at the beginning.

Dr. André

851. Just a comment, one major risk for these hormones is the risk associated with management of an hormone, an active hormone imported directly in the feed on the farm. That's a real risk I think. In this hormone is very different from the others, but no more comment on this.

Dr. Lucier

852. Well I'm not saddled with the same amount of information my colleagues are so it's difficult for me to make a comment because of lack of information. There is some, there is a report that it produces an equivocal increase in mammary tumours, a long-term study and that it's a very potent progestational agent. The information that I could get is that it's about 30 times more potent than progesterone and orally active so it's an extraordinarily potent progestant. So that raises some concerns toxicology

just for that reason. But I haven't seen the toxicology studies that apparently are available but I would have some concern based on these two pieces of information.

Chairman

853. Would it be possible to get this information for the Panel or is this too difficult?

Dr. Ritter

854. No, but the issue Mr. Chairman, is that in the case of five of the six, I think the view that you've heard from all of us participating, not necessarily agreeing, but that there has been a substantial amount of information on which we have based our opinion. In a number of cases we have arrived at different opinions, but we have all agreed that there has been a substantial amount of information. In the case of MGA because it has not been subjected to an international review thus far, a JECFA review, and because information submitted in support of these sorts of petitions to national regulatory authorities is generally proprietary, I think none of us would have had the benefit of the depth of the review that would be available for the other five. So I think that the cautionary note that you are hearing, at least from Dr. Arnold, Professor McLean and myself, is that the most accurate thing we could say is that we simply don't know. I mean that not one way or the other but that I on my own, would not venture a guess one way or the other because I have not seen one per cent of the information on MGA that I've been able to examine for the others.

Chairman

855. Thank you very much. I'd like to come to the final tour de table on the side of the experts and I'd like to link this to question seven here, I think that this will be at heart of the, also of the legal issues to be discussed in this case. Dr. Liehr has provided to us what is called the new evidence on the potential genotoxicity of the hormones. Other experts have questioned the relevance of this evidence. I would like to have your personal views on what is the relevance of this new evidence for veterinary drugs other than the hormones at issue, such as carbadox, and for the use of natural hormones, especially oestrogens, for therapeutical purposes. If this new evidence would be a reason to ban hormones added for growth promotion, would it also be a reason to ban all other uses of these hormones or to ban other veterinary drugs? And perhaps before you address this, we are not very clear on the Panel on your fundamental views to what extent one should, a scientist should or should not consider when he consider the risk for hormone residues, to what extent he should really take into account the genotoxic effects. There seems to be different, slightly different views. But if you could state again your position on the genotoxic effects and then perhaps follow this up. How would you advise the Panel to take into account this new evidence which has been presented particularly yesterday to us. Maybe we'll start with Dr. Ritter and then go through the Panel.

Dr. Ritter

856. Just very quickly, I won't take much time Mr. Chairman. I think, I'm reminded that Dr. Liehr may have captured the reference point on this information that he presented better perhaps than anyone else. When he suggested himself yesterday, I think quite correctly, that in order to establish the direct relevance of his preliminary findings, he was seeking additional research funding. I think he said that the parties to the

dispute would have made a better investment, if they would have funded him to examine the relevance of these findings at the low levels which are being present, than they have expended in coming to this hearing. I am paraphrasing a little bit, but I think that was the gist of his comments. I think he has put it better than anyone else. I think the findings are interesting but he himself I think has suggested that they are not in the form or of the nature where they can be directly applicable to the nature of the deliberations here. The nature of scientific investigation is that it goes forward. And if we were to meet again in a year, I dare say you would be looking at evidence which you didn't have available today. I mentioned to you yesterday Mr. Chairman, that I know of no scientist who has ever said on any issue, because we are all looking for funding, I know enough, please don't provide any more money on this issue. I know I've never done it. So I think just very quickly in the context of the relevance, that would be my view, it's interesting, but I like the way Dr. Liehr phrased it.

857. In terms of the relevance in a larger sphere to other veterinary drugs, again I think the only way to answer that question is to apply the same technology to other drugs. It is conceivable that if one applied the new methodology that we heard described yesterday to a range of other veterinary drugs, pesticides, other food contaminants, that it might raise the very same degree of concern that it seems to have generated in this debate over the last couple of days. I don't know the answer because it hasn't been done. But if you'd like to provide the funding Mr. Chairman ... . And finally I think on the issue of carbadox specifically, if I read this to be the third issue if you like, I think in the case of carbadox there is already general agreement that it is a genotoxic agent, so to subject that specific example to further investigation, I think would contribute little to our knowledge because we have already concluded that it is capable of this type of action. Subjected to further studies would only confirm what we have already all agreed on. So I'm not looking for more funding on that one.

Chairman

858. Thank you very much. Professor McLean.

Dr. McLean

859. Yes Mr. Chairman, the way that I read it was that Dr. Liehr was putting forward an interesting, along with a number of other people, were looking at the mechanism of carcinogenesis if I could put it that way and therefore genotoxicity was important. That he had a hypothesis, he had made a series of observations and he was testing that hypothesis and that may or may not be significant, when it's finally worked its way through, to this particular group of hormones. Dr. Arnold did point out that there were other hypothesis being tested with similar sorts, at this stage, of strength, if you like. And so therefore I think in relation to the new evidence, the jury is really still out and until the hypothesis firms up, if I could put it that way, then there is little we can do. And it would be unfortunate if the hypothesis didn't stand up and other hypothesis came forward and were tested and shown to be effective if they do that we'd made a mistake there. In relation to other veterinary drugs, many of them are carcinogenic in animals. Just to name a few, dimetridazole, metronidazole which is widely used in humans is quite carcinogenic in animals, yet it is still used, the sulphonamides are quite carcinogenic in rodent carcinogenicity tests, carbadox, we know is carcinogenic and that's to name four. And to go that next step, we don't have the mechanism of toxicity in all of the cases. And we could develop a hypothesis and

test it and then we might arrive at the precise mechanism. So I think we have a similar situation with other veterinary drugs although, with the hormones, they do have a very serious human health effect in producing for example breast cancer and so we're putting a lot of money in the area to work that through. Because it is an important human health activity and I would support continuing research with the other drugs, they don't assume that importance and so we don't put the money in.

Chairman

860. Thank you very much. Dr. Arnold

Dr. Arnold

861. I don't want to add very much because I largely agree with the two previous speakers. But should it happen that, for example, oestradiol would be identified as genotoxic carcinogenic and should this then cause a ban of this substances for growth promotion, I would say from the viewpoint of a consumer, I could then not understand its use for zootechnical purposes For example, then one should do research to replace this and use other substances which could be available for the same purpose. And also I would say then the substance should be restricted in veterinary therapy to a more narrow definition of therapeutic use. We have a very broad, as a consumer, I cannot agree with this broad definition of therapeutic uses. And it would have severe consequences in human medicine because then it would be very difficult to justify the use of this substance in oestrogen replacement therapy, for example, for the prevention or treatment of osteoporosis where millions of women take one microgram, in the order of one microgram of micronized and bio-available amounts of oestradiol every day. So it would have severe consequences in many areas.

Chairman

862. Professor André.

Dr. André

863. Yes, I think that Dr. Liehr gives us new results in the mode of action of these oestrogens in their carcinogenic effects, but he is not alone to give these results. We have many different ways to understand how they act. The difference here is it a complete theory which seems very understandable and the relation between oestrogens and DNA seems to be more identified that it was earlier, for this it's clear. But I think that if we admit that these hormones are genotoxic, it's two very different things to ban them as growth promoters, as I said yesterday, in a large scale for all populations and it is very different for their use as to therapeutic use. It's the same difference as I tried to explain with my example. As therapeutic use, they are used in one animal for one time and usually for reproduction purposes, so it's a completely different thing. So they can be banned for growth promotion and they can be used for drugs. But I agree with Dieter Arnold on the fact that there is some problems in the definition of what is therapeutic use and also how to evaluate really a drug for therapeutic use, as is done classically for years now by different committees, and the use of compounds for other purposes than really therapeutic use. And in this case, to my opinion, the evaluation has to be maybe different.

Chairman

864. Thank you very much. Dr. Lucier.

Dr. Lucier

865. My comments will be a bit different. I think the work that Dr. Liehr is doing, I think it's important to point out, as he has, is that it's not just himself. There is a group of scientists who are looking at the role of oxidative damage and genotoxicity of oestrogens, himself and several other folks throughout the world. And I think this activity is very important to our understanding of how oestrogens and how hormones may cause cancer. So I'm a strong supporter that kind of work, I actually have a couple of publications in it myself. But for this narrow purpose that we are talking about today, about the influence of this on additional risk from oestrogens from eating, consuming meat containing oestrogens from growth promoted animals, it doesn't have too much consequence. If I did a calculation of risk as I've done, this one in a million thing how that has been much discussed, I would come up with the same calculation whether or not oestradiol was genotoxic. That would bear no influence on the carcinogenic risk as the assumption is we are already on a linear part of the curve in terms of amount of oestrogen, the magnitude of oestrogen and the magnitude of response, say for breast cancer. I would come up with the same answer either case; there would be no difference in the risk. So I think in that respect whether or not oestrogen is genotoxic, has less consequence then what we talked about up to this point in time.

Chairman

866. Well thank you very much for your final statements. This brings us to the end of this expert hearing, I come to procedures, which brings us to the end of this two-day meeting. In my view, the combination both of your excellent papers, and I know you took pains to write them in a way that the normal person can read it, together with your oral presentations and the questions and comments on the parties, I think have exceedingly helped to inform the Panel on the scientific side. A side which is very difficult and very complicated. It is almost as complicated as the procedural one, but not as much. So thank you very much for your tremendous effort and also the effort you put in such a short time to assist the Panel which is operating under these very strict rules. Thank you also to the delegations for assisting in these proceedings. Thank you in particular also for the scientists who sat with the EC delegation and came here to present their views and their convictions and inform us as well.

867. So this brings us to the final procedural point. With a view to the meeting tomorrow, which is the second substantive meeting, the Panel has reflected and in the light of the fact that this has been a joint meeting today and we had difficulties to make decisions about what is new evidence, what is a new argument, and so on, and also in light of the fact that all the papers have been exchanged in the two proceedings, the Panel has taken a decision to come back to its right which it reserved before and we decided to invite the United States delegation to attend the meeting tomorrow. Do you have any other points on procedure?

Mr. Brinza (US)

868. Mr. Chairman, you anticipated correctly the question I was going to ask, thank you

Chairman

869. Professor André

Dr. André

870. Just on behalf of my colleague experts, I would like to thank you for the excellent level of this debate, due mainly to an excellent chairmanship.

Chairman

871. Thank you very much. So the meeting is closed, good night. I'm sorry, ... Mr. Christoforou, you wanted the floor.

Mr. Christoforou (EC)

872. Yes Mr. Chairman. I would also like to thank the experts, and it is not usual procedure but we would appreciate if it is possible to get the typed version of what was discussed here today. I know it is not usual, but I think it would be very useful if we can get the discussions today typed and circulated to the parties.

Chairman

873. Yes, this is underway, but it will of course take some time. But this will be done yes.

Mr. Thompson (Canada)

874. I too would like to thank again the experts for participating, I was wondering what time we are reconvening tomorrow and is it in this room.

Chairman

875. Thank you very much, the meeting will be a 10:00 in this room here. So the meeting is closed.